Psychology in 1

C000217618

Psychology in Britain

Historical Essays and Personal Reflections

Edited by
G. C. Bunn, A. D. Lovie *and* G. D. Richards

Published in association with the Science Museum

First published in 2001 by BPS Books (The British Psychological Society), St Andrews House, 48 Princess Road East, Leicester LE1 7DR, UK.

© Board of Trustees of the Science Museum, 2001

All rights reserved. No part of this publication may be reproduced or transmitted in any form or by any means, without permission.

This book is sold subject to the condition that it shall not, by way of trade or otherwise, be lent, resold, hired out, or otherwise circulated without the publisher's prior consent in any form of binding or cover other than that in which it is published and without a similar condition including this condition imposed on the subsequent purchaser.

A catalogue record for this book is available from the British Library.
ISBN 1 85433 332 1

Typeset by Ralph J. Footring, Derby
Printed and bound in Great Britain by Biddles Ltd,
www.biddles.co.uk

Whilst every effort has been made to ensure the accuracy of the contents of this publication, the publishers and authors expressly disclaim responsibility in law for negligence or any other cause of action whatsoever.

Contents

Tables and figures

Contributors

Michael Argyle is Emeritus Reader in Social Psychology at Oxford University (where he has been since 1952), an Emeritus Fellow of Wolfson College, and now is also an Emeritus Professor of Psychology at Oxford Brookes. He directed the Oxford Social Psychology Group over many years. He helped to found the *British Journal of Social and Clinical Psychology* and was its first social psychology editor. He was an early chairman of the Social Psychology Section of the British Psychological Society, and started that Section's annual conferences. He is the author of many books and papers, such as *The Psychology of Interpersonal Behaviour* (fifth edition 1994), *Bodily Communication* (second edition 1988) and *The Psychology of Happiness* (second edition in press). His interests are in social interaction, non-verbal communication, social skills, social relationships, and the psychology of religion and happiness. He has spread this good news abroad by lecturing in 35 countries.

Alan Baddeley is Professor of Psychology at the Department of Experimental Psychology, University of Bristol. After graduating from University College London and spending a year in Princeton, he moved to the Medical Research Council's Applied Psychology Unit in Cambridge, where he completed a PhD. In 1967 he moved to the Department of Experimental Psychology at the University of Sussex, moving some five years later to a Chair at Stirling University. In 1974, he succeeded Donald Broadbent as Director of the Applied Psychology Unit, a post he held until moving to Bristol in 1995. His interests are in cognitive psychology, both basic and applied, and in particular in the psychology of memory, where his work has included the study of normal adults and children, as well as people with neuropsychological deficits.

Karen Baistow lectures in psychology in the Department of Social Work, Brunel University. Her teaching and research interests lie in the field of child and family welfare, and she has been involved since 1992 in comparative European research on child protection practice and policy. In addition to this, her research has focused on the role of behavioural psychology in the field of child welfare, in particular the historical and contemporary influence of behavioural approaches in conceptualising and intervening in parent–child relations. She has published in the journals *Critical Social Policy*, *Children and Society* and *History of Human Sciences* and is co-author of *Positive Child Protection: A View from Abroad* (1995) and *The Welfare of Children with Mentally Ill Parents: Learning from Inter-Country Comparisons* (forthcoming).

Margaret Boden was a Major Scholar at Newnham College, Cambridge, graduating in medical sciences before qualifying in philosophy (1955–1959). After lecturing in philosophy at the University of Birmingham, she studied cognitive and social psychology at

Harvard Graduate School (1962–1964). Besides her PhD, she holds an ScD from Cambridge. Appointed by the University of Sussex in 1965, she is now Professor of Philosophy and Psychology there, and was founding Dean of Sussex's interdisciplinary School of Cognitive and Computing Sciences. She has been elected Fellow of the British Academy, Academia Europaea, the American Association for Artificial Intelligence and the European Coordinating Committee for Artificial Intelligence, and Life-Fellow of the Society for Artificial Intelligence and Simulation of Behaviour.

Joanna Bourke is Professor of History at Birkbeck College, University of London. She is a Fellow of the Royal Historical Society and Fellow of the Royal Society for the Encouragement of Art, Manufacture, and Commerce. Since 1991 Dr Bourke has given over 120 conference papers and invited lectures. Her research interests include: domesticity and gender; war and disability; and gender and warfare. She is the author of *Husbandry to Housewifery: Women, Economic Change and Housework in Ireland 1890–1914* (1993); *Working-Class Cultures in Britain, 1890–1960: Gender, Class and Ethnicity* (1994); *Dismembering the Male: Men's Bodies, Britain and the Great War* (1996); and *An Intimate History of Killing: Face-to-Face Killing in Twentieth-Century Warfare* (1999). The last won the Fraenkel Prize for Contemporary History and the Wolfson History Prize in 2000.

Geoff Bunn was the British Psychological Society Research Fellow at the Science Museum, London, 1998–2001. Dr Bunn curated the History of Psychology exhibition at the Science Museum that marked the centenary of the British Psychological Society in 2001. His current research interests include the history of industrial psychology and the psychology of aesthetics. He has published in the journal *History of the Human Sciences*. Dr Bunn completed his doctoral dissertation *The Hazards of the Will to Truth: A History of the Lie Detector* (York University, Toronto) in 1998.

Alan Collins is a Lecturer in Psychology at the University of Lancaster. His main research interests are in the history of psychology and psychiatry. He is particularly interested in the emergence of psychological concepts and categories.

Alan Costall is Reader in Ecological Psychology at the University of Portsmouth. In 1995 he was appointed the Simon Senior Research Fellow at the University of Manchester, where he researched the history of the Manchester Psychology Department and relations between British psychology and anthropology. A member of the Board of Directors of the International Society for Ecological Psychology, he is also an Associate Editor of the *British Journal of Psychology*. Dr Costall is a member of the editorial boards of *History of the Human Sciences* and *History and Philosophy of Psychology*, among others. A member of the founding committee of the British Psychological Society's History and Philosophy Section, he has published widely, in journals such as the *Journal of the History of the Behavioral Sciences*, *Theory and Psychology* and *Human Development*. He is a co-editor of *Against Cognitivism: Alternative Foundations for Cognitive Psychology* (1991).

Maarten Derksen was a Postdoctoral Research Fellow in the Faculty of Social Sciences at the University of Groningen, The Netherlands. His PhD thesis was titled *We Psychologists: Rhetoric and Demarcation in the History of Dutch Psychology* (University of Groningen, 1997). His research interests include: the relation between psychology and common sense; the rhetoric of science; boundary work; science and technology studies. He is currently undertaking comparative research on the history of the early development of clinical psychology in England and The Netherlands.

David Conochie Duncan is a Chartered Occupational Psychologist who has so enjoyed his chosen career that after 50 years he has no intention of giving it up. In 1946, experience of poor morale and redundancy in RAF Aircrew made him decide to become an industrial psychologist. He read philosophy, psychology and economics for the MA of the University of St Andrews, and by 1957 the National Institute of Industrial Psychology had provided him with his competencies in applied psychology, which he has used ever since. For the British Psychological Society he helped to establish its Standing Committee on Test Standards, its Standing Press Committee and its Division of Occupational Psychology. In the business world he has been a chief executive since 1965.

Fay Fransella is Director of the Centre for Personal Construct Psychology, London, Emeritus Reader in Clinical Psychology, University of London and a personal construct psychotherapist. She took her first degree in 1961 as a mature student at University College London. Taking early retirement from the University in 1981, she set up the Centre for Personal Construct Psychology. She has written and edited ten books, including *Inquiring Man* with Don Bannister (1971, third edition 1985); *PCP Counselling in Action* with Peggy Dalton (1990) and *George Kelly* (1995). Her research work has mainly been into problems to do with weight and speech. She currently directs the Centre's distance learning programme and its diagnostic and other work within organisations.

Richard Gregory is Emeritus Professor of Neuropsychology at the University of Bristol. Following a lecturership at Cambridge University, when he designed and then ran the Special Senses Laboratory, he moved to Edinburgh in 1967 to set up the Department of Machine Intelligence and Perception with Donald Michie and Christopher Longuet-Higgins. He moved to Bristol in 1970 to direct the Brain and Perception Laboratory in the Medical School. His main work has been developing a general account of visual perception, with emphasis on a variety of phenomena, including various 'illusions' for suggesting and testing theories of brain mechanisms and cognitive processes. Founder of the Exploratory Hands-on Science Centre in Bristol, he was awarded the Royal Society Faraday Medal for work on the public understanding of science. He has eight honorary doctorates and Honorary Fellowships of Corpus Christi and Downing Colleges, Cambridge. He is a CBE and Fellow of the Royal Society. Publications include *Eye and Brain* (1966), *The Intelligent Eye* (1970), *Mind in Science* (1981), *The Oxford Companion to the Mind* (1987) and *Mirrors in Mind* (1997). He is founder editor of the journal *Perception.*

Lyubov G. Gurjeva is a Researcher at the Centre for the History of Science, Technology and Medicine, University of Manchester. Her interests in the history of psychology include: the relationship between lay and professional psychological ideas and practices; the development of psychological education; and the role of material objects in psychological practice. Her expertise includes the history of child study and late-nineteenth-century British psychology, particularly the work of James Sully. Dr Gurjeva completed her doctoral dissertation *Everyday Bourgeois Science: The Scientific Management of Children in Britain, 1880–1914* (University of Cambridge) in 1998. Her publications include 'Scientific motherhood' (*Studies in the History of Biological and Biomedical Sciences*, 1998); and 'James Sully' (for the forthcoming *New Dictionary of National Biography*).

Rom Harré studied mathematics and physics and then philosophy and anthropology at Auckland and Oxford. His published work includes studies in the philosophy of the natural sciences, including *Varieties of Realism* (1986) and *Great Scientific Experiments* (1981). He has been among the pioneers of the 'discursive' approach in the human sciences. In *Social Being* (1979), *Personal Being* (1983) and *Physical Being* (1991) he explored the role of rules and conventions in various aspects of human cognition, while in *Pronouns and People* (1990) he and Peter Mühlhäusler developed the thesis that grammar and the sense of self are intimately related. His most recent work, *The Singular Self* (1998), follows further ramifications of the grammatical thesis. He is Emeritus Fellow of Linacre College, Oxford, and currently Professor Psychology at Georgetown University, and Adjunct Professor of Philosophy at American University, Washington, DC. He holds honorary doctorates from the universities of Helsinki, Brussels, Aarhus and Lima, and is Honorary Professor of Psychology, University of East London.

Rhodri Hayward is Research Fellow at the Wellcome Unit for the History of Medicine at the University of East Anglia. He studied at the University of Edinburgh and the University of Lancaster, where he completed a doctorate on *Popular Mysticism and the Origins of the New Psychology, 1880–1910* (1995). In 1996 he began research with Roger Smith on the brain sciences in Britain, 1920–1960 (funded by the Wellcome Trust). Dr Hayward has published on the psychological interpretation of prophecy in Edwardian Britain, in B. Taithe and T. Thornton (Eds) *The Power of Prophecy* (1997) and the politics and psychology of Victorian dream interpretation in the *History Workshop Journal* (2000). He has contributed a number of articles on the history of psychology to *The Reader's Guide to the History of Science* (2000), the forthcoming *New Dictionary of National Biography* and the *Oxford Companion to the Body* (forthcoming).

Gustav Jahoda is Emeritus Professor of Psychology at the University of Strathclyde, where he founded the Department in 1964. He has been Visiting Professor in several European countries as well as in Africa, the United States and Japan. A former President and now Honorary Fellow of the International Association for Cross-Cultural Research and Membre d'Honneur of the Association pour la Recherche Interculturelle, he has also been elected Fellow of the British Academy and of the Royal Society of Edinburgh.

Sandy Lovie is Senior Lecturer in Psychology at the University of Liverpool and Visiting Research Fellow at the Centre for the History of Psychology, Staffordshire University. His current research interests include: psychological statistics, factor analysis and the work of Charles Spearman. Since the early 1980s he has been the British Psychological Society's Honorary Archivist, and in 1984 he founded (with Norman Wetherick) the Society's History and Philosophy of Psychology Section. The Section's first Secretary/Treasurer, he is now its Chair. He has published widely on the history of psychology. Dr Lovie was the Editor of the *British Journal of Mathematical and Statistical Psychology*. He is also editor and co-editor of two books on recent developments in statistics (for the British Psychological Society) and author of a book on the psychology of science (*Context and Commitment*, 1992).

Francis Neary is Research Fellow in the Centre for Medical History at the University of Exeter. He has recently completed his doctoral thesis *Consciousness, and Coherence and Control of the Self: Thomas Henry Huxley, William James and the Human Automatism Debate in the Late Nineteenth Century* (Lancaster University, 1999). His research interests include: psychology and religion; evolution and ethics in late-nineteenth-century psychology; the relationship between philosophy and psychology; William James; and scientific biography.

John and Elizabeth Newson established the Child Development Research Unit in the Psychology Department of the University of Nottingham in 1957, when they began their longitudinal study of 700 children in Nottingham. They refined the naturalistic methodology of interviewing, and their inclusive sampling gave a voice to a broad spectrum of parents, which highlighted social class as a major factor in child-rearing principles and beliefs. Their core study led to many other studies of special groups, including the upbringing of children with different disabilities, and the attitudes of very young fathers. They both held chairs in Developmental Psychology at Nottingham, continuing to direct the Research Unit until 1994; John extended his research interests to mother–baby interaction, while Elizabeth specialised in clinical method and diagnostic understanding of pervasive developmental disorders. Since retiring as Emeritus Professor, Elizabeth has worked full time in clinical research and practice, and has been awarded an OBE for services to children with autistic spectrum disorder and an Honorary Fellowship of the Royal College of Paediatrics for services to paediatrics. Their many books and other publications include two books for parents, and they have always been concerned to establish a 'language of partnership' between parents and the professionals who serve them.

Graham Richards is Director of the Centre for the History of Psychology at Staffordshire University. He has published numerous books and academic papers, including *Mental Machinery Part One: 1600–1850* (1992); *Putting Psychology in its Place: A Critical Overview* (1996) and *'Race', Racism and Psychology: Towards a Reflexive History* (1997). Professor Richards was Chair of the British Psychological Society History and Philosophy of Psychology Section 1991–1994.

Martin Roiser is a Senior Lecturer in Psychology at Thames Valley University. He completed a doctorate on attitude measurement at the University of Bristol but became critical of those techniques. He went on to study public opinion in terms of social representations and has developed an interest in the public understanding of science and the psychology of shared knowledge. His interests in the history of psychology include: Marxism and psychology, the Mass-Observation movement of the 1930s, and the Authoritarian Personality study. He has published in the journals *History of the Human Sciences*, *Papers on Social Representations* and *The Psychologist*.

Michael Rutter is Professor of Developmental Psychopathology at the Institute of Psychiatry, King's College, London. He is a Fellow of the Royal Society, a Foreign Associate Member of the Institute of Medicine of the US National Academy of Sciences, a founding member of Academia Europaea, a Foreign Honorary Member of the American Academy of Arts and Sciences, and an Honorary Fellow of the British Psychological Society. Throughout his career he has had an interest in spanning developmental and clinical research in psychology and psychiatry. His 38 books span education (*15,000 Hours: Secondary Schools and their Effects on Children*, 1979), developmental psychology (*Developing Minds: Challenges and Continuity Across the Lifespan*, 1993), social policy (*Cycles of Disadvantage: A Review of Research*, 1976), psychosocial risk factors (*Maternal Deprivation Reassessed*, 1972), genetics (*Behavioural Genetics*, 1997) and psychopathology (*Antisocial Behaviour by Young People*, 1998).

Janet Sayers (née Toulson) graduated in experimental psychology from Cambridge, trained as a clinical psychologist at London's Tavistock Clinic, and now teaches gender studies and psychoanalysis in the Sociology Department of the University of Kent at Canterbury, where she also works part time as a psychotherapist both privately and for the National Health Service. Her books include *Mothering Psychoanalysis* (1991), *Freudian Tales* (1997), *Boy Crazy: Remembering Adolescence* (1998) and *Kleinians: Psychoanalysis Inside Out* (2000). She is currently doing research towards a book provisionally called *Unconscious Gods.*

Roger Smith took early retirement from Lancaster University in September 1998 and is now Reader Emeritus in the History of Science. He is the author *of Trial by Medicine: Insanity and Responsibility in Victorian Trials* (1981), *Inhibition: History and Meaning in the Sciences of Mind and Brain* (1992) and *The Fontana History of the Human Sciences* (1997), and a co-editor *of Expert Evidence: Interpreting Science in the Law* (1989). A past President of the European Society for the History of the Human Sciences, he is currently a consultant to the Institute for the History of Science and Technology, Moscow. He is currently coordinating a European Union INTAS project on comparative historical studies, in Britain, The Netherlands and Russia, of science and belief about human nature.

Mathew Thomson is Lecturer in the Department of History at the University of Warwick. In addition to *The Problem of Mental Deficiency: Eugenics, Democracy and Social Policy in Britain, 1870–1959* (1998), he has published a series of articles on the same theme and on the mental hygiene movement. For the last few years he has been researching the popular and cultural impact of psychology in Britain during the first half of the twentieth century. He has recently published essays on psychology during the First and Second World Wars, while essays on the consciousness of modernity, psychology and race, the socialist early psychoanalyst David Eder, and the psychological body in the twentieth century are placed in forthcoming volumes. He regularly reviews new publications on the history of twentieth-century psychology.

Peter Wason was a Liaison Officer in the 8th Independent Armoured Brigade between 1942 and 1945. After the war, he read English literature at Oxford before embarking upon a career in psychology. Having been a member of the scientific staff of the Medical Research Council's Industrial Psychology Research Unit between 1953 and 1965, in 1974 he was appointed Director of the Psycholinguistics Research Unit at University College London. His main research interest has been the psychology of reasoning. He devised the Wason Selection Task in 1960. With Phillip Johnson-Laird he published *Psychology of Reasoning: Structure and Content* in 1972. Dr Wason was appointed Reader Emeritus at University College London in 1983.

David Wilson is a senior lecturer at Cumbria College of Art and Design, where he administers the joint honours degree programme and postgraduate studies in cultural and heritage management. He had spent the earlier part of his career in the museums world, becoming principal curator at Bristol Museums and Art Galleries before his career change and move to Carlisle in 1991. In 1999 he completed his doctoral dissertation on *Encouragements and Constraints in the Development of Experimental Animal Behaviour Studies in Great Britain since the Late Nineteenth Century* (University of Leicester).

Foreword

'To advance scientific psychological research, and to further the co-operation of investigators in the various branches of Psychology.' Such sentiments are no less important today than they were in 1901, when ten people first met at University College London and founded the Psychological Society. The British Psychological Society now has over 30,000 members. They work in many modern institutions: in health and social services, in universities, schools and prisons, and in industry and the media. In addition to traditional areas such as cognitive, educational, and occupational psychology, the British Psychological Society also supports newer interests such as consciousness and experiential psychology, and sports and exercise psychology. From modest beginnings, psychology has become a vast, diverse and influential discipline, and the British Psychological Society has grown accordingly.

Produced to mark the centenary of the British Psychological Society, this collection of essays not only gathers together pre-eminent historians of psychology, but also contains contributions from distinguished senior psychologists. The first major study of the history of psychology in Britain for over 30 years, the book investigates such topics as the prehistory of twentieth-century psychology and the connections between professional and popular psychology. It also examines cross-currents between psychology and war, education and politics. The origins of social psychology, comparative psychology and clinical psychology, and the relationships between psychology and other disciplines, such as psychoanalysis, psychiatry and physiology, are also explored. In a stimulating reversal of the orthodox view of the importance of history, the book demonstrates that the history of psychology is a crucial component of the discipline's self-understanding.

The Society's centenary slogan is 'Bringing Psychology to Society'. This book not only vividly underscores the historical roots of this ambition, but also argues that to undertake the task requires developing a deeper, more factually grounded appreciation of psychology's place in British culture than we currently possess. I am delighted to recommend it to anyone interested in understanding the associations between psychology, its neighbouring disciplines, and society.

Professor Vicki Bruce, OBE
BPS Centenary President

Acknowledgements

Psychology in Britain was produced during Geoff Bunn's tenure as British Psychological Society Research Fellow at the Science Museum, 1998–2001. Thanks are due to Allan Sakne and Stephen White of the British Psychological Society, and to Robert Bud and Tim Boon of the Science Museum, for their far-sighted vision in initiating the process that led to the three-year sponsorship arrangement between the two organisations. The British Psychological Society Centenary Sub-Committee nurtured the book through the early stages of planning and supervised its development thereafter. Joyce Collins of BPS Books and Ela Ginalska of Science Museum Publications both demonstrated exemplary professionalism and skill in bringing the project to fruition. This book would not have taken the form it has without the encouragement of John Groeger and Steve Newstead. We are also grateful to Ingrid Lunt and Vicki Bruce, who made timely interventions at important junctures. Tim Boon was an unflagging source of enthusiasm and support. Finally, we would like to thank all our contributors who have so generously shared their time, energy and expertise during the past three years.

Geoff Bunn
Sandy Lovie
Graham Richards
October 2000

Introduction

Geoffrey C. Bunn

> The adoption of a historical point of view does not appear to the psychologist as something to be borrowed from history but rather as an internal necessity of his field, linked to the fundamental nature of human psychology. (Vernant, 1965/1991: 264)

1   Psychology in Britain, 1901

Psychology was a modest enterprise in Britain in 1901. Laboratories for experimental research had been established in London and Cambridge, and elementary psychophysiology was being taught at Liverpool. A lectureship in comparative psychology had been created at Aberdeen and Oxford had appointed a Reader in Mental Philosophy.[1] An informal psychology discussion group had been formed at University College London. It was here, on 24 October 1901 that the Psychological Society was founded. The aim of the Society, its members quickly decided, was 'to advance scientific psychological research, & to further the co-operation of investigators in the various branches of Psychology'. The ten founders resolved 'that only those who are recognised teachers in some branch of psychology or who have published work of recognisable value be eligible as members' (Lovie, Chapter 4). It is quite possible that the strict eligibility criteria for membership expressed the Society's desire to distance itself from the London Psycho-Therapeutic Society, which had also been founded that year as an ecumenical organisation for those associated with the 'Mental Science' movement.[2]

Although a variety of attempts had been made to institutionalise the subject during the previous quarter of a century, the 'new psychology' nevertheless remained the activity of but a few specialists.[3] Alexander Bain had first broached the idea of bringing out a new philosophical journal in 1874. The principal aim of the new venture, editor George Croom Robertson declared in the first issue of *Mind: A Quarterly Review of Psychology and Philosophy*, was to 'procure a decision of this question as to the scientific standing of psychology'. The first attempts at creating a formal institutional setting for psychology were made by Edward Cox in 1875, who established the Psychological Society of Great Britain (PSGB) to investigate the workings of 'psychic force'. In 1877, James Ward unsuccessfully lobbied the Cambridge University Senate to establish a psychophysical laboratory. Fourteen years later he was given a small grant for apparatus (Hearnshaw, 1964: 171–172).

Shortly after the PSGB's demise in 1879, some of its members formed the Society for Psychical Research to gather information on telepathy, hypnotism, hauntings and hallucinations (Hearnshaw, 1964: 158). A year after publishing his *Inquiries into Human Faculty and Its Development* (Galton, 1883), Francis Galton set up an anthropometric laboratory at the International Health Exhibition in London, which continued at the South Kensington Museum until 1891 (Hearnshaw, 1964: 59). Galton's laboratory provided James McKeen Cattell with a base for applying methods he had learned as a student in Germany to anthropometric testing. Having brought experimental apparatus from Leipzig, Wilhelm Wundt's American research assistant was also able to run an unofficial and short-lived psychological laboratory at Cambridge between 1887 and 1888 (Sokal, 1972).[4]

In 1897, W.H.R. Rivers established a psychological laboratory at Cambridge in a room donated by the Physiology Department (Slobodin, 1978/1997: 16). That same year, Henry Wilde, a successful electrical engineer, offered the capital to Oxford University to endow a Readership in Mental Philosophy. The holder was obliged to lecture 'on the illusions and delusions which are incident to the human mind' and 'on the psychology of the lower races of mankind, as illustrated by the various fetish objects in the Anthropological Museum of the University' (Oldfield, 1950: 346). George Stout, whose *Manual of Psychology* was to became the standard text book for generations of students (Stout, 1898), was appointed to the position. With assistance from Galton, James Sully opened an experimental psychology laboratory in early 1898 at University College London. Appointed to undertake the teaching of students, Rivers managed to obtain experimental apparatus from Hugo Münsterberg's laboratory in Freiburg (Valentine, 1999).[5] A Department of Experimental Psychology had also been set up in 1901 in connection with the Pathological Laboratory of the London County Council Asylum at Claybury.[6]

As the British Psychological Society's first historian, Beatrice Edgell, later recalled, the most outstanding feature of British psychology at the turn of the century 'was the development of experimental and of quantitative methods.' Edgell had herself pioneered experimental psychology at Bedford College, London, on her return from Würzburg in 1901 (Valentine, 1997, forthcoming). 'In Germany and in America psychology was already established as an independent science with laboratory courses. This country was awakening to the importance of this new development' (Edgell, 1947: 113). One indication of the enthusiasm was the creation, in 1904, of the *British Journal of Psychology*. James Ward and the ubiquitous Rivers were the founding editors.

Membership of the British Psychological Society increased steadily until the First World War. On his return from serving in the Royal Army Medical Corps in November 1918, Charles Myers, the editor of the *British Journal of Psychology*, initiated changes that would have revolutionary consequences for British psychology. Myers proposed that the British Psychological Society should support sections for specialised aspects of applied psychology. He noted that medical, industrial and educational psychology groups were already moving to establish separate organisations. In 1918, when the Society had almost 100 members, recognised scholars or teachers were still the only people eligible to join. But following the acceptance of Myers' proposal that anyone merely 'interested in psychology' should be allowed to join, by the end of 1920 the Society's membership had increased to over 600. Myers was duly elected the Society's first President.

Myers' career spanned the period during which British psychology emerged as a recognised speciality. The trajectory of his career was, to a considerable extent, indicative of some of the changes that British psychology experienced during the first half of the twentieth century. With ecumenical interests that reflected the variegated character of the new discipline, he had a comprehensive knowledge of his subject that would be impossible to acquire today. An enthusiastic advocate of experimental psychology, he also wrote on the philosophy of mind. He was particularly fascinated by the psychology of hearing and music, an enterprise that was no doubt assisted by his musical expertise. The research for his first scientific paper – 'An account of some skulls discovered at Brandon, Suffolk' – was undertaken before he had taken his Cambridge BA degree. One of his last publications, some 50 years later, was his 1946 report *Attitudes to Minority Groups* (for a bibliography, see Bartlett, 1945–1948: 774–777). 'He passed on to us his own deep and wide love of human studies,' his student and protégé Frederic Bartlett recalled, 'and a complete freedom from that dogmatic theorizing which has been the bane of psychology. He taught us how to treat psychology as a biological science without forgetting the wide human world beyond the laboratory' (Bartlett, 1945–1948: 774).

In terms of 'his *flair* for organization', as Bartlett (1945–1948: 769) put it, Charles Myers was certainly the most important British psychologist of the first half of the twentieth century: 'He built a laboratory, a society, an institute' (Bartlett, 1965: 9). Myers was one of three psychologists on the famous 1898 anthropological expedition to the Torres Strait (Herle and Rouse, 1998; see also Richards, 1997: 41–64); he settled in Cambridge in 1902 after further foreign research. He proceeded to advance the cause of experimental psychology by establishing a laboratory at King's College, London, writing a series of textbooks (Myers, 1909, 1911, 1914) and lobbying for the replacement of the 'damp, dark, and ill-ventilated cottage' that then served as the Cambridge laboratory (Myers, 1936: 221). Funded largely from his own considerable wealth, the new laboratory opened in 1912 (on Myers and the 'Cambridge school' see Crampton, 1978). An advisor to the *British Journal of Psychology* since its inception in 1904, Myers became its sole editor in 1914, the year in which it was acquired by the British Psychological Society. In 1915, he was given a commission in the Royal Army Medical Corps to supervise the treatment of functional nervous and mental disorders occurring in the British Expeditionary Force. Although he later came to regret it, it was Myers who coined the term 'shell shock'.[7]

Myers' most important contribution to the establishment of psychology in Britain was undoubtedly the National Institute of Industrial Psychology (NIIP), which he co-founded in 1921 with Henry Welch, a director of a company of East India merchants. The Institute's mission was to promote 'the application of psychology and physiology in industry and commerce' (Anonymous, 1926a: 14). During the interwar period, when university psychology departments and jobs in educational and clinical psychology were rare, the NIIP was the chief source of employment for psychologists in Britain. 'Its service to British psychology was of incalculable importance,' wrote L.S. Hearnshaw, 'without which the expansion of psychology in the Second World War and after would have been virtually impossible' (Hearnshaw, 1964: 277). Welch and Myers recognised how important the NIIP was to become. 'We may envisage a future,' they predicted in 1932, 'when every large factory, store and office, and every university, will have an industrial psychologist immediately or indirectly attached to it' (Welch and Myers, 1932: 138).

That future has now arrived – and in a manner that even the prescient Myers could not have envisaged. Industry is not the only beneficiary of psychological expertise. Psychologists now work in every type of institution of modern life, from hospitals, schools and prisons, to the armed forces and government departments, to advertising agencies, the media and multinational corporations. Psychologists advise the police and act as consultants to the legal profession. Entirely new fields have emerged in recent years, such as environmental psychology, community psychology and traffic psychology. In addition to the traditional areas of cognitive, educational and occupational psychology, the British Psychological Society supports the activities of consciousness and experiential psychology, lesbian and gay psychology, and sports and exercise psychology, among many others.[8] As British psychology's first historian, Leslie Hearnshaw, quaintly put it nearly 40 years ago: 'In more ways than one psychologists today are in the public eye. Their work is frequently referred to in the press, on the air, even in Parliament, and it excites a variety of reactions and prejudices. Psychologists are no longer rare specimens in the community' (Hearnshaw, 1964: v).

According to Nikolas Rose, whose influential *The Psychological Complex* (1985) shifted the parameters of scholarship in the history of psychology, the rise of the psychological is a characteristic feature of modern existence:

> Psychological experts, psychological vocabularies, psychological evaluations, and psychological techniques have made themselves indispensable in the workplace and the marketplace, in the electoral process and the business of politics, in family

life and sexuality, in pedagogy and child rearing, in the apparatus of law and punishment and in the medico-welfare complex. (Rose, 1992: 351)

From sexual attraction to the waging of war; from the shop floor to the shopping mall; from neurones to neurosis; from the cradle to the grave: there is indeed hardly an area of human subjectivity that has yet to come under psychology's critical gaze.

2   The history of psychology

Although Hearnshaw and Rose both agree that psychology has become a significant feature of contemporary British society, their theoretical approaches to its history are very different. This section reviews these historiographic differences by discussing some of the changes that have occurred in the history of psychology in the last 30 years or so (the best introduction to the field is Smith, 1997b, which includes an extensive bibliographic essay). The history of psychology has always had a special relationship with its parent discipline and there is every reason to believe that this will continue to be the case.

It may come as a surprise to those unacquainted with the field to learn that the history of psychology is almost as old as the discipline itself. By 1914 a variety of historical texts had already been written.[9] In the struggle to establish psychology as a scientific discipline independent of philosophy, the first generation of writers were faced with the difficult task of demonstrating that psychology had an ancient and respectable lineage as well as a more recent experimental origin. Psychology was thus presented both as being a worthy heir to Scottish common sense or Baconian philosophy and as having an independent scientific status. According to Mitchell Ash (1983), the first histories of psychology helped to establish the discipline in its academic context. The history of psychology was, in effect, an 'agent of socialisation' for the first generation of psychologists.[10]

Mainly written by psychologists for psychologists, the enterprise was fuelled by what Ash called the requirements of pedagogical self-presentation. Edwin Boring's famous text *A History of Experimental Psychology* (Boring, 1929/1957), for example, attempted to align experimental psychology with sensory physiology while dismissing the importance of applied psychology. Boring sought to demonstrate that experimental psychology had freed itself from metaphysical allegiances and was now a model of linear continuity and cumulative scientific progress. In accordance with their underlying positivist philosophy, many older texts assumed that human nature was universal and that science progressed according to a linear teleology of discovery. The existence of competing 'schools' of psychology was thus a source of great anxiety for Boring as it was for later textbook writers: if human nature had a natural and thus universal basis, then why was psychology divided into apparently irreconcilable approaches? In order to answer this question, some authors argued for the existence of a unity underlying the competing schools. Others considered the discipline as yet too immature to demonstrate conceptual coherence (see, for example, Murphy, 1929; Woodworth, 1931; Heidbreder, 1933).

Such themes were evident in the first British contribution to the history of psychology, J.C. Flügel's *A Hundred Years of Psychology, 1833–1933* (Flügel, 1933). According to Flügel, although psychology had made great progress over 100 years, it remained ineffective and inadequate on account of being divided into numerous competing schools. Only when the detailed discoveries of the various approaches had been 'linked up in some more comprehensive system' could 'further systematic advance on a united front' occur. 'In this way there may come into being one "psychology" with many methods,' Flügel hoped, 'in place of the several "psychologies" that exist to-day' (Flügel, 1933: 361). Although psychology had 'made for itself a place, though still a humble one, in the hierarchy of sciences', its lack of unity was not merely a cause for concern for the discipline alone:

> Intolerance, fear, hatred, cruelty, misunderstanding, the results of which have so disfigured human history in the past, are likely to have even more terrible consequences in the future, now that science has put extremely dangerous weapons in man's hands, without at the same time teaching him how best to use them. Only psychology can perform this latter task. If it is true, as the old adage says, that *tout comprendre, c'est tout pardonner*, then we may reasonably hope that an increased general understanding of the workings of the human mind will really produce some increased measure of human kindness, toleration and co-operation, which may prevent that collapse of civilization with which, according to many authorities, we are genuinely threatened. (Flügel, 1933: 358)

As the threat of fascism in Europe became apparent during the 1930s, the belief that a suitably unified psychology could contribute to human welfare became an increasingly widely held sentiment.

'What the future holds we cannot tell,' Hearnshaw counselled in the conclusion to his *The Shaping of Modern Psychology*, 'but what we can affirm is that psychology has not only become of central importance in the intellectual cosmos, but also, in the rapidly changing and turbulent circumstances of the contemporary world, of great practical relevance' (Hearnshaw, 1987: 304). Like Flügel before him, Hearnshaw was worried that psychology had yet to achieve conceptual unification: 'Cognitive processes, innate structures, imagery, consciousness, competencies and dispositions have been restored to respectability. But unification is still but a dream. To dream, however, is not an unscientific activity, unless dreams are mistaken for contemporary reality' (Hearnshaw, 1987: 298). What was needed was a 'metapsychology', a synoptic overview to discipline vagaries and reconcile differences of approach. Drawing upon Stern's personalistic psychology, Hearnshaw argued that only the 'complex unity' of the person, conceived as a 'psycho-somatico-ideological unit', could furnish psychology with the unification it apparently required (Hearnshaw, 1987: 300).

The history of psychology, as originally conceived by such pioneers, thus served its parent discipline in a variety of ways. It attempted the difficult task of squaring psychology's long philosophical past with its short experimental history. Demonstrating the fact that psychology had degenerated into numerous competing schools, it attempted to reconcile differences by pointing to underlying unities. In short, historians of psychology wished to reassure psychologists that their discipline was scientific and progressive, had practical consequences for everyday life, and rightly adhered to a universalistic conception of human nature.

3   'An historiographic revolution'

In recent years, however, it has become evident to a new generation of scholars that many of the assumptions that launched their discipline are problematic. Beginning in the 1960s, the history of science began to experience 'an historiographic revolution', according to Thomas Kuhn, one of its chief architects (Kuhn, 1964: 3). Writing in the first volume of the *Journal of the History of the Behavioral Sciences*, the editor, George Stocking Jr, welcomed this development and predicted the demise of the anachronistic 'search for "firsts" and "founders" – for the agents of cumulative forward progression' (Stocking, 1965: 214). Kuhn's analytic categories of 'normal science', 'paradigm' and 'revolutionary science' would provide historians of psychology with alternative roles to that of 'chroniclers of incremental progress', as Stocking put it. Energised by this revised philosophy of science, the history of psychology began to emerge as a distinct scholarly discipline. The Archives of the History of American Psychology were established at the University of Akron, Ohio, in 1965. The following year saw the creation of the American Psychological Association's Division 26, History of Psychology. The first meeting of Cheiron: The International Society for the History of the Behavioral and Social Sciences took place in 1969. By 1970, three-quarters of the colleges and universities in the United States offered at least one course in 'History and Systems' of psychology (Ash, 1983: 161). The European Society for the History of the Human Sciences originated at a meeting held in Amsterdam in 1982.

Yet in comparison with activity in the history of science, the quality of research in the history of the behavioural sciences in the 1960s was extremely variable, as Robert Young (1966) pointed out in an extensive contemporary review of the field. Endorsing the 'new historiography' of Kuhn and others, Young (1966: 15–16) argued that having 'passed through the useful but limited stage of amateurism,' the time had come 'to insist upon rigorous standards of scholarship.' The history of psychology had, until that point, been written primarily by psychologists and because the field was reliant on the textbook as the primary mode of publication it suffered from 'a sad absence of the intimate acquaintance with the primary sources' (1966: 18). One of the chief problems of didactic, expository history was that it avoided asking provocative questions. But by joining forces with the history of science, the history of psychology could itself experience a paradigmatic change of scholarly standards. Young suggested that research should concentrate on detailed studies of individuals and concepts in their historical contexts. All general surveys should be abandoned, he argued, and the 'presentist' tone abolished.

4   Centenary legacies, 1979

The first issue of the *Journal of the History of the Behavioral Sciences* also contained a reflection by E.G. Boring 'On the subjectivity of important historical dates: Leipzig 1879' (Boring, 1965). Young read it with dismay, considering it 'symptomatic of three limitations from which the history of psychology has suffered: great men (whom to worship?), great insights, and great dates' (Young, 1966: 36). Nevertheless, the centenary of the founding of the world's first psychological laboratory became a cause for celebration. The American Psychological Association designated 1979 psychology's 'centennial year' and the International Congress of Psychology was held in Leipzig to mark the occasion. Yet in spite of the celebratory impetus, a number of historians had already begun to criticise the traditional image of psychology's 'founding father'. Reflecting on this period, the Canadian historian of psychology Kurt Danziger recalled that, having acquainted himself with the original literature, it became clear that there was a discrepancy between the primary and secondary sources: 'My experience at that point was a bit like a subject in an Asch conformity experiment because what I was reading didn't seem to jibe with what I had previously read in secondary sources like Boring and some others' (Brock, 1995: 14).

The subsequent reappraisal of Wundt was one of the first achievements of the new critical scholarship and 'the beginning of an important shift in psychology's view of its history' (Ash, 1983: 171). Arthur Blumenthal (1975) listed a number of false characterisations of Wundt, such as his reputation as a dualist and elementaristic introspectionist. Ash (1980) demonstrated that, contrary to the received view, Wundt was, in fact, strongly opposed to the separation of psychology from philosophy. Adrian Brock (1992) revealed that the spurious association between Wundt's *Völkerpsychologie* and fascist racial typologies could be traced back to American personality psychologist Gordon Allport. Danziger (1979) argued that not only had a severely caricatured account of Wundt's work been uncritically accepted in history of psychology texts, but also that the distortion had originated with one of Wundt's most influential students, Edward Bradford Titchener, the 'Englishman who represented the German psychological tradition in America' (Boring, 1929/1957: 410). Wundt had imposed strict limitations on the use of the experimental method, arguing that only basic psychophysiological processes were amenable to laboratory investigation. His American students, however, disregarded these methodological proscriptions in an attempt to institutionalise psychology in the utilitarian context of the American university system. *Völkerpsychologie*, Wundt's historical, ethnographic and comparative analysis of language, myth and custom, did not find favour in the United States, where an antimetaphysical positivism was in the ascendant (Danziger, 1979, 1990: ch. 3). Summarising these developments, Brock (1993) showed that Wundt's reputation as psychology's 'founder' was a useful – if mythical – resource for generations of polemical textbook writers (see also Brock, 1998).

5   The psychological complex

In subsequent years, historical scholarship informed by social constructivism and other post-positivist philosophies of science further extended understanding of the interrelationships between investigative practice, social and political contexts, and psychological knowledge.[11] But, perhaps inevitably, during the 1980s it became less clear what the history of psychology actually was and what its relationship was to psychology on the one hand and to the history of science on the other.

The formation of the British Psychological Society's History and Philosophy of Psychology Section in 1984 inspired Graham Richards (1987) to ask 'Of what is history of Psychology a history?' Although the history of psychology had certainly benefited from employing concepts developed in the history of science, Richards argued that some important issues were not being confronted precisely because of that reliance. Although historians of science could arguably avoid confronting a particular scientist's biographical characteristics, for example, this could not be sustained in the history of psychology. Was William James' famous account of habit to be interpreted as reflecting his disciplinary position within American psychology or as an expression of his own personal psychological characteristics? Was his work representative of late-nineteenth-century American psychology or the late-nineteenth-century American psyche? In other words, the appropriate level of analysis was a matter for historical scrutiny and could not be settled in advance of analysis.

In his *The Psychological Complex*, Nikolas Rose offered a critique of the distinction between 'the social conditions within which psychology emerged and functioned' and the domain 'external to that of its concepts and theories' (Rose, 1985: 7). Instead of assuming that the normal individual mind was a transhistorical object waiting to be discovered by experimental psychology, Rose argued that modern psychology was itself made possible by the emergence, in the late nineteenth century, of an assemblage of administrative requirements and techniques of statistical analysis and measurement:

> Psychology's role as an administrative technology cannot be understood as the application of a psychological knowledge of normality, gained through theoretical reflection or laboratory investigation, to a domain of practical problems. On the contrary, it was through attempts to diagnose, conceptualise and regulate pathologies of conduct that psychological knowledge and expertise first began to establish its claims for scientific credibility, professional status and social importance. (Rose, 1985: 226)

Turning the distinction between 'pure' and 'applied' psychology on its head, Rose argued that techniques devised to regulate pathological conduct in the late nineteenth century were central to the emergence of psychology in the twentieth century. Individual psychology was made possible by the combination of judgements concerning social abnormality with the theory of normal distribution. The resultant of this amalgamation – the intelligence test – was an attempt to meet the pragmatic needs of schools, prisons and factories. As late as 1940, many more psychologists worked in education, industry and medicine than were employed in university positions. Indeed, when the Second World War broke out, there were only six chairs of psychology in the entire British university system (Hearnshaw, 1964: 208).

Rose's analysis helped to explain why psychology quickly became such a deeply fragmented enterprise: psychological knowledge is the product of a complex amalgamation of heterogeneous 'practices, techniques, institutions and agencies'. Although such a conclusion is profoundly unsettling to a positivist psychology that assumes the existence of a unified subject matter – the transcendental self – it nevertheless helps to explain why the history of psychology was initially employed to seek synthetic harmony on behalf of its parent discipline. 'The objects of scientific discourses are historical and not ontological,' Rose concluded, critical of earlier strategic attempts to employ history to placate disciplinary anxieties; 'history itself cannot provide any tranquil and unifying antidote to the fractious condition of contemporary psychology' (Rose, 1985: 223).

The lack of a transhistorical subject matter formed the basis for Roger Smith's call to abandon one approach to the history of psychology altogether. Writing in the first volume of the *History of the Human Sciences*, Smith concluded that it no longer seemed possible 'to conceptualize a continuous and unitary subject to set the tasks of such a history' (Smith, 1988: 162). To attempt the history of psychology prior to the middle of the nineteenth century would be anachronistic because it would be ignoring the very conditions of possibility that enabled psychology to come into being in the first place (Smith, 1988: 156). Thus it seemed as if historians of psychology had to face the possibility of either not studying the period before about 1850 or undertaking studies of psychology only 'in clearly circumscribed local circumstances'.

If psychology was not a transhistorical enterprise, and if its subject matter did not posses transhistorical unity, then what could historical work involve? Smith's solution to the problem of striking a balance between 'finding psychology everywhere and finding it nowhere' was provocative. Echoing Robert Young's criticism of textbook histories of psychology, Smith called for a history 'in which representation of "the psychological" is bound up with distinctive, local characteristics of time and place, not with the authority of modern "psychology" communities' (Smith, 1988: 165). Contemporary psychological categories, in other words, could not be assumed in advance to have an eternal transhistorical existence; in philosophical parlance they were not 'natural kinds'. Such a form of history would thus necessarily involve a reflection upon the status of those psychological objects – such as self, emotion, intelligence and personality – that have usually been regarded as having a naturalistic ontology (see also Danziger, 1993, 1997a,b). The psychological maps of the present may not be particularly useful guides with which to explore the psychological terrain of the past.

'If one views psychological objects as inherently historically constructed, within certain divisions made possible by an adjacent field of discourse,' Lisa Blackman concurred, 'the question for critical psychologists is to describe the divisions and their conditions of possibility, and not the description of an ontological object and its gradual evolvement from obscurity to truth' (Blackman, 1994: 502). Influenced by Michel Foucault's 'archaeology of knowledge',[12] Blackman argued that historians might profitably investigate how psychological objects are brought into being through assemblages of knowledge, power and practice. Such an approach eschews teleological, social interests and sociocultural accounts of historical change in favour of one based on *discourse*:

> Discourses are not discrete entities which function for certain interests. They are made up of shifting networks of associations, bodies of knowledge, expertise, agencies and problems. Discourses do not merely legitimate and perpetuate 'reality', but actually constitute new ways of thinking and acting, where power is productive, inciting and inducing desire and a subjective commitment to certain 'ways of making sense'. (Blackman, 1994: 496)

Because the notion of discourse has enabled historians and psychologists to investigate the ways in which psychological objects have been constituted historically, it has also greatly expanded the sorts of problems they can address.[13] It has further challenged many of the traditional ways of undertaking the history of psychology.

6   The reflexive science

Diametrically opposed to a form of history that considers psychological categories to be unproblematic entities that may be uncritically imposed on the past,[14] the discursive approach regards the psychological not as a resource to be utilised, but rather as a problem to be explained. As the historian Jean-Pierre Vernant eloquently explained nearly 40 years ago:

> In the past, the psychological has been a principle of historical explanation. To interpret institutions, works, and the interrelations of human acts, the historian has gladly turned to a psychology of man, considered as a constant, evident, and universal given. For the historian of today, the psychological no longer constitutes a principle of intelligibility, a self-evident norm to be imposed. Rather it has become one aspect among others of historical material, one of the dimensions of the subject, a problem that needs to be accounted for in the same way as all the rest of the data. (Vernant, 1965/1991: 262)

Assisted by the 'linguistic turn' in critical studies, the rejection of the assumption of 'a traditional conception of an immutable human nature' (Vernant, 1965/1991: 262) has energised the history of psychology by vastly enlarging the sorts of problems it can engage in. Fruitful work has been undertaken on the metaphorical basis of psychological knowledge (G. Richards, 1989; Leary, 1990) and on the historical dimensions of psychological discourse (Graumann and Gergen, 1996). Danziger (1997b) has traced the historical emergence of common psychological terms like intelligence, behaviour and attitude. Smith (1992) has demonstrated that because a category like inhibition can simultaneously express both scientific and moral meanings, it can mediate between scientific and non-scientific communities.

In one of the boldest formulations of these new possibilities, Rose (1992) has suggested that psychology has made itself indispensable to the liberal democratic capitalist societies of the West (see also Miller and Rose, 1988, 1994). This it has done, Rose argues, by inventing and endorsing practical techniques that foster privacy, rationality and autonomy. Although analytical tools such as ideology, social control and social interests have certainly proved their utility to the revised historiography of psychology, these very categories have themselves begged many questions. As Rose argued, psychology does not oppress its subjects by exercising 'social control'. On the contrary,

> the ethical technologies in which psychology participates, and within which psycho-logical expertise is so deeply enmeshed, provide a means for shaping, sustaining, and managing human beings not in opposition to their personal identity but pre-cisely in order to produce such an identity: a necessary reciprocal element in the political valorization of freedom. (Rose, 1992: 366; see also Rose, 1996a)

The modern soul is thus governed through freedom (Rose, 1989). Conceptualising psychology as a productive rather than a repressive enterprise, this approach is particularly interested in the consequences of psychological theory and practice for human subjectivity. Certain areas of psychological activity, such as the psycho-therapies and educational and occupational psychology, axiomatically assume that their mission is to effect change: the depressed are to be restored to happiness; the unruly are to be disciplined; the fatigued are to be made efficient. Some scholars have become fascinated by the processes by which individuals, groups and populations are changed in such ways, or even brought into being, as a result of becoming the subjects of psychological scrutiny.

The philosopher of science Ian Hacking has called this process 'making up people' (Hacking, 1986). Because it involves both the creation of a psychological category as well as that category's assimilation by the subject of the inscription, Hacking calls this process 'dynamic nominalism'. Calling a spade a spade is one thing, but diagnosing someone as a 'sexoesthetic invert' (Foucault, 1978/1990: 43) is quite another:

> The claim of dynamic nominalism is not that there was a kind of person who came increasingly to be recognized by bureaucrats or by students of human nature but rather that a kind of person came into being at the same time as the kind itself was being invented. In some cases, that is, our classifications and our classes conspire to emerge hand in hand, each egging the other on. (Hacking, 1986: 228)

Hacking is particularly interested in 'human kinds' such as people diagnosed with multiple personality disorder and fugue (Hacking, 1995, 1998), although many psychological terms could, in principle, operate according to these 'looping effects' (Hacking, 1994; Danziger, 1997b). Similarly, Graham Richards (1989, 1992a) has argued that psychological language is a reflexive derivative of language used to describe the world. According to this formulation, psychology is merely the latest expression of a process of assimilation 'by which our changing knowledge of the world is mediated into changed conceptions of ourselves' (G. Richards, 1989: 102).

The problem of reflexivity is central to Roger Smith's discussion of the problem of 'the big picture' in the history of psychology (Smith, 1998; see also Smith, 1997a). How, Smith wondered, might it be possible to attempt to write a general and synthetic history of psychology when the new historiography has rejected it in favour of analytic studies of particular historical episodes? He concludes that only by broadening the definition of psychology to encompass all of the 'human sciences' might it be possible to attempt a general overview. In effect, Smith is arguing that the history of psychology should be a part of the history of reflexivity, the history of the interplay between science and the self-fashioning of human nature. Thus 'the history of ways of life is an essential part of the history of the human sciences' (Smith, 1998: 4).

Smith's argument explains why it is that despite repeated attempts to ensure 'the methodological rigour of observation', psychology has remained a protean enterprise composed of many competing approaches. In short, psychology is an instantiation of the many forms of life that human beings have adopted in certain societies. 'The history of the human sciences is not so much about uncovering the truths of human nature,' he suggests, 'as about adventures of human expression of such power that they have acquired the status of truths' (Smith, 1997b: 14). The historian's task is thus to trace these 'adventures of human expression' and to explore their effects.[15] Smith's more provocative point, however, is that insofar as the history of the human sciences is a history of these expressions or forms of life, then the history of the human sciences thus becomes a part of the scientific enterprise. Following Jean-Pierre Vernant, Smith concludes that because the history of the human sciences is knowledge of what human beings are, then that history becomes a contribution to the human sciences themselves (Smith, 1998: 9). The historian is a psychologist whose experimental domain is the laboratory of the past.

If psychology's subject matter is historical, then historical studies can contribute to the development of the discipline. This argument is also at the heart of Danziger's call for historians of psychology to resist attempts to distance themselves from their parent discipline and instead explore 'the historicity of human functions' (Danziger, 1994: 479). 'The increasingly polycentric structure of the field, the growing awareness of agonistic relationships within it, and the resulting loss of moral cohesion,' he argues, 'create a more complex situation than the one allowed for by the stark opposition between scientific and historical sensibilities'

(Danziger, 1994: 479). Danziger suggests that a critical historiography could affect psychology's conceptions of its subject matter, the understanding of its practices and the nature of its social contribution. Again, the issue of reflexivity is at the heart of the analysis:

> Human beings, as has often been noted, are self-defining. What we are is expressed in the categories of psychological discourse, so that, as we change, the categories we use to describe ourselves to ourselves also change. This means that two fields of study, the history of psychological functions and the history of conceptions about those functions, have considerable relevance for each other. (Danziger, 1994: 479)

Reflexivity implies that psychological functioning as experienced and exhibited by humans is affected by changes in conceptions about those functions. Because categories of self-description 'are historically constituted and culturally variable', the self and its contents are therefore historical rather than natural objects (Danziger, 1997a: 157).

According to the phrenologists, 'Self-Esteem' was one of the 'affective sentiments', 'common to man and some animals' (A Member of the Phrenological and Philosophical Societies of Glasgow, 1838: 111; for the history of phrenology, see Cooter, 1984). Although the category of 'Self-Esteem' has experienced a revival in recent years, the discursive conditions that led to its current popularity are clearly quite different from those that produced 'Organ No. 10' and its associates in the nineteenth century. A society which organises a 'Task Force on Self-Esteem and Social and Personal Responsibility' and employs 'Self-esteem and Personal Safety Co-ordinators' is a very different one to that which explained character in terms of some 30-odd mental faculties located on the surface of the skull.[16] Investigated by fashion magazine questionnaires and explored in television talk shows, self-esteem appears to be one of the most insubstantial of all contemporary psychological discourses. Yet, as Barbara Cruikshank has argued, the category carries a burden of immense responsibility:

> Self-esteem is but one in a long line of technologies of citizenship.... The constitution of the citizen-subject requires technologies of subjectivity, technologies aimed at producing happy, active and participatory democratic citizens. These technologies rarely emerge from the [United States] Congress; more often, they emerge from the social sciences, pressure groups, social work discourses, therapeutic social service programs, and so on. Their common goal, nevertheless, is to get the citizen to act as his or her own master. (Cruikshank, 1993: 340)

Cruikshank's demonstration of how to connect the microhistory of psychological categories to the macrohistory of liberal democratic society points to the kinds of enquiry the historian-psychologist might undertake (for an introduction to governmentality, 'the conduct of conduct', see Burchell *et al.*, 1991).

In contrast to earlier approaches to the history of psychology, which attempted to find a 'tranquil and unifying antidote' to the discipline's lack of conceptual coherence, the new historiography endorses and attempts to contribute to psychology's protean character. Following the linguistic turn, the acceptance of post-positivist philosophies of science, feminist challenges and the emergence of a range of investigative strategies that do not axiomatically assume the universality of psychological truth – such as cultural psychology (see Cole, 1996) or discursive psychology (see Potter and Wetherall, 1987; Harré and Gillett, 1994; Edwards, 1997) – the history of psychology is now, at the start of the twenty-first century, set to make an important contribution to the discipline itself. It need not be claimed that the history of psychology is 'marginal to the mainstream'; after all, it has become increasingly difficult to know what 'the mainstream' is. Rather, the history of psychology has the potential to exist at the centre of psychology, addressing many of the same issues as contemporary psychology. Whereas historians of the natural sciences may seek independence from their parent disciplines (Forman, 1991), the history of psychology is, by contrast, a legitimate part of psychology.

It is widely accepted that it is no longer possible to write encyclopaedic 'grand narratives' of the history of psychology. This volume, published to mark the centenary of the British Psychological Society in 2001, is therefore emphatically not an attempt to write the definitive account of the history of British psychology. Rather, what follows are detailed studies of particular episodes in the history of psychology in Britain. The ambition was to bring together, in a single collection, some of the best historical scholarship currently being undertaken in the field today.

7   Psychology in Britain: historical essays

The brief to contributors to Part I: Historical essays, was to produce a chapter which, even if focusing on a relatively narrow topic or episode, nevertheless bore upon more general issues that linked psychology to the wider society. All those involved were eager that the volume's intended readership should extend beyond the community of historians of psychology. It was the intention, indeed, to offer something which psychologists might find not only interesting but also helpful and challenging. Another intended readership is the wider community of historians concerned with twentieth-century British social and cultural history. The work showcased in this volume will doubtless inspire further historical studies. For those who have long been striving to raise the profile of the history of psychology, the centenary of the British Psychological Society presents a timely opportunity to demonstrate that the topic has important things to say about issues of contemporary relevance.

In Chapter 1, 'Edward Cox, the Psychological Society of Great Britain (1875–1879) and the meaning of an institutional failure', Graham Richards discusses what might be called the prehistory of British psychology. Richards argues that the story of the rise and fall of the Psychological Society of Great Britain is instructive of the nature, definition and social location of psychology in late-Victorian

Britain. No institutional support existed for psychology in the early 1870s, although a variety of people were writing on the subject. Somewhat autonomous and unconnected with universities, these were either men of independent means, writers or medical professionals. Edward Cox, lawyer, publisher, occasional politician and author of psychology texts, had a lifelong interest in phrenology, hypnosis and spiritualism. He first suggested forming a psychological society in 1871.

The Society's membership was somewhat detached from the evolutionary thinking which informed the psychological theorising of the metropolitan intellectual elite. The Society thus appeared to suffer from both social and intellectual exclusion and it was finally abandoned in 1879, shortly after Cox's death. Richards concludes that his account of the Society illuminates 'the peculiarly transitional nature of psychological thinking in the 1870s'. Psychology could not yet assume a disciplinary form at this time because of the social distance between its amateurs and elites, coupled with an intellectual confusion about the definition of what psychology actually was.

As Francis Neary shows in Chapter 2, the nature and definition of psychology were critical questions for those behind the establishment of *Mind* in the mid-1870s. In 'A question of "peculiar importance": George Croom Robertson, *Mind* and the changing relationship between British psychology and philosophy', Neary demonstrates that the early history of the journal can be seen as a microcosm of the relationship between British philosophy and psychology. In contrast with previous accounts that depict *Mind* as the first stage towards the professionalisation of British psychology, Neary argues that the journal's eclectic character reflects local contingencies, and not large-scale forces. Its editor, George Croom Robertson, declared in the first issue of *Mind* that the principal aim of the new publication was to 'procure a decision of this question as to the scientific standing of psychology'. Because one of the principal ambitions was to discover upon what foundations a scientific psychology would rest, the journal's pages necessarily included a great deal of philosophical discussion.

The discussions surrounding the definition of psychology were reflected in the social networks the editors of *Mind* built around themselves. Both amateurs and professionals contributed to the enterprise, although the meaning of the distinction was itself a matter for debate. The journal was a collaborative enterprise of an elite group of philosophers, physiologists and intellectuals and its form and content were actively negotiated from the outset. The contents of early issues of *Mind* show how well Croom Robertson acted on his demand for a breadth of philosophical positions. Neary argues that not only is Croom Robertson's academic work important in its own right but that it provides a record of the relationship between British philosophy and psychology towards the end of the nineteenth century. On Croom Robertson's death in 1892, James Sully took over his post at University College London, where he later succeeded in establishing an experimental psychological laboratory. The announcement that appeared in the journal Croom Robertson had done so much to create expressed the hope 'that the name of George Croom Robertson may in some way be connected with the laboratory'. It would have indeed been an ambiguous epitaph for a man who insisted that the scientific status of psychology should always remain a matter for philosophical discussion.

Whether inclusive or exclusive of historical actors, social networks can exert powerful effects on scientific knowledge. In Chapter 3, 'James Sully and scientific psychology, 1870–1910', Lyubov Gurjeva argues that Sully's social position shaped his approach to psychology. During the 1870s, Sully gained an entree to London's intellectual and scientific elite through journalism. Although he had travelled to Germany to work with Dubois-Reymond and collaborated on *Mind* with Croom Robertson, he found it difficult to gain an academic position until 1892, by which time he was nearly 50 years old. But Sully turned his marginal status to his advantage. Not only did many of his academic texts originate with ideas and arguments first made in periodicals like the *Cornhill Magazine* and the *Westminster Review*, but, because they constituted his primary audience, he was able to ask parents and teachers to assist in studying the development of children's minds. In the course of his work, however, he was obliged to make methodological concessions to the conventions of upper-class domestic life.

Gurjeva uses Sully's career as a case study of the professionalisation of psychology in relation to popular cultures of psychological observation. She argues that although Sully is now largely remembered for being the founder of the Psychological Laboratory at University College London and leader of the British Child Study movement, both reputations are historically problematic. Sully's view of the institution of the psychological laboratory, for example, acquires a new meaning given his pedagogic ambitions. Gurjeva demonstrates that mediators like Sully play important roles in the processes of defining and professionalising psychology. Although the boundaries between academia, science, journalism and teaching might have appeared insuperable to Sully, in fact they became fruitful opportunities for knowledge production.

It was Sully who invited a group of interested persons to University College London in 1901 to form the Psychological Society. In 'Three steps to heaven: how the British Psychological Society attained its place in the sun' (Chapter 4), Sandy Lovie discusses some of the struggles that animated the Society during the first half of the twentieth century. When the Psychological Society was initially established, only teachers of psychology or those who had 'published work of recognisable value' were eligible to join. Because of these exclusive criteria for membership, the Society grew slowly and had barely 100 members by 1918. But when Charles Myers initiated changes in the aftermath of the First World War, membership of the Society rapidly increased to over 600 (see also Lovie, 1998).

A tension persisted during the ensuing years between the wish for an exclusive Society devoted to the progress of a scientific psychology, on the one hand, and the equally potent demand, on the other, 'for an identifiable physical presence'. Some members thought that Myers' crusade to reform the Society was hindering the advance of scientific psychology.[17] Although the Professional Status Committee was little more than a 'short-lived registration device' intended for Members and Associates actually engaged in psychological work, it nevertheless moved the Society during the mid-1930s towards increasing the degree of professionalism of British psychology. The campaign for incorporation, which came to fruition in October 1941, was the first step towards the application for a Royal Charter (which was eventually granted in 1965). Divisions of Professional Psychologists (Educational and Clinical) were finally created in 1958, thereby finally resolving the professional–public tension, initiated by Myers in 1919, in favour of the vision of the Society's original founders.

In 'The popular, the practical and the professional: psychological identities in Britain, 1900–1950' (Chapter 5), Mathew Thomson argues that in order to understand the development of British psychology, attention must be paid not only to the emergence of the psychology profession but also to what he calls the 'practical psychology movement'. As an expression of a deeply entrenched British self-help tradition with its roots in the nineteenth century, practical psychology aimed to effect self-reliance and personal transformation with a heterogeneous array of psychospiritual techniques and exhortatory strategies. The British Psychological Society and the London Society of Psycho-Therapeutics were both founded in 1901, but their constituencies – academic and practical psychologists, respectively – initially regarded each other with hostility.

Academic psychology scorned the confused mysticism of this 'eccentric fringe'. Practical psychology in turn dismissed mental measurement as vulgar reductionism and challenged industrial psychology's anti-libertarianism. Yet the two enterprises were not separated by impermeable barriers. In publications such as the *New Thought Journal* and *The Thinker*, practical psychologists claimed their ideas were based on sound laboratory science. Likewise, academic psychologists such as Cyril Burt, William McDougall and Tom Pear not only sought practical applications for their psychologies but also popularised their ideas to mass audiences in books and radio broadcasts. Thus in spite of their oppositional positions, the two enterprises came to exert considerable influence over each other. By the late 1930s, over 50 practical psychology clubs were actively catering for an alternative psychological world of New Thoughters, Mental Scientists and creative thinkers.

According to Thomson, a history of psychology that restricts itself to recounting the story of the theoretical and professional development of the discipline alone will have grave limitations. Ultimately, he provocatively suggests, orthodox psychology's ambition 'to shape and inform everyday life' can be traced to its relationship to a far broader movement than the discipline itself. The history of practical psychology demonstrates that what Nikolas Rose (1985) called the 'psychological complex' is far more complex than historians have hitherto suspected.

The mutual relationship between two professional groups provides the focus of Joanna Bourke's chapter, 'Psychology at war, 1914–1945' (Chapter 6). Bourke demonstrates that British psychologists expressed few reservations about assisting the military in the prosecution of warfare. In fact, psychology made increasingly important contributions to the waging of armed conflict during the twentieth century. The First World War was a catalyst. Not only was modern warfare impersonal and unpredictable, but armies were composed of millions of conscripted and inexperienced men. As the psychologists argued, because modern battle stimulated extreme emotions without the possibility of their release, repression ensued. By 1917 one-third of all discharges were due to emotional disorders. Although psychologists like Myers campaigned for the recognition of 'shell shock', the pathologising of emotional reactions actually made it harder for men to return to society after the war because, unlike physical ailments, psychological illnesses were popularly believed to be under the control of an individual's will.

Psychology was also employed to stimulate aggression during military training, to forge 'man-the-weapon'. Although its influence had diminished in psychology by the Second World War, 'herd instinct theory' continued to be used by the military, who used it to justify 'blood training' – the realistic creation of battlefield conditions. By 1941, psychology was also beginning to be used extensively to screen personnel. Bourke argues that although war proved very productive for psychology, the 'psychologists faced immense pressures to change their own values to pull them in line with those of the military'. The influence was reciprocal: psychology enabled the armed forces to control and direct the emotional as well as the material lives of its recruits with great effectiveness.

The impact of war is also a central theme in Alan Collins' discussion of 'The psychology of memory' (Chapter 7). Collins discusses the variety of ways in which an important psychological category, memory, has been scientifically conceptualised and historically shaped. Four very different approaches to memory emerged in four quite different locations. Systematic experimental studies of memory initially arose during the early years of the century in response to concerns regarding the effectiveness of formal training in schools. Following the horrors of the First World War, however, forgetting could no longer be understood in terms of the then popular theory of 'trace decay'. Although not amenable to experimental investigation, psychoanalytic concepts of meaning and repression seemed far more appropriate constructs to employ at a time when the reclamation of meaning through remembrance was a crucial component of society's response to the tragedies of war.

Frederic Bartlett's theory of remembering was not psychoanalytically oriented, but many of its ideas were also formulated in the aftermath of the First World War while the wider culture was preoccupied by myth, superstition and rumour. Conceptualising memory as a reconstructed activity through the action of schemata, Bartlett's work may be seen as a transitional text between the social-ethnographic psychology of his earlier writings and his individualistic later psychology. Bartlett was also instrumental in establishing the Applied Psychology Unit (APU) in Cambridge during the Second World War. A new category of memory emerged there in the mid-1950s: short-term memory. Initially constructed to account for the memory of telephone numbers, it has come to have an immense influence in cognitive psychology. Collins concludes that the techniques, practices and aims of memory research all vary in accordance with the broader sociocultural context. Different sets of social practices and cultural preoccupations produce different investigative traditions.

The influence that society can have on psychology is also a central theme in Martin Roiser's chapter, 'Social psychology and social concern in thirties Britain' (Chapter 8). Roiser argues that a politically engaged social psychology arose in Britain during the 1930s in response to mass unemployment, poverty and the emergence of right-wing political movements. Social psychology had developed little during the early decades of the twentieth century and it was certainly not noted for its social or humanitarian concern. William McDougall's version, for example, although extremely influential, was essentially a theory of biological instincts inspired by eugenics.

In the summer of 1935 a small group of academics met in Cambridge 'to discuss informally what steps could be taken to direct the application of the more reliable methods of psychology, anthropology and sociology to a study of the problems of complex societies'. The group was interdisciplinary, with psychologists, anthropologists and sociologists making contributions. The result of the discussions was an influential volume, *The Study of Society: Methods and Problems*:

> There is to-day widespread recognition of the fact that the future of human civilization depends to a high degree upon Man's capacity to understand the forces and factors which control his own behaviour. Such understanding must be achieved, not only as regards individual conduct, but equally as regards the mass phenomena resulting from group contacts, which are becoming increasingly intimate and influential. (Bartlett *et al.*, 1939: vii)

One participant, O.A. Oeser, had called for an 'anthropology at home' in the pursuit of such objectives. His plea proved particularly influential for Tom Harrisson, Charles Madge and Humphrey Jennings, who subsequently formed the Mass-Observation movement. As social psychology of the 1930s became concerned with social issues, Mass-Observation created new ways of conducting social psychological research. Transcending disciplinary boundaries, it pioneered a participative methodology and maintained a 'democracy of method'. Insisting that its research be relevant to contemporary social problems, the movement employed street surveys, diarists and media analysis, and undertook surveys of public opinion. Although an applied, interdisciplinary, socially concerned social psychology was created, there was, unfortunately, little postwar continuation of the radical agenda. Mass-Organisation itself became a market research company. Nevertheless, as Roiser points out, recent approaches to social psychology have once again taken up Mass-Observation's pioneering methodologies.

Radical sentiments did survive in some quarters. In his 1939 contribution to *The Study of Society*, Manchester's Professor of Psychology, T.H. Pear, offered a prescient list of topics that social psychology might usefully investigate: unemployment, attitudes, radio, television and the cinema, propaganda, war and conversation. As Alan Costall demonstrates in 'Pear and his Peers' (Chapter 9), Pear was an 'intentionally peripheral psychologist', forever proposing new research topics that were grounded in their relevance to everyday concerns. Despite attaining the Presidency of the British Psychological Society in 1942, Pear was dissatisfied with mainstream British psychology. He made overtures towards anthropology and social theory and advocated the breaking down of disciplinary barriers.

During the First World War, Pear had assisted Myers on the selection of hydrophone operators at HMS *Crystal Palace*. But it was his experiences with shell-shocked soldiers that had the most impact on him. In his 1922 book *Remembering and Forgetting*, Pear repudiated the nonsense-syllable laboratory approach to memory for an account based on intimacy and personal meaning. After the war, his continuing insistence on the importance of the emotions and his emphasis on social psychology's practical significance marginalised him from the increasingly narrow mainstream of British academic psychology.

Frederic Bartlett and Tom Pear had parallel but very different careers. Almost exact contemporaries (both men were born in 1886 and Pear outlived Bartlett by three years), both were protégés of C.S. Myers. Pear was appointed the first full-time professor of psychology in Britain in 1919 and Bartlett became chair of the Cambridge Psychological Laboratory in 1922. Costall (1992, 1995) has argued that Bartlett's position as chair of the Cambridge department – and the attendant responsibilities to institutionalise the discipline – conflicted with his conviction that psychology was essentially a social science. The cost of his astute promotion of psychology, 'in the light of the existing opportunities and prejudices, as a *natural science* of industrial and military relevance', was the marginalisation of social psychology (Costall, 1992: 633, original emphasis). Myers' departure from Cambridge had presented Bartlett with a Faustian bargain: the discipline could be advanced and promoted within the British university system but only at the expense of an intrinsically social psychology.

It was a deal Pear was not prepared to strike. Whereas Bartlett was obliged, tactically, to play down his interests in social psychology in order to promote psychology as a laboratory science, Pear became increasingly committed to the exploration of ordinary experience. Bartlett's successor at the APU, Kenneth Craik, regarded the laboratory in an almost spiritual light, 'a place of infinite possibilities and far horizons, full of pathways leading me into the unknown'. In contrast, Pear came to regard the laboratory as a place of contrived problems, 'an ideal refuge' for those uninterested in the 'social psychology of everyday life'. Instead, he was fascinated by English social differences and the dynamics of how impressions of people's personalities are formed on hearing their voice. Consequently, while Bartlett produced 'a brilliant crop of students who, after the Second World War, held the lion's share of the Professorships of Psychology in Britain; and indeed quite a number elsewhere in the Commonwealth' (Broadbent, 1970: 3), Pear's Manchester department averaged an intake of one student every two years before the end of the Second World War (Costall, Chapter 9).

One of Pear's first students at Manchester was Susan Isaacs, the subject of Chapter 10. In 'British psychology and psychoanalysis: the case of Susan Isaacs', Janet Sayers argues that Isaacs combined the data collection methods she acquired as a psychology student with the clinical methods of psychoanalysis. Isaacs 'enormously advanced academic and public understanding of, and provision for, children, particularly through highlighting the fantasies mediating their inner and outer worlds'. After a period of psychoanalysis she decided to become a non-medical lay analyst. In 1924 she obtained a position at the experimental Malting House School in Cambridge; it became a rich source of non-clinical data on children's fantasies. Influenced by John Dewey, Isaacs disagreed with Maria Montessori and Jean Piaget's philosophies, arguing instead that 'development involves a continuous process of increasing synthesis of children's knowledge and skills through their changing interests and phantasies'.

Under the pseudonym Ursula Wise, Isaacs popularised psychoanalysis and child development in magazines and books and on radio. Having worked at the London Institute of Education during the 1930s, Isaacs moved back to Cambridge at the outset of the Second World War, where she investigated the effects of evacuation on children. This work became influential in the postwar period, when government policy on institutional and foster care was being formulated. Throughout her career, Isaacs was very much a bridge-builder, attempting to traverse the gap between a child's inner and outer worlds, between psychology and psychoanalysis, between different approaches within psychoanalysis, and between expert knowledge and lay audiences. The concept of fantasy was, for Isaacs, the category that could not only bridge thought and reality, but also mediate the inner and outer aspects of psychology, studied, respectively, by psychoanalysis and non-analytic psychology.

As Roger Smith demonstrates in 'Physiology and psychology, or brain and mind in the age of C.S. Sherrington' (Chapter 11), Charles Sherrington was also concerned to reconcile two apparently conflicting domains – those of mind and brain. The influential physiologist was supportive of psychology and believed the separation of the two disciplines was a barrier to scientific progress. Sherrington's concept of integration referred to a process controlling movement and posture. It thus framed an approach to the nervous system as the controlling centre of unified action, with mind and body as joint participants in a unified individuality, and physiology and psychology as partners in a unified biology. 'It was indeed the power of one concept to encompass both the sensory and motor dimensions of the nervous system, and the perceptual as well as conative side of psychological life,' Smith notes, 'that justified the reputation Sherrington acquired as a philosopher of organic wholeness.'

Alas, what Sherrington called the 'last and final integration' was never achieved. The disciplines of physiology and psychology were separated by language, by subject matter and by experimental technique. In showing how Sherrington attempted to bridge the two sciences, Smith demonstrates that the history of the philosophical relations of mind to brain is linked to the history of the disciplinary relations between physiology and psychology. Sherrington's values of the integrated person have now been called into question by a variety of enterprises ranging from information technology to drugs and deconstruction. Although made possible by the work of Sherrington and his generation, contemporary neuroscience has decidedly rejected the values upon which it was founded.

According to David Wilson's assessment, comparative psychology has also had a frustrating history in Britain. In 'A "precipitous *dégringolade*"? The uncertain progress of British comparative psychology in the twentieth century' (Chapter 12), Wilson argues that progress in the field has been characterised by 'confusion and controversy along an uncomfortable and uncertain path'. The first promising period of British comparative psychology came to an end with the publication of Hobhouse's *Mind in Evolution* in 1901. Initially inspired by Darwin's evolutionary theory, this 'tradition in the making' had more of an influence in the United States than in Britain, where behaviourism came to sustain animal work. In Britain, industrial psychology and medical psychology were stimulated by the First World War, but the lack of a 'market' for comparative psychology meant that little work could be undertaken in the field until after 1945.

In the postwar period, new opportunities for comparative psychology work arose in pharmacology, psychiatry and agriculture, and the later expansion of the universities in the 1960s also stimulated research. Beginning in the 1950s, a wide variety of books and radio and television programmes brought the animal world to an enthusiastic mass audience. This in turn gradually encouraged the development of a populist environmental ethics. Although the government had continued to regulate animal work after the Second World War, by the end of the 1970s sources of hostile pressure, especially to the use of animals in the psychological laboratory, had emerged, and the academic societies responded with internal investigations and the promulgation of codes of practice. Ethical concerns about the use and treatment of experimental animals prevented psychological research along lines which are tolerated outside Britain, and statutory controls were rapidly reinforced in the 1980s. Wilson demonstrates that external influences, like the political, economic and academic climate, as well as more recently articulated ethical concerns about the welfare of animals, have affected the development of British research in comparative psychology in the twentieth century.

In 'Science in the clinic: clinical psychology at the Maudsley' (Chapter 13), Maarten Derksen discusses the establishment of clinical psychology at the Maudsley Hospital, the most influential of the three places where the field first developed in Britain. Behaviour therapy, a novel therapeutic technique pioneered there in the late 1950s, opened up a new field of professional activity and led to the rapid growth of clinical psychology. It had itself been made possible by the development of two interlinked approaches.

Invited to establish a Department of Psychology at the Maudsley Hospital, London, at the end of the war, Hans Eysenck argued that psychology could be to psychiatry what physiology was to medicine: a basic science. Opposed to the widespread practice of employing psychologists as either IQ test administrators or purveyors of 'mystical' psychotherapy, Eysenck argued that clinical psychologists should be independent scientists, not subservient technicians. Psychiatric instruments such as the Rorschach test were consequently subjected to 'devastating critical analysis' (Jones, 1980: 25, quoted by Derksen, Chapter 13) and the dimensional theory of personality was proposed as an alternative to the traditional psychiatric categories of hysteria and schizophrenia.

One of Eysenck's colleagues at the Maudsley also devised a model of the laboratory in the clinic. It was based not on a theory of personality, however, but rather on the experimental investigation of individuals. Unlike Eysenck's model, which emphasised research, Monte Shapiro's was therapeutic in orientation. Derksen concludes that Shapiro's paradigm of attuning science to the unique individual ultimately triumphed over Eysenck's dimensional theory of personality as the paradigmatic technique of clinical psychology. As pioneered at the Maudsley, behaviour therapy and clinical psychology emerge from this study as products of both demarcations and alliances forged between psychology and psychiatry. Derksen makes a strong case for regarding the concept of the boundary as a productive site of innovation, not as a prohibitive or restrictive entity. Both practical and rhetorical 'boundary work' prove immensely fruitful sources of both novel practices and new knowledge.

In Chapter 14, '"Our friends electric": mechanical models of mind in postwar Britain', Rhodri Hayward is concerned with understanding how new knowledge emerges on the boundaries between theoretical and practical models and between philosophy and engineering. The chapter's focus is the rise – and ultimate reification – of Kenneth Craik's 'speculative hypothesis' that human beings are model makers. It has hitherto been argued that this 'man–machine identity thesis' arose in the United States during the Second World War. But as Hayward demonstrates, these new conceptions of behaviour and purpose as feedback-governed mechanisms were pioneered in Britain. The work of Craik and Ross Ashby can thus be seen as a counterpoint to the thesis that the origins of cybernetics can be found in the military. For Craik – whose practical skills enabled him to recast philosophical questions as engineering problems – modelling was no mere heuristic: it was the basis of the human mind.

Craik stimulated the development of a programme of research which subsequently had an immense influence within British psychology (see Baddeley, Chapter 17; Gregory, Chapter 21). Proposing that 'stable equilibrium' was the key to behavioural adaptation, Ashby built electrical machines based on the concept of feedback and used them to model psychological health. His 'homeostat' was a mechanical vehicle for the promotion of Craik's hypotheses. Grey Walter's work with the electroencephalogram (EEG) and his famous 'tortoises' similarly acted as a bridge between the feedback hypothesis and neurological data. The tortoises in turn provided material representations of Craik and Ashby's cybernetic speculations. The model-making heuristic eventually became the key to a whole series of activities. The computer, artificial intelligence and cognitive psychology came to be regarded as modellers, and not mere models of human cognition. British psychology came to define thinking – highly reduction-istically – as 'problem solving'. From starting out as a 'speculative hypothesis', Craik's theory became an idea which maintains a strong discursive presence today.

In 'Behavioural approaches and the cultivation of competence' (Chapter 15), Karen Baistow follows the movement of psychological concepts from one discursive regime to another. Despite the reputed 'death of behaviourism', behavioural management techniques are thriving in certain sectors of British society. Baistow argues that the current widespread deployment of practical behavioural approaches in the fields of child health, welfare and education can be ultimately traced to challenges to behaviourist theory that took place in the United States in the 1960s. Humanist and cognitivist critiques of behaviourism shifted the goals of behavioural intervention from 'social control' and behaviour modification to-wards an emphasis on self-empowerment and 'optimising potential'. This was accompanied by an expansion of the types of subjects and actions considered amenable to behavioural interventions. This happened most noticeably in the 'well' community and, in particular, to children, whose behaviour at home and in the classroom was targeted, from birth onwards, by the new techniques.

Although the behaviour of children has long been the object of reform, their normative regulation using techniques for the behavioural cultivation of com-petence were novel insofar as they primarily emphasised freedom and were promulgated by a heterogeneous array of professionals and lay authorities: health visitors, parents, community psychologists, teachers and social workers. The systematic focus on positive behaviour was also embodied in legislation as Local Education Authorities drew up 'behaviour support plans' and 'parenting' became the object of government policy. Such developments, Baistow argues, would not have been possible were it not for changes in the political and economic landscape of the late 1970s and 1980s. Driven by neoliberal political innovations and an ethical emphasis on self-regulation, fundamental changes in the provision of health, welfare and education – demanding cost-effectiveness, evaluation and evidence – provided fertile territories for the expansion of these new behavioural techniques.

8 Psychology in Britain: personal reflections

In Part II of the book, Personal reflections, we have included personal professional reminiscences of 12 senior psychologists. Such testimonies are a long-established practice within psychology, the best-known example being the *History of Psychology in Autobiography* series started in 1930 by Carl Murchison (Murchison, 1930). The autobiographical accounts are important for several reasons. First, they help preserve the kind of 'implicit knowledge' which each generation possesses but rarely writes down and which is therefore usually lost to history. 'It is difficult now to understand the social and academic climate in which we were attempting this work,' John and Elizabeth Newson report, discussing their use of unconventional methodologies in their research on child-rearing practices. 'We had two major problems to contend with: the belief (of the middle class) ... that "social class no longer exists"; and the very low esteem accorded to interviewing as a methodology at that time.' Particularly striking in Michael Rutter's account of his work is the extent to which science is a collaborative activity on both a local and an international level, involving networks of individuals, research groups and institutions. Michael Argyle gives a similarly reflexive description of how social cohesion helped to sustain a social psychology research group in Oxford. With influences ranging from new material technologies to ethology, Argyle recalls how the hugely influential field of non-verbal communication and the social skills model emerged from quite unpromising beginnings.

The autobiographical essays also constitute primary source material in their own right for future historians. For example, a number of the psychologists reveal how important anthropology was to the development of their thinking. Gustav Jahoda recalls how repeated lack of success in replicating traditional experiments in the Gold Coast gradually led to his disenchantment with Western social psychology. He subsequently became convinced of the culture-boundedness of experimental social psychology and the artificiality of disciplinary boundaries. Having worked on Ashanti day names, Jahoda applied his ideas to the investigation of Scottish children's beliefs. John and Elizabeth Newson were influenced by the anthropological ideas of Margaret Mead and Gregory Bateson, having also discovered that their academic training had provided inadequate resources with which to answer the questions that arose in the course of studying the everyday practices of parenthood. Anthropology was likewise an influence on the nascent Oxford social psychology group, as Michael Argyle indicates, 'though not really Oxford anthropology, which was unsympathetic to psychology at the time'.

Rom Harré began his career at Oxford but he perceived mainstream social psychology's understanding of causality to be fundamentally misconceived, particularly because it paid insufficient attention to anthropology. 'It soon became clear to me,' he reports, 'that most social psychology had no claim to be a science in the sense of laying bare universal aspects of human social interaction. It was the anthropology of the local tribe.' Although departmental rules insisted that doctoral dissertations had to include statistical analyses, the regulations could be met by making use of the methodology of George Kelly's personal construct psychology. Kelly's work has had a great impact on certain sectors of British psychology, an enterprise that Fay Fransella has done much to promote. The repertory grid has proved itself a valuable tool in a wide range of applications, she shows, from workforce training to the treatment of stuttering and eating disorders.

A number of our authors disclose unexpected philosophical influences. Margaret Boden regarded the inimitable William McDougall 'not as an unchallengeable guru, but as an intellectual sparring partner'. His ideas about novelty, purpose and creativity proved important to her work on artificial intelligence. Peter Wason suggests that science is itself an inherently creative enterprise. 'An experimental idea is like a poem,' he says, implicitly exhorting historians not to overlook 'the affinity of discovery between arts and science'. In his development of the logical problems he devised to study thinking, Wason admits to being influenced by the philosophies of science developed by Karl Popper and Imre Lakatos. 'We've read everything you have written, and we disagree with all of it,' said Lakatos one day; 'do come and give us a seminar'! Alan Baddeley similarly discusses the influence of the philosophy of science on his work, although this was soon matched by that of Kenneth Craik. 'There was … a feeling of real intellectual excitement. We felt that we were at the forefront of a revolution, a revolution inspired by Kenneth Craik's insights.'

The influence of Craik's engineering ideas is likewise a central theme in Richard Gregory's chapter; he also communicates how exhilarating scientific research can be. Through his writings and the famous Bristol Exploratory Science Centre, Gregory has done much to convey the thrills of science to a wide public. Although David Duncan goes as far as to title his chapter 'The joys of psychology', it is clear from his account of his career that industrial psychologists regularly confronted unforeseen frustrations. Visiting a tyre factory some years after studying its inefficient practices, he discovered that his report 'lay in a drawer for two years, but was then fully implemented'. Selection tests employed at another organisation verged on the bizarre: 'You put a mirror under their nose,' said one employer: 'If it clouds, hire her, then allocate.' Such accounts indicate that these autobiographies can give a much better idea of what it was actually like to be a practising psychologist, especially during the middle years of the twentieth century, than the historian can usually achieve.

9 Psychology in Britain, 2001

Although the relationship between psychology and society is complex, many of the contributors to this book have nevertheless endeavoured to comprehend its features. As all the chapters demonstrate, the process of bringing psychology to society has been far from straightforward. The emergence of 'the psychological' profoundly changed numerous aspects of British society in the twentieth century. In turn, society has exerted powerful influences on psychology. The twenty-first century will certainly witness further explorations of the possibilities for this reflexive science. New domains of expertise will emerge; theories of human action will be revised, innovative techniques of intervention will be developed. Novel psychological categories will be mapped; others may be rediscovered; yet others still could vanish from the landscape of subjectivity. Psychology and society will doubtless exert mutual influences in as yet unforeseen ways. If this volume inspires historians and psychologists to reflect further upon the interdependence of psychology and society, then it will have fulfilled its purpose.

Notes

1 See Hearnshaw (1964: ch. 11) and Boring (1929/1957: ch. 20) for British psychology's experimental and institutional beginnings. For an extensive but accessible history of the human sciences, see Smith (1997b). Richards (1996) provides a critical historical introduction to psychology.

2 As the British Psychological Society's first historian later recalled, the change of name from the Psychological Society to the British Psychological Society in 1906 'was not due to any sudden uprising of imperial pride, but to the fact that members had discovered another body of persons who were using the former title. To prevent confusion with this unacademic group the change in title was agreed to' (Edgell, 1947: 116).

3 According to the American historian of psychology E.G. Boring, 'From 1890 to 1920, when Germany and America were teeming with laboratories and professional experimental psychologists, Great Britain was advancing slowly in the new science only by way of the work of a few competent men' (Boring, 1929/1957: 460).

4 In London, an informal Psychological Club sprang up around *Mind* editor George Croom Robertson in the late 1880s. 'The meetings this winter are to consider original psychophysical research,' Cattell told his parents in November 1886, 'and to discuss how psychological terms are used and should be used' (J.M. Cattell to Parents, 19 November 1886, in Sokal, 1981: 236). Sophie Bryant, who would later become one of the founder members of the Psychological Society, also attended these meetings.

5 It was James Sully, Grote Professor of Mind and Logic at University College London, who had called the meeting that led to the founding of the Psychological Society. W.H.R. Rivers was also a founder member. For biographical sketches of all ten original members of the Society, see Steinberg (1961).

6 Three of the original founder members of the Psychological Society were associated with the Asylum: W.G. Smith, F.W. Mott and R. Armstrong-Jones. See Steinberg (1961).

7 Myers recounted his work in the First World War in Myers (1940).

8 For an account of the work of the British Psychological Society and its Divisions, Sections and Special Groups, see *The 1999 Annual Report*. Leicester: The British Psychological Society.

9 For example Brett (1912–1921), Dessoir (1912), Hall (1912), Klemm (1914), Rand (1912) and Baldwin (1913). James Mark Baldwin, one of the pioneers of psychology in North America and co-founder of the *Psychological Review*, certainly deserves a mention in any history of British psychology for his claim to the establishment of the first psychological laboratory in the British Empire. On the founding of the *Psychological Review* see Sokal (1997).

10 The third paper to be published in the first issue of the *British Journal of Psychology*, for example, was titled 'A sixteenth century psychologist, Bernardino Telesio' (McIntyre, 1904).

11 The history of German psychology has been well served by the new historiography (see Geuter, 1992; Ash, 1995; Kusch, 1995, 1999).

12 Foucault (1972). Useful introductions to the work of the French historian of the human sciences are Foucault (1980, 1988).

13 On the invention of the psychological in the context of North American culture, see Pfister and Schnog (1997).

14 For a recent example of the genre of studies known as 'psychohistory' see the special issue of the *British Journal for the History of Science* devoted to 'Psychoanalysing Robert Boyle' (Hunter, 1999).

15 American historian of psychology Jill Morawski has argued that 'Historians of psychology have a special opportunity (and obligation) to explore the reflexive dynamics

of [those] investigative practices' that psychology has systematically 'recognized and then neglected, covered over, or denied' (Morawski, 1992: 281).

16 On the Task Force on Self-Esteem, see Cruikshank (1993: 328–334). Wolverhampton Council's Education Department advertised for a 'Self-Esteem, Personal Safety Co-ordinator' in March 2000. *The Guardian*, 22 March, 2000, p. 65.

17 The suggestion to create an elite 'Psychological Club' was one response to this criticism, which, to some extent, animated the Society until the late 1950s. As Oliver Zangwill later recalled, the formation of the Experimental Psychology Group in October 1946 (the Experimental Psychology Society from 1959) 'owed something to misgivings felt by a number of us about certain tendencies current in British psychology at the time' (Zangwill, quoted in Mollon, 1996: 3).

Part I

Historical essays

1

Edward Cox, the Psychological Society of Great Britain (1875–1879) and the meanings of an institutional failure

Graham Richards

It is a truth increasingly acknowledged that a discipline seeking a cultural presence is in need of an institutional base. If, in the latter part of the nineteenth century, the achievements of Psychology's[1] intellectually autonomous British pioneers (such as Alexander Bain, Francis Galton, Herbert Spencer, James Ward, James Sully and W.B. Carpenter) were to assume a disciplinary form and the various Victorian modes of hostility towards a 'science of the mind' neutralised, then that discipline would require an organisational structure. In the 1870s James Ward's efforts to create one at Cambridge foundered on rock-like theological resistance (see Crampton, 1978). Bain's journal *Mind* (launched in 1876) provided an invaluable publishing outlet but could not serve the discipline's other institutional requirements, nor was promoting scientific Psychology its primary aim.[2] Only in 1879, in the long canonical version of Psychology's history, did its institutional history begin, with Wilhelm Wundt's creation of a laboratory at Leipzig University. With a journal and opportunities for doctoral research,[3] Leipzig remained Psychology's institutional hub until the 1890s.

Britain's situation contrasted with those in Germany, the United States and France in one crucial respect – the effective absence, outside Scotland, of universities which could provide institutional sites able to nurture the new discipline. The extensive German university system was long established and had been radically overhauled early in the nineteenth century. Psychology's German pioneers, from E.H. Weber, Hermann Helmholtz, Gustav Fechner and Wundt to G.E. Müller, Hermann Ebbinghaus and Carl Stumpf, were all university based. The number of universities and colleges in the United States had been continuously expanding since the late eighteenth century, the post-Civil War period seeing an acceleration of this trend and an increasing move away from identification with specific Christian denominations, as had previously been typical. In these the mental and moral philosophy course had been a cornerstone of the curriculum since the turn of the century and it was from this which American Psychology eventually evolved in a fairly direct fashion, as evidenced in the academic lineages from Noah Porter to G.T. Ladd, James McCosh to J.M. Baldwin, even John Bascom to G.S. Hall (O'Donnell, 1986; Richards, 1995). In France, while the university system was less extensive, the Sorbonne provided a congenial Paris home for Théodule Ribot, while for other Psychological pioneers (such as Charcot) clinical settings supplied a secure base.[4] In England, however, Oxford and Cambridge retained a virtual monopoly and were both essentially con- servative Anglican institutions, jealously guarding ancient privileges and sharing an intense and powerful theological opposition to the scientific study of the mind or 'soul'. A strong Scottish philosophy tradition, which often assumed a clear proto-Psychological character (see Richards, 1992b: chs 3–5), had flourished at Aberdeen, Glasgow and Edinburgh (to which we should, in effect, add Belfast) from the early eighteenth century but had, by the 1860s, largely lost its vigour, Sir William Hamilton being its last major representative, excepting James McCosh, who emigrated to the United States in 1868.

Among British Psychology's major founding figures only Bain, at Aberdeen from 1860, and Ward – in vain – at Cambridge were operating within university settings during the 1870s. Of the rest, some, like Galton, Charles Darwin, Sir John Lubbock and Sully (until 1879) were of independent means, others such as Spencer, Sully (after 1879) and G.H. Lewes largely survived by their literary labours (supplemented in Lewes's case by those of his partner, George Eliot).[5] Another group were medical professionals, either neurologists and physiologists (such as Carpenter and David Ferrier) or psychiatrists (like Henry Maudsley), inheritors of the tradition of the 'Queen Square' neurologists of the 1840s and 1850s (which included Benjamin Brodie, Henry Holland, Robert Dunn and Thomas Laycock).[6] Only in the 1890s would English Psychology establish a formal university presence (at London and Cambridge). The intellectual action in the 1870s centred on a London metropolitan elite, whose members ranged from progressive scientists such as T.H. Huxley to literary lions like George Eliot. This elite had its own informal institutions in the form of clubs, salons and societies such as the Metaphysical Society and the more exclusive X Club, while the Royal Society, the Royal Institution and annual meetings of the British Association for the Advancement of Science provided more formal centres and occasions of social and intellectual activity. Magazines like *The Contemporary Review*, *Fortnightly* and *Nineteenth Century* served as their main public vehicles. But in each of these forums the issues of interest were wide-ranging and eclectic, and none could have served as a base devoted solely to promoting Psychology, even had anyone wished to do so. This intellectual elite included the majority of Britain's most eminent physical scientists, Darwinians, doctors, literati, philosophers, even some liberal church intellectuals, poets and politicians. Most importantly for us, regarding matters scientific, philosophical and psychological they were generally self-con- sciously contemptuous of what they saw as 'amateurism' (a theme which will also thread through the next two chapters). The intellectual richness of this milieu perhaps contributed to their failure to consider it necessary to found a Psychological Society similar to those serving natural history, anthropology and geography, for example,[7] and in the early 1870s they rarely even countenanced a formal discipline of 'Psychology' at all. During the 1870s, any attempt to create a British institutional base for Psychology would, clearly, have to involve factions and forces beyond either this select coterie or the universities.

This was indeed so, for there was a third, long-forgotten, move, besides Ward's and Bain's, on the British scene, and one with which it is particularly appropriate to begin this volume: the Psychological Society of Great Britain (PSGB) founded in 1875 and wound up on the last day of 1879, following its founder's death a month earlier.[8] The PSGB's published legacy consists of a single volume of 19 selected *Proceedings* (1880)[9] plus various other works issued under its auspices or authored by its members. This has received virtually no coverage at all in histories of Psychology, figuring only as a footnote in histories of spiritualism. Janet Oppenheim (1985) considers it a little more extensively, but also solely in that connection. Besides simply rescuing this project, and its progenitor, from historiographic limbo, this chapter will use it as a focus for considering the broader questions raised by its failure. These relate to the nature, place and definition of Psychology in late-Victorian Britain and the background against which the (British) Psychological Society was more successfully launched in 1901. We must begin though with the PSGB's founder himself.

1   Edward William Cox (1809–1879)

The PSGB was one of the numerous strings in the harp-like bow of Edward William Cox (1809–1879), lawyer, publisher and occasional Conservative politician. '[A] shrewd observer, a clever little man', according to one associate,[10] Cox, a manufacturer's son, was born in Taunton and first entered print in verse in 1830, but the law, not poetry, proved his main vocation. Called to the bar in 1843, he practised little as a barrister, becoming instead responsible for a volume of *Reports of the Court of Common Pleas* (1844), the *Reports of the Courts of Law and Equity* (5 volumes, 1846–1867), and 24 volumes of *Laws and Statutes* (1849– 1856).[11] The *Dictionary of National Biography* (*DNB*) catalogues various recorderships and court posts, the last being Chairman of the 2nd Court of Middlesex Sessions, which he held from 1870, along with being recorder for Portsmouth (from 1868). Made a serjeant-at-law in 1868, he is often referred to thereafter as Serjeant Cox. But aside from unsuccessfully contending four elections as Conservative candidate (Tewkesbury in 1852 and 1857; Taunton in 1865 and 1868[12]) he early on began a parallel career in publishing, beginning with the *Law Times* in 1843. While legal journals continued to figure prominently in his portfolio, he became proprietor variously of *The Field*, *The Critic* and *The Queen* as well as launching *Exchange and Mart* and *The Country, A Journal of Rural Pursuits* (alongside *The Magistrate*, *The Joint Stock Companies' Law Journal* and *The County Courts*

Chronicle and Bankruptcy Gazette). Over the years he additionally published other books relating to law and some political pamphlets.[13] Only in his sixties did he begin actively promoting what had in fact been another long-standing interest – Psychology – the first full fruit of which was the two-volume *What Am I? A Popular Introduction to the Study of Psychology* (1873, 1874, a second edition appearing in 1876 and a third edition of volume I only in 1879).

This interest dated back to the 1830s and 1840s, when he had had some connection with John Elliotson[14] and become intrigued by 'artificial somnambulism' (hypnotism), as well as by George Combe's phrenology.[15] In 1870 or early 1871 the eminent chemist William Crookes co-opted him to witness his experiments on spiritualistic phenomena, regarding which Cox was initially sceptical. As a result, he became convinced of the authenticity of these phenomena but ascribed them to what he called a 'Psychic Force'[16] originating within the human organism rather than to spirits of the dead.[17] At his Russell Square residence he subsequently hosted numerous séance sessions, at one of which Mary Showers (a friend of the famous medium Florence Cook) was exposed as a fraud. Francis Galton – a friend and admirer of Crookes – was also present on one occasion.[18]

This experience seems finally to have spurred Cox into promulgating his long-gestating ideas on the nature of the human mind. At any rate, turned 60, and presumably also feeling time's wings at his heels, he now became infused with almost evangelical ardour in propagating the case for a branch of science devoted to investigating 'psychic force'. This science he called Psychology.[19] In a letter to Crookes dated 8 June 1871 he mentions the need to form a Psychological Society for this purpose (see Crookes, 1926). Oppenheim (1985) quotes F. Podmore (1902: vol. 2, p. 170) (who became a major adversary of spiritualism) to the effect that Cox's Society was a reaction against the 'slovenly acquiescence' of spiritualists to the belief that spirits of the dead were solely responsible for the phenomena produced in séances. This, however, is to define its character – and Cox's own position – too narrowly, as we will see, while his interest in Psychology long predated his encounter with spiritualism.

The project finally came to fruition at a meeting at his house on 22 February 1875, by which time *What Am I?* had seemingly established his credentials as an authority in the field. Eight people including Cox were present: Crookes; George Harris (a barrister and anthropologist); the Rev. W. Stainton Moses, who was to become one of the most successful mediums and, initially under the pen-name 'M.A.(Oxon)', a regular contributor to the spiritualist magazine *Light*; Frederic W.H. Myers, best remembered for *Human Personality and Its Survival of Bodily Death*, 1903, but also the first British writer to refer to Freud in print (see Myers, 1893b); Professor C.J. Plumptre (Britain's leading elocutionist and expert on 'the voice', also a barrister[20]); Francis W. Percival (another barrister); and Francis K. Munton (a solicitor who acted thereafter as Honorary Treasurer and Secretary). George Harris, the PSGB's Vice-President until its demise, was Cox's main active ally in the enterprise. Vice-President of the Anthropological Institute, Harris was, according to his *DNB* entry, dissatisfied with the level of attention it was giving to psychological issues. On 14 April 1875, the inaugural meeting at 9 Conduit Street, London, was, to Cox's surprise and gratification, so packed that people had to be turned away. A council of 11 members (in addition to Cox and Crookes) was now formed, including (as well as most of those previously identified) the solicitor and anthropologist C. Staniland Wake, the Indian barrister Gunnendo Mohun Tagore,[21] Sir John Heron Maxwell and P.W. Clayden. Cox, naturally, was appointed the Society's President. Within three months the PSGB had 64 members and in his November 1875 Sessional Address Cox was boasting that 'Names of world-wide fame have been permitted to grace our roll of honorary members, and already many corresponding members have volunteered in other countries'; 'lying before me' are communications from France, Germany, New York, San Francisco and Melbourne (*Proceedings of the Psychological Society of Great Britain*, 1880, pp. 94/8).

When Cox unexpectedly died in November 1879 (after giving 'a reading from the works of a popular novelist at a local entertainment') the PSGB was promptly wound up and its surplus funds used for publishing the *Proceedings*.[22] 'After much consideration the Society came to the conclusion that the President's death was an irrecoverable blow to the undertaking' (*Proceedings*, p. xii). By its demise it could list 113 people who had at some time been members (eight of them were women 'subscribing members'; a full list is provided in the *Proceedings*, pp. xiii–xvi). Expansion did not, apparently, maintain its initial momentum, nor achieve the international character which Cox anticipated, only seven being based overseas. We may now explore a number of issues arising from this episode.

2   The PSGB agenda

Despite the catalytic role of Cox's experiences with spiritualism in triggering the project, only about a fifth (10 of 49) of the titles listed among the papers (most unpublished) and topics discussed at the Society's meetings obviously pertain to such subjects as hypnotism, apparitions and paranormal phenomena (*Proceedings*, pp. xiii–xvi). Others included memory, sleep, the hereditary transmission of endowments and qualities, wit and humour, comparison of human and animal faculties, character as expressed in handwriting and 'the Psychology of Hindoos'. The PSGB published such papers as 'Psychology Proved by Physical Science' (by the eminent James Croll[23]), 'Cerebral Psychology' and 'Natural Law, Automatic Mind, and Unconscious Intelligence' by Charles Bray, and Harris's lectures on 'The Psychology of Memory' and 'Caligraphy [*sic*] Considered as affording a Test of Character'. Cox himself separately published *Heredity and Hybridism. A Suggested Solution of the Problem* (1875a), *Spiritualism Answered by Science, with Proofs of a Psychic Force* (1871/1872), *The Psychology of Memory and Recollection* (1875b) and *Monograph on Sleep and Dream: Their Physiology and Psychology* (1878). While a substantial number of PSGB presentations were by Cox (these dominating the *Proceedings* published posthumously in his honour) the Society's active members were clearly also engaging with psychological topics we would now consider fairly orthodox. In the preface to his inaugural address, Cox proclaimed that the PSGB:

> embraces no creed, supports no faith, contemplates no theory, has no latent designs, but proposes only to collect facts and investigate psychological phenomena, precisely as other scientific societies investigate the phenomena of Magnetism or the Laws of Astronomy, with no foregone conclusions. (*Proceedings*, p. v)

Had it continued it is possible that the more orthodox (to our eyes) concerns could have come to the fore and the Society been able to catch the experimentalist mood of the subsequent decade. One might go further and argue that, Galton aside, the first manifestation of experimental methods in British Psychology came in the investigations of spiritualist phenomena undertaken by Crookes, his colleague Dr Huggins, and Cox, in which indeed Galton was occasionally involved.

Three years after the PSGB's demise the Society for Psychical Research (SPR) was founded (1882), involving several of those prominent in the PSGB (notably Crookes, F.W.H. Myers and Stainton Moses), which was more specifically focused on empirical 'scientific' investigation of 'psychic' phenomena (the term largely introduced by Cox himself). The SPR was in effect Britain's first institution successfully to implement what amounted to a Psychological research programme. The historiographical sidelining of the role of psychic research in the founding of Psychology is unfortunate, but not perhaps surprising given the traditional celebratory pedagogic role of history of Psychology[24] – O'Donnell (1986) notes how in the United States G. Stanley Hall used funds from the American equivalent of the SPR to establish the American Psychological Association and William James' fascination with it is – exceptionally – now well known, but in Britain too such leading twentieth-century psychologists as William McDougall, J.C. Flügel, Cyril Burt, Charles Spearman, C.A. Mace, R.H. Thouless and, later, H.J. Eysenck, continued to take the topic seriously and were involved in various ways with the SPR.[25] British SPR members were also among the first to take notice of Freud before the First World War.[26]

The PSGB was, however, more than a short-lived precursor to the SPR. Its agenda was far broader, and Cox's own Psychology, which he used the PSGB to promote, genuinely sought a comprehensive account of human nature.

3   Cox's Psychology

Cox's concept of the subject matter of Psychology is curiously complex. In his 1878 fourth Presidential Address, 'Claims of Psychology to a Place in the Circle of the Sciences', he defines Psychology as 'the Science that investigates the forces by which the motions of the material Mechanism of Man are directed and determined' (*Proceedings*, p. 242/4). While not exactly conventional, this definition would, on the face of it, surely not be entirely unacceptable even today and could even, at a stretch, be given a behaviourist reading. As it stands, its dualism is far less overt than in more orthodox founding definitions, such as the 'Science of Mind'. The devil, however, is in the word 'forces'. He saw the project as beset on three fronts: by theologians, materialist scientists and 'metaphysical' philosophers – none of whom, for their different reasons, were prepared to countenance empirical investigation of psychological phenomena as he conceived them. He adamantly insists that the project is not theory guided but will initially at least be based on gathering 'facts'; in his Inaugural Address he even states 'we contemplate the periodical publication, not of a mass of essays, but of *Psychological Facts* collected from all parts of the world, which being first duly authenticated, will be narrated without note or comment' (*Proceedings*, p. 34, italics in original), and again in 1875 his Sessional Address as President outlines plans for a 'Psychological Record' 'as soon as our funds permit' (p. 96/10). Although he apparently fails to see that taking the operations of 'Psychic Force' as Psychology's primary subject matter itself constituted a fundamental theoretical commitment to a form of dualism, the existence of such a force had, in his view, already been empirically demonstrated, as we will see shortly.

Cox's full exposition of his views in *What Am I?* fuses Combean phrenological faculty Psychology (although not the strict phrenological theory of brain functioning), interest in 'abnormal' phenomena in the Elliotson tradition ('artificial somnambulism', 'psychic' phenomena, trance, insanity, etc.), concern with the 'duality of mind' implications of brain morphology, a rhetoric of dogmatic empiricism, ambivalence over evolutionism and exploitation of the haziness of contemporary atomic theory. This last he takes as implying the possibility (verging on inevitability) of 'non-molecular' – and hence invisible – 'arrangements' of atoms (thereby converting 'immaterialism' into a variety of non-materialist physicalism).

He returned to this in his inaugural address. His case is worth elaborating on a little further since, given the time at which it was written, it is far from lacking in power, and it is essential to appreciate it if the character of his Psychology is to be understood. Matter, which alone can directly affect our senses, is, he asserts, constructed of molecules. Physiology deals with the 'material structure, with the whole visible and palpable mechanism of Man' (*Proceedings*, p. 5). Psychology deals with 'the potencies or entities, whatever they be, whence proceed the forces by which this mechanism is moved and directed, and which, being immaterial – that is to say, *non-molecular*, are imperceptible to human sense' (p. 5, italics in original). He continues: 'our conception of [Mind is] merely a function of the brain, for, as the brain is, so is that mind' (p. 7). And then: 'We protest that the potencies with which we deal are as capable of actual demonstration as are the Electricity and the Magnetism of the Physicists' (p. 8). It is these 'potencies' to which the term psychic force refers. Like electricity and magnetism these are 'not substances, not matter, not things', merely (quoting Tyndall) 'modes of motion', known only via their effects on molecular structure 'when it impedes their passage' (p. 8). A science of Psychology, he concludes at this point, 'is at least as possible as is a Science of Electricity or a Science of Magnetism' (pp. 10–11).

Only as he proceeds further do we see him arguing himself towards a more radical dualism. Mind or soul ('in popular conception') is 'that conscious self which receives and takes cognizance of those brain actions, which to it are sensations' (although these are not all 'conscious' – he also accepts Carpenter's notion of 'unconscious cerebration') (*Proceedings*, p. 24). For Psychology, 'soul' is 'the definite entity which has the consciousness of individual identity and which constitutes the individual Man' (p. 25). 'Psyche' would be a better term – 'the *intelligent* motive force that directs the mechanism of Man' (p. 25, italics in original). 'Psychic force' becomes 'the instrument by which "Psyche" operates upon the material mechanism of the body, and upon the external world' (p. 26). Which leads us to ask '[is] *this thing that is conscious* something other than the material organism of which it is conscious?', a question 'surely of overwhelming interest to every human being', but one which 'can only be answered by *facts*' (p. 26, italics in original). Hence he is led to argue (p. 28) that if psyche is something other than matter then it must stem from some intelligent being other than a person's physical structure.

That he aspires to an account in which immortality of the soul can be salvaged, if not the strong spiritualist agenda, is more apparent elsewhere in passages such as: 'we are Souls, clothed with a molecular mechanism necessary for communication with the molecular part of creation, in which the present stage of being is to be passed' (Cox, 1878: 50). While not actually contradicting the statements so far given, in referring to a 'present stage of being' and a soul 'clothed with a molecular mechanism' he inevitably highlights the potential affinities of his doctrine with those of the spiritualists. Even so, this remains anchored in the earlier, only semi-immaterialist, case that this does not so much consist of some immaterial spiritual substance as of some submolecular stuff, only knowable, like magnetism, via its molecular-level effects. In arguing for the 'Duality of Mind' he cites Carpenter, Brown-Séquard and Ferrier. He saw their several claims regarding the differential and separate functioning of the cerebral hemispheres as immensely significant, for this suggested that the 'material mechanism' alone could not account for the evident unitary purposiveness of the psyche, but rather served only to put its intentions into effect. Although his statements are not entirely consistent, Cox appears to envisage consciousness or mind as the self-disclosing product of the effects a personal 'Psyche' exerts – via 'non-molecular' psychic force – on the 'molecular' brain.

Obviously, from our perspective, he seems to fall between two stools – he definitely does not want to be identified with spiritualism, and yet defines Psychology's subject matter in such a way that it has to be differentiated in principle from the subject matters of the orthodox natural sciences. It must, though, be conceded that he quite plausibly fudges the boundary by invoking electricity, magnetism, gravity and heat as phenomena studied by orthodox physical sciences which are nonetheless similarly 'immaterial', known only indirectly by their effects. Acceptance of his view of Psychology implies, nonetheless, a prior rejection of hard 'materialism' of the kind being, as he saw it, advocated by Tyndall, whom he specifically attacked (*Proceedings*, pp. 99–106/1–8), and T.H. Huxley. A serious, if slightly tangential, consequence of this was that it meant his supporters in the PSGB were at best semidetached from evolutionary thinking,[27] exacerbating the perceived divergence of their position from that being explored by the rising Darwinian (and often Spencerian) intellectual elite.

While clearly deeply intrigued by spiritualism, its phenomena were, for Cox, but one segment of a spectrum of phenomena for which physical scientists could not account. But these other phenomena were not 'paranormal' in the current sense; rather they included many which had long been of interest to now canonical proto-psychologists and medical writers – hypnotism, sleep, trance states, 'automatism' and various symptoms of mental illness for example, as well as more familiar riddles regarding the mind–body relationship.

Most importantly, this highlights the extent to which the meaning of the term 'Psychology' was, until the late nineteenth century, still undecided (a theme which will recur in the next two chapters). Spiritualists, for example, were attempting to co-opt it and published a journal with the word in its title.[28] 'Mental Philosophy' or 'Mental Science' were still, for many, the preferred terms for the discipline concerned with the 'human mind'. Mental and Moral Philosophers frequently, moreover, placed within 'anthropology' many topics now considered as Psychological – restricting their concerns to the nature and structure of the mind *sensu stricto*.[29] Cox was desperately trying to define a proper subject matter for this putative discipline – something tangible like electricity or magnetism which could constitute the target of conventionally scientific empirical investigation. The psychic force which he believed must underlie phenomena such as those just listed provided this subject matter. For Cox, psychic force was a demonstrably existing province of nature, amenable to rigorous scientific investigation, which contemporary science was wilfully neglecting.

Unfortunately for him, most elite Psychological thinkers were starting to pursue a rather different line of attack – the implications for human nature of evolutionary thought. In the early 1870s, however, this trend was less clear; after all, *Mind*'s progenitors Bain and George Croom Robertson were both at best lukewarm about evolutionary theory. In Lakatos' terms, this would soon, however, provide a much richer research programme in which identifying a distinct psychological subject matter was of less interest than how evolutionary perspectives might illuminate everything pertaining to human nature from childhood to neurology, sex differences to idiocy, emotion to madness, its evolutionary roots to its possible destiny.[30] It is reasonable to conjecture that by December 1879 their awareness of the gathering, irresistible, momentum of the evolutionary programme, as evidenced by the rapidly increasing number of such Psychological works being published in Britain and the United States, was one of the factors leading the PSGB's surviving members to lay Cox's project to rest along with him. Much had, in fact, transpired since early 1875 to render Cox's 1875 protestations of a general scientific neglect of Psychology out of date[31] (although in truth they were somewhat overstated from the outset). Those more interested in spiritualist phenomena would henceforth pursue their own path[32] and the remainder, even if they wished, may well have felt unable to readjust a society so identified with Cox's doctrines to the rising materialist evolutionary tide. In most scientific discussions on the 'evolution of mind', the ontological status of 'mind' was of ancillary interest – arising only at the point where material evolutionary-biological and neurological accounts seemed insufficient. And this point appeared to be ever receding. The questions of whether 'Man' was possessed of some special spiritual status, and whether an irreducible non-material residuum would remain when physicalist accounts were completed, were not so much answered as parked while more immediately interesting and profitable enquiries were pursued to the limit.

In the early 1870s the direction of events had been less clear. Cox's alternative conception of scientific Psychology was neither intrinsically 'unscientific' nor bizarre. To use a musical analogy, its relationship to the main note was that of a harmonic rather than a discord. Much in his research agenda would subsequently be reincorporated into mainstream Psychology, while some current theorising about the mind–body relationship (such as Roger Penrose's) is oddly reminiscent of Cox's views (invoking as it does, in Penrose's case, subatomic – 'non-molecular' – quantum processes[33]). Moreover, in some of his statements at least, Cox's 'psychic force' concept possesses certain affinities with the Freudian unconscious in being a covert, transpersonal, source and grounding of conscious psychological phenomena. PSGB member F.W.H. Myers' subsequent notions of a 'subliminal self' and 'subliminal action' certainly provide a clear link between Cox's formulation and the general acceptance of an 'unconscious mind', which – partly through Myers' efforts – was in place by the early 1900s (Myers, 1886, 1893b). Expounded less stridently by one of the elite, Cox's arguments may well have been accorded far more respect in those circles than they actually received, and his name have retained some kind of acknowledged place in subsequent Psychological discourse. His case for 'psychic force' was not so much answered as simply ignored. Cox's failure was not then due to intellectual factors alone – there was an important social dimension too.

4   The social position of the PSGB

The social character of the PSGB membership was an especially significant factor in its fortunes, illuminating its patent failure to engage the sympathetic attention or involvement of the metropolitan intellectual elite. Cox himself, as mentioned earlier, achieved some kind of association with Galton, although Galton did not feel this significant enough to mention in his autobiography (Galton, 1908). He also knew A.R. Wallace (with whom he testified, unsuccessfully, in defence of 'Dr' Henry Slade, a 'notorious' American 'spirit writer' accused under the Vagrancy Act after exposure by E. Ray Lankester and Horatio Donkin in 1876 – see Oppenheim, 1985: 22–23). But even as a major publisher and senior lawyer, Cox managed, at best, to hover on the fringes of the circles in which the intellectually eminent moved. The PSGB's active members were, in truth, firmly in the 'amateur' camp which Bain and Croom Robertson were so keen to exclude from involvement in *Mind* (Neary, this volume). As a keen Conservative, Cox's politics may have further handicapped him. The Society's membership were men ('Ladies' could not become full members, but could acquire admission tickets for half the usual annual subscription) drawn from the urban professional ranks, often with a penchant for anthropology, lawyers being especially prominent, along with higher-ranking military figures and doctors.[34]

From the membership list we can clarify the nature of the PSGB's supporters a little further. The prominence of the legal profession is demonstrated by the fact that 23 of the 105 full members were barristers, solicitors or judges. Of the others whose professions may be ascertained, nine were doctors or otherwise involved with medicine, seven military officers (one also a judge) and five clergymen (25 are simply given as 'Esq.'). While 12 members had MAs and two others were 'Professors' (including Plumptre), only two were members of the aristocracy. A couple of diplomats, an MP, an alderman and an architect also appear, while 13 are given as 'Fellows' of other learned societies – six of the Royal Geographical Society, but a mere three of the Royal Society.[35]

Men such as these had long been welcome in societies such as the Linnean, the Geographical and the Anthropological, where their labours and observations provided invaluable data for the more 'professional' specialists, and their subscriptions a major source of funding.[36] Those, such as Bain and Croom Robertson, struggling to promote rigorous discussion of human nature were, by contrast, acutely conscious of the need to police admission into their debates. By its very nature it was a topic on which every literate person might feel entitled to hold forth. Progress – 'self-professionalisation' as it were – seemingly required restricting participants to those with acceptable intellectual credentials, and in the enduring shadow of the now venerated John Stuart Mill (who died in 1873) the standard was high. While an Oxbridge philosophy degree might help, it was not necessary or perhaps even sufficient: what was required rather was to persuade the gatekeepers – by writings, talk and social mores – that one was 'one of us'.[37] This was a world in which, while desirable, formal qualifications as yet played a relatively minor role. Unusually for the time, social class origins per se were less important than perceived intellectual calibre or value to the intellectual community – Herbert Spencer and Alexander Bain, for instance, had both clawed their way up from poverty by dint of sheer workaholic single-mindedness. The label of 'amateur' was, nonetheless, often as much a reflection of lack of social connections as of intellectual quality.

Reporting a new species of spider to the Linnean Society was one thing, it was quite another to expect the editors of *Mind* to warmly receive what one believed were original musings on human nature. Besides, elite Psychological thinkers had enough on their hands fending off attacks from the religious party, who felt human nature to be their own legitimate preserve. In this context, the PSGB constituency found itself on the receiving end of what appears to have been a deliberate exclusion policy. Only three of their works were briefly noticed in Mind: Cox's *Monograph on Sleep and Dream* received a sarcastically deadpan dismissal and George Harris's *A Philosophical Treatise on the Nature and Constitution of Man* (1876) – a two-volume magnum opus – fared little better; only C.S. Wake's *The Evolution of Morality* (1878, also two volumes) was honoured with a haughtily dispensed crumb of praise – 'A sufficiently conglomerate production, yet withal a valuable collection of facts'.[38] *Nature* rarely mentioned the Society's meetings in its weekly notices of learned society meetings and took little notice of its members' writings.[39] Yet it is worth remarking that if *Mind* and *Nature* were unimpressed by Cox, the provincial press could, in contrast, be more enthusiastic. The advertisement for *What Am I?* among the pages preceding the *Monograph on Sleep and Dream* quotes laudatory puffs from 14 regional papers, ranging from the *Brighton Guardian* to the *Ayr Advertiser* and *Irish Daily Telegraph* (*Lloyds Newspaper* was also enthusiastic). Cox (1875a) complained that *What Am I?* 'received but scant notice from the reviewers' but was consoled by the fact it 'found such favour with the public that an edition of 750 copies was exhausted in nine months' (p. vi) (and, as mentioned earlier, it was subsequently reissued).

It is against this background that we should read Cox's prefatory polemic to the first volume of *What Am I?*, especially the following passage, in which he appears to be trying to 'pull rank' on the entire scientific community:

> To a Lawyer, who has imbibed from his youth up the Principles of Evidence, and who has been trained, by experience in Courts of Justice, to the almost instinctive recognition of what does or does not constitute *proof*, there is nothing so surprising, and at the same time so vexatious, as the almost entire disregard of the plainest Principles of Evidence by the votaries of Science, who assert and deny facts, apparently without the slightest conception of the nature or degree of *proof* necessary to be produced before any asserted fact can be either accepted or rejected.... This disregard of the most elementary rules of evidence is especially remarkable in works that treat of Physiology, Medicine, and Psychology. (pp. xii–xiii, italics in original)

A little later he even mooted the possibility of a legal-style 'Tribunal of Science' to determine disputed facts (pp. xiv–xv). Coupled with the high proportion of lawyers in the PSGB's active membership, this inevitably makes one wonder whether the situation had a more circumscribable source than has so far been considered: frustration on the part of legal professionals regarding claims by theologians, philosophers and scientists to expertise on human nature. This certainly fits Cox's own case – was he then voicing feelings widespread among his legal colleagues? They were, after all, dealing with human nature every day and having to make judgements on the basis of empirical evidence alone.[40] This passage does in fact touch on profounder issues regarding the respective natures of 'scientific' and 'jurisprudential' methodological rationality which cannot be pursued here. The point does, nonetheless, demand to be flagged.[41]

This impression of marginalisation is reinforced when we further examine Cox's tenuous connection with Galton. Not only is it unmentioned in Galton's autobiography, but even in Karl Pearson's monumental *Life, Letters and Labours of Francis Galton* it figures only briefly in the second volume (1924) in connection with Galton's transient flirtation with spiritualism in the early 1870s.[42] A letter from Galton to Charles Darwin dated 28 March 1872 mentions his attending, with Crookes, 'a noisy but curious séance at Sergeant [*sic*] Cox's' (this occasion was alluded to previously) and in another dated 19 April 1872, describing a séance with Home[43] 'in full gaslight', at which an accordion held by its base under the table apparently played itself, he says, 'The playing was remarkably good and sweet. It played in Sergeant Cox's hands, but not in mine, although it shoved itself, or was shoved under the table into them' (cited in Pearson, 1924: 63–64). The tone certainly suggests that Darwin would have known who Cox was without further explanation.

Inattention to Cox's Psychological efforts was not due to mere ignorance regarding them. Oppenheim (1985) identifies two further occasions on which Galton and Cox were both present at séances: in January 1873 and some time in 1875 when Crookes tested the medium Annie Eva Fay.[44] The only other context in which I have so far identified their co-presence is an Anthropological Institute meeting in 1874 at which Galton presented a 'Proposal to apply for anthropological statistics from schools'. Tanner (1993: 110) notes 'Also in the discussion Serjeant Cox said that Quételet, "in his recent work (that is *Anthropometrie*) [published in 1870] has made an extensive and valuable collection of statistics … of this kind which would form a basis for comparison." To this remark Galton did not reply, presumably because he was not acquainted with the reference.' Galton of course was steeped – none indeed more so – in Quételet's earlier work, so this inadvertent and unwelcome exposure of the master's ignorance may well not have helped Cox's cause! Bearing in mind the adage that absence of evidence is not evidence of absence, it is nonetheless also difficult not to read some significance into the fact that the copious Galton correspondence at University College London contains not a single communication to or from any of the PSGB figures identified earlier with the sole exception (M&G, no. 289/1) of an 1891 letter from F.W.H. Myers proposing a role for Sully in the impending Congress of Psychology. For whatever reason, acceptance by the metropolitan intellectual elite forever eluded Cox despite his high profiles in legal and publishing circles, familiarity with the literature and attendance at meetings of learned societies.

Even less successful were his most productive associates, C.S. Wake (1835–1910) and George Harris (1809–1890). Only F.W.H. Myers would eventually prove the exception, while the Rev. W. Stainton Moses ascended into ever more ethereal realms of spiritualistic mysticism.[45] Wake's case is perhaps the most poignant. Prominent in the Anthropological Society of London and its successor the Anthropological Institute, his works such as *Chapters on Man* (1868) – which had urged the creation of a 'comparative' (i.e. cross-cultural or cross-'racial') Psychology – and *Serpent-Worship, and other Essays, with a chapter on Totemism* (1888) were ignored by his contemporaries and hardly even known to posterity until Rodney Needham reissued *The Development of Marriage and Kinship* (1889) in 1967.[46] And yet, as Needham demonstrates at length, his writings were fully professional: technically competent, original, sophisticatedly argued and immensely learned. The non-moralising style and careful formulation of conceptual issues in this work, in contrast with his famous contemporaries (John Lubbock, E.B. Tylor and J.F. McLennan) again bear the hallmarks of a legally trained mind cautiously evaluating the evidence. (Needham also sees him as approaching a Durkheimian, as opposed to routinely evolutionary, position.) In 1889 or 1890 he emigrated to the United States, continuing his involvement with anthropology, but soon became obsessed with developing what he called 'vortex philosophy'. Having lost a 600-page manuscript in a fire, the poor man privately published a brief account of this in 1904 (reissued 1907). Alas, it is one of those bizarre, borderline psychotic, Theories of Everything, hinging on the notion of vortical connections between all levels of reality, replete with complicated coloured plates of spirals and other geometrical figures. He died 'in lonely poverty' in Chicago in 1910. A prolific, assiduous, original and erudite man of 'unusually retiring and unassuming character' (Needham, p. viii), Wake was effectively air-brushed from the histories of both Anthropology and Psychology. Even the *Journal of the Anthropological Institute*'s obituary notice of its sometime Director and Council member got his initials wrong. No portraits, and none of his papers, have survived.

Harris is also worth further comment. *His Supernatural Phenomena. Tests Adapted to Determine the Truth of Supernatural Phenomena* (1874) displayed his own concern to place investigations of the subject on a sound empirical basis. In the promotional pamphlet for his mighty A *Philosophical Treatise on the Nature and Constitution of Man* (bound in before the title page in one of the copies in the British Library) he lists 'the gentlemen who have so kindly aided the undertaking' (p. 3) – an impressive roll-call including Darwin, Galton, Gladstone, Lubbock, Huxley, Maudsley, Quatrefages and Wallace as among those with whom he had 'been in correspondence … and consulted'. This cannot save him, however: as we have seen, *Mind* roundly dismissed this product of (according to the *DNB*) 43 years' labour. As in Cox's case, the provincial press was, by contrast, more enthusiastic (as were some popular magazines).[47] The entry in the *DNB* (itself of course an elite project) also says of it that 'he completely ignored the methods and conclusions of modern scientific psychology'. This is a travesty of the truth – among others he cites or quotes Bain, Carpenter, Darwin, Galton, Huxley, Lewes, Maudsley, M. Müller, James Mill, John Stuart Mill, and Spencer. It is true that he believed in a spiritual realm, and in a somewhat cruder fashion than Cox, but he was patently striving with all his might to engage with the elite. As the Anthropological Institute's Vice-President he might reasonably have had high hopes of succeeding; instead he too could but linger on the threshold.

There was in fact a third level of psychological concern below the PSGB in this hierarchy, which Psychology would eventually have to come to terms with – a process even yet incomplete (see Thomson, Chapter 5). This is the popular 'self-help' and 'self-improvement' tradition, now identified most prominently with Samuel Smiles (see Smiles, 1859), but also reflected in the persisting popularity of phrenology as well as other genres such as those concerned with memory improvement (e.g. J.H. Bacon, 1889) and moral instruction regarding sex (e.g. T.L. Nicholls, n.d., *c.* 1873). Little in the PSGB literature suggests, however, that this topic ever featured in its discussions (a possible exception might be Plumptre's involvement with elocution, but there is no reference to his having addressed the Society on this). They are thus neatly sandwiched between the elite and the practitioners in this popular, but scientifically disdained, field.

5   Conclusions

The psychological constituency which the PSGB represented in the late 1870s had not yet seen its psychological interests and concerns being properly addressed by 'science'. Despite the rhetoric to the contrary, their basic anxieties remained, for the while at least, quasi-theological – the wish to affirm and demonstrate the inadequacy of 'materialism' in accounting for human nature, coupled with a perception that the scientists (who had heightened these anxieties in the first place) were either ignoring those phenomena which might challenge materialism or failing to acknowledge their true significance. If only briefly, in the new scientific temper of the times, Cox's campaign and conception of Psychology touched a chord, as he proclaimed that 'for centuries mental science has made no progress whatever, while all other sciences have been advancing with great strides' (*Proceedings*, p. 14/3). Progress was being especially hampered by vain metaphysical philosophising on the one side and dogmatic scientific materialism on the other – and he could show a way through the impasse. Even by 1880, however, this was becoming a position difficult to sustain, while over the next two decades or so this constituency's psychological concerns would also change – shifted in no small part, ironically, by the evolutionary ideas of Spencer and Galton. The social-managerial tasks with which many of them (not least the lawyers) were directly concerned became increasingly problematic in the face of ongoing urbanisation and industrialisation, placing them under ever greater pressure to create ways of handling the tasks of education, mental health and maintaining law and order – and of these it was its bearings on education and child-rearing (ignored by the PSGB) that proved most crucial to Psychology's institutional emergence (see Chapter 3). As these tasks assumed an ever-higher priority, so their potential commonality with the practical interests of those in the 'psy' disciplines (as Nikolas Rose calls them) would come to the fore, and the issue of contesting 'materialism' would cease to be a major preoccupation. Spiritual anxieties yielded to eugenic ones.

The PSGB episode thus exemplifies the peculiarly transitional nature of Psychological thinking in the 1870s. The need for a discipline of Psychology is becoming accepted but what it is actually about is still a matter of contestation. Cox's *What Am I?* and Harris's *A Philosophical Treatise* thus emerge as intriguing transitional texts in which educated 'amateurs' are earnestly endeavouring to keep up to speed with scientific developments, in each case nurturing and evolving over many decades their own 'scientific' visions of human nature. While able to lay these before the public under the imprints of reputable publishing houses, and despite their best efforts at participation in the scientific debate, their wisdom is now being spurned by the elite gatekeepers, even if retaining some authority in the world at large. The PSGB, despite its promise as an institutional base from which to forge connections between Britain's pioneer Psychologists and the educated professional intelligentsia, was in the end too bound up with promoting Cox's alternative project and serving as a vehicle for that group's own psychological wrestlings to be able do so, especially in a climate in which the 'professionals' were increasingly hostile to such connections being forged in the first place. (The *mentalité* represented by the PSGB membership is perhaps most sensitively conveyed in F.W.H. Myers' later essay 'Science and a future life'; Myers, 1893a.)

Were this group's initiatives entirely in vain? It is undoubtedly regrettable that they have been totally ignored by disciplinary historians, as they obviously enjoyed some contemporary success and had some, albeit now unascertainable, impact in furthering popular cultural acceptance of the idea of a discipline called Psychology. Even so, it must be conceded that (Myers excepted) they have left virtually no traces by way of remembered texts, theories, concepts or findings. (The popular self-improvement genre has fared better in this respect, since modern cultural historians rightly see it as providing an index of and entrée into Victorian mass psychology.) *Mind*, we saw, condescended to notice, dismissively, three of their publications and otherwise ignored them entirely. How then are we to interpret an episode like this and the works of such writers? We can, I think, improve on sterile anticipation spotting. Rather, they constitute data in their own right regarding the hitherto historiographically invisible psychological conditions of that section of society within which British Psychology would eventually have to strike root in order assume a clear disciplinary form. They clarify first why, during the 1870s, these conditions were as yet unripe for such a development, but also enable us to spot some of those strands which did subsequently facilitate Psychology's emergence, most obviously the adoption of experimental methods for investigating 'psychic' phenomena, a general insistence on empirical study of psychological matters and concern with psychological issues among those engaged in social-managerial professions. It is also suggested that Cox's notion of psychic force might, via the involvement of F.W.H. Myers in the PSGB, have played a previously unnoticed role in the complex late-nineteenth-century evolution of the notion of the unconscious. Less obviously, the concerns of this group perhaps manifest a psychological shift towards 'interiorisation' and 'inwardness' among the British middle-classes, analogous to that which recent scholars have been identifying in the nineteenth-century United States – although this point cannot be explored further here (but see, for example, the papers by Joel Pfister, Nancy Schnog and David M. Lubin in Pfister and Schnog, 1997). Moreover, they direct our attention to further questions regarding how, when and why these conditions changed. How and when did British psychologists manage to 'self-professionalise' themselves? And when did the Rosean agenda of a discipline geared to the 'inscription' and management of subjectivity in an applied 'governmental' fashion (Rose, 1985) really come to the forefront within British Psychology? (Did this in some respect involve a meeting between the popular and the professional over the heads, as it were, of the PSGB group, providing a further reason for the latter's neglect?)

Finally, from the historiographical point of view, this episode demonstrates how important it is to focus on relatively brief timeframes; crucial and significant events are often fleeting, and sweeping expressions like 'the late-Victorian world view' or 'late-nineteenth-century British Psychology' fail to capture the real subtlety and complexity of events. The years 1873–1879 were ones during which Psychological thought in Britain underwent fundamental change. The intellectual trees in this neck of the wood are thus vital for an understanding of its eventual shape, and clearly constitute a Site of Historical Scientific Interest in which further rare specimens and missing links may yet be discovered. Our image of the dynamics of the late-Victorian intellectual scene is fundamentally flawed and incomplete if we exclude the now forgotten under-swell of writers and events such as those we have been discussing and ignore the roles they played in the quotidian social psychological and intellectual life of the times. From my reflexive perspective, this quotidian psychological life is the very subject matter to which Psychology as a discipline owes its origin. If the labours of Cox and his associates have been deemed (unfairly in my view) to fail in qualifying for the status of Psychology, their status as significant psychological phenomena in their own right surely has to be acknowledged.

To return to the chapter's title: the meanings for us of the PSGB's failure lie in what it signifies about the intellectual climate and wider psychological context from which British Psychology emerged and why, despite the number of canonically eminent pioneers who were publishing in the 1870s, the discipline could not yet assume an institutional form. The evidence presented here suggests that at least three factors were in play: first, intellectual confusion about how Psychology's subject matter should be defined; second, the social distance and the incongruence of psychological concerns between such pioneers and the psychological constituencies (most prominently middle-class men in professions such as the law and medicine) upon whom institutional success depended in the absence of a university base; and third, the peculiarly pervasive effects of the spiritualism craze.

The first of these is additionally significant in reinforcing the message of much recent history of Psychology that, in a more direct fashion than in the physical sciences, Psychology's understanding of what constituted its appropriate subject matter was itself something which had to be forged within specific historical and social contexts (Richards, 1996; Pfister and Schnog, 1997). The second also draws our attention to the way in which the distinction between professional and amateur was as yet as much a social distinction as one of intellectual calibre, resulting in the enduring exclusion of some quite important and significant work from the historical canon. Regarding spiritualism, the effect was, again, temporally extended, for while it was certainly being viewed by most of the scientific elite of the time with a degree of suspicion,[48] its later decline into more serious disrepute led to its systematic neglect by traditional heroic historians of Psychology. The roles of figures and organisations in any way cast as associated with it thus fell even further from view. We have shown here that such a casting is seriously misleading as far as Cox and his Society were concerned. If marking the centenary of the British Psychological Society must inevitably involve celebration, surely we might generously extend our celebratory hospitality and belatedly welcome to the fold its long and unjustly forgotten predecessor, the Psychological Society of Great Britain – which fell so foul of the pride and prejudice of the discipline's canonical British founding fathers.

Acknowledgements

This chapter ultimately originated in the chance discovery of Edward Cox's *Monograph on Sleep and Dream* in the stock of London bookseller Eric Korn, which included details of the Psychological Society of Great Britain at the end. I would like to acknowledge the comments on earlier drafts by Francis Neary, Lyuba Gurjeva and Sandy Lovie.

Notes

1 In this chapter, 'Psychology' and 'Psychological' refer to the discipline, and 'psychology' and 'psychological' to its subject matter. This has long been the author's own practice since, without it, unambiguous reference to the relationship between the two becomes extremely cumbersome.
2 On the initial aims and wide-ranging content of *Mind* see Francis Neary (this volume).
3 British universities did not at this time operate doctoral research programmes; the standard postgraduate qualification was the masters degree, which entitled one to teach the subject. Doctorates (if not honorary) were awarded only in recognition of sustained academic achievement. The PhD was subsequently introduced in Britain in order to compete with the German universities in attracting overseas, primarily US, research students. The distinction persists in the difference between the now conventional thesis-based PhD and the DLitt, DSc, DPhil group of awards made on the basis of published work.
4 This did, nonetheless, have the consequence that French nineteenth-century Psychology, in particular, was dominated by psychiatric and 'abnormal' concerns, such as hypnotism.
5 This could happen in France too, as in the cases of Gustav Le Bon and, to some extent, Alfred Binet (who was a sometime dramatist). On James Sully see Lyuba Gurjeva (this volume).
6 See Danziger (1982) for a discussion of this group which advances on Hearnshaw's (1964).
7 These were also widespread imperial intellectual preoccupations of direct political and economic significance, which could hardly be said of Psychology at this date.
8 Hearnshaw (1964) fails to mention either the PSGB or its founder, though briefly touches on spiritualism and Crookes.
9 Cited henceforth as '*Proceedings*'. This is doubly paginated from p. 38 (i.e. after Cox's inaugural address), conventional pagination being coupled with separate pagination for each paper. Citations to subsequent material indicate individual paper pagination

second. An editorial introduction and Cox's preface to his inaugural address are separately paginated in roman (i–xvi, i–vi, respectively).

10 W. Stainton Moses – see Oppenheim (1985: 30) and her footnote for original source. An obituary in *The Athenaeum* also commented that 'even his opponents admired the kindliness and honesty of the man' (No. 2718, 29 November 1879, p. 695).

11 I may I hope be forgiven for not including these in the references!

12 Although he was in fact elected MP for Taunton in 1868, he was unseated by petition.

13 One of these enjoyed longer success than anything else he wrote – *The Arts of Writing, Reading, and Speaking. Letters to a Law Student*, first published in 1863; a reprint of the third, 1878, edition was issued as late as 1909. The publisher was Horace Cox – a relative?

14 The controversial London physician famed for pioneering the anaesthetic use of mesmerism and founder of the journal *The Zooist*.

15 See Cox (1873, 1874: vol. 2, pp. iii–x) for his own account of the origins of his views. Intriguingly he claims that the work is 'in outline the same' as a lecture written for a scientific society 42 years previously (i.e. *c.* 1832!). Another early influence was a work by Dr Arthur Ladbrooke Wigan '30 years ago', *A New View of Insanity. The Duality of the Mind Proved by the Structure, Functions and Diseases of the Brain.*

16 The *Oxford English Dictionary* (*psychic* A3b) credits Crookes with the phrase giving the date as 17 July 1871 (*Quarterly Journal of Science*), with Cox using it two days later in his letter to him; however, Cox's letter is actually dated 8 June 1871 (see next paragraph of main text). Cox is, however, credited with the substantive form of '*psychic*' (B1a) – a person susceptible to psychic influence – in the same letter. The phrase 'psychical research' (*psychical* 3) starts with the founding of the Society for Psychical Research (1882) although '*psychical*' as 'of or pertaining to the human soul' (*psychical* 1) dates back to Henry More (1642). It appears reasonable to grant Cox the major role in promoting the current usage of the term 'psychic' as referring to paranormal psychological phenomena during the 1870s, and 'psychic force' was clearly his.

17 The immediate upshots of this collaboration were two publications: Crookes *et al.* (1871) (a 15-page pamphlet) and Cox (1871), the 1872 revised edition of which really introduces his 'psychic force' notion publicly for the first time.

18 For Galton's involvement with spiritualism during this period, largely ignored in his own autobiography, see Oppenheim (1985: 294–529) and Pearson (1924: 62–67). See below for more on the Galton connection.

19 Oppenheim (1985: 30) observes that 'Psychological' in the PSGB's title did not mean what it means now, but that is really to beg the question.

20 Was he, one wonders, the source of the expression 'plummy voice'? The *Oxford English Dictionary* dates it from *Punch* in 1881 as being a figurative usage equivalent to 'fruity'; however, Plumptre published several editions of *King's College Lectures on Elocution* (1870–1886) and was the author of *The Principles and Practice of Elocution* (1861) and *The Culture of Voice and Speech* (1874). This would fit in very nicely with an 1881 origin if his identification with the topic had, as seems likely, become widely established in London society.

21 I have been unable to ascertain whether he was related to the more famous poet Rabindranath Tagore. He is not mentioned by Sykes (1947).

22 *Proceedings* Introduction p. xi.

23 Croll is best remembered for his cosmological and evolutionary theorising (*Stellar Evolution*, 1889; and *The Philosophical Basis of Evolution*, 1890).

24 See Smith (1988) for a now classic attack on this approach. The immediate point is that approaches aimed at celebrating Psychology's rise to scientific respectability will be disinclined to attend to embarrassing earlier connections with such things as spiritualism.

25 As well as J.B. and Lousia Rhine, Gardner Murphy was among the prominent American psychologists to sustain an interest in the topic.

26 See Ellesley (1995: 267), who lists seven reviews of Freud from the *Proceedings* and *Journal of the Society for Psychical Research* between 1910 and 1913.

27 A. R. Wallace's own association with spiritualism, and belief that evolution could not fully explain human consciousness, are well known. While some, such as Lord Balfour, felt that psychic abilities could somehow be fitted into the evolutionary scheme of things (as atavistic survivals of once prevalent capacities, or seeds of future evolutionary developments), others became ever more firmly convinced otherwise (for an aggressive stance, see for example Bozzano, 1937: ch. 1).

28 *Psychological Review: A Cosmopolitan Organ of Spiritualism and Psychological Research*, which ran from 1878 to 1883. The struggle for intellectual ownership of the term 'psychology' between spiritualists, purveyors of popular self-improvement books and academic psychologists was also a feature of the US situation at this time.

29 This more limited agenda may be seen, for example, in the work of the leading American figure in mental and moral philosophy, Noah Porter, notably in his highly influential *Human Intellect* (1868/1872). It is more explicit in, for example, Samuel Bailey (1858).

30 See Lakatos and Musgrave (1970). R.J. Richards (1987) is the most thorough treatment of the role of evolutionary thought in Psychological thought.

31 In Britain these included, among much else, the founding of *Mind* in 1876, Bain's *Education as a Science* (1878) (and a new edition of *The Emotions and the Will*, 1875), H. Calderwood's *The Relations of Mind and Brain* (1879), successive editions of W.B. Carpenter's *Principles of Mental Physiology* (which, first appearing in 1874 was into a fourth edition by 1876 – and continued to flourish thereafter) and his hostile *Mesmerism, Spiritualism &c. Historically and Scientifically Considered* (1877), W.K. Clifford's *Seeing and Thinking* (1879), and the second to fifth (final) volumes of G.H. Lewes's *Problems of Life and Mind* (1875–1879). The impacts of Darwin's *Descent of Man* (1871) and *The Expression of the Emotions in Man and Animals* (1872) were also escalating throughout the decade, as was that of the second, much enlarged and revised, edition of Herbert Spencer's *Principles of Psychology* (1870). The hugely influential *International Scientific Series*, founded by Spencer's American disciple Youmans in 1871, was also getting into its stride (see Macleod, 1980).

32 It should of course be stressed that the SPR was (and is) not dogmatically pro-spiritualist and has always also been concerned with the full range of so-called 'paranormal' phenomena. Many members were, like Cox had been, profoundly critical of the spiritualists' own 'theory' and sceptical of séance phenomena.

33 See Penrose (1990a). Admittedly Penrose's position is generally considered somewhat eccentric but, as the fact that a summary and peer commentary appeared in the highly prestigious *Behavioral and Brain Sciences* (Penrose, 1990b) testifies, it was accorded the fullest respect by his scientific peers.

34 See Oppenheim (1985: 28–29) on the professional middle-class character of spiritualism's supporters at this time. Spiritualism nonetheless appealed to a rather broader spectrum than the PSGB, whose members were mostly metropolitan and towards the upper end of the middle-class social scale, while spiritualism had a huge provincial following penetrating to the lower middle class.

35 The absence of anyone clearly identifiable as associated with education is also to be noted in the light of subsequent events discussed by Gurjeva (Chapter 3).

36 Note, for example, Charles Darwin's own extensive cultivation of amateur contacts as a source of information, including the circulation of a questionnaire. In the 1870s the majority of even the most 'professional' botanists, zoologists and geographers were still not actually earning their livings in these capacities. In the more advanced disciplines, such as physics and chemistry, the amateur was, however, rapidly being

left behind and had long since disappeared from medically related disciplines such as neurology and physiology.

37 See Chapters 2 and 3 for Sully's 'apprenticeship'. Bain had previously followed a similar route involving, for both of them, what was basically hack journalistic and general dogsbody work for the elite's favoured periodicals.

38 See *Mind* (1878), Vol. 3, pp. 289–290, for the reviews of Cox's and Wake's books, *Mind* (1876), Vol. 1, pp. 438–439, for the review of Harris's. Reviewers are not identifiable but Sully is an obvious candidate (see Chapter 2).

39 One exception is mention of George Harris's lecture on 'caligraphy' and a mention of impending reissue of volume I of Cox's *What Am I?* (11 February 1875, p. 294). I have been told that *Nature* also gave this work a hostile review, but have been unable to locate it in volumes 9–14 (covering late 1873–1876).

40 Lawyers were indeed prominent among those believing in spiritualism at this time, precisely because they felt the evidence being presented was weightier than that considered sufficient in a court of law (R. Noakes, personal communication).

41 In late-twentieth-century philosophy of science this broader issue was raised by Toulmin (1972), for example.

42 The University College Galton papers also, however, contain a curious 14-page (but unpaginated) handmade booklet entitled *Spirit Rappings at Mrs Hayden's*, dated 1853. This contains a number of what appear to be scrawled (in the dark?, under mediumistic control?) nonsense words with occasional neater notes (e.g. 'right little finger on hand of neighbour' on p. 7). Merrington & Golden (1978) list no. 173.

43 D.D. Home was the most famous and impressive of all those associated with spiritualism and supernormal powers during this era. See Wyndham (1937) for a full account of his strange career.

44 On the former occasion the mediums were the Americans Mr and Mrs Nelson Holmes, exposed as fakes two years later in Philadelphia (Oppenheim, 1985: 294). On the second occasion Crookes' long-time colleague Dr Huggins and the physicist Lord Rayleigh were also present (p. 346).

45 An ascent that may be tracked from Moses (1877), via Moses (1889) to Moses (1902). A selection of his writings was also published after his death in Moses (1930).

46 Needham's introduction contains the only attempt at a biographical account of Wake (pp. viii–xiii), though he does not spot his PSGB membership. Wake's opposition to Lubbock's and McLennan's views on the evolution of marriage may not have endeared him to the establishment but, as Needham observes, Lubbock (1911) does not refer to Wake in answering his critics, despite the very high calibre of his arguments. See references for details of Wake's publications, including Westropp and Wake (1875/ 1972).

47 The promotional pamphlet includes puffs from the Scottish press particularly – both the *Perthshire Courier* and the *Perthshire Constitutional*, the *Dumfries Standard* and the *Dundee Advertiser*. The *Journal of the Anthropological Institute* naturally supports its Vice-President, but so too did *John Bull*, *Criterion* and *Literary World*.

48 W.B. Carpenter (1877) was already becoming thoroughly contemptuous of what he saw as an 'Epidemic Delusion', although, significantly, he ignored Cox's by then well aired position.

2

A question of 'peculiar importance': George Croom Robertson, *Mind* and the changing relationship between British psychology and philosophy

Francis Neary

In January 1876 the first issue of the journal *Mind: A Quarterly Review of Psychology and Philosophy* finally appeared. Over a century later *Mind* has firmly established itself as a seminal journal in the philosophy of mind and language. In 1974 it finally abandoned the psychological epithet and now proudly calls itself a quarterly review of *philosophy*. But this is not how it began. In retrospect, its early title and contents may seem an obvious result of the pressing need for a systematic record of contemporary psychological researches in Britain, but its form and content were heavily contested in the two years before it went to press.[1] This chapter gives a broad picture of the relationship between British philosophy and psychology in the last quarter of the nineteenth century, using the early years of *Mind* as a microcosm of this relationship. The agenda from the outset was to keep something distinctly British from the old discipline of mental philosophy but to subject this to the rigours of empirical research that had been seen on the continent.

 Mind occupies an ambiguous position in the history of psychology. Writers of general histories are keen to mention it, usually as one of the achievements of Alexander Bain, its founder, or as the first psychological journal in the world (see, for example, Flügel and West, 1964: 150; Murphy and Kovach, 1972: 103; Murray, 1983: 120; Leahey, 1980: 170; Hothersall, 1995: 74). They then either leave it at that, or praise it as a unique publishing outlet for works in philosophy and physiology in the period, before moving on to an analysis of the significance of Bain's work. There is, in these accounts, a real sense of not knowing what to do with *Mind*, nor how to incorporate it into a progressive history of the discipline of psychology.[2] So what sort of story should we tell as to its significance to the history of psychology? Neither the claim of Bain's solo achievement nor that of the journal's originality is particularly helpful beyond the domain of heroic and whiggish histories that tend to look for origins of present psychological concepts, ideas and institutions in the work of 'great men' (but see Richards, 1996, ch. 1, for a clearly expressed antidote to this approach).

Mind cannot be described as the *original* journal of psychology[3] because, when it was founded, there was no professional discipline of psychology in Britain to support it. Indeed, one of the principal aims of *Mind* was to discover what exactly psychology was and upon what foundations it should be built to make it scientific. It had the word 'psychology' in its title but articles using the word had earlier appeared in *The Zoist* (1843–1859), the *Journal of Mental Science* (1855–) and some popular monthlies.[4] In fact, the term had been used so extensively in these periodicals that, as we shall see, there were worries about using 'psychology' in the title for a journal which wanted to distinguish itself as a serious, scholarly investigation into the possibility of a science of mind. Nor was *Mind* merely Bain's achievement alone: it was from the outset a collaborative enterprise between Bain, George Croom Robertson and an elite group of philosophers, physiologists and intellectuals who negotiated its form and content and became its first contributors. Bain financed *Mind* with his own money but relied heavily on the well established institutional base of philosophy to establish its academic status and credibility.[5]

As Roger Smith has recently pointed out:

> [The] German-language world did not have a monopoly on psychology, though it did have an academic infrastructure able to support experimental activity on a scale not possible elsewhere – until laboratories were established in the United States in the 1890s. Psychology differentiated as a separate subject area in other places but it did so piecemeal and with distinctive local characteristics. (Smith, 1997b: 494)

Mind can be seen as an example of this differentiation subject to the local contingencies of the British context. This process cannot be seen teleologically, as though the journal somehow anticipates the present state of the discipline. Rather, its development was contingent on the personalities, institutions and wider context in late-nineteenth-century Britain. The purpose of this chapter, then, is not to fit *Mind* into a progressive narrative, but rather to tell a story that identifies the contingent factors which contributed to the journal's development.

A.W. Brown (1947: 197–203) claimed that *Mind* was a response to the failure of the Metaphysical Society of London's generality. That society's elite cocktail of clergymen, philosophers, scientists, artists and politicians who met throughout the 1870s had demonstrated, if anything, that they shared little common ground in their approaches to ultimate philosophical questions such as the relationship between science and religion. Specialisation, with agreed ground rules and agendas, was needed, away from general societies and periodicals, if any progress was to be made. *Mind* thus represented one attempt to specialise, along with Shadworth Hodgson's Aristotelian Society and the journal *Nature*, which were founded about the same time.

R.M. Young (1985: 65) points to the fact that psychological and physiological issues were rarely included in the general evolutionary debates, unless they were treated polemically. Those upholding the traditional picture of nature and society did not wish to attend to the sciences of mind and brain because their position depended on denying that the human mind lay within the domain of science. *Mind* is thus seen by Young as an expression of psychologists frustrated with being ignored. Instead of perpetually treating mind and brain metaphysically, *Mind* intended to procure a decision as to the scientific standing of psychology once and for all.

While Brown uses a thesis of *specialisation* from general debates to explain *Mind*'s inception, Young suggests a thesis of *separation* from the traditional picture of nature and society. The two arguments are not mutually exclusive because, as Young suggests, the separation brought about a fragmentation in the common intellectual context of the nineteenth-century periodical which itself led to the birth of specialist journals. In the late nineteenth century, the common intellectual context of natural theology – which had hitherto provided the framework for discussions of science and religion – was split apart by developments in the natural sciences, particularly by biology and physiological psychology (Young, 1985: ch. 5). On this reading, the failure of the Metaphysical Society in the 1870s to find common ground for intellectual debate becomes a symptom of the fragmentation process.

As a partial corrective to these general positions, this chapter argues that the development of *Mind* can be seen as contingent on the personalities and specificities of exchanges as they unfolded, rather than seeing it against the backdrop of a large-scale social or a general political current. The actors themselves felt most acutely the tension between scientific psychology and the older, associationist philosophical tradition from which they came. In this chapter, I focus on the work and correspondence of George Croom Robertson (1842–1892) to explore the peculiarly British process of how psychology divorced itself from philosophy to become an autonomous discipline. This process of separation and specialisation was not written into the agenda of *Mind* from the outset. In fact the opposite was the case, because the backgrounds and ideas of the key players in the journal's development made them disposed towards keeping philosophy and psychology together.

Croom Robertson is a lesser-known figure in the history of psychology. If he is mentioned at all it is usually as footnote to the work of his mentor and friend Alexander Bain (1818–1903).[6] One purpose of this chapter is to show Croom Robertson's importance as both a builder of extensive networks in his role as the first editor of *Mind*, and to draw attention to his academic work in its own right as a systematic record of the relationship between British philosophy and psychology. The last quarter of the nineteenth century was not only the period when psychology became an autonomous professional discipline, but also the period when psychology's scientific credentials were most intensively questioned and debated. The process of the professionalisation of psychology in Britain took longer than in Europe or the United States. This lack of synchronisation of Britain with other countries is partially due the philosophically minded actors at the helm of the scientific psychology movement, who refused to allow psychology scientific status until critics had been heard and fundamental underpinnings had been fully questioned.[7] Croom Robertson was instrumental in this project in the breadth of positions he allowed into the first journal of philosophy and psychology in Britain and his constant reflections upon them. However, unlike the case of Bain,[8] Croom Robertson's work has not enjoyed a contextual treatment. This chapter sets out to encourage this endeavour, and for this reason I sometimes indulge myself in a modicum of edification.

Croom Robertson attended Aberdeen's Marischal College in the late 1850s and, after the colleges were merged into the United University of Aberdeen in 1860, he won a two-year scholarship in classics and mental philosophy.[9] He used the money wisely and, following a brief spell at University College London, he went to Germany, where, in addition to studying metaphysics, Kant and Hegel, he attended the classes of Du Bois Reymond and Rudolf Wagner in physiology and of Trendelenburg in psychology. In Göttingen, Wagner introduced him by letter to Broca in Paris, where he spent the summer of 1863. On his return to Aberdeen it was this privileged schooling in psychology, physiology and German philosophy on the Continent that made him of use to Bain in aiding the revisions for the second editions of *The Senses and the Intellect* (Bain, 1865a) and *The Emotions and the Will* (Bain, 1865b; see also Bain, 1904: 277). Bain and Croom Robertson continued to collaborate on many projects throughout the 1860s and early 1870s, including Bain's *Mental and Moral Science* and the editing of the George Grote's posthumously published *Aristotle*. A lifelong friendship was forged and Bain was of great importance in Croom Robertson being awarded the chair in Mental Philosophy and Logic at University College London in 1866 over his rival James Martineau (Bain, 1904: 282; and Robertson, 1890, for a more complete account). Croom Robertson made many important connections in the capital, mainly through becoming a member of the Metaphysical Society of London (on which see Brown, 1947). It was in these monthly meetings of London's intellectual elite that he met some of the thinkers who were to become the staple contributors to *Mind*. They included Henry Sidgwick, Shadworth Hodgson, Leslie Stephen and William Kingdom Clifford. It was this extensive network that Croom Robertson forged in London, coupled with Bain's philosophical contacts all around Britain, that led Bain to suggest further collaboration on a new journal. As the latter recalled in 1894:

> In 1874, I broached to him the founding of a Quarterly Journal of Philosophy; explaining my notions as to its drift, and asking his opinion on the project. My desire was that he should be editor in the fullest sense of the word; and, on that condition, I undertook the publishing risks. After full consideration he approved of the design, and accepted the editorship on the terms proposed to him. The subsequent steps were to obtain the concurrence and approbation of active workers in the field. (Bain and Whittaker, 1894: xv; see also Bain, 1904: 327–328)

It is to this process of 'design' and 'concurrence and approbation of active workers in the field', with specific reference to the relationship between philosophy and psychology, that we now turn.

1 The early plans for *Mind*

The early plans for what was to become *Mind* were shrouded in secrecy. It was only in July 1874 that Bain felt 'surely at the point of mentioning the thing to all parties that will assist' (letter to Croom Robertson dated 13 July).[10] The plan was to go to press the following August with enough material in hand for two numbers to make an apt selection for the first, by June or July 1875. Herbert Spencer (the prominent evolutionary philosopher) was approached to do the lead article, on perception, and Henry Sidgwick (the Cambridge critic of utilitarianism and the ethics behind the new 'Scientific Naturalism') to reply to it. Care was to be taken in letting Spencer see the proof of Sidgwick's article so he could comment – they went out of their way not to offend their star contributor. David Ferrier was also sounded out to see if he could think of anything that would make a rounding off paper for the first issue and to assist with psychological notes on brain research. James Sully was to deal with the German networks and Croom Robertson himself was instructed by Bain to do a historical article on associationism and 'to put Hamilton right about Aristotle' (*ibid.*).[11] By August 1874 Sidgwick had so fully traced out Spencer's handling of perception that he was completely set up for the subject. Bain's worries about offending their big name were assuaged, and he stated: 'It is not [Sidgwick's] way to be unkind, and he knows our amity with Spencer sufficiently well to be the opposite of offensive' (Bain to Croom Robertson, 8 August 1874). Bain took great pleasure in the journal dealing with the subject of perception early on but it was agreed that the area was too wide to admit a reply from Spencer in the first number. Sully was already prepared to turn down reviews for established journals like the *Contemporary Review* and work with his friends on the new periodical.[12] Bain busied himself with writing to Irish philosophers at Trinity College, Dublin, to see what they could contribute. Still only a few were in the know about the new venture: despite receiving an article on free will from W.G. Ward, editor of the *Dublin Review*, Bain kept him in the dark about the new journal (*ibid.*). Bain wanted to contribute research on James Mill to the first issue and in a subsequent series, and prepare some smaller notices.

In the summer, a prospectus was issued announcing the forthcoming periodical by its working title, the *Quarterly Review of Mental Science*. It was to provide a great register of progress of the scientific investigation of mind in Europe and the United States. It stressed how the mind had become the subject of positive scientific enquiry, despite all the efforts of speculative reason to deal with it otherwise. But it also emphasised the doubts as to the possibility of a phenomenal science of mind expressed not only by representatives of older philosophical schools but also by scientific specialists. By publishing a continuous record of fresh results, the new review was to do something to determine the answer to this question of highest moment for science.

In defining 'mental science', the prospectus stressed that it should be seen as independent from other sciences, but related to them through biology. Nonetheless, the science of mind was to be seen as distinct from biology, as biology itself was distinct from chemistry. However, mental science was to be seen as much more distinct by virtue of the unique character of its data from subjective consciousness. All objective researches on functions of the nervous system were to be reported in the review, but the interpretation of these data must be seen as subjective. Equally, results from the subjective side must submit to an objective expression where one could be found. This first prospectus thus relied on an elaborate fudge between subjective and objective in defining mental science, so as to include the widest possible scope for researches into the mind, without including any details of specific researches done or underway.

The review was to be a scientific journal but also had to include general philosophical discussion, because psychology did not have the limited scope of any of the other sciences:

> Psychology so to speak, faces all the other sciences, because its subject, Mind, does, literally and in every other sense of the word, comprehend the subjects of them all. The psychologist cannot work out his special results, but these are at once seen to have general import, involving the conditions and aims of all other special knowledge. The question, then, is not how the discussion of properly philosophical topics may be excluded, for it cannot be excluded, where mind is concerned, but in what manner it should be included in a review professing to be scientific. (Robertson, 1874: 2)

Aesthetics, logic and ethics, because of their important bearing on the psychological categories of feeling, knowing, and willing, were thus all seen as important to the study of scientific psychology. The history of reason was also singled out as an important topic for the review to cover:

> What more profitable or encouraging task for enquirers who would cleave to scientific experience than to mark its steady encroachment on the ancient domain of reason? And what better means of preparing the way for their own ulterior (never ultimate) expressions, than by weighing with the utmost care and openness of spirit, those speculations concerning the universe of thoughts or things which eager minds, in every age have been impelled to frame. (Robertson, 1874: 2)

From their initial definition of a review of mental science, Bain and Croom Robertson gradually widened the scope to include all the philosophical researches of themselves and their colleagues. Through stating the uniqueness of psychology and its distinctions from the other natural sciences, in their prospectus they tortuously grappled with the issue of whether psychology could ever become a science. By setting up the journal in this way, it was difficult to see the philosophical topics that could be left out. The agenda was so comprehensive and all encompassing that the definition of mental science was almost redundant.

Herbert Spencer and the writer and expositor of popular science George Henry Lewes were prominent among the in-crowd allowed to see the prospectus and they were both extremely critical. 'Take the tortuous elaboration out', 'assume a more man-of-the-world style' and 'cut down the length' were their cries. Lewes wanted to see more minute details of actual psychological researches, which were totally absent from prospectus. But by far the most unanimous criticism was of the title. The physician and pioneering psychiatrist Henry Maudsley dreaded the criticisms of 'mental science' and Spencer characteristically found the term difficult to swallow (Bain to Croom Robertson, letter dated Thursday evening, October 1874). Spencer also pointed out to Croom Robertson (17 November 1874) that the title would be confused with the existing *Journal of Mental Science*, stating that a greater distinction from it needed to be established and feeling 'convinced that some confusion would result, even in the minds of the most instructed, and much confusion in other minds'. 'The Psychological Review' was suggested,[13] which Bain felt could not interfere with anybody but would be caviar to the multitudes (Bain to Croom Robertson, Thursday evening, October 1874). Bain was keen to see his new journal distinguished from the psychological articles in the popular monthlies by much greater rigour and argument in the contributions.[14] It was for this reason he agreed early on to out-pay the *Contemporary* and *Westminster* reviews for contributions. A title was needed that would suggest a rigorous, quality publication. Croom Robertson came up with 'Mind'. Bain's response was that it was on a par with the structure in everything except being perhaps a little more affected and assuming, and open to sarcastic wits. On the prospectus as a whole Bain concluded: 'Every expression you leave in to please the critics, cuts you loose at some point or other; and is a compromise for the sake of the vulgar, who must to a certain degree be courted' (*ibid.*).

On 6 August, Bain responded to Croom Robertson's rewrite of the prospectus. He was concerned that the inverted commas around the word 'Mind' gave it an even greater affectation. He also worried about putting the editor's name on the cover. The prospectuses bore only the name of the publisher, through which the editor could be contacted. They did not bear Croom Robertson's name because Bain was zealous in avoiding any suggestion of partisanship. He added, 'with the prevalence of catholicity our list of ambitions taken by itself will quickly show institutions. There might be a certain gain not exposing [them] anymore to the highest degree of prominence'. However, Bain left the design of the cover of the journal in Croom Robertson's hands, stating that it would build his reputation in the field to have his name on it. He even worried about a successor should Croom Robertson fall ill. He knew him to be of sickly disposition and the fact that he could think of no one else fit for the job made him intensely anxious. He continued to worry over those inverted commas all summer and by December they were still debating the title. 'Mind' was eventually decided upon, but what of the subtitle? 'Mental science and philosophy', 'Scientific philosophy' and

'Scientific psychology and philosophy' were all considered. At last, in January 1875, the new prospectus was issued. The title of the new journal was to be *Mind: A Quarterly Review of Scientific Psychology and Philosophy.*

The new prospectus was much slimmed down, with less discussion of definitions. With some of the old material on the distinctions between biology and psychology, the text came to an explicit statement of the journal's contents: 'All special lines of investigation affording insight into Mind, in dependence on the main track of psychological inquiry, will receive attention in the Review: e.g. Language, Primitive Culture, Mental Pathology, Comparative Psychology' (Robertson, 1875: 2).

The general philosophical parts were justified as being broad debates that the investigator of mind would inevitably be engaged in. The scientific status of the journal was re-emphasised: *Mind* would publish the work of positive psychological research and labour to encourage such philosophical thinking as would be consistent with a full and ungrudging recognition of the methods of modern science. The scope was still very broad but science rather than philosophy became the journal's focus in the amended prospectus. Copies of the prospectus were sent out to a chosen few in Oxford, Cambridge, Edinburgh, Dublin and London and this time it was met with approval. Bain began to worry about the money he had invested and set up advertisements in all the major newspapers in England and Scotland. Lists of potential subscribers were meticulously drawn up. The secret was out.

The catholicity of the journal was severely tested when Bain was seen to be fobbing off anti-mechanistic clerics who wanted to contribute and give the journal their blessing. Most notable and persistent among them was James Martineau. His critiques of mechanism and materialism through the existence of God (for example Martineau, 1876) threatened the scientific character of the new journal, and his name had to be politely excluded from the journal at all costs. Martineau was sent a copy of the second prospectus and – much to the relief of Croom Robertson and Bain – wrote: 'I fear [neither] my health nor my engagements will permit me often to put to the test your editorial catholicity'. He gave his assent to the project but was one of few to object strongly to the name 'Mind':

> I dare say my taste in these matters is old-fashioned; but I cannot take kindly to the practice of adopting the subject matter of a publication for its title; nor should I feel quite comfortable to walk into a bookseller's shop and ask for 'Mind'. An astronomer would hardly designate a treatise on his science as 'Stars'. Some words would be added, otherwise than as a mere 2nd title, to show that the thing named is a book. No doubt the example of 'Nature' opens the way to this method; but whether it is an example which is expedient to follow seems to me a little doubtful. (Martineau to Croom Robertson, 29 January 1875)

Towards the end of 1875 Bain was becoming obsessed with expenses and kept very detailed accounts. With the contributors to the first issues out in the open in September 1875, Croom Robertson's concerns were more about getting the seal of approval from the German star experimentalists Wundt and Helmholtz. When he finally replied (26 December 1875), Helmholtz's response was brief and frosty, but at least he promised a paper, 'The origin and meaning of geometrical axioms'. Such was Croom Robertson's eagerness to secure Helmholz's support that he wrote back in a nervous and apologetic tone shortly after the publication of the first issue: 'I hope the first number of the journal, if you have had time to look at it, will not have disappointed you. The English public must be very gradually accustomed to a philosophic diet. Hence the mixture of some lighter matters' (5 January 1876).

Wundt was much more warm and positive in agreeing to contribute to subsequent issues (letter to Croom Robertson, 25 June 1875). To the first two volumes he contributed articles on 'Central Innervation and Consciousness' and 'Philosophy in Germany'. The Continental indifference to British psychology loomed large in Croom Robertson's prefatory words to the first issue (Robertson, 1876: 2). The journal was going to do away with the image of British psychology as done by philosophers in their spare time, with amateurish tinge. It would represent the new generation of British psychology, not tainted with the names of Locke, Hobbes, Hume, Berkeley and the Mills. The irony was that many of Croom Robertson's own contributions to the journal dealt explicitly with the work of these figures. By the time the first issue went to press, the adjective 'scientific' to qualify the word 'psychology' had been dropped from the subtitle. This final amendment could be seen as being in the interests of brevity and crispness or as an indication that both Bain and Croom Robertson were transitory figures, sympathetic to the new scientific psychology but still steeped in the old traditions of mental philosophy. To both of them a declaration of scientific psychology from the outset begged the very question that the journal had been set up to investigate.

2   George Croom Robertson and the relationship between philosophy and psychology

Although Croom Robertson has often been portrayed as a puppet editor carrying out Bain's instructions in his shadow, there is little truth in this characterisation.[15] No one devoted more energy to the question of the relationship between psychology and philosophy in short articles and reviews than Croom Robertson. From as early as 1866, he saw psychology as having a 'peculiar importance' to philosophic teaching (Bain and Whittaker, 1894: 1). Psychology for Croom Robertson was a proper and desirable preliminary to philosophy. As he later stated in his inaugural lecture at University College London:

> The real and natural beginning is a rigorous investigation of the phenomena of mind. If all philosophy must be essentially philosophy of mind, because it views nothing except in express relation to Thought, the question as to the innermost nature of mental action must surely be taken first…. Psychology then is, and must

still be for a long time to come, the only true point of departure in philosophy. (Robertson, 1866/1894: 3)

Two years later he addressed his students with an introductory lecture arguing for the coupling of science and philosophy, with many examples from the history of science of how scientists have benefited from a wider philosophical culture. The lecture was in part a celebratory justification for studying philosophy in London but it is striking how it integrated psychology, philosophy and science.[16] He stated that 'the teacher will do well to have been led by psychological study to reflect upon the subject of education, and to conceive that at least the manner of instructing dare not be unscientific' (Robertson, 1868/1894: 23). Conscientiousness, labour and rhetorical gifts were not enough to appreciate the weight of conflicting evidence, comprehend the springs of human action and to conceive of human destiny with large vision. These gifts required the analysis of the psychologist and the wide conceptions of the philosopher. In Croom Robertson's early thought, philosophy, psychology and science found harmony together. He attempted to incorporate this rhetorical resonance into the plans for *Mind*, but the experience of editing the journal proved these elements to be too discordant for practical synthesis.

In the first issue of *Mind*, Croom Robertson argued for the inclusion of psychological material in a defensive way, by insisting that the journal would not be composed entirely of the speculative differences of individual thinkers. With a Baconian spirit he hoped for cumulative, cooperative work on the nature of mind. He also encouraged the widest range of philosophical positions. Despite his own broadly empiricist position of the school of the Mills, he went out of his way not to be partisan. His time in Germany had allowed him to break from Bain sufficiently to see Hume as needing some Kantian correction (Quinton, 1976: 9). He was also far too widely read in the history of philosophy to be a zealot of any particular point of view. If he had a bias at all, it was against the amateur nature of British mental philosophy and for the new professionalism in academic departments.

The contents of early issues of *Mind* show how well Croom Robertson acted on his demand for a breadth of philosophical positions. The four major late-nineteenth-century schools of British philosophical psychology were all well represented. There were the naturalists, who were not enchanted by the theory of evolution, including Bain, Fowler (the Oxford Baconian) and, most importantly, Henry Sidgwick. Then there were those for whom evolution was central to their philosophical outlooks, like Spencer, Lewes, Leslie Stephen, W.K. Clifford, Karl Pearson and the British pragmatist F.C.S. Schiller. The idealists could also be found: T.H. Green, F.H. Bradley, Bernard Bosanquet, Edward Caird and, in a less orthodox way, Andrew Seth and James Ward. Last, there were the realists, Robert Adamson and the two Oxford Aristotelians Thomas Case and Cook Wilson (Quinton, 1976: 14). Croom Robertson had certainly cast his net widely.

The editor's first scoop and extensive piece of 'psychological' data came from Charles Darwin. On receiving the prospectus in 1875, Darwin had written: 'I have so much work in Nat. History half-completed which I desire to finish that I am sorry to say I have resolved not the time to any other subject, so that it is extremely improbable that I can ever be a contributor to your journal' (letter to Croom Robertson, 19 February 1875). Yet the author of the theory of natural selection produced his 'Biographical Sketch of an Infant'[17] for the journal in 1877. The piece was short and anecdotal, taken from notes on his son William, but was significant in that it represented an early example of infant biography. It also suggested a thesis of rapid recapitulation in human individual development and touched on grand themes he had developed in his other works, such as 'the roles of instinctive reflexes, habits, emotions and other sensibilities in an increasingly effective adaptation to the world' (Fancher, 1990: 203).

Francis Galton's much more systematic work on 'Generic images and automatic representation' was one of the few articles to follow Darwin's empirical lead.[18] During this period, only two British books containing empirical psychological research were noticed in *Mind*. These were Edmund Gurney's *The Power of Sound* and James Sully's *Illusions*. James Mckeen Cattell's 1886 paper 'On the Time It Takes to See and Name Objects' (*Mind*, vol. 11, pp. 63–65) was a much shortened version of one he had submitted to Wundt's *Philosophische Studien* the year before. Its clarity and brevity immediately made it an important contribution to experimental psychology (see Hothersall, 1995: 118–119).

In the journal's first issue, Croom Robertson (1876: 3) had declared that the principal aim of the new publication was to 'procure a decision of this question as to the scientific standing of psychology'. Psychology was to be on trial in the journal to prove itself as a science or nothing at all. After such boldly ambitious pronouncements, he expressed disappointment in 1883 that there had been few positive contributions to psychological science in its pages. With a few notable exceptions, the journal had not succeeded in fostering 'such habits of specialist investigation in psychology as are characteristic of the workers in other departments of science' or 'work on such special lines of psychological research as other countries have given evidence of' (Robertson, 1883/1894: 250). He did not feel that psychological activity in Britain could have been increased by the publishing opportunity afforded in the first seven years of the journal's existence. He felt that the reasons for this lay both in the lack of academic posts and in the multifarious duties attached to them, which did 'not favour the concentration required for this kind of work'. In addition, and more crucial to Croom Robertson, was the disposition of 'English psychology'. While maintaining the interest in the positive investigation of mind, it did not 'tell in a way of stimulating special inquiry' and 'has never been remarkable for its elaboration in detail' (Robertson, 1883/1894: 251). 'Historic circumstances' meant that British work continued to be psychological in its import but philosophical in its application, concerning itself with 'Treatises on Man or Human Nature, Essays or Inquiries on Understanding generally [and] Analyses of Mind in all its aspects'. This tradition had been translated into the present to produce work that either reconsidered the general psychological point of view with reference to philosophy or the newly enlarged biological principle of evolution, or reordered the whole psychological field with new facts from physiology, or applied psychological facts to the practical work of education.

Croom Robertson took nationalistic pride in British achievements and despaired that 'we shall soon fall too far behind in the scientific race if we have not our own record of positive results to show'. Yet he still defended *Mind*'s catholic editorial policy, stating that comprehensiveness did not mean philosophical indifference and calling for 'mutual understanding' rather than 'agreement' (Robertson, 1883/ 1894: 252). He continued to reflect upon the relationship between philosophy and psychology and psychology's relationship to science in Britain until his premature death in 1892 (see Robertson, 1876/1894, 1878/1894a, 1878/1894b, 1882/1894, 1887/1894).

Croom Robertson's posthumously published lecture notes on psychology (*Elements of Psychology*) may not have added a great deal to Bain's work (Hearnshaw, 1964: 175). Nonetheless, he had not only enriched Bain's volumes (Bain, 1865a,b) with his knowledge of Continental physiology and philosophy, but with his broad knowledge he had also made a sustained contribution to the debate over the relationship between British psychology and philosophy. When, on his death in 1892, James Sully took over his post at University College London and set up a psychological laboratory in October 1897, the notice that appeared in *Mind* hoped that it would be connected with Croom Robertson's name (Hearnshaw, 1964: 134). Such an epitaph would have been an ambiguous monument to a man who intensively questioned the scientific status of psychology, both in his work and in the catholicity of his editorship of *Mind*.

3   George Frederick Stout's editorship

When George Frederick Stout took over the editorship in 1892 he started a new series but made only minor changes to the form of the journal. He endeavoured to continue the catholicity and impartiality so dear to his predecessor and was excited that the mutual understanding and cooperation that now existed among professional philosophers would enable him to carry out Croom Robertson's wishes in producing a thoroughly representative and professional journal (Stout, 1892: 1).

However, his attempts were continuously marred by rivalries between the three main centres of research, London, Cambridge and Oxford. Oxford thought London and its Aristotelian Society to be too charitable to the work of amateurs, while London thought Oxford too high-minded and patronising. The bitter disputes between Oxford and Cambridge made matters worse. After the death of Sidgwick, the Cambridge philosopher, the Mind Association, which had been set up to support *Mind* financially, came to be dominated by Oxford scholars (Passmore, 1952: xxix). The larger faculty in Oxford thus thought it had dealt the decisive blow in its vying for the control of *Mind*. There was even an internal dispute in Oxford between the most voluminous contributors during Stout's editorship: the idealist Bradley at Merton College on the one hand and the pragmatist Schiller at Corpus Christi on the other. Despite their geographical proximity, it is not clear that they ever met. Stout's job as editor was not made easy by the fact that they continued to snipe at each other's work in the pages of *Mind*, as well as in private correspondence, in a very unguarded way.

Stout hoped that *Mind* would be the journal not only of professional philosophers but also of psychologists and sociologists. Bradley, McDougall, Spearman and Titchener all contributed to lively philosophical psychology debates around the turn of the century.[19] Titchener (1898) even contributed an article on the art of setting up a psychological laboratory. However, by 1904, when the *British Journal of Psychology* appeared, times were changing. Despite Stout continuing to send out review copies of the leading works in psychology, articles like W.D. Morrison's 'The study of crime' began to disappear from *Mind*'s pages. By 1910 articles by experimentally minded psychologists were almost entirely absent from *Mind*. Against Stout's will, *Mind* gradually became a journal of philosophy by philosophers (Passmore, 1952: xxviii). This was aided by various attacks on psychology as an explanatory science in the first decade of the twentieth century. The most famous was H.A. Prichard's 1912 paper 'Does moral philosophy rest on a mistake?', which put forth the view that if psychology was anything it was descriptive philosophy and that Plato and Aristotle were the best psychologists. The rivalry between Oxford and Cambridge again came into play here. Stout and James Ward, both of Cambridge, continued to be sympathetic to the new science of psychology,[20] whereas the younger generation at Oxford vigorously questioned its worth. As Passmore has pointed out:

> the general intellectual atmosphere, with on one side scientific psychologists trying to free themselves from philosophy and on the other side philosophers denying not only the relevance but even the possibility of a science of psychology, was scarcely conducive to fulfilling Stout's hope of editing a journal of philosophy and psychology. (Passmore, 1976: 23)

The complex and fraught relationship between philosophy and psychology in the teens of the twentieth century was reflected in *Mind*. Because of the very short notice needed to give the publisher articles in this period, one gets a real sense of current and vibrant debate over scientific psychology, and H.W.B. Joseph and Prichard (the key players in the anti-psychology movement) were rebuffed by a series of speedy replies from Stout and Ward. Joseph attacked the whole enterprise of psychology as pretending to make an advance towards a scientific understanding of the facts, when in large measure it had merely found new names for them. He saw it as at best a collection of more or less detailed inquiries as distinct from a particular science about one sort of thing. Ward's contribution to the last number of *Mind* under Stout's editorship specifically attacked Frege's and Husserl's ignorance of and contempt for psychology, arguing for the very psychological epistemology which Joseph and Prichard had attacked. In this period *Mind* also became more British in character as the number of critical reviews of foreign works declined. The international flavour and the scientific psychology element of Croom Robertson's days were fading. Although Stout tried hard to be true to Croom Robertson's original prospectus, various contingencies made it gradually more difficult.

When G.E. Moore took over the editorship in 1921, scientific psychology was almost entirely absent, and personal idealism and system building were greatly out of fashion. C.D. Broad's articles were a notable exception. The emancipation of psychology from philosophy had taken a considerable time in Britain and still was not entirely complete. The first four decades of *Mind* give a blow-by-blow account of this peculiar relationship. Only local contingencies and the relationships between the personalities and institutions in the story can fully account for it.

4   Conclusions

We have seen both in the work of Croom Robertson and in the debate over the title of *Mind* (and the contents of its prospectuses) that the relationship between psychology and philosophy was heavily contested in this period and constantly rewritten. There was no single sense of what psychology was and no particular philosophy that could inform the diverse psychologies that existed in parallel and turn one or more of them into a science.

Similarly, the apparent distance between work in Britain, the United States and on the Continent can be called into question by a historical study of *Mind*. The autonomy of these foci for psychological research is challenged by the dialogue between them. The attempt to separate the British context for this chapter seems somewhat arbitrary, as we have seen that figures like Wundt, Helmholtz, James and Dewey (along with many others from abroad) made important contributions to the British debate. *Mind* established itself as an international journal that reviewed foreign works and reported foreign researches. In fact, Croom Robertson praised these researches highly and used them as a model for what he thought should be going on in Britain. The fact that British empirical research was hardly facilitated by *Mind* was more to do with the history of English approaches to the study of mind and the lack of an institutional base for them than any conscious separation of Britain from the Continent and the United States.

Nor was it the case that *Mind* was simply an exercise in the professionalisation of philosophy or psychology. Although Croom Robertson could be seen to be biased towards research conducted in academic departments of universities, he neither excluded the work of amateurs of independent means nor the writings of professional philosophers who wanted to deny the possibility of a science of mind. George Henry Lewes, Herbert Spencer and Shadworth Hodgson are just a few examples of instrumental contributors who did not hold professional posts.

They were amateurs in the sense that they did not have any institutional backing and were either men of independent means or, like James Sully and Bain himself before they acquired academic posts, men who sustained their work through publishing articles in the periodical press. What was important was not so much having a university position as being prepared to engage in debates over the possibility of a science of mind. Most important of all was being a privileged member of Croom Robertson's and Bain's intellectual community. Because Croom Robertson and Bain wanted to encourage a lively debate, membership of their court of elite thinkers was much more important than professional background or a particular philosophical point of view. Consequently, our contemporary categories of 'professional' and 'amateur' do not apply in any straightforward manner in the case of *Mind*. Even the best candidate for defining the category of 'professional' in the context of *Mind*, commitment to scholarly rigour, is problematic.

The problematisation of each of these apparent dichotomies in turn (including, perhaps, the rivalry between idealist Oxford and pro-science Cambridge) lends weight to the thesis that the history of *Mind* is notoriously difficult to fit into neat categories; it defies being slotted into a neat and simple progressive historical narrative. In short, it is extremely difficult to find a general category that captures the early contributors to *Mind*, beyond membership of the intellectual community that Bain and Croom Robertson created. The case of *Mind* supports the thesis that psychology in Britain did not develop along the lines of a specific agenda or plan. Instead, its development was sporadic and piecemeal, and it partially came out of the debate contributed by a diverse range of actors in the pages of the periodical. Brown's and Young's general argument of specialisation and separation cannot do justice to these local contingencies. *Mind* in its historical context did not have such an agenda from the outset and its diversity of contributions hardly created a common intellectual context to replace the fragmentation that occurred in the 1860s and 1870s.

Daston (1982: 111–112) has argued that the late-nineteenth-century debates over the science of mind involved more than psychology. They pushed to breaking point the movement to explain all phenomena of the universe in natural terms (referred to by historians as Scientific Naturalism) and strained the old methods of the philosophy of science, facilitating new ones. This drama was partially played out in the pages of *Mind* in the last quarter of the nineteenth century. This chapter has also indicated a social dimension to these debates that goes beyond the ideas and theories themselves. With specific reference to physiological psychology, Jacyna (1981) has argued that much more was at stake than the philosophical theories and movements themselves – they also had great political significance. The supplanting of a spiritual controlling agent for the mind with a naturalised, spontaneous nervous system became an important political metaphor in the Liberals' struggle against the Anglican establishment. The metaphor fuelled the Liberals' argument for reform of, and freedom from, centralised elite power. It was popular among the aspiring professional middle classes who formed the main body of the readership of *Mind* and many of its contributors. This linkage of the theories in psychology and physiology to political movements not only adds a political dimension to the debates in *Mind*, but acts as metaphor for the free-thinking and catholic editorial policy, and the diversity and spontaneity of the journal's contents. The debates in the journal were not subject to centralised control or pre-established agendas. In future work it would be interesting to look at the Liberal politics of Bain, Croom Robertson[21] and their close social group to see how this fed into how the journal was organised and how it subsequently progressed.

Paying detailed attention to a specific historical episode and attempting to place it in its social and political context show how complex and contingent histories of psychology are. The history of the journal *Mind* resists being slotted into a progressive, linear narrative moving towards contemporary psychology. A history that is overtly preoccupied with present concerns cannot do justice to the subtleties and ambiguities of the context of late-nineteenth-century debates over the nature of mind and psychology itself. This is a period in Britain when questions were being asked about psychology's method, its subject matter, its relation to the natural sciences and philosophy, and its potential status as a professional and academic discipline. *Mind* is a testimony to these debates and, consequently, its history evades the convenient modes of historical narrative expression such as origin myths, stories of professionalisation and heroic tales of scientific or philosophical endeavour. By the same token, George Croom Robertson was a paradoxical figure in the centre of these important debates, reflecting upon them with conflicting agendas, goals and aspirations for defining psychology in terms of its future relations with science and philosophy.

Notes

1 See my 'Making up *Mind*: mental philosophy, psychology and the negotiations behind setting up a journal in the late nineteenth century' (forthcoming) for these negotiations and their wider implications for periodical management in the period.

2 This is hardly surprising since most of them are written for an American audience and focus on American psychology. The American context was very different to the British one during this period (see O'Donnell, 1986). The *American Journal of Psychology* (1887), the American Psychological Association (1892), *The Psychological Review* (1894) and many laboratories and departments (in the 1890s) had been set up much earlier in America than had their counterparts in Britain. Despite Britain having few such institutions until the turn of the century, there is a tendency to project the American context on to *Mind* and expect it to fit. Part of *Mind*'s significance is that it was the only vaguely psychological institution in Britain until a few laboratories were established in 1890s – excepting the long-forgotten Psychological Society of Great Britain (1875–1879), discussed by Richards in Chapter 1. The [British] Psychological Society (1901) and *The British Journal of Psychology* (1904) did not follow until after the turn of the century.

3 See Smith (1997b: ch. 14) for a critique of origin myths, a sense of the diversity of the roots of what became psychology and its fragmented, family resemblance status in the twentieth century.

4 The *Psychological Review: A Cosmopolitan Organ of Spiritualism and Psychological Research* was published between 1878 and 1883. The term 'psychology' was heavily contested in this period, with a diverse range of groups, from spiritualists to metaphysicians all vying for its use. For a sense of the problems faced by William James over this issue see Valentine (1991).

5 Bain and Herbert Spencer reformulated the psychology of experience in the 1850s and '60s without academic support, but by the time Bain set up *Mind* he had established himself as Professor of Logic at Aberdeen.

6 For examples of this marginalisation see Hearnshaw (1964: 14) and Cross (1970: 1, 10–11). For Bain see Hearnshaw (1964: ch. 1).

7 In fact, those early psychologists in the United States, like William James and John Dewey, who were consumed by the philosophical underpinnings of psychology, found a home publishing numerous articles in *Mind*.

8 For a contextual treatment of Bain see, for instance, Young (1970: ch. 3).

9 Further biographical information on Croom Robertson can be found in Bain and Whittaker (1894: ix–xxiv); Bain (1893) and Stephen (1892, 1896).

10 All the letters in this chapter are quoted from the George Croom Robertson Collection (MS add. 88), held in the Manuscripts and Rare Books Department of the Science Library at University College London. I acknowledge the kind help of the archivist and staff in finding relevant materials, and the permission to reprint extracts from the collection.

11 William Hamilton (1788–1856) was a Scottish common-sense philosopher who defended a faculty-based view of psychology.

12 See Gurjeva (Chapter 3) for an insight into Sully's extensive journalistic enterprises in this period.

13 Lewes also suggested *The Annals of Psychology* and *The Archives of Psychology* (Lewes to Croom Robertson, 'Friday' October 1874?), but they were both rejected, probably because Bain wanted to keep the term 'psychology', with its populist associations, out of the main title.

14 For a sense of the amateur articles and figures from which Bain and Croom Robertson wanted to distinguish their new journal see Richards (Chapter 1).

15 Letters regarding *Mind* often went back and forth across the Scottish border several times a week but Bain (in Aberdeen) hardly demanded the final say on matters relating to the journal.

16 In fact, Croom Robertson could boast a progressive programme of study, where mental philosophy had been chiefly interpreted as psychology since 1860. See Robertson (1876/1894: 174).

17 *Mind*, vol. 2, pp. 285–294. Darwin would never have thought of sending the manuscript had he not seen a translation of Taine's report 'The acquisition of language by children' (Darwin to Croom Robertson, 22 April 1877). This is evidence that the 'Reports' section, which contained brief pieces on a diverse range of psychological topics, such as sleep, trance, deafness, colour blindness, canine suicide and language acquisition, by prominent figures like Francis Galton, John Lubbock, G.J. Romanes, James Sully, Edmund Gurney and G.M. Beard, were reaching an audience in the natural sciences. However, after 1878 the section was dropped and the empirical content of the more demanding 'Notes and Discussions' section that replaced it was greatly diminished. The new section was chiefly concerned with debating philosophical issues. The re-naming of the section to 'Research and Discussion' in 1884 did not greatly change matters.

18 Galton's research is noticed in *Mind* (1879), *4*, 551–556, and the article appears in *Mind* (1880), *5*, 301–317.

19 See, for instance, McDougall's three part 'Contribution Towards an Improvement in Psychological Method' (*Mind*, NS *7*, 15–33, 159–178 and 364–387), Titchener's

'Simple Reactions' (*Mind*, NS 4, 74–81) and Bradley's 'Some Remarks on Memory and Inference' (*Mind*, NS 8, 145–166).

20 However, despite Stout making use of, and being greatly interested in, experimental psychology, it remained to him 'a source of information' and 'not a substitute for thinking' (Passmore, 1952: xxxvii).

21 Croom Robertson supported many Liberal causes and had a significant involvement in the National Society for Women's Suffrage, along with J.S. Mill.

3

James Sully and scientific psychology, 1870–1910

Lyubov G. Gurjeva

1   Sully's career in histories of psychology

In *My Life and Friends: A Psychologist's Memories* (1918), James Sully (1842–1923) explicitly identified himself as a psychologist, yet histories of psychology acknowledge him only in passing. This by itself is not remarkable – many British pioneers have been absent from the intellectual map of the discipline, and this book will only partially rectify the situation. What is remarkable is that Sully has been remembered either for something he did not do, such as found the British Child Study Association (BCSA), or for something he considered marginal to his psychological work, namely the organisation of the psychological laboratory at University College London (Gould, 1977; Rose, 1985: 115–116). Although these two roles fit well into the narrative of the enduring rise of scientific psychology, they provide little insight into Sully's career and do not do justice to the complex processes of discipline formation.[1] Robert Thomson gives a more perceptive, though brief, characterisation, which emphasises two contradictions in Sully's work: 'although not an original thinker ... he did branch out into new fields of inquiry'; 'although he was no experimentalist, Sully established a laboratory in University College, London' (Thomson, 1968: 174). Later historians must have been perplexed by the seeming disparity between Sully's role as one of the founders of the laboratory and his disregard for experimental work[2] and, similarly, between the acknowledgement he received from contemporaries and the scarcity of research publications, in the modern sense of 'research'.

A key to explaining these apparent contradictions is an examination of Sully's psychological concerns and career in relation to the wider questions of discipline formation. Between 1870 and 1910, one of the central questions for aspiring psychologists was the relationship between professionals and amateurs. In this chapter I focus on how Sully defined and negotiated this relationship, especially in the area of child psychology, where the contradictions between professionals and amateurs was compounded by tensions between male and female practitioners and domestic and laboratory settings. I begin with a brief examination of the questions entertained by the new mental science and the data with which Sully and others hoped to answer them.

2   Evolutionary mental science and the study of children

The sentiment that the theory of evolution – which had proved so fruitful in biological sciences – also had much to offer to the sciences of the mind was commonplace in the last two decades of the nineteenth century. Scholars of human development saw recapitulation as a central tenet of evolution theory.[3] Hence, for them the study of children was the study of the inception of the human mind. For psychologists, studies of children were in this sense similar to the studies of primitive forms of life by biologists. Children were to students of human evolution what sea urchins and mosses were to zoologists and botanists: the simplest representatives of the kind. Darwin considered writing the natural history of babies (Barrett *et al.*, 1987: 157).[4] He compared the skills of his baby son William Erasmus with those of the orang-utan, Jenny, at London Zoo (Desmond and Moore, 1991: 287). Once, he suggested to his friend and student of mental evolution George Romanes that he should 'keep an idiot, a deaf mute, a monkey and a baby' in his house (Romanes, 1896: 78).

The evidence for mental evolution available from fossils and other remains was partial and indirect. Hence the study of children and indigenous peoples, who were seen as 'savage' and believed to occupy lower stages of the evolutionary ladder, was critical to research into the evolution of mind. James Sully was one of the most high-profile advocates of mental evolution. According to him, the key to understanding the human mind was understanding its functioning at lower stages, and its development. 'The psychologist,' Sully wrote, 'cannot dispense with the young unformed minds of infants. His business, like that of all scientific workers, is to explain the complex in terms of the simple, to trace back the final perfectly shaped adult mind to the first rude beginnings' (Sully, 1885: v). Sully called his project 'genetic psychology' and contrasted it with experimental projects aimed at studying psychological phenomena outside developmental and evolutionary contexts. Ethnographers and psychologists frequently considered evidence on 'primitive people' and children in parallel. W.H.R. Rivers had procured drawings from A.C. Haddon's children before going on the Torres Strait expedition and asking the islanders to draw comparable objects (Schaffer, 1994: 33). Likewise, Sully used the ethnographic materials collected by A.H.L. Pitt-Rivers in his analysis of children's drawings.[5]

Proponents of genetic psychology and ethnography had to rely on observations and data collected by diarists, travellers and teachers. There were two problems with the information obtained in this way: first, material procured by untrained people was unreliable; and second, unorganised observation produced results which were not comparable. The pressure to amass comparable observations of mental phenomena was growing. A number of Galton's publications – eventually collected in the book *Inquiries into Human Faculty and Its Development* (1883) – emphasised the peculiarity of individual mental life, and thus brought into doubt all extrapolations from individual observations to humankind at large. Sully was well aware of the dangers of unwarranted extrapolation when he wrote, in a review of Wilhelm Preyer's *The Mind of the Child*, that it was risky to draw generalisations from a single model (Sully, 1882b: 416).

Some ethnographers increasingly relied on new instruments, devising methods of information gathering that would tackle the problems of unreliability and lack of organisation, and live up to the standards established in the biological sciences (Schaffer, 1994: 30–32). Sully approached the problems of data collecting in a different way. He was cautious about the use of instruments and questionnaires, for fear of imposing the experimenter's patterns of thinking on the spontaneous mental phenomena he wanted to record. He believed that the main method of psychology was introspection (Sully, 1884: v). As it was unavailable for the study of infant mental development, this aspect of the science of the mind was to rely on information procured through observation. Therefore he cultivated contacts with potential observers of young children and took an active part in the work of the Child Study Association, the national federation of child study societies formed in 1898 by teachers and parents interested in child development. He tried to ensure the reliability of data on child development by using the social organis-ation of child study. At the same time, he tried to give his own project a guise distinct from the works of amateur observers of childhood, for his ambitions were scientific. While ethnographers resorted to fieldwork by trained practitioners, he had to defend a science relying on amateurs before the scientific community.[6]

The tensions between amateur and professional, domestic and scientific, female and male were the axes of Sully's reflections on his position in science. He resolved the tensions by mapping these categories on to the terrain of people, practices and places, laying down boundaries between science and the public, and between scholarly work and domestic pursuits. He located his ideal child study outside the domain of science proper but in immediate proximity to it. For him, child study was a movement of dedicated amateurs, who pursued the observation of children by applying scientific method under the guidance of scientists. Sully is widely believed to be the founder of the British Child Study Association and the leader of the child study movement (see, for example, Rose, 1985: 115). In fact, most child study societies were founded by teachers, and Sully was invited to serve as one of several vice-presidents of the London Child-Study Society, founded in 1894 (Cockburn, 1908: 1–3). The misrepresentation of his role is not least due to his careful self-fashioning as the leader of child study and a go-between scientists and child study activists. Sully saw practitioners of child study as 'general students' of science and a potential large audience for psychology. Elaborating the notion of child study as an applied science, at the same time he also defined the new science of psychology as one of the sciences which were applied in child study.

3   Genres of Sully's work

At the time when Sully was writing on scientific psychology, the status and content of this discipline, also called the science of the mind, were hotly debated in Britain and America. The words 'scientific' and 'science' are of vital importance here, for they had come to mean 'true' and 'truth' in turn-of-the-century Britain.[7] Consequently, discussions of scientific psychology addressed the questions of what was true knowledge and what agents and practices created it. This social and moral dimension is the key to understanding the formation of scientific psychology and Sully's own project. In the previous section, I characterised Sully's project as evolutionary and described the kinds of evidence this commitment called for. In this section, I focus on the scope of Sully's project and look at the kinds of publication in which Sully developed his version of psychology.

Sully published in *Mind*, the journal sponsored by Bain and edited by Robertson. But he also published a serialised novel in *Harper's Magazine* and contributed to the *Journal of Education* and to *The Baby*, a magazine, for parents, devoted to child care. How should we limit the range of publications to consider here in order to determine the scope of Sully's psychological project? I suggest that we do not need to make such an *a priori* decision. By following his career in the next section, we will understand the range of Sully's literary activities and their relevance to psychology. In this section, I describe the genres of his publications and examine his works in relation to the conventions and exemplars available within those genres.

According to Ludwik Fleck, vade mecums and textbooks – of which Sully wrote three – as well as articles for a general readership – which Sully wrote regularly – are distinct socio-intellectual forms of science. Aimed at a wider readership than journal science, they define esoteric science from the outside, by laying its limits and indicating the areas of scientific certainty (Fleck, 1939/ 1979: 111–112). Mustering these genres, Sully posed himself as a spokesman for modern psychology. As Sully took a moderate position on most debates in turn-of-the-century psychology, his works constituted a convenient point of reference for people not directly involved in psychological research, as well as a suitable introduction for psychology students. Thus, the apparent contradiction between Sully's insignificant contribution to research and his prominence in defining the boundaries of psychology loses its force, while his career becomes a case study of the uses of popular scientific genres in constituting a professional science.

Sully developed his style as a freelance journalist, a common occupation for many Victorian public figures, writers and politicians.[8] While the boundaries of specialised 'modern science', as described by Fleck, had not yet been established, many men of science also wrote for general interest periodicals. Authors writing on scientific topics for different sorts of publications were effectively constructing different scientific genres. In the context of the new science of psychology, Sully's engaging and accessible journalistic writing was particularly well suited for textbooks.

Writers for a general educated audience not only established the boundaries of science, but also identified the main directions within it and classified them in order of relevance to various sections of the audience, such as teachers or parents. Sully, for instance, identified both experimental psychology and the philosophy of the subconscious as least relevant to teachers, and at the same time the most obscure areas of psychology. Although Sully's position on many issues of the science of the mind was moderate, if not reconciliatory, he also expressed antagonism to certain currents of psychological research. The areas disregarded by Sully and other writers who undertook to speak for science were not presented to the wider audiences.

His orientation towards an audience of teachers and students is most obvious in the composition of Sully's books. *Outlines of Psychology* (1884) was written for students of psychology and teachers. The book uneasily combines an exposition of the mental science research covering the study of sensation, intellect, volition and action, with chapters on attention, memory and mental development, which Sully deemed of special interest to teachers. He used a combination of three different typefaces to distinguish between the main body of the text and the sections aimed at teachers and advanced students (Sully, 1884: vii).[9] Despite this technique, the book was difficult to read, because it was not written with one audience in mind. Philosopher Robert Adamson found Sully's 700-page book at once too long and detailed for a beginner and too short for an advanced student, owing to the omission of difficulties in the subject. The most conspicuous omission, according to Adamson (1884: 429), was the question of psychological method.

Heeding this criticism, Sully wrote three separate books on the basis of *Outlines of Psychology* between 1884 and 1892 (Table 3.1). In 1886 he published *The Teacher's Handbook of Psychology*, considerably reducing the volume and limiting the scope of the original book. Looking at the index, one can see that 'Taine', 'Helmholtz' and 'evolution' were replaced by 'Rousseau', 'boyhood and girlhood' and 'toys'. The index was simplified by cross-referencing such unusual terms as 'tactual perception' with more common ones, such as 'touch'. The addition of several general index entries, such as 'method of psychology', 'the relation of science to art' and 'science as orderly classification of things', shows that definitions of science and its attributes were elaborated in the exoteric areas of science. The genre of books for neophytes or outsiders, such as teachers, enabled and constrained Sully to put forward a comprehensive, if somewhat schematised, view of psychology and its history. The schematism of textbooks was conventionally determined by didactic priorities. Comprehensive expositions for different levels of students relied on schemata and simplifications to a greater or lesser extent.[10]

Having dealt with psychology for teachers in a separate book, in 1892 Sully prepared a revised edition of *Outlines of Psychology*, which was about two-thirds the length of the original edition. The new edition was divided into four parts. The main body of the book was organised in three parts, on intellection, feelings and volition, which followed a more general introduction to psychology and a

Table 3.1 *James Sully's publication pattern*

Books	Year	Earlier publications on the same topic
Illusions	1881	Articles on illusions of memory and perception in *Cornhill Magazine* (1880) and *New Quarterly Magazine* (1880)
Outlines of Psychology with Special Reference to the Theory of Education	1884	'Evolution' in the ninth edition of the *Encyclopaedia Britannica* (co-authored with T.H. Huxley); *Sensation and Intuition* (1874)
Teachers' Handbook of Psychology	1886	*Outlines of Psychology* (1884 edition)
Aesthetics. Dreams and Association of Ideas	1888	'Aesthetics' in the ninth edition of the *Encyclopaedia Britannica*; 'Aesthetics of human character' in *Fortnightly Review* (1871)
Teacher's Handbook of Psychology (3rd revised edition)	1891	*Teacher's Handbook of Psychology* (1886); *Outlines of Psychology* (1884 edition)
The Human Mind: A Text-Book of Psychology	1892	*Outlines of Psychology* (1884 edition); *Teacher's Handbook of Psychology* (1891 edition)
Outlines of Psychology (new revised and largely rewritten edition)	1892	*Outlines of Psychology* (1884 edition); *The Human Mind* (1892 edition); *Teacher's Handbook of Psychology* (1891 edition)
Studies of Childhood	1895	'Babies and science' (1881) and 'A learned infant' (1887), in *Cornhill Magazine*; 'Children's fears' (1888), in *The Baby*; 'The new study of children' (1895), in *Fortnightly Review*; 'George Sand's childhood' (1889) and 'The story of a child' (1891), in *Longman's Magazine*
Children's Ways	1897	*Studies of Childhood* (1895); 'The child in recent English literature' (1897), in *Fortnightly Review*

Illusions, *Aesthetics* and *Outlines of Psychology*, like the majority of Sully's books, were preceded by articles on closely related topics. The first edition of the *Outlines* served the basis for three new publications: *Teacher's Handbook*, *The Human Mind* and a revised edition of the *Outlines*. (This table does not include all of Sully's books; neither does it mention all the editions of the titles featured.)

chapter on the general view of the mind. Although this edition had a more clearly defined readership than the first, Sully still used various founts to organise material in the book. He introduced more subsections, clearly set out in bold. Main concepts and definitions were printed in italics. Another innovation of this edition was the inclusion of 'references for reading' at the end of each chapter.

Although the new edition of *Outlines of Psychology* still did not focus on any conceptual difficulties of psychology, in his own way Sully evidently addressed Adamson's criticism of the omission of the psychological method. Where the readers may have expected discussion of the nature of mental phenomena and research into them, Sully pitched the description of the comparative method, analysis and synthesis at a general philosophical level. In revising *Outlines of Psychology*, Sully drew not only on the *Teacher's Handbook* but also on a new book, published earlier in 1892. Having started it as a new edition of the *Outlines of Psychology*, he turned it into a two-volume 'advanced text-book', on the advice of William James (Sully, 1918: 228). This book, entitled *The Human Mind*, surpassed all its predecessors in volume, level of detail and complexity. It opens with a provisional definition of psychology, addresses the 'problem of psychology' and then goes on to discuss data and method, as well as the physical basis of mental life. Part II, 'General view of the mind', while sharing the title with the corresponding part of the 1892 edition of *Outlines of Psychology*, starts with a discussion of the 'problem of dividing the mind' in relation to psychological analysis. Thus, in *The Human Mind*, Sully for the first time in his textbooks tackled psychological controversies: 'an effort has been made,' he wrote in the Preface, 'to illustrate the obscurity and debatableness of many of the problems of the science.' Furthermore, Sully aimed to 'aide the reader at arriving at a judicial conclusion on these points by a historical reference to the main diversities of the doctrine' (Sully, 1892b: v). This book, addressed to advanced students, could also serve as a reference volume for psychologists, which puts it into the vade mecum genre.

4   Psychological career outside academia

4.1 *Journalism*

Sully's autobiography gives one the idea of the social circles he inhabited and the networks in which he participated, placing him in the London socio-intellectual landscape of the second half of the nineteenth century. The analysis of Sully's career affords a comparison with other writers and scientists, and emphasises the ways in which he complied with and enriched various genres of science.

Upon the recommendation of Alexander Bain, his examiner for the University of London MA in philosophy, Sully started his literary career in 1871 in the world of London 'higher journalism' as an assistant to John Morley, the editor of the liberal *Fortnightly Review*. Morley, who earned his living by freelance journalism between 1860 and 1863, remarked later that a young graduate 'in pursuit of a literary calling, had little choice but journalism' (quoted in Collini, 1991: 39). Coming from a Baptist family, Sully was educated outside ancient Anglican schools and universities, earning his London MA in Göttingen, Germany. He became interested in educational reform and tried his hand at teaching, first at the Birmingham League and then at the Baptist College in Pontypool (Sully,

1918: 127, 132). Dissenters, secularists and radical liberals, like Morley, were united in their outrage over the 1870 Education Bill, which turned Anglican schools into a national education system. While his family cherished the hope that Sully would take holy orders, he prepared himself to join the unholy army of London journalists and gravitated towards the circles of London's intellectual and scientific elite. The invitation in 1873 from Spencer Baynes to contribute an article on 'Aesthetics' to the ninth edition of the *Encyclopaedia Britannica* is an indication of Sully's success as a writer. Like many aspiring intellectuals, Sully got an entrée to London literary circles through journalism.[11] His friendship with George Meredith started during these years. Having made acquaintance with Leslie Stephen (on whom see Annan, 1984), the editor of the *Cornhill Magazine*, Sully became a regular contributor to it.

With new publications, Sully's circle of acquaintances broadened and by 1877 included several proponents of what Frank Turner called 'scientific naturalism' (Turner, 1993). He became intimate with Huxley and his family and got to know George Romanes and John Tyndall. The Sullys even moved to St John's Wood in order to stay close to his new friends and participate in their meetings. Sully co-authored with Huxley an article on evolution for the *Encyclopaedia Britannica.* Tyndall lent him optical instruments for lectures on art and vision at the Royal Institution. In 1881 Sully published a psychological study of illusions in the *International Scientific Series* to which Tyndall, Norman Lockyer and T.H. Huxley had also contributed (see MacLeod, 1980: 63–93).

Like many other British and American students of psychology, in 1871 and 1872 Sully travelled to Germany to further his knowledge of physiology. In Berlin he pursued anatomical studies in Emil Du Bois-Reymond's laboratory and attended Helmholtz's lectures on physiological optics. The studies undertaken in Germany enabled Sully to claim proficiency in laboratory work and experimentation. They also strengthened his personal connections with other British psychologists who studied in Germany and identified themselves with the 'German school', most notably with George Croom Robertson. Sully was introduced to him by Frau Hentze, his German hostess, at whose pension Robertson had also lodged. Sully and Robertson, as shown by Francis Neary (Chapter 2), closely collaborated in the *Mind.* In 1892 Sully succeeded Robertson as the Grote Professor of Logic and Philosophy of Mind at University College London (UCL). Until 1892, however, the support of Robertson and other friends did not help Sully get the chairs of philosophy for which he applied. He first applied to Trinity College, Dublin. Then, in 1880, he was a candidate for the Chair of Logic at Aberdeen University, which had fallen vacant upon Bain's resignation. Bain encouraged Sully to stand as one of the representatives of his own school, but the chair went to William Minto, Bain's former assistant. In the following year Sully reluctantly applied for the newly endowed Chair of Philosophy at University College, Liverpool. He was unsuccessful again and for a long time thereafter sought no further academic posts. He saw the lack of an Oxbridge education and membership of an unorthodox school of philosophy as two serious handicaps in any academic competition.

Nevertheless, Sully pursued his interest in psychology outside academia. Most of his philosophical and psychological works were published before he got a university appointment: *Sensation and Intuition* in 1874, *Pessimism* in 1877, *Illusions* in 1881, *Outlines of Psychology* in 1884, *The Teacher's Handbook of Psychology* in 1886 and *The Human Mind* in 1892. Even his acclaimed *Studies of Childhood*, published as a book in 1895, was first serialised in the British and American periodical press from 1881 onwards, and a popular selection from it was issued in 1897 as *Children's Ways*. His work was well received and its importance acknowledged by the leading authorities in evolution and psychology, such as Darwin and James. Darwin thanked Sully for a copy of *Sensation and Intuition* and regretted that it had not been published earlier, for his own work would have profited from it. James was particularly interested in Sully's work on evolution.[12] Thus, Sully's election to the UCL Professorship in 1892 came as recognition of his contribution to psychology. After a decade of financial problems, exhausting teaching and much writing, Sully characterised his accession to the chair as 'slackening the pace'.

Sully first formulated most of the ideas and arguments which subsequently appeared in his books and other publications in the pages of the *Fortnightly Review*, *Contemporary Review*, *Cornhill Magazine* and other general interest periodicals. The invitation to write an article on aesthetics for *Britannica* followed Sully's publication in the *Fortnightly Review* on the same subject. In the autumn of 1873 he set about 'stringing together some papers for a volume', which was to be his first book, *Sensation and Intuition* (1874) (Sully, 1918: 145). Later in his career Sully reversed this pattern and as far as possible tried to write articles which covered the same subjects as the books he was working on. In preparation for *Illusions* (1881) he published two articles on illusions of memory and perception in *Cornhill Magazine* and *New Quarterly Magazine* (Table 3.1).

Publications in the periodical press ensured discussion of Sully's work by his acquaintances and correspondents before its appearance in book format. Sully used these discussions to gauge the level of consensus among a broad group concerned with the investigation of the mind; in his own words, he sought to 'produce a view of psychology which should give prominence to what [he considered had been] ... firmly established in our rather shapeless science'. He articulated this objective in an argument with James, who urged him to make his writing 'more polemic, more careless of including all truth' (Sully, 1918: 317).

The career of a man of letters was the most likely way of pursuing philosophy and psychology for a man of independent means in the 1870s. Scientific institutions were few, and much research was supported by private incomes. The careers of several other Victorian men of science illustrate the same point.[13] Sully's ideal was to be the wise man extolled by Aristotle – one of those 'who have [a] strong bent towards the intellectual life and at the same time sufficient independence and leisure for its full fruition' (Sully, 1918: 267). Sully's lifestyle was not far from implementing this ideal, and was typical of the circle he joined in London.

Sully possessively protected his working hours. He had a daily routine which was seldom interrupted: 'From three to three and a half hours in the morning were my best hours and these I allotted to writing, while reading and business were relegated to what I always found to be a good second best, an hour or two after tea.' He always put his lectures in the afternoon, securing mornings for writing. The Sullys had two children, and the whole family must have fastidiously observed his working hours. Sully was a 'light' worker: the smallest noises disturbed him. 'To me such stories as that of Mrs. Somerville's writing scientific books in a room where children were at large,' he wrote, 'read like the superhuman exploits of Greek and mediaeval heroes' (Sully, 1918: 171). The work schedule left Sully with plenty of time for open-air physical exercise, long walks with 'Sunday Tramps' and visits to scientific and literary friends. Family holidays in the Swiss Alps were also shared with parties of London friends.[14]

This routine was sustained by the support of Sully's father. When in 1879 the father had to stop his allowance owing to financial problems, Sully was obliged to search for an income to complement the earnings from journalism and occasional lectures. By this time some of his more specialised writing did not pay at all. Bain generously supported *Mind* and initially paid for all contributions but later had to restrict the honorarium to book reviews. Sully had to try his pen at more lucrative writing. He received his largest-ever honorarium for a fictional story, 'Friendly Rivalry', in *Harper's Magazine*. Further income came from examining in philosophy and moral sciences in London, Cambridge and Manchester. But his financial affairs were most notably improved by his first long-term teaching appointment as a lecturer on the theory of education at the College of Preceptors, one of London's teacher training colleges.

4.2 *Teaching*

Sully's engagement with teacher training started in 1879 and continued until his retirement in 1903. Never losing touch with the audiences of teachers and parents, Sully continued lecturing at the College of Preceptors and at the Maria Grey Training College even after his UCL appointment.

Teachers were an important constituency for turn-of-the-century researchers of human evolution. From the point of view of scholars, teachers were the most qualified and best organised group of people in regular contact with children.[15] After the enactment of the 1870 Education Bill, primary education became increasingly common, and teachers began to deal with children from various social groups. Teachers were, therefore, targeted as potential informants by both researchers into human development and those investigating the health of the nation (Warner, 1897). Many measurements were carried out at schools and a substantial proportion of those was done by teachers. Karl Pearson appealed to teachers and parents through the *Educational Times* in early 1901 for 'aid in the measurement of children'. Pearson was engaged in research on the strength of hereditary influences in brothers and sisters. When he wrote to the *Educational*

Times, he already had obtained the measurements of some 1,600 children from schoolmasters and schoolmistresses and was therefore convinced that this was feasible. 'The measurements and observations I require,' he wrote, 'can only be obtained from the teacher.' Not wanting to put any willing teachers off by the complexity of the task, he continued: 'The observations ... can easily be made by any thoughtful teacher who is well acquainted with his or her pupils, and the measurements are not difficult to make' (Pearson, 1901). As a lecturer at teacher training colleges, Sully had an extensive knowledge of and contacts with teachers. However, the role of the teaching profession and educational institutions in relationship to psychology was more comprehensive than that of a potential source of data: school was a major institution in relation to which psychology was defined as a discipline.[16]

Sully wrote textbooks in defiance of long exclusion from academia. 'I asked, should I not make myself still more independent of the University authorities by becoming a teacher through my books?' (Sully, 1918: 189). He reckoned that the only accessible textbooks in psychology were Bain's works, but even they were 'not particularly well adapted to the needs of the general student, while for those who were studying the subject as teachers they were practically useless' (Sully, 1918: 189). Sully based his criticism of Bain and others on the requirements of the 'general student' and teachers, while crafting his own books to the demands of these audiences. At the same time, by introducing new concepts such as 'general student', Sully redefined his audience and the science of psychology in relation to it.[17] The bearing of the *Outlines of Psychology* was quickly appreciated in the United States, where the book was pirated and issued as a psychology textbook for teachers before Sully prepared his own American edition. *The Teacher's Handbook of Psychology* was born out of the effort of Sully and his New York publishers to secure their royalties and profit. In its fifth edition by 1909, it had even larger sales, both in Britain and America, than the first textbook.

With the help of teachers, Sully gained better access to schoolchildren than most scholars. However, children of preschool age and babies were particularly interesting subjects for an evolutionist. If middle-class babies were to be observed and measured in domestic settings, the understanding and cooperation of parents were needed. Sully observed his own two children from infancy and availed himself of friends' replies to his queries. In fact, many parents who knew Sully only from his articles sent him observations of children. Sully was in touch with the audience of parents through correspondence with his readers and through writing for publications like *The Baby*. In *The Baby*, Sully was presented to parents as a scientist, psychologist, evolutionist and leader of the British Child Study Association. These were the categories in which his work was typified for the audience of parents and which, therefore, became prominent in his writing. Claims for scientific psychology based on the data supplied by amateur observers, advanced by Sully and his supporters, were hotly contested by their opponents, of whom Hugo Münsterberg was one of the most formidable figures.

5   Münsterberg versus Sully

The child study movement could undertake two related tasks of data collection for scientists. First, it could launch observations of children in homes and schools, and channel them to scientists. Second, it could be a vehicle of educating parents and teachers so that their observations did not discredit the psychologists who used them. Scientists had to motivate parents and teachers to contribute observations in order to amass the required stock of anecdotes and data amenable to statistical analysis. At the same time, the scientific community had to be satisfied that observations of such provenance were admissible and could form the empirical basis of a science. In Britain, Sully dominated the discourse on the boundaries of science and child study, and on the relationship between science and domestic practices more generally. Addressing teachers and parents, Sully identified with science and grounded his authority in it. At the same time, he created a niche for his version of psychology using the discussions of the boundaries of child study and science, and of the relevance of psychology to education.

Sully's view of psychology, particularly its relevance to education, is highlighted through his differences with Hugo Münsterberg, Professor of Psychology at Harvard University. Both Sully and Münsterberg agreed that psychology could be applied to education, but their understandings of what 'applied psychology' meant differed significantly. Sully conceived applied psychology as the application of psychological methods to solving practical problems. Münsterberg conceived applied psychology as the application of the results of laboratory research to practical situations. Rejecting the possibility of the use of psychological methods by lay people, such as teachers and parents, Münsterberg sought to undermine the programme of applied psychology and child study advocated by Sully.

Sully's interest in the study of children centred on its implications for genetic psychology; he wished to elaborate a theory of the 'mind as a whole in its connected phases and stages of development' (Sully, 1886: 15–16). Münsterberg conceived psychology as an abstract and analytical study of the elements and laws of mental life common to all stages of life (Münsterberg, 1899: 115). He objected to the use of the term 'development' on the grounds that it demanded a value judgement, and was not 'given in the facts of science' (Münsterberg, 1909: 24–27).[18] Unlike Sully, for whom the study of children was a major way of studying mental development, he limited the relevance of the study of children to a few phenomena inaccessible in adults. Having a strong preference for direct observation in controlled experimental situations – or collective self-experimentation by a group of psychologists (Danziger, 1990: 49–52) – he found it futile to study any phenomena available in his own mind by 'the doubtful means of indirect observation' (Münsterberg, 1899: 115). Sully, conversely, relegated experiment to a relatively unimportant position. The value of experiment, according to him, was limited to the study of simpler, artificially induced mental processes, and it was useless in tracing the path of the development of the human mind. Thus, after inheriting Münsterberg's laboratory equipment, which was acquired by UCL upon Münsterberg's move from Freiburg to Harvard (Valentine, 1999), Sully put it to a different use.

Sully and Münsterberg concurred that the technical work of the laboratory was not relevant to teachers. However, each interpreted this conclusion in accordance with his own view of psychology. Sully expounded other areas of psychology to teachers, paying particular attention to mental development, phenomena of attention and memory, and the stages of thinking. Münsterberg challenged Sully's work by questioning the availability of a reliable body of experimental work that could form the foundations of sound psychological recommendations for education. The 1894 debate between Münsterberg and G. Stanley Hall, the central figure in American child study, before the Boston Schoolmaster's Club, in which Münsterberg rejected the research programme of child study supported by extensive connections between scientists and teachers, could not but reflect on Sully.[19] Münsterberg admonished those who made teachers believe that their observations were useful for psychology and branded child study 'seductive but rude and untrained and untechnical gathering of cheap and vulgar material, … a caricature' of psychology (Münsterberg, 1899: 116).

During the 1890s, Münsterberg also contested the need for psychology in teacher training and even declared its inclusion in the curriculum harmful. He argued that analytical scientific categories were detrimental to the values of practical life in general and teachers' work in particular (Münsterberg, 1899: 131). Postulating that psychology was not of any use to teachers, he nevertheless believed that education could benefit from the conclusions of psychology and other sciences with the mediation of the theory of education, which should elaborate the means by which educational goals can be best achieved.

Despite acute differences, in their books for teachers Sully and Münsterberg expounded similar psychological phenomena. A major difference between them consisted in their perception of teachers' ability to apply psychological knowledge. Sully, whose book is almost twice the size of Münsterberg's, led the reader into the study of psychology. Münsterberg, who by 1909 was satisfied that psychologists had material adjusted to the needs of the teacher and other practical professions, offered to teachers his own conclusions as to the relevance of psychology to their work (Münsterberg, 1909: viii) (on the wider context of this shift see O' Donnell, 1979a, especially chs 8–11).

A further contentious issue was whether psychology for teachers belonged to the psychological science or to an applied discipline, such as theory of education or educational psychology. Although Sully reserved 'more speculative parts' of psychology, such as the definition of the unconscious, for men of science, other areas of psychology were open to study by teachers and 'general students'. The hierarchy of practitioners of the science, so clearly articulated by Münsterberg, although present in Sully's writing, is less rigid. Drawing characteristically 'sharp, hard and fast'[20] distinctions, Münsterberg restricted the sciences to a professional activity, and warned against the application of cursory scientific knowledge by the 'thoughtless public' (Keller, 1979: 52, n.42; Hale, 1980: 72). Satisfied that reliable information had been accumulated in laboratory research, he personally undertook to explain its relevance to education.

Münsterberg justified the need to interpret the results of psychology for outsiders, such as teachers, by the difference between the realities constructed by science and common sense. In *Psychology and the Teacher* (1909), Münsterberg warned against the illusion, entertained by the philosophy of common sense, that everyday experiences were compatible with scholarship. Again, it was the vision of science as 'organised common sense', with which Sully aligned himself, that Münsterberg attacked. Sully, like Huxley and Lockyer, saw an educational value of scientific instruction in the acquisition of logical rigor and mental discipline. Adepts of this view, although clearly distinguishing between professional practitioners and others, encouraged scientific training, laboratory work in particular, in the education of various specialists (Gooday, 1990; Jardine, 1992: 304–323) and the general public.[21]

The view of the sciences as organised common sense was fundamental to Sully's journalistic writing and textbooks. In *The Teacher's Handbook of Psychology*, he explicitly treated the relationship between psychology and child study in introductory and methodological statements, and implicitly reflected on this relationship in the comments on observations provided by parents and teachers. His discussion of this relationship can be considered under two rubrics: the definition of child study as an applied science, and the teaching of science to parents as an element of the preparation for child study.

6   Uses of Sully's psychology

6.1 *Child study as an applied science*

Sully stated the following objective for the child study movement: to promote studies of human development in childhood and to provide a scientific basis for child management and education. 'A vital point in this bearing of psychology on education,' he wrote in *The Teacher's Handbook* in 1886, 'is that the adequate grasp of it delivers us from the old unscientific view of our work' (p. 14). The editorial in the first issue of *Paidologist* (the journal of the British Child Study Association) in 1899 also emphasised that child study was an applied activity, in contrast to the fundamental study of psychology. G.S. Hall, in a contribution to the *Paidologist*, maintained that, despite the fact that child study used scientific methods, those psychologists and physiologists who thought that the child study movement was doing their work were wrong because 'child-study is at present largely an applied science; it is prosecuted for the most part by parents and teachers who want knowledge that can be used in the development of the children for whose future happiness and usefulness they are immediately responsible' (Hall, 1899: 9). Child study, according to its professional proponents, used scientific methods but did not replace or challenge the sciences. The champions of child study sought to situate themselves without encroaching on any academic establishments.[22]

However, they came in conflict with Münsterberg, who denied child study the status of an applied science, reserving it for the theory of education. While commending the work of Hall, Preyer and Sully, he dismissed any attempts of parents or schoolteachers to contribute to science. His separation of psychology and practical life protected the monopoly of experts on knowledge, whether theoretical or applied (Hale, 1980: 74).

Illustrating the idea of child study as an applied science, Hall compared the relationship between child study and psychology to that between horticulture and botany. Surely, the relationship between horticulture and botany, and indeed between child study and psychology, was more complex than Hall implied. One aspect of this relationship, not embraced by the notion of application, was the dependence of Sully's and Hall's psychology on child study for data. 'If the reader is induced to study children for himself,' wrote William Drummond, child physician and lecturer to Edinburgh schoolteachers, ' … these pages will not have been written in vain' (Drummond, 1907).

Although child study writers valued lay observation, the term 'applied science' often rendered the work of laypersons invisible. In London in 1900 there were three child study 'Centres of Practical Work', each focusing on one of three themes: children's fears, pleasures and occupation as seen by country children. All three groups were led by lay members – Miss Crees, Miss Young and Miss Crombie – and met at the homes of these women. It was groups like these which gathered and summarised observations for scientists like Sully or Earl Barnes, Professor of Education at Stanford University in the United States and a visiting member of the British Child Study Association. Barnes was assisted by the members of the BCSA London branch in gathering and tabulating information for at least three studies between 1898 and 1900.[23] The 1898 'Schemes of Work' illustrate the level of cooperation between professional and lay members of the London branch. The experimental subcommittee, comprising professional researchers, parents and teachers, 'drew up a list of experiments which might be made with a view to submitting them to Mr. Francis Galton for his advice'.[24] They selected a number of experiments by C. Lloyd Morgan, each member preparing information on one of the experiments. This work required a full command of recent anthropological and psychological literature.[25]

The Schemes of Work Committee also analysed over 1,300 children's drawings, collected and annotated by parents, and over 2,500 responses to an association test. In their report to the Association, the Committee deliberated on the technical aspects of the mass survey, and concluded that for future investigations more detailed and unambiguous instructions were needed; they therefore suggested that the next assignment be limited to one simple test. In their textbooks and articles, Sully and other professional child study writers did no justice to the complex work carried out by lay enthusiasts. In the guidelines for those who wished to embark on the study of children they emphasised the humanistic value of scientific training, rather than the achievement of technical competence.

6.2 Preparation for child study

The novelist George Meredith commended Sully on his *Studies of Childhood* (1895) shortly after its publication. Meredith, a young father himself, promised to send Sully observations of his baby. The first one (in a letter dated 4 April 1896) was that the baby 'has already begun to observe with interest the motions of his great toe when he is in the bath'. Meredith jested that '[t]he nurse, the mother, and the father are pencil in hand about the infant for your behoof' and then, possibly, reflecting on his own experience as much as on Sully's, added: '[s]eriously indeed let me say that concerning the length of time you have devoted to the observation of these little ones and your devout intentness, the marvel is that you did not sink midway into the condition of the infant mind. It is a triumph of the philosophical …' (Cline, 1970: 1255). Sully and his colleagues firmly believed in the virtues of the philosophical and, indeed, scientific training. They generally indicated two groups of desirable results of students' exposure to science: the knowledge of certain facts, and the general strengthening of the mind, 'scientific mood', or 'passion for facts' – akin to that admired by Meredith in Sully.

On the factual side, mastering the theory of evolution was essential in the preparation for child study. Evolution was identified by Sully as the 'fore-knowledge' that should guide observation of child development and as the source of 'scientific imagination'. '[W]hile it is a commonplace,' he wrote, 'that theory must proceed to build on a basis of observation, it is also true, though less obviously so, that the finest observation is guided by scientific conjecture' (Sully, 1882b: 416). Child study activists developed an original body of writing pertaining to the attainment of the scientific state of mind, in other words, to the acquisition of the scientific method.

The mastery of scientific method was the key to carrying out scientific observation. According to its proponents, such observation could have been practised by almost everyone (though in a different fashion), given due preparation. Scientific training was conducive to a 'scientific mood', characterised by 'a great passion for facts', which could be acquired through a course of laboratory work of some kind.[26] 'Some faithful work of weighing, or measuring, or dissecting, or analyzing, may be warmly recommended,' wrote Drummond (1907: 9–10). During laboratory exercises participants learned to make and record observations, and to separate observations from interpretations.[27] Sully attributed Preyer's observational skills to his experience in physiology (Preyer was Professor of Physiology at Jena, Germany). But even Preyer, according to him, occasionally gave 'too much rein to the natural impulse to interpret observed facts' (Sully, 1882b: 416).

In preparation for child study, laboratory learning was to be complemented by 'careful study of a scientific work of a related field'. Drummond recommended the manual *Practical Biology* by Huxley and Martin.[28] It did not matter which branch of biology was chosen for study or what kind of laboratory work was performed by the student, for these exercises were aimed at the acquisition of general skills of observation and reasoning. The requisite preparation for child study is considered here separately from the question of whether these guidelines were followed. This analysis of postulated requirements suggests that proponents of child study believed in the efficiency of a unified scientific method. This method and generic laboratory practice were the ground on which various experts – for instance Sully, ex-student of Helmholtz, and Drummond, a physician – could unite and define themselves as scientists in relationship to parents and teachers. While providing experts with a common ground, scientific method also sanctioned their position within the movement and provided learning goals for aspiring practitioners.

In this connection, Sully's involvement in the establishment of the laboratory at UCL acquires a new meaning, and can be seen not to contradict his lack of interest in (and occasional scepticism towards) psychological experimentation. Laboratory practice was a token of scientific privilege and aptitude. At the time when the actual practice of child study was based on observation and anecdote, animal dissection was recommended for aspiring practitioners. Proponents of child study shared the emphasis on laboratory training with the adepts of the late-Victorian 'public science', who believed that laboratory work enhanced individual virtues and was, therefore, beneficial for society at large.

7   The practice of Sully's psychology

7.1 *Scientist–mother opposition*

The female sex of most lay practitioners of child study, as well as the perceived feminine nature of child care, constituted a major difficulty for those who, like Sully, believed that child study was a source of data for scientific psychology. Scientists featuring in popular narratives of the second half of the nineteenth century were men. Whether female practitioners of the sciences and engineering had stepped outside the roles properly available to middle-class women was an issue of public debate (Benjamin, 1991: 1–23; Broks, 1996: 87–89). Conversely, the practical engagement with children demanded by child study was strongly associated with the domestic role of women, despite the growing attention of the adult public of both sexes to the world of the child. Sully used two strategies in dealing with these difficulties. In order to circumvent the biases introduced by unreliable female observers, he proposed a hierarchy of child study practitioners, in which women were supervised by men. Aiming to divorce child study from the connotations of domestic child care, he constructed the child as a scientific object, contrasting it with the child as an object of maternal adoration.[29]

The nature of child study, particularly its direct relationship to children, had two ramifications for its gender identity. On the one hand, the focus on the home underscored the potential conflict faced by mothers, between their roles as carers and observers. On the other hand, immediate connection with the home and the raising of children made psychology a science of prime relevance to women, and child study a women's pursuit. Unlike other scholarly pursuits, the study of children was not perceived as a threat to the femininity of its practitioners or as a distraction from their domestic duties. Child study fitted well with the prevalent sentiment that mothering had to be learned, and with the practices of motherhood being increasingly mediated by experts, books and child care gadgets. However, doubts about the compatibility of care and study came from within the child study movement itself.

Sully's heroes were male students of child development: Darwin and Preyer. He used their names to attract more male practitioners into child study. Darwin 'deemed the child worthy of study' because he saw in its development 'nature's spectacle' of 'humble inception' and 'proud maturity' of man (Sully, 1895/1903: 4). His anti-heroes were 'perennial baby-worshippers', mothers whose affection for their child stood in the way of scientific observation. Sully used his accounts of female shortcomings to buttress his case for male intervention. It has to be noted that, at the same time, Sully held liberal views on education, taught at the Women's Training College in Cambridge and contemplated starting a private hostel for women students with the assistance of Cambridge philosopher Henry Sidgwick (Sully, 1918: 191, 278; see, however, E. Richards, 1989: 253–284, on Huxley's liberalism and anti-feminism). Sully's doubts over women's involvement in child study are, therefore, to be taken as earnest.

> The average mother can hardly be expected to do more than barely tolerate the experiments.… One may be bold enough to hazard the prophesy that women who have had scientific training will, if they happen to become mothers, hardly be disposed to give their minds at the very outset to the rather complex and difficult work … of making an accurate scientific inventory. (Sully, 1895/1903: 17–21)

Hence, Sully concluded, it was the job of the father to record the development of the child. Thus women's knowledge of children and the scientific knowledge of children were dissociated and the former was exposed as lacking, because it was conducive to unscientific approaches to upbringing and teaching.

Sully emphasised only the mental side of the juxtaposition of scientific observation and the mother–child relationship. Mothers were deemed unable to give their *minds* to scientific work and men trained in science were 'guided by fore-*knowledge* … to what is essential in the phenomenon and its surroundings' (Sully, 1895/1903: 11, emphasis added). Although Sully stressed the difference between the attitudes of a scientific observer and a mother, he believed that both engaged with the child mentally. Clearly, he drew on the lifestyle of a well-to-do mother who was emotionally but not necessarily physically involved with her child,[30] thus constructing child study on the foundations of upper-class daily life.

7.2 *Conflicting loyalties*

The roles of female servants and mothers were understated in the descriptions of ideal child study. It is, however, evident from the actual accounts of child behaviour analysed by Sully that women actively participated in observations and experiments. Even the reviewer of Preyer's *The Mind of the Child* could not fail to note that he 'was enabled by the cooperation of a sympathetic and intelligent wife'.[31] According to Darwin's own account, the nurse participated in his experiments (Darwin, 1877). Psychologist Charles Wilfred Valentine, who started close observation of his own children in 1912, took turns in keeping the diary with his wife. In a few years his children took to filling in the notebooks with test results and recording each other's performance.[32] Conversely, the absence of women's cooperation put the completeness of observations at risk: the father's diary appended by Sully to his *Studies of Childhood* contains a gap of over five weeks during which 'the child was very cross and not a good subject of observation' (Sully, 1895/1903: 402).

Women, who had prime responsibility for children's welfare and attended to them whatever their temper, were indispensable when it came to dealing with children. Underplaying women's participation was a rhetorical device, and a close reading of child study materials rehabilitates the role of women in child study in particular and in the popularisation of science in the home in general.[33] It also explains why women were, despite the rhetoric, targeted by popularisers. Both the inclusion of the famous names of scientists and the exclusion of women worked to enhance the authority of child study in the eyes of the general public and other scientists. Nothing illustrates this point better than the administration of the British Child Study Association and its constituent societies (the BCSA itself became the Child-Study Society in 1907). Women were extremely powerful within child study organisations: they were the founders of the movement in Britain, held offices and contributed funds. Professor Barnes, the visiting American psychologist and a BCSA Vice-President, had to seek the support of the majority of the Advisory Committee in his confrontation with Mary Louch, a fellow Committee member, who had allegedly tried to define the policy of the Association's journal, *Paidologist*, single-handedly. Despite the strong position of women inside the BCSA, its presidents and most vice-presidents were men. These men represented child study in the press.

Scientists interested in child study in Britain were poised between an audience of interested amateurs and professional scientists. Unlike ethnographers, who, with the advent of fieldwork by trained practitioners, were no longer dependent on the reports of travellers, psychologists could not circumvent the parents of those children who were deemed normal.[34] At the same time, they had to maintain the scientific status of the data supplied by parents in the eyes of peer scientists. The separation of the male science from the female home was a way of defining science by scientists vis-à-vis various audiences. The arcane journal title *Paidologist* was chosen over several more common alternatives which would have had a broader appeal precisely for its esoteric air, in order to sift out all but the most serious and devoted of amateurs.[35]

The efforts of scientists involved in child study add up to a consistent tendency to mould the identity of child study through differentiation and certification of its practitioners by experts. This policy was relevant to the consolidation of one brand of scientific psychology in three ways: psychologists positioned themselves as professionals vis-à-vis amateur child study practitioners; they carved an area of application of their expertise; and they tried to guarantee the validity of their data. This is why attacks on child study were so painful to many psychologists. What was at stake in the discussions about the utility of parents' education and the validity of their observations was the shape of psychology as a new area of scientific expertise, the status of its method, its facts and, not least, the jobs for new experts. In the discussion on the status of scientific psychology, Sully aligned himself with the English tradition of naturalism, laid a heavy emphasis on the humanitarian value of the scientific method, and elaborated this postulate in relation to psychology and education.

8   Conclusion: Sully and the role of the mediator

After more than 30 years of writing on a range of topics and teaching a variety of subjects, Sully called himself a psychologist in his autobiography. Many contemporaries corroborated such an identification, as is evident from ample references to his work. Yet, by the standards of our own day, Sully is hardly a classic. Why, then, would a historian turn to this name? Can a practising psychologist learn anything from the examination of the paradoxes of Sully's career?

   Through this examination of his career, we have resolved the contradictions between his lack of experimental work and his responsibility for the psychological laboratory, and between the scarcity of his specialised psychological publications and the tributes of contemporaries. As is apparent from the analysis of Sully's views on the subject matter and methods of psychology, he saw a limited role for the laboratory in psychological research; a comparison of the views of Sully and Münsterberg highlights this feature. Sully saw, however, a major role for the laboratory as a place of general scientific training, which he regarded as requisite for the pursuit of psychology. The requirement of laboratory training for the practice of psychology enhanced the scientific status of the new discipline. Moreover, in the context of child study, laboratory experience was used to construct a hierarchy of its practitioners. Being a professor at the UCL, Sully did not take an earnest interest in the basic laboratory training of students, but saw it fitting to be associated with the laboratory and act as the secretary of the organising committee. Thus, the understanding of the place accorded by Sully to experimental work explains his apparently ambiguous relationship to the laboratory.

   Sully sought to justify this vision of scientific psychology in the eyes of other scientists and of the public, and to create a niche for himself personally and for such a profession more generally (for Sully's role in the organisation of the British Psychological Society, see Lovie, Chapter 4). As other contributions to this volume testify, Sully was not the only spokesperson for psychology. The aim of this chapter was not to plead for Sully's special merit, but to relate his way of defining psychology to his specific position in the British social and intellectual landscape. Being a Baptist, Sully was educated outside the mainstream Anglican institutions. Despite good academic references and the ever-growing circle of influential acquaintances in London, he failed at first to secure an academic job. Having started as a writer and a person of means, Sully was soon forced by financial difficulties to take up any writing and teaching job he could get. Thus, by 1892, when Sully became the Grote Professor of Logic and Philosophy of Mind at UCL, he could move comfortably between writing and lecturing for different audiences.

Only a minority of Sully's readers and listeners would have called themselves psychologists. A narrowly defined professional psychological community did not exist during the last three decades of the nineteenth century. Sully regularly wrote articles for teachers and parents as well as for the general educated audience; he published four different textbooks for beginners, teachers and advanced students, two of which went through several editions. It was the focus on Sully's social and intellectual position that allowed me to analyse his role as a mediator between the nascent profession and the public, and to conclude that such mediators have a very important role in the process of professionalisation.

The position of a writer and lecturer who shared much of his social world with the academic community and yet, professionally, remained on its margins, deserves special attention. Sully continuously crossed the boundaries between academia, science, journalism and teaching. Having achieved university tenure, he continued his involvement with teacher training and the work for the audience of parents. His position in the child study movement was manifestly borderline. He was a nexus between academic researchers and lay enthusiasts for the study of child development. In the efforts to nurture the practices supporting the collection of data, he made methodological concessions to the conventions of domestic life. Maintaining contacts with lay audiences, namely teachers and parents, Sully popularised the new science, secured a flow of data, and created prestige and, possibly, demand for psychology graduates. Despite being a marginal figure in academia for most of his life, Sully was influential in defining the boundaries of psychology.

Acknowledgements

I am grateful to Jim Secord and Graham Richards for comments on drafts of this chapter and to Sandy Lovie for locating papers relating to child study in the archives of the British Psychological Society.

Notes

1 For the analyses of various aspects of this process, see contributions to this volume by Graham Richards (Chapter 1), Francis Neary (Chapter 2) and Mathew Thomson (Chapter 5).
2 W.H.R. Rivers came down from Cambridge to give practical classes in the UCL laboratory (Thomson, 1993: vi).

3 Bowler (1988: 6–13) examines the relationship between growth, evolution and re-capitulation.

4 Darwin's interest in the observation of children is outlined by Bradley (1989: 1–27).

5 Sully refers to the drawings exhibited in Room 7 of General Pitt-Rivers' Museum at Farnham, and acknowledges 'friendly help in studying the drawings of savages' extended to him by the General and Mr H. Balfour of the Oxford Museum. Sully (1895/1903: introduction and 336; 1897: 188).

6 On the branding of the Ethnographic Society as a 'ladies' society' after the admission of women, and Huxley's anxiety over this, see E. Richards (1989: 253–284).

7 On the moral dimension of the definition of science at the end of the nineteenth century, see Daston (1982: 99).

8 On the careers of Victorian public figures, see Collini (1991), especially pp. 25–50.

9 For an example of an earlier textbook using this device, see Porter (1870).

10 On the history of philosophical textbooks, see Schmitt (1988).

11 On careers of men of letters see Heyck (1982); on Morley see Gross (1991: 112–125).

12 Letters of 23 December 1875 and 3 July 1880, respectively. Sully collection, University College London, Archives, MS Add. 158.

13 Darwin, for instance, was a gentleman of means; Huxley was not, and it took him so long to find a job that enabled him to support a family that his engagement lasted over 12 years (Desmond, 1994: 211–214).

14 On the role of 'Sunday Tramps' and the Alpine Society in intellectual and literary life, see Annan (1984: 90–98). See also Sully (1912).

15 On the history of the study of human growth and specifically on the role of teachers, see Tanner (1981), especially p. 180.

16 At the same time, the psychologising of the relations between pupils, teachers and families transformed schools. Rose (1985: 112–145).

17 Steven Sturdy (1992) has described a similar strategy on the part of hospital consultants to appeal to private patients in a bid to strengthen their position in hospitals dominated by traditional physicians, and thus redefine medicine. See also Lawrence (1985).

18 The distinction between facts and values was central to Münsterberg's philosophy (Hale, 1980: ch. 6). Hale (1980: ch. 7) positions Münsterberg in relation to German and English-language philosophical traditions.

19 Rose (1985: 241) shows that British head teachers drew up record cards and tested the characters of pupils in 1885 and 1886, and apparently used a scheme of tests similar to that of Galton's, with whom Sully subsequently collaborated at University College. Münsterberg (1899: 6, 17) criticised this way of collecting data. See also M. Münsterberg (1922: 49).

20 John Dewey, review of *Eternal Values* by Hugo Münsterberg, in *Philosophical Review*, vol. 19 (1910), p. 110, quoted in Hale (1980: 85).

21 On Norman Lockyer and scientific training for rational citizenship see Turner (1993: 201–228).

22 Drummond (1907: 1) also characterised child study as an applied science.

23 British Child Study Association, London Branch Minute Book, 1897–1907, British Psychological Society Archives, Staffordshire University.

24 British Child Study Association, London Branch Minute Book 1897–1907, British Psychological Society Archives, Staffordshire University.

25 On C. Lloyd Morgan and his contribution to animal and comparative psychology, see David Wilson (Chapter 12) and Costall (1993).

26 On laboratory training as a liberal education in rational and accurate reasoning, see Gooday (1990).

27 *General Instructions on the Scheme of Work*, no date, 1898 (?), inserted into the minute book of the London branch of the British Child Study Association, 1897–1907, British Psychological Society Archives, Staffordshire University.

28 Drummond was probably referring to T.H. Huxley's *A Course of Practical Instruction in Elementary Biology* (1875, with the assistance of H.N. Martin) or his *A Course of Elementary Instruction in Practical Biology* (1879).
29 For a broader survey of male experts and their roles in the promotion of 'sexual romanticism', see the classic study by Ehrenreich and English (1979).
30 On the differences in upper- and working-class experiences of motherhood see Ross (1993: ch. 5).
31 The review was probably written by Sully (1882a), who also reviewed the book for *Mind* (Sully, 1882b).
32 Charles W. Valentine papers, British Psychological Society Archives, Staffordshire University.
33 On the rhetoric of separate spheres, see Vickery (1993).
34 On the study of mentally retarded children in relation to human evolution, see Zenderland (1998).
35 Editorial, *Paidologist*, 1 (1). In 1907, during the Association's amalgamation with the Childhood Society (originally called the Society for the Promotion of Hygiene in School Life) to form the Child Study Society, the journal was renamed *Child-Study*.

4

Three steps to heaven: how the British Psychological Society attained its place in the sun

Sandy Lovie

There are a thousand stories in the naked city. (*The Naked City*, Jules Dassin's motion picture, 1948)

1   Step 1 (1901–1919): birth, a near-death experience and resurrection (courtesy of C.S. Myers)

The Britain of 1901 was not, on the face of it, a particularly propitious place in which to plan for the future: Queen Victoria had died at the start of the year, aged 81, only to be succeeded by her eldest son, the Prince of Wales (famously described by Henry James at the time of the Queen's death as 'fat vulgar Edward'). Meanwhile, the socially divisive and morally bankrupt Boer War (which had seen the British pioneering the use of mass concentration camps for civilians) still had another year to drag its broken carcass around South Africa until finally collapsing at the Peace of Vereeniging in May 1902. Furthermore, the continuing and costly arms race between Britain and Germany to see who could construct the biggest and most deadly ironclads seemed to offer only the horrifying certainty that what had been built would inevitably be used. It must have been a remarkably optimistic group of ten assorted academics, intellectuals and educationalists, therefore, who gathered on a day in late October in 1901 at the Godless College of Gower Street (University College London) at the express invitation of James Sully, then Grote Professor of Mind and Logic, in order to create 'a psychological Society' (minutes of the general meeting on 24 September 1901).[1]

The present chapter outlines some of the consequences of the choices made at this first meeting. I concentrate particularly on the decisions regarding the Society's aims and membership criteria, which helped shape the early years of the Society and which, paradoxically, eventually led to what was effectively its rebuild in 1919 by C.S. Myers, one of the Society's more far-sighted and pragmatic members. I also cover the contradictions and opportunities which arose from this pivotal event in 1919, among the latter being the eventual professionalisation of much of British psychology by the Society.

There were ten people, nine men and one woman, at this first meeting of the Society (originally referred to as the Psychological Society, the word 'British' did not come until a little later, in 1906; see also Richards, Chapter 1, for an earlier attempt to found a psychological society). Although anyone knowledgeable about the history of British psychology would have been able to recognise the names of three of the ten, specifically James Sully, W.H.R. Rivers and William McDougall, the others would have been much less familiar, although one of them (the physiologist F.W. Mott) had been elected a Fellow of the Royal Society in 1896 and was later to concern himself with the treatment of shell shock during the First World War, while the one woman, Mrs Sophie Bryant, was headmistress of the North London Collegiate School, a place made famous in the nineteenth century by the presence there of Miss Frances Mary Buss.[2]

The other five came from a variety of professional backgrounds, ranging from R. Armstrong-Jones, who trained as a physician, to W.G. Smith, F.N. Hales and W.R.B. Gibson, who added a more general philosophical, moral sciences and psychological flavour to the mix, while the tenth, A.F. Shand, had legal training, although he never practised, devoting himself instead to the service of the Society. (It is perhaps also worth noting that Mott, Armstrong-Jones and Smith were all associated with the Claybury Asylum, where their careers overlapped during 1901.)

Together these ten people announced the creation of the Society with all the self-conscious flourish of a nineteenth-century company of touring thespians:

> At a meeting held at University College London on October 24th 1901 … it was proposed by Dr. Mott and seconded by Mr. Shand that 'a psychological Society be formed on the same lines as the Physiological Society, as originally formed', the motion was carried unanimously.
>
> Dr. Smith then proposed & [blank] seconded 'That it is the aim of the Society to advance scientific psychological research, & to further the co-operation of investigators in the different branches of Psychology.' The motion was carried unanimously.
>
> Mr. Shand next proposed & Dr. Mott seconded 'That all present at this meeting be ipso facto members of the Society.' This motion was also carried unanimously. (Minutes of the general meeting, 24 September 1901)

This ambitious programme went further, in that it was also proposed that a fairly lengthy list of the great and the good (and possible future stars) who were not actually present should nevertheless be approached to become 'original members' of the Society. Among these were 'Prof. James Ward, Dr. Stout, Prof. Alexander, Mr. Francis Galton, Prof. Lloyd Morgan, Prof. Sherrington … Miss Edgell … Mr.

Carveth Read'. It is worth noting that all approached agreed to become original members of the Society, with the exception of Francis Galton (minutes of the general meeting, 14 November 1901), although not all are recorded as having been formally elected, including the Society's own official historian, Beatrice Edgell (see Edgell, 1947, for example)! However, it was only when Galton was offered an Honorary Fellowship in 1905 that he decided to associate himself with the Society. Although such Fellowships, which had been created in January 1904, were very occasionally awarded to existing members of the Society, for instance James Sully, Honorary Fellows were invariably distinguished figures in psychology who had little or no connection with the Society.

However grandiloquent the aims of the Society, it was the decisions made during the latter, more prosaic portion of this first meeting which were to shape the Society for the next 17 or so years of its existence. Here the strict criteria for membership of the Society were spelt out, as was the elaborate voting system under which those proposed would be actually elected into the Society. Together these two hurdles made it almost impossible for anyone at the time to become a member: 'Mr. Shand next proposed and Mrs. Bryant seconded "that only those who are recognised teachers in some branch of psychology or who have published work of recognisable value be eligible as members," carried unanimously.' And 'Mr. Shand proposed & Dr. Rivers seconded That noone be elected a member of the Society unless his name be first approved by the executive committee & thereafter receive a two-thirds majority at a general meeting of the society – carried unanimously' (minutes of the general meeting, 24 September 1901). Since there were no university departments of psychology in Britain at the time, or indeed any undergraduate or postgraduate degrees in psychology, and there were few people employed to teach psychology at any level, or journals to display their research, the target group for Society membership was tiny, and was to remain so in Britain for nearly five decades (although I am sure that the original Committee would not have agreed *at the time* that this was a plausible future scenario).

One point that will have struck the reader about these first minutes is the high degree of coherence achieved between the aims of the Society and the membership criteria. This was undoubtedly not accidental, as the Society seemed eager from the start to define the nature and practice of psychology as a scientific discipline, like physiology, with which it felt a kindred spirit, hence the Society's use of the Physiological Society as a model rather than, say, the recently founded American Psychological Association. It is also the case that many of the earliest members of the Society had extensive formal training in physiology and, because psychology and physiology have a shared interest in the material circumstances of the individual body, looked to physiology as a source of ideas about the direction in which psychology should progress. Such a commitment to a particular world view and a belief that it was also shared by the tiny number eligible for election to the Society in turn supplied the criteria for deciding who should be defined as a psychologist, and hence who would be eligible to join. This mutually self-supporting position meant that the Society was never going to be a best seller among the public at large, even if the same public was as fascinated then as it is now by the subject (see Richards, Chapter 1, for an assessment of the popularity of psychology among the psychological laity). Notice too (and in line with this last comment) that the minutes have nothing to say about the propagation of the subject to the wider public: the only communications from the Society were to be directed (and even then only by implication) at those currently engaged in the Great Game. Finally, the only doubts aired early on against the direction that the Society seemed hell bent on travelling was at a 1906 meeting of the (executive) Committee of the Society, when the following semi-formal proposal was debated: 'the possibility of establishing a Psychological Society with wider membership and more popular interests, the present Society remaining as a Research Branch' (Committee minutes, 14 July 1906; see below for more about the nature of the committee). Not too surprisingly, the Society did not pursue this suggestion any further, but it is worth noting for what happened in 1919 that both Rivers and Myers were present at this 1906 gathering.

All in all, then, this first meeting of the Society looked like a well engineered and highly successful effort to create a certain kind of psychological collective and to give it a formal and public face. If I were a betting person, I would have put my money on William McDougall as the organising force behind the Society's foundation, particularly as May Smith (quoted in Steinberg, 1961) has claimed that he was hosting informal meetings about psychology in University College London in the year before the Society's appearance, and that many of the people who attended these gatherings were to form the original corpus of the Society.

Although I do not have the space to cover the next 17 or so years of the British Psychological Society (BPS) in any detail, it is worth making one or two comments about its life up to 1918, since its progress up to that year helps to explain why it might have ceased to exist as a separate body after that date. The simple problem was that, in spite of the enthusiastic start to the Society and its early success in recruiting high-profile academics, including the neurologist Henry Head, the physiologist J.S. Haldane (the well known father of J.B.S. Haldane) and the philosopher R.H. Bradley (and a paper contributed by a certain L. Wittgenstein in 1912), the long years of the 1910s, particularly the war years from 1914 onwards, saw the Society growing at only a snail's pace. Indeed, by 1918 the gross membership was only 98, a mere fourfold increase of its original size over 17 or so years, with the war years themselves contributing virtually nothing to the total (see Figure 4.1). To cap it all, the attendance at general and annual meetings of the Society was sparse: for example, between 1914 and 1918 the audience at such meetings averaged only about 25 people, including visitors. Of course, the major problem was the highly exclusive membership rules, which effectively guaranteed that the membership would be limited to the London and Oxbridge academic elites who had originally founded the Society in their own image.

Now this would not have been a difficulty for the Society if it had wished to stay small (and select), but it became pretty clear by 1917 that what the BPS

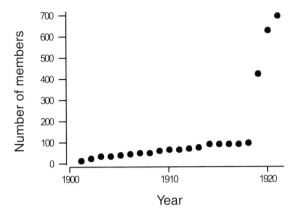

Figure 4.1 *Scatterplot of reported growth in membership over the first 20 years of the (British) Psychological Society's existence.*

really wanted was to be much larger (but still as selective). However, since still no one was setting up departments of psychology in any British university at the time, or was radically increasing the number of research and teaching posts in psychology, and as the Society showed little sign of wishing to liberalise its membership rules, so the BPS was forced to deal with the unpalatable contradiction of size versus exclusivity as best it could.

> The Secretary then raised the question as to the desirability of taking steps to increase the membership of the Society. It was decided that no changes should be made in the rule relating to membership, but that certain qualified persons who were considered desirable as members should be approached by members of the Committee acquainted with them with a view to their becoming members of the Society. (Committee[3] minutes, 12 December 1917 – so noted 'Jack' Flügel at the start of the revolution)

The next but one Committee meeting, on 20 November 1918, saw C.S. Myers, the major player in the drama and a long-term BPS insider, taking the members to the top of the mountain and showing them the promised land:

> Col. Myers brought before the Committee the question of the desirability of extending the membership of the Society with a view to the possibility of obtaining such advantages as (a) permanent headquarters, an increased library, a paid librarian, the establishments of definite sections for the study of special aspects of psychology & [blank].

But then we encounter the near-death experience, prefaced by the usual bureaucratic move:

> The question was discussed at length & at the conclusion of the discussion a Subcommittee consisting of Mrs Ballard, Jones, Myers, & Rivers – was appointed to investigate the matter further, with particular reference to questions of finance & to the possibility of co-operation or fusion with certain other societies, this Subcommittee to report to the Committee of the Society before the next Annual General Meeting of the Society.

There is no name recorded in association with the question of whether the BPS should in effect perform an act of self-immolation, but I believe that it was no coincidence that the only common member of this and the very first ordinary meeting of the Society in 1901 was Shand, who had (it will be recalled) proposed both of the restrictive membership rules which had helped shape the nature of the BPS for so long. However, irrespective of whether Shand was actually the hidden hand behind the invitation to jump, there were clearly people on the committee for whom the effective suicide of the BPS as an independent entity was more acceptable than the weakening of the membership rules.

In the event, this self-terminating term of reference was ignored, with the next meeting of the committee hearing an alarming paper from Myers which spelt out the dire consequences facing the Society if it did no proceed to rebuild itself (Committee minutes, 8 January 1919):

> The consideration of schemes for the extension of the work & membership of the Society was then resumed. A report drawn up by Col. Myers to serve as a basis of discussion was read and discussed. It was decided that Col. Myers should read an amended form of this report at the following Annual General Meeting in order that members of the Society might have an opportunity of expressing their views on the proposed changes at that meeting.

Although there is no surviving copy of Myers' report in the Committee minutes, a copy of the amended version can be found with the minutes of the extraordinary general meeting (of 19 February 1919) to which the hapless Annual General Meeting (of 25 January 1919) had passed the buck.

This brief report from Myers outlined a threat to the future of the Society in the form of three groups of people external to the Society who were either interested or actually engaged in certain specialist areas of psychology (in medicine, industry and education), and who were actively proposing to set up organisations and journals to further their sectional pursuits (see also Myers, 1936: 224–225). Together, these three groups would outnumber the Society's current membership by roughly four to one and (in Myers' eyes) would have constituted an almost instant drain on the Society's numbers and funding if their ambitious plans were to be realised. On the other hand, as Myers argued, if these outside people were brought into the Society through the creation of sections catering to their more specialised needs, so the land of the BPS would flow with milk and honey (or at least secure the possibility of a permanent London base for the Society and a larger library, etc.). The extraordinary general meeting voted a resounding and unanimous yea for both the new sections and, equally importantly, for a key but seemingly minor alteration to the memberships rules, which Myers had also drafted for the meeting: thus, in place of 'engaged in psychology' in the old Rule 2, Myers and the Committee suggested the substitution of 'interested in psychology'. The changes to the membership rules went even further in that while the Committee (and its proposed makeover, the BPS Council) could still elect people to the Society, the sections themselves were now able to nominate their own adherents, who, if accepted, would become *ipso facto* members of the Society as well. Collectively, these two alterations to the rules represented a massive shift of power away from the centralising and professional members in the old Society to the amateurs running the three sections. At one fell stroke, the BPS had abandoned its exclusive and elitist membership, and had opened its doors to the hordes of the unwashed (or so it seemed to some members), although interestingly the grade of Honorary Fellowship was retained (it might actually have been very impolitic to have done otherwise!).

Myers had already grasped with both hands the opportunity presented to him by these menacing if somewhat shadowy groupings of people outside the Society, and even before either the Annual General Meeting or the extraordinary general meeting of the Society, he had convened a session of the Committee (on 22 January 1919) at which the outline for the new golden age was sketched in and the troops allocated to their positions. Thus, at the imminent Annual General Meeting, Myers was to read out the report and to present the Committee's suggestions for changing the rules of the Society, while the educationalist Professor T.P. Nunn (another member of the Committee) was to take the chair. The Committee meeting of 22 January also discussed the route (and cost) whereby existing Society members could become members of the future (and as yet unsanctioned) specialist sections, and the governance of these sections – all this *before* even the Annual General Meeting had met, never mind the extraordinary general meeting whose date, time and possible venue the Committee had already pencilled in!

In addition, since the Committee could also recommend new members to the Society (provided, of course, that they could find a proposer and seconder, and were not black balled by having their names crossed out by the existing members), so they used this power to pack the Society with their own nominees, and not just on a small scale either, but at a rate never dreamed of by the old Committee. Thus, at a Committee meeting on 7 March 1919, the names of 109 people (that is, 11 more than there were in the Society at the end of 1918) were nominated for membership of the Society, while at the next two meetings (30 April and 31 May 1919) no less than 145 new names were proposed, seconded and then forwarded by the Committee for consideration at the appropriate BPS general meetings, and so on and so forth for the next two years.

One of the reasons that Myers was able to recruit so many new people for the Society was that his extensive wartime service in treating shell-shock cases, first in various hospitals in France and then, in 1917, as overseer of the many new units in England and Scotland set up to treat the condition, meant that he came into daily contact with a large number of fellow medics from the Royal Army Medical Corps, whose day-to-day work was almost exclusively of a psychological nature and who would be potential recruits for the BPS. In addition, a quick perusal of the serried ranks of members of the Royal Army Medical Corps (overwhelmingly either proposed or seconded by Myers himself) who made up the bulk of this list of 250 people also reveals that while all of them are given a rank and an address, none of them is credited with any formal expertise in psychology, or time in service at the teaching coal face, or the publication of some *magnum opus psychologicus*. In other words, while it is the case that the extraordinary general meeting of 19 February supported the creation of sections and the rule changes, this did not amount to their formal adoption by the Society, since the fashionably named Reconstruction Committee (which, while nominally an off-shoot of the Society's general meeting, was in actuality yet another of the Committee's many hydra heads) was *still* working on a draft version of the Society's rules, one which they did not present for final adoption until a further extraordinary general meeting of the Society on 1 May 1920! However, Myers and the Committee seem to have assumed after 19 February 1919 that the creation of the sections and the changes to the membership rules were a *fait accompli*, and thus warranted any of their subsequent actions.

For instance, the Committee at the 7 March meeting, having agreed a notice to be circulated to all existing members informing them of the recent changes to the rules, then decided on which dates the inaugural meetings of the three sections – educational, medical ('provided this suited the convenience of Dr Rivers') and industrial – would be held and, for two of them, the venues for this first meeting. On 7 February 1919, some 15 days before the extraordinary general meeting, at a session of the four-person subcommittee of the Committee (no prizes for guessing the name of one of the participants), we see at the end of the unsigned minutes the following: 'The Secretary was instructed to approach Dr. Rivers & Prof. Nunn with a view to ascertaining whether they would be willing to deliver an inaugural address on the occasion of the first meeting of the medical & educational sections respectively.'[4] Seemingly Myers *et al.* took their own commitment to reform as enough of a warrant for their actions *even before* the various formal (and public) rounds of annual and extraordinary general meetings.

Be that as it may, by the 1920 Annual General Meeting, which was held in Kings College, London, on 2 October, the revised rules had already been accepted, the sections and their separate secretariats were up and running, and the membership flow (and finances) had started to resemble Niagara after a particularly heavy cloudburst (Francis Aveling, the new BPS Secretary, had claimed 631 members in his end-of-year report). The Reconstruction Committee had also proposed to the extraordinary general meeting of 1 May 1920 that the Society be governed by a Council, consisting of a President, Vice-President, Secretary, Treasurer, representatives from the sections, and Uncle Tom Cobley an' all. This, in effect, meant renaming the old Committee 'the Council' (the heading for the Committee meeting of 8 May 1920, for example, has the name Committee scored out and the word Council inserted above it) but, more immediately, this also meant that to the victor the spoils, as Myers was named the very first President of the BPS at the 1920 Annual General Meeting. From Myers' position at the start of the first decade after the war, therefore, the Society (which still recorded an increased membership at the end of 1921) had been saved and seemed en route to even greater success. So what happened next?

2   Step 2 (1919–1933): challenges, challenges, challenges

Even before the dust had settled on Myers' triumph, both the Committee and the Reconstruction Committee were negotiating for more permanent premises for the BPS than the peripatetic accommodation offered by Committee members' houses, or the grace-and-favour rooms that they had managed to squeeze from their respective universities. Thus, early in 1919:

> Major McDougall undertook to approach certain bodies represented by the Conjoint Board of Scientific Societies with a view to ascertaining whether it would be possible to share the expenses of a meeting room, offices etc.(?) with some other Society or Societies. (Committee minutes, 30 April 1919)

The Reconstruction Committee (which vanished after the Committee turned into the Council) also became a little twitchy over the lack of progress in finding permanent London premises (minutes, 12 December 1919). All of this house hunting (which finally paid off when, at the end of 1926, the Society rented a limited amount of accommodation in the Royal Anthropological Society's new building at 52 Upper Bedford Place, Bloomsbury), together with the growing feeling that there was indeed a longer-term future for the Society, was no doubt helped along by the welcome and predicted increase in funds to the BPS. This, in turn, meant that the Society was faced with the pleasurable if somewhat urgent task of considering where to invest the surplus (Committee minutes, 15 November 1919). Such a welcome release from the genteel penury of the past looked like it would never be reversed as the Society and the sections flourished, with the addition of the Aesthetics Section in 1922, the creation of regional branches starting in 1923, and the expansion of the BPS's stable of publications, with the addition of the *British Journal of Medical Psychology* in 1920 to the *British Journal of Psychology* which the Society had acquired in 1914, some ten years after its foundation by James Ward and Rivers.

Unfortunately, this new-found openness did not satisfy those elements of the BPS for whom the tension between the wish for an exclusive and controlled Society devoted to the progress of a scientific psychology, on the one hand, and the equally potent demand, on the other, for an identifiable physical presence which only a large and growing BPS membership could bring, had not been resolved by the Myers settlement of 1919. This led to a rather clumsy attempt as early as 1925 to force the Society to reverse some of the effects of the settlement of 1919, mainly on the grounds that under the Myers rules the Society had become little better than a set of psychological groupies, complete with embarrassing T-shirts – a Society, in other words, open to all who had the price of the subscription. According to some of the new Society's critics, the only way forward was to split the BPS, with a tiny elite providing the scientifically respectable base for the Society, and the less technically qualified bankrolling this intellectual effort through their subscriptions. The Council's uncompromising response to this suggestion (and one which uniquely was attached to the original proposal) was to throw it out unreservedly, and then to counter-recommend a more elitist tier to the relatively flat structure originally conceived by the Reconstruction Committee and subsequently adopted. Thus, in a printed pamphlet included in the minutes of an extraordinary general meeting held on 21 March 1925, the case, its rebuttal and the counter-recommendation were set out as follows:

1. The Society in its present form … differs from the old Society as to qualification or membership. The old Society only admitted to membership persons who had made signal contributions to the advance of Psychology.

2. It has been felt in some quarters that that the waiving of this qualification, while it throws membership in the Society and participation in its Journals and meetings open to any persons interested in Psychology, has not made for that advance in the Science which the original constitution fostered, and accordingly:

3. A proposal was suggested for the formation of a Psychological Club on the lines of the original Society, with a view to the communication and discussion of papers of a more technical nature than those calculated to interest the members of the present Society as a whole. It was also suggested that, in such a Club, certain psychological ideas might be discussed informally, with a view to their subsequent presentation, in the form of communications, to Sections of the Society.

4. The Council feels that the formation of such a Club would be very disadvantageous to the welfare of the Society as a whole, and is of the opinion that no such movement, independent of the Society, should be encouraged; but, on the contrary, that the Society should be advised to attempt to guide it in the direction of formation within, and as an integral part of, the Society. Accordingly, the Council recommends:-

5. That the Society should institute Fellowships, and that Fellows of the Society should be elected on grounds of psychological eminence and standing from amongst the Members of the Society....

10. That the Fellows of the Society should have no especial privilege or rights in regard to the government of the Society.

The history of this the first (and unsuccessful) attempt at recasting the Society in a more hierarchical mould, and its twisty progress before and after the Council meeting of March 1925, is of some considerable interest, but I can only hint at its complexity here.

First, at the end of the Council meeting of 9 October 1924, Myers, in what looked like the next move in his careful crusade to reform the Society, had suggested that the BPS might consider setting up a new tier of membership called Fellowships, which would be comparable to the grade of Honorary Fellowship in that they would be awarded for high attainment in a recognised area of psychology, except that Fellows could come only from the existing membership of the Society. Discussion of this matter was postponed to the next Council, of 13 November 1924, where, after much toing and froing among the members, Myers (who was unfortunately not present) was drafted in as convenor of a committee to consider Fellowships, with the six people who were actually at Council making up the rest of the committee.

What happened next is not very clear but in my opinion the work of this committee was hijacked by some of its members, who were also those responsible for the barely veiled attack on the Myers settlement of 1919 contained in the first three paragraphs of the printed proposal. However, the attitude to the whole issue among the Society at large (including Myers himself, and for rather obvious reasons) must have been lukewarm at best and hostile at worst, since at the March extraordinary general meeting the business of Fellows was put on hold for a year (a decision reaffirmed at the following Annual General Meeting, on 12 December 1925), while the idea of a separate Psychological Club sank without trace. This was in spite of the fact that an earlier version of the proposal from the Myers committee on Fellowship had been discussed, and its contents amended and approved at a Council meeting of 12 February 1925. There is, however, something odd about the matter, in that the paragraph numbering scheme (and the contents) used by Council when the proposal was amended at that meeting only agrees with the printed version of 21 March for the first three paragraphs. My hunch (and it is no more than that, since Myers' initial report has not survived) is that sometime between 12 February and 21 March, certain members of Council had inserted both the new paragraph about rejecting the idea of a Psychological Club, and the possibility of Fellowships as the counter-recommendation, into the printed version of the proposal.

Whatever is the case, the notion of Fellowship, never mind the Psychological Club, had proved to be a membership move too far for the Society, as the dismal history of the former idea after March 1925 shows. Although the Council revived the idea much less than a year later (Council minutes, 8 October 1925), that meeting postponed any consideration of Fellowships until the February Council of the following year, while all that was done at this latter session was the creation of yet another subcommittee (but this time without Myers as its convenor) to look into the matter (Council minutes, 11 February 1926). This subcommittee did little more than exhume the original report (complete with the Psychological Club, the Council's rebuttal and the counter-offer of Fellowships) at a Council meeting on 14 October 1926, but only with the rather feeble aim of suggesting that it be circulated to the sections for comments. Finally, the whole enterprise was ignominiously dropped at the Council meeting of 11 November 1926. This unexpected setback to Myers' longer-term plans for the Society seems to have had the effect of turning him against the notion of Fellowships, as his negative reactions to their later recreation showed. However, the unresolved tension which had sparked off the rising of '25 between those who wanted a Society for psychologists only, and those who perhaps thought (or wished) that the Society could survive and have a strong presence on the ground only if it remained as a general interest group was still there, festering away beneath the surface.

Although the 'new' Society was as active after 1926 as it had been from 1919, there is little to interest the constitutional historian until 1934, when a move to inject considerably more professional oomph into the Society was begun, a change of direction freighted with dire consequences for the settlement of 1919 which, in the end, neither Myers or his supporters could resist.

3   Step 3 (1934–1958): future proofing

One of the triumphs of the Myers settlement was the sevenfold increase in membership over the three years 1918 to 1921. This, as we have seen, was also used by Myers and his friends as one of the levers to topple the old Society of 1901. Unfortunately, as the 1920s turned into the 1930s, the membership of the Society barely moved from the figure of 700 that Spearman had so loudly proclaimed at the 1921 Annual General Meeting. Thus, while in 1927 the membership had stood at 717, this had fallen back to 677 during the early part of the Depression in 1933, to recover only a little, to a figure of 750, in 1936. (The latter is the last firm number that I can get hold of before the 811 members recorded for the end of 1941, the date that the BPS has habitually used in its annual reports to benchmark membership changes.) There was, it seems, simply no readymade or prolific source of new members to exploit, nothing comparable to the large pool of medics from the Royal Army Medical Corps that Myers had used to such devastating effect in 1919 and 1920. The main reason for this is simple: only a tiny handful of new departments of psychology were created in the 1920s and '30s, and even then their output of straight psychology students was low (see Hearnshaw, 1964, for more details here). If the Society had been seduced into thinking that the country could somehow be spared the economic downturn that invariably accompanies the ending of any major conflict by the fatuous postwar cry that Britain would become a land fit for heroes, then their experiences of the decade after 1918 must have come as a great and sobering shock. And there was, of course, the Great Crash of '29 and the consequent Depression, whose effects in Britain at least had been made considerably worse by economic incompetence of the kind that had kept the country on the Gold Standard long after most other countries had jumped off.

Against the background of a static or even a falling resource base, therefore, it is not too surprising to find that any proposed changes to the nature and direction of the Society were low key and were adopted in a gradual and consensual fashion. In this section, I briefly cover the early days of two of these developments, whose eventual flowering changed the direction of the Society: these are the work of the Professional Status Committee and incorporation. The former laid a little of the groundwork for the eventual professionalisation of most areas of British applied psychology, while the latter finally finished off the 1919 Myers settlement of an interest-only Society, while also eventually ensuring that the Society's bid for its Royal Charter in 1965 would succeed.

On 3 March 1934, the Council received a report from Dr Philpott of University College London, a long-time member of the Society and its Treasurer at the time, that the Society should recognise in some appropriate fashion the existence of a distinct group of people both inside and outside the Society for whom 'Psychology is rapidly becoming a profession,' with 'people making it their vocation and livelihood.' Consequently 'the question of an organisation to look after their corporate interests is arising.' After warning of the possible interprofessional conflicts that such a body might have to negotiate its way around, and suggesting that the body could be either wholly independent of the Society or semi-independent, or could exist within the BPS as a Section or a Committee, Philpott then threw down a scarcely veiled gauntlet to Myers and others of similar mind: 'But whatever its origin, its functions should be those of a professional body, Membership should be of people actually *engaged* in recognised psychological work, or who are academically qualified' (emphasis added). Contrast the term 'engaged' used here and in the first set of membership rules for the Society dating from 1901, with the term 'interested' from the membership rules drawn up by Myers and the Reconstruction Committee in 1919. Philpott concluded by declaring that 'A register should be maintained; an eye kept on matters of professional status, and so on' (Council minutes, 19 March 1934).

Although the next move was to create a Professional Status Committee to deal with the report, its wings were severely clipped from the start. Consequently, this was given only the vaguest of briefs, without any firm commitment to any of the more radical of Philpott's proposals. Nevertheless, this Committee duly reported to the Council meeting of 26 June 1934 that 'the time has come to take some steps towards the organisation, recognition and registration of professional psychologists, and that the British Psychological Society is the most appropriate body to act in this manner.' Of the three possible actions, registration would clearly be the least costly and least intrusive (and least likely to arouse Myers, who was present at both Council meetings). Thus the Committee recommended that the first step was to set up a register, which would hopefully be self-financing, since psychologists wanting their name placed on it would need to pay a non-refundable fee of one guinea (£1.05 in today's debased coinage) for their initial entry, with an extra subscription (also non-returnable) charged for each change of professional address. In return, the list would be 'open to inspection by individuals and public bodies requiring the services of trained workers in the various branches of psychology' (Council minutes, 26 June 1934). Equally clearly, the next issue for the Council and the Committee was to find ways of reassuring those 'individuals and public bodies' that the BPS was not foisting assorted flim-flam merchants of the 'Let-me-cure-your-smoking-habit-through-hypnotism-at-a-distance' type on to them.

What was needed, in other words, was a pretty efficient sheep-from-goat detector, which the ad hoc Committee duly supplied: 'Inclusion in the register would be open to all persons possessing the requisite qualifications and would not be confined to members of the British Psychological Society.' There would be two classes of professionally defined persons on the register, Members and Associates, where the former were deemed superior to the latter, since they had to be:

A) Those holding senior Posts (roughly corresponding to the position of 'recognised teachers') in Psychology in one of the Universities.

B) Those who have contributed to the advancement of Psychology by original research.

C) Those who hold an Honours Degree (or its equivalent) in Psychology and who are employed in work for which a knowledge of Psychology is an essential qualification.

Associates, on the other hand, would be:

A) Those who hold an Honours Degree (or its equivalent) in Psychology, but who are not yet engaged in Psychological work, though desirous of doing so.

B) Those who are engaged in psychological work, but who do not posses an Honours Degree (or its equivalent) in Psychology.

(Note that it is unclear from the report whether these criteria for Members and Associates should be interpreted as 'either/or' or 'and'.)

To anyone familiar with the selection system which the BPS has operated in basically the same format from 1958 onwards, many of the Committee's criteria will look very familiar indeed, particularly if you substitute today's Associate Member for Member, and Graduate Member for their Associate. Clearly, the criteria used in 1958 had evolved from those proposed here, but what is perhaps even more interesting is the overlap between them and those laid down in 1901, where (it will be recalled) Shand had proposed 'that only those who were *recognised teachers* in some branch of psychology or who had published work of a recognised value would be eligible as members' (emphasis added). Consequently, insofar as the BPS has over a considerable period of time moved towards adopting (and augmenting) the Philpott Committee membership rules, so this 1934 report at least represents the first serious break with the Myers rebuild of 1919, and a return to the essentially exclusive and controlling tendencies of the old Society, but one, of course, now replete with the attractive honeytraps of specialist sections and other goodies to snare the unwary (a legacy which was also, ironically, bequeathed to the Society by Myers).

But it was only a beginning, and a pretty poor beginning at that, since, at the same Council meeting, Myers and the others present gave the newly named Professional Status Committee one task only, that of compiling the register, thus effectively denying it the more proactive roles suggested by Philpott's drafting

Committee; but even with this reduced role, the new Committee was allowed to employ only a rather watered down and somewhat ambiguous set of criteria for registration, thus:

> I.   Registration is desirable.
> II.   It seems desirable to have one category only of registered members, for inclusion in which the Committee should ascertain an applicant's competence in theoretical knowledge of psychology and its applications.
> III.   That qualification should be based on professional training but not necessarily paid employment. That the degree in psychology should not necessarily be an Honours degree. etc. (Council minutes, 26 June 1934)

Although this seemed in theory to represent something of a triumph for those hankering for the old, pre-1919 Society (the Professional Status Committee became, for example, a permanent Committee of the Council in 19 March 1935), in practice the newly created body became no more than a short-lived registration device of marginal use to the Council, receiving only a slight boost in the period just before and during the early years of the Second World War, when it was renamed the Register Committee and instructed to assemble a list of psychologists for the war effort (see, for example, the Council minutes for 1 February and 1 June 1939, and for 26 October 1940). Clearly, the new Committee was not to be the powerhouse for change (or counter-revolution) that some of its supporters might have hoped for; perhaps this was due not just to the hostility within certain, still powerful sections of the Council, but also to the rather windy brief given to it in 1934, where it was instructed 'to study the general conditions affecting the professional practice of psychology in this country and to report to the Council matters of interest thereto' (Council minutes, 19 March 1935; see also the Council minutes of 3 December 1935, where a questionnaire for circulation to potential members of the register was proposed and accepted).

However, the rather more subtle importance of the new Professional Status Committee to the story of the BPS was not just that it augured, however slightly, a change in direction for the Society, but what direction this would be, that is, towards increasing the degree of professionalism of British psychology. This was in addition to the exclusivity implied by an intake only of psychology graduates which the rules for the new register had as their final logical outcome. Perhaps it was for these somewhat conflicting reasons, therefore, that Myers, who had created the National Institute of Industrial Psychology in the early 1920s, and those of a like mind, did not actually block the creation of the Committee, but instead weakened the exclusivity of the selection criteria for the register with, as we have seen, the increasing diminution of the Committee's role in the Society.

Something much more potent than the Professional Status Committee was going to be required if the Society was to change in the direction that an increasing number of BPS members seemed to want. That something turned out to be the Society's bid for incorporation, whose completion in October 1941 also galvanised those with professional concerns in the Society into taking over where the hamstrung Professional Status Committee had left off.

In the context of the BPS's bid, incorporation meant that the Society would become a sort of business or legally defined company, although not one enjoying a limited legal liability, but one which nevertheless endowed its newly recast constitution with a legal status, and one which could also create new types of legally defined membership with legally prescribed entry criteria. It also allowed the Society to buy land at any time of up to two acres in area, although that was not a matter of primary concern to the BPS of the 1930s! It also held out the tempting longer-term possibility that the Society might one day aspire to a (Royal) Charter, for which incorporation was the major initial step. Incorporation also implied a higher degree of financial probity, in the sense that the Society would have to have its accounts professionally audited each year, although this was not a difficulty. The possibility of incorporation had actually first arisen as early as 1921, when it had been summarily rejected by the Council.[5]

However, the next time that the Society considered incorporation it had a much more weighty purpose in mind: it was determined at last to be taken seriously by the British establishment and the British public. Consequently, at a Council meeting held on 30 November 1936, in the Society's rooms at 55 Russell Square, 'The President [James Drever, Senior] opened a discussion on the desirability and practicability of establishing a Fellowship of the Society, and of the desirability of seeking to secure for the Society either a Charter or incorporation'. Right from the start, therefore, the two aims of creating an all-psychologist grade of Fellowship (augmented by subsidiary but linked membership categories as the business advanced) and achieving incorporation were run in tandem, with the possibility of a charter dangled like a carrot in front of the horses.

It should also be noted that, unlike all the other unsuccessful attempts to change the BPS, this one had the weight of the BPS Presidency behind it. This meant that Myers (and his supporters) never really had a chance, even though he twice tried to slow down the process. At a Council meeting on 19 May 1937, he successfully proposed that the discussion on Fellowship should be postponed to the next Council meeting 'owing to the lateness of the hour'. He was present also at a Council meeting in November of the same year, where it was collectively agreed not to proceed with the discussion on the report of the Incorporation–Fellowship Committee, partly because of the seriousness of the policy issues raised by certain clauses of the report, and partly because 'of the small attendance of Council, members of the Committee itself being in the majority' (Council minutes, 10 November 1937). But these were mere pebbles under the wheels of the juggernaut. So the President, at a meeting in February 1937, successfully requested that Council should place the possibility of a Charter before the Society's solicitors (Council minutes, 3 February 1937) while at the next meeting, after having received the solicitors' advice, the Council first affirmed its desire to incorporate and then, as usual, set up a committee to draft a constitution for Fellowship, where one of the aims of the exercise was 'to raise the status of Psychology and to protect the public' (Council minutes, 7 June 1937; it is of some relevance here that the motion from which this extract has been taken was seconded by Philpott, who, as Treasurer of the Society, was also appointed to the Committee for the new constitution). From then on, everything started to snowball, slowly but surely.

Again, I can give only the bare outlines from the Council minutes of the progress of incorporation, which was meticulously pursued by the Council, with the creation of Fellowships (and the other new, all-psychologist membership category of Associateship) now subsumed within the more general processes of incorporation. Thus the Council meeting on 1 July 1937 saw and commented on the first draft of the constitution 'drawn up by Dr Philpott', while at its meeting on 15 February 1938, the final draft was circulated for additional comments, with the final, final draft being sent to the Society's solicitors for their *initial* comments sometime after this meeting. A note that the final final final final draft (I have left out at least one further turn here) had been placed in the hands of the Board of Trade's Incorporation Committee for *its* initial comments was included in the Council minutes for 1 February 1939. However, after several short hiccups in the proceedings, including the outbreak of real wartime hostilities and the Board of Trade's unsuccessful attempt to get the BPS to change its name on the frivolous grounds that it had already registered the British Institute of Practical Psychology as an incorporated body (see the Council minutes for 30 March 1940, and Thomson, Chapter 5), the BPS finally cleared the last hurdle and officially became an incorporated Society on 1 October 1941.

And the recreation of the Society now began in earnest, with the new, all-graduate psychologist grades of Fellowship and Associateship on offer for the first time in the same year as incorporation, with the first elections being in 1942 – not 1943 as Knight (1961) has it (see the Council minutes for 1 November 1941 and 31 July 1942). Although incorporation had forced the Society to heavily revise its early constitution, the detailed rules for membership (and the administration of the Society) were still pretty much as they had been, with Ordinary Membership (but not Associateship or Fellowship) still open to people with an interest in psychology, but with no formal qualifications in the subject. Again, the tension between those of the Myers tendency and members who were resolved to create a Society of only graduate psychologists had not been completely resolved by incorporation, with Fellowship and Associateship being viewed as little more than the thin end of what the latter group hoped would become a very fat wedge. What this group also realised was that they could recycle some of Myers' original tactics to their advantage: there were, for example, increasing numbers of Associates and Fellows either transferring from Ordinary Member status or being directly elected into the Society in 1942 and 1943, as against a somewhat slower rate of recruitment of Ordinary Members at that time (see, for instance, the Council minutes for 31 July 1942, or those for 3 October of the same year).

However, the pool of eligible members for these all psychology graduate categories had been nearly drained by the end of 1943 and recruitment into their ranks stayed almost static for many years. Although the success of incorporation had clearly stiffened the resolve of an increasing portion of the Society for a root-and-branch reform, the same numbers game that had held back all such rapid or radical changes in the past was still in place: was there, in other words, a sufficiently large, but as yet untapped, pool of psychologists to offset the number of interested non-psychologists whose subscriptions were still essential to the continuing existence of the Society? The answer in the 1940s and much of the 1950s was, unfortunately, no, as it had been in the 1920s, and for pretty much the same reasons of economic stringency. And while universities, after the Second World War, had established many more departments of psychology than had been the case in the 1920s, their output was still tiny (my Leeds graduating class of 1961, for example, contained only 12 people). Indeed, on the evidence of the BPS's own snapshot figures, total membership in 1950 stood at a mere 1897, rising only to 2655 in 1960, with the psychological (*sic*) barrier of 10,000 being breached only in 1982. Incorporation must have seemed in hindsight a pretty risky move in 1941!

The reformers had therefore little option except to move cautiously so as not to frighten off the non-psychologist members with their essential subscriptions. Consequently, the Council did not set up the Articles and By-Laws (Revision) Committee until 1953 (Council minutes, 4 June 1953), which then took almost five years to put the final draft of the new rules for approval at a general meeting of the Society on 19 April 1958. Even with these now in place, the ghost of the Myers settlement (or its *raison d'être*) had still not been fully exorcised from the Society, since the new rules also allowed that any Ordinary Member elected before the general meeting of 19 April could still continue in that grade (but only, of course, if they paid their subscription!), although everyone elected to any of the significant membership categories after that date would have to have an honours degree in psychology as a minimum qualification, or be undertaking such a degree at the time of application. It might also be argued that the redefinition of the category of Subscriber (also dating from the rule changes of April 1958) represented a bow in the direction of Myers' shade, since people elected to this grade did not now need the formal or technical qualifications required by any of the other categories. It has not, however, proved to be a popular choice.

Meanwhile, in addition to encouraging the Society to picture itself as a collective solely of psychology graduates, complete with club tie and secret handshakes, incorporation had also prompted a burst of activity from 1943 onwards which was associated with that other (barely) detectable change of direction originating from the 1930s, namely that the BPS should also attempt to dominate the professional side of psychology. Consequently, and either as a result of some entirely uncharacteristic initiative-seizing by Council or because its hand had been forced by the various memoranda submitted by Margaret Lowenfeld early in 1943 (which had independently suggested that the Society should set up a section devoted to child psychology), a small group of professional psychologists employed in child mental health (called the Fildes Committee, after its convenor L.G. Fildes) was able to negotiate the creation of a Committee of Professional Psychologists (Mental Health) within the Society (Council minutes, 4 September 1943). Although the Committee was initially concerned only with those engaged in professional work with children, in order to achieve its more ambitious aims it successfully petitioned Council in 1950 that the target group of professionals for recruitment and oversight by the Committee should be broadened to include psychologists involved professionally with adults in the mental health field (Council minutes, 1 July 1950).

Meanwhile, the Committee of Professional Psychologists had, from the start, briskly co-opted an increasing number of graduate-educated and professionally experienced psychologists in a way more reminiscent of a section than a committee of Council. It also extended its remit to include psychologists engaged in educational practice, while early on also splitting into separate regional Committees of Professional Psychologists for England and Scotland. Finally, these inappropriately named Committees transformed themselves into regionally based Divisions of Professional Psychologists (Educational and Clinical) in 1958 after the new rules had been accepted by the Society's membership, although the English Committee had unsuccessfully tried to restyle itself as 'the Clinical Division' as early as 1951 (Council minutes, 3 February and 3 March 1951). However, what in the end turned out to be crucial for this move from Committee to Division was the encouragement given to it by the Articles and By-Laws (Revision) Committee, whose second (interim) report (dated 7 February 1955) had argued that a Professional Committee with over 300 members occupied an entirely anomalous status within the Society and should therefore consider turning itself into a division as soon as possible.

The 1919 Myers settlement of a BPS membership open to everyone who was interested in psychology and could pay the price of admission had now all but been swept away by pressure from at least two formidable groups arguing for a highly selective entry to the Society, although from slightly different perspectives. Thus, it was the *final* triumph of the ten people who set up the Society in 1901 to have shaped the modern face of the BPS.

Postscript: *The Death of Nelson*

THE LATE DR. C.S. MYERS. The President paid tribute to the late Dr. C.S. Myers, referring to his work in experimental and industrial psychology and to the services that he had rendered the Society. The President reported that on behalf of the Society he had sent a letter of condolence to Mrs. Myers and had attended the funeral and the Memorial Service. The Council stood in silence in tribute to the memory of Dr. Myers. (Minute 788 of the Council minutes for 2 November 1946)

In my admittedly still limited experience of Council minutes, a letter of condolence to the relatives on the occasion of the death of a prominent member of the Society was not unusual, although attendance by the President at the funeral was, while the Council standing in tribute was almost without precedent.

Notes

1 In writing this chapter, I have drawn heavily on many of the minute books of the Society and some of the supporting material, all of which are now held in the BPS Archive associated with the Centre for the History of Psychology (CHOP) at Staffordshire University. Where necessary, any quotations from this Archive have been acknowledged.

2 Frances Buss, a pioneer of women's education, had co-founded the North London Collegiate School for Ladies. I am irresistibly reminded at this point of the little rhyme that the pupils of Miss Buss and her contemporary Miss Dorothea Beale of Cheltenham Ladies' College made up about them: 'Miss Buss and Miss Beale / Cupid's darts do not feel / How unlike us / Miss Beale and Miss Buss'.

3 The Committee was set up at the first meeting of the Society as the executive or working arm of the Society, with the general and annual meetings increasingly treated as the Society's more public face, whose major purpose was to rule on proposals brought to it by the Committee and to elect new members of the Society, again where these were increasingly supplied by the Committee. Therefore, if one controlled the Committee and its various subcommittees, then one also controlled the BPS. The Committee itself became the Council of the BPS on 8 May 1920.

4 Although the birth of the Reconstruction Committee is not completely recoverable from the existing minutes of the Committee (the first mention that I can find of it is in the Committee minutes of 15 November 1919), I suspect that the subcommittee mentioned above, which also contained Myers, was actually one of its immediate parents.

5 For more on this first brief encounter with legality see the Council minutes for 23 June 1921 and 6 July 1921, where incorporation is also taken to be equivalent to being registered as a scientific society with the right to purchase land, where this latter privilege no doubt owed something to the early days of the Royal Society, which Charles II had exceptionally granted the right to acquire property up to a certain acreage.

5

The popular, the practical and the professional: psychological identities in Britain, 1901–1950

Mathew Thomson

Writing from the perspective of the 'psychological society' – a society which is psychological in its everyday language and its common assumptions about human action, and in which psychological advice and therapeutic strategies in magazines, books and television attracts mass audiences – the history of psychology can no longer rest content with telling the story of the theoretical and professional development of the discipline alone (Pfister and Schnog, 1997). Two other subjects have to be addressed if we are to move beyond a history of psychology to a history of the psychological. First, we need histories of the organisations (and their languages and practices) which emerged outside the boundaries of the discipline to colonise and contribute to the constitution of the psychological and give birth to a host of unorthodox but still explicitly psychological identities. Second, we need histories of the ways in which the psychological reached even further into the social fabric to shape and inform everyday life and turn all identity into something which was self-consciously psychological. Focusing on the first half of the twentieth century, this chapter concentrates on the first of these subjects, though of course both, as well as the narrative of discipline itself, are deeply interrelated and this also must be the subject of analysis.[1] To a certain extent, this period can be seen as one in which the vigour of an associational, alternative psychological culture reached its height, subsequently to fall away as the profession cemented an authoritative position within British society and as the psychological culture reached out – as common sense – to a much broader and less actively committed audience. It may be noted that such a narrative of the persistence of a pluralist, associational, self-help psychological culture – which in some ways reached back to nineteenth-century movements like phrenology (Cooter, 1984) – conforms to the broader interpretation from a number of historians that a Victorian intellectual and social culture persisted into the 1950s (Harris,

1993); at the same time, it implicitly questions those who have emphasised the role of psychology during this period in a Foucaultian restriction of liberty and normalisation of identity (Rose, 1985).

In his classic *A Short History of British Psychology 1840–1940*, Leslie Hearnshaw devoted only the last page and a half to what he dismissed as the 'eccentric fringe': leaving it the object for diagnosis – 'interesting social psychological phenomena' – rather than a subject for serious historical analysis (Hearnshaw, 1964: 296). The whole thrust of his narrative was to chart progress, away from the 'wave of mystery-mongering and credulity' associated with movements like mesmerism, spiritualism and phrenology in the early- and mid-nineteenth century, towards the emancipation of psychology not only from mysticism but also philosophy, as marked by the founding of the British Psychological Society in 1901 (p. 182). It was his belief that as facilities for psychiatric treatment extended within the National Health Service, 'the more esoteric cults and movements should decline' (pp. 296–297). Indeed, he suspected that such a trend was already in place by the 1950s, thanks to the maturation of the discipline: 'The best safeguard against credulity and its exploitation is the progress of a broad and soundly based psychology, theoretical and applied' (p. 297). This chapter suggests that there is a case for this periodisation, though in doing so it will call for a very different approach to the history of the popular–professional dualism. It attempts to demonstrate not only that popular strands were present and vibrant at the time of British psychology's emergence as an organised discipline, but also that the development of the discipline itself can be fully understood only within the evolving context of this relationship. It concentrates on how this dual identity was understood, how it shaped psychology and how it evolved over the first half of the century.

1   Lay interest in psychology

At the start of the century, an organised discipline of psychology was only in embryo. Science was predominantly sceptical about claims that mental force could exert power over matter and body or could have a meaningful existence beyond consciousness. And the medical profession was generally hostile towards the role of psychology within therapy. In such an environment, it is unsurprising that those who did believe in such 'psychic' phenomena, and who attempted to develop practices using them, came to see themselves as the embattled pioneers. This identity was also based on a sense of tradition, reaching back to the struggles of figures like Mesmer and Elliotson, whose interest in mental force and attempts to harness its power for therapeutic effect had been suppressed by the scientific and medical establishment (see for example Lovell, 1902). Although 'psychology' was not always the term they chose to describe their field – the language was more likely at this date to have been that of 'Psychic Research', 'Mental Science', 'New Thought' or 'Practical Psychology' – such groups effectively saw themselves as the psychologists of the era.

Projecting our own conceptual frameworks into the past, it is tempting to classify and in turn dismiss these movements as examples of 'popular psychology'; to see them, like Hearnshaw, as a distinctly different, and perhaps even a polar opposite, to the emerging discipline and profession (Hearnshaw, 1964: 295–297). However, this was not the way these movements usually articulated, nor the way they necessarily conceptualised, their own identities. Moreover, although they appealed to a lay rather than an academic or professional audience, this audience was invariably committed and well defined, scarcely 'popular'. Indeed, in terms of appeal to the general public, academic psychologists might in fact have reached significantly further when they chose to broadcast their ideas in an intentionally popular form. The third reason for being cautious about a too-ready use of the label is that it risks obscuring the fact that the contemporary titles taken by these groups – for instance 'Practical Psychologists' – served as much more than mere signifiers of popular status, and as such it seriously limits our understanding of the heterogeneous nature of psychology at the time. Finally, the concept of the 'popular' tends to occlude a deeper understanding of non-academic psychology, since it encourages us to dismiss it too readily as ephemeral, faddish and without a serious theoretical basis. It deserves to be taken more seriously.

The main area of early-twentieth-century popularisation which has attracted attention from historians is the diffusion of interest in Sigmund Freud and psychoanalysis. It has been pointed out that the British medical profession was initially cautious and sometimes hostile to his ideas, particularly when set against a more favourable reaction in the United States, for instance (Hale, 1971, 1995). There was a feeling that he overemphasised the role of the sex instinct and this was paralleled by a concern that techniques like hypnotism might be liable to abuse in the wrong hands; unsurprisingly, such anxieties were shared by guardians of public morality (Oppenheim, 1991: 304–311; Pines, 1991: 206–231; Turner, 1996: 144–155). Through studies of the negative and positive coverage in the press and magazines and in a profusion of books, it is now recognised that among the educated reading public, not simply a Bloomsbury elite, there was certainly a hitherto unrecognised awareness and probably also an underestimated enthusiasm to find out about these exciting new ideas (Rapp, 1988, 1990; Ellesley, 1995; Richards, 2000a). Unfortunately, these studies tend to stop here, limited by their still largely canonical focus on Freud and psychoanalysis. Although they recognise in passing that much of the interest and debate went well beyond this terrain – that Freud, for instance, was one among many of the psychologists who attracted attention and that the debate seemed to flow over into other fields, like occultism, religion and alternative therapeutics – the significance of this has not been properly explored. Instead, these studies implicitly support the dismissive view that British popularisation was weak, superficial and descended into faddism and parlour games (Chesterton, 1923; Graves and Hodge, 1971: 98–100). As such, this literature goes only part of the way in challenging a history of psychology which locates the discipline and its theories at the centre, and leaves the popular on the outer, neglected margins.

In the first decade of the century there was a surge of lay interest in psychology in Britain. 'Psychology is everywhere' reported a commentator in one lay psychological journal: 'week by week it is more and more in evidence. In almost every walk of life, and in wider and still wider circles. It is frequently on the lips of public speakers ... Psychology is going with a bang' (Anonymous, 1925).

Among those drawn to the subject were people from all social classes looking to reform a spiritual view of life in the light of modern science.[2] This can be traced through the evolution of one periodical, the *Talisman*, an occult publication which relaunched itself in 1904 as the *New Thought Journal*. 'New Thought', adopted by a loose collection of groups at the time, was a signifier of the popular excitement that modern psychology made all 'old thought' redundant and limiting. The journal, like others catering to this audience, was stridently populist. In theoretically primitive psychological language, it aimed to reach out to 'men and women who are not scholars, but those who have a strong desire to know more of their own selves, what they are, how they may forward their evolution' (Anonymous, 1904). It would be devoted to 'practical idealism'. Dedicated to self-reliance, it opposed hypnotism and in its place advanced the value of auto-suggestion. With this technique, readers could train their own minds and 'forward their evolution' through the simple daily exercise of concentration, following the lessons provided by the journal. Two decades of psychology as a professional discipline would, by 1924, do little to dim this populism:

> Too many seem to think that it needs special gifts, or cleverness, to demonstrate the blessings of New Thought or applied psychology, but this is far from being the case. It is true that it means some knowledge of mental laws, but this is soon gained. Generally the big stumbling block in the way is want of confidence.

Although the journal went on to change its name to the apparently more orthodox *Applied Psychology*, this was more an indicator of the emphasis on the practical than of an acceptance of the authority of the psychological profession: after all, 'the individual', as far as the journal was concerned, 'may be his own psychoanalyst' (Anonymous, 1926b). Indeed, professional psychologists were still criticised for their limited conceptualisation of the psychological: they might understand mind; they did not understand the full self (Anonymous, 1930).

An anti-establishment tone, this time in a language of 'mental science' rather than 'new thought', was also adopted by *The Thinker*, a journal dedicated to 'true healing in all its branches and upliftment of all materially, mentally and spiritually'. It counterposed the 'new and the old thinking' and attacked not only doctors but also ministers of the church for their opposition to new thought and mental science. And as to those members of the two professions who were beginning to show interest in the subject:

> [these were the real] irregular practitioners.... They have no right to do so seeing they have in the past decried it. The true mental healers are those who have brought it to its present state of perfection through all the difficulties that have to be

encountered and the dangers to themselves in the days when it was despised and its advocates regarded as unsound in mind and mere cranks. (Anonymous, n.d.)

Looking to act as an ecumenical site for the development of the 'psychic' interests of Spiritualists, Theosophists, the Mental Science, Christian Science and Divine Science Movements, the London Psycho-Therapeutic Society was founded in 1901. From the start, its relationship to the medical profession – that 'popish institution' ('A vegetarian clergyman', 1905) – was particularly tense, since it aimed not merely to investigate psychic and mental forces, psycho-magnetics, hypnotism and mesmerism, but also to apply them therapeutically. Paying close attention to Continental psychology's interest in psychopathology and to its use of hypnotism and suggestion, these new techniques were fitted unproblematically into a therapeutic armoury which already embraced mesmerism and psycho-magnetism: all, after all, were examples of psychic power and all were opposed by most of the British medical establishment. Much emphasis was placed on the training of 'operators' to extend therapy to the poor. In an area like the cure of cancer, doctors had revealed the limitations of a therapeutic armoury of drugs and surgery, and the Society set out to prove the power of nerve force in over 4,000 treatments by the First World War. Ultimately, however, the most radical potential of psychotherapeutics was to make people aware of their own latent vital force and to demonstrate how this power could be accessed through healthy living, self-control and auto-suggestion. In line with this, there was a shift in enthusiasm away from hypnosis towards auto-suggestion, with its radical potential for self-implementation in everyday life.[3]

There was also tension with the religious movements which the Society had looked to build upon. An increasingly secular emphasis on mind and body rather than spirit alone (as could be the case, for instance, among Christian Scientists, who rejected medicine altogether) was mirrored in the shift of title of the Society's magazine from the *Psycho-Therapeutic Journal* to the *Health Record*. And it became clear to the Society's Secretary and driving force, Arthur Hallam, that the tying of psychic theory to particular religious positions had led to a confusion which undermined the credibility of the Society's science. In its own way, it was just as bad as the monopoly of the medical profession:

> For any body of people to arrogate this power to themselves and apply it as proof of the truth of their particular religious beliefs, as many have done in the past and are trying to do to-day, is only sign of ignorance and blind presumption. (Hallam, 1910: 66)

The way forward, instead, was to conceptualise mental force as part of 'natural law', a truth which stood above any single religion and which could account for the spiritual and healing power that was a product of all faith.

As this shift suggests, the idea that psychology brought new tools for 'self-mastery' was not necessarily directly tied to religion. It was also, for instance, central to the popularity of the writings of Emile Coué in the early 1920s, which advanced a preference for auto-suggestion over suggestion imposed by some expert intermediary. Most famously, individuals were advised to channel the power of subconscious imagination over body and mind through the repetition of positive-thinking mantras, such as his 'every day in every way I am getting better and better'.[4]

By the 1920s, a large number of these lay movements were conceptualising their identity as 'Practical Psychologists'. Again, this was far more than a mere synonym for the popular. One definition was offered by Anna Maud Hallam,[5] the founder of the Practical Psychology Clubs of England and Life President of the Federation of Practical Psychology Clubs of Great Britain, in the first issue of the *Practical Psychologist* in 1925:

> PRACTICAL psychology is a scientific effort to unfold and understand the laws operating in human life.… This great study of human life brings new enlightenment, new education, new and clearer understanding of the phenomena of every-day life. It is an effort based upon unbiased investigation, research, experiment and observation, with just one motive underlying it – to assist the individual in knowing himself. (Hallam, 1925: 1)

Clearly, as far as the Practical Psychologists were concerned, the key distinction between the academic and the practical was neither that of a gulf in the scientific sophistication of the two, nor one of the theoretical emphasis of the former to the non-theorised position of the latter. Science, Hallam asserted, was in fact increasingly supporting the claims of Practical Psychology:

> Twenty-five years ago about the only available proof of this statement [the ability to harness the power of mind over body] was the practical teaching of religion on behalf of the productive power of faith. To-day, we have the authority of laboratories, tests and experiments, also a clearer and more practical understanding of the psychic phase of personality. (*Ibid.*: 5)

Instead, she drew attention to a difference in theoretical viewpoints:

> Academic psychology will centre the cause of these mental conflicts in the various human instincts. The student of practical psychology will explain them under the caption of the subconscious mind where all instincts, emotions and inclinations have their origin. (*Ibid.*: 2)

Thus, as far she was concerned, the key factor distinguishing the two was their open-mindedness about the powers of the subconscious and of mind over body. She acknowledged that attitudes were changing in academic psychology and did not reject the importance of its work:

> [A]cademic psychology deals primarily with the natural instincts of the individual and the development of reason. Such men as Herbert Spencer, Professors Wright, Kant, McDougall, William James, Schiller, Hume and Huxley have done much to

stimulate and encourage the study of mind power and its influence upon individual conduct. Some authorities of the academic world have gone so far as to say that the neurotic person suffers from a mental cause as well as a physical cause. (*Ibid.*: 2)

But this paled beside Practical Psychology's promises of self-transformation through harnessing the immense energy of the subconscious mind. The second key to Hallam's definition was that her psychology was to centre on the practical application of this new understanding of the mind's power, particularly in the sphere of self-management and therapy of the body: it was to provide the theoretical key not only to a series of explicitly psychological practices such as auto-suggestion and mind concentration, but also through its appreciation of the holistic relationship of mind and body to regimes of what one ate, how one exercised and even what one wore.

The final distinction was that Hallam's Practical Psychology, despite the emphasis on science and the practical, remained at the same time intensely spiritual in both its idiom and its goals. For instance, Sir G. Walter Roffey, Vice-President of the Federation of Practical Psychology Clubs of Great Britain, welcomed the new journal in a language which was unable to break free from a deeply entrenched Christian framework for conceptualising self-elevation:

> Its publication cannot but help to spread the blessings which P.P. brings to all who embrace its philosophy from the high motives of improving their own lives and of passing on to others the means of advancement in the daily struggle to find Truth and overcome difficulties, thus enabling many, who 'want' without realising what they need (and so drift through life without making it better for their having lived it) to find their feet firmly placed on the rock of conviction and thereon build or rebuild their character, step by step, until they have qualified for some more noble functioning in another plane after they have passed on from this one. (Roffey, 1925)

This was not merely an issue of language. The practical tools of psychology offered a path towards a higher form of consciousness, which was akin to that gained by the religious mystic, and a creative consciousness analogous to the creative role of God. In recasting the claims of religion in these scientific and humanist, but also open-ended, terms, Practical Psychology made itself attractive to a broad spectrum of people, ranging from convinced Christians to those looking for a wholly secularised religiosity. To Charles Wase, Chairman of the School of Practical Psychology, 'Practical Psychology, as taught in this school, is "Practical Religion". It is a Gospel of Healthy-Mindedness, relating the inner life of the spirit, to the world in which we live.'[6] And though his school aimed to reach out to agnostics, the religious and the scientific alike (Watkins, 1927), it maintained an, albeit reconfigured, Christian theology as a constant source of inspiration and demonstration.

A similar positioning of psychology was to be found in another journal, *Practical Psychology*, based in Blackpool, and drawing mainly on an audience of practical psychology clubs in Lancashire and Yorkshire. Again, there was the counterposing of the merely theoretical and academic against the practical, powerful and emancipatory: 'Academical Psychology as a branch of knowledge was intensely interesting, but Practical Psychology developed the latent powers within' (Rees, 1925). There was the spiritual: it 'enabled us to affirm and realize our oneness with the Creative Spirit of God.... The fundamental truths of Christianity were faith, love, peace, joy, power, truth, spiritual healing; and Psychology came along to show us how to turn these ideals into realities' (*ibid.*). And there was the claim that this did not mean that it was not also scientific: 'Practical Psychology is the application to the problems of everyday life of the scientific principles discovered after long periods of scientific investigation and laboratory research' (Anonymous, 1925).

There were signs also of a new way in which the two identities would be contrasted: we begin to see attention being paid to the practice of professional psychology reaching beyond medical therapy to a new terrain of mental measurement and industrial psychology – what Nikolas Rose has termed the emergence of the 'Psychological Complex' (Rose, 1985). This appears to have been viewed with considerable suspicion by Practical Psychologists. There were two main grounds for this. First, it was likely to infringe that liberty of the individual which was so fundamental to the self-help ethos of this constituency. And second, it appeared to reduce psychology to crude measurement, whereas the whole thrust of practical psychology had been to develop an expansive understanding of the self (see for instance Myddleton, 1925).

In 1936, to take up the mantle, the *Practical Psychology Magazine* was founded by the British Union of Practical Psychologists, which represented 34 groups scattered around the country. The opening editorial set out the aim of being of value to those with little psychological knowledge and emphasised 'creative thought', in which 'as a man thinketh, so he is'; it adopted both a positive-thinking ideology and a less challenging position to the profession than had been the case with earlier claims to a superior and more radical insight into psychology a decade earlier (Anonymous, 1936). In the same opening issue, H. Ernest Hunt again attempted to draw the distinction with academic psychology:

> In contradistinction to the purely academic study of descriptive and analytic psychology, our movement has adopted the title of 'Practical Psychology'. This indicates that it is intended to be applied by the ordinary individual to the everyday purposes of life in very actual fashion. (Hunt, 1936: 3)

Yet, this increasing ordinariness still went side by side with fairly bold, unordinary, albeit less overtly transcendental, claims about self-development: 'practical psychology is one of the ways in which one may study to become one of the few in a world of many' (*ibid.*). Now with regular columns in its specialist press explaining the latest ideas in 'academic psychology' and 'modern psychological theory', and with articles contributed by Adler, Practical Psychology appears to have been in a transition in the 1930s towards a less oppositional and combative position: one which more readily recognised its subordinate theoretical position to the academic. However, an undercurrent of tension clearly remained, particularly towards the perceived restrictions of academic psychology, the subject for attack once again in 1937: 'We are of the opinion that the study of psychology, and by that we mean the structure of the mind and its technique in action, is of incalculable benefit to the ordinary individual' (Anonymous, 1937). This tension continued to be at its most acute when it came to restrictions over practice, particularly in medical therapy, an area now being colonised by qualified medical psychologists (Scarff, 1938). Even this was shifting, however. Though still the official organ of the British Union of Practical Psychologists, the 'practical psychology' epithet was dropped from the title of its magazine in 1938 and it became the more punchy *You*. This populist shift was paralleled by the adoption of a pocket-book format, suggesting that the material to be conveyed was less serious and instead more personal. No longer was there such a strong evangelism for a particular and radical theoretical position. And although the attacks on professional monopolism were still there, they continued to be toned down. Now the defining spirit was one of presenting psychology to the public as a fascinating, entertaining and personal (rather than, as earlier, a transformative and therapeutic) facet of everyday life:

> "You", the Magazine of Practical Psychology, recognizes psychology in a comprehensive sense. Not as the monopoly of any priesthood, but devoid of ritual – as a subject related to all human behaviour – and of importance to each individual, however intelligent and learned he may be. "You" does not regard psychology as a complicated and gloomy issue. (Anonymous, 1938)

Though the London-based journal may not have fully represented the views of the clubs scattered around England and Scotland, with over 50 by the end of the 1930s, it probably did point and perhaps lead the way: the vigour and radical nature of an anti-establishment movement for self-realisation and transcendence were running out of steam. Traces of this ideology remained, but the role of populist intermediary between the profession and the public (rather than an audience of already convinced Practical Psychologists) was taking over. In line with this trend, Practical Psychology, which had earlier criticised theories like psychoanalysis for focusing on the pathological rather than self-realisation and elevation, now began to produce advice manuals of its own covering many of those very areas which had been delimited as 'problems' by academic theory and professional practice: the expert was now accepted into the popular fold, to guide the reader in the path of adjustment to cope with anything from parents' and children's problems, inferiority complexes and nervous tension, to loneliness (for instance 'Psychologist', 1936; Northfield, 1940; Teear, 1939, 1941). Thus, the nature of popular psychology had shifted in the first four decades of the century; one might put it that popular psychology, in a form recognisable to later-twentieth-century eyes, had in fact emerged, and earlier but different manifestations – spiritual psychologies and Practical Psychology – were beginning to give way.

In sum, the psychological world of the first decades of the century was certainly not confined to the profession or discipline; nor was the emergence of a normalising and liberty-restricting 'psychological complex' the sole or perhaps even the dominant feature on the landscape. There was also a rich, highly active and independent-minded alternative psychological world of New Thoughters, Mental Scientists and Practical Psychologists, as well as a much greater number who adhered to none of these faiths in a strict sense but whose lives nonetheless were changed – liberated and opened up, more often than restricted – by their ideas, activities, publications and their development of new languages of self. The changing relationship with the profession was of fundamental importance to the identity of this other psychological world. Particularly at the start of the century, these groups often believed that they were in the vanguard of psychological progress and, as such, were the true psychologists. Though academic psychological theories of the subconscious and psychic were read with sympathy, the emergence of claims to exclusive expertise in practice from the medical profession, which had traditionally denied the power of mind over body and had attacked lay mental science, was viewed with understandable suspicion and at times hostility. This dichotomy would become a central feature of the way Practical Psychologists viewed the particularity of their psychology: it was common sense, rather than a mystery open to the professional expert alone; and it was a knowledge whose true power was fulfilled only when it was practised by individuals on themselves.

By the end of the interwar period, this tension had dissipated to a considerable degree. Practical Psychology was more comfortable about the now well established claims of academic and professional psychology. As a consequence, it became less oppositional and instead forged a position as populariser for its counterpart's ideas. Part of the explanation for this transition lies in this evolution of popular attitudes towards the profession. But it was a two-sided process. We also need to understand how the profession's attitude shifted and how this affected the relationship. This is the subject for the second half of this chapter.

2   Professional psychology

Both the vigour of popular movements at a time when British academic and professional psychology was so poorly developed, and the unorthodoxy of their psychological views, suggest that it would be hard to explain the emergence of such movements by a simple model of ideas flowing down from above. It must also be seen as the response to demand: demand for therapy in a society where this was still very limited by a lack of both scale and expertise on the part of medicine, but where rising prosperity created the conditions for the commodification of health care; demand for strategies of interiorised self-development to satisfy a deeply entrenched self-help culture which was negotiating the transition towards a more individualist society; and demand for a new scientific pathway for transcendence of self in a secularising world. Such demand was not yet satisfied by a psychological profession which was emerging into this already occupied world only in the first decades of the century. Since the shaping of the modern psychological discipline and profession would take place within this context, their relationship to the popular was a subject which could hardly be avoided.

For a discipline which felt insecure about its own scientific reputation (Wooldridge, 1994: 154–155), a popularisation which might further undermine this, associated as it so often was with a vague mysticism or a zealous enthusiasm, was viewed with understandable alarm, not least because the popularists so stridently asserted that their psychology was scientific. As E.S. Waterhouse pointed out in a radio broadcast in the late 1920s, 'Psychology is a very popular science at present, and it is rather dangerous to be popular'. For the very fact of its popularity would lead 'scornful people [to] tell us it isn't a science at all' (Waterhouse, 1930: ix). Waterhouse, a Methodist, was himself another example of the move to extend psychology beyond the discipline, one of a movement of theologians during this period who attempted to popularise an integration of psychology and Christianity (Hearnshaw, 1964: 293–294). Though he defended the subject's status as a science, his argument that psychology was a science, since 'science, after all, is common sense made exact', would have done little to alleviate the discipline's anxieties. It simply framed the problem in a different form, suggesting as it did the prospect of accessibility to all with the lifting of an obfuscating veil of technical language, and as such the potential redundancy of the expert (Hearnshaw, 1964: 293–294). As one Practical Psychologist put it: 'One of the surprising things about Psychology, just as about electricity, is that it is not necessary to know a great deal about the subject' (Blain, 1932).

A common response was to position the popular variant as having little or nothing to do with real, scientific psychology. Its theoretical basis was condemned as no more than confused mysticism. And its entry into practice, particularly when this involved therapy on mind and body, was attacked as a serious danger to the individual. Since protection of the individual mind and body was such an obvious area for concern, the medical wing of psychology was to the fore in attempting to police Practical Psychology and its therapeutic claims. In 1907, the General Medical Council had investigated what it felt to be a worrying profusion of unqualified persons engaged in medical practice, and undoubtedly this anxiety had been fuelled by the coming together of unorthodox religion and an interest in psychic force. The government responded by setting up a survey, which found an increase in unqualified practice in 82 of the 217 towns responding, with a further 75 reporting a significant level (General Medical Council, 1910: 3). Undoubtedly, this context of heightened policing was an important factor in the emergence of an oppositional and at times radical tone within the popular movements of the day. The difficulty was that nothing could be done unless these practitioners were on the medical register or claimed to be medically qualified.[7] Such concern persisted throughout the interwar period.[8] Of course, not only did it have implications for Practical Psychology, but it also acted as a restraint on the entry of non-medically trained psychologists into this sphere of practice. As such, to some extent they would share the identity of being on the margins.

Fury at the effect of a bastardisation of psychological theory was still evident at mid-century, with psychiatrist Henry Yellowlees trying to steer a lay audience away from misguided psychological populism:

> [The] inability to realize that a vast volume of abstract theoretical knowledge cannot be dished out in pleasant little teaspoonful doses, is pandered to by the publishers of the stream of booklets and magazines dealing with popular psychology which floods our shops and bookstalls. Very often, though by no means always, there is nothing much wrong with the particular little point which the writer tries to expound, but when he appears to regard his remarks as a complete summary of all psychological truth, and encourages his readers to elevate them into a kind of rule of conduct or way of life, it becomes a different matter … it is fatally easy for almost anyone to acquire from the above-mentioned literature a few catch-phrases and striking illustrations, and to pose thereafter as a competent lay psychologist, incapable of realizing the folly and the risk of playing about with a few superficialities of a great subject in which he has had no training, and to which he has not devoted so much as a week of honest study. (Yellowlees, 1955: 53)

The encounter with the popular appeal of the alternative psychological movements could sometimes lead to a more positive response from the profession. It highlighted their subject's potential for reaching out to the public. Clearly, this had its dangers, as evident in the popular movements, but safely in professional hands it might bolster the still beleaguered discipline. Indeed, Maarten Derksen has argued that the fragile scientific status of the discipline has drawn it inexorably into what he terms 'boundary work':

> It is not enough for psychologists themselves to be convinced that their practice is far removed from the doings of ordinary mortals; those very mortals need to be convinced of the fact. Only then can the discipline reap the rewards of funds, clients, students and trust. In order to demarcate, therefore, one has to popularize, and thus cross the boundary. (Derksen, 1997: 436)

Yet of course, as Waterhouse had pointed out, the paradox is that in crossing the boundary the discipline may once again open itself to claims of populism, which weaken its status within the broader scientific community.

The balancing act of making an overture to the common people and yet at the same time reasserting the discipline's authority is exemplified in the figure of Cyril Burt. Since he was such a leading light of the profession during this period, Burt was both unavoidably and probably by choice in the position to play a significant role in projecting an image of psychology to the public. He reached a fairly broad audience with books like *The Young Delinquent*, first published in 1925, entering a fourth edition by 1944, and reprinted a total of eight times by the end of the 1940s. In the preface to the first edition, he imagined an audience which included a schoolmaster and probation officer, and undoubtedly such groups – as well as the emerging profession of psychiatric social workers – would have provided him (like many other psychologists in the period) with an enthusiastic and growing readership midway between the scientific and the lay (Burt, 1925: ix). The way that he brought the lives of delinquent or backward child alive in the case studies of his books suggests that this audience may have reached even further. But it was through his contributions to newspapers and magazines, his lectures and interventions in debates, and his use of the new medium of radio that he would reach a much broader public and become the best-known British psychologist of his day (Wooldridge, 1994: 106). In 1930 he delivered a series of radio talks which provide us with an insight into his strategy in popularisation:

> The plain man now at last has started to inquire, what is this novel, self-styled science of which he is hearing so much? Is it quackery? Is it a fad? Or is it just sheer common sense?

But once implicitly invited into the study of mind, the public are now firmly told where the real authority lies:

> It is sometimes said that that 'we are all of us bound to be psychologists'. The proper study – indeed the inevitable study – of mankind is man. Yet for the most part we commonly assume that human nature is a thing about which any reasonable person can generalize and reach a satisfactory view. To manufacture or repair a lifeless machine – a motor-car, a microphone, a submarine – expert knowledge is essential. But to follow the workings of the growing mind, to guide its development and correct its faults, for that we imagine, nothing but common sense is needed. *No view could be more mistaken.* (Burt, 1945: 8)

In sum, the profession should broadcast its views and educate the public, but in a way that convinced these readers and listeners of the expert nature of psychological knowledge and practice. Psychology was science, it was difficult and it was certainly not, as Waterhouse had suggested it might be, plain 'common sense'. This was 'boundary work' in Derksen's terms. And in crossing the boundary, Burt positioned himself as prone to a peculiarly intense attack when the credibility of his work was placed in question in the 1970s (Joynson, 1989; Fletcher, 1991; Wooldridge, 1994: 340–358).

Another way to reach the public was to appropriate the language and genres of the lay movements. Thus, many of the leading psychologists of the day wrote popular advice books with titles which echoed those of their popular counterparts. For instance, William McDougall's *Character and the Conduct of Life* of 1927 was subtitled *Practical Psychology for Every Man* (McDougall, 1927; see also Glover, 1914). And this concept of 'every man' or more often of 'everyday life' was to be a constant refrain in announcing the popular relevance of the subject (for example Drever, 1921). Psychology's success as, above all else in this period, an applied discipline takes on a new light when set within this context. In a sense, academic psychology, under pressure as a science on the one hand and from populism on the other, took the same route as the populists: it became a practical discipline. This was the case in sites such as the school, the factory and the army. However, for the purposes of this argument, of particular significance was the profession's construction of a role for itself in 'mental hygiene', both because of its necessarily more direct engagement with the public and because its therapeutic intent mirrored that of practical psychology.

British mental hygiene has generally been seen as a strategy for extending the power of the psychological and psychiatric professions. Using arguments about the relationship of mental health to the eugenic health and efficiency of the nation, they were able to gain state backing for the extension of a 'psychological complex' to survey and measure minds, establish normative standards, and weed out or adjust the abnormal (Rose, 1985). However, mental hygiene also needs to be set in the context of psychology's relationship to the public and the popular, and this has attracted less attention.

The term was imported from the United States in the 1920s. There, a clear conflict had arisen over the nature of mental hygiene: was it to follow its founder, Clifford Beers, a layman who had come to the subject through his own mental suffering and envisaged a crusading and evangelising popular movement; or was it to concentrate on the more limited and professionally circumscribed role of extending psychological medicine beyond the closed institution into new sites in the community, such as the child guidance clinic? This conflict was never as marked in Britain, where the movement was always firmly in the hands of the professionals.[9]

The limited success of the British mental hygiene movement was intimately related to the way in which professional psychologists struggled with the issue of popularisation. If mental hygiene was to become a truly effective strategy of fostering mental health in everyday life – its hugely ambitious target – it would have to go beyond establishing clinics for treatment, measurement and surveillance in isolated sites such as the school, the court and the factory, not least because it was all too apparent that expansion within these sites faced opposition from other professional groups, with their own claims to expertise, and that resources in terms of personnel and finance were wholly inadequate and would remain so for a long time to come. Mental hygiene, despite its conservative professional ethos in Britain, had to consider the strategies of those it scorned: it had to address the public more directly. This was exceedingly sensitive territory. Henry Yellowlees believed that it could have the opposite effect of that desired:

> There is, I think, nothing so maddening to the thoughtful man, and certainly nothing more inimical to mental hygiene than this utterly vicious principle of 'every man his own psychologist', or rather, 'every man his own psychological broadcaster'. The extent to which we aid and abet the public in this game of fads, slogans, and short cuts, is a blot on our profession. (Yellowlees, 1943: 77)

He was less damning of the kind of activities undertaken by the National Council for Mental Hygiene – organising lectures, courses and conferences open to the public, and issuing books, pamphlets and circulars. Indeed, he recognised the profession's ultimate duty to enter this territory to combat the occupying populists and 'the flood of hints, tips, slogans, shortcuts, epigrams, devices, gadgets and theories, with which the spoonfed public is overwhelmed' (Yellowlees, 1943: 75). However, he still felt that such a strategy was probably 'doomed to futility from the start' (*ibid.*).

Speaking on behalf of the National Council for Mental Hygiene, Dr Maurice Craig unsurprisingly presented a more positive view of popularisation: 'the knowledge of the mind and its working should,' he ventured, 'be available for the young and the old, for both must understand it.' However, this ran alongside a persistent ambivalence when it came to popularising theory. There was, after all, no need to tax the (limited) minds of the public by 'adding one more subject to an already overburdened mass of material, for the subject is part of our life whether we try or neglect to understand it' (Craig, 1933: 61). The crucial role for the mental hygienist was to tell the public how to lead a psychologically healthy life – not struggle to explain the theory which lay behind this: 'Our aims are to teach persons how best to handle their lives.… It is action which should follow words that I am seeking. [And to see] to it that this action is a right action' (*ibid.*: 64).

Understandably, supporters of a more individually liberating psychology could view the discipline's entry into the therapeutic field as a form of pacification and appropriation. As D.H. Lawrence observed in 1921:

> No sooner had we got used to the psychiatric quack who vehemently demonstrated the serpent of sex coiled round the root of all our actions, no sooner had we begun to feel honestly uneasy about our lurking complexes, than lo and behold the psychoanalytic gentleman reappeared on the stage with a theory of pure psychology. The medical faculty, which was on hot bricks over the therapeutic innovations, heaved a sigh of relief as it watched the ground warming under the feet of the professional psychologist. (Lawrence, 1921/1971: 201)

It would be wrong, however, to see the entry of professionals into the popular and practical arenas simply in terms of deliberate appropriation. The parallels also reflect the fact that professional psychology was nurtured in the same environment as its popular counterparts and was shaped, whether it was aware of it or not, by the same set of cultural dispositions. This is perhaps most striking when we recognise how many of the leading psychologists of the era, both religious and secular, shared the popular interest in marrying psychology with spirituality, not simply to rationalise its attractions but to seek in mental development a scientific basis to support the idea that people could transcend the limitations of an individualist self (Richards, 2000b).

Towards the end of the interwar period, a number of psychologists began to reformulate the problem of their discipline's relationship to the popular. In part this paralleled that shift within the popular psychology of the late 1930s which had been epitomised by the ambition of *You* to develop a new popularism through a psychology of everyday life. Psychologist Tom Pear, albeit a somewhat isolated figure in the discipline, called for the same reorientation in research, noting the

neglect of such central features of everyday existence as common speech, conversation, manners and fashion.[10] If psychology were to justify its social role, it
surely had to pay attention to the issues which really mattered to the public in
its daily life. Influenced by anthropology as much as psychology, the Mass-
Observation movement was in favour of a similar reorientation. Moving out of
the laboratory and into the field, it was to establish the lives and pastimes of
normal Britons as its subject of study. This type of populism was linked to a
second, for observation was to move out of the hands of the experts and into the
hands of the citizen: 'observation by everyone of everyone, including themselves'
(Harrisson and Madge, 1937: 9; see also Roiser, Chapter 8; and Pandora, 1997,
for the situation in the United States). The scale of the project demanded this.
But it was also recognised that there was a problem of cultural distance between
the expert and the public. Ultimately, the shift in the role of observer also had a
consciousness-raising agenda (Harrisson and Madge, 1937: 29). And since the
whole aim of the project was to make the public more self-aware – more socially
conscious – the findings would have to be delivered in plain, non-scientific
language (*ibid.*: 40). Unsurprisingly, such a project found little support from the
psychological profession. However, the rise of Nazism and the descent into another
world war was forcing the discipline both to examine the psychological roots of
democracy and to apply its science in its defence. The study of popular feelings
and a therapeutics which incorporated the individual and group and recognised
the importance of freedom of expression were therefore all encouraged. As such,
the discipline was pointed towards a more open relationship with its public (this
is explored at more length by Thomson, 1998a).

3   Conclusions

The popular is clearly a fundamentally important and problematic category for
any history of British psychology in the first half of the twentieth century, not
only because there was such a flourishing body of writing and activity beyond
the boundaries of the discipline – well before the psychotherapeutic society of
the postwar era – but also because the discipline itself cannot be fully understood
apart from this context of popularisation. The two, indeed, were to a considerable
extent mutually constitutive. In arguing this, however, I do not want to paint a
picture in which the popular and the professional were poles apart. Rather, I
hope to have demonstrated that there were conflicts over strategies of popularisation, and over the balance between science and spirituality and theory and
practice, throughout what is better conceptualised not as two poles but as a
spectrum of overlapping and interacting psychologies. My second aim has been
to set out a narrative of the changing relationship between the professional and
the popular in Britain between 1901 and 1950, and indeed the changing nature
of what constituted the popular.

   The chapter has argued that the first half of the century saw a transition in
the nature of popular psychological movements, from an emphasis on the spiritual,

to an oppositional emphasis on the practical, and finally towards an accommodation with the profession. Ultimately, popular psychology expanded beyond its associational roots to become a much more broadly influential dimension of lifestyle management. At the same time, and reinforcing these trends, there was a shift in professional attitudes, from outright condemnation of the popular towards the development of professional strategies to position psychology as a popular science. Ironically, therefore, popularisation can be seen as coinciding with a consolidation of power in professional hands, making way for what has been termed the 'governing of the soul' (Rose, 1989). The final point which needs to be re-emphasised is that both the vibrancy of often highly independent popular cultures in a period in which the organised profession was only beginning to establish itself, and some of the striking similarities between the popular and academic – in particular their common orientation towards the practical and the spiritual – suggest that we need to be very cautious about explaining either the popular simply in terms of a diffusion-from-above model or the academic in terms of theoretical progress alone. Both popular and academic psychology emerged in part because of the common conditions which created both the demand and the space for development. As this suggests, not only must a history of psychology in early-twentieth-century Britain now go beyond the narrow horizons of the discipline to embrace a more complex set of psychological identities and their interrelationship, but it must also go beyond internalist debates about the development of theory, practice and institutional settings to appreciate the significance of broader social and cultural forces in shaping and reshaping these identities.

Notes

1 For a preliminary attempt to address the second subject see Thomson (forthcoming).
2 This was not the only force driving popularisation – it also drew on a well entrenched culture of self-help and was encouraged by a flourishing culture of commodification. For a fuller exploration see Thomson (forthcoming). In Hearnshaw's view popularisation was intimately related to religion (Hearnshaw, 1964: 292–297). For a study which does recognise this attraction to psychology see Hayward (1995).
3 See, for instance, Hollander (1912). Dr Bernard Hollander was Britain's leading phrenologist and a regular contributor to the *Psycho-Therapeutic Journal/Health Record*.
4 For instance Emile Coué's, *Self Mastery Through Conscious Autosuggestion* (1922); and C. Harry Brooks' *The Practice of Autosuggestion* (1922), both published in 1922, the year of Coué's visit to England, had reached their sixteenth impressions by 1956 and 1954, respectively. In a slightly earlier form, Coué's ideas had reached the British public in Charles Badouin's *Suggestion and Autosuggestion* (1920), reprinted twice in 1921 (see also Coué and Orton, 1924; Macnaghten, 1922). W. H. Auden was heavily influenced by these ideas in his youth – see Davenport-Hines (1995: 70–73, 84–85).
5 It is not clear whether Anna Maud Hallam was related to Arthur Hallam, though the coincidence of this unusual name recurring suggests this might be the case.
6 Quoted from the cover page of *Thought and Action*, No. 1. September 1927.
7 British Medical Association papers held at the Contemporary Medical Archives Centre, Wellcome Institute for the History of Medicine, London (CMAC), SA/BMA, C. 378.

8 *Ibid.*, CMAC SA/BMA/B.89, 'Psychological Medicine Group: status of non-medical psychotherapists, 1938–53'.
9 On Beers and the United States see Dain (1980). On the international spread of mental hygiene see Thomson (1995: 283–304). In Britain the main challenge to the professionals came from the charitable groups which had already colonised this area but which were generally willing to accept a subservient role. See Thomson (1998b: ch. 4).
10 For instance Pear (1940b). He was heavily influenced by an article by the American psychologist Hadley Cantril (1934). On Pear see Costall (Chapter 9).

6

Psychology at war, 1914–1945

Joanna Bourke

Social and clinical psychology received a significant boost from the First World War. Out of that conflict, there emerged a new branch of the profession: that is, military psychology. It was not an inevitable occurrence. Indeed, many senior military personnel remained sceptical about the utility of psychological theory in wartime. Because its scientific status was looked at suspiciously and its predictive possibilities questioned, it did not win institutional influence until the Second World War. However, from 1916, when the first consultant psychologist was appointed to accompany the consultant neurologist with the British Expeditionary Force, psychologists have increasingly made an important contribution to the waging of armed conflict. Their roles have been diverse. This chapter focuses on only a few of their interventions – specifically the debates between medical psychologists and psychiatrists about the nature of trauma in wartime, the role of social psychologists in reducing levels of malingering, and the ways in which psychological thought contributed to shifts in training regimes.[1]

It was the unique aspects of modern warfare that convinced many senior officers in the first half of the twentieth century that the conventional emphasis on the military 'arts' was becoming misplaced. The burgeoning discipline of psychology was increasingly seen as offering a 'scientific' paradigm, which was more suited to 'man management' in the twentieth century. As the instruction manual entitled *Courses in Psychology for the Students' Army Training Corps* (*Psychological Bulletin*, 1918) admitted, it was no longer sufficient for an officer to be familiar with the inanimate materials of battle: 'he must also be taught to understand the human factors with which he has to deal', it noted. The highly technological aspects of modern warfare had, paradoxically, heightened the importance of the 'human material'. To make its point, the instruction manual provided an example based on the most important of all branches of modern warfare, the artillery. It observed that:

it is not enough that an artillery officer should understand the operation of his gun, range finding, spotting, sight setting, the effect of atmospheric conditions, ballistics, etc.; he must also know how to organise, control and develop a competent gun crew. Unless he can do this, all the rest is useless. In no military task is the human factor absent. With the complexity of modern warfare, it is increasingly important.... Doubtless young officers will eventually acquire more or less facility in handling men, but in the present exigency, all preparation must be condensed to essentials and systematised to save time and to eliminate waste.

Thus, psychological instruction was imperative: 'We cannot wait for prospective officers to get the necessary information by accident or by the costly methods of trial and error' (*ibid.*). Such sentiments were repeated time and time again in the interwar years. As Field Marshal Archibald Wavell (an influential British infantryman who played a large part in military education in the interwar period and then went on to command troops in the Middle East and the Pacific during the Second World War) rhetorically asked in a lecture given in 1933 calling for the establishment of a branch of the Intelligence Directorate to study the psychology of soldiers in battle: 'We have a manual on "Animal Management"', he asserted, 'is not "Man Management" just as important?' (Wavell, 1948: 103–108). It was a slow process, but by 1943 psychologists had made major inroads into the military establishment. By that time, a Senior Psychologist was a member of the staff of the Second Sea Lord (Chief of Naval Personnel). In addition, there were ten individual psychologists (aided by around 300 assistants) working in other parts of the Admiralty. At the War Office, 19 psychologists were employed in the Adjutant-General's Department. An additional 31 officers in that department had received psychological training. Hundreds of non-technical and non-commissioned officers had also received psychological training in selection processes. Other psychologists were employed at the Directorate of Biological Research in the War Office's Medical Department and in the Directorate of Scientific Training. At the Air Ministry, four psychologists were employed to advise on training methods and 31 officers had been specially trained in the psychology of personnel selection. They were assisted by around 100 psychologically trained assistants.[2]

1   Trauma in wartime

Calls for the application of psychological insights within the military context had many origins. The chief reason for this acknowledgement that psychologists were better than senior military officers well versed in military history and literature in understanding human reactions in battle was related to an awareness that warfare had undergone dramatic shifts from 1914. There were two significant changes: first, in the modern battlefield; and second, in the nature of the personnel. The very nature of modern battle was a potent reason why the military needed a new 'science' of human motivation. No longer was war a face-to-face encounter in which 'natural instincts' could be brought into play. For instance, by the end of the Second World War, the ratio of soldiers to space was one man to every

27,500 m^2 (Macksey and Woodhouse, 1991: 111). In the words of T.H. Pear, a lecturer in experimental psychology at the University of Manchester (see Costall, Chapter 9), in a book written with G. Elliott Smith, a professor of anatomy in Manchester and keen amateur psychologist and anthropologist:

> A man has seldom a personal enemy whom he can see and upon whom he can observe the effects of his attacks. His anger cannot be directed intensely night and day against a trench full of unseen men in the same way in which it can be provoked by an attack upon him by an individual. And frequently the assaults made upon him nowadays are impersonal, undiscriminating, and unpredictable, as in the case of heavy shelling. One natural way is forbidden him in which he might give vent to his pent-up emotion, by rushing out and charging the enemy. He is thus attacked from within and without. (Elliott Smith and Pear, 1919: 9–10)

Or, in the words of John T. MacCurdy (psychology lecturer in Cambridge and Fellow of Corpus Christi College by the Second World War), the problem with modern warfare was that men were exposed to long periods of intense bombardment yet may 'never once have a chance to retaliate in a personal way'. As a result, the thrill of 'giving some satisfaction in active hand to hand fighting, where they might feel the joy of personal prowess' was 'more difficult to maintain than in any previous war' (MacCurdy, 1918: 14).

It was this strange and especially terrifying environment that caused the behaviour of combatants to change. The military establishment found that it could no longer take the behaviour of men in battle for granted. There had always been cowards and malingerers in war – the difference was that it became increasingly difficult to control them and force them to conform. For the first time, the British army mobilised millions, rather than tens of thousands, of men to fight. From 1916, they consisted of men who had been conscripted to fight, not of loyal regular servicemen or eager volunteers. A large proportion came from middle-class homes and were educated. This was an entirely different cohort of servicemen, and they brought with them the prayers, aspirations and anxieties of an entirely different cohort of family and friends. Officers had to study psychology because they were no longer dealing with a professional army. Even the officer class was inexperienced and could not be depended upon to 'act promptly on sound lines in unexpected situations' (Kiggell, 1916: 2). The British public school system was widely regarded as the most fertile recruiting ground for well disciplined, effective officers, yet by 1945 only one-third of British officer army cadets were former public school boys.[3] So-called 'human factors' were important because those doing the fighting were no longer 'socialised warriors'.

Social psychology and medical psychology were crucial because they took the expectations and experiences of this new cohort of combatants seriously. Instead of pretending that emotion was irrelevant to warfare, they placed it centre stage. Furthermore, they insisted that the study of human behaviour was their unique speciality. In the words of E.F.M. Durbin and John Bowlby immediately before the start of the Second World War:

> Our attempt has been rather to describe and analyse the general psychological
> forces lying behind the timeless and ubiquitous urge to fight and kill. Just as it is
> the task of the physicist to study the general laws governing the behaviour of forces,
> such as electricity or gravitation, and of others, the astronomer to engineer, to study
> their particular manifestations, so do we conceive it to be the task of the social
> psychologist to isolate and understand the instinctive forces lying behind all human
> conduct. (Durbin and Bowlby, 1939: v)

This sentiment had been forged in the context of the First World War. In 1919,
the *British Journal of Psychology* had published an article summarising this unique
role of psychology in wartime. It was written by Alfred Carver of the Birmingham
Psychoneurosis Clinic and was a transcript of a paper read before the British
Psychological Society on 11 June 1919. The article dealt with the 'problem' of
emotion. The first sentence simply observed that 'the fact that emotion plays a
capital role in the genesis of the psychoneuroses has long been recognised; but
recently increased attention has been drawn to the subject owing to its importance in connexion [sic] with the war neuroses'. Carver then set out to survey
psychological knowledge concerning the emotions. Unquestionably, he insisted,
psychologists agreed that emotions were linked to instincts. He defined the
'interest' of an instinct as 'the affective tone which accompanies the whole
instinctive process when it is carried through in a normally satisfying manner',
while emotion was defined as 'the subjective experience which develops when
gratification of the instinctive impulse is held in check by higher level control'
(Carver, 1919). This view was in harmony with that of William McDougall, but
even William James, whose *Principles of Psychology* (1905) treated instinct and
emotion separately, added that 'every stimulus that excites an instinct excites
an emotion as well'. According to Carver, it was clear that psychoneurotic
problems were likely to arise when the strong emotional stimulus was continuously applied yet the organism was denied satisfaction:

> Emotion, having as its function the reinforcement of the 'interest' associated with
> an instinctive process, it is ... only natural that, when the issue of the impulse in
> satisfying response is continuously withheld while the stimulus remains active either
> in actuality, in memory, or in imagination, the result can only be injurious to the
> organism ... the unprecedented conditions of modern warfare are just such as are
> calculated to arouse intense emotion by withholding satisfaction from the instinctive
> processes so violently stimulated. (Carver, 1919)

Consequently, the emotional tension had to seek a different outlet, and would
attempt to escape by a process of repression. This seldom occurred successfully,
'for when the focus of attention sweeps on to some associated object or idea the
energy properly belonging to the original process, instead of disappearing, has a
tendency to attach itself to the latter'. In other words, the person would develop
a phobia or would suffer severe general anxiety. This was a common occurrence
in modern warfare, where the solider was exposed to incessant danger yet was

only rarely able to respond. For this reason, he concluded, psychoneuroses were far more common in modern warfare than they had been in 'the old days of open warfare and hand-to-hand fighting'. This was why psychology was imperative to the modern military in a way never known before.

Senior military personnel tended to agree. It was patently clear to everyone that large numbers of combatants could not cope with the strain of warfare. By the end of the First World War, the army had dealt with 80,000 cases of 'shell shock'. As early as 1917, it was recognised that war neuroses accounted for one-seventh of all personnel discharged with disabilities from the British army. Once wounds were excluded, emotional disorders were responsible for one-third of all discharges (Salmon, 1917: 509). (During the Second World War, between 20% and 50% of all discharges were the result of psychological trauma.) Even more worrying was the fact that a higher proportion of officers were suffering in this way. According to one survey published in 1917, while the ratio of officers to men at the front was 1:30, and the ratio of wounded officers to wounded men was 1:24, among patients in hospitals specialising in war neuroses, the ratio of officers to men was 1:6 (Salmon, 1917: 514–515). Since officers tended to come from a higher social class than privates, the correct way to treat such casualties was particularly problematical.

As a consequence, the military turned to psychologists to find a way of ensuring that men predisposed to mental defects were eliminated from military service at an early stage. Along with psychiatrists, medical psychologists were needed, not only to cure such persons, but to ensure that fewer men were placed in situations where they might endanger the military enterprise by breaking down at crucial moments of battle and subsequently use up valuable medical resources that were more urgently needed to help the physically wounded. Pension implications were also never far from the minds of the War Office and the government. The list of men who should not be allowed to enlist was lengthy, and included such diverse groups as epileptics, homosexuals, those suffering from venereal disease, those with a history of insanity in their family or in their own past, men frightened by trains and men incapable of micturating in public (Savage, 1916). Undeniably, though, the chief screening device consisted of ensuring that people who had a 'neuropathic or psychopathic soil' were identified (Mott, 1919: 110). Clinical psychologists had a duty to ensure that men with a dubious psychiatric family history were identified and excluded from military service.

Once a serviceman did suffer psychiatric collapse, it was the responsibility of medical psychologists and psychiatrists to describe and explain the particular problem and to attempt a cure. Their diagnostic conclusions were strongly structured around class assumptions. For instance, officers who broke down in combat were typically diagnosed as suffering from anxiety states. They were rarely diagnosed as hysterical. In the words of some researchers: 'Any soldier above the rank of corporal seemed possessed of too much dignity to become hysterical' (MacPherson *et al.*, 1923: 18). The private soldier was allegedly predisposed to hysteria because military training increased his suggestibility. In contrast, the officer was liable to anxiety reactions due to the weight of responsibility placed upon him. Officers found the solution to the conflict between instinct and duty provided by hysteria as too crude. In addition, their class background – particularly education in public schools and at games – was apt to emphasise the importance of repression of fear (Rivers, 1918: 526–527; Mott, 1922: 684). As Alfred Carver told a meeting of the British Psychological Society, anxiety states arose 'at a higher mental level' than conversion hysteria: 'The higher ideas and greater responsibility for an officer cause him to repress all manifestations of fear and to endeavour so to act before his men as to set them an example.' In the end, the effort would prove too great and he would suffer extreme general anxiety. Among privates, 'the conflict between self-preservation and those forces which have been summed up under the term "herd instinct" is, as a rule, fought out at a lower mental level and the tendency is for somatic rather than psychic symptoms to develop' (Carver, 1919: 60).

Such diagnostic assumptions had strong implications in terms of the treatment and reception of these men when they returned home. Officers clearly fared much better than privates. The different theories applied to men suffering from various war neuroses have been described in many other books (see Bourke, 1999a) – suffice to say here that in the British armed forces between the First and the Second World Wars there was a shift in treatment from 'hardness training', physiotherapy, persuasion and hypnosis to group therapy, chemical sedation, narco-analysis and modified insulin therapy. In all cases, it was crucial to ensure that the proportion of men who could be 'cured' and sent back to the front lines was as high as possible.

2   Malingering

Madmen were not the only military problem. In wartime, psychologists were seen as essential in controlling another group of men as well. While some servicemen broke down in war, others recognised their weakness 'in advance' and were successful in feigning all kinds of physical ailments in order to avoid the antici-pated slaughter. The problem was recognised by Sir John Collie, President of the Special Pension Board on Neurasthenics. He first published his book *Malingering and Feigning Sickness* in 1913. When a revised version was published during the First World War, it was nearly twice the size of the first, with entirely new chapters added on self-inflicted injuries and 'shell shock' (Collie, 1917). To the horror of the military establishment, everything from feigning poor eyesight to self-inflicted injuries was countenanced by some men (see Bourke, 1996: ch. 2). Even the stigma of madness could be preferable to going into battle. As one unnamed First World War volunteer recalled, one of his comrades 'used to whimper to me and ask me if I thought it was any use for him to sham madness'. This young soldier 'had tried every other complaint on the M.O. [Medical Officer] except leprosy and womb trouble' (Ex-Private X, 1930: 97–98).

Thus, one of the roles for psychologists within the military was to prevent and police malingerers. The problem was that many forms of malingering and self-inflicting wounds were difficult, if not impossible, to control. After all, a hand wound could be got by waving at the enemy from the trench. Another problem involved the relationship between neuroses and malingering. It is no coincidence that the wartime edition of Sir John Collie's book *Malingering and Feigning Sickness* included a new chapter on shell shock (Collie, 1917). As Arthur M. Hurst cynically put it in 1918:

> malingering may end in hysteria; a man who pretends to be paralysed for a sufficiently long period may end up genuinely believing he is paralysed, just as the German people have repeated the official line as to the cause of the war so frequently that many now doubtless believe in the truth of what they originally knew was untrue. (Hurst, 1918: 28–29)

Millais Culpin, Lecturer in Psychoneurosis at the London Hospital Medical College and Lecturer in Medico-Industrial Psychology at the London School of Hygiene and Tropical Medicine, observed that, in May 1916, there was such concern that a memorandum was sent to every medical officer 'in a certain area of the South of England' warning them that many cases of 'hysteria or malingering' were being recorded as organic disease. This practice must stop, it warned (Culpin, 1931: 17).

Medical psychologists often expressed harsh attitudes towards men they suspected of being malingerers. The most influential expert on malingering – Sir John Collie – had no scruples about the lengths officers should go to 'detect' malingerers. At one stage in his book on malingering, he described how he successfully persuaded a man to stop pretending that his arm was paralysed. Collie made a promise to the man:

> if he recovered within 14 days I would arrange for him to be again brought before the travelling medical board, when I would use my influence to have him classified for home service only. Before the 14 days had elapsed, in my presence, he suspended his weight on a trapeze and pulled himself up to his chin on it, and lifted a 28-pound weight with his paralyzed hand. In short, he wholly recovered. He is now doing full duty in his unit … I did not scruple to tell him quite frankly that, in my opinion, he was an arrant coward. (Collie, 1917: 376)

This was not an aberrant attitude. Dr Wilhelm Stekel had been placed in charge of a large neurological station during the First World War. In a paper he read before the Medical Society of Individual Psychology in 1940, he recalled that the first question he would ask himself about his patients was whether or not they could be malingering. He gave one example of a patient who was allegedly suffering from a heart disease. Heart specialists had confirmed the diagnosis, but Stekel reported that he had known immediately that the man was malingering.

After forcing him to confess, Stekel explained to the patient how he had known he was malingering:

> By merely looking at you I was suspicious. You looked at me in such a cunning, perhaps I should say, superior manner. I could read it in your face … because I am a psychologist I could read the truth in your face. The look on the face of an ill man is quite different from that of a malingerer. You see I am not only a Neurologist, but a Psychologist too. (Stekel, 1943: 22)

In this example, Stekel did not describe exactly what technique he used to get this heart patient to confess, but later in his lecture he described a technique that he found effective. He noted that it was common knowledge that some hospitals treated patients suspected of malingering with faradic brushes. It was 'like torture to the poor soldiers,' he admitted. In his hospital, 'if a malingerer was stubborn and in spite of explanation did not admit or give up his simulation, I threatened to send him to another hospital where this electrical torture was used. Mostly this threat was sufficient to induce the patient to give up his simulation' (Stekel, 1943: 22–24).

Psychologists who had specialised in the detection and prevention of malingering in the wartime context rapidly switched their newly honed expertise into industry after the war. Just as they had accused military selection boards of performing perfunctory examinations in order to pass into the army all willing recruits, so they alleged that employers were failing to ensure that proper recruitment processes were in operation within factories (Myers, 1918; Muscio, 1920; Earle and Macrae, 1929; Earle and Gow, 1930; Woodward, 1938). Selection had to become 'scientific', and the psychological discipline was essential. Wartime needs for increased production had signalled this shift. During the First World War, it had become increasingly obvious to the government that the excessively long hours of work put in by munitions workers had failed to increase production. The emphasis that psychologists placed on 'human factors' came to be seen as holding a solution to the problem of productivity. Not surprisingly, Charles S. Myers, the prominent psychologist who coined the term 'shell shock' and a leading expert on malingering in war, was a founder member of the Industrial Fatigue Research Board and founder of the National Institute of Industrial Psychology (as well as being the Director of the Psychological Laboratory at Cambridge University and consulting psychologist to the British Expeditionary Force). The Board had been set up under the auspices of the Department of Scientific and Industrial Research and the Medical Research Committee in 1918, as a result of the shock when the Health of Munitions Workers' Committee released its final report on low productivity and the increase in accidents and absenteeism. Three years later, the commercially orientated National Institute of Industrial Psychology had been established. For both, the human body was to be understood as bipolar, or as consisting of both a physical and a psychological 'pole' that needed to be balanced.[4] As they had done in wartime, psychologists noted that negative incentives had a limited effectiveness. Instead, managers were advised to analyse working conditions 'scientifically' and to pay particular attention to the psychology of the workers. Malingering and shirking could be eradicated by the better 'handling of men' (Casson, 1928: 96; Lawe, 1929: 227; Myers, 1933: 152–153). While American industrialists were adopting Taylorist principles (or the application of efficiency practices such as time management to industry), British employers drew from their war experience and stressed 'human factor' psychology.

3   Military training

There was one further area where psychologists made a major impact: military training. The psychological disciplines were increasingly regarded as crucial in training men to act aggressively in battle. Before the First World War, the British armed forces had not needed to place undue emphasis on the problems of enticing men to kill in battle. There were always malingerers and cowards, but it was believed that the vast majority of combatants would carry out their duty when necessary. In contrast, from 1916, the British forces were faced with having to motivate a largely conscripted group of service personnel and were forced to justify their actions to a much wider civilian public than ever before. The task of converting civilians into effective combatants required more than merely training them to name the various parts of the rifle and teaching them how to throw grenades. These men had to develop distinctive military traits, such as toughness, loyalty and discipline. Psychology came to be seen as the way to forge 'man-the-weapon' (Shirley, 1916: 23).

Admittedly, in many instances, the military merely adopted the *language* of psychology in order to justify conventional military practices to a much more sensitive middle-class population back home. Thus, by the Second World War, the frustration–aggression formula of the psychologist John Dollard and others – which argued that aggressive behaviour could be fostered by increasing levels of frustration – was used to legitimise some of the more sadistic aspects of military training. Similarly, by this time, the language of transference and displacement could be used to replace cruder military vocabulary without necessitating any change in the behaviour of instructors.

Others used psychological insights in a more constructive way in order to train men for combat. From the First World War, military training was influenced, consecutively, by three theoretical approaches. Instinct theories encouraged drills geared at stimulating reversion to primal passions and promoting automatic movements. By the Second World War, character or personality theories inspired the instigation of drills designed to develop certain character traits, particularly in leaders. Environmental theories assumed that most men would make suitable soldiers, but that appropriate combat behaviours needed to be instilled in every man through socialisation.

The first of these theories (that is, instinct theory) clearly made the greatest impact on training regimes. Military instructors found ideas arising out of the more popular psychological writings of William McDougall compatible with the established military ethos. McDougall's *Introduction to Social Psychology* (first published in 1908 and going through 30 editions by 1950) was immensely influential. As William James asserted in his renowned paper 'The moral equivalent of war', 'Our ancestors have bred pugnacity into our bone and marrow, and thousands of years of peace won't breed it out of us' (James, 1910/1971: 5). In terms of training men for war, the practical implications of instinct theory involved adopting techniques aimed at stripping away the civilised veneer of recruits in order to expose the 'beast within'. Bayonet drill was a central method used to 'awaken savage instincts'.[5] Thus, a 'scientific' rationale was found for dehumanising rituals and repetitive, aggressive drills.

At the same time, instinct theory reminded military personnel that there was another instinct that they had to deal with – the instinct of self-preservation. In order to reconcile the 'fight or flight' choice in the interests of martial valour, military instructors turned to crowd psychology. In Britain, Wilfred Trotter's ideas were those most commonly cited (Trotter, 1916; Conway, 1915: 305–306; Eltinge, 1918; Maxwell, 1923: 46 and 57–58; Murray, 1940: 13–14). Humans were herd animals, with strong gregarious impulses. In a crowd – and the army was only a trained crowd – the 'group mind' would take over, bestowing the individual with a sense of almost limitless power and even immortality. Group solidarity led to a return to primitive forms of behaviour, including reliance on the leader as the father substitute. Crowd psychology also promoted automatic movements: group drills, with emphasis on monotony and everyone doing the same thing together, enabled men to carry out the required movements almost without conscious thought, all the time as strong as the group. Wilfred Trotter and John T. MacCurdy both placed emphasis on the 'herd instinct' in enabling men to act 'effectively' (that is, aggressively) in battle (Trotter, 1916; MacCurdy, 1917). The practical implications of this were well understood by military personnel.

Instinct theory lost popularity after 1918. Individual psychologists criticised the theory and, in the 1930s and the 1940s, the *British Journal of Medical Psychology* and the *British Journal of Educational Psychology* published extensive attacks upon it.[6] However, it never died out completely, especially within military psychology. A particularly crude form of instinct theory was used to justify introducing 'blood training' into the 'battle schools' of the British army in 1941 and early 1942, in which animals' blood was squirted on faces during bayonet drill and men were taken to slaughterhouses and encouraged to test the 'resistance of a body' by using their 'killing knives' on the carcasses. As part of their training, recruits had to go through a gruelling, mile-long assault and obstacle course. Loud speakers relaying chants of 'Kill that Hun. Kill that Hun' and 'Remember Hong Kong. It might have been you' taunted and disorientated recruits following the course. There were explosions and, as the soldiers waded through water and mud pits, they were shot at with live ammunition. They were instructed to fire their own weapons at imitation German and Japanese soldiers. When they arrived at the section which involved a bayonet charge, recruits were showered with sheep's blood. At another stage in their training, recruits were taken to slaughterhouses and they were exposed to a 'hall of hate', consisting of pictures of German atrocities in Poland.[7]

Of course, such 'misuse' by the military of psychological principles was not supported by the psychological profession. When such training methods became public knowledge, psychologists were at the forefront of the arguments against it, pointing out that anything which made recruits faint and vomit was dangerous and suggesting that comparing the battlefield to slaughterhouses was neither relevant nor inspiring.[8] It was noted that previously keen recruits became depressed (Rees, 1945: 80–81). Such training was 'so crude and artificial that it could only be a product of an abnormal and infantile mind' and would be more liable to stimulate unconscious guilt and depression than heightening morale.[9] Attempts to 'work up hot blood in cold blood' were psychologically damaging: the use of real blood was even worse.[10] Blood training undermined the 'foundation stones of morale – human self-respect' (Ahrenfeldt, 1968: 189–190). The schools were based on an incorrect notion of human nature as innately sadistic and bloodthirsty (*ibid.*). Such comments by social and medical psychologists were instrumental in getting the training stopped.

Crowd theories had a longer life within the military. The ability of the crowd to produce actions antithetical to individuals was regarded as justifying the army's emphasis on leadership or the 'father figure', who could 'sway' the unit by his personality. The *character* of the leader was the central feature: he had to embody aggression, courage, strength of mind and physique, and responsibility. This continued to be the central use made of crowd theories during the Second World War. However, group dynamics were increasingly substituted for crowd theory: in particular, emphasis was placed on the cohesion of the wider group and the need for reassurance. The 'primary group concept' and 'group identification' came to dominate psychological discussions on combat motivation. The displacement of love from the self to the group was clearly desirable in military units. It enabled even weaker servicemen to adopt the aggressive stance of the group.

Briefly, it must be noted that psychoanalysis never gained much favour within the armed forces in Britain. Freudian ideas had appeared in English only in 1913 and by the time of the First World War there was still widespread uncertainty about its usefulness. Even after many of these ideas had become popular as a clinical discipline, psychoanalysis was too time-consuming for the military. Furthermore, it required highly trained personnel and was inappropriate given the transient nature of military relationships. As John T. MacCurdy acknowledged, if individual attention was to be paid to men who had problems coping with the act of killing, time would have to be 'taken from somewhere else' (MacCurdy, 1943: 45). Psychoanalysis was much more important in dealing with *breakdown* rather than training, precisely because although violent passions lay just underneath the surface, the chief problem was that of sublimation afterwards. Despite the attractive pension implications for the military (some military psychoanalysts argued that since emotional problems could be shown to have been based in infancy or early childhood, the military should not be found liable for compensation), it remained a marginal influence.

In practical terms, the uses made of certain psychological theories can be seen by examining the writings of J.F.C. Fuller. Fuller was arguably the most prescient military philosopher of the twentieth century (Reid, 1987: 1). He believed that the 'spirit of the offensive' could best be inculcated by a process of slow, continuous and almost imperceptible indoctrination. Human psychology was crucial (after all, he sensibly pointed out, 'the firer and not his weapon' was 'affected by the fear of death'). In developing his argument, Fuller drew on his own brand of instinct theory and crowd theory. According to him, the character of an individual depended on his impulses and his will which, in turn, depended for their nature on the spirit or ego. Everything that the individual came into contact with produced within him a sentiment for good or for evil. If repeated frequently enough within the individual, these sentiments became habits; if repeated frequently enough within the race, they became instincts. Although the army could not change a man's instincts, it could 'so bombard him with warlike impressions that his acquired tendencies, his reflexes, become wholly warlike'. In addition, the army itself acted as a crowd and, as such, was governed by the same laws which governed a crowd. Like the individual, crowds were ruled by voices from the past. Examining the army 'as an entity', Fuller lectured,

> we find that that part of it which we call its mind is swayed by that part of it which we call its soul; and that in this soul the dominating impulses are those drawn from the substratum of unconscious acts, and in particular from the inherited instincts. Under certain circumstances the conscious personality of the individual evaporates, and the sentiments of each man are focused in the same direction: a collective soul is then formed, and the crowd becomes a psychological one, and henceforth acts as an individual in place of a mass of individuals. (Fuller, 1914: 111–117)

In other words, the 'army-crowd' would be swayed by the voice of training, 'for uniformity of environment creates uniformity of character and of spirit'.

Bombarding the individual and the crowd with 'warlike impressions' was crucial – yet, Fuller recognised, training regimes did not do this because they ignored the one vital ingredient of battle: bullets. Without this ingredient, recruits could easily be trained to act appropriately – but they would not act similarly under real battle conditions. In order to simulate the presence of bullets, he proposed using a series of coloured flags. A red flag meant that the fire of the enemy was superior to that of the attackers; blue signalled equality; and white indicated inferior firepower of the attackers. Through a series of manoeuvres, recruits would have to respond in different ways to combat situations, depending upon the risk. They could be taught to advance under cover, make appropriate choices of fire positions and act calmly under pressure. In contrast to company drill, which stressed perfect order and absolute precision to the word of command, combat drill placed emphasis on tactical order and adaptation to the ground (Fuller, 1914: 7–29, 103–117).

By the Second World War, this emphasis on the psychological importance of 'realism training' had taken vast steps forward, with the introduction of infiltration courses, which required crawling over rough ground under live gunfire. These courses were a much milder variation of the 'blood training' mentioned earlier. Variously called 'blitz courses', 'village fighting courses' and 'close combat courses', they were regarded by nearly everyone as an effective means of training since they provided soldiers with more realistic expectations of combat, increased their motivation to learn combat skills, accustomed them to loud noises and enabled men to practise psychological techniques for distracting themselves in terrifying situations.

In addition, psychologists were important in improving training regimes by applying to them the principles of learning (Valentine, 1943: 27–38). The most important principles included spreading the practice of a particular skill over a few days instead of excessively concentrating it into one long period of drill, renewed stress on active participation, the use of varied material, accurate record-keeping combined with positive reinforcement, and systematic lesson plans. These were, indeed, all introduced as mainstream training principles (Valentine, 1942: 13). By 1942, a special 'method of instruction' wing was opened at the British Army School of Education, which provided courses in methods of teaching (Gibb, c. 1942: 23).

4   Personnel selection

Personnel selection was relatively unimportant during the First World War since a professional elite was not in place to administer a complex system and (until conscription was introduced in 1916) volunteers were able to choose their own corps and (it was considered) were sensitive to their own strengths and weaknesses. It was only from 1941 that psychologists were extensively used to screen personnel and even then it was generally considered a failure, since although it led to the army rejecting men for mental and emotional reasons at a rate almost seven times that which prevailed during the First World War, the rate of separations for these causes was five times higher than it had been during the First World War.[11]

There was one aspect of personnel screening that caused much debate in military and psychological circles, and that was the relationship between sexuality and combat. Ernest Jones (Freud's disciple and the chief promoter of psycho-analysis in England) in 1915 mused over whether it was possible that sexual desire was one of the most important factors in 'darkly impelling' men to enlist (Jones, 1915: 177; see also Hopkins, 1938: 119). Similarly, as Gerald H. Fitzgerald confessed to his colleagues at the British Psychological Society's conference in February 1921, he found that 'tougher' soldiers in the army coped with the enforced segregation from the opposite sex by 'resorting openly to perverted practices' (Fitzgerald, 1922: 109). The debate continued throughout the interwar years. In 1937, the *British Journal of Medical Psychology* published a detailed exposition of this subject by R.E. Money-Kyrle, in which he noted that 'unconscious inverts' actually made good combatants. Those who turned their aggressive urges inwards were capable of heroic displays of self-sacrifice in defence of their comrades, while those who turned their aggression outward were exemplary in battle (Money-Kyrle, 1937: 235). During the Second World War, Charles Berg followed up this argument, again in an article published in the *British Journal of Medical Psychology*. According to Berg, war itself was a 'dramatization' of 'unconscious phantasies'. War was a kind of 'homosexual substitution … an emotionally all-powerful (an orgastic) dealing with *men* rather than with women' (Berg, 1942: 185).

Of course, they admitted, there was a 'downside' to the retention of homosexuals (whether of the 'unconscious' variety or not) in the armed forces. In 1945, the *British Journal of Medical Psychology* published an article by Charles Anderson (of the E.M.S. Wharncliffe Neurosis Centre) which delineated the value of different types of homosexuals. There were, he argued, two main varieties of homosexuals. Those he labelled 'active inverts' were militarily desirable. They found it relatively easy to express aggressive urges and were dangerous to their comrades only during periods of inactivity. In other words, if they were kept on the front lines, they made good soldiers. There was another type of homosexual, though. These he called 'passive inverts'. Such men found battle unbearable, since they found it difficult to externalise their aggression and were 'expected to perform a psychic volte-face, to visit upon others what he wants to have visited upon himself'. There was a great risk that 'passive inverts' would suffer psychiatric collapse. Even worse, they might rush 'in an animal panic' to surrender to the enemy. It was almost impossible to 'cure' either of these two groups of 'inverts', Anderson discovered to his chagrin, since they tended to regard their sexual orientation as 'an integral part of their make-up' (Anderson, 1945: 162–163 and 172–174).

5   Conclusions

As this last discussion implies, much of the work of psychologists in wartime consisted of attempting to persuade people to act in ways that conformed to a military ethos. It was this role that earned them much dislike among the rank and file, who responded by attempting to subvert the power of this group of professionals. As noted earlier, some men did fake madness in order to be reclassified or dismissed from the services. One well documented example is that of Edward Casey, who pretended to be shell shocked in order to get back to England. As a result, however, he also had to pretend to be hypnotised:

> The Doctor who put me to sleep, examined me again, I had to tell him every thing I remembered before the barrage. Talking and telling him lies, while he wrote every

word I spoke, in a book, telling me my complaint of shattered nerves was becoming very prevalent. (Bourke, 1999b)

He was not alone in this. According to at least one psychiatric survey, faking shell shock was not uncommon – and the psychologists and psychiatrists had a duty to stop the practice (Southard, 1919: 106). In the words of Lieutenant Colonel John Philip Stewart:

> My experience of army psychologists [in the First World War] was disappointing. Most lived in cuckoo land without having experienced the reality of life. A period serving as a ranker would have been of the utmost value, fully-educating them in the diversity of man. They were too often deceived. I have personal knowledge of brother-officers, perfectly healthy in body and mind, who to evade being drafted to the War Zones in the second War [*sic*], were able to dodge the draft by giving information completely false.[12]

Patients resisted in other ways as well. Many refused to accept the psychological arguments given for their ailments. Thus, Lieutenant A.G. May refused to accept the slur of cowardice that he believed had been fixed to him with the diagnosis of shell shock. He had been shot during the Messines push and had been sent back to England. As he recalled:

> A few days later I started to have uncontrollable jerking and shaking of my legs. I was quite upset because I was unable to stop it. The doctor came and told me I had shell shock but I didn't believe this. That afternoon I was moved to a room by myself and this was not nearly as nice as being in a ward with six and eight other chaps.[13]

According to the historian Janet Oppenheim:

> The widespread assumption, after the war, that neurotic illnesses were wholly psychological in origin encouraged popular belief that they were, somehow, under the patient's control and therefore a source of discredit to people who allowed diseased thoughts to dominate their lives. (Oppenheim, 1991: 15)

Freudian ideas in particular were thought to clothe the sufferer in a mantle of disgrace that had been absent when more somatic explanations were accepted. Pathologising emotional reactions to killing and ascribing psychological weakness to men who disliked (or disapproved of) military life made it even more difficult for combatants to discuss their experiences in war to their families and friends when they returned.

In conclusion, although military psychology in the first half of this century was an integral part of the broader psychological community (and, as this chapter has suggested, was instrumental in forging many branches of social, clinical and industrial psychology), it retained a distinctive character. After all, military psychology was more 'military' than 'psychological'. Some psychologists expressed doubts about their role. For instance, in 1919, T.H. Pear and G. Elliott Smith admitted to feeling uneasy about declaring that a man suffering shell shock as a reaction against the horrors of killing had 'lost his reason or senses'. His senses were 'functioning with painful efficiency', they dryly observed (Elliott Smith and Pear, 1919: 2). However, the majority of psychologists – like the majority of professionals in other fields – had little difficulty adapting to the demands made of them in wartime and then readapting to civilian mores afterwards.

The extent to which military psychology was swallowed up by the 'military' half of its title has been explained in many ways. The sociologist Arlene K. Daniels described this in a series of articles written in the 1960s and 1970s. Although her particular focus was on psychiatry, her conclusions were equally applicable to medical psychology. She noted that military psychology and psychiatry were not simply special arenas in which these scientific discourses were applied. In contrast, the practitioner resolutely had to advocate 'denial' and the philosophy of 'you can make it'. This 'firm attention to the practical questions of adjustment to present circumstances belies the classical importance of introspection and self-awareness' (Daniels, 1972: 160). Daniels employed the notion of 'role conflict' to explain the process, arguing that the conflict between the military and the psychological discipline was resolved by compartmentalisation (Clausen and Daniels, 1966: 281; Daniels, 1969: 255). In Daniels' words, the discipline was 'particularly vulnerable' to the needs of the powerful military organisation. It offered a 'value-orientated' service:

> Normally, when everyone agrees about the value (e.g. health), no problem arises. The problem of the value orientation arises when the professional practitioner is employed to mediate between conflicting sets of values. The value of heath, for example, may be in conflict with the need for available manpower…. In such situations the practitioner is subject to pressures by the groups represented; and he is likely to make decisions which favour the client who has the most power. (Daniels, 1969: 257)

In other words, psychologists faced immense pressures to change their own values, to pull them in line with those of the military. For this act, they were rewarded with an unprecedented, large and docile community of experimental subjects.

In addition, there were more prosaic reasons for the accommodations made within military psychology. Conditions of work in modern conflicts provided little time for introspection. The military as an institution was exceptionally powerful and provided very strict limits within which psychologists could operate. Even the psychoanalytically sympathetic Myers said that in times of war medical psychologists and psychiatrists were simply forced to tell the patient to 'pull himself together and resume control over himself' (Myers, 1918: 41).

Finally, the military and the burgeoning discipline of psychology enjoyed a symbiotic relationship. Psychology did not simply serve the military, but was crucial in actually defining and expanding military power so that the armed forces could control and direct the emotional as well as the material lives of its recruits with great effectiveness.

Notes

1 Readers interested in other aspects of their role, such as intelligence testing and man–machine efficiency regimes, can turn to Carson (1993). For a broader discussion, also see Bourke (1996, 1999a).
2 Ministerial Committee on the Work of Psychologists and Psychiatrists in the Services. *Report by the Expert Committee*, 31 January 1945, 17, in the Public Record Office, London, CAB 21/915.
3 The estimate was based on the analysis of 1,218 candidates accepted for training for commissions in July and August 1945 (Sparrow, 1949: 22).
4 Leonard P. Lockhart, 'Industrial problems from the standpoint of general practice', August 1931, 3, in the National Institute of Industrial Psychology Papers, London School of Economics.
5 For a First World War discussion, see Meredith Logan (1923: 72).
6 For instance, see Money-Kyle (1937); Perry (1918); Pear (1943); and the contributors to the *British Journal of Educational Psychology*, November 1941, February, June and November 1942, and February 1943.
7 'Realism in Army Training. The Spirit of Hate', undated newspaper clipping, in the Public Record Office, London, (PRO) WO199/799; 'Realism in Training', *The Times*, 27 April 1942, 2; 'The New Battle Drill', *The Times*, 25 November 1941, 5; Bellah and Clark (1943: 72–75); 'Object of Battle Inoculation', undated but after 1 May 1942, p. 3, in PRO WO199/799; Rees (1945: 80).
8 'Battle Inoculation', 1944, 2, in PRO CAB 21/914. See also Jones (1945: 15).
9 Undated and unsigned report in PRO WO199/799.
10 Letter from A.I.M. Wilson (of the War Office) to Lieutenant Colonel Briton ('G' Training, Home Forces), May 1942 (no day), in PRO WO199/799.
11 For a discussion, see the minute by the Director-General, Army Medical Services, in PRO WO32/11974; see also Ungerson (1953).
12 Lieutenant Colonel John Philip Stewart, 'Tallest on the Right', n.d., p. 19 of the prologue, in Contemporary Medical Archives Centre, London.
13 Lieutenant A.G. May, 'Personal Experiences of the War Years 1915–1917', 32, in the Imperial War Museum, London.

7

The psychology of memory

Alan Collins

Memory and remembering are not issues on which only psychologists claim to speak with authority. Nevertheless, memory has become so firmly part of the discipline of psychology that it can be difficult for psychologists to appreciate that it was an object of enquiry and expertise before science, let alone psychology, came into being (Yates, 1966). Famous examples of writings on memory from before the existence of psychology abound: Aristotle, Cicero, Augustine, Aquinas, Bruno, Locke, Vico and Wordsworth are frequent citations, and there are many others. All of these writers discussed memory and remembering as something special, as an essential aspect of the experience of being human and so deserving of explanation and exposition. The views on memory in ancient and mediaeval times were radically different from contemporary scientific and cultural ideas about memory (Carruthers, 1990). A good memory was enormously valued during the mediaeval period and regarded as something integral to the merit and worth of a person. Those deemed to possess a good memory could construct arguments by rearranging or recombining things such as biblical texts to produce insights or to correct error. In mediaeval times a good memory facilitated knowledge and understanding of scriptures, laws and the nature of proper conduct, and in this sense memory was essential to being an esteemed member of the community. If there is a continuity between mediaeval and contemporary psychological views of memory, it lies in the perception of memory as an integral part of everyday human life and of human nature.

Memory is an accepted part of contemporary academic psychology and the literature on it is vast. In psychology, memory was – and is – frequently taken to be a natural object that can be studied without reference to social conditions.[1] In experimental psychology and in histories of psychology this assumption is rarely seen as problematic, and it appears equally natural that psychologists are properly the modern experts on memory. Leaving aside the thorny issue of the ontological status of entities existing independently of the means of studying and depicting them, this chapter discusses how the study of memory and the claimed nature of memory itself have been tied to particular social and cultural conditions. The chapter is not an exploration of the origin of the concept of memory or even the origin of the psychological category 'memory'; it does not consider memory's elevation to a 'natural kind' nor its recruitment into the classifications, practices and expertise of the discipline of psychology. An exploration of such issues would take one well beyond the bounds of Britain and the twentieth century. However, the chapter concentrates on how various psychological depictions of memory emerged in different domains: the classroom, the clinic, the university department and the applied psychology research unit. In each case the concept of memory and the means of studying it that emerged were different, sometimes strikingly so and sometimes more subtly so. The accounts of memory produced were not simply reactions to previous accounts, nor were they necessarily refinements and advancements on what had gone before. Instead, the changes in the conceptualisation of memory were profoundly affected by attempts to negotiate between the various and sometimes conflicting demands and opportunities of the contexts in which they emerged.

1   Memory in the classroom

References to studies of memory conducted before the 1950s rarely include any British researchers other than Francis Galton, Frederic Bartlett and, perhaps, Philip Ballard. Yet at the end of the nineteenth century and in the early part of the twentieth century, British academics such as James Ward, George Frederick Stout and James Sully had published theories on the nature of memory. Each of these men was a key figure in the emergence of a university-based discipline of psychology in Britain. It was Ward who succeeded in obtaining money for psychophysical apparatus for research at Cambridge in 1891 with the laboratory opening, after efforts by Michael Foster, in 1897. His article on psychology in the 1885 edition of the *Encyclopaedia Britannica* was particularly important in shaping the beliefs and practices of early generations of British psychologists, including Bartlett (Ward, 1885; Bartlett, 1936). Sully established the experimental psychology laboratory at University College London in 1898 and he wrote several important texts, including *The Human Mind* (Sully, 1892a; see also Gurjeva, Chapter 3). One of Stout's texts, the *Manual of Psychology* (1898/1904), was the psychology text most widely used in British universities for the first quarter of the twentieth century (Hearnshaw, 1964).

All of these major figures were steeped in philosophy and their writings on memory were philosophical in tone, but they also advocated empirical investigation as a means of understanding memory. They also thought the potential social roles for a discipline of psychology were important. Sully and Ward in particular were concerned with the place of memory in matters of pedagogy and the improvement of the child. The British Child Study Association was formed largely by teachers in the late nineteenth century and Sully was invited to become a vice-president of the London Child-Study Society. Sully's *The Teacher's Handbook of Psychology* (1886) was a standard text in teacher training colleges and his textbook publications were important in bringing psychological research to the attention of non-psychologists, especially teachers (see Chapter 3). Ward's interest in the importance of psychology as it related to education was evident in the lecture series he delivered in the 1880s (though they were not published as a text until 1926). Both Ward and Sully emphasised the role of psychology or mental science in establishing better ways of educating and improving the child, and memory was given prominent treatment as part of this aspiration.

By 1914, experimental psychology was only tenuously established in British universities and even in Germany and the United States, where the bulk of experimental psychology was being conducted, its position was not secure (Hearnshaw, 1964; Smith, 1997b). There were occasional empirical studies of memory in Britain in the nineteenth century. In the 1880s Galton and Jacobs had conducted studies of 'prehension', essentially a test of memory span, in collaboration with Sully, Read, Bryant and Bain (Galton, 1887; Jacobs, 1887). Galton had also done work on autobiographical memory (Robinson, 1986). When the *British Journal of Psychology* began in 1904, experimental studies were reported from the outset and, occasionally, these included studies of memory. In 1913, Beatrice Edgell reported experimental investigations into the effects of different forms of association on children's remembering – a study based on theoretical distinctions made by Stout (Edgell, 1913, 1924; Valentine, in press). In the same year Philip Ballard produced his monograph *Oblivescence and Reminiscence*, which was much cited subsequently (Ballard, 1913). These were important contributions but it is not possible to review them all in detail. Instead, I want to highlight the research of W.H. Winch, not only because he used experimental methods but also because his research was probably the most sustained empirical programme looking at memory in pre-1914 Britain.

William H. Winch worked as an inspector of schools in London. He was an interviewee for the job with London County Council that was given to Cyril Burt – thereby coming close to being the 'first official psychologist in the world' – and he was an early member of the British Child Study Association (Keir, 1952; Wooldridge, 1994). His main interest was in finding the best means of educating children and he regarded psychology as informing scientific pedagogy, something which was being advocated by American psychologists such as G. Stanley Hall during the same period (Zenderland, 1998). His specific concern with memory lay in whether or not good remembering could be promoted in schoolchildren using reproducible methods. The method on which he concentrated his research was formal training. In formal training, children practised remembering set material in the belief that practice would result in a general improvement of memory that would transfer to other material and other tasks. Winch's theoretical justification for his studies referred back to earlier claims for a faculty of memory improvable by practice and to Bain's claim that 'the retentive faculty is the faculty that most of all concerns us in the work of education' (Winch, 1910: 96). This was not an interest limited to Winch: there had been other experimental investigations examining the possibility of a transfer of improvement in memory (see, for example, Fracker, 1908).

Winch's opinion on memory and formal training was far from being a universal one. For example, William James, Stout, Sully, and Ward had each expressed doubt that memory could be much improved by practice of any form. In these accounts, memory was inherited and its essence was retention and recollection. James supposed that the ability to store memories, what he called 'native retentiveness', was a physiological given that was not susceptible to improvement through practice, any improvement in remembering being attributable to better acquisition, that is, better learning (James, 1890: 663–664). Ward wrote of a constitutional allocation of 'adhesiveness' which was not susceptible to change by training (Ward, 1926). Sully also assumed that 'the whole retentive power of the individual's brain ... [was] a definite quantity not susceptible of being increased by exercise' (Sully, 1886: 191–192). Sully used the metaphor of energy to explain retentiveness and proposed that there were separate forms of memory (for faces, music, places and so on). He concluded that the retentive quality could be 'channelled' into particular forms of memory and so memory for some material could be improved through training but overall retentiveness could not.

Such scepticism over improving general memory function promoted a distinction, found in many writings of the period, between learning as the acquisition of knowledge or skill and memory or remembering as the retention and recovery of that knowledge. The relationship between learning and memory was an intimate one, in that memory as existing knowledge was also a prerequisite for the process of learning, which, in turn, produced changes in memory.[2]

Winch was undeterred by the doubts over formal training and he conducted a series of experiments aimed at showing that practice on one form of memory improved memory in other domains (Winch, 1908, 1910, 1911). Clearly, memory was not here understood as a fixed capacity, though Winch's theoretical views on the nature of what was improved and how it was susceptible to improvement are obscure. Winch's studies were conducted using schoolchildren, who were split into two groups matched on the basis of their scores on a test of their verbatim recall of a prose passage. After this initial matching, the two groups of children underwent a training period of two weeks in which one group, the formal training group, practised remembering poetry verbatim while the matched group practised algebra. At the end of the two weeks the groups were given a test of verbatim memory for history or geography. Winch found better remembering of the test material in the formal training group and concluded that there were spin-off benefits from training of recall in one domain (poetry) to other domains (history or geography). On the basis of his studies, Winch claimed that formal training or training oriented towards memory improvement was beneficial for the child.

The rationale behind Winch's experiments contrasted with the idea of memory as a fixed retentiveness, but it was in accord with the doctrine of 'formal discipline', proposed by a number of psychologists, which held that training the mind on whatever subject would facilitate thinking in all domains (Angell, 1908). The novelty of his experimental methods was well recognised, especially his introduction of the notion of matched or equivalent groups (Woodworth, 1938). Together, these innovations led Danziger (1990: 149) to conclude that 'a new era of psychological experimentation had been ushered in by the English school inspector W.H. Winch'. However, Winch's methods and his statistics, and by implication his conclusions, were soon severely and persuasively criticised by William Sleight of University College London (Sleight, 1911). After presenting his critique and a wider review of the existing literature, Sleight described his own series of experiments on formal training that provided no evidence of transfer. Sleight concluded that there was no general memory function that could be improved by practice and hence formal training would not lead to transfer.

When interpreting his findings, Winch stressed the physiological nature of memory. In such a framework formal training was likened to exercising a muscle: there were inherited limits on the strength of memory but, in contrast to James's opinion, its realised strength could be improved by exercise. However, the disputes around formal training did not treat memory *only* as a physiological entity. On the contrary, formal training and the efficiency of memory were intimately connected with educational concerns and the production of more effective citizens. Winch was an inspector of schools who ran his studies in schools and his express aim was to discover whether it made sense to devote school time to improving children's recall. Equally, opponents of formal training argued that it detracted from what was important in schooling, in particular that it removed attention from understanding the material. For example, Ward argued that formal training and rote remembering were of little value: what mattered was good understanding, because it was this that would ultimately ensure good remembering (Ward, 1926). And Sully, despite having some sympathy for the idea of improving memory, felt that rote memory was a 'mere knowledge of words' and not of ideas and for this reason regarded it as a worthless exercise (Sully, 1886: 201).

The literature on formal training treated a good memory as a desirable quality in children. Such knowledge was produced not so much to deepen understanding of memory as to find the best means of improving the child, that is, it was knowledge having potential utility. Psychological science presented a means of assessing what could be improved in the pupil and how it could be improved. This was not a one-way process, with science simply responding to sociopolitical conditions or needs: rather there was a mutual interplay whereby psychology also informed views of the child, such as whether or not the child possessed capacities, if so what they were, whether they could be measured and whether they were open to improvement (Walkerdine, 1984; Rose, 1985). Winch's studies were not solely the product of grand movements such as producing a better-educated and more efficient workforce, they were also the product of local opportunities, with his position as school inspector allowing access to schools and large numbers of schoolchildren. After the First World War, Winch concentrated on other matters. Yet despite Sleight's attack and the later critical overview by Woodworth (1938), research on and speculation about transfer of memory improvement did not disappear completely (see, for example, Valentine, 1960). More broadly, transfer remained and remains an issue for psychology. For example, in the cognitive psychology of problem solving and expertise, considerable effort has gone into attempting to specify whether or not transfer occurs between problems and if so under what conditions and as a result of what mental representations and processes (see, for example, Singley and Anderson, 1989).

2   Remembering as pathology and as cure

In an autobiographical piece written in 1936, Bartlett remarked that, after the First World War, 'Psychology, everybody found, had changed' (Bartlett, 1936: 40). He was referring to the way in which psychology became a more independent discipline in the postwar years, but there were other changes, too, and some of these were apparent in the psychology of memory.

In 1918, Charles S. Myers gave notice of a shift in psychological views on memory in his series of lectures on *Present Day Applications of Psychology* (Myers, 1918). In these lectures he noted that 'our conception of the psychology of forgetting has undergone a very radical change' (p. 30), which, he went on to explain, necessitated abandoning the idea that learning and recall were merely functions of association and trace decay, respectively. He urged experimental psychologists to reintroduce notions of feeling and meaning when explaining remembering and forgetting. He also encouraged them to contemplate the Freudian idea that all memories were preserved, with their recurrence depending on current conditions. Most importantly, he emphasised the importance of repression as an explanation of forgetting, characterising it as a natural and not necessarily conscious process.[3] Myers was not rejecting experimentation and his lectures were full of references to claims based on experimental work. However, he was clearly making an attack on experiments in the tradition of Ebbinghaus, Müller and Meumann that had dominated the experimental psychology of memory in Germany and the United States before the war (Müller and Pilzecker, 1900; Ebbinghaus, 1913/1964, Meumann, 1913).

In his autobiographical text *Shell Shock in France, 1914–1918*, Myers presented a number of clinical cases he had encountered in the war and in all of them forgetting and remembering were given a central role (Myers, 1940: 42–48). In the case histories, as elsewhere, Myers outlined how in psychotherapy what he described as 'restorative measures' frequently required the 'revival of forgotten memories' (p. 56) through analysis or mild hypnosis. Such revivals of memories were necessary for overcoming destructive repressions or dissociations, a therapeutic aim in line with psychoanalysis and with the recommendations of many others who had worked with soldiers (see, for example, Head's and Rows's evidence to the War Office Committee of Enquiry into 'Shell-Shock', 1922).

Other British psychologists writing around this time were similarly doubtful about the adequacy of explanations of forgetting that relied on decay. Even before the war, Tom Pear had argued that decay could explain only the least interesting of forgetting phenomena – it just was not sufficient as an account of all forgetting. For him the most interesting memory lapses were those where subsequently the experience was remembered, a phenomenon not easily explained by decay (Pear, 1914a; for more on Pear see Costall, Chapter 9). After the war, Pear's conviction was strengthened. In his *Remembering and Forgetting* (1922) he discussed experiments on nonsense syllables, but his doubts about their value are apparent: 'Such investigations have resulted in valuable knowledge concerning the laws governing the economy and training of the memory for relatively meaningless material' (p. 135). The implication was that such laws were hopelessly inadequate for understanding memory of complex, meaning-laden experiences undergone by people who themselves differed greatly on all sorts of dimensions.

For Pear, ordinary and extraordinary forgetting needed richer explanations than decay theory provided and, like Myers, he turned to the concept of repression. Repression had been introduced in the work of Freud and Breuer, and although arguably it had had earlier manifestations in the works of Bachofen and Nietzsche, it was as the 'cornerstone' of psychoanalysis that it gained prominence (Freud and Breuer, 1895/1974; Ellenberger, 1970; Billig, 1999). While many things lay outside consciousness, repression prevented certain things entering consciousness; in other words repression ensured forgetting. Pear saw repression as a biological mechanism, but one that was also tied to social convention and to the urging that one should try to forget unpleasant experiences – an imperative he thought common to many societies but one that was especially prominent in Victorian Britain. Any attempts to obey this imperative to forget were assumed to be revealing of morality and class and, in Pear's account, the weakling drank to forget, the slightly stronger sought to forget through excitement and the strongest turned to work. During the war, similar class-based assumptions as well as rank informed the conclusions drawn about the nature and origin of troubles caused by war experiences (Bourke, Chapter 6).

A third prominent member of the British psychological community writing on memory shortly after the war was William H.R. Rivers.[4] Like Myers, Rivers was heavily involved in treating soldiers. Also like Myers and Pear, Rivers wrote in a psychoanalytic vein about memory. In his book *Instinct and the Unconscious*, first published in 1920, he distinguished between repression (the witting act of forgetting), suppression (the unwitting act of forgetting) and dissociation (where what was forgotten was an alternate, active conscious state). For Rivers, repression and suppression were aspects of memory present in the healthy person and each of them usually contributed to the person's health by eliminating from consciousness memories which would interfere with everyday living. That is, in everyday life, health and normality were assisted by maintaining the appropriate balance between remembering and forgetting (see also Roth, 1989). Only in the face of extreme experiences, such as those encountered in the trenches, did repression and suppression become problematic facets of memory.

Rivers argued that repression and suppression were grounded in biology and in our evolutionary past. Referring to his own work with Henry Head, he linked suppression to physiological inhibition. He used Head's concepts of protopathic and epicritic sensation to illustrate how two physiological systems could exist together with some aspects of the systems being fused while other aspects of the cruder and more primitive system (the protopathic system) were ordinarily suppressed and became apparent only if the systems suffered some trauma – as in Head's experiments on the nerves in his own arm (Head and Sherren, 1905; Head, 1920). Rivers claimed that some general system of suppression existed in most animals. For example, when animals experience conflicting states – such as the classic flight-or-fight conflict – one way of dealing with them was for one of the states to be suppressed. To illustrate the idea further, he argued that something like suppression must exist in the frog, where, during development, the muscular movements of the earlier tadpole stage are suppressed (Rivers, 1922: 69). Rivers' experience of working with soldiers during the war provided him with apparent evidence of suppression through the recurrence of previously inaccessible memories.

Alongside repression and suppression, Rivers considered dissociation, something also addressed by Myers and William Brown. All three of these writers argued that the key characteristic of dissociation was an independently active consciousness. Rivers speculated that the possibility for such dissociation stemmed from a general requirement to keep different modes of existence separate. In particular, he linked this to amphibian modes of life and argued that this lies behind the tendency to dissociate: for the full-grown frog, for example, it is necessary to keep the movements associated with land and with water separate. In British psychiatrists' descriptions of double personality in the mid-nineteenth century, it was the alternate consciousness rather than forgetting that was emphasised, but this changed in France in the 1870s when a science of memory began to emerge and thereafter memory was a central issue in understanding multiple personality (Hacking, 1991, 1995). Rivers' explanation of dissociation was a complex one: consciousness remained the focal issue but the explanation of the dissociation depended upon some account of forgetting. Consequently, forgetting was hardly incidental to understanding dissociation.

As a final example of this genre, in 1927, in his address as President of the Psychology Section of the British Academy for the Advancement of Science, William Brown chose to speak on 'Mental unity and mental dissociation' (see also Brown, 1928). This is the same Brown who had written the dry but seminal work *Essentials of Mental Measurement* with Godfrey Thomson (Brown and Thomson, 1921; the first edition was by Brown alone in 1911). But Brown had also served as a neurologist to the 4th and 5th armies in France and had given evidence to the 1922 War Office Committee of Enquiry into 'Shell-Shock'. In his address, Brown paid attention to dissociation as pathology, as in amnesia and

multiple personality, explaining them using the concepts of repression and extrusion. He was careful to argue that the processes of repression and extrusion
were not in themselves pathological but were essential for a rich understanding
of disorders associated with the war. Like Myers, Pear and Rivers before him,
Brown argued that such processes were the norm and he claimed in a remarkably
(post)modern manner that 'the most normal mind is a multiplicity. We are all
many selves' (Brown, 1927: 170).

For those psychologists who lived through the war or who were involved in
the treatment of its victims, encounters with loss of memory and with the persistence of painful memories became dreadful commonplaces. The American
psychologist G. Stanley Hall commented (1919: 217) that 'Hering, Simon and
Loeb tell us that the central thing in the soul is memory' and whereas his point
was that memory was one among many contenders for the essence of the soul, I
am claiming that, in the aftermath of the First World War, for many British
psychologists the claims for memory's centrality were considerable. While the
experiences with soldiers from the front were critical in promoting such an
orientation, there was also another factor that pressed the case for a psychoanalytic theory of memory. Alan Costall has described how, during the war, Myers,
Pear, Rivers and Brown – and many others – shared time working at the Maghull
Hospital in Liverpool under the guidance of Rows (Costall, 1998). Costall mar-
shals evidence showing how the hospital acted as a kind of academy where the
curriculum was dominated by psychoanalytic ideas and the participants appear
to have been persuaded that such ideas offered a guide to therapeutic intervention
and to understanding memory (though it should be pointed out that Maghull
was not their first exposure to psychoanalytic ideas – see Pear, 1914b, for example).

The wider story of the First World War and shell shock has been much rehearsed and has been used to argue for shifts in understanding of mental illness
and the status of the psychiatric profession (Stone, 1985). Histories of shell shock,
neurasthenia and war neuroses have highlighted the importance of these concepts
for tempering the extreme physicalist theories of prewar psychiatry and psychological medicine (Feudtner, 1993). My claim is of a similar kind, namely that the
First World War made remembering and forgetting central to psychological
accounts of human experience and that a turn to psychoanalytic ideas on memory
was understandable within a culture where such ideas were gaining currency,
both in the psychological community and much more widely (Hearnshaw, 1964;
Richards, 2000a). For Brown, Pear, Myers, Rivers and others, memory was something much richer and more central to our conception of self than associationism,
decay theory and experimental work had suggested. Repression and suppression
not only provided richer conceptual alternatives – they also suggested aims and
methods for therapy that hinged on remembering and forgetting.

Memory and remembering were at the heart of social and cultural responses
to the First World War (Fussell, 1975; Hynes, 1990). The matter of how to
remember the war and the war dead became a preoccupation. War memorials
had been erected after previous wars, notably to the soldiers of the Boer War,

but now the memorials generally took on a new (though not entirely unprecedented) form, with the dead being individually commemorated by name (Bushaway,
1992). Individual gravestones were erected by the War Graves Commission and
the individual stones set in cemeteries of thousands emphasised the poignancy
of the loss of a particular soldier set among the vast losses of nations (Laqueur,
1994). Ceremonials or rituals such as the silence on Armistice Day and wearing
the Flanders poppy were introduced and, in 1927, the British Legion festival of
remembrance was created to temper the spirit of celebration and emphasise
remembering. Memory and remembering became important as they offered the
possibility of a better understanding of the war as well as being some form of
salve for collective grief in what became a national obligation to remember
(Bushaway, 1992). Similarly, in therapy with war victims, many psychologists
offered remembering as a necessary step both in understanding and in achieving
a cure and explained these using concepts that had a resonance with cultural
concerns of the immediate postwar years.

Sometimes the inadequacies of remembering the dead and commemorating
them fuelled a desire to go beyond memory and to make contact with the dead.
The spiritualist movement gained momentum during the war and in its immediate
aftermath. Parents of dead soldiers consulted mediums as a form of solace and
reports of spiritual experiences in the trenches were common (Winter, 1995).
The movement had wide appeal and the psychical claims and research that
formed part of it engaged the interest of academics as well as members of the
public from all classes and with various degrees of religious belief (Oppenheim,
1985).[5] For example, Henri Bergson, Cyril Burt, W. Boyd Carpenter and William
McDougall were all members of the Society for Psychical Research and as academics they were hardly exceptions in a Society that was littered with scientists
(including several Fellows of the Royal Society and Nobel Prize winners). The
period of intense interest in spiritualism during and after the war can be construed
in many ways, but in the context of this chapter it can be seen as a means of
transcending memory's limitations. Remembering was simultaneously and paradoxically valuable, dangerous and to be encouraged. But memory was a defining
aspect of loss, whereas spiritualism offered something more than memory: a
coming together of the living and the dead. Spirit photographs, for example, were
offered as proof that the act of remembrance really was something more, that
through an act of remembering a more intimate encounter was possible.[6]

3   Ordinary remembering and experimentation

The early and often powerful writings on memory by major figures in British
psychology did not give rise to a systematic and sustained programme of experimental research. Repression and suppression were not readily susceptible to
investigation either by mental test or by laboratory experiment. A key turning
point in the empirical study of memory came with the publication of Sir Frederic
Bartlett's *Remembering: A Study in Experimental and Social Psychology* (1932). As

I hope I have made clear already, this was far from being the start of psychological work on memory in Britain but it did represent a break with what had been done previously.

Where Myers, Pear, Rivers and Brown all made use of psychoanalytic ideas, Bartlett hardly discussed them. In *Remembering*, he considered only Jung's notion of collective unconscious at any length and he was clearly unsympathetic to both the content and style of Jung's writings. In the same text he cited Freud only twice and elsewhere displayed a lack of sympathy for psychoanalytic explanations of one of his major interests, folklore (Bartlett, 1920, 1932). He largely finessed the idea that memories might persist in the unconscious and in some passages of *Remembering* he seemed deliberately to avoid psychoanalytic terms. For example, a persistent 'unexpressed tendency' was something that Bartlett believed required 'critical consideration', yet he made only passing reference to suppression (Bartlett, 1932: 92–93).

Freud's comparative absence in Bartlett's writings appears as a form of repression through language (Billig, 1999). When he did mention Freud he was critical of his rather static view of memory, where memories continued to exist in a relatively unchanged state in the unconscious. Commenting on Bartlett's attitude to psychoanalytic ideas, Pickford said:

> At Cambridge [where Bartlett spent most of his academic career] psycho-analysis was very much under a cloud…. In fact, I suppose it is in a sense the only real gap in Bartlett's understanding of Psychology from my point of view … that he had no use for psycho-analysis and no insight whatever into its importance.[7]

Having been unable to enter active service due to previous ill health, Bartlett was also less engaged in therapy with soldiers than many of his contemporaries and although he attempted to work with shell-shocked soldiers, he did not find the work satisfying (Oldfield, 1972). Instead, during the war Bartlett concentrated his efforts on experimental work into the effects of fatigue and into the detection of submarines. One can only speculate on whether or not Bartlett's comparative lack of contact with shell-shocked soldiers made it easier for him to reject psychoanalytic theories of memory and to develop instead his view of memory as a constructive activity.

Bartlett's approach to remembering has been quoted as the antithesis of Ebbinghaus's and it has been cited with approval as an alternative, cognitively based way of understanding and studying memory (Neisser, 1967). Rather than memory as a faculty or capacity, Bartlett emphasised remembering as an active, dynamic process influenced by a host of conditions, from personal appetites to social background; memories were not retrieved from a store but reconstructed through the action of schemata (Bartlett preferred the term 'organised settings') and the social contexts in which remembering took place. While his book *Remembering* has been described as a forerunner of much in cognitive psychology, it has also been claimed as anti-cognitivist and a forerunner of discursive approaches to remembering (Edwards and Middleton, 1987). What is not disputed is that

Bartlett insisted that remembering was a pervasive activity. Some philosopher-psychologists had separated out memory by defining it narrowly as 'ideal revival', that is as a conscious and sometimes effortful attempt to revive past experiences, making it clear that these qualities distinguished memory from mere repetition or habit (Stout, 1898/1904; Bergson, 1911).[8] Bartlett thought that such a definition reduced memory to 'an exceedingly small and rather unimportant field' (Bartlett, 1932: 312) but more fundamentally he refused to accept that mental processes were so easily separated; he regarded the isolation of the high-level mental processes one from another as an impossible and dangerous simplification (pp. 12 and 186). Instead, Bartlett regarded memory as something that had to be understood in relation to other mental functions. In part, this orientation was a legacy of his attempts to develop a sociocultural psychology and his earlier work on perception, where he had introduced the phrase 'effort after meaning' to illustrate how perception was not simply a product of the material presented but also of the conditions under which something was perceived (Bartlett, 1916: 231; Costall, 1998). Bartlett's widening of the scope of memory and his emphasis on interconnectivity presented a difficulty that persists, namely that of drawing a boundary around what is and what is not memory.

In his studies for *Remembering*, Bartlett used four main methods: the method of description, the method of repeated reproduction, the method of serial reproduction, and the method of picture writing. The method of description was used for studies carried out during the early part of the First World War (Bartlett, 1932: 47) and consisted of presenting people with a series of cards, each of which had a drawing of a face on it. After an interval of about 30 minutes, he then asked the subjects questions relating to the cards shown. In the studies using repeated and serial reproduction, several of which began during the war, Bartlett presented subjects with materials – most famously stories – that were then recalled repeatedly at intervals. The main difference between the two methods was that in repeated reproduction the same person did the recalling on each successive occasion whereas with serial reproduction each recall was relayed to someone else who then had to recall it for someone else and so on. In the method of picture writing, Bartlett presented people picture signs, each of which was paired with a word. Subsequently, they were asked to write a passage to dictation. Where the passage contained one of the words paired with a picture, participants had to try to write down the sign instead of the word.

Among the materials he used in the reproduction experiment, the most famous and the one that Bartlett used most to exemplify his claims was 'War of the ghosts', a North American folk-tale translated by the anthropologist Franz Boas. The story was regarded as a rather strange one by a number of participants and there were a number of unconventional elements to the tale, particularly the lack of specification of causal links between events that were temporally close together (Mandler and Johnson, 1977).[9] The strangeness of 'War of the ghosts' for British readers was something of a paradox, given Bartlett's objection to researchers such as Ebbinghaus using experimental materials devoid of meaning (Costall, 1991).

Also paradoxical was Bartlett's neglect of the role of the listener in his discussion of the results of his repeated and serial reproduction experiments, despite having emphasised the importance of 'auditors' when discussing the effects that different audiences would have on the form and content of the folk story (Bartlett, 1923). He made the same point towards the end of *Remembering* when he wrote: 'There is social control from the auditors to the narrator' (p. 266). Edwards and Middleton (1987: 86) have pointed out that: 'It is clear that Bartlett's subjects were not simply reporting their mental processes [or contents], but doing so in the context of a dialogue with Bartlett'. Nevertheless, in his discussion of what was recalled in the repeated and serial reproduction experiments, Bartlett hardly considers the role of the listener, treating the 'auditor', himself, as though he were a silent and neutral recipient, having no effect on what was said. Whereas such a form of report might be ideal for someone committed to the experiment and laboratory as properly divorced from everyday circumstances, it did not fit with Bartlett's theoretical account of memory, his methods or his commitment to 'ordinary remembering' as the object of investigation.

There is a tension in *Remembering* regarding the main object of psychological enquiry: the individual mind, or social interaction (Costall, 1991). A similar tension is reflected in the place of *Remembering* in Bartlett's career, where it can be read as a transitional text between the thoroughly social psychology that he outlined in his *Psychology and Primitive Culture* of 1923 and the increasingly individualistic psychology of his later writings (Bartlett, 1958; Shotter, 1990). Finally, there was a tension between his interests in and views on psychology and the kind of psychology he sought to promote. Bartlett's position in university psychology was historically unique: he occupied the Cambridge chair at a time when psychology was being established as a discipline in British universities, yet when the community remained sufficiently small to be known and significantly shaped by an individual (Costall, 1991, 1992). Costall has argued that Bartlett skilfully promoted a narrow, experimental psychology somewhat at odds with his early theoretical orientation, his own methods and his continuing interest in social psychology. If Bartlett was concerned with too narrow a definition of memory as making that topic 'unimportant', it was also clear early on in his career that he regarded too individualistic a psychology as being subject to exactly the same criticism (Jahoda, 1982).

How are we to explain these ironies? The most obvious answer is that Bartlett himself was involved in two forms of activity that were not easily reconciled: the active researcher and the advocate of a new discipline. The opportunities that existed for the establishment of an academic discipline of psychology required a certain expediency on his part. In particular, the promotion of psychology as a science may have been facilitated by apparent methodological rigour, even if that rigour required setting to one side what Bartlett himself may have regarded as best practice.[10]

If the writings on memory by Rivers, Brown, Myers and Pear had been explicitly shaped by their wartime experiences, the impact of war on Bartlett's work is less obvious. His training in anthropology and his interdisciplinary interests and friendships were proximal effects on the research, as were institutional constraints and opportunities. However, as one might expect from his general theoretical stance, he was sensitive to the general social context in which his experiments were conducted, commenting several times on his materials and the salience of the war to the participants in his studies. For example, in the presented version of 'War of the ghosts', one of the 'excuses' for not fighting offered by a character in the story was that the potential combatant's family would not know where he had gone. In the course of serial reproduction, Bartlett reports that this 'excuse' became transformed into one more in accord with the war, namely that of having elderly relatives 'who would grieve terribly' if the potential combatant did not return (Bartlett, 1932: 129). Bartlett was also interested in the supernatural element of 'War of the ghosts', especially its ending, where the death of a character was marked by 'something black' coming 'out of his mouth' (p. 65). Although he makes little of this subsequently, he does comment on the way in which the episode becomes rationalised into the more familiar idea of soul or spirit leaving the dead man's body – something consistent with a period when the issue of life after death and the idea of spirit had a renewed salience.

The fact that *Remembering* was published in 1932 should not obscure the fact that much of the work and many of the ideas were formulated during and shortly after the First World War (Bartlett, 1958). The considerable cultural interest in remembrance has already been discussed and there are aspects of it echoed in Bartlett's work. From early on, Bartlett demonstrated an interest in how conventional modes of representation were developed within groups and transmitted from one group to another, so much so that he originally planned *Remembering* as a book on conventionalisation (Bartlett, 1932, 1958). For Bartlett, folk stories and their transmission were an integral part of conventionalisation, and Paul Fussell has argued that one of the effects of the war was to reinstate or strengthen the un-modern themes of myth, superstition, legend and rumour in the literature arising from the conflict (Bartlett, 1920, 1923; Fussell, 1975). For survivors of the war, remembrance became an essential component of ritual, be it the annual pilgrimage to the Somme or the more public acts of ritual such as two-minute silence on Armistice Day, when people were required to remember as a group but, simultaneously, to be alone with their private memories. Bartlett's account of remembering was also one that sought to understand it as something both individual and social. One final aspect of this wider cultural setting is important. Bartlett's depiction of memory as reconstructive made remembering and forgetting inseparable, each necessarily implying the other. A similar symbiosis exists in other writers, notably Freud, and Roth (1989) has argued that at various periods the balance between remembering and forgetting has been a matter of intense concern not only within psychology and psychoanalysis but also in society more widely (see also Billig, 1999). Bartlett offered a rich means of understanding this balance without recourse to the psychoanalytic ideas preferred by his immediate predecessors such as Myers, Brown, Rivers and Pear.

The richness of Bartlett's work on memory did not lead to a major and sustained programme of research. However, it would be too extreme to claim that his seminal work led to no research on memory. Soon after the book's publication, Oliver Zangwill, as a postgraduate student, conducted experiments at Cambridge looking at Bartlett's ideas in relation to recognition rather than recall. He also conducted experiments investigating the effects of attitude on recognition, which, although discussed in relation to Koffka's trace theory, were clearly related to Bartlett's ideas (Zangwill, 1937a,b, 1938, 1939). Other researchers in the 1930s and 1940s, not always in British universities, also used Bartlett's ideas when justifying their experiments and interpreting the data (examples are Taylor, 1947; Ward, 1949). Many of the articles in the early volumes of the *Quarterly Journal of Experimental Psychology*, the outlet of the recently founded Experimental Psychology Group, revealed Bartlett's continuing influence (see Belbin, 1950; Davis and Sinha, 1950a,b; Hall and Oldfield, 1950; Zangwill, 1950a; but see Kay, 1955). The fact that many of these researchers worked with Bartlett at Cambridge clearly played a part, but it does highlight the extent to which experimentalists oriented towards his work and its 'brilliant suggestion' (Oldfield and Zangwill, 1942a,b).

4   Memory and human performance

The Second World War was a watershed in the growth of British psychology (Hearnshaw, 1964; Rose, 1989; see also Bourke, Chapter 6). Techniques of personnel selection, the measurement and promotion of morale, performance under extreme conditions and the dynamics of groups were all topics profoundly affected by the war and psychology's engagement with it. In the First World War, British psychologists had been involved in research on how suited men were to particular tasks and on the abilities of men to perform certain tasks. The increased complexity of the weaponry and equipment used in the Second World War made it more urgent to consider how to design machines and tasks that took human capabilities into consideration. Although the importance of this new perspective was voiced by several key figures in British psychology, it was put most crisply by Cyril Burt:

> Training may be regarded as a method of adapting the man to the machine. But the need for speed and efficiency may also at times be better satisfied if the machine is adapted to the man. It is a principle that is well recognised in industrial psychology, yet constantly overlooked by the inventor and constructor. (Burt, 1942: 108)

Here was a potential role for experimental psychology, that is, the systematic exploration of how war technologies could be best designed given the psychological qualities of the person. The strengthened emphasis on studying the capacities of the human operator during the war was apparent in the early research at the Applied Psychology Research Unit in Cambridge (hereafter APU), one of the most important research institutions in British psychology after the Second World War.

The APU was founded in 1944 by the Medical Research Council (MRC) with Kenneth Craik as its first Director. Unsurprisingly, given his pivotal role in British academic psychology, Bartlett pushed for the establishment of such a unit beginning in 1943, at the Industrial Health Research Board.[11] From the outset, Bartlett made it clear that although he saw the work of such a unit as being a form of industrial psychology, he did not see vocational selection as a suitable topic for industrially related research. Instead, he highlighted work by Mackworth on the design of displays and by Craik on the design of machines as examples of the kind of psychological research that such a unit could undertake. He also emphasised the neglect of social aspects of industrial work when he argued that 'very nearly everything is yet to be done'. The fact that the APU became dominated by the experimental study of individual qualities, with very little being done on social psychology, is a further demonstration of the gap between Bartlett's advocacy of a socially grounded psychology and his activities in encouraging experimentally based research.

By 1944, the Psychology Department at Cambridge University had already been active in war-related research, looking, for example, at inspection of radar screens. When the APU was founded, it resided within the Department and its staff took on war-related research. After the war, much of the APU's research continued to be prompted by problems with a military aspect. In a paper in *Nature* announcing the founding of the unit, Craik described the early research of the APU as focusing on problems of display and control (Craik, 1944). Craik, and all his successors as Director, argued that although the problems studied were sometimes of an ad hoc nature, the scientific purpose of the unit was to extract from these apparently local problems more general principles concerning psychological capabilities.

Early on at the APU, little research was done on memory in and of itself. The war encouraged the approach adopted at the APU rather than a specific interest in human memory. Of the first 150 publications emanating from the unit, just two mention memory explicitly in their title: a paper by S.R. Nixon in 1946 (Nixon was not listed as a member of the APU staff at the time) which reported 'Some experiments on immediate memory' and a paper by Eunice Belbin in 1950 on the effects of interpolated recall upon recognition (Nixon, 1946; Belbin, 1950). In the 1949–1950 progress report for the APU,[12] almost certainly written by Mackworth, who became the second Director, the unit's principal research areas were listed as: bodily and mental skill, climatic psychology, problems and methods in the use of mental tests, and road research problems. A more detailed breakdown gave: experiments on thinking and perceiving, researches on skilled muscular movements, visual display problems, effects of abnormal environments, new devices, temperament and social studies, and, finally, statistical investigations. Little had changed in the report for 1950–1953 except, importantly, the word 'information' appeared in defining two of the main areas of interest and information theory was acknowledged as 'a potentially important new approach especially in the quantitative treatment of skill'.

Within the APU in the early 1950s, memory was not a separate topic of research but one which received scrutiny only to the extent that remembering was a component of a skilled task. For example, memory was discussed in the reports of some experiments by Harry Kay and Christopher Poulton, but these looked at memory as part of the general problem of anticipation on a task (Poulton, 1950; Kay and Poulton, 1951).

The real emergence of memory as a key area of the research programme of the APU appeared to come in the mid-1950s and arose in two ways: first, through increasing attempts to explain the performance of tasks using the information processing approach; and second, through the practical demands of research projects such as that sponsored by the Post Office on remembering telephone numbers, conducted by Reuben Conrad and later Alan Baddeley (see Baddeley, Chapter 17). In a short period of time memory became a perfect fit for the stated objectives of the APU, namely to observe and measure human behaviour in order to establish general principles of healthy human performance and to obtain knowledge of practical value. Tasks such as remembering telephone numbers required memory for short periods, and the intricate information processing models being constructed by Donald Broadbent gave a central role to short-term memory (Broadbent, 1958). When the 1960 report on the APU was published, Broadbent was typically cautious in his remarks when he concluded that:

> tentatively one may say that all these results, taken together with work from other laboratories, suggest the presence of a mechanism for short-term memory quite different from that used for long-term memory. Such a distinction has of course long been familiar in theories of the brain put forward by cyberneticists, since computing machines often have two types of memory. (MRC Applied Psychology Unit Progress Report, 1956–1960)

The 'work from other laboratories' referred to research such as that conducted by John Brown in the main department at Cambridge (and then Birkbeck) and in the United States by the Petersons (Brown, 1956, 1958, 1959; Peterson and Peterson, 1959). Crucially for memory research, by the late 1950s the APU had a new object to explore: short-term memory.

Short-term memory promised to be tractable and amenable to experimental work. It represented a circumscribed 'component' that could be described in terms of information theory and which, through its relation to physical devices and quantitative measurement, appeared an appropriate object for an experimental psychology. At least a part of memory was now defined and delineated in such a way that it seemed divorced from social contexts, and this allowed the experiment to be deployed, apparently unproblematically, as the method of investigation, while at the same time these laboratory-based studies promised some practical utility. The combination of memory as natural object, the experiment as the best investigative technique and the resulting knowledge as having utility was a seductive one and by the 1960s memory research was firmly established at the APU and continued to have a central role in the activities of the unit, and British experimental psychology, thereafter (Baddeley, 1976).

5 Conclusions

In this chapter I have traced in general outline some of the major shifts and changes in memory research in Britain until the late 1950s. I have claimed that the forms taken by research on memory and the proposed nature of memory itself were profoundly shaped by local and distal contexts. The innovative methods of Winch were markedly different from the clinical method that inspired the psychoanalytic writings on memory by Rivers, Myers, Brown and Pear. Similarly, the conceptualisations of memory produced in these two sites – the classroom and, for want of a better term, the clinic – were very different. Even though they apparently shared the experimental method, Bartlett's studies on remembering and studies at the APU of short-term memory conceived of memory very differently and conducted experiments of very different styles. Bartlett saw remembering as a richly contextualised activity, whereas short-term memory was regarded as a fixed and universal object; Bartlett's experiments expressly rejected statistics, whereas experiments on short-term memory were littered with them. The rhetoric used and the kinds of evidence recruited in these projects on memory varied considerably and the knowledge claims and the practices informed by them were not the same. The memory studies by Winch provided a view of memory that could affect practices in the schoolroom and his studies promised to guide such intervention if successful. The clinical experiences (rather than studies) of Myers, Pear, Brown and Rivers provided a view of memory that saw the balance between remembering and forgetting as essential to a person's sanity and offered remembering as evoked through talk as being a cure. The short-term memory investigated at the APU promised a means of designing technologies so that they could be used more efficiently, and when memory came to be a topic central to operating a technology so it became an object of investigation through experimentation and measurement.

Kurt Danziger has claimed that the tying together of psychological kinds, often interpreted as biological entities, with certain kinds of use in social practices has been crucial in establishing psychological experts and expertise (Danziger, 1997b). The same claim is being made here. Memory and formal training, psychoanalytic accounts of remembering and forgetting, and the properties of short-term memory were all studied in domains that were an interface between psychology and a set of social practices. In each of these cases there was not some hard-and-fast division between an isolated discipline and social practices and events (see also Thomson, Chapter 5). Rather than a reified separation of academic discipline from social settings, there was a permeable membrane between the activities of the psychologists and a variety of social practices.

Acknowledgements

I would like to thank Alan Baddeley, Alan Costall, Susan Condor, Graham Hitch, Sandy Lovie and Tom Ormerod for comment and discussion of the material in this chapter.

Notes

1 Roger Smith (Chapter 11) discusses this point in more detail in the context of Charles Sherrington's research. In psychology there are exceptions to the generalisation – see, for example, Middleton and Edwards (1990). See also the early work of Bartlett and early work by the sociologist Maurice Halbwachs, who regarded memory as something intrinsically social, where the rememberings of an individual could be understood only within the thought and rememberings of the groups to which the individual belonged (Halbwachs, 1980).

2 The relationship between learning and memory is a complex one and deserving of historical analysis. To address it adequately would require an international perspective and a separate chapter. However, the distinction outlined here is one that still holds sway in some quarters. For example, the influential cognitive psychologist John R. Anderson recently defined learning as 'the process by which long-lasting changes occur in behavioral potential as a result of experience' and memory as 'the record of the experience that underlies learning' (Anderson, 2000: 4–5). Such a distinction begs as many questions as it answers. For example, it clashes with all those views of memory that emphasise the processes of encoding and retrieval as part of memory's domain; it prompts disputes over memory as consisting of records that are accessed rather than memory as reconstructive (see below on Bartlett) and it finesses a whole set of issues around the concept of the memory trace (see Crowder, 1993; Sutton, 1998, for some discussion of these issues).

3 Disputes over what Freud meant by repression, and whether or not repression is wholly unconscious, have been conducted both by psychoanalysts and commentators on psychoanalysis. The issues are not of immediate concern here, but see Billig (1999) and references therein.

4 Recently, there has been something of a Rivers revival through Pat Barker's trilogy of novels *Regeneration*, *The Eye in the Door* and *The Ghost Road*, the associated film *Regeneration* and activities and publications arising from the anniversary of the Torres Strait expedition. See Herle and Rouse (1998).

5 For more on the important topic of psychological organisations 'outside' the discipline, see Thomson (Chapter 5).

6 Spirit photographs were claimed to capture on film the ghosts of the dead. Frequently, they were taken at funerals or services of commemoration. Some of the most famous were taken by Mrs Ada Deane of the Armistice Day in Whitehall, 1922, which claimed to show the ghosts of dead soldiers above the crowd. Although spirit photography preceded the war, interest in it became particularly widespread afterwards (Winter, 1995).

7 Interview with R.W. Pickford by J. Kenna, 4 June 1973. British Psychological Society Archive, Centre for the History of Psychology, Staffordshire University.

8 Beatrice Edgell (1929) made a somewhat similar claim in her contribution on 'Memory' in the *Encyclopaedia Britannica*; see Valentine (in press).

9 Bartlett himself commented on this issue. See Bartlett (1932: 85–86).

10 Given the relative paucity of private papers from or to Bartlett, that this was a strategy he deliberately adopted can only be speculation.

11 Letters from F.C. Bartlett in the minutes of the Industrial Health Research Board, Technology Sub Committee, 1943. Public Records Office, London, FD/1/4143.

12 These unpublished reports are held at the Applied Psychology Unit, Cambridge.

8

Social psychology and social concern in 1930s Britain

Martin Roiser

1   Social concern in postwar social psychology

The idea that psychologists might involve themselves in the study of social problems and issues in an endeavour to contribute to their solution is now well established. In British social psychology, we can turn to examples such as Michael Billig's (1978) study *Fascists*, and David Milner's (1975) work on children's ethnic identity. This sense of concern is also found in American social psychology, for instance in *The Authoritarian Personality* (Adorno *et al.*, 1950) and in the Readers in Social Problems series, which includes *War and Its Prevention* (Etzioni and Wenglinsky, 1970).

Dennis Howitt's (1991) book *Concerning Psychology: Psychology Applied to Social Issues* discusses the psychology of social problems and issues, and the differences between pure and applied psychology. He argues that pure, academic psychology has too high a status, tending to set the agenda for applied psychology, which may be, in consequence, of little relevance. He argues for a real-world psychology which rejects the 'inside-out approach' where psychology sets the agenda, in favour of:

> [an] outside-in approach, where the key features of psychology are the needs of the outside world beyond the individual and, perhaps more importantly, beyond the discipline. From this perspective psychology becomes significant only to the extent that it helps understand matters of real world interest. (Howitt, 1991: 4)

This characterisation is helpful in understanding the difference of approach between early social psychology and the social psychology of 1930s Britain and, more recently, that which became concerned with social issues and problems.

In this chapter I examine the emergence of a concerned social psychology in 1930s Britain. I look at the work of the Mass-Observation movement, which developed new ways of conducting social psychological research, in which large numbers of ordinary people 'spoke for themselves' and recorded their experiences of everyday life. I discuss its participative methodology, its relevance to contemporary social problems, its democracy of method and its interdisciplinary approach. However, I first examine the influences from the historical development of three social science disciplines – social psychology, sociology and social anthropology – which came together during the 1930s to form this socially concerned interdisciplinary tendency both in Mass-Observation and in more formal academic circles. I argue that previous social psychology lacked this sense of social concern, and that postwar social psychology has only gradually recovered it.

2   The development of social concern in the social sciences

2.1   *From social psychology*

The earliest psychology was firmly rooted in physiology and its relation to cognitive processes. Wundt's early writings, for instance, lacked a social dimension. In Wundt's (1920) later *Völkerpsychologie*, however, he sought to extend the scope of psychology beyond the physiological and the cognitive and into the social area. He argued that social psychology should deal with phenomena such as 'language, religion, custom, myth, magic and cognate phenomena' (Farr, 1996: 21). Defined in this way, it was clearly theoretically close to anthropology, and associated with the study of ancient society. The early academic intent of this social psychology was to establish that there was a social dimension to the emerging discipline of psychology. Its applied aspect was minor, as was its orientation to social problems.

French crowd psychology of the same period had a more obviously applied aspect. Gustave Le Bon's (1896) *The Crowd: A Study of the Popular Mind* made a number of practical points and recommendations following from his views about the irrationality of the crowd. He expressed grave concern about all forms of crowds. The jury was prone to emotional persuasion, and even voting was a dangerous collective activity. The fear of mass society and the principled opposition to democracy derived from Le Bon's conviction that the primitiveness of human society was just below the surface and could be easily and dangerously evoked by unscrupulous leaders and collective situations. Le Bon was concerned to discourage crowd phenomena as much as possible. It was social concern, but of a reactionary kind.

William McDougall's *An Introduction to Social Psychology*, initially published in 1908, was the first textbook in the discipline, although its contents differ dramatically from today's social psychology texts. In the introduction, he stated the ambition that psychology be recognised as the basis of the social sciences, and the book is devoted to an exposition of this argument. It was a successful publication, enjoying almost annual editions between 1908 and 1931. The text discusses the motives underlying human social life. Indeed, the front cover of the twenty-second edition of the book advertises it as:

[the] first successful attempt to replace the philosophies of Bentham and Mill by a consistent theory of human motives. In the first part the principal motive forces that underlie all the activities of individuals and societies are defined. The second part illustrates the way in which each of them plays its part in the life of society. (McDougall, 1931: front cover)

McDougall argued that there was a need to give the social sciences a better psychological foundation. His list of social sciences was long, and included ethics, economics, political science, philosophy of history and jurisprudence (McDougall, 1931: xxi). The book is taken up with lengthy discussion of general innate tendencies, the major instincts and the structure of character. It does not deal with the kind of research topics now associated with social psychology; indeed, remarkably little empirical research is considered. Certainly, there is no discussion of the application of research findings to the study and resolution of the social problems of human society.

His later book *The Group Mind* (1920) was intended as a sequel and recognised a weakness of the *Introduction to Social Psychology* in being insufficiently social in its approach. But this did not mean that the new book addressed the social psychological problems of everyday life. The opening chapters dealt with the social nature of mind, collective consciousness and the crowd. But the argument then developed in a more disturbing direction. Later sections of the book discussed the formation of races, nations and national character. He argued that:

> races bred in the tropics, are in fact incurable lotus eaters, their chief desire is for the afternoon life or, as is commonly said of the Malays throughout the Eastern Archipelago, they are great leg-swingers…. Contrast with these the Northerly races, in Asia and Japan…. But more especially contrast them with the English people [whose] taste for and habit of effort, must be regarded as the most essential attribute, the profound and spontaneous quality of the race. (McDougall, 1920: 220–221).

Here he was influenced by the climatological determinism of Buckle, who is quoted five times in *The Group Mind*. Thus hot climates encouraged indolence while the warm Mediterranean gave space for the intellectual advances of Greece and Rome. McDougall noticeably neglects to offer an explanation for Rome's military prowess, but does attempt to apply the theory to northern Europe. Apparently, the backward, northern Celts, struggling against the cold climate, created a collective national consciousness from which they advanced with speed (McDougall, 1920: 223).

Richards (1997: 198) points out that McDougall maintained a scientific racist position, was a supporter of the eugenics movement, and wrote about 'eugenics and national decay'. It should be noted that he drew ideas from both Darwin and Lamark. He argued that collective mental advancement could occur and be passed on:

> We have found reason to believe that during the historic period the peoples of Europe have made no progress in innate qualities, moral or intellectual; yet that

the period has been characterised by immense mental development, a development essentially of the collective mind.... It is not to be regarded as a biological problem. It cannot be treated as a problem of economics or of politics; these sciences only touch its fringe at special points. (McDougall, 1920: 270)

However, McDougall (1920: 136) did not abandon biological determinism so much as elaborate it. He noted, for instance, that all races included individuals of high intelligence, evidenced by larger than normal skull sizes, quoting from the work of Le Bon. And he concluded that any racial group was thereby capable of generating a purposeful national consciousness that could lead to rapid social and economic progress. Nor did he abandon eugenics. In the concluding page of *The Group Mind*, he said that a modern nation may hope to progress:

> not only in respect of the intellectual and moral tradition, but also in respect of racial qualities; for a better knowledge of the factors at work and of the laws of heredity will enable them to put an end to the influences now making for race deterioration and to replace them by others of the opposite tendency. (McDougall, 1920: 301)

His racial theory thus combined climatological, biological and social psychological elements. It is of some reassurance that his writings in this area were considerably less influential than the textbook *Introduction to Social Psychology*, which continued to be republished. In 1931 he added a chapter on 'hormic psychology', which sought to explain behaviour in animals and man in a way which was both instinctive and purposive. In 1936, he wrote a final preface, in which he expressed the hope that the differing schools of psychology would move towards agreement, 'provided, of course, that our civilisation shall contrive to endure for so long a period' (McDougall, 1943: xxii). This dour proviso was appropriate. The period following witnessed the rise of the most deadly and extreme form of racism and nationalism. Fascism took hold over some of the most advanced nations, culminating in the Second World War and the Holocaust.

McDougall did not live to witness these events. He died in 1938. In his obituary in the *British Journal of Psychology*, J.C. Flügel (1939: 328) commented that, 'Early in his career he determined to devote himself to pure research into the secrets of human nature. This course he consistently pursued to the end.' This hints that a more applied social psychology might now develop. Thouless's textbooks *Social Psychology* (1925) and *General and Social Psychology* (1937) were in a sense sequels to McDougall's. Both books were designed to meet the syllabus requirements of the psychology section of the BSc (Econ) at London University. They may be seen as a systematic statement of the contemporary content of social psychology. In the preface of the later book he indicated a reduced use of the concept of instinct and an awareness of the importance of social class: 'The class system in modern civilised societies seems to me of the greatest practical importance for social psychology and to be strangely neglected by social psychologists' (Thouless,

1937: vi). However, the book is still structured around an instinctual physiological theme, with much discussion of instincts as the bases of social behaviour. While it includes chapters on language, warfare, religion and morality, the stress is still on the determinants of social behaviour rather than its flexibility, autonomy or the study of its everyday detail. It is noticeable that the chapter on social groupings, the topic most recognisable to a contemporary social psychologist, still begins with a discussion of herding animals, and goes on to discuss leadership, manners and national consciousness. Even eugenics gets a brief mention. The conclusion must be that social psychology in Britain had developed little in the early decades of the twentieth century. However, awareness of the need to apply social psychology to social problems and to study everyday life soon became evident in Bartlett *et al.*'s (1939) collection *The Study of Society: Methods and Problems*.

2.2 From sociology

Sociology advanced more rapidly in addressing social problems. Its development in nineteenth-century Britain was dominated by the study of poverty. The initiative for this came largely from outside academia. Friedrich Engels' *The Condition of the Working Class in England* (1845/1969) was one of the first studies, written in 1844 and based on official data and on his own meetings with workers. Charles Booth (1902/1980) studied poverty in London. His account was that of a wealthy ship-owner shocked by the extent of poverty and its threat to the social order. He used truant officers as informants. Seebohm Rowntree's (1901/1980) study of poverty had the approach of a social administrator. These studies were concerned to describe in detail the facts of poverty, especially urban poverty, and to propose solutions.

Engels' book was published in Germany long before it appeared in English. It was probably read by the worker-intellectual Adolf Levenstein (1912), whose book contains no references. He carried out a questionnaire study which examined the attitudes and feelings of German workers in a surprisingly modern psychological manner and concluded that factory life was psychologically debilitating. His work was quoted by Erich Fromm (1984: 41) as 'a social psychological enquiry which used a questionnaire like our own to capture attitudes and behaviour'. It was seminal to Fromm's work and in turn to the authoritarian personality study carried out in postwar America (Adorno *et al.*, 1950).

This sequence of studies, from Engels to Adorno, links periods of social crisis in mid-nineteenth-century England, Germany at the turn of the century and in the late 1920s with postwar America. Over time, the studies became less sociological and more social psychological. This shift focused attention on particular social problems, such as prejudice and authoritarianism. The authoritarian personality researchers saw their work as 'action research', and recommended liberal childrearing and educational practices to create open-minded and unprejudiced individuals (Adorno *et al.*, 1950: 972; see also Roiser and Willig, 1995).

2.3 From social anthropology

Social anthropology was orientated towards social application, though in a different way and in a distant arena. As the European empires expanded, social anthropologists were sent to study far-off societies and advise on their government. This research also took on a more academic aspect, as the study of human social evolution.

An intriguing idea developed that techniques of social anthropology might be of value in studying the problems of modern society. Social anthropology had two methodological strengths often lacking in other social sciences. First, it examined the detail of everyday life, using systematic observation. Second, it sought to encapsulate the whole of the society it was examining, its entire culture, while other social sciences tended towards their own particular topics, like poverty or prejudice. Its weakness was that it was prone to an elitist approach which saw peoples and cultures arranged in a hierarchy from primitive to advanced. This approach was clearly evident in the writing of McDougall. But such an attitude was not obligatory, as we shall see.

3   The shock of the 1930s and the dilemma of social psychology

The period of the First World War saw psychologists gainfully employed in government and military service (see Bourke, Chapter 6). In the postwar period, it seemed that their skills could be used in the better running of society. The boom of the 1920s encouraged such optimism. However, by the end of the decade things were not going well. The societies of America and Northern Europe seemed destined to repeat the crises and collapses of the earlier part of the century.

Social and psychological science seemed to have little to offer those addressing social problems. Eugenic writing like McDougall's was unhelpful and R.B. Cattell's (1937) *The Fight for Our National Intelligence* was alarmist and its recommendations retrograde. In Britain, Thouless's later textbook showed some shift towards practical social concern. But, in America, Murchison's (1935) *Handbook of Social Psychology* starkly illustrated its lack of social relevance. Eight of its 23 chapters concerned social behaviour among animals and plants. Another four concerned the social history of the 'Negro', 'Red Man', 'White Man' and 'Yellow Man'. None of these chapters made much contact with the problems of contemporary society. Only about one-third of the chapters (such as that by Allport, on attitudes) concerned topics of social relevance. The problem was clearly evident to Murchison, whose preface said:

> The social sciences at the moment stand naked and feeble in the midst of the
> political uncertainty of the world. The physical sciences seem so brilliant, so clothed
> in power by contrast. Either something has gone all wrong in the evolution of the
> social sciences, or their great day in court has not yet arrived. It is with something
> akin to despair that one contemplates the piffling, trivial, superficial, damnably

unimportant topics that some social scientists investigate with agony and sweat. And at the end of all these centuries, no one knows what is wrong with the world or what is likely to happen to the world. (Murchison, 1935: ix)

This is a sad and poignant statement. Even its faith in the physical sciences was brought into question during the following decade, after the experience of the Second World War and the development and use of nuclear weapons.

But it was just at this period that people began to turn to the social sciences for possible solutions to the problems of society. In Britain in the 1930s, a number of social scientists began to show an increasing concern with contemporary social problems: poverty and mass unemployment, the growth of irrational opinions and right-wing movements, the crisis of government and the drift towards war. The impetus for these studies came from several social science disciplines and also from outside academia. Of the trio of social psychology, sociology and social anthropology, social psychology seemed unlikely to form the basis of an inter-disciplinary joint effort to study contemporary social problems. However, a paper by O.A. Oeser, entitled 'Methods and assumptions of field work in social psy-chology', given at the 1936 meeting of the Psychology Section of the British Association for the Advancement of Science, put forward the idea of an inter-disciplinary 'anthropology at home'. The paper was published in the *British Journal of Psychology* in April 1937. The editor, F.C. Bartlett, thought the matters raised sufficiently important to add an appeal for further discussion, saying that the article:

> deals with fundamental aims and methods in a series of coordinated social researches in a Scottish area which are being carried out under the general direction of the author, Dr. A. O. Oeser. It is considered desirable to publish this contribution forthwith in the hope that it may stimulate discussion and research, since the methods and ideas put forward appear to possess a very wide application. (Bartlett, 1937)

However, over the next three years, there was no response to the editor's request. It was not that Oeser was an outsider – he had contributed a long review of Koffka's *Gestalt Psychology* (Oeser, 1936) in a previous issue of the journal. But social psychology was a minority research interest. Most papers were about statistics, psychometrics and perception. Though McDougall was still contributing, he was concerned with Lamarckian inheritance. It was not until 1941 that social psychologist Marie Jahoda, at Cambridge University, contributed a paper giving 'a descriptive analysis of the factory situation as experienced by the factory girl', in which she referred to Oeser's paper (Jahoda, 1941).

But there was a much faster response from elsewhere. Oeser's paper at the British Association meeting had been noticed by anthropologist Tom Harrisson. He was intrigued by the idea of an 'anthropology at home' and directly set out to implement Oeser's proposal under the heading of 'Mass-Observation'.

4   Mass-Observation: a new form of social psychology

4.1 *Origins, allies and techniques*

In 1934 Tom Harrisson, schooled at Harrow and a student of zoology at Cambridge, went on an expedition to the island of Malekula in the New Hebrides. His original purpose was to study ornithology, but he soon became more interested in the local humans. He wrote a book about them, ironically called *Savage Civilisation* (Harrisson, 1937), which was successfully published by Gollancz. He praised their ability to sustain their own culture despite successive waves of colonial invasion, which had brought disease, death and semi-slavery. Harrisson returned to Britain in 1936 to find 'advanced' society in a state of social and economic crisis. Short of money and out of work, he took a job in a textile factory in Bolton. In this differently strange culture he found himself continuing to make observations of everyday life in the manner of a social anthropologist. At this time he encountered Oeser's article calling for an 'anthropology at home' and considered that this was just what he was doing. He joined with journalist Charles Madge and pioneering documentary film-maker Humphrey Jennings and together they wrote a letter to the *New Statesman and Nation* which outlined their research topics and appealed for volunteer diarists and field workers.

They argued that the concept of Mass-Observation developed 'out of anthropology, psychology and the sciences that study man'. The initial topics suggested reflected an anthropological bias:

> behaviour at war memorials, the aspidistra cult, football pools, anti-semitism, diffusion and significance of dirty jokes, funerals and undertakers, female taboos about eating and the private lives of midwives. (Harrisson *et al.*, 1937)

While this was an odd list, the anthropological influence in Mass-Observation's work was generally an advantage. It led Harrisson, Jennings and Madge to attempt a comprehensive study of British society. And their lack of funding ensured a participative approach. They rapidly recruited a panel of 1,500 diarists and a number of full-time volunteers. Though their work was in a sense amateurish, they were insistent on their commitment to scientific method:

> The subject demands the minimum of prejudice bias and assumption; the maximum of objectivity. It does not presuppose there are any inexplicable things. Since it aims at collecting data before interpreting them it must be allowed to doubt and re-examine the completeness of every existing idea about humanity while it cannot afford to neglect any of them. (Harrisson *et al.*, 1937)

Mass-Observation did not regard itself as a lone organisation. There were others engaged in similar activities, some of whom are listed in Madge and Harrisson's programmatic book *Mass-Observation* (Madge and Harrisson, 1937: 60):

1 Institute for Social Research (Frankfurt School)
2 Folklore society

 3 Institute of Sociology
 4 St Andrews University Group
 5 Social Psychologists Group
 6 Edinburgh Group of Physical Anthropologists
 7 Peckham Health Centre
 8 Political and Economic Planning
 9 Industrial Welfare Society
10 National Institute of Industrial Psychology
11 National Council for Mental Hygeine

The list is intriguing. Social psychology is well represented, with the Social Psychologists group from Cambridge and London Universities, the St Andrews University Group, coordinated by O.A. Oeser, and the Frankfurt School, which had a London office at the time. Anthropology, both social and physical, is represented. The presence of the Edinburgh Group of Physical Anthropologists suggests that physical anthropology, often associated with the pseudo-science of racial classification, could be put to more useful purposes, along with the Peckham Health Centre, which was described as studying 'health and behaviour in a free environment'. Families could register for free health care if they participated in a health survey. The Folklore Society is also included, though it is dismissively described as concerning 'obvious relics of the past'. The inclusion of Political and Economic Planning, subtitled in their account as 'fact-finding for social reconstruction', indicates Mass-Observation's hope that government would take note of their findings.

4.2 Asking questions and 'speaking for yourselves'

The researchers wanted to involve the people they were studying. They encouraged people to 'speak for themselves' and asked their panel of diarists to give accounts of everyday life and to respond to set questions on a monthly basis. There was a democratic principle at work, that an informed public and an informed government would lead to a better society. In addition, they carried out street surveys on particular topics, such as people's attitudes to crisis, war and science. In this respect, their activity might be seen as similar to that of the standard opinion pollster. But there were important differences. For example, their questions were often open-ended and so the responses were phrased in the respondent's own terms. Thus, the resulting report would typically quote individual responses, prefaced by, for example, 'Woman, middle class, said…' as well as percentages of responses in given categories, such as those expecting war and those expecting peace. They also set their work in a reflexive context. Thus, when the British Association for the Advancement of Science issued an appeal for 'popular science', Mass-Observation went on to the streets and asked what ordinary people thought about science and scientists.

Interestingly, it was exactly at this time that the opinion poll, developed in America by social psychologists Gallup and Allport, was brought to England. The British Institute of Public Opinion (BIPO) was set up in 1937. For a while, both organisations' findings were published in the *News Chronicle*. While the BIPO was more methodologically precise, Mass-Observation painted a rich and more immediate picture. Angus Calder, introducing a new edition of *Britain by Mass-Observation*, argued as follows:

> Whatever reservations must be expressed about their use of statistics, this chapter remains extremely gripping. It surely provides the first comprehensive and sophisticated account of British public opinion in rapid flux. If it did not exist, BIPO polls of the day would tell us something about that stage of opinion – but Gallup's techniques do not provide that means of recreating, as 'Britain' does so vividly, the atmosphere of the Munich period. (Harrisson and Madge, 1939/1986: xi)

4.3 Observation, estrangement and intervention

The standard advice given to the anthropological observer was to regard the observed situation as strange and unfamiliar, to 'pretend you are a man from Mars'. This was not hard in the New Hebrides, but was more difficult in Britain. However, sometimes this problem was readily overcome. Some full-time observers had been educated in public schools and universities. They found Bolton and Blackpool very strange. The difference was that their observations were conducted across a gulf of class, rather than of culture, as in the New Hebrides. For instance, Mass-Observation's photographer, Humphrey Spender, said he would have been afraid to talk to those he observed: 'I would have been terrified. The whole difficulty for me there was what happens when you talk to them. They are total

Table 8.1 *Observational techniques used by Mass-Observation*

Category	Techniques
Observation	Accounts of people's behaviour and appearance, together with descriptions of locations and conversations
Overheards	Heard items of conversations on specific topics
Follows	The practice of following an unsuspecting subject
Counts	Counting people entering or leaving premises or wearing a particular item
Participant observation	An observer would attend a meeting or take a job
Indirects	Accounts of conversation engaged in where the observer would steer the discussion towards a researched topic
Directs	A standard street or door-to-door interview
Informals	Open and unplanned interviews of people with particular knowledge

Adapted from Varley (1987: 11).

foreigners, it was acutely embarrassing' (Spender, 1987: 6). Nonetheless, the pictures he took are now regarded as a valuable and sympathetic documentation of 1930s working-class life. Halla Beloff (1985: 146) commented: 'Although Spender characterises himself as a spy from another planet and tells how his language and accent diverted him from the people, there seems to be no "distance" or patronage in his pictures.'

Mass-Observation developed a list of observational techniques, which are summarised in Table 8.1.

In anthropological research into an ancient society which was assumed to have been static for many generations, effort was made to leave it unchanged. This was intended to protect that society and to leave it available for future researchers. In Mass-Observation's study of British society, that ethic was largely discarded. It was a society in rapid flux, indeed in social crisis. The researcher and the researched were members of the same society and the research process was intended to inform them both.

4.4 *Media analysis*

Mass-Observation was fascinated by the media. Harrisson was an able writer and journalist and could not forget the ridicule heaped upon him by his Melanesian hosts when he wrote down his notes at the end of each day. This made him acutely aware of the peculiarly cultural nature of writing and of the importance of the media in modern society. By the same token, he was intrigued that modern newspapers continued ancient practices such as astrology and horoscopes. Mass-Observation's reporters would ask people about their attitudes and their reactions to the media, whether they relied on them for information and whether they trusted the papers.

5   Studies carried out by Mass-Observation

5.1 *People's attitudes*

In a study entitled 'Crisis' in September 1938, Mass-Observation asked people's views on the danger of war (Harrisson and Madge, 1986). They first asked how people formed their views: 35% said newspapers, 17% said friends, 13% said radio, and 8% said 'own opinion'. But they noted that people distrusted the papers; a woman of 33 said, 'I read all the papers on it. I don't understand the politics of it, but they are all different. That's why people have less faith in the papers' (p. 30). They asked people whether they thought there would be a war (Table 8.2).

5.2 *Everyday lives, Worktown and Holidaytown, 12 May*

The major field studies were carried out in Bolton (termed 'Worktown') and Blackpool ('Holidaytown'). A fieldwork team hired premises and set to work.

Table 8.2 *Examples of responses to Mass-Observation's question 'Will there be a war?*

Respondent	Comments
The majority thought there would not:	
A taxi driver, 40	There'll not be a war. It's all paper talk. Its serious, though the papers make it worse
Man, 60, lower middle class	No possibility of war, we're building up a huge army, etc., only for defence
Worker, 50	I think the present policy will keep us out of trouble
Curate, 30	We are quite safe
Others were less certain:	
Worker, 17	Reckon we're in for a war
Worker, 50	There's trouble brewing, these armaments are not for nothing
Worker, 25	Not yet. If Czechoslovakia is invaded there will be a war
Other responses illustrated uncertainty and even fatalism:	
Man 45, landlord of pub	I can't think, I hope it comes to nothing
Woman, 40, worker	If the bomb has got your name on it, it's all up with you. That's that, I don't read the newspapers

Source: Harrisson and Madge (1986: 54–55).

People were observed going about their everyday lives: they were interviewed in their homes; they gave accounts of their working lives and family experiences; they were observed in pubs, shops, in the street, shopping, attending church, at football matches. Notes were made, interviews were taken down. Humphrey Spender discreetly took photographs.

From the study in Bolton there emerged a sympathetic picture of a strong and confident working-class community. Its industry was in decline and many families were not well off. But the rhythms of work and leisure continued. People discussed and argued, went to the shops and cinemas, attended football matches and voted in elections.

The study of leisure in Blackpool used similar methods. Here the observers were looking at people whose lives were briefly freed from the daily routines of working life. The theme of the observations concerned entertainment, superstition and sex. This last aspect has been reasonably criticised for intrusiveness. Nonetheless, the study reached the unexpected conclusion that 'in relation to the number of persons on holiday in Blackpool, the amount of extra-marital actual sexual intercourse is negligible, less than on a Saturday night in Worktown' (Calder and Sheridan, 1985: 60).

A further research study examined people's experiences of the coronation of King George VI on 12 May 1937 (Jennings and Madge, 1937). This study was full of anthropological redolence. It was a king-making ceremony, and one in which heads of state from other countries were invited to witness the crowning of an imperial majesty. It was an opportunity to study the whole of British society for a single day, to take a snapshot of an entire culture. All the members of Mass-Observation were asked to record their activities and experiences. These were collected and assembled by Humphrey Jennings, who used the skills of a modern film editor to create a coherent report of the entire day. It included those present at the coronation and those far away in the countryside, patriots and peace campaigners, monarchists and republicans.

For scientific comparison the observers were also asked to carry out the same exercise on an ordinary day, 12 March. Interesting comparisons emerge. On 12 May there was a sense of coherence and common reference to the coronation. All minds were focused on this one event, even those not interested or sympathetic were drawn into the common experience. On 12 March, there was a much greater sense of individuals going about their daily lives, with a mixture of separate and shared experiences.

5.3 Superstition, media and science

Mass-Observation was aware that there was a complex relationship between the views of the ordinary person and those circulating in the media. They criticised the papers for attributing particular, and sometimes contradictory, opinions to the entire public, with no scientific justification and with the danger of creating a crisis mentality. They were particularly critical of journalists and politicians who encouraged anti-scientific attitudes and belief in horoscopes. They noted that interest in horoscopes increased at times of social crisis. They recorded the horoscopes on the day of the Munich crisis, 30 September 1938:

> 'Be discreet' / 'don't repeat scandal' / 'take care you do not betray secrets through lack of thought' / 'rumour and scandal are abroad which you can ignore' / 'keep your own counsel about immediate plans' / 'pay no heed to rumours or scandal they are probably false' / 'you can't depend on the accuracy of news or information' / 'defer important decisions' / 'take care what you put in writing' / 'not a good day to sign a business agreement' / 'be on guard against fraud' / 'defer important journeys if you can' / 'not a good day to sign documents'. (Harrisson and Madge, 1986: 20)

But it was to no avail. Chamberlain signed the Munich agreement. Harrisson and Madge railed against the fatalism that the media encouraged in their audience.

During the war the media played a crucial role in national life. Mass-Observation felt that the hostility of the media to science generally, including social science, was a serious problem. They followed the media coverage with care. For example, the archive contains an interesting collection of clippings of editorial comments from four national newspapers on the deployment of radar. Harrisson notes the differing attitudes of the journalists to this important scientific and technical development. Most sympathetic to the scientists was the *News Chronicle*:

> It is authoritatively stated that the new anti-aircraft barrage is based on new methods of prediction which have proved an undoubted success. As time goes by and the experience is gained that success is likely to grow. The nation's thanks are due in no small part to the scientists whose labour in comparative obscurity will help to lighten the burden of the war for millions.[1]

Much less sympathetic was the *Sunday Times* (29 September 1940), which pronounced:

> Just as the long-bow overcame the heavy armour the depth-charge the submarine, and the tank trench warfare, so will the effective answer to the night raider be forthcoming. Public optimism, so admirably maintained, will doubtless continue steadfast until ideas, only rudimentary three weeks ago are translated into destructive action. A great deal of ingenuity is being devoted to this subject since scientists have had their own rest, convenience and comfort to consider. Germany, by its persistence and brutal attacks on London may find that it has stimulated a reply to this form of warfare which will cost it dear.[2]

Harrisson's clippings illustrate the range of attitudes to science held by different newspapers. Indeed, Mass-Observation became involved with a campaign to popularise science and to impress upon government the importance of science in the war effort. Although the media image of scientists improved during the war, the public discussion of scientific matters was limited for security reasons. Scientific matters were considered to be 'very hush-hush'. This attitude was relaxed somewhat when the radio programme 'The Brains Trust' included among its panellists the biologist Julian Huxley, who was an able populariser of science and a keen supporter of Mass-Observation. The risk of his revealing any scientifically sensitive material was slight, as he was not involved in research of military importance. Feelings of ordinary people about science and writings of journalists were monitored by Mass-Observation before during and after the war.

6   The development and decline of Mass-Observation

Between 1937 and 1939, Mass-Observation grew rapidly, published widely and courted controversy. It founded and promoted a democratic do-it-yourself social science with considerable success. It was part of a wider documentary and interventionist movement within the social sciences and it gained supporters in the academic world. But the war profoundly affected the movement. It became harder to conduct street interviews. One member of Mass-Observation, Nina Hibbin, recalled that she was arrested while interviewing (*New Statesman*, 31 May 1985). She produced a list of their academic sponsors, whom the police regarded as 'rather foreign', but was released once her credentials had been checked.

Although panel members continued to write, publication was curtailed. In 1941 Harrisson wrote:

> Every bit of stuff is read, filed and put well out of bombs way. We can't publish much now. After the war we promise to tell a unique almost incredible story. Your help is making, and will make the piecing together of this story possible. (*Mass-Observation Bulletin*, October 1940)

Their numbers were reduced. Harrisson volunteered for active service and Charles Madge joined National Institute for Economic Research (Varley, 1987: 20). However, in another respect, Mass-Observation was a beneficiary of the war. The Ministry of Information began to commission studies, for instance on morale during the Blitz and popular feeling about rationing. Towards the end of the war, Mass-Observation began to conduct anticipatory market research, which became the basis of a commercial market research organisation after the war. In the postwar period, Mass-Observation declined. Harrisson went to the Far East to curate an anthropological museum, though still remained in contact. The panel ceased activity, publication tailed off and the movement almost entirely disappeared from view. Awareness of its activity was revived with the publication of Angus Calder's (1969) *The People's War* and the establishment of the Mass-Observation archive at the University of Sussex in the 1970s. It is not surprising that the social historical aspect of Mass-Observation then took precedence over its social science aspect.

7   Convergence of social psychology and Mass-Observation

In 1939 a collection was published, *The Study of Society: Methods and Problems*. Edited by Bartlett, Ginsberg, Lindgren and Thouless, it sought a synthesis of the social sciences and addressed itself to the problems that society faced towards the end of the 1930s. The leading discipline was social psychology. Indeed, the 23-strong group of authors whose discussions led to the book called itself 'the social psychological discussion group' (p. xi), although its membership included sociologists and anthropologists as well as clinical, industrial and experimental psychologists. The group began meeting in the summer of 1935 and took four years to complete the book. The ethos was democratic; draft chapters were circulated among the group and revised following discussion. The editors remarked that:

> the contributions in their final form represent views concerning which a very substantial degree of agreement has been achieved. It is not infrequently said that when psychologists, anthropologists or sociologists meet little but disagreement emerges. This book may be regarded as a practical rebuttal of such a charge. (p. viii)

The departure from the group of R.B. Cattell to go to America was briefly mentioned (p. ix) and it is possible that he did not share the group consensus.

His eugenic views were clearly set out in *The Fight for Our National Intelligence*, published in 1937, while the group was still meeting. He might, for instance, have disagreed with Nadel's discussion of anthropological objections to the cross-cultural use of intelligence tests in his chapter, 'The application of intelligence tests in the anthropological field'.

T.H. Pear's opening chapter, 'Some problems of social psychology', argued that there were certain social problems that psychologists had not, until recently, addressed; indeed, they had been avoided. His list included: social stratification; the inevitability of war; and propaganda in cinema, radio and television and in the coronation of 1937. Oeser, contributing to this chapter, discussed Lazarsfeld and Jahoda's pioneering social psychological study of unemployment in Marienthal, a one-factory Austrian village where the factory had closed, and the later studies it inspired in London and Dundee. Methodological issues of systematic and unsystematic observation, interviews and indirect questionnaires were included, and the role of the amateur investigator was discussed.

What takes place in this book is the kind of discussion which Bartlett called for in the *British Journal of Psychology* in response to Oeser's 1937 article, and which so evidently did not take place in the pages of that journal. The convergence of topics and techniques with those of the Mass-Observation movement is striking – such as the use of field work, the blend of observation and interview, the reference to the coronation, and the reference to Jennings and Madge's 12 May survey.

The book is also critical of conventional social survey techniques. A.F. Wells' chapter on social surveys gives an account of the studies of poverty by Booth and Rowntree. He complains that these studies did not deal with the whole of society, but only with one section of it: 'these studies are incomplete without a study of the middle-class' (Bartlett *et al.*, 1939: 430). This point exposes the nineteenth-century assumption that the working class was the object of research by the middle class, from whose ranks came the researchers. This is a weakness that Mass-Observation did their best to avoid, with their use of participative techniques.

Thus, during the 1930s, a broad, applied and socially concerned social psychology was created which was partially merged with sociology and social anthropology. Mass-Observation represented the more popular and interventionist wing of this activity, seeing social research as a participative activity with rapid feedback of findings through newspapers and bulletins. Their books were published within months of writing. The Bartlett *et al.* collection represented the voice of leading academic figures of the time. Their discussions were more drawn out, and their approach less participative. But both brought together the social sciences of social psychology, social anthropology and sociology in a concerted attempt to address the problems of British society at the time.

But, as with Mass-Observation, this initiative went into decline. Postwar social psychology seemed largely to forget the role that it had played in the interdisciplinary movement of the 1930s. Oeser emigrated to Australia. The *British*

Journal of Psychology remained the main outlet for the publication of social psychological research. Only in 1962 was the *British Journal of Social and Clinical Psychology* launched. Prominent on the editorial board were psychologists whose interests spanned the clinical and social areas, for instance Hans Eysenck and Michael Argyle (see Argyle, Chapter 16). British social psychology did not have its own journal until 1981.

Nonetheless, some applied interdisciplinary activity continued. In 1962 a book was published entitled *Society: Problems and Methods of Study*, edited by Welford, Argyle, Glass and Morris. Despite the striking similarity of title with the earlier *The Study of Society: Methods and Problems*, there is no reference to it. Nor is there any feel of collaborative activity and social purpose. The later book was addressed to a more professional and academic audience. The cover boldly proclaimed that 'No student of sociology, social psychology or social administration will be able to do without this volume'. It provided 'an authoritative introduction and outline to the main areas in which knowledge of social behaviour exists' (Welford *et al.*, 1962: 1). This contrasts with the earlier book's 'recognition of the fact that the future of human civilisation depends upon Man's capacity to understand the forces and factors which control his own behaviour' (Bartlett *et al.*, 1939: vii). The future of civilisation now seemed more assured and social science became more concerned with issues of social administration. The chapters on social surveys and censuses are interesting but conventional and uncritical. There is also a striking academic shift in the later book: only two of the 30 chapters are concerned with social psychology and social anthropology gets barely a mention. Somewhere the intellectual concerns and radicalism of 1930s British social science had been lost.

8   A new tradition

However, in the postwar period, a new focus of radical interdisciplinary social science developed, in North America. This drew considerably on the work of exiled European social scientists, who joined forces with American scholars. A number came from the Frankfurt Institute of Social Research. Others included Paul Lazarsfeld and Marie Jahoda, whose research on Cambridge factory girls was part of the British 1930s tradition. There was intensive study of prejudice and authoritarianism, the major example of which was *The Authoritarian Personality* (Adorno *et al.*, 1950). This research was subsequently strenuously attacked by the American political theorist E.A. Shils and the British psychologist Hans Eysenck. Indeed, some American psychologists, such as Martin Brewster Smith (1986), suffered political oppression in the Cold War atmosphere of the time. However, the tradition survived and continued. Indeed, its influence returned across the Atlantic.

A new trend in British social psychology emerged in response to the problems and concerns of the 1960s and drew inspiration from this tradition to create a new psychology of social concern. For instance, Billig (1978) described *The*

Authoritarian Personality as a landmark in the study of prejudice and David Milner (1975) refers back to the work of Clark and Clark (1958) on the identity of black children. The work of American social anthropologist Erving Goffman was also influential. His studies of behaviour in public places and the organisation of social gatherings (Goffman, 1961) are reminiscent of Mass-Observation.

And, as in the 1930s, there are two sides to the new movement, the one more academically orthodox, seeking to apply social scientific techniques to understanding and hopefully the resolution of social problems. Such a description applies to the experimental studies of intergroup discrimination carried out by Henri Tajfel (Tajfel *et al.*, 1971), to the subsequent flowering of work on intergroup behaviour (Turner and Giles, 1981) and to critiques such as *The Context of Social Psychology: A Critical Assessment* (Israel and Tajfel, 1972). On the other hand, some of those involved in this new trend in social psychology have adopted a more radical attitude. This has involved participating in the movements of the time, for instance anti-psychiatry (see, for instance, Sedgwick, 1982), and adopting a much more strenuous philosophical critique of contemporary social psychological theory and methodology (Ibanez and Iniguez, 1997) and the adoption of more qualitative and participative methods.

An interesting difference with the 1930s is that while Harrisson and the members of Mass-Observation were concerned to insist on the scientific nature of their work and sought to defend themselves against accusations that their techniques were less than scientific, the new radical social psychology offers a critique of science. But in other ways there are many similarities. Many of the methodological aspects of this new work are prefigured in Mass-Observation – techniques of observation, of informal interview, of participant observation, of media analysis and a concern with everyday language, discourse and social interaction. Indeed, some of these techniques have found their way into mainstream social psychology, such as Manstead and McCullogh's (1981) content-analytic study of sex-role stereotypes in television advertising. The recent interest of social psychologists in the public understanding of science is also reminiscent of Mass-Observation (see, for example, Evans and Durant, 1989).

These new developments in social psychology have happened in almost entire ignorance of the history of Mass-Observation. Awareness of its work has come about only recently and indirectly – perhaps through Halla Beloff's (1985) book, *Camera Culture*, which provided a sympathetic account of Spender's photography; perhaps through the republication of several Mass-Observation publications during its fiftieth anniversary in 1987 and the revival of its panel of diarists; perhaps through social psychologists at the Bolton Institute of Higher Education celebrating the important role their town played in Mass-Observation's earliest field research by organising an interdisciplinary conference there to mark its sixtieth anniversary. One way or another, the social scientific aspect of Mass-Observation's work is now becoming better known, and it is becoming not just a part of social science history but making a contribution to contemporary social psychology and to its relations with social science generally.

Acknowledgements

The author acknowledges financial support from a British Academy grant, AN 606APN/607, which helped the research for this chapter.

Notes

1 *News Chronicle*, 13 September 1940. Mass-Observation Archives, University of Sussex, Falmer, TC 34.
2 Mass-Observation Archives, TC 34.

9

Pear and his peers

Alan Costall

1   Getting started

Psychology, the new 'upstart subject',[1] was slow getting established within the British universities.[2] By 1939, there were just six chairs of psychology in all the universities of Britain, and three of these were in London. Of the small number of movers and shakers on behalf of the new discipline of psychology, most had trained as physicians, gone to Cambridge and met at St John's College. This tight social network was consolidated during a ramshackle expedition, organised by the Cambridge anthropologist A.C. Haddon, to the Torres Strait, in 1898 (see Kuklick, 1991; Herle and Rouse, 1998; Costall, 1999). Among this small group were two Cambridge students of psychology, Charles Samuel Myers and William McDougall, and their teacher, W.H.R. Rivers. McDougall, who became the Wilde Reader in Mental Philosophy at Oxford in 1904, has described the awkward position facing the new psychologists within the traditional university system:

> It was, I think, T.H. Huxley who said that, if he had to devise a punishment for a very wicked scientist, he would condemn him to be a professor of science at Oxford. If I had been recognized as a teacher of science, my punishment would have been light; for by that date science was well established at Oxford. But I was neither fish, flesh, nor fowl.... The scientists suspected me of being a metaphysician; and the philosophers regarded me as representing an impossible and non-existent branch of science. (McDougall, 1930: 207)

McDougall was explicitly forbidden by the terms of the Wilde Readership from conducting experimental work, although, according to his student, William Brown, a laboratory was established for a short time, until the space was taken over during the First World War 'for more urgent business' (Brown, 1936: 274).

Cambridge, often held to have been a model of scientific enlightenment compared with Oxford, also presented its problems. When Myers became the Director of the new Laboratory of Experimental Psychology in 1913, this was more an honour Myers bestowed – imposed – upon Cambridge, than the reverse: 'He planned it, to a very large extent in detail he designed it, he himself, his family and his friends, mostly paid for it. With some air of reluctance the University accepted it' (Bartlett, 1965: 4).

On returning to Cambridge after the First World War, Myers was keen to apply psychology to medicine, industry and education. He had become 'increasingly disgusted, after my very practical experience during the War, with the old academic atmosphere of conservatism and opposition to psychology' (Myers, 1936: 224). When the University insisted that his Readership should be restricted to *experimental* psychology, his dissatisfaction was complete (Myers, 1936; Bartlett, 1965), for not only was he keen that psychology should be applied to practical problems, but he also regarded scientific psychology itself as extending beyond the purely experimental.[3] Myers had already begun to make plans to found a National Institute of Industrial Psychology in London as early as 1918. His new Institute opened in 1921, and, after a year of leave from Cambridge, he resigned, once he had made sure the promised Readership would be handed on to his assistant, Frederic Bartlett.

Manchester was different. According to Denys Harding, the University of Manchester offered a friendly place for psychology, when 'psychology had such precarious footholds in the British universities'.[4] In fact, the ground was well prepared, long before the University came to appoint an experimental psychologist in 1909. Samuel Alexander, who joined the Philosophy Department in 1893, was already committed to what was then called the 'new psychology'. He had travelled to Freiburg to study experimental psychology with Münsterberg, during the academic session 1890–1891. He, along with Ward, Sully, Lloyd Morgan and Rivers, was one of the small number of early members of the (British) Psychological Society. One of Alexander's early students, May Smith, went on to became one of Britain's foremost industrial psychologists. By 1902, Alexander had already established an advanced laboratory class in experimental psychology, which took place in the basement of the main university building. Winifred Hindshaw has recorded her experiences as one of the five members of that class:

> I belonged to a small class doing Advanced Psychology with Professor Alexander (not to mention his famous terrier Griff) in the basement of the old building. We studied the special senses intensively, and did experiments relating to reaction times and attention. I think the apparatus in 1902–3 must have been rather simple. But we had a beautiful thing called a Plethysmograph which indicated pulse-changes, and therefore pleasure or pain according to the stimulus…. He was very interested in colour vision, and very precise about recording impressions…. He did not do hypnosis experiments with us, but he was interested in that side of inquiry. He had been to Nancy and knew about the work there.[5]

There were also other sources of support for psychology at Manchester. Several people connected with the Medical School, such as Lorrain Smith, the Professor of Pathology, were attempting to introduce reforms in the training of mental hospital superintendents, and were keen to institute a new course, the Diploma in Psychological Medicine. It also helped that for several years (from 1895 to 1913) the eminent physiologist Charles Sherrington had been based nearby at Liverpool, once affiliated with Manchester. Sherrington was an important source of support for psychology within Britain. He was one of the original members of the newly formed Psychological Society (later, in 1906, to become the British Psychological Society) and had appointed several psychologists to his own department (W.G. Smith in 1905, H.J. Watt in 1906, Cyril Burt in 1907). He was very encouraging about Manchester's plans to establish a new department of psychology: 'With Education and Medicine for your practical clients in addition to some B.Sc. men, your new department will find work enough at once I feel sure.'[6]

On 22 February 1907, the Senate Committee on Experimental Psychology recommended that a lectureship or readership should be established, arguing that it would be valuable to several existing departments:

> (a) *In Science* it would enable the subject to be treated thoroughly as a degree subject for pass and class....
>
> (b) *In Medicine*, in connection with the development of psychiatry and neurology....
>
> (c) *In Education*, in connection with the study of school children normal and abnormal and of the conditions of school life.
>
> (d) *In Philosophy*, in connection with the more extended study of Psychology for Honours and M.A.[7]

This report closed with the warning that the number of suitable candidates would be extremely limited. Alexander put a great deal of effort into seeking out an appropriate person, and his correspondence further demonstrates Alexander's own standing among within the new psychology. There are replies from, among others, William James, Hugo Münsterberg and James Ward about possible candidates. The Americans R.M. Yerkes and E.B. Holt were seriously considered for the post. James Ward wrote back that there was no suitable person available at Cambridge, because 'C.S. Myers, who is – I think – first rate, has just been snapped up by King's College'.[8] At one point, the Senate resolved to offer the new position, as a readership, to the subsequently eminent Charles Spearman, but evidently nothing came of that. Instead, in 1909 the post was offered to an undergraduate student, Tom Hatherley Pear, the subject of my chapter.

Pear is now a largely forgotten figure in British psychology, but I think his career is of historical significance for the following reasons. First, as a very young psychologist, he was exceptionally well 'placed' within early British psychology, and mixed with the central figures. Second, he spent his long career not in Oxbridge or London but in 'the provinces'. Third, he was genuinely interested in people, and was prepared to take on interesting issues shunned by most of his psychological peers. Finally, he was already being 'forgotten' even during his lifetime. And that is the most important point. Given his auspicious entrance into the discipline, the fact that Pear became increasingly marginalised surely tells us as much about British psychology as about Pear himself.

2   Getting networked

Pear had initially been a student of physics at King's College, London, but became convinced, when attending Myers' lectures, of the crucial psychological issue underlying all science, that scientific observation implies an *observer*:

> a great change suddenly happened to my 'world-view' [and] this caused a swing over from a belief that the essence of everything was physical and chemical, to one that physical scientists, in their attempts to penetrate the reality of the known, were deliberately ignoring the knower. I fell out of love with physics and chemistry, liking them now as friends. Henceforth the psychological point of view seemed all-important. As yet I took no interest in social psychology. The textbooks one read, Stout's *Manual* and *Analytic Psychology*, stretched the mind, but a long vacation, when I was absorbed in James's beloved *Principles*, made me realize that 'warmth' and 'intimacy', as he would have said, is a necessary part of genuine psychological treatment. (Pear, 1948a: 110; see also Pear, 1922: viii)

Furthermore, Myers had caught Pear's imagination as an unusually attractive person, interested in, and well liked by, other people:

> Myers was unusually many-sided: doctor, anthropologist, musician, Alpinist, traveller. Few psychologists had seen so many places. Though a fine experimentalist, he never believed that the most important things in life could be experimentally investigated or measured. There would never have been any need to remind him that all human psychology is social psychology or that society is made up of individual persons. (Pear, 1960: 233)

Half way through Pear's degree course, Myers left England, as Pear quaintly put it, to 'winter' in Egypt, and Spearman, based at University College London, kindly agreed to take him on. Pear attributed his own non-dogmatic approach to psychology to the fact that he had two such contrasting teachers, though, it seems Spearman failed to create the same positive impression. Spearman's military background tended to show through:

> I felt that his tone was that of any army instructor rather than of a lecturer; that for him the mind, like a rifle, had parts, the names and functions of which must be learned before one proceeded to the noegenetic principles – Army Council Instructions on the ways in which the mind ought to work. (Pear, 1962: 224)

Pear, along with the Cambridge psychologist Frederic Bartlett, became Myers' protégé. His arrival at Manchester, as Pear himself put it, 'resulted from a simultaneous push from Myers and a pull from Alexander' (Pear, 1962: 226). In fact, Pear was appointed to the staff at Manchester in the way that graduates, especially those from Cambridge, are supposed to have been enlisted to either the British or Soviet secret services:

> One dark winter afternoon I was walking along the corridor of the lab at University College with Shepherd Dawson ... he said 'Don't look round, but coming up behind us is one of the world's greatest philosophers'. Samuel Alexander was only about 50 then, but in his old black wide-brimmed professor's hat ... his shapeless overcoat and wide trousers fluted in Jacobean style, he looked 80. I little thought that Myers and this Rembrandt figure were about to shape my life. Soon after this meeting I sat for the final examination. About 4 days before the results were due to appear I received an express letter, at my lodgings in Bedford Park, from Alexander. It asked me to have coffee with him that morning in Hampstead, and to discuss 'without prejudice' ... the possibility of starting a department of psychology in Manchester, if I had got a 'first'.[9]

Pear obtained his first-class degree, but was not even subjected to an interview for the post. He was simply invited to stay with Alexander at his home, while important Manchester figures, such as W.H. Perkin, H.B. Dixon and Ernest Rutherford, dropped in and, as Pear put it, 'looked me over'.[10]

The University made Pear an offer he could hardly refuse. It undertook to complete his psychological education at its own cost. It arranged for him to go to Germany to study with Oswald Külpe at Würzburg, and also to learn German, though evidently Külpe was somewhat bewildered to be sent such an 'unfinished' psychologist.[11] After a few months back at Manchester, teaching his first six students there (one of whom he later married), Pear was off again to Germany, this time to spend the summer term studying with Robert Sommer at his psychiatric clinic at Giessen in Germany, to learn about innovations in the early treatment of the mentally ill.[12]

Pear arrived at Manchester in 1909. It was an especially exciting time. The Germanic culture of the town had not been dispelled by the First World War (Pickstone, 1992), nor, for that matter, had the war seriously depleted the University of student fees. The depression in the cotton industry was yet to come. Manchester was altogether an attractive place:

> Those were the days of trams and bicycles, when the nearby suburbs housed the University staff. The internal combustion engine had not yet begun its calamitous destruction of culture, of which the centrifugal trek from the cities was an early feature ... a *milieu* of easy 'dropping-in'. (Pear, 1939a: 317)

Pear found himself drawn into a 'wonderful community'.[13] He met with such figures as Elliot Smith, Rutherford, Weizmann and Bohr, for discussions about the latest developments in science, and they would continue their conversations at the French restaurant then at the Midland Hotel (Pear, 1960). He also quickly entered into the social life of the Medical School, being made a member of the 'Pathological Tea Club' (which, as Pear noted, fortunately failed to live up to its title). Through this society, and also through his close links with Lorrain Smith, he came to know two pathologists based in the region, David Orr and R.G. Rows. Although conducting basic pathological research with Lorrain Smith, Orr and Rows were later to make significant contributions to the reform of psychiatric treatment and education. Grafton Elliot Smith, who arrived at Manchester shortly after Pear, as the new Professor of Anatomy, had already developed an interest in both anthropology and psychology, thanks to his earlier contacts with Rivers. From the outset, Smith was prepared to take Pear seriously, and immediately agreed to act himself upon Pear's tentative proposal that the psychology students might benefit from lectures on the brain and the sense organs (Pear, 1931a: 5).

Pear's remarkable success, as a young man in his early twenties, in entering into the wider intellectual community at Manchester depended upon a number of factors. As a result of his visits to Germany, he had developed a distinctly cosmopolitan outlook. Also, as his son has explained to me, the Pear family had not been prone to the anti-Semitism then prevalent among many Anglican families. Furthermore, Pear's exceptional grounding in the new Continental developments in psychiatry was to prove an important asset in relation to his medical colleagues.

Pear was elected to the British Psychological Society in 1909, through the patronage of both Alexander and Myers. At that time, membership was supposed to be restricted to established researchers and teachers. Pear did, however, go on to make a promising start, publishing a sequence of papers in the early issues of the *British Journal of Psychology*. In 1911, there were two papers on the psychology of music, which related to the work by Myers in that field (Pear, 1911a,b). In 1914, there were three papers. One was on the role of repression in forgetting (Pear, 1914a). Another was a substantial study, conducted by Pear and one of his former students, Stanley Wyatt, on the reliability of children as witnesses (Pear and Wyatt, 1914):

> Pear, disguised as a salesman of educational material, came to Fielden School in the middle of a science lesson and, with the deftness of a conjuror, proceeded to extract a weird assortment of articles from a large black bag. The next day the children had to describe the event and then they were cross-examined in the best legal manner. (Wyatt, 1950: 66)

Pear was not really a dedicated experimentalist, however. Among his early papers, it was his evaluation of Freud's theory of dream interpretation that attracted most attention (Pear, 1914b). For one and a half years, Pear had engaged in what he described as an 'auto-analysis', an intensive study of his own dreams. His paper, based on analyses of just two of his dreams, while demonstrating many of Freud's proposals, did challenge the general claim, made by Freud, that the wishes fulfilled in dreams were necessarily of infantile origin and unconscious (see also Pear, 1922). When Pear arrived to speak about his work on dreams at the 1913 meeting of the British Association at Birmingham, the attendant, after conveying the good news that the room was completely full, then barred his entry, refusing to believe that the young man could be the speaker (Pear, 1955b: 24).

The First World War, although it put an end to the intimate, interdisciplinary community that had existed at Manchester, immediately thrust Pear into an even more intense intellectual environment, the Military Hospital established at Maghull near Liverpool. Not only the military authorities but also traditional psychiatry were generally antagonistic to the new psychology, as is very clear, for example, from Myers' account of his appalling experiences in France trying to rescue from execution soldiers suffering from so-called 'shell shock' (Myers, 1940). The contrast with Maghull could hardly be more extreme. From the very outset of the war, the hospital was converted for the psychiatric treatment of troops, both officers and 'other ranks', on an enlightened basis. The Medical Research Council (MRC), established in 1911, had close links with the War Office and Liberal politicians, and evidently regarded the war as a welcome opportunity to make its mark. The MRC took steps to set up the centre at Maghull, and appointed Ronald Rows as the Director. Rows invited Elliot Smith to join him, and Smith, in turn, enlisted Pear. Pear stayed there throughout the war and was engaged not only in teaching the medics but also in the therapeutic work with the soldiers.

Maghull quickly achieved the status of a psychiatric academy (Shephard, 1996).[14] The extensive list of psychiatrists and psychologists who came to be based at Maghull is impressive. They included Bernard Hart, John MacCurdy, Charles Seligman, C.S. Myers, William McDougall, William Brown and Millais Culpin. Elliot Smith also arranged for W.H.R. Rivers to join them, and it was at Maghull that Rivers had his first experience of working with shell shock and his first serious encounter with the ideas of Freud. Here is Pear's own account of working with Rivers at Maghull:

> An hour after his arrival, [Rivers] got down to work. He told me that his recent absence in the Pacific had prevented him knowing much about Freud. He was sure that Freud was a great thinker, whose concepts of the unconscious were overdue…. With impressive modesty, he suggested to my surprise that for a time I should direct his reading, and that we should go for afternoon walks and hammer things out together. So now I connect Freudian concepts, not with the Bergasse or with that city whose attractive culture and charm hid much envy, hatred and malice, but with the dull country of South Lancashire and the inspiring companion-ship of a traveller excitedly trying to supplement a life hitherto spent chiefly with dons and primitives. Round the fire in the evenings I listened avidly to Rivers and Elliot Smith discussing 'the mother's brother', the Oedipus complex and what Malinowski might say when he returned [from his field work] about the relations between sons and mothers in those distant lands. As a consequence, I never joined the 'all or nothing' band when thinking of Freud.[15]

In addition to his work at Maghull, Pear was later involved in research on auditory localisation to deal with the new military problem of detecting submarines, and Pear arranged for Myers to be brought back from France to help in this work at HMS Crystal Palace. Within the Navy, however, it seems that psychology was still the science that dare not speak its name. Furthermore, even though the research concerned *listening* for submarines, the authorities in their wisdom decided to give Pear and Myers the title of '*oral* specialists'.[16]

Pear, along with both Myers and Rivers, believed that British psychology had had a good war. At the end of the First World War, he published a paper in *Nature* setting out how he believed psychology had contributed to the war effort, and confidently predicting that psychology, as a result, would itself be transformed:

> greater emphasis will be laid upon the importance of instinctive and emotional factors and upon the power of non-rational beliefs to influence conduct…. 'Individual' and 'social' psychology can no longer be regarded as separate departments. The rather exclusively intellectualistic viewpoint of psychology will be enormously modified and supplemented. (Pear, 1918: 89)

The same air of confidence pervades *Shell Shock and its Lessons,* by Elliot Smith and Pear (Smith and Pear, 1917). As far as these authors were concerned, the experience of dealing with the war neuroses clearly indicated the need for two reforms: a restructuring of the hospital system to deal with mental disorders at the earliest stage, and the recognition by the medical profession of the importance of psychological factors in mental disorders and 'bodily troubles'.

However, British psychology did not undergo the transformation or achieve the influence so confidently anticipated by Pear. His continuing commitment to the importance of emotional and non-rational factors, and of the social, marginalised him from the increasingly narrow mainstream of British academic psychology.

3   Becoming marginal

Pear stayed on at Maghull for a year after the war, training officers of the Royal Army Medical Corps (RAMC) for service on the pension boards. Although Pear had maintained contact with Manchester throughout the war, this was on a part-time basis. In 1919, when he returned to Manchester, he was promoted from lecturer in experimental psychology to Professor of Psychology, to establish the new department. Pear thus became the first full-time Professor of Psychology in Britain.[17] The creation of the Psychology Department, however, did not itself mark the beginning of the honours course. As the University calendars reveal, Pear, Alexander and Elliot Smith had already been offering an impressive range of courses as early as 1910, and by 1913 their courses, along with supplementary ones offered by the Education Faculty, were advertised as part of the entry for Philosophy as components of an Honours School in Psychology.

Pear described his new department as autonomous from the start. This autonomy had its costs. By 1919, Elliot Smith had moved from Manchester to University

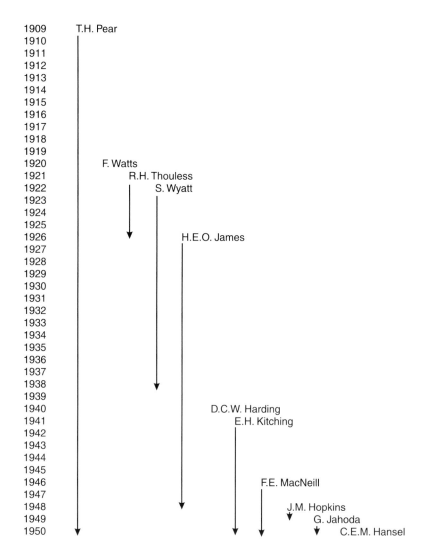

Figure 9.1 *Manchester University Psychology Department staff, 1909–1950.*

College London, and Alexander was happy to turn his psychology teaching over
to Pear. After the intense intellectual companionship of Maghull, Pear now found
himself largely alone, as the sole member of his new department, and faced once
again with building up psychology teaching at Manchester. I have pieced together
the details of the staff during Pear's long period as Professor, from 1919 to 1951.

For most of that period, there were just three members of staff (see Figure 9.1). For most of the time, there was Pear himself, Harold James, who was in charge of the experimental laboratory, and Stanley Wyatt, a part-time lecturer in occupational and industrial psychology. And there were even fewer honours students than staff (see Table 9.1). In fact, it was only through the enterprise of Florence MacNeill, when she joined the department at the close of the Second World War, that the number of honours students began to increase. Until that time, there had been just 14 honours graduates over that whole period, though more than a third of them obtained firsts (a good argument, perhaps, for a return to extremely small class sizes).

The class of 1939, namely Arthur Harrison, in his 80s at the time of writing, has described his own experiences at Manchester:

> During that time I was, truly, the one and only undergraduate studying for the B.Sc. Hons degree in Psychology at Manchester. At times odd lectures boasted 4 of us, sometimes Marie Jahoda from Vienna, a mature student sponsored by the WEA for a short period and from time to time the odd dropper in! ... Dr. Wyatt lectured as the part-time semi-evening lecturer in Industrial Psych. as it was then called.... The degree course included Nervous Anatomy with the medics, and the B.Sc. Ord. degree in Physiology, including the full lab. experimental work, taken at the end of Year 2. Just to make things more difficult, I had to take the anatomy and physiology in 3 terms of a 5 term medic course, taking term 1 and term 4 at the same time! ... Pear was almost never in the lab. That was left to H E O James, full time lecturer. The course included a period at Prestwich Hospital and the Royal Infirmary.[18]

Those readers long used to honours teaching as the focus of psychology departments may well suppose that Pear must therefore have spent most of his time drumming his fingers on his desk, waiting the next inrush – every other year or so – of yet another student! But, of course, there were plenty of students to be taught, including the medical undergraduates and those taking the postgraduate Diploma in Psychological Medicine, a course established at Manchester in 1910 (shortly after Pear's arrival at Manchester) and based in the Faculty of Medicine. And Pear's activities were not confined to teaching. He was a prominent figure within the University, becoming Dean of Science and later Pro-Vice Chancellor. He also remained locked into the wider academic and professional community. For example, he served as President of the Psychology Section of the British Association in 1927 and, in 1942, became President of the British Psychological Society. He (along with Bartlett) was on both the Administrative and Scientific Committees of Myers' National Institute for Industrial Psychology from its inception in 1921 (Welch and Myers, 1932), and Manchester provided a base for some of its industrial research. Indeed, it was Pear who first alerted Myers to the new field of industrial psychology (Hearnshaw, 1964: 276; Bartlett, 1965: 5). Much of Pear's own work focused on human skills and transfer of training (see Pear, 1948a). According to David Duncan, one of the scientists at

Table 9.1 *Manchester University BSc honours graduates in psychology, 1921–1951*

Year	Student	Grade
1921	Cicely J. Parsons	2 (no division)
1922	S.C. Jackson	2.1
1923	H.E.O. James	1
	Ethel Wilkinson	1
1926	Edna M. Yates	2.1
1932	Joan M. Attenborough	2.1
	Miriam Farber	2.1
1933	J.J. Webster	1
1935	Reginald Marriott	1
1936	Ruth H. Manson	2.1
1937	W.E. Moore	1
	Margaret L. Davidson	2.2
	P.W. Kippax	2.2
1939	A.L. Harrison	2.1
1948	Betty P. Fearnley	1
	Joyce B. Bradshaw	2.2
	Sylvia Fletcher	2.2
1949	Edgar Howarth	1
	Alan Crawford	2.1
	Jane D. Hewitt	2.1
	A.B. Rowse	2.1
	Joyce S. Levene	3
1950	E.S. Howe	1
	Jeffrey Caine	2.1
	Trevor Simm	2.1
	D.H. Lewis	2.2
	Enayat Z. Mohamed	2.2
		BA (Hon)
	D.B. Bromley	1
	Margaret Livingstone	1
	B.A. Maher	1
	K.W. Tilley	1
	Vera Cutting	2.1
	K.P. Murphy	2.1
	Elizabeth G.J. Orme	2.1
	John Petro	2.1
	Edward Bowskill	2.2
	Robert Henthorne	2.2
1951	Patricia E. Kingerlee	2.1
		BA (Hon)
	A.C. McKennell	1
	J.E. Orme	1
	Joan Dudley	2.1
	G.M. Hindle	2.1
	V.W. Meyer	2.1
	J.L. Worsley	2.1
	D.B. Worthington	2.1
	Hilary A.D. Evans	2.2
	Una P. O'Neill	2.2

From 1950 students could also graduate with BA (Hon).

the National Institute for Industrial Psychology, 'the visits of Tom Pear … were always a delight. He was a genuine systematic observer of the social scene.'[19]

Pear's first main book, *Remembering and Forgetting* (1922), adopts a distinctly anti-intellectualist approach to what is still largely regarded as a purely 'cognitive' issue, that of memory. Like Bartlett's later text on *Remembering* (Bartlett, 1932), Pear contrasted his new approach with Ebbinghaus's reliance on nonsense syllables. Yet Pear's contrast takes quite a different turn, emphasising the *intimate, personal* quality of our memories:

> Few of Ebbinghaus's investigations will help us to understand the manifold processes which have resulted in our present memory of that morning, when with smiling face and shivering inside, we first left home for boarding-school, or of that tremendous moment when we became quite certain we were in love. (Pear, 1922: 35)[20]

In this early book, Pear identified himself with what he believed to be the new mainstream emphasis upon the affective aspects of our lives (see Collins, Chapter 7), and attempted to build a bridge between the separate worlds of academic psychology and psychological medicine. Indeed, he regarded the practical perspective of medicine as an important corrective to the 'methodolatry' and abstractions of academic psychology:

> medically trained psychologists (the rigid concept of 'scientific medicine' had not complicated matters) like Rivers, Myers, and McDougall knew from hospital experience that not all important facts could be measured, that a patient's account of himself was sometimes all there was to act upon, that a persistent thought or image was a fact even if a subjective one. In them there was no obsessive quest for objective, measurable events. (Pear, 1954: 23)

Working in the special environment of Maghull, Pear would have been relatively isolated from the wider antagonism within the medical and the military establishments to the psychological approaches being developed there. Indeed, as Millais Culpin, who had trained at Maghull with Pear, Hart and Rivers, was to complain, the staff there had failed to warn their students about the 'hostility' to the new views (Culpin, 1949).

After the war, Pear had not only left the supportive environment of Maghull, but found his relations with the Medical Faculty less congenial than before. The concept of 'scientific medicine' had, indeed, come to complicate matters. Pear was dependent upon a physiologist, Professor A.V. Hill, for space for his own department, and Hill's outlook could not have been more 'materialistic':

> Hill's scientific interests were at the opposite end from mine. It would be too easy and crude to write that his 'angle' on life was almost purely extravert, but though he deemed many of the psychologist's interests, and many ways of satisfying them, rather comic, he believed that Nature had a right to her little jokes, which as a natural scientist he took seriously. Personally, he preferred to study measurable,

especially micromeasurable, things. So from Hill 'medicals' learned about hydrogen-ion concentration, from me about the wide bounds of normal human behaviour and some psychological aspects of psychiatry. (Pear, 1948a: 111)

Teaching psychology under these conditions to medical students, especially the 'excessively extraverted athletes' (Pear, 1944: 412), was not the most satisfying experience. By the time the clinical psychologist J.C. Kenna joined the Medical Faculty, in 1950, he found that 'P[ear] always spoke of doctors with a certain disdain, with that characteristic pursing of lips'.[21] Pear came increasingly to look back to Maghull as a golden age, a lost opportunity:

Here R.G. Rows, a pathologist, converted from a simple materialistic faith by studying Dèjerine, Janet and Freud, had collected a group of doctors whose belief in the importance of mental factors in disease was rapidly intensifying, as hundreds of cases, many complicated by months of neglect or purely physical treatment, presented their protean symptoms.... Perhaps never before or since has such con-centrated, many-sided interests been taken by a group of widely travelled doctors, in somatic and psychological medicine, anthropology and ethnology. Had they not dispersed in 1919, part of the history of psychological medicine might have been differently written. (Pear, 1947: 3)

Pear turned instead to social psychology, regarding himself as a 'pioneer' in this field.[22] In these more popular publications, he positioned himself quite differently with respect to both the discipline of psychology and his readers. He reached out over the heads of his psychological colleagues, as it were, to appeal to a wider public and tried to convince them of the importance of problems his fellow psychologists were refusing to address.

Pear's approach to social psychology involved two interrelated themes. The first was 'culture-pattern' theory, which was being promoted within American anthropology (e.g. Benedict, 1935), but which Pear believed had been anticipated by Rivers, Myers, Seligman, and Elliot Smith in their discussions at Maghull (Pear, 1960: 235). As Julian Blackburn (1947: viii) has noted, Pear was almost alone in examining the implications of this theory for social psychology (e.g. Pear, 1942, 1945). The other theme derived from the title of a paper by Hadley Cantril (1934), 'The social psychology of everyday life'.[23] According to Pear, this paper 'changed my life' (Pear, 1948b: 279), and led him to examine many topics neg-lected, or even shunned, by most psychologists.

For example, Pear became fascinated by the psychological issues raised by the new medium of radio, such as the remarkably vivid imagery that can be provoked by radio dramas, and the compelling impressions of personality conveyed by the disembodied radio voice (Pear, 1931b).[24] In one intensive study, he arranged with the BBC to have broadcast, on three successive evenings, the voices of nine different speakers, each reading the same short passage. Around 4,000 listeners returned the answer sheets provided. Judgements of age, regional origin and occupation were often quite impressive. Several listeners, for example, correctly identified one of the speakers as a clergyman, though, interestingly, they went on to report that he sounded like a clergyman trying hard *not* to sound like a clergyman.

Among Pear's many other publications was a book on the psychology of conversation (Pear, 1939b) and one on English social differences (Pear, 1955a), which managed to upset not only the psychologists for raising the question of class, but also the sociologists for failing to mention Marx. Pear's purpose in these publications was to open up new directions for research, raise new questions, rather than pretend to provide definitive answers.

He believed that psychologists should turn from the contrived problems of the laboratory to a study of the psychological problems of everyday life. And, in the face of the resistance of his fellow psychologists, he also came to reflect upon what might be wrong both with psychology and psychologists that they should shy from what he regarded as the genuinely interesting problems. Indeed, as far as Pear was concerned, their resistance itself posed 'an interesting psychological project' (Pear, 1953: 116). In 1939, he wrote poignantly of 'those facts which follow the behaviourist around, like sad neglected animals, with sad, reproachful eyes: synaesthesia and eidetic images, memory images, hallucinations, dreams' (Pear, 1939a: 319). In 1942, he complained that the attempt by psychologists to take a 'middle-of-the-road' approach and a classless attitude was destined to 'result merely in a middle-class account of the middle-class mind' (1942: 78).

Towards the end of his career, evidently failing to persuade his fellow psychologists that psychology could be interesting and indeed relevant to everyday life, Pear developed contacts instead with anthropologists and social theorists. For example, he came to work closely with Morris Ginsberg, the sociologist, and Ethel Lindgren, the Cambridge anthropologist, and, in 1951, he became one of the small number of founder members of the British Sociological Association. In the end, Pear came to question the very idea of disciplinary divisions within the human sciences and, in the process, his own identity as a psychologist:

> There should be much more co-operation between anthropologists, sociologists, political scientists, economists and psychologists; sectionalism has already gone too far. The functions of different university departments and sub-departments might benefit by serious consideration of their usefulness in 1948. (Pear, 1948b: 294)

4   An intentionally peripheral psychologist

Pear invited, if not relished, the opposition of his peers. At a time when the laboratory had become the definitive site of scientific psychology, Pear was insisting that there was something deeply wrong not merely with laboratory psychology, namely its triviality, but also with laboratory *psychologists*. Noting that so many of them made a point of shunning public holidays to pursue their work, he suggested that the laboratory had become for them a retreat from real life and real people, 'an ideal refuge for thinkers whose affection for human beings is subnormal' (Pear, 1940a: 107). Yet his own research, which he offered as an example of humanly relevant psychology, can be disappointingly sketchy and incomplete in execution, if intriguing in its promise. Not surprisingly, he was not always warmly received. For example, at a British Psychological Society conference at Birmingham in 1940, the outraged audience rallied against him, subjecting him to heated retaliation late into the night (Harrower, 1983: 243–244).

What did Pear think he was up to? In his book *Philosophy and the Mirror of Nature*, Richard Rorty (1980: 359) made a contrast between systematic philosophers, who create grand, coherent systems, and 'edifying philosophers', such as Wittgenstein, 'who are reactive and offer satires, parodies, aphorisms'. Edifying philosophers, as he put it, are *intentionally* peripheral. Are there 'intentionally peripheral psychologists'? I want to suggest that this is the kind of psychologist Pear eventually became. The teasing, admonishing style is just right, as is the nature of his various forays into 'everyday research', which are best regarded as tentative demonstrations of what psychology might become.

But, of course, the cost of being peripheral – in psychology, if not philosophy – is to become marginalised. Pear was born in 1886, the same year as Bartlett, and their careers both got off to a good start as protégés of C.S. Myers. Bartlett went on to develop a unique power base within psychology (Broadbent, 1970); for example, nearly all of the new chairs established in Britain in the 1950s and 1960s were taken by his students. Bartlett, with his eye to the main chance, jettisoned his hopes for a truly social psychology. Pear continued to live by his hopes for the new science. And he has been duly forgotten. His name hardly appears even in the history books. His old university holds no archival materials and the main memorial within his own department, 'The Pear Lecture Theatre', is consistently mispronounced.[25] But the most striking example of his marginalisation is also the most poignant. Because of his early close links to so many influential psychologists, Pear became a prolific contributor of many fine obituaries in the academic journals. When Pear died in 1972, there was no obituary in any of the psychological journals, not even the *British Journal of Psychology*.

Acknowledgements

A version of this paper was presented at the opening of the extension to the Manchester Psychology Department, 4 November 1995. The research reported here was conducted while the author was a Simon Senior Research Fellow at the University of Manchester. At a very late stage in this project, I was exceedingly fortunate to make contact with J.C. Kenna, who not only knew T.H. Pear as a colleague at Manchester but had been archivist for the British Psychological Society. His information and suggestions have been especially valuable to me. The help of the following people is also gratefully acknowledged: Michael Argyle, K.R. Dearnaley, David Duncan, the late Dorothy Emmet, Nora Firth, Sebastian Halliday, Arthur Harrison, Alistair Heron, Tim Ingold, Gustav Jahoda, Terence Lee, Ivan Leudar, Geoffrey Leytham, Stephen MacKeith, Florence MacNeill, Wolfe Mays, Laura Miles, Audrey Moir, Richard Pear, John Pickstone, James Reason and Ben Shephard.

Notes

1 Frederic Bartlett to Albert Michotte, 27 December 1931. Letter kindly made available to the author by Baron Fritz Michotte.

2 Scotland was more receptive – see Hunter (1998).

3 'Experimental psychology has sometimes been styled the "new" or "scientific" psychology. It has been spoken of as if it were quite distinct from, and independent of, the older or "general" psychology, in which experiment finds no place. Now these are manifest errors. For experiment in psychology is at least as old as Aristotle. And scientific work is possible (e.g. in astronomy, geology, and natural history) under conditions which preclude experiment. We must regard experimental psychology as but one mode of studying psychological problems, not all of which, however, can be approached from the side of experiment. Far from being independent, experimental psychology has arisen as a refinement, of general psychology' (Myers, 1909: 1).

4 Denys Harding to Sebastian Halliday, 2 July 1980. Harding was based in the Philosophy Department at the University of Liverpool, and set up a psychological laboratory there. He served as a part-time lecturer at Manchester during the Second World War, as a stand-in for Stanley Wyatt, who was involved in war work. He later became Professor of Psychology at Bedford College, University of London.

5 Winifred Hindshaw, 'Reminiscences' (1938), Samuel Alexander Papers, John Rylands Library, University of Manchester.

6 Charles S. Sherrington to Samuel Alexander, 14 February 1907, Samuel Alexander Papers, John Rylands Library, University of Manchester.

7 Senate Committee Book II, 28 July 1906 – 21 July 1908.

8 James Ward to Samuel Alexander, 19 March 1907, Samuel Alexander Papers, John Rylands Library, University of Manchester.

9 T.H. Pear, 'Reminiscences', 25 April 1959, p. 4. Typescript, with a few modifications and additions, from notes made for a recording to be kept in the archives of the British Psychological Society, 10 May 1957, at the request of James Drever Junior and John C. Kenna, the Society's first Archivist.

10 T.H. Pear to J.C. Kenna, 30 June 1953, letter held in the British Psychological Society Archives, Centre for the History of Psychology, Staffordshire University.

11 O. Külpe to Samuel Alexander, 25 December 1908, Samuel Alexander Papers, John Rylands Library, University of Manchester.

12 Pear (1955b) dates this visit to the summer of 1911, whereas the account given in 1959 (see note 9) implies that this visit took place during the summer of the academic session following his visit to Külpe's laboratory. J.C. Kenna, commenting on an earlier version of this chapter, raised the important question of why the British students of psychology, unlike the Americans, rarely travelled to Germany to complete their education, by obtaining a PhD. 'Why didn't Burt, Pear, Valentine, Bartlett, etc. do the thing properly?' (J.C. Kenna to Alan Costall, 6 February 1996). He suggests that the Oxbridge degree was regarded as a complete preparation for further university study, while, in the USA and Australia, there was 'an intellectual, academic sense of inferiority'.

13 Richard Pear, personal communication, 4 July 1995.

14 Maghull was no 'ivory tower'. Rowlands (1980, 'A mental hospital at war', unpublished manuscript), basing his account on the hospital records, makes it clear that the hospital was run-down, with shortages of food and staff, and (as far as the military authorities were concerned) poorly disciplined patients.

15 Pear, 'Reminiscences', p. 16 (see note 9).

16 T.H. Pear, Reminscences of Würzburg, and some International Congresses of Psychology. Recorded on 20 August 1960. Archive of the British Psychological Society, Centre for the History of Psychology, Staffordshire University.

17 In 1901, C. Lloyd Morgan was appointed Professor of Psychology and Education at Bristol. From 1903 to 1909, Myers held a part-time Professorship in Psychology at King's College, London. In 1911, Spearman had taken up a chair at University College London, but as Grote Professor of the Philosophy of Mind and Logic. Although his work was predominantly psychological, it was not until 1928 that he became Professor of Psychology. J.C. Kenna (n.d.), 'Brief psychological chronology 1875–1950', manuscript held in the British Psychological Society Archives, Centre for the History of Psychology, Staffordshire University, and J.C. Kenna to Alan Costall, 19 August 1995. See also Hearnshaw (1964); Kenna (1969).

18 Arthur L. Harrisson to Alan Costall, 23 September 1995.

19 David C. Duncan to Alan Costall, 10 July 1995. In contrast, Duncan regarded Bartlett's influence as 'negative and harmful, in opposing any ventures into applied social psychology…. His social psychology was that of the ivory tower, cut off from the people'.

20 You don't get any of that kind of 'nonsense' from Bartlett!

21 J.C. Kenna to Alan Costall, 6 February 1996.

22 Alastair Heron to Alan Costall, 20 February 1996.

23 Cantril's important point was that psychologists had let method define their problems, rather than the reverse: 'Instead of selecting full-bodied problems from everyday life and attempting to create new techniques or to adjust existing ones which would elucidate the problems with the least amount of distortion, investigators have tended to reverse the order and have adapted their problems to fit standardised laboratory methods. The choice lies between thorough studies on authentic problems, conducted with the best techniques that can be devised, and controlled laboratory experiments on problems which have no relation to life itself' (Cantril, 1934: 298).

24 Pear's interest in radio was provoked by his own early involvement in broadcasting. He also wrote for the *Manchester Guardian* and *Manchester Evening News*, contributing a regular column for the latter under the name of Tom Hatherley.

25 'Pear' should be pronounced like 'peer' not 'pair'.

10

British psychology and psycho-analysis: the case of Susan Isaacs

Janet Sayers

Psychology is still often popularly equated with psychoanalysis. Yet psychoanalysis is now almost totally marginalised or absent from British university-based psychology. But this was not always the case (see for example Richards, 2000a). In this chapter I highlight the point with the example of Susan Isaacs. In particular, I recount her life and work chronologically to show how her determination to protect others from suffering the unhappiness she experienced as a child led to her major contributions to British psychology and psychoanalysis. Not only did she contribute to pioneering university-based teaching, research and policy regarding children's nursery and primary school years, but she also contributed to psychoanalysis by emphasising – much more than did Freud and his immediate followers– the early appearance and ubiquity of phantasy in bridging our inner and outer worlds.

1   Childhood unhappiness

Born Susan Sutherland Fairhurst on 24 May 1885 near Bolton in Lancashire, Susan was the ninth child of Miriam and William Fairhurst. She was weaned suddenly when the next oldest child, William, became ill with pneumonia and soon after died. His death left her mother free to give Susan more of her attention. But this soon ended when she gave birth to another child, Alice, when Susan was four years old. After the birth, Miriam was an invalid until her death two years later.

Susan's unhappiness at her dying was compounded, she later wrote, by Miriam accusing her shortly before she died of lying in suggesting that Susan's father, William, was having an affair with the nurse. But it was true. Soon after she died he married the nurse. The family's fortunes now improved as a result of William, a lay preacher and journalist, being appointed editor of the *Bolton Journal and Guardian*. They moved to a large house, Monksfield, on the outskirts of Bolton. But Susan was unhappy and, still aged only six, ran away to the house of a friend of the family who had several times playfully suggested they marry. He welcomed her, took her in and sent a note to her family telling them what had happened. They replied by sending a parcel saying, if she was going to marry, she would need clothes. Opening the parcel, however, she discovered it was stuffed with newspaper. It left her feeling utterly mocked and humiliated. It was this, she later wrote, that first decided her to specialise in child psychology, to help others better understand the children in their care.

More immediately she took 'refuge from the tragedy at home' in the council primary school which she now attended with her younger sister, Alice. But this compensation was short-lived and she soon felt hemmed in by, and rebelled against, the school's 'manifold constraints and inadequacies' (Anonymous, 1948a). Moving on from this school, when she was 12, to attend Bolton's recently opened secondary school was not much better. Here, among other unhappiness, she suffered the indignity of the boys teasing her because of the short dresses her stepmother insisted she continue wearing into her teens.

Worse still, she suffered her father's rigid discipline, including sentencing his children to bread and water for even such minor infringements as making grammatical errors. Now he punished Susan by withdrawing her from school when she was 14: through her brother, Enoch, she had become interested in agnosticism, at which William declared that 'if education makes women Godless, they are better without it' (Gardner, 1969: 31).

Describing this period of her life as though it were that of a patient, Susan later wrote that it was:

> characterised by obstinacy, noisiness, insubordination, seeking after boys, occasional stealing. At seven years she ate chalk (just as some younger children insist on drinking their bath water). She used in school to blow her nose very loudly in order to annoy a woman teacher whom she much admired and loved. In early adolescence she became an intellectual rebel against everything her father believed in and had frequent feelings of utter despair, with strongly marked suicidal tendencies. (Isaacs, 1934/1948: 34)

She also described feeling miserably guilty lest her jealousy of her younger sister, Alice, had contributed to their mother's long illness and to the family being so 'disorderly and unhappy' (Isaacs, 1934/1948: 35).

Whether or not her childhood unhappiness contributed to her teenage rebelliousness and agnosticism, her father withdrawing her from school was followed by her working briefly as an apprentice photographer. She also helped keep house with her older 'mother-sister', Bessie (Gardner, 1969: 21), read a great deal, played the piano, supported the suffragette leaders Mrs Pankhurst and Mrs Despard, refused to wear corsets, declared herself a socialist, and joined the Fabian Society. When she was 16 she persuaded Alice to join her in giving up butter so as to send the money thus saved to support the striking cotton mill workers. She also earned money teaching a delicate boy at home, worked for a year as a nursery governess with an English family in Morocco, and taught in a small private school in Bolton.

2   Further education and early career

Meanwhile her sisters, Alice and Miriam, went to teacher training college. Eventually she persuaded her father to let her go to college as well. He agreed grudgingly, saying 'young children were, after all, the province of women' (Gardner, 1969: 37). To prepare herself as a teacher she joined a course at the University of Manchester for infant school teachers run by Grace Owen, an advocate of the 'learning by doing' progressive education ideas of Froebel and Dewey. Impressed by Susan's 'quite unusual intelligence' (Gardner, 1969: 37), Owen arranged for Findlay, the University's Professor of Education, to encourage Susan to take a degree and, when Susan said her father would refuse to let her, Findlay used his influence to persuade him to agree.

Susan's cousin, William Sutherland, coached her in the German she needed for the entrance examination. He might also have been her first boyfriend. Certainly, he and Susan made enquiries about cousins marrying (Gardner, 1969). And he was evidently impressed by Susan, particularly by the ability and hard work she put into securing a university place.

Within a year of her becoming an undergraduate – when, among many other activities, she became a founder member of the University's Socialist Federation – her father died. Having left no will, his estate was divided between his widow and daughters. This enabled Susan to repay her grant and thus free her from its requirement that she become a teacher on graduating, which she did in 1912, with a first in philosophy.

It was then that her research in child psychology began. One of her Manchester professors, the psychologist Tom Pear, recommended her to Charles Myers at Cambridge. Like Pear, who taught W.H.R. Rivers about Freud (see Costall, Chapter 9), Myers was also familiar with psychoanalysis, though not a staunch advocate. He persuaded Susan to investigate children's spelling difficulties and after completing her MA on the subject, during which time she lived in Newnham, she returned north where, from 1913 to 1914, she lectured in infant school education at Darlington Training College and, from 1914 to 1915, taught logic at her old university, Manchester.

In 1914 she married one of her University teachers, a botanist, William Brierley. Following his 1915 appointment as a researcher into plant diseases at Kew Gardens in London they moved to a top-floor flat overlooking Richmond Park, and she began work teaching psychology for London County Council, the University of London, and for the Workers' Education Association (WEA). She also wrote up her MA research (Brierley, 1918) and completed her first book, *An Introduction to Psychology* (Brierley, 1921a), in which she emphasised the biological roots of psychology. By now, however, she had also become interested in psychoanalysis. In 1921 she began a long analysis with J.C. Flügel (a close friend from Oxford of Cyril Burt), who combined teaching psychology at University College London (UCL) with being one of the founder members of the British Psycho-Analytical Society (BP-AS). It was at UCL that, after the First World War, he had been the first to teach psychoanalysis in a British university psychology department. At the same time, he was Secretary of the International Psycho-Analytical Association (for further details see Jones, 1956).

Susan, too, combined administration, psychoanalysis and psychology. From 1919 to 1921 she was Honorary Secretary of the Education Section of the British Psychological Society (BPS), served on the editorial board of the BPS's *Journal of Educational Psychology*, and worked from 1921 as an assistant editor on the *British Journal of Psychology*. She also wrote about industrial psychology (Brierley, 1920, 1921b), and from 1921 to 1929 served – like Myers and the future psychoanalyst Marion Milner – as a member of the Council of the National Institute of Industrial Psychology, for which she also served from 1923 to 1931 as a member of its advisory committee on vocational guidance.

During the early 1920s she also became involved with one of her WEA students, Nathan Isaacs. Born in Frankfurt-am-Main in 1895, Nathan had fled with his Russian Jewish family from Warsaw to Basel and settled in England when he was 12. He left school when he was 14 and became a junior clerk to a button merchant before starting work in the metal business. Keenly interested in philosophy and psychology but dissatisfied with the orthodox approach to 'mental philosophy' of the Aristotelian Society, he instead pursued the subject through Susan's WEA class, to which an economist friend, Lionel (later Lord) Robbins, introduced him. Soon, it seems, he courted Susan with endless questions and wrote her a 95-page essay (Lawrence, 1960). Susan was initially reserved and offputting. She went abroad and had a brief analysis with Otto Rank, but finally eloped with Nathan to Austria, and got a divorce from William. (William later became Professor of Botany at the University of Reading and, after retiring, settled in the Lake District with his second wife, Marjorie, who, like Susan, also became a psychoanalyst.)

In 1922 Susan and Nathan married and settled in a flat in 53 Hunter Street, Bloomsbury. Because of the scandal of her becoming involved with Nathan while still married to William, the WEA stopped employing her as an adult education teacher. Instead, she decided to devote herself to working with children. She never had any herself: neither William nor Nathan wanted them; and by the time she got over her fear of childbearing (due to her mother's illness and death after her sister's birth) it was too late (Wooldridge, 1994). Her determination, nevertheless, to devote herself to children remained and she decided to serve them by becoming a medically qualified psychoanalyst. She took the necessary preliminary examinations but, having burdened Nathan with the cost of their Bloomsbury home, she was loathe to burden him still further with the cost of her medical training. So she abandoned it and instead trained as a non-medical lay analyst. Having become an associate member of the BP-AS on 13 October 1921, she qualified for full membership on 3 October 1923.

The same year, the *British Journal of Medical Psychology* published her first article combining her BPS and BP-AS involvements and interests. In it she argued that forwarding the cause of sex equality depended on empirically and psychoanalytic-ally addressing children's phantasies about sexual difference. To illustrate the point, she described an example, perhaps gleaned from her own childhood, of a 4½-year-old girl who persuaded her older brother to cut off her hair, proclaimed herself a boy, and then swallowed her brother's whistle, saying 'I didn't like the noise, so I hid it in myself' (Brierley, 1923: 300). The little girl thereby acted on the phantasy that she could literally take inside herself what represented the outward privileges accorded her brother as a boy. Having thus drawn attention to the way phantasy bridges inner and outer reality, Susan began studying children's phantasies further through the job she obtained the next year as a progressive school headmistress.

3   Progressive school headmistress

On 22 March 1924, a full-page advertisement appeared in the *New Statesman*:

> WANTED – an Educated Young Woman with honours degree – preferably first class – or the equivalent, to conduct education of a small group of children aged 2½–7, as a piece of scientific work and research ... someone ... who has hitherto considered themselves too good for teaching and who has probably already engaged in another occupation.... Preference will be given to those who do not hold any form of religious belief. (Rickman, 1950: 279)

The advertisement was an expanded version of an announcement which had appeared in the 1 March 1924 issue of the *New Statesman*, in *Nature* and in the *British Journal of Psychology*. It had been placed by a Mr Geoffrey Pyke, an investor on the London Stock Exchange. He lived near the Isaacs in a flat in Gordon Square, which he had taken over from the economist John Maynard Keynes (Lampe, 1959).

Like Susan, Geoff Pyke had had an unhappy childhood. His father, a Jewish lawyer, died when Geoff was 5 years old. Geoff was then sent to Wellington, where his mother insisted he wear the dress and observe the habits of the orthodox Jew, despite there being no other Jews at the school, where most of the boys were sons of army officers and mercilessly instituted 'Jew hunts' against him. After a couple of years he left and was educated at home before going to Pembroke College, Cambridge, where he studied law. But he never finished his degree. Instead, he persuaded the *News Chronicle* to employ him as a war correspondent in Berlin, where he was almost immediately captured and imprisoned near the Charlottenburg Palace, in the Ruhleben district, from where he made a dramatic, or at least much publicised, escape.

The miseries he suffered in prison, he later maintained, were nothing to those he suffered at Wellington. Determined to protect his offspring from the unhappiness he had suffered as a child, he prepared himself for fatherhood – when his wife, Margaret, became pregnant with their son, David – by going into analysis with James Glover, who was then practising in Wimpole Street, London. Subsequently, in 1923, when David was three, Geoff asked an American economist friend at Cambridge, Philip Sargant Florence, to send one of his sons to live with them to keep David company. Nor surprisingly, Florence refused. So Pyke decided instead to provide David with companions by opening a school. With grand plans for it to become a research institute revolutionising children's education by freeing them to pursue whatever interests they liked (Van der Eyken and Turner, 1969), and believing Cambridge was therefore a particularly suitable setting, he decided to house this venture in Cambridge's Malting House, which he had rented for his family in 1923.

Nathan Isaacs was intrigued by Pyke's advertisement in the 1 March issue of *New Statesman*. Susan, however, was more cautious. She suspected it was the work of a crank. But Nathan – together with Glover and Pyke, who visited the Isaacs in their Hunter Street flat – persuaded her to take on the post to which she finally agreed on condition that she was given sole charge of running the school. It began some months later, on 6 October 1924, with an initial intake of ten boys, the youngest of whom was the 2½-year-old son, Tim, of the Cambridge philosopher G.E. Moore. Soon the school expanded to include a few girls, with some of the pupils boarding in nearby St Chad's, in Grange Road. As well as G.E. Moore's sons, Tim and Nicholas, the school's pupils included Sue Foss (who later became a Kleinian psychoanalyst, known as Sue Isaacs-Elmhirst), Lord Rutherford's grandson, Lord Adrian's daughter, the Florences' younger son Tony and, of course, the Pykes' son, David.

Recalling Susan's first appearance in Cambridge, the psychoanalyst John Rickman (who had worked with W.H.R. Rivers as a psychiatrist at Fulbourn mental hospital near Cambridge – see Payne, 1952) described her as sturdy, chubby, rather short, challenging, friendly, dumbfounding but also forbearing and 'rather cold'. The psychoanalyst James Strachey was much more critical. He dismissed her as 'conceited beyond words' (Meisel and Kendrick, 1986: 136). As for her school – dubbed by some a 'pre-genital brothel' (Rickman, 1950: 281) – Strachey wrote of its pupils as follows:

All that appears to happen is that they're allowed to do whatever they like. But as all they like doing is kicking one another, Mrs. Isaacs is obliged to intervene in a sweetly reasonable voice: 'Timmy, please do not insert that stick in Stanley's eye'. There is one particular boy (age 5) who domineers, and bullies the whole set. His chief enjoyment is spitting. He spat one morning onto Mrs. Isaacs's face. So she says: 'I shall not play with you Philip' – for Philip is typically his name – 'unless you have wiped my face.' As Philip didn't want Mrs. Isaacs to play with him, that lady had to go about the whole morning with the crachat upon her. Immediately Tony appeared Philip spat at him, and in general cowed and terrified him as had never happened to him before. (Meisel and Kendrick, 1986: 205)

Isaacs herself also noted the children's behaviour. She kept detailed records, particularly of her pupils' biological interests and phantasies, including the following observation of their playing while dissecting mice:

> 20.7.26 Christopher, Dan, and Priscilla dissected one each. While dissecting, Priscilla and Dan carried on a play of 'mother' and 'doctor', with the dead mice as children. They pretended to telephone to each other about it, saying, 'Your child is better now', and so on. Priscilla telephoned to Dan, 'Your child is cut in two'. Dan replied, 'Well, the best thing to do would be to put the two halves together again.' … Presently Dan said, 'Now I'm going to put some water on it, and make it come alive again'. Priscilla joined in this … Priscilla gave Mrs. I. a dead mouse to hold, and said, 'Now it is alive again,' and pretended to make it walk. Mrs. I. said, 'Is it?' Dan: 'Well, we are only pretending'. (Isaacs, 1930: 188–189)

Eventually Pyke employed a secretary to keep these and other notes. In September 1926 he also hired Nathan Isaacs, who had previously commuted from Cambridge to continue working in the City, to write about the theory of knowledge (this later being incorporated as an appendix to Susan's 1930 book about the school). In 1926, Pyke also hired a London School of Economics (LSE) graduate, Dr Evelyn Lawrence (who many years later became the second Mrs Isaacs), to teach in the school. Other appointments included a Russian-born teacher from New York, Richard Slavson, hired in 1927 to introduce the children to science and scientific method. Meanwhile, Pyke also ensured publicity for the school by arranging for a film about it to be shown in the Marble Arch Pavilion on 24 July 1927. It received wide press coverage, including an article in *Nature* (Anonymous, 1927).

But at the end of October 1927, Pyke's metal market investments crashed. The school became increasingly dogged by financial problems. Nor was this helped by the failure of an appeal – signed by Sherrington, Burt, Piaget, Haldane, Moore and others – to the Laura Spelman Rockefeller Trust. By the end of July 1929, the school was finished. Susan, irritated by Pyke not leaving the running of the school to her as he had initially agreed, had meanwhile left with Nathan at the end of 1927 for London. Here she went into analysis again, this time with Joan Riviere. She also used her Malting House experience to further child psychology through drawing academic and public attention to the place of phantasy in children's early lives.

In her first book about the school, *Intellectual Growth in Young Children*, which she dedicated to those she referred to as her 'child companions', she took issue with then current psychological theory, including Maria Montessori's claim that child development is essentially biologically determined. She also took issue with the child psychology claims of Jean Piaget, with whom she entered into critical academic debate in *Mind* and the *Journal of Genetic Psychology* (see for example Isaacs, 1929a, b, 1931, 1934; Piaget, 1931).

Piaget, who visited the school, maintained that children's development proceeds through a step-wise sequence of stages. Isaacs, by contrast, argued that
development involves a continuous process of increasing synthesis of children's
knowledge and skills through their changing interests and phantasies. Adopting
the example pioneered by Dewey in the United States, she organised the Malting
House School to maximise the chance of young children pursuing whatever most
immediately engaged and caught their attention, phantasy and imagination.
Phantasy, she insisted, crucially bridges thought and reality. It inspires children
to experiment and test out the outer reality of their inner ideas. Illustrating the
point, she described her pupils' reaction to the death of the school's pet rabbit:

> 14.7.25 ... Dan found it and said, 'It's dead – its tummy does not move up and
> down now'. Paul said, 'My daddy says that if we put it into water, it will get alive
> again'. Mrs. I. said, 'Shall we do so and see?' They put it into a bath of water. Some
> of them said, 'It *is* alive'. It floated on the surface. One of them said, 'It's alive,
> because it's moving'. This was a circular movement, due to the current in the water.
> Mrs. I. therefore put in a small stick, which also moved round and round, and
> they agreed that the stick was not alive. They then suggested burying the rabbit,
> and all helped to dig a hole and bury it.' (Isaacs, 1930: 182–183)

Phantasy, Isaacs added, is also a starting point for logic. The following is a case
in point:

> Jessica (4;0) and Lena (4;2) were building castles in the sand, and told Mrs. I. that
> they were going to 'build castles as high as the sky'. But Jessica soon added, 'If we
> did, the aeroplanes would knock them down'. (Isaacs, 1930: 106)

In his book *The Scientific Outlook*, Bertrand Russell characterised Isaacs'
approach as the 'application of psycho-analytic theory to education' (Isaacs, 1933:
19n). Isaacs, however, disagreed. Her research, she said, was not educational but
psychological. Above all, she maintained, it was addressed to 'the desperate need
of children themselves to be *understood*' (Isaacs, 1933: 13). It was a need to which
she particularly addressed herself in her second Malting House book, *Social
Development in Young Children*.

In it she again maintained that children's phantasies impel their scientific
learning about the physical world around them. She also insisted that children's
phantasies impel them to learn about their social world. As evidence she cited
the work of her psychoanalytic colleague, Nina Searl. Most of all, however, she
cited the work of the psychoanalyst Melanie Klein, who had been to the school
while visiting England in 1925 to give lectures in London.

Klein's lectures subsequently formed the basis of her 1932 book, *The Psycho-
Analysis of Children* (Klein, 1932/1975). In it she gave many clinical examples of
children's phantasies of oral loving and hating, eating and biting. Isaacs followed
this up in her 1933 book with non-clinical, Malting House examples of children's
phantasies, bearing on their everyday occurrence. They included the following:

25.2.25. Harold had accidentally kicked Mrs. I.'s foot under the table, and this led him to say, 'I'll undress you and take off your suspenders, and gobble you all up' …

11.10.25. In the garden, Tommy ran after Mrs. I. and caught her. He said, 'I'll kill you,' and called Christopher and Penelope to 'come and help me push her down and kill her – and make her into ice-cream!'

2.2.26. At lunch there was some talk about 'cutting Mrs. I. up' and 'having her for dinner'. (Isaacs, 1933: 113, 114–115)

As well as describing children's oral phantasies, Klein also described their urethral phantasies. Again Isaacs provided everyday non-clinical examples, including:

19.11.24. At lunch the children had a conversation as to what people were 'made of', and spoke of people being made of pudding, pie, potatoes, coal, etc., and of 'bee-wee', 'try', 'do-do', 'ah-ah', 'bottie' …

24.11.24 … Frank said, 'Shall we make Benjie drink bee-wee water?' 'Yes,' Harold said, 'and poison him'. And another time, 'and make spots come out all over him'. (Isaacs, 1933: 121, 122)

Klein (1921/1975, 1932/1975) also gave examples of her child patients' phantasies about adults and their sexuality, as, again, did Isaacs:

16.1.25. While modelling, Frank said, apropos of a long piece of plasticine, 'Somebody's climbing up the lady's ah-ah [lavatory] house' …

2.2.26. The children said they were 'going to have a wedding', and there was much talk as to whether Priscilla would marry Frank or Dan … Frank said, 'You *can't* marry Dan, because daddy must be bigger than mammy' … we asked each child in turn whether his mammy or his daddy was the bigger. Christopher reported quite accurately that his mammy was; but Dan denied this of C.'s parents … [and] said, stamping his foot, 'Yes, you see, I *shall* be bigger than Priscilla,' thus twisting Frank's argument to suit his own phantasy.

13.12.26. While Jane, Conrad and Dan were drawing with crayons, Conrad asked Jane whether she had 'seen Dan's mummie's penis' – but at once corrected himself and said, 'No, she hasn't got one. Have you seen her overs?' (ovaries? vulva?) Jane replied, 'No, I haven't, but I've seen my mummie's.' Conrad: 'So've I.' (Isaacs 1933: 143, 158, 142)

Isaacs was warned against publishing these examples lest they damage her reputation. Less likely to be damaging were her observations of children's phantasies about what she called 'cosy places'. These phantasies, she said, signify children's longing to protect their inner world from outer danger and attack, as in the following example:

5.2.26. The elder children arranged chairs and tables round themselves in the summer-house, while they were modelling, 'to keep the tigers out'. They asked Mrs. I. to 'be a tiger and come' – and to 'come from a distance, so that we can hear you growling'. (Isaacs, 1933: 170)

Klein attributed her patients' phantasies about similar 'growling' figures in their external world to fears about their parents as punishing superego figures within them. Again, Isaacs provided everyday examples, including:

> 8.10.24. The children were standing at the door, watching a heavy shower of rain. They heard the rustling noise of the rain on the leaves, and when something was said about this, George remarked, 'Perhaps it's God saying He will punish us for doing things we shouldn't.' …
>
> 20.1.25. After the children had played Harold's game of running round the room, saying that they were 'going to blow up' the tower of bricks which he had built, they presently asked Mrs. I. to say, 'I'm going to tell the policeman'; and soon Frank begged her to 'go and *pretend* to tell the policeman'. (Isaacs, 1933: 172, 173)

Klein often provided examples of just such phantasies of 'blowing up' and destruction. She less often described children's frequently less untoward, constructive and more contented phantasies, perhaps because, as Isaacs observed, 'The happiest days with children, as the happiest women's lives, are those that have no history' (Isaacs, 1933: 93). Making good their absence in Klein's writing, Isaacs recounted several examples of children's phantasies of happy, loving and generous concern for others, including:

> 25.11.24. Dan's father came into the school room, and sat down beside Dan and Benjie, who were modelling. Benjie asked him, 'What have you come for, Mr. X.?' 'To talk to you and Mrs. I.' Benjie made a basket with eggs in it, and gave it to Mr. X. Then he made a motor boat and gave that to him, and then another basket.…
>
> 10.12.24. Harold and Benjie were pushing the large table to the other side of the room, and accidentally bumped Paul with it. Paul flung himself on the floor crying … Harold ran to get his own handkerchief for Paul, and sat down beside Paul with his hand on Paul's head, comforting him. He kissed him, and sat by him until Paul stopped crying and got up.…
>
> 23.3.25. Dan cried at lunch-time because he had not been given a brown plate, and when Harold, who had a brown plate, had finished his pudding, he took his spoon off and passed it to Dan – 'You can have my brown plate.' He stroked his hand affectionately several times, and Dan said to him, 'I love you, Harold, I love you.' …
>
> 4.6.26. When Priscilla shut Dan up as a 'puppy', and he began to cry with boredom, Alfred said to him, 'Don't cry, Dan – I'll be your nurse,' and Priscilla agreed. (Isaacs, 1933: 94, 99, 106)

With these and other examples, Isaacs laid the groundwork for her work in the interwar years furthering public awareness of, research into, and policy related to children's psychology in their early years. She did this through her popular and academic writing, lecturing and research, particularly influentially through heading England's first university-based child development department.

4 Child development writing and research

Following her and Nathan's 1927 return to London, when they settled in a flat in Primrose Hill, Susan became involved in academic teaching and research through her work as a lecturer at Morley College and through supervising Burt's advanced psychology students at UCL. She also gave public lectures about psychology and psychoanalysis, including a BPS lecture on 27 June 1927 in which she reiterated Klein's May 1927 defence of her method of child analysis against that of Anna Freud (Klein, 1927/1975). Klein emphasised the early disjunction between children's inner images of their parents and their parents' outer behaviour. She noted how this disjunction contributes to neurosis. So too did Isaacs (1928/1948). In another talk, Isaacs (1929/1948) added that children often construe the losses involved in weaning and potty-training as punishment by outer figures constructed out of inner phantasy figures punishing them for imagining destroying their mothers by biting and eating them, or by robbing them of their faeces.

At a more readily accessible level, Isaacs gave radio talks and wrote guides to early child development. Particularly successful in this respect was her 1929 book *The Nursery Years. The Times* later dubbed it 'a classic of popular exposition' (Anonymous, 1948b: 6). In it she included an engaging account of the inner meaning the baby gives to what happens to him externally:

> He not only eats, but thinks with his mouth … we can see too that the baby *loves* with his mouth, and feels his mother's love in her gift of the breast…. But if the mother withdraws the breast how quickly the picture changes! His face puckers and reddens, he screams with distress and anger, his fists clench and his body stiffens in protest…. Thus are little children in these critical early years torn and tossed between their loves and their hates, between the delights of possession and the fears and anxieties of loss. (Isaacs, 1929c: 24, 92)

Isaacs followed this book – her most enduringly popular – with a book about primary school children called *The Children We Teach* (Isaacs, 1932). She dedicated it to Klein and Searl, and included examples gleaned both from her Malting House work and from those sent in by readers (which had prompted articles about 7–11-year-olds which she contributed to the magazine *Teacher's World*). Both books became a major influence on education policy in England and abroad through the ensuing decade (Pole, 1948).

As well as shaping education policy and popularising child psychology through her books and contributions to *Teacher's World*, Isaacs, who began writing for magazines in her early twenties (Brierley, 1916), also popularised child psychology through her contributions to *The Highway, The Forum of Education, The New Era, The Spectator* and *Twentieth Century*. From 1929 to 1936 she also wrote articles for *Nursery World*. They dealt variously with children's phantasies about where babies come from, about smacking, masturbation, reading, writing and other topics in child psychology (Smith, 1985).

She adopted Nathan's suggestion that, as a journalist, she write under a pen-name, Ursula Wise. Ursula was also the name she gave to the only child she described at length in her second Malting House book. Perhaps she would have written more about this little girl had she written her third intended Malting House book, *Individual Histories*. As it was she confined herself in her second Malting House book to writing about the phantasies (recounted by Ursula's mother) through which Ursula managed her feelings about her mother's pregnancy with Ursula's younger sister (born when Ursula was four years old, just as Susan's younger sister Alice was born when she, too, was four).

As well as writing about children's phantasies, Susan continued working administratively for the BPS. She was chair, from 1928 to 1931, of its Education Section. In 1931 she also rejoined the editorial board of the *British Journal of Educational Psychology* and in 1936 joined the editorial board of the *British Journal of Medical Psychology*. From 1931 she was also appointed as a staff psychologist to the London Clinic of Psycho-Analysis. The WEA also now hired her again, this time to run a class at Toynbee Hall – work she later transferred to Marion Milner when she took on the post of heading England's first university-based child development department, others already having been established in Geneva by Piaget, in New Haven by Gesell and in Toronto by Bott.

The Director of London's Institute of Education, Sir Percy Nunn, wanted her for the post. In designing it for her, he insisted that the post required 'an able and qualified woman' who could both teach and inspire research (Gardner, 1969: 168). Initially, Susan was uncertain whether to accept the post. But she finally accepted it on 11 May 1933, and began that autumn with an initial intake of five full-time students. Their lecturers included the paediatrician and psycho-analyst Donald Winnicott. He also provided a student placement in his outpatient department at Paddington Green Children's Hospital. To this, Isaacs added other clinic and nursery school placements, as well as arranging educational visits, including a spring 1934 visit to a progressive school, Dartington Hall, in Devon.[1]

She also advanced child development policy through consultative work to various central and local government departments. This included answering departmental enquiries, including one from an inspector at the Board of Education about children's fairy tales. She answered by dwelling on their mixed benefit in both externalising children's 'phantasies in a form that robs them of their individual terror' while also risking seeming to make real what the child most dreads (Gardner, 1969: 101).

Isaacs also talked about these and other topics in child psychology in lectures at the Institute of Psycho-Analysis. They included a 1934 lecture about the ways in which children become defiant, as she had been as a child. Sometimes, she said, defiance is a means by which children protect themselves against wanting anything from their mothers. Or they become defiant because they feel they have insufficient goodness inside to enable them to take responsibility for putting right damage done actually or in phantasy to their mothers. Others justify their defiance by imagining their mothers as hateful and bad, and as therefore fully warranting the attacks they make on them. Or they use defiance to test out whether their parents are as bad as they phantasise and fear them to be. Alternatively, children are defiant to confess and bring to their parents' attention the bad people they imagine themselves to be inside. Or they are defiant and bad to make themselves look outwardly as big and powerful as they inwardly phantasise their parents as being (Isaacs, 1934/1948).

In addition to summarising these causes of children's defiance, Isaacs also contributed to a 1934 symposium of the BPS's Medical Section, of which she was the first non-medical woman committee member. In her contribution, she illustrated and supplemented Kleinian psychoanalysis with examples of children imagining greedily robbing and enviously spoiling what is inside their mothers (Isaacs, 1935/1948). In another talk she dwelt on children's thumb-sucking, masturbation and so on, which she analysed in terms of their phantasies of having their sexually coupling parents inside them (Isaacs, 1935).

This may seem far-fetched. More readily recognisable were the bodily ills Isaacs now endured. Suffering from cancer, she was treated with radium in December 1935, which in turn resulted in pleurisy-like symptoms, for which she was treated the next month. Despite these problems, however, she continued to be immensely productive. She compiled a teachers' record card system in 1936 for Wiltshire's education committee (Hamley *et al.*, 1937). Helped by Ilse Hellman (1990), a recently arrived developmental psychology graduate from Vienna, she also continued answering readers' letters to *Nursery World*, as well as to the magazine *Home and School*, edited by George Lyward, for whom she also edited a number of pamphlets (for example, Shepherd, 1937; Guttridge, 1937; Isaacs, 1937). And in 1937 she gave lectures in New Zealand and Australia, where she was awarded an honorary DSc in Adelaide. She edited further books, including *The Human Problem in Schools*, which reported Marion Milner's (1938) research for the Girls' Public Day-School Trust. And in the autumn of 1938, after being rehoused with the Institute of Education in the University of London's new Senate House building, her Child Development Department reopened with much of its playroom furniture supplied by Paul Abbatt, whose father she had phantasised marrying when she was six.

5   Child analyst

Through the 1930s Susan Isaacs continued developing her major contribution to British psychology and psychoanalysis through her work as a child analyst. In 1934, for instance, she spoke to the Education Section of the BPS about a 3½-year-old boy (Isaacs, 1938/1948). Since Isaacs did not give him a name, I will call him Colin. Isaacs writes that Colin blamed his extreme dirtiness and temper tantrums, for which he was referred for analysis, for a succession of 14 nurses leaving him, the first when he was one year old, when his younger brother was born. To control this outward behaviour he got Isaacs to bind a wooden doll tightly round and round with string and paper in pursuance of an inner phantasy that this would stop him screaming and dirtying himself and driving her and his current nurse away over the Christmas break.

To this example Isaacs added that of another boy – a 4-year-old whom she called Jack, whose father had died of tuberculosis when Jack was still less than a year old. Through analysis it turned out, according to Isaacs (1938/1948), that the tantrums for which he too was referred involved various phantasies: screaming for his dead father to come and help his mother in her hard life bringing him up alone; identifying with his father as an alive, loud and violent figure within him; and inwardly attacking and fighting his father for being 'bad' in not being alive and still around to help his mother. Perhaps Isaacs was also thinking of Jack in a talk she gave to the 1938 Paris Psychoanalytic Congress (Isaacs 1939/1948b). In it she described how a boy's phantasy about his mother attacking him was lessened by the phantasy being put into words.

She also spoke about Jack in another 1938 talk, this time to the BP-AS, in which she described him putting one railway coach in front and another behind an engine, and then anxiously and repeatedly asking, 'Engines *do* go like this, don't they?' (Isaacs, 1943/1948: 145). She linked this with Jack living with 'one Daddy and two Mummies' (his uncle, aunt and mother) and with his image of his mother attacking his masculinity through insisting ladies go first. By putting into words his fear of his mother, Isaacs claimed, his anxiety lessened and she became more benign in his mind.

In a second paper to the 1938 Paris Congress, Isaacs returned to the above-mentioned 3½-year-old, Colin, to illustrate further the notion of children inwardly representing in phantasy form figures in their outer world. She described Colin's tantrums as the means by which he attacked an inner image of his mother. She also described how, in one of his treatment sessions, he ate some sugar and then took a ball of plasticine and got her to make the plasticine into lots of little balls corresponding to the number of patterned daisies on her dress. It represented his phantasy, she claimed, of eating her up as he had eaten the sugar. But then, fearing she might retaliate by eating him up, he sought to allay his fear by externalising it through getting her to punish and drag him around the room at the end of a skipping rope.

Or so Isaacs (1940/1948) maintained. She went on to speak more about Colin at a 7 December 1938 talk to the London Institute of Psycho-Analysis. In expanding it for publication, she detailed further examples of children's phantasies, including the phantasy she had long ago described of a 4½-year-old swallowing her envied older brother's whistle. She also noted how – in imagining internalising others whom they envy, love and fear – children seek to control them (Isaacs, 1940/1948).

She reiterated this theme in a 30 April 1939 talk to British and French psychoanalysts in Paris. In her talk she took up the 'depressive position' theory put forward a few years earlier by Melanie Klein (1935), in which Klein claimed we control figures in our minds to defend ourselves against dependence on, and loss of, their outward counterparts. Reiterating Klein's claim, Isaacs maintained that analysis serves to free children from these inwardly controlled and controlling figures, through attending to the good and constructive as well as bad and destructive feelings involved. 'What we are always concerned with in our work,' she emphasised, is the inner '*meaning to the child* of the person in question or the external events which impinge upon him' (Isaacs, 1939/1948a: 102, original emphasis).

In another paper she emphasised a related theme: namely the means by which children and adults control their inner world through enacting it outwardly. She illustrated the point with the example of a 15-year-old patient who, following his parents' separation when he was 7, lived with his grandmother, whom his mother later bitterly criticised in trying to persuade him to come and live with her. In his analysis he externalised the situation. He became preoccupied with making a parachute attached to a basket in which he planned to put the family cat so as to lower it gently from an upstairs window to the ground below. In doing this, wrote Isaacs (1939/1948c), he represented externally a phantasy he could not bear internally of vomiting out his grandmother made bad by his mother's criticism of her. Putting such phantasies into words, she concluded, helps restore links between their inner and outer reality.

6 Wartime contributions

Arguably, however, Isaacs' most long-lasting contributions to British psychology, and certainly to British psychoanalysis, occurred during and just after the war. While Nathan worked in Warwickshire, where his securing wartime supplies of tungsten and molybdenum later earned him an OBE, Susan returned to Cambridge, where her LSE colleague Sibyl Clement Brown asked her to join her when the LSE was evacuated there. Susan found a flat for them, and together with Clement Brown, R.H. Thouless, the psychoanalyst John Bowlby and others she investigated the effects on children of being separated from their families after evacuation there from Tottenham and Islington in North London. In the resulting report she criticised government agencies for being so concerned with practical details – train timetables, housing and so on concerning the children's evacuation – they overlooked its inner psychological impact on the children involved (Isaacs, 1941). She illustrated the effects by quoting the children, such as an 8-year-old who wrote: 'I miss my tortoise in LanDon he is Robert Taylor he bit me once he bit me. And I tod [told] him he wac [was] a note [naughty] boy and I fod [fed] him a lost [lots] of tam [times]' (Isaacs, 1942: 159). Another evacuee, aged 15, wrote: 'I miss my relations, parents and friends who are in Tottenham. And I often wish our foster mother wasn't so particular' (Isaacs 1942: 160).

Meanwhile, Melanie Klein, with whom Isaacs had evidently become friends, joined her in Cambridge before going north in 1940 to Pitlochry in Scotland. Soon after, in 1941, Isaacs returned to London, where the Ministry of Education urged her to reopen her Child Development Department. She negotiated for her post there to be made full time, but then found someone else – one of her department's first students, Dorothy Gardner – to fill it. Although she continued giving lectures in the department, her most long-lasting legacy to British psychology – at least to British psychoanalysis – resulted from her wartime account of phantasy which she contributed to what are now known as the BP-AS's 'Controversial Discussions', in which she and others defended Klein's work against its Freudian detractors.

The discussions began on 27 January 1943 with Isaacs' pre-circulated essay 'The nature and function of phantasy'. In it, Isaacs reiterated Klein's extension of Freud's concept of phantasy to include not only dreams but everything mediating between inner and outer reality. She also went further. She insisted on the omnipresence of phantasy. 'There is no impulse, no instinctual urge,' she declared, 'which is not experienced as (unconscious) phantasy' (Isaacs, 1943/1990: 276–277). Phantasy, she asserted, not only involves the sexual impulses described by Freud but also involves the destructive impulses, anxieties and inner–outer defences of introjection and projection described by Klein. Taking issue with Robert Wälder, Anna Freud and other psychoanalysts from Vienna who claimed that representation of our parents as phantasy figures within us begins only with the Oedipal conflicts of later infancy, Isaacs maintained that this process begins much earlier. After all, she pointed out, Freud himself noted that his grandson, when he was only 18 months old, already represented his mother in phantasy by a spool of thread which he played at throwing away and retrieving in dealing with his inner feelings about her going away and wanting her to come back.

To this example, Isaacs added others she had learnt about from her work as a headmistress, analyst, journalist, child development researcher and policy adviser. From her resulting data she chose the following example:

> A little girl of one year 6 months saw a shoe of her mother's from which the sole had come loose and was flapping about. The child was horrified and screamed with terror.... At two years and 11 months (15 months later), she suddenly said in a frightened voice to her mother 'Where are Mummy's broken shoes?' Her mother hastily said, fearing another screaming attack, that she had sent them away. The child then commented, 'They might have eaten me right up!' (Isaacs, 1943/1990: 308)

At 18 months, Isaacs concluded, there was already evidence that the little girl had a phantasy, which she could not then put into words, that her mother's shoes might devour her. This phantasy, Isaacs claimed, stemmed from a still earlier phantasy that her mother might bite her in revenge for her imagining biting and eating her up.

In her book *The Nursery Years*, Isaacs (1929c) had described a toddler waking up when he was 14 months old terrified of a white rabbit biting him. Now, in this 1943 essay, she linked this little boy's biting phantasy to a game he played when he was 16 months old, in which he would shout 'Quack, quack' as he shooed imaginary ducks into the corner. By shooing them and their enormous beaks away, Isaacs wrote, he sought to quell his earlier nightmare of the biting white rabbit.

It represented, she claimed, a still earlier phantasy of his mother biting him in retaliation for his wanting to bite her. This was evident, she said, from his reacting, aged seven months, to being weaned by rejecting and refusing the milk his mother gave him.

As further evidence of the early origins of children's phantasies, she described an example she had previously recounted in a talk promoting nursery school education (Isaacs, 1937/1948). She now elaborated this example in another contribution to the BP-AS's Controversial Discussions. She wrote it jointly with Paula Heimann (who later recalled Susan working so closely with her husband, Nathan, they even shared the same double desk; see Gardner, 1969). In their paper, presented on 7 December 1943, she and Isaacs described the phantasies involved thus:

> A girl of sixteen months often plays her favourite game with her parents. She picks small imaginary bits off a brown embossed leather screen in the dining-room, carrying these pretended bits of food across the room in her finger and thumb and putting them into the mouth of father and mother alternately. She chooses the brown screen, with small raised lumps on it … to represent the 'food' she wishes to give her parents. (Heimann and Isaacs, 1943/1990: 690)

The little girl, they claimed, thereby turned into a pleasurable game the anxiety and guilt she felt when, aged 12–16 months, she was reprimanded by her parents for smearing herself with her faeces and putting them into her mouth while lying in her cot in the morning.

Heated discussion continued in the BP-AS as to whether such examples constituted evidence of the early occurrence of phantasy. As well as writing further on the subject in the following years, Isaacs (1945) also secured the future of her contribution to psychoanalysis through her wartime and immediate postwar membership of the London Institute of Psychoanalysis's Training Committee from 1944 to 1946, as a member of its Board from 1945 to 1947, and through serving on the Council of the London Clinic of Psycho-Analysis from 1946.

She also continued contributing to child development policy. She pleaded for better provision for children who had lost their fathers – through their death or absence during the war – and for better understanding of their responses to this (Isaacs, 1945/1948a). Of much more general and long-lasting importance, however, was her use of her wartime Cambridge research into the psychological effects of evacuation to oppose children being brought up away from home. Her memo to this effect was, according to one authority, 'the most important single document' consulted by the government's Curtiss Committee in deciding England's postwar policy regarding institutional and foster care for children (Anonymous, 1948b: 6). In her memo, as ever, Isaacs included an illustrative phantasy, this time of a 15-year-old orphaned servant girl, who, she wrote, filled a drawer with photos the teenager stole from her employers as a means of meeting her inner 'longing to be a member of a family and to have kind and loving parents and brothers and sisters of her own' (Isaacs, 1945/1948b: 234).

The memo was published in 1945. The previous winter the Isaacs' Primrose Hill flat had been bombed. Shortly afterwards, still ill with the cancer that had first afflicted her in 1935, Susan suffered pneumonia. In January 1946, she gave up the teaching she had undertaken at LSE and that she had continued to provide at London's Institute of Education. She also gave her last public lecture. In it she paid tribute to Grace Owen, who had first introduced her in her early twenties at the University of Manchester to the progressive-education ideas of Dewey, which Isaacs had subsequently developed so much in her own work.

In late 1947 she underwent surgery for the removal of an ulcer and soon after was awarded a CBE in the 1948 new year's honours list. It was testimony to her achievement in and for British psychology and psychoanalysis. Her achievements continued with the 1948 publication of her last childhood psychology advice book, *Troubles of Children and Parents* (Isaacs, 1948a), her collected papers, *Childhood and After* (Isaacs, 1948b), and an *International Journal of Psycho-Analysis* article (Isaacs, 1948c) – a version of her January 1943 contribution to the BP-AS's Controversial Discussions – which remains one of the single most formative influences on psychoanalysis today. In it she recounted further phantasies, including one recounted by the BP-AS's first President, Ernest Jones, of a small boy who, seeing his mother breastfeed the new baby, exclaimed 'That's what you bit me with' (Isaacs, 1948c: 88).

It was almost the last thing Isaacs wrote. After holidaying in the summer of 1948 in the Scottish Highlands – the childhood home of her mother – she died in her and Nathan's London flat on 12 October 1948. Earlier that day she told her one-time student and colleague, Dorothy Gardner, of her lifelong quest for understanding. It was the counterpart of children's longing to be understood, of which she had so often written.

7   Conclusions

I have sought to demonstrate how children's longing to be understood, and Susan Isaacs' concern to enable parents and others better to understand children so as to protect them from the unhappiness she suffered as a child, fired her pioneering university-based child development research and policy making. They also underpinned her major contribution to psychoanalysis in insisting on the ubiquity of phantasies mediating between our inner psychology and outer behaviour, as well as their occurrence from earliest infancy. Her achievement was immense. Would that academic psychology and clinical psychoanalysis – which, since Isaacs' death, have often been severed from each other in England – could again become conjoined in the next hundred years of British psychology to as productive effect as they were by her in the early decades of its previous century's history.

Note

1   S. Isaacs-Elmhirst, interview with the author, 22 June 1998. See also Young (1982).

11

Physiology and psychology, or brain and mind, in the age of C.S. Sherrington

Roger Smith

> Only by continual modification of its ancestral powers to suit the present can … [the organism] fulfil that which its destiny, if it is to succeed, requires from it as its life's purpose, namely, the extension of its dominance over its environment. For this conquest its cerebrum is its best weapon. It is then around the cerebrum, its physiological and psychological attributes, that the main interest of biology must ultimately turn. (Sherrington, 1906: 393)

Claims for success in breaching 'the last frontier' of knowledge, the mind itself, redoubled in strength and confidence in the last decade of the twentieth century. At least three substantial intellectual shifts appeared to support this optimism, shifts which transformed the sciences of mind and brain developed a hundred years earlier.

The first change realigned science and philosophy. Many neuroscientists and philosophers of mind rejected a clear-cut distinction, which an earlier generation vehemently maintained, between analytic and empirical argument. There was still sometimes dispute about what is properly a philosophical and what is properly a scientific question, but a generally bullish atmosphere in science placed philosophers uninformed by science on the defensive. The change brought a host of topics, earlier thought to be conceptual, logical or in some sense purely mental, under the empirical and entirely naturalistic worldview of science. It was a change which made progress in knowledge appear inevitable.

The second change was the elaboration of scientific theories of consciousness, however speculative, controversial or even misguided some judged them to be. The hope that a biological theory of consciousness was just around the corner became a driving force at the end of the century. By contrast, before the 1970s, reference to consciousness as a topic for scientific research, let alone reference to a theory of consciousness, was alien or even reprehensible to psychologists and physiologists alike. While, of course, there were many earlier claims that mental properties can be fully explained as properties of biological systems, such claims were speculation, the stuff of science fiction rather than the subject of research.[1] Belief in the reducibility of theories of mind to theories of matter was perhaps widespread in scientific circles in earlier decades. But the belief was informal and most scientists avoided the topic of mind and brain. By and large, they left it to philosophers or to colleagues put out to graze in retirement.

The social, material and intellectual context of these two changes was the revolution in information technology based on computing. Computing was a seemingly ever-enlarging framework of possibilities for the representation of all aspects of life.[2] The computing revolution was fundamental for the notion and growth of cognitive psychology; and computing processes suggested the terms and concepts (notably 'distributed processing') for scientific theories of consciousness.

The new technology also underlay a third profound transformation – the shattering of a general belief in a unitary selfhood. While literary theory and cultural studies, which influenced academics and an intellectual elite, entertained the deconstruction of what was often called 'the self', the experience of computing and cyberspace, and indeed drugs, brought dissolution of a conventional sense of selfhood into very many Western households. The result was a personal and social culture in marked contrast to earlier years. Many scientists and writers about science had believed in science as a humanistic undertaking which enhances human dignity and freedom. In effect, whether with conscious intent or not, they sustained a belief, in historically Christian terms, in the sanctity of the person. L.S. Hearnshaw's comment about the interwar years is pertinent: 'No responsible British psychologist questioned the existence of a conscious subject or self. This was a primary fact of experience. It was as [F.A.P.] Aveling put it, "a centre or focus of all that is felt, known or actively performed"' (Hearnshaw, 1964: 213, quoting Aveling, 1931: 16–17). The disruption of this view of the self was pivotal in the late-twentieth-century debate about postmodernity.[3]

This chapter looks at part of the background to these changes. It discusses views of the relations between mind and brain in the 1920s, 1930s and 1940s, and it links these views to the disciplinary relations of psychology and physiology. As I discuss, the relation between physiology and psychology was of great importance for psychology's social identity; it was also a troubling intellectual question, most sharply posed by the apparent conundrum of the mind–body problem; and it implicated open-ended questions about the future of values in the modern world. We must bear in mind that for many psychologists these were distant issues.[4] Most psychologists were in practice faced by demands to establish objective methods and social credibility in relation to local, delimited projects, not to establish the authority and coherence of the discipline in general. When scientists did mention the mind–body relation, however, it was frequently in terms of some kind of dualism which left the precise relationship unspecified or even classed as unknowable. This looked pragmatic; but it put psychology in a philosophically incoherent and socially awkward position in relation to its claim to be a natural science. If, as was often claimed, psychology is a discipline with 'the mental' as its subject matter, what relationship could this discipline have to the natural sciences? Hearnshaw quoted G.F. Stout's assertion that, since 'mental processes cannot be explained as special complications of processes which are not mental', psychology must be radically distinct from physiology (Hearnshaw, 1964: 230, quoting Stout, 1896: vol. 1, p. 6). And if, by contrast, it was claimed that psychology does not have 'the mental' as its subject matter, what claim has it to be a science independent of physiology?[5]

1   The relations between psychology and physiology

The course of modern psychology as a scientific area of activity has been bound up with its relation to physiology.[6] Whereas experimental physiology achieved unquestionable status as a natural science in the mid-nineteenth century and, by the end of the century, as a considerable institutional presence, the same cannot really be said for European psychology before 1945. Psychology, in most settings, had questionable status and an insecure situation for the first half of the twentieth century.[7] There were times when it was a concern for psychologists to say why psychology, if it is indeed a natural science, should have autonomy and not simply exist as a branch of physiology. In the United States, the only country at the turn of the century where there was substantial institutional support for the creation of a distinct discipline of psychology, psychologists felt under pressure to demonstrate that psychology has its own non-physiological subject matter, methods and social applications (O'Donnell, 1986). There were reasons why psychology could be thought a subordinate subject: its experimental methods originated with research on the physiology of the senses;[8] and everyone touched by scientific ideas had agreed since the early nineteenth century that the brain is the organ of mind. Why, then, psychologists felt obliged to ask, should the science of brain not encompass the science of mind? Indeed, the same question, in revised form, gained new life in the second half of the twentieth century, with the result that it seemed appropriate to attach the prefix 'neuro-' to every field.[9]

  This chapter examines the topic through the work of C.S. Sherrington (1857–1952). It may at first glance appear discrepant to make Sherrington the principal figure in an essay on British psychology, since no one, least of all Sherrington himself, described him as a psychologist as opposed to a physiologist. Yet he addressed the mind–body relation and the relation of psychology to physiology throughout his long life. His concept of integration, with which he brought order to a mass of research on nervous processes, and specifically to the control of posture and movement, applied to the organism as a whole. As others have noted, Sherrington envisaged neurophysiology as part of a biology of behaviour.[10] He certainly intended, as science made progress, that this biology should include human beings and mind.

The general perception at the time and later was that British psychology and physiology were not in constructive relation in the first half of the century. Hearnshaw observed:

> To the fields of physiology and comparative psychology British psychologists made few contributions between the wars…. According to Spearman 'the renunciation of physiology' was as important an ingredient in the development of psychology as 'the renunciation of philosophy'. (Hearnshaw, 1964: 230, referring to Spearman, 1937: vol. 1, chs 2 and 3)

This chapter might therefore be said to be about the absence of physiological psychology – about a state of affairs which enabled psychologists to act independently but which was intellectually unsustainable.

A survey of the contents of the *British Journal of Psychology* from its inception in 1904 to the late 1930s suggests that physiological psychology was indeed absent. There are a few papers (for example, Watt, 1910) that might come into this category before 1920, but thereafter there are almost none.[11] But it is not obvious that physiological psychology formed a recognised subspeciality at the time, either in Britain or elsewhere: the search for it may be anachronistic. If we extend the search to include scientists who did not call themselves psychologists, the picture is a little different. In particular, a number of medical men, some eminent – like Henry Head (a neurologist), John Herbert Parsons (an ophthalmic surgeon) and W. Russell Brain (President of the Royal College of Physicians in the 1950s) – maintained a physiological approach to psychological questions. Their interests, and the interest in health and wellbeing generally, kept the topic of mind and brain at the forefront of a medical and popular literature on psychology. Further, there were physiologists – notably Sherrington (who trained as a physician and maintained his medical contacts) and E.D. Adrian – who held cooperation between physiology and psychology in view. Thus, there was a powerful constituency for the view that the separation of physiology and psychology was a barrier, that there was a need 'to destroy the bulkhead which has appeared between psychology and physiology, a partition that has created, artificially, two watertight compartments' (MacCurdy, 1928: 3).

The significance of medical writers is well illustrated by the symposium on 'The conception of nervous and mental energy' held at the International Congress of Psychology in 1923. Head here introduced his concept of 'vigilance', developed in studies of aphasia, when 'we are compelled to ask ourselves how a diminution in physiological activity can be associated with specific psychical defect' (Head, 1923: 127). Head used 'vigilance' to name a physiological state of 'high-grade physiological efficiency' in the central nervous system which he supposed to be the base of consciousness and higher (mental) adaptation. He drew on his reading of both John Hughlings Jackson and Sherrington: 'Conscious processes bear the same relation to the life of the higher centres of the nervous system as purposive reflexes to the vitality of those lower in the neural hierarchy. All alike are the expression of physiological vigilance' (Head, 1923: 147). If, as Frederic C. Bartlett later observed, Head had not, as he hoped, solved the mind–body problem, he had perhaps opened up a more integrated view of the organism. Head showed that:

> the dualism which we commonly make of bodily and conscious processes, and which is still at the basis of most accepted psychology and physiology, is all wrong and raises entirely spurious problems.... We have instead the gradual building up of more and more complex integrations and more and more complicated adaptations. (Bartlett, 1926: 159)

A similar hope for the unification of physiology and psychology, mediated by the replacement of dualism by a concept of integration, was evident in E.C. Grindley's early paper on 'The neural basis of purposive activity'. Grindley, whose primary affiliation was certainly psychology, thought it necessary to preface his experimental studies of learning by an apology for physiological psychology: 'Since, however, "physiological psychology" of this kind has lately become unpopular both with psychologists and with physiologists, it is perhaps necessary to say a word about this more general subject ... ' (Grindley, 1927: 169).

These references to 'integration' alluded to Sherrington's contribution. There was widespread agreement that *if* psychology were to be brought into relation with physiology, it would be by building on his work. The word 'integration' served to refer both to the organism and to the intellectual unification of physiology and psychology in the study of the organism. Parsons, who tried to construct a general physiological psychology on the basis of his specialist medical knowledge of sight, observed:

> It is only of comparatively recent years that physiology has made substantial contributions to psychology.... One of the greatest contributions to psychology has been made by an Englishman in Sherrington's *Integrative Action of the Nervous System.* (Parsons, 1928: 103)

The other major contributions he had in mind were those of Karl S. Lashley and of I.P. Pavlov.[12] Elsewhere Parsons wrote:

> The epoch-making researches of Sherrington on reflexes and their integration reveal principles which throw a flood of light on instinctive and other reactions, and are in many cases directly applicable to integrations of a higher order than those actually observed. (Parsons, 1927: v)[13]

Sherrington, in fact, staunchly supported the growth of scientific psychology, and he had hopes for it both as an academic discipline and as an applied occupation. He joined the British Psychological Society, contributed a paper for the first issue of its journal (Sherrington, 1904) and remained on the masthead as an advisory editor (though it is not clear to what degree he refereed for the journal). Owing to his major book on integration, published in 1906, and his social standing – he was, for example, President of the Royal Society, 1920–1925 – he was in a position to make his views count. 'It is to the psychologist that we must turn to learn in full the contribution made to the integration of the animal individual by mind' (Sherrington, 1923: 12).

Sherrington's early life spanned the period during which the natural sciences, in their modern form, became consolidated as academic disciplines, with career structures and professional standards. Physiology in Britain achieved an institutional position by simultaneously gaining a degree of autonomy from medicine and claiming to provide medicine with a scientific foundation. By 1901, physiology was firmly established, was very self-conscious of its standards and had high status as an experimental science.[14] The rigour of the field depended in part on recognition of how difficult it actually was to carry out experimental work with any authority. This was exemplified by the difficulties of studying the brain, and the result was scepticism about the immediate prospects for knowledge of brain and mind. Discussion of the relation of mind to brain, which was widespread in the early to mid-Victorian period, appeared to the newly professional physiologists to be characteristic of just those activities – philosophy and metaphysics in one direction, and popular speculation in the other – from which they wished to distant themselves.

Psychologists did not attempt to solve the mind–body problem or to achieve what physiologists thought beyond the capacities of contemporary science. Instead, they stressed psychology's distinctive subject matter – whether understood to be individual differences, mental capacities or behaviour – and distinctive techniques, such as testing, statistical analysis and introspection involving report of conscious contents.

All the same, there were occasions when discussion of the relations of mind and brain, or of psychology and physiology, came to the fore. This was certainly so in the medical area, as I have already suggested, and as the literature on instincts, sexual life, 'shell shock', pain and emotion testifies. A wider consideration would also have to deal with the reception in Britain of psychoanalysis. The common interests were exemplified in the work of William McDougall, who left Oxford for Harvard in 1920, and of W.H.R. Rivers, whose premature death in 1922 was felt to be such a loss to psychology.[15]

Within the academic natural sciences, the experimental study of sensory perception posed questions about the relations of psychological and physiological events in the most direct way. Scientists working in this area – as Sherrington's own activity shows – struggled with conceptual as well as factual issues involving mind's relation to brain. At Cambridge, what began as the grafting of new German approaches to sensation on to physiological research led in the interwar years and beyond to the rich experimental activity led by Bartlett and, later, Oliver Zangwill. This was a setting in which the import of physiological observations for psychological ones, and vice versa, received attention. The focus, however, was experimental rather than speculative. For example, R.C. Oldfield tried to study the simplest and most elementary forms of cortical arousal and dispersion of excitation through research on psychological inhibition. He stated:

> By doing so we may make no immediate contribution to the understanding of intimate cortical mechanisms. On the other hand it would seem plain that at every level of our mental life, states suspiciously reminiscent of internal inhibition constantly play a part.... If we cannot hope to find out *how* the brain *does* work, we may at least discover something about *why* it sometimes *doesn't*. (Oldfield, 1937: 37)[16]

Before turning to Sherrington as a research scientist, we should recall that he was also both a physician and a staunch advocate of the contribution of science to human wellbeing. While Professor of Physiology at Liverpool (1895–1913), he was very active in advocating a scientific approach to school hygiene.[17] He wanted society to provide the right physiological conditions for children, and he took it upon himself to communicate the necessary information to teachers. He also became involved with fatigue and lighting conditions in factories.[18] At Liverpool he created opportunities for his assistants, W.G. Smith, H.J. Watt and Cyril Burt, to do psychological work.

During the First World War the government asked him to investigate conditions in the munitions industry, and he contributed to the work of the committee that became the Industrial Fatigue Research Board (which he chaired). After the war, he supported C.S. Myers when the latter founded the National Institute for Industrial Psychology (of which Sherrington was for a while a Vice-President), and he held high hopes about what individual testing might do for the efficiency of personnel and career selection. A notice in *Nature* (Anonymous, 1923: 439), paraphrasing Sherrington, stated that 'Most boys have no chance whatever of getting into an occupation that suits them best; unguided, they drift into any trade'. Like so many physicians, scientists and other professional people of his generation, he took for granted the significance of heredity for differences in individual capacity, and he looked for a social mechanism by which people could find a place in society appropriate to their capacities.

2   Sherrington's researches and the mind

Much of Sherrington's research appears to exemplify physiological analysis independent of psychological questions. This is especially so with that side of his work which concentrated on the neurone, nervous conduction and synaptic connections.[19] Yet, from the time when he acquired his experimental outlook at Cambridge in the early 1880s to the humanistic writings of his years of retirement (though he retired only in 1935, aged 77), he also referred to mind or psychological questions, albeit in carefully circumscribed ways. He aspired to include mental functions and the values he thought inherent in mental life in knowledge of integration.

> There remains yet another type of integration [in addition to nervous integration] which claims consideration, although to saddle it upon nerve may perhaps encounter protest.... Though our exposition kept these two systems [the physicochemical and the psychical] and their integrations apart, they are largely complemental and life brings them co-operatively together at innumerable points.... For our purpose the two schematic members of the puppet pair which our method segregated require to be integrated together. Not until that is done can we have before us an approximately complete creature of the type we are considering. This integration can be thought of as the last and final integration. (Sherrington, 1961: xv–xvi)

This was the summation at the end of his life, added to a reprint of his book, and it indicated the most general sense in which he looked to physiology and psychology to serve a common goal. Within this framework, he had long had a rich engagement with particular psychological topics.

Sherrington's research concentrated on the spinal level of motor control. He hoped to isolate and hence gain precise knowledge of the elementary units of nervous integration. But he had an acute appreciation of the abstraction intrinsic to this approach. Though the achievement of methodological precision as a physiologist required him largely to exclude brain and mind, all his work supposed the reality of a nervous hierarchy with the brain – the organ of mind – as the controlling centre. He thought it too difficult for the most part to address the brain directly in experimental terms. How psychology and physiology would contribute to each other was therefore a matter for the future. It was this sense of the inaccessibility of the brain that changed in the 1930s, creating modern brain science, opening up possibilities for a new physiological psychology, and leaving much of Sherrington's work behind.

He did make a considered attempt to extend his research to the brain, since his theory clearly required tying together a hierarchy of cerebral and spinal levels of control. As he wrote, 'the cerebral cortex augments the motor solidarity of the creature' (Sherrington, 1906: 306). He therefore undertook work, much of it in collaboration with A.S.F. Grünbaum (who changed his name during the First World War to Leyton) on the motor cortex of the higher apes. They used ablation and excitation to extend the localisation studies begun by David Ferrier (to whom Sherrington dedicated his book on integrative action). On one noteworthy and rare occasion, they investigated a gorilla, supplied at great expense.[20] They hoped that this work with the higher apes would make research more relevant to clinical neurology than the investigation of rabbits or cats, the usual subjects. In fact, Grünbaum's and Sherrington's studies revealed the extent of inter-specific and individual variability, as well as the lability, of the cortex, and thus tended to restrict rather than encourage belief in the value of localisation research to psychology.

The power of Sherrington's exposition depended on the concept of integration, the conceptual means with which he related 'abstract' reflexes to the 'whole' organism. The way Sherrington conceptualised the nervous system was more influential than specific research on the cortex. Thus, according to one assessment, British neurology was transformed between 1910 and 1915, when physicians began to use his neurophysiological ideas to bring order to the mass of observations derived from clinical examinations, thus giving neurology a scientific as opposed to merely an empirical base (Anonymous, 1947).[21]

When Sherrington set out to study the nervous system in the early 1890s and deliberately isolated spinal reflexes, his decision enabled him to work with decerebrate animals. Animals thus prepared, with the higher brain centres divided from lower levels, were – scientists agreed – unable to feel pain. The imperatives of vivisection imposed their own requirements on the separation of psychology and physiology. Physiologists had fought a fierce battle in the 1870s to legalise vivisection, the immediate occasion for the founding of the Physiological Society of London.[22] Sherrington's work created standard experimental subjects, which scientists agreed did not suffer pain, but the cost was that they also did not exhibit mind. He demonstrated heroic patience in mapping the peripheral nerves in different species in order to delineate the anatomical substrate of the reflexes, which he wished to study as physiological units. He turned the macaque monkey into an anatomically and physiologically known land. But the manner in which he did this could not directly include mind. Later, however, especially in the laboratory which his student John F. Fulton established at Yale, and when there were new techniques, the monkey became the surrogate for human beings in studying the mind's relation to brain (Pressman, 1988, 1998). This later work opened up neuropsychology.

In the book on integrative action, in the midst of a seemingly rigorous empirical discourse, Sherrington drew speculative analogies between brain processes and mental activity. About attention, for example, he wrote: 'The interference of unlike reflexes and the alliance of like reflexes in their action upon their common paths seem to lie at the very root of the great psychical process of "attention"' (Sherrington, 1906: 234). The summative and inhibitory action of reflexes on each other at a central site, he suggested, may be the means by which the organism focuses on one mental performance, just as it achieves one motor performance through routing the outcome of summations and inhibitions along one 'common path' to muscle. For Sherrington, as for C. Lloyd Morgan and Head, it was the mental ability to focus attention, unifying activity, which seemed to be mind's biological function. Thus, the speculative parallel between mental attention and nervous integration made it possible to imagine the utility of mind in the evolutionary process:

> But … [man] is a machine with a mind. Does that make a difference? Yes, it enables him to do, in addition, things on a different plane of cognition and intent from those other [automatic] ones; it enables him to do 'main' things. But only one at a time. (Sherrington, 1963: 158)

In such ways, while fully accepting the reality and value of active human consciousness, Sherrington promoted a fully evolutionary view of human existence.

In summary, 'our inference would be that one use of mind in the individual is to control and modify the individual's motor act' (Sherrington, 1963: 167).

Sherrington's vision was broad. When it came to extending claims beyond the very limited range of experimental results, however, he hedged with qualified expressions and conditional phrases. In a summary of the functions of the motor cortex, he wrote:

> As to the meaning of this whole class of movements elicitable from the so-called 'motor' cortex, whether they represent a step toward psychical integration or on the other hand express the motor result of psychical integration, or are participant in both, is a question of the highest interest, but one which does not seem as yet to admit of satisfactory answer. (Sherrington, 1906: 307)

All the same, whatever the qualifications, he made clear his interest in psychology, and indeed at this point in his discussion he expressed hope for the new methods of studying comparative psychology developed in the United States by S.I. Franz, Edward Thorndike and Robert Yerkes.

The concept of integration originated as an approach to movement and posture, the motor side of the organism. But Sherrington was clear from the beginning that the concept in principle also encompassed the sensory side of the organism. It was, indeed, the power of the one concept to encompass both the sensory and the motor dimensions of the nervous system, and the perceptual as well as conative side of psychological life, that justified the reputation Sherrington acquired as a philosopher of organic wholeness.

Sherrington tried to extend experiment and theory alike from the motor to the sensory side of neurophysiology. 'Can we at all compare with the simultaneous co-ordination of the nervous factors in a motor reflex the synthesis of the nervous elements whose combination underlies a simple sense-perception?' (Sherrington, 1906: 357). As he was well aware, with this question he entered into the border-land between psychology and physiology.

His approach relied on a conventional but powerful metaphor: the head is 'at the head' of the body and is the high point of evolution. He believed that the brain evolved in the head, at the front, since this is where sensation at a distance takes place. He thought of the evolving brain as the coordination site for what he called 'the distance-receptors'.[23] The integration of sensations, he argued, was a major step in the achievement of integration between organisms and surrounding conditions, that is, of adaptive behaviour. While he thought the sensory side 'too difficult for me to expect much success' in research terms (Sherrington, 1906: 308), he had hopes that the study of sensory integration might open up a route to knowledge of higher integration, the integration of mental and physiological processes. This was to be Sherrington's royal road to the study of mind.

He kept abreast of current work in sensory psychophysiology, though his own attempt to study sensory integration experimentally was made in the 1890s. The last lecture of his book on integrative action discussed sensory fusion, drawing on his own research on binocular vision, as a tentative point of entry into the study of higher integration.[24] His conclusion, which he recognised went against established opinion, was that the fusion of images from the two eyes cannot be attributed to the geography of nerves and brain but depends on the psyche.

> It is not therefore a physiological conjunction in space but a temporal conjunction in 'mental' space. It is not spatial conjunction of cerebral mechanism which combines them. Identity in time and in perceptual space suffice. It instances the 'now' as an integrating factor of the finite mind.... It is as though the right-eye and left-eye perceptions are elaborated singly, and then psychically combine to one. The synthesis is a mental one in which the finite mind uses 'time' as synthesiser. (Sherrington, 1963: 214)

This experimentally based conclusion, as Sherrington well understood, entangled scientific theory in the puzzle of mind's relation to body. His approach to an answer presupposed evolutionary continuity and utility – these must be the presuppositions in understanding mind and body alike if they are to be explained by natural selection. We can observe that even when physiological or psychological language distinguished mind and body as states or entities, evolutionary language united them again as functions.

The topic of perception made Sherrington explicit about his ambition that the concept of integration would one day make possible the collaboration of psychology and physiology. For the present, however, he felt progress was hamstrung by both the paucity of scientific knowledge and the mystery of mind's relation to body. The result was some tortuous expressions when he lectured to a general audience on the sensory side of integration. Sherrington referred to 'the first and greatest problem vision faces … [as] doubtless that attaching to it as part of the matter–mind relation. How is it that the visual picture proceeds – if that is the right word – from an electrical disturbance in the brain?' (Sherrington, 1963: 109). He moved back and forth between terms proper to a physiological and to a psychological analysis. Significantly for psychology as a discipline, he accepted the value of empirical descriptions of the psychological dimension as on a par with descriptions of the physiological dimension. He just was not sure that psychology had yet achieved its promise.

This discussion of the brain as the site of higher integration, of mind with body as well as of sensory-motor processes, related to a larger vision of evolution and of 'man's place in nature'. This aspect of Sherrington's thought became well known through the Gifford lectures, which he gave in Edinburgh in 1937 and 1938. He then allowed himself a degree of poetic expression and visionary writing which he would never have countenanced in a scientific paper. All the same, there was continuity between his treatment of integration in the earlier physiological work and the later thoughts. He took the opportunity of retirement to speak to an audience, wider than the scientific community, about the image of human nature which made sense of his life's work. He remained extremely circumspect, however, about what he actually claimed.

He took it to be fact that human beings are the most advanced organisms of the evolutionary process. He thought that the brain, by virtue of its highly elaborated connections with distance-receptors, laid the basis for this success. In the adaptive flexibility that the brain makes possible, he found a criterion for the identification of progress in evolution and thus, speaking more abstractly, for a hierarchy of value in nature.

> If we ask a test for which among living forms are 'higher', range of dominance of the environment is one of the features to which the term 'higher' can be accorded. Since mind is one of the great keys to dominance of the environment, 'higher' in that sense in biology is almost graded by degree of mind. At the present time no range of domination of life's environment is so great as that of man. On that ground we can acclaim him the 'highest' of all living forms. (Sherrington, 1963: 132)

In this manner, he followed earlier evolutionary naturalists like G.J. Romanes and Lloyd Morgan, and he linked his work with that of many other scientists – in Britain, the most conspicuous was Julian Huxley.[25] Sherrington wrote: 'A touchstone for rank of a centre in this neural hierarchy [i.e., the nervous system] is the degree to which paths from separate loci and of different receptive modality are confluent thither' (Sherrington, 1906: 314). He conceived the higher forms of integration to be 'higher' in an evaluative sense.

For Sherrington, the question of mind was a question for the scientific theory of evolution and the scientific theory of integration. He looked to the future development of psychology to provide answers.[26] Meanwhile, in the context of his presentation for a public audience, Sherrington wanted to say something direct about the mind's relation to the body. As the existence of a large literature testifies, the question of how the mind and body relate was one which the public expected scientists and philosophers to answer.[27] Sherrington felt it necessary to accept the common-sense position that mind and body constantly interact, even though this position could not be formulated in scientific terms.

> But indeed, what right have we to conjoin mental experience with physiological? No scientific right; only the right of what Keats, with that superlative Shakespearian gift of his, dubbed 'busy common sense'. The right which practical life, naïve and shrewd, often exercises. (Sherrington, 1933: 22–23)

Sherrington's position was unexceptional. As an experimentalist, he looked back for inspiration to Ferrier, rather than to the neurologist Hughlings Jackson. It is perhaps noteworthy that Ferrier was not very circumspect about the language with which he related psychological and physiological functions in the brain; Hughlings Jackson, by contrast, was famous for his attempt to impose distinctions supported by a philosophy of psychophysical parallelism.[28] Sherrington's language, as well as his theory of integration, implied the interaction of mental and nervous processes. In *Man on His Nature* (1940), he wanted to make clear what his position was, but he had to overcome the difficulty that he thought almost nothing was known about this interaction. In obscure but evocative prose, he tried to find words to describe a topic of paramount scientific importance, not to mention public interest, about which it appeared impossible to say anything in a scientific way.

3   The philosophy of the mind–body relation

Sherrington had no 'philosophy', in the sense of a systematically elaborated theory, of the mind–body relationship. His reference point, as for the scientific theory of integration, was the unity, or individuality, of the organism. Of mind and body, he wrote: 'To separate the one as "action" the other as "thought", the one as physical the other as mental, is artificial because they both are of one integrated individual, which is psycho-physical throughout' (Sherrington, 1963: 212). When he discussed the mind–body relationship – often enough in dualistic terms – he referred to their 'liaison' (Sherrington, 1963: Lecture VIII; 1961: Foreword). The 'how' of that 'liaison', he was clear, is unknown. 'No attributes of "energy" seem findable in the processes of mind. That absence hampers explanation of the tie between cerebral and mental' (Sherrington, 1963: 247). Judith Swazey's conclusion appears just: 'It was a position he felt constrained to adopt because the sciences of his day offered no evidence, no means, for bridging the gap between mind and brain' (Swazey, 1969: 27–28).

Many of his contemporaries were not so reticent. There was a substantial academic as well as popular literature, by people like the philosopher C.D. Broad and the psychologist C.S. Myers, which discussed, or even purported to solve, the mind–body question. Broad's catalogue of 17 varieties of answer (or C.K. Ogden's mere seven) was something of a dry exercise in comparison to R.J.S. McDowall's collection of popular lectures by scientists on the sciences and mind (Broad, 1925; Ogden, 1929; McDowall, 1927).

Myers, a dedicated psychologist and Sherrington's contemporary, also turned later in life to write on the mind–body relation. Myers was much more positive than Sherrington that it is possible to understand the relation, once it is grasped – as he thought modern physics makes clear – that the mechanisms described by physicists and physiologists are abstractions.[29] Following Herbert Spencer, Myers argued that reality should be viewed as a complex system with 'direction'. The facts of 'conservation' of energy in the universe, of 'self' and of 'the various individual sub-systems within the "universe" of the individual mind' indicate a wholeness in reality prior to the particularities which the sciences describe in terms of abstract concepts (Myers, 1937: 175). The different levels of reality have evolved by specialisation. What we refer to as the self, Myers claimed, is the manner in which the primary unity of existence is re-expressed by the evolved complexity of specialised but integrated levels. This melange of physics and philosophy, half Spencer and half philosophical idealism, did not command authority. By contrast, Sherrington preferred to play with an epigram from Marvel: 'Our loves so truly parallel though infinite can never meet' (Sherrington, 1963:

243), or to pose rhetorical questions: 'But this last, not the eye, but the "seeing" by the brain behind the eye? Physics and chemistry there are silent to our every question. All they say to us is that the brain is theirs, that without the brain which is theirs the seeing is not. But as to how?' (Sherrington, 1963: 113).

Given the variety and confusion of opinion about the mind–body relation in Sherrington's lifetime and later, his modesty might be counted wise. But it was surely an uncomfortable position for a scientist whose authoritative account of integration was incomplete without the unification of physiology and psychology. The sign of this disunity was dualism of mind and body. How could knowledge of integration be achieved if the very terms in which physiology and psychology expressed themselves were predicated on an incomprehensible relationship between different kinds of stuff?

Discussion generally referred to mind and body as natural or ontological entities, without social content. Nowhere did Sherrington consider the view that language, culture and history, that is, the social dimension in which the human mind–body relation exists, might be constitutive of the problem at issue. The debate to which he contributed, like many subsequent debates, was essentially abstract, as it treated mind and body as natural entities independent of the social life in which statements about them were utterable. The poetry of Sherrington's writing took him from abstraction to concrete experience; but the lack of a discourse about the social dimension left the argument substantially empty. As a physiologist, he did not say how psychology as a natural science could advance understanding of real human beings, with their consciousness and language of values, as opposed to advancing a physiological psychology of local processes abstracted from human life as a whole. As a humanist, he had not so much an answer but the poetic means of re-expressing the goal of living as a whole person.

Poetic language was a striking part of Sherrington's retelling of the story of evolution, full of the wonder of man's encounter with his nature. He struggled to find expression for an evolutionary account of the origins of mind and consciousness.[30] This involved several elements. First, the reality of evolution means that mind must have utility: 'The mind is utilitarian. By evolution it is bound to be so. Each step of its development has had to justify itself *ad hoc*. What evolution looks to is use to the individual as a going concern' (Sherrington, 1963: 149). Second, we should be able to trace the presence of mind down the animal scale. Unfortunately, this left him making vague surmises, rather as earlier evolutionary naturalists like Romanes had done: 'Let us seek where we can first trace mind, or where we last lose it. Does it not begin with urge to live? Zest to live which is part and parcel of life?' (Sherrington, 1963: 158). And third, again like his Victorian forebears, he had to say something about how to reconcile the presumed continuity of the evolutionary process with the apparent duality of mind and body as entities in the world: 'What has evolution had to evolve mind from?' (Sherrington, 1963: 209). Sherrington did not really answer his own questions, though he somewhat inclined to the view that 'mind', in some sense, has always been present in the universe, though it is recognisable only in the later stages of evolution: 'It is as though the elementary mental had never been wanting; as though evolution in dealing with the brain had taken that elementary mental and developed it until it blossomed into evidence' (Sherrington, 1940: 266).[31] With such expressions, Sherrington vividly located the human mind in nature. Nevertheless, 'to man's understanding the world remained obstinately double' (Sherrington, 1940: 251).

4   Conclusions

The example of Sherrington suggests that there was sympathy in the early-twentieth-century scientific establishment for psychology's aspiration to become a natural science. Sherrington, indeed, required a psychology, and his theory of integration was incomplete in its absence.

> It is that want of knowledge [of mind's relation to brain] which today is the greatest obstacle to progress in biology, because the two sciences which should cooperate together, biochemistry and psychology, remain not intelligible one to the other. Their attitude is for each practically to ignore the other.[32]

At the same time, the practical skills required for achieving empirical rigour in both physiology and psychology diverted energy away from such large questions. People outside the scientific community, however, thought they mattered. A different literature, written sometimes with scientific content and sometimes not, for general rather than specialist audiences, sought to fill the gap. Psychologists and physiologists alike had ambivalent feelings about this situation. They wanted the public to share the scientific outlook, but they were conscious that this outlook appeared incoherent in relation to 'busy common sense'. Ordinary language, if not always scientific language, grasped the integration of mind and body.

There was a significant direct philosophical response by Broad, John Laird, Samuel Alexander and many others (Broad, 1925; Laird, 1925; Alexander, 1920/1966). There was also a response which subsequently influenced the practice of the history of psychology. A number of writers thought the mind–body problem symptomatic of a situation in which there was progress in scientific knowledge but lack of progress in human values. The achievements of neurophysiology exemplified the progress of science, but the lack of integration of these achievements with the science of mind, that is, with psychology, appeared to leave human interests outside science and hence, in a scientific age, with no foundation. E.A. Burtt and A.N. Whitehead argued in the 1920s that the problem could be traced to the scientific revolution.[33] The mechanistic worldview, they argued, was predicated on a metaphysics, a view of reality, in which qualities attributable to mind and characterising humanness could have no place. This banished knowledge of the secondary qualities (the 'qualia' of recent discussions) – will and judgements of value and significance. Descartes' convoluted attempt to say how the non-spatial mind and the spatial body interact appeared to be a sign of this intellectual and moral failure. This failure, it was suggested, was bequeathed to the twentieth century as the mind–body problem.[34] When scientists like Myers and Sherrington took up the question, they did so, then, with awareness of very deep issues at stake.

Sherrington followed convention and believed that Descartes founded the modern physiology of the nervous system. He took it for granted that knowledge of the reflex, the core of his own research, began with Descartes.[35] His own intellectual career similarly took him from the study of minutely ordered mechanisms to bemusement about their relation to mind. When encouraging a science of psychology, he had to face the question of how such a science could be achieved. His response, the theory of integration, was one of the most creative and fruitful.[36] But it did not solve the mind–body problem. In the eyes of supporters and critics alike, he was thought to be one of the most eminent proponents of dualism in the modern age, dualism's greatest spokesman since Socrates and Descartes, according to one enthusiast (cited in Penfield, 1957: 410).

To conclude: 'the absence' of physiological psychology in Britain in the 1920s and 1930s is part of a much larger picture, with implications for the very nature of knowledge of human beings. To be historically accurate, reference to this 'absence' needs to be qualified. There was considerable medical interest in the relations of psychology and physiology, and scientists were concerned that the mind–body question blocked the progress of biology, progress which required the joint efforts of neurophysiology and psychology. The disciplines of physiology and of psychology were, nonetheless, separated by language, by subject matter and by experimental expertise. This chapter uses Sherrington's life and work to illustrate these points. It also suggests how, with the concept of integration, he framed an approach to the nervous system as the controlling centre of unified action, to mind and body as joint participants in a unified individuality, and to physiology and psychology as partners in a unified biology. Sherrington's central place in British science, as well as the intellectual riches of the concept of integration, makes his work important in the history of academic psychology. He also contributed to the large literature on psychology and mind–body questions written for lay audiences. This literature made clear that people, Sherrington included, thought of a science of psychology as ultimately answerable to values associated with the idea of the self and the individual person. But the new neuroscience, which the physiology and psychology of Sherrington's generation made possible, appeared to call these values and concepts, as once understood, into question. When, in the postwar years, the full impact of new techniques for the experimental study of the brain, and new conceptual analogies for brain function, began to take effect, the very notion of what it is to be human appeared to shift.

Acknowledgements

This chapter is informed by research undertaken, with Rhodri Hayward, on 'The brain and the self: the public understanding of science and medicine, c.1925–1955', funded by the Wellcome Trust. Much of the reading on which the chapter is based was undertaken while I was a Resident Scholar, Dibner Institute for the History of Science and Technology at MIT. I am grateful to these institutions and to Rhodri Hayward and the editors for suggestions and support.

Notes

1 H.J. Eysenck is an example of a British psychologist who took for granted the biological base of psychological processes but did not spend time discussing the mind–body relation; see especially Eysenck (1967). Pavlov was an inspiration – and Pavlov left the mind–body question to those who liked that kind of thing (see Joravsky, 1989: 122, 134–139).
2 The way in which tools – material practices in all their forms – structure knowledge is an important theme of the sociology of science. For psychology see Gigerenzer (1992) and, more widely, Danziger (1990). The notion that there was a 'cognitive revolution' is, at least for Britain, highly questionable (for the United States see Gardner, 1985). It was commonplace in British psychology to refer to 'internal' states – for example Bartlett's use (1932: 198–214) of Head's notion of the 'schema' – while before 1945 there was little sympathy for US behaviourism.
3 An influential thesis about the relations between psychology and discourses of selfhood has been elaborated by Nikolas Rose (1996a, 1999). The argument, which locates the site of modern liberal government within the internal mental world of the individual, makes questionable the belief that only late-twentieth-century psychology shattered belief in the unified self. The sources of this sense of 'dissolution' or 'deconstruction' are indeed many and diverse. It is likely that further argument about psychology and 'the self' will have to take account of the so-called 'popular psychology' embedded in British life alongside the 'official psychology', as discussed by Mathew Thomson (Chapter 5).
4 The attempt to define the scope and nature of psychology appears almost entirely in the early years of the British Psychological Society, as in James Ward's opening article for the *British Journal of Psychology* (Ward, 1904).
5 David Wilson (Chapter 12) refers to fears for psychology's independence, given the degree to which Zangwill, after 1945, directed experimental psychology towards research on brain functions. See also Alan Collins' comments on Zangwill and research on memory in Chapter 7.
6 Sandy Lovie (Chapter 4) points to the Physiological Society of London as a model for the elite, scientific purposes of the founders of the British Psychological Society.
7 I have attempted to summarise this state of affairs in Smith (1997b: chs 14, 16, 17), which also gives an extensive bibliographic essay. Rose (1985) highlights the response of psychologists to local needs. It is a tribute to Hearnshaw (1964) that his book still provides the best overview for Britain; it well conveys the eclectic and diverse nature of British psychology – and this, as Mathew Thomson writes (Chapter 5), while still excluding the vast realm of 'popular psychology'.
8 There was research on sensory perception in Britain at the beginning of the century, but it declined – or, at least, physiological and psychological approaches separated. Articles in the area published in the *British Journal of Psychology* increasingly cited only psychological methods – see for example the papers by Shepherd Dawson (1917) and H.J. Watt (1911, 1913, 1920); the latter had begun his career in Sherrington's Liverpool physiology laboratory. In 1927, Sherrington lamented to Lloyd Morgan the lack of interest in psychophysics and had hopes to rectify the situation (letter, Sherrington to Morgan, 29 March 1927, Bristol University History Collection: DM 128/394 – I owe this reference to David Wilson). Alan Collins (Chapter 7) also comments on the feeling that psychology had gained autonomy after the First World War.

9   The term 'neuroscience' itself was introduced in 1962 by F.O. Schmitt as part of a concerted effort at the Massachusetts Institute of Technology to unite and hence transform research across medical as well as scientific specialities (Schmitt, 1992).

10 Swazey (1969) examines Sherrington's research up to the synthesis of 1906. Sherrington was an influential teacher, a figurehead of British science and an inspiration to medical neurology. The result is a large and often eulogistic literature on his achievements, but there is no proper biography. I examine Sherrington's status in Smith (2000).

11 The situation is confirmed by the absence of a chapter on physiological psychology in the postwar survey by Mace and Vernon (1953).

12 The British reception of the work of these scientists would be the subject of another chapter, and it would be one way to initiate a more comparative history. Karl Lashley was one of the most cited of all North American psychologists in Britain, while H.J. Eysenck and other psychologists created new interest in Pavlov's work, but only after Sherrington and his school had dismissed it for outdated neurophysiology. On Lashley, see Weidman (1999). For criticism of Pavlov, see Denny-Brown (1932).

13 Parsons (1927) tried to advance a comparative physiological psychology of perception, in a book strongly influenced by his reading of Sherrington.

14 The most extensive study is Geison (1978); see also Butler (1988) and, for data, O'Connor (1988, 1991).

15 Recent work on the 'popularisation' of psychoanalysis is referenced in Mathew Thomson (Chapter 5). McDougall was so individualistic, and his solution of the mind–body question in terms of animism so unusual in Britain, that it may be unwise to use him for any generalisation. Though he has not attracted a biographer, see Boden (1972; see also Chapter 18) and Soffer (1978). For Rivers, see Myers (1923) and Alan Collins (Chapter 7), who also points to the significance of the medical dimension for studies of memory. It is not possible here to compare the interrelations of psychology and physiology in other countries, but it differed in interesting ways. Thus, one of the texts most directly on 'physiological psychology' to be published in Britain was a translation from the leading French psychologist Piéron (1927).

16 For the background of the concept of inhibition, and its importance to relations between physiology and psychology, see Smith (1992).

17 He chaired the committee of the British Association for the Advancement of Science appointed to enquire into 'the conditions of health essential to the carrying on the work of instruction in schools' (British Association for the Advancement of Science, 1903: 483–496; 1904: 455–464; 1905: 348–352; 1907: 433–438; 1908: 421–422; 1909: 458–463), and he contributed chapters on physiology to a new edition of a manual (Hope *et al.*, 1913). He was on the Departmental Committee on Sight Tests of the Board of Trade (Sherrington, 1913). For his lectures to teachers, see, for example, the *British Medical Journal*, 1902.

18 British Association for the Advancement of Science (1911: 212–217; 1912: 174–175); Sinclair (1984); and for a summary of fatigue work, Vernon (1921). See also Joanna Bourke (Chapter 6) on psychologists and the First World War. For the psychology of work, see Rabinbach (1992) and Vatin (1999).

19 This topic, which provides a model success story of scientific understanding, has attracted historian-scientists. See, for example, the articles in Hodgkin *et al.* (1977); Worden *et al.* (1975); Samson and Adelman (1992).

20 The American surgeon Harvey Cushing witnessed the incident with the gorilla: see his diary and letters to his wife (July 1901) quoted in Fulton (1946: 197–198). The gorilla, already cold and ill, died.

21 See also Walshe (1947). These articles are from an issue of the *British Medical Journal* marking Sherrington's ninetieth birthday.

22 Legislation, which provided the framework for the next century, was passed after much agitation against physiologists, in 1876. See French (1975).

23 Sherrington later also used Pavlov's term, 'the analysers' (Sherrington, 1963: 150).

24 The significance of this lecture for psychology was pointed out by Swazey (1969: Appendix F). Sherrington also discussed other topics of significance to psychology, notably the emotions (Sherrington, 1906: 255–268).

25 See Boakes (1984) and R. J. Richards (1987). The extent to which evolutionists believed in 'progress' is examined in Ruse (1996).

26 Adrian similarly hoped that the progress of psychology would solve problems which physiology could not address (Adrian, 1950: 6).

27 The *British Journal of Psychology* noticed a large number of such books but took few seriously; papers directly on the topic were absent from its pages after the First World War. Physiology journals, it hardly needs saying, excluded the topic.

28 Ferrier (1876: ch. 10), on the cerebrum, was very speculative – and substantially cut in the second edition of 1886; see also Jackson (1931–1932) and Young (1970).

29 Myers believed that new ideas in physics also made untenable one old objection to psychology becoming a science, the argument that the subject matter of consciousness cannot be measured. He thought that this followed in some way from belief about the observer's interaction with what is observed; but his thought was obscure. See Myers (1932, 1937). Myers' 1931 address began with a brief account of the founding (1920) of Section J, Psychology, in the British Association for the Advancement of Science, and he indicated that physical scientists had resisted this step, on the grounds that 'the mental' could not be measured.

30 It is indicative of Sherrington's difficulties in balancing his subject, mind's place in nature, with a desire to avoid speculation that he cut much of what he said on the topic (Sherrington, 1940) in the second, 1951, edition of his Gifford lectures (Sherrington, 1963). He evidently thought, and in my view thought rightly, that he had repeated himself rather than deepened what he had to say by trying to nail down unanswerable questions.

31 Sherrington referred in this context to 'subconscious' events. He drew on psychological theories about sensory fusion and memory rather than theories of psychoanalysis (which Sherrington ignored). The importance of this sense of unconscious activity for disruption of views of the self is traced by Gauchet (1992). Sherrington's sensibility towards gradation in mind led him to be wary of the concept of emergence, used, for example, by Alexander (Alexander, 1920/1966: vol. 2, pp. 3–30), since a claim about emergence might be thought to posit a break in evolutionary continuity (see Sherrington, 1940: 266). For theories of emergence, see Blitz (1992).

32 This is the conclusion to an unpublished note on the mind–body relation as the highest integration: small memorandum book, University of British Columbia, Woodward Biomedical Library, II.A.2, dated 1946–7 according to the archive; it appears to be draft elements of the foreword to Sherrington (1961). I am grateful to Lee Perry of the Woodward Biomedical Library for permission to use this material.

33 See Burtt (1924/1932) and Whitehead (1926/1953). These views inspired Robert M. Young who, in the 1960s, fostered a new approach to the history of psychology (Young, 1966, 1985, 1989). Another dimension was the debate about the direction of British culture in the 1920s and 1930s (see, for example, Lepenies, 1988).

34 It is not to the purpose here to debate the historical veracity of this view of Descartes or of his legacy. The symbolic significance of Descartes to modern debates, down to recent linguistics and research in cognitive psychology, can be noted. There appears to be much confusion between claims about the world and historical claims about what Descartes wrote. For historically informed literature on Descartes' relevance to modern psychology see Hatfield (1992) and Sutton (1998).

35 Speaking precisely, and in the face of common opinion, Descartes had no concept of the reflex; he portrayed only possible mechanisms for automatic actions. (Of course, it might be possible to use 'reflex' as a synonym for 'automatic', but this is both vague and makes any search for 'the discovery' of the reflex rather pointless.) See Canguilhem (1955/1977). A standard picture of Descartes' significance was given by T.H. Huxley (1894a,b).

36 For the interwar interest in holist theories in science and medicine, see Ash (1995); Cross and Albury (1987); Harrington (1996); Lawrence and Weisz (1998).

12

A 'precipitous *dégringolade*'?[1] The uncertain progress of British comparative psychology in the twentieth century

David Wilson

1   The lead is lost

The year 1901 marked not only the birth of the British Psychological Society, but also the end of a unique phase of highly original and influential work in British comparative psychology. This work had been inspired by the possibilities revealed by Darwinian theory,[2] and, apart from Charles Darwin himself, Douglas Spalding, George Romanes, Conwy Lloyd Morgan, John Lubbock and Leonard Hobhouse undertook in the last quarter of the nineteenth century a range of pioneering experimental work that seemed to be a tradition of British comparative psychology in the making. But after Hobhouse's *Mind in Evolution* of 1901, the British lead in comparative psychology was lost to the United States, where, following earlier British influence (largely through Lloyd Morgan), new, procedurally precise, laboratory-based experimental work had begun with Edward Thorndike, continued with Willard Small, John Watson and others, and soon led to a neglect of the role of evolutionary theories in favour of the experimental study of short-term, observable learning behaviour, mainly in the rat and under various artificial environmental conditions. In Britain in subsequent decades, having at first almost vanished without trace, the subject became eclectic, often rubbing shoulders with ethology or applied forms of general animal psychology, and sometimes being put to work to serve another discipline.[3] A gradual importation of ideas from abroad took the place of British innovation. Continental ethology reinforced existing domestic enquiries, especially after the Second World War, but in the meantime American-style comparative psychology was never fully accepted as an adequate substitute in Britain for evolution-based research. It is a paradox that, as Britons, Lloyd Morgan provided the theoretical justification and practical means, and William McDougall the motivation, for the American behaviourists to reinforce their methods and beliefs, and for the resulting differences between theirs and the British outlook to be highlighted. Lloyd Morgan's 'Canon' was applied excessively in the United states, while McDougall's neo-Lamarckian views provoked an American reaction to what appeared to be violations of the principles of parsimony and empirical verifiability, so that attention was turned away from instinct theory generally (R.J. Richards, 1977).

If a rise in British comparative psychology was a clear feature of the late nineteenth century, the twentieth century witnessed a decline resulting from a variety of influences which are examined in this chapter. Although George Bernard Shaw's 'precipitous *dégringolade*' was an expression of his disdain for a version of Darwinian materialism and the 'laboratory mind' as represented by the 'simpleton Pavlov', it might also serve as a description of the faltering progress of comparative psychology in Britain for much of this century. There has not been a movement to sustain or direct it, as in the case of American behaviourism, which for many became akin to a religion. It is worth noting, too, that Shaw's lay comments on the value and ethics of comparative psychology presaged the growing range of external influences that would affect the course it could take after the Second World War.

Indeed, not much happened in Britain until after the war, but among limited numbers of laboratory workers in animal psychology, a leading part in keeping a British grasp on the subject was played by women, including E.M. Smith at Cambridge and Victoria Hazlitt, on the staff of Beatrice Edgell at Bedford College for Women. It is clear that Smith, before the First World War and encouraged by Charles Myers, helped, through her experimental work, to make known in Cambridge the nature and potential of Pavlovian conditioning and American learning theory, but that in the light of the knowledge afforded by her work, opportunities to develop it fully were not taken.[4] Lack of interest could not therefore be attributed to lack of knowledge, and Smith's later marriage to Frederic Bartlett did not result in any greater enthusiasm on his part for animal psychology or its theoretical products.

Hazlitt's new and pioneering work in the laboratory study of animal learning had no doubt been stimulated by discussions of the work of Thorndike and other American scientists during her time at Colorado State University between 1912 and 1914, when she had the opportunity to consider learning theory according to the American methodologies then developing. But Edgell soon had to focus the attention of her department on other areas because there seemed no prospects for appropriate facilities: 'Three years ago we dropped our attempts to carry on a first hand study of Comparative Psychology. The time and effort which it required without trained assistance and special accommodation seemed disproportionate when taken in relation to other claims.'[5] Such work and the facilities it needed came to depend on a 'market': education and the social sciences provided one in the United States, but one did not come into being in Britain until the time of the Second World War.[6] This perhaps explains why Thorndike was able to make such progress and why a demoralised Hazlitt had to give up her animal work.

The general lack of research facilities contrasted strongly with the position in the United States,[7] and improvements would first benefit the better-established research areas. In any case, the nature of British society perhaps made it less predisposed to embrace science-based opportunities for social and political control as represented by conditioning or behaviourism. On the other hand, Pavlov soon became politically most correct in his post-revolutionary homeland, and in the United States people like Thorndike, Watson and then B.F. Skinner were encouraged to develop their ideas as newly professionalised specialists working for an appreciative cosmopolitan society which was willing to invest in and respond to scientific solutions or proposals.

The First World War made the British public, if not at first the British establishment, aware of a new dependence on applied science, through which, according to H.G. Wells and others, victory would be achieved by invention. The only attempt actually to apply a scientific understanding of animal behaviour to the war effort consisted of a project of the Admiralty's Board of Invention and Research to train sea lions and seagulls to detect submarines, as a secret measure to counter the U-boat threat of 1916–1917.[8] This was not an encouraging experience – it resulted in failure – and did nothing to persuade the services that the assistance of civilian science in this area was indispensable. In the Royal Navy, the most conservative of the services, the sea lion project caused a severe sense of humour failure among senior officers. Still smouldering in 1931, Admiral Sir Alexander Duff, formerly Director of the Anti-Submarine Division, said of the idea: 'Valuable time, personnel, and money had in fact to be wasted to prove the futility and childishness of this contention' (Marder, 1969: 78). In any case, a marine biologist, physicist and music-hall trainer were in charge of the sea lion programme, and psychologists were neither directly involved nor consulted. The First World War did not, therefore, create a 'market' for this branch of psychology as it did for others in personnel selection or the analysis of 'shell shock' (see Bourke, Chapter 6).

As Hazlitt turned to other aspects of psychology in the 1920s, G.C. Grindley took up work which maintained slender links with developments across the Atlantic and in Russia. He worked from Bristol and Cambridge, undertaking conditioning and learning work with chickens and guinea pigs, when he received frequent advice from Lloyd Morgan as well as the attention of Sir Charles Sherrington, who kept him in mind in case an opportunity arose to create a new post to develop physiological psychology. Grindley experimentally tested and criticised Pavlov's theories, and O.L. Zangwill later commented that he anticipated much subsequent work on what came to be called instrumental or operant conditioning, earning due acknowledgement from Skinner (Zangwill, 1977). Grindley's pupil and colleague G.C. Drew carried on the same interests at Cambridge and Bristol, using rats as his subjects and achieving support from the Medical Research Council and the Rockefeller Foundation in the 1930s.[9]

Lloyd Morgan remained at the centre of a network of correspondence on matters concerning animal behaviour long after he ceased his own experiments, and, until his death in 1934, his desk became a forum for most of those involved in psychological research with animals in Britain. All types of investigator as well as some foreign workers corresponded with him: these included Sherrington, Henry Head, Margaret Washburn, C.S. Myers, E.B. Poulton, William McDougall and J.A. Thomson.[10] Lloyd Morgan's circle included those who also studied the behaviour of animals outside the laboratory and who were preparing the ground for the thoroughgoing introduction of ethology into Britain after the Second World War. For example, W.P. Pycraft introduced him to the work of the ornithologist Eliot Howard, and a strong friendship developed between Howard and Lloyd Morgan, as between Howard and Julian Huxley.[11] Other correspondents, like F.B. Kirkman and E.S. Russell, combined observational with experimental work, and believed strongly that they were interdependent.[12]

This integration of the 'soft ethological' with the 'hard psychological' approach was expressed in the Institute for the Study of Animal Behaviour (ISAB), founded in 1936 by individuals representing a variety of research methods, such as Grindley, Kirkman, Zuckerman, Russell and Julian Huxley. There has always been some spirit of tolerance of alternative viewpoints among British students of animal behaviour: the postwar conflict between laboratory psychology and field ethology was relatively short-lived (and contrary to the objectives of the ISAB), as it was defused by W.H. Thorpe, Nikolaas Tinbergen, Robert Hinde and others. There has been, on the other hand, a regular and widespread opposition, stronger in those with field tendencies, to extreme behaviourism (which has sometimes been associated by onlookers with all laboratory psychology). Scepticism and caution about their own as well as their colleagues' work has not led to the confident and, perhaps, as Bartlett alleged, ill-judged promotion of a single and competitive movement like behaviourism. As a result, British work has appeared eclectic, uncoordinated, uncertain and lacking in vigour, failing to attract regular funding or fashionable status for any of its aspects. Civilised disagreements here have centred on the extent to which animal studies can interpret human behaviour, the relative emphasis to be put on genetic and environmental determinants, the comparative role of observation and experiment, and the extent to which experimenting psychologists should acquire the understanding of the zoologist or the knowledge of the naturalist (see, for example, Russell, 1934).

2   Postwar revival: application and fragmentation

From the late 1930s, comparative psychology and ethology began to show promise as applied research areas, and while ethology has perhaps retained its status as the study of animal behaviour for its own sake, comparative psychology, often becoming better described as more general animal psychology, has increasingly taken on the role of an applied science, occasionally even a secondary technique, serving another primary research-based discipline's programme. In this way, pharmacology and psychiatry as well as agriculture came to represent those new 'markets' which had been lacking, and studies of animal behaviour began increasingly to diversify across academic boundaries, sometimes in an industrial environment.

At the time of the founding of the ISAB, E.S. Russell was based at the Ministry of Agriculture and Fisheries Laboratory at Lowestoft, while the work of W.H. Thorpe at Cambridge on the olfactory conditioning of parasitic insects was directed at the practical problems of economic entomology. As a conscientious objector, Thorpe then applied entomology to the war effort for self-sufficiency in food production, contributing to a project on wire worms, which were causing serious agricultural damage. The war itself enabled students of animal behaviour to advise on a variety of subjects (Hindle, 1947) and analogies were drawn between the adaptations of animals in their natural environment and human invention:

> Almost every invention … has its counterpart in the modifications and behaviour of various wild creatures. To realize the truth of this we have only to think of the use, by squids, of jet propulsion and smoke-screens; of poison gas by skunks and many insects; of chemical warfare by various termites…; of armour, by tortoises and armadillos; and of the recently discovered system of echo-location in bats … [and] the use of those devices [colour resemblance, obliterative shading, disruptive coloration and shadow elimination] which serve for concealment, for disguise, or for bluff. (Cott, 1948)

Postwar developments in applied studies of animal behaviour were varied. For example, Solly Zuckerman was asked from 1948 to 1956 to study the capacity of dogs to be trained reliably to detect buried explosives in non-metallic casings, as they did buried bones. This resulted in the training and assessment of 'mine-dogs' and 'tracker-dogs', and the findings remained of relevance in the 1980s in the aftermath of the Falklands War. Using the principle of conditioned response in their training of dogs, Zuckerman, together with J.T. Eayrs and Eric Ashton, studied the process by which dogs discriminated between different smells and reacted to disturbed ground (Zuckerman, 1988: 150–153).

Soon after the war, a post in animal behaviour was created at the Agricultural Research Council Poultry Research Centre in Edinburgh, and efforts were made to bring veterinarians and animal behaviourists together. Thorpe laid great emphasis on the opportunities for workers in veterinary science and animal husbandry to employ animal behaviour studies, not just for industrial and economic reasons but also for understanding the changes in instinctive behaviour which took place with domestication. Meanwhile, industrial and economic pressures on the natural environment soon required urgent investigations of a variety of ecological processes, such as the movement of animal populations on the land and in the sea.

Commercial interest and agenda setting started to become evident after the war, too, as in sponsorship by the Glaxo pharmaceutical company of Michael Chance's work in 1946. During the 1950s animal colonies for behavioural work became established in the research departments of other pharmaceutical companies in Britain, but by the end of the decade only a few results had been published. Chance's Pharmacology Department at the University of Birmingham was especially concerned with the analysis of exploratory behaviour in the rat (Mead, 1960) and with social influences on the effects of drugs in rodents (Chance, 1956a), as well as the evolutionary significance of seizures (Chance, 1957).

Finally, clinical psychology, introduced to Britain after the war and vigorously promoted by H.J. Eysenck of the Maudsley Hospital's Institute of Psychiatry (Gwynne Jones, 1969; see also Derksen, Chapter 13), was another new field in which some people thought that researches into animal behaviour would be advantageous. Eysenck believed that individual animals as well as humans possess introvert/extrovert and stable/neurotic characteristics; that these vary according to the individual subject and can be measured; and that animals, for example rats, can be bred as experimental aids to express a particular level of emotionality, and conditioned to behave in a desired manner.

P.L. Broadhurst and Irene Martin carried out a survey by questionnaire of all university departments engaged in animal behaviour studies and found that by 1960 there was special interest in exploratory behaviour in the rat, brain lesions (using species not usually associated with this type of work, such as birds and octopus), in the 'traditionally British' study of individual differences, and in the role of hereditary determinants in behaviour (Broadhurst and Martin, 1961). During this postwar period, the ISAB became the Association for the Study of Animal Behaviour; it now attracted a significant international membership and represented many interests in addition to ethology (see Durant, 1986). Also, the Experimental Psychology Group (later Society) came into being in 1946, with the aim of encouraging international communication. These associations soon largely replaced the limited academic involvement in animal behaviour of the British Psychological Society, an involvement so far represented only by the occasional publication of relevant papers in its journal.[13]

By 1960, the study of animal behaviour in Britain was still frequently absent from psychology and zoology courses and was not yet well established as a regular research subject within the universities. At that time, there were university psychology departments wanting to provide the necessary facilities but still deterred by the cost of special buildings and staffing for animal laboratories and by the competition for scarce funds. The work of existing animal laboratories was meanwhile only irregularly assisted by government grants, research foundations and other private or semi-private bodies (Broadhurst and Martin, 1961). With the practical worth of such work nevertheless well recognised and public interest in behavioural topics beginning to be stimulated by the broadcast media, the climate was benign when the recommendations, in 1963, of the Robbins Committee led to a rapid development of higher education.[14] Under a new Labour government, the Science and Technology Act of 1965 brought into being the Science Research Council and Natural Environment Research Council. In this new phase, research into animal behaviour, especially of the laboratory-based kind, was able to take advantage of the opportunity to expand into new university departments and new research areas. The study of animal behaviour was more than ever before spread across the boundaries of academic disciplines, and this sometimes increased the size, role and status of the psychology department, as in the case of the University of Sussex. However, the number of undergraduates involved in these developments remained small and animal behaviour studies continued to grow mainly as a subject for graduate research (Pritchatt, 1966). Furthermore, legislation did not allow for the licensing of invasive laboratory work for teaching purposes.

In a survey of animal behavioural work in a *Supplement to the Bulletin of the British Psychological Society* in 1969, Sluckin noted current interest in operant conditioning, discrimination learning, motivation, behaviour genetics, effects of various prenatal and infantile experiences, imprinting, and mother–infant interaction (Sluckin, 1969).[15] But as behavioural experimentation in the 1960s and 1970s increasingly became a tool for research in medicine, genetics, toxicology, nutrition, pharmacology, and many other areas, the validity and survival of comparative psychology as a truly independent research area were therefore often questioned, as at the same time investigators from other disciplines, such as physiology, biochemistry and neuroendocrinology, influenced the course of behavioural studies in the laboratory and helped to create neuroscience. Some came to think that psychology was becoming entirely dependent on neurophysiology (e.g. Joynson, 1970), much as others later wondered whether it was not mortally threatened by sociobiology. (E.O. Wilson also later felt that ethology itself was likely to be torn in half and consumed by physiology and sociobiology – Wilson, 1975, cited in Slater, 1979.) Developments in neurophysiology had promised since the war to illuminate the observations of ethologists and psychologists and, at Oxford, R.C. Oldfield believed that 'psychology would be much better advised to attract the interest of able young men and women trained in the various fields of natural science than to set itself up as an exclusive and self-contained academic discipline' (Zangwill, 1972).

A joint conference between the Association for the Study of Animal Behaviour and the Society for Experimental Biology in Cambridge in 1949 had been devoted to a consideration of 'Physiological mechanisms in animal behaviour' and it brought together for the first time leading representatives of animal behaviour study in Britain, Continental Europe and North America. Zangwill expressed his optimism in 1950:

> It is my belief that the foundations of an empirical psychology have been securely laid during the past sixty years … a central biological science of psychology is in process of formation … [but] it is urged that the elucidation of central nervous mechanisms in relation to behaviour is a central problem in modern psychological research. (Zangwill, 1950b: 20)

Zangwill believed that 'the neurology of today may well provide the psychology of tomorrow with its basic principles' (1964: 130).

After the Second World War, studies of psychology generally became more fragmented, and Broadhurst and Martin later said that their survey of 1961 could not discern any general trends in the pattern of research. In the sphere of animal behaviour studies, rivalry within a 'reputational system' was seen in some lingering disagreements between laboratory psychologists and ethologists. But beyond this simple division, many others reflected the wide-ranging purposes and methods related to the subject. As professionalism and institutional organisation increased, the whole field became a great variety of specialist activities, groups and individuals, as often competing as cooperating in what remained scientifically a comparatively new as well as uncertain subject area. Many of the components of this broad subject area had also remained of interest to those outside the immediate centres of research activity, and external influences on progress and direction were therefore strong.[16] Studies of animal psychology and behaviour existed in a loosely structured field marked more by innovation and new avenues of interest than the cautious and conservative development of conventional, well established theories. This meant that, though healthier and in greater evidence after the war, professionalisation and institutionalisation were fragmented processes and, as a result, comparatively restricted; and excessive innovation has also at times brought into question the identity and relevance of an entire subject (that of comparative psychology, for example).

3   The effect of ethology and internationalisation

In the late 1940s, laboratory-based research in 'comparative' psychology had found a new impetus, resulting from a revival of interest in neo-behaviourist ideas from the United States. But concentration there on the laboratory rat had produced an experimental psychology which could no longer convincingly be described as comparative. Ethology came to represent the study of animal behaviour as a possible means of interpreting human behaviour, and its appearance helped to restore attention to those Darwinian theories which had been neglected after the turn of the century. W.H. Thorpe believed that ethology and comparative psychology could help humankind understand its own nature, circumstances and prospects, much as did Julian Huxley (and, to a lesser extent, E.S. Russell), whose support and influence provided the main assistance for the establishment of ethology in Britain after the war.[17]

Laboratory-oriented work, which owed much to the procedural refinements developed in the United States in the previous 40 years, now helped to make ethological field studies of animal behaviour for their own sake more distinct. Kurt Danziger has commented: 'During that period [1949–1951] the influence of one or two people outside psychology was very much more important than anything within the discipline. Dr Chance of the University of Birmingham was doing animal work that aroused interest among some of the younger generation.'[18] In the mid-1950s, Michael Chance, a zoologist, had begun a new wave of research on rhesus monkeys at London Zoo: he attempted to improve the assessment of the nature of their social structure, following the conclusions that Solly Zuckerman had drawn in the late 1920s, incorrect owing to the effects of overcrowding

(Chance, 1956b). Furthermore, after the war, certain key figures of the academic establishment, whose interests dictated the nature of research programmes, changed. For example, the highly influential Frederic Bartlett did not share those interests of his wife (as mentioned above) and had done little to encourage animal psychology at Cambridge before the war.[19] When Oliver Zangwill took over in 1952, research priorities were transformed.

The willingness of those such as Thorpe and Tinbergen to recognise its value and use its methods meant that laboratory work in the study of animal behaviour in Britain reappeared after the Second World War in a new and invigorated form by courtesy of ethology. Tinbergen later recalled:

> We learnt a great deal from the American psychologists who criticized us and they also came to see the value of the sort of evidence we had. Now, for example, you have two zoologists teaching here at the Institute of Experimental Psychology and plenty of psychologists have developed an interest in animals other than the white rat. There's been mutual traffic … many psychology departments now employ zoologists on their staff. Here in Oxford zoology and psychology share the same building. (Cohen, 1977)[20]

Tinbergen and Thorpe had soon come to an informal agreement that the Cambridge group should concentrate on mechanisms and development of behaviour while the Oxford group should focus on behavioural functions and evolution. The establishment of the Animal Behaviour Research Group at Oxford in 1949 and the Sub Department of Animal Behaviour at Madingley, Cambridge, in 1950 facilitated this cooperative arrangement.

By the early 1960s, the distinction between some of the work of ethological stations and psychological laboratories was becoming blurred, and explicit attempts were being made by people such as Robert Hinde to bridge the gap in outlook between them as it became realised that animals' habits were learned within the constraints imposed by genes.[21] Deutsch (1963), for example, admitted his surprise at discovering the natural burrowing behaviour of the rat in its natural environment outside the laboratory. Because so much had been learnt about the rat over the course of the century, it seemed difficult to discard it, although many researchers, especially ethologists, were recommending the diversification of species interests as well as of the kinds of behaviour studied. Thorpe, meanwhile, remained sceptical about comparative psychology,[22] and Broadhurst stated:

> Emphasis on learning alone, that is, on one aspect of the environmental determinants of behaviour, to the neglect of genetic variables as well as other influential background variables, often environmental but liable to interact with the genetic ones in affecting behaviour, and this emphasis limited to results from one species alone, created a climate inimical to the study of psychogenetics which is only now being eroded. (Broadhurst, 1963: 69)

Work both in the laboratory and in the field had begun to be internationalised soon after the war's end. Tinbergen had written to David Lack in 1940: 'There are so few really serious students of animal behaviour and yet there is so much to do. When the war is over, it will be highly necessary to reconstruct international co-operation in our science as soon as possible.'[23] The period between the end of the Second World War and the 1960s witnessed a considerable expansion in the output of research, matched by new key research areas, centres of research, professional associations and scientific journals. British work in the early 1960s (W.D. Hamilton, 1964) led to developments in genetic theories[24] which contributed to the growth of interest in sociobiology as a new international subject emanating from the United States. By the 1970s, the internationalisation (at least between Continental Europe, Britain and the United States) of the various forms of field and laboratory studies of animal behaviour was complete, achieved through a new level of publications, communications, conferences, collaboration, visits, residencies and exchanges. Such internationalisation included Western, Westernised and developed, democratic countries and, in common with other pure and applied sciences and with the environmental issues often related to them, the subject, typically from the late 1960s onwards, came to be regarded by the research workers of the relevant nations as a global one. Individual scientists from these nations might contribute now to an international discipline, not one linked to or dependent on the domestic conditions of a particular nation. The sharing of the Nobel Prize for Physiology and Medicine in 1973 by Nikolaas Tinbergen, Konrad Lorenz and Karl von Frisch demonstrated the transnational status of this and other scientific areas. When E.O. Wilson's *Sociobiology* was published in 1975 to offer new theories to develop ethology (Wilson, 1975), reactions to it were therefore given by an international readership concerned with an international subject. If there were, in the postwar years, any cultural barriers, they were erected within the scientific community itself, and they were not related to national cultural predispositions or to political influences.

4   External influences: popularisation and ethical controversies

4.1 *Popularisation*

Following the tradition set by Julian Huxley in the 1930s, aspects of field research were brought increasingly into the public eye from the 1950s onwards, assisted by the advent of television to many homes and by the popularising work of individuals such as James Fisher and Desmond Morris (see, for example, Morris, 1958; see also Hinde, 1971). Morris in particular used comparative themes to produce popular works which sharpened public attention on animal behaviour and its alleged significance in understanding that of humans, and Tinbergen's popular books, films (such as *Signals for Survival*) and talks on radio and television brought ethology and animal behaviour study to the general public. Coinciding with these developments was the intensification of science coverage in the broadcast media, for which subjects related to natural history were especially suited. Amateurs were still involved to an appreciable extent and represented a link between the professional scientists and the public, blurring the distinction between the two. There was also a threefold increase in science coverage by BBC television, through programmes such as *Horizon*, which was charged with exploring the 'scientific attitude' and being 'more concerned with ideas and philosophies of science than with techniques, or even discoveries' (Jones *et al.*, 1978).

Television has, since the 1960s, engaged and promoted the public's interest in animal behaviour, primarily in natural contexts, through a growing number of natural history documentaries.[25] These have often served to encourage the notion of human kinship with animals and have effected an 'ethical bridge-building' (Serpell and Paul, 1994: 129). They have also drawn attention to the vulnerability of animals in terms of the behaviour of humans towards them (threatening extinction, destruction of habitat, commercial exploitation, and so on).[26] The new media coverage was based more on ethological studies than on comparative psychology. Public interest in and knowledge of animals was no longer restricted to pets or working animals, and media attention, mainly to animals in the wild, generated a new public sympathy with them that frequently became anthropomorphic and stimulated a widespread, if poorly articulated, environmental ethic.

4.2 *Ethical controversies*

The contemporary proliferation of laboratory-based animal research work then became subject to intense public scrutiny and ethical criticism; during this period, ironically one of highly sophisticated, objective and complex scientific analysis, philosophical commentary and the old questions about the moral basis of the 'man–animal relationship' began to reappear.[27] The renewed evolutionary emphasis of animal behaviour studies of the 1970s underscored these questions.

In the 1930s, E.S. Russell had stressed the value of observation and recording as opposed to exploitative collecting or the use of unnatural control in the artificial conditions of the laboratory. His was a philosophical approach to practical studies in animal behaviour which was in many ways compatible with the environmental ethics of the 1960s and 1970s, a period when there was a tendency anyway to question the establishment and conservative viewpoints. In the mid-1970s, some scientists began to lend support to the social and philosophical concerns over the morality of certain forms of animal behaviour study, concerns often based, ironically, on those Darwinian theories which had been neglected as sources for experimental programmes in Britain because of the constrictive sociopolitical environment of science at the turn of the century, and in the United States because they had been less relevant to the growing interest there in new learning theories. Such concerns were absent in earlier decades. N.J. Mackintosh recalls that, at a practical level, suffering in laboratory animals was avoided in the late 1950s because it might spoil the results of experiments, 'but this belief was not translated into any formal procedure for soliciting ethical concern or monitoring the treatments and procedures we adopted'.[28] A change of outlook in the 1970s led to a spate of overt self-regulation on the part of the specialist societies[29] and a redrafting of controlling legislation, which became a feature of the 1980s.[30]

At the end of the Second World War, it was commonly accepted that scientists should help secure the postwar economy, and no serious public suspicion of science appeared in Britain until the organised protests against the atomic bomb in the late 1950s and the general questioning of establishment values that developed in the 1960s (c.f. Jenkins, 1979). Since then, science has occupied a paradoxical position both as the object of criticism, often from liberal and 'environmental' sources concerned with a variety of ethical issues, and as the source for the public of fascinating discovery and media-friendly speculation, if not for the solutions to the problems which it was accused of creating.

For laboratory-based animal behaviour studies, a great deal of negative public attention has been brought to bear since the mid-1970s, resulting from the perception of a non-medical science dependent supposedly on sinister (rather than simply painful) experimental procedures often serving seemingly trivial or questionable ends. It came to be argued that if an animal were psychologically like us, there might be more scientific reason to experiment but less moral justification to do so. In response to this dilemma, some scientists denied it existed, saying that although there were scientifically valuable similarities between humans and animals which made experimentation worthwhile, humans were at the same time fundamentally different. This outlook was, ironically, typical of the pre-Darwinian era. (Another irony was that debate about these issues facilitated the participation once more of philosophers in questions concerning experimental psychology.)

In Britain, certainly more so than in the United States, ethical constraints have prevented the development of psychological research with animals along certain routes, and the professional and academic societies have over the past 20 years published for their members codes of conduct and guidelines that are intended to respond to public concern about the welfare of animals in the psychological laboratory. Ethical considerations arose as a consequence of the acceptance of legitimacy of comparability, a consequence with, therefore, a scientific basis rather than one resulting only from philosophical arguments, or from emotive and subjective traditions of common-sense morality.

By the end of the 1970s, the public debate about the perceived value, processes and moral significance of animal behaviour studies had been brought into the open by some vociferous members of the British Psychological Society and by an array of hostile pressure groups, among which the longer established were turning attention to psychology only for the first time. For example, there is no evidence in the archives of the British Union for the Abolition of Vivisection of any earlier concern about this area of scientific work, and until the Second World War the main objects of criticism were physiology and vaccination.[31] However, in 1948 the Duchess of Hamilton, together with the British Union for the Abolition of Vivisection, the National Anti-Vivisection Society and other anti-vivisection societies, had presented a coordinated petition to the Home Secretary demanding a Royal Commission to investigate animal experiments, and using in support of the petition seven examples of licensed research which was deemed unacceptable. The petition was rejected because the Home Secretary believed that the legislation was working adequately, but only after the Home Office had sought explanations from the relevant scientists to put alongside the Duchess of Hamilton's seven statements. One of the seven examples was an experiment for which G. Ungar and S. Zuckerman had received a licence on 3 April 1943, to study, in relation to the Blitz, traumatic shock, using a rotating drum and other methods, and involving rats, guinea pigs and other animals. By 1948 Ungar had returned abroad again, but Zuckerman explained that the animals were under anaesthetic at the time.[32] It was not made clear, however, whether the animals were allowed to recover from the anaesthetic instead of being destroyed, which would have been the normal requirement of the Act, but which would have presumably compromised this behavioural experiment. The 'rotating drum' referred to was probably what came to be known as the 'Noble–Collip drum', a new device perhaps used in Britain for the first time by Zuckerman, which had been invented the year before by the two eponymous Toronto scientists. They first described it in 1942 as 'A quantitative method for the production of experimental traumatic shock without haemorrhage in unanaesthetized animals'. The animal would be traumatised by placing it in a revolving drum 'in which are projections or bumps.... The number of animals dying showed a curve in proportion to the number of revolutions' (Noble and Collip, 1942). This enduring method, alongside the American studies of 'learned helplessness' developed by Martin Seligman, was later classed as unacceptable by W.D.M. Paton (1979), chairman of the Research Defence Society.

The effect of hostile external influences on the progress of academic and research programmes is usually denied by those whose work appears to be under threat, and justification and defence of such work is reaffirmed internally through the editorials of societies' periodicals, the establishment of codes or the inauguration of specialist groups within societies, such as the Psychobiology Section of the British Psychological Society. However, signs that organised and sometimes militant opposition was affecting the content and administration of academic research programmes appeared from the 1980s, when some prospectuses announced the optional status or absence of animal work, and university departments introduced extra security measures. The University of Bristol displayed a public notice outside its city-centre Department of Psychology in Berkeley Square which announced that animals were not used there. In some cases, controversial work was simply exported.

4.3 *Regulation*

By 1980, it had become clear that the 1876 Cruelty to Animals Act, the traditional reference point for discussions on animal research of all kinds, was to be replaced.[33] Although well regarded by the scientific community, its reform would be the inevitable outcome of protracted public argument, over the decades, based largely on the Act's regulation of physiological work. During the 1970s, it had been generally agreed that the Act was inappropriate for much psychological work on stimulation, deprivation or motivation rather than on surgical intervention. It was designed to regulate vivisection rather than experimentation, and no psychological work had been mentioned in the annual reports of the Home Office Inspectorate before the Second World War. The attachment of the special certificate A to a licence, enabling experiment without anaesthetic, required that 'no operative procedure more severe than superficial venesection or simple inoculation may be adopted in any of the said experiments', but, taken literally, this would place no restriction on stressful psychological procedures. Furthermore, the Act stipulated that 'if an animal appears to an Inspector to be suffering considerable pain, and if such Inspector directs such animal to be destroyed, it shall forthwith be painlessly killed': an equivalence of pain and mental suffering was not addressed.

Psychologists had worked within the spirit of the 1876 Act and had recognised specific advice given by the Research Defence Society in its *Notes on the Law Relating to Experiments on Animals in Great Britain (The Act of 1876)*, first published in 1950. This was reprinted in 1967 and 1969, but in 1972 was superseded by *Guidance Notes on the Law Relating to Experiments on Animals*, which was based on guidance notes compiled by the Home Office Inspectorate.[34] When designing an experiment, much depended on judgements made by psychologists (and others studying behaviour) about whether it fell within the Act and so required description, submission, approval and a licence.[35] A full and representative record of the process of submission, approval and report-back is provided by the work of Dennis H. Chitty between 1950 and 1955. A biologist and Deputy Director of the Bureau of Animal Population, he planned to apply behavioural experimentation in a primary study of the 'physiological mechanisms involved in population control by intraspecific competition', testing Selye's adaptation syndrome by keeping voles under conditions likely to result in fighting for the establishment of a social hierarchy.[36] Chitty and Selye were Canadians who shared an interest in studies of stress and the means of experimentally producing it. Selye published widely on stress and his work, which was particularly criticised by anti-vivisectionists, led to the identification of a stressed-induced hormone which was later reproduced synthetically for use in medication (adrenocorticotrophic hormone and cortisone). Chitty worked in Britain in circumstances in which the law and the Advisory Committee on the Administration of the Cruelty to Animals Act 1876 applied greater restrictions than those experienced in the prosecution of this sort of work by his Canada-based counterparts.

4.4 *Public and professional reactions to animal behaviour experimentation*

On 2 November 1946, a letter had been sent by the War Office to the Home Secretary seeking confirmation that no licence was needed for the War Dogs

Training School of the British Army of the Rhine, where Royal Army Veterinary Corps officers were designing experiments on dogs trained in mine detection in which the olfactory nerves would be cut and other operations carried out in order to determine how the dogs detected mines. The response of the Home Office was to indicate that the experiments could proceed because they were to take place abroad, but that if they were to have been conducted in Britain a licence might well have been refused. The Home Office also noted that if the work in Germany was made known in Britain, there could be a public outcry, and it would then be up to the Secretary of State for War to provide an explanation.[37]

After the war, the Universities Federation for Animal Welfare (UFAW) began to turn its attention to the position of laboratory animals, when, as an organisation consisting largely of scientists and academics, it was seen as competent to comment authoritatively on carefully examined issues of experimental suffering, issues inevitably connected with factors related to sensation and behaviour. In November 1947, the inaugural meeting of the Cambridge University branch took place at St John's College, when Sir Frederic Bartlett took the chair and accepted the branch presidency. Following a circular, 100 applications had been made to join the branch within a week, and in February the following year it organised a symposium on pain at which Bartlett and E.D. Adrian spoke, with James Gray in the chair, and when, according to the Twenty-Second Annual Report of UFAW, the house was packed. Bartlett soon became a Vice-President of the Federation. At the annual general meeting of the Cambridge branch in October 1949, again under Bartlett's presidency, George Humphrey and R.E. Rewell spoke on 'Fear in animals'.[38] In 1959 the Association for the Study of Animal Behaviour invited C.W. Hume of UFAW to address it on the question of anthropomorphism (Hume, 1959). Scientific societies have not often encouraged animal welfare organisations to lecture them, especially on a topic of routine familiarity, and the speaker being from without the discipline scientifically most competent to understand it. However, the nature of the topic of anthropomorphism allowed for some philosophical argument, and Charles Hume was an extremely articulate author (the strength of his articles often let down by their trivial titles – for example Hume, 1949).

Factors related to but not part of the experiment itself, such as the suitability of accommodation, have come to have equal status in animal welfare issues, and are better addressed in later legislation.[39] Writing in 1977, W.H. Thorpe believed that ethology could help in solving the problems of animal welfare that existed in animal experiment and husbandry: 'The problem of determining what treatment is to be allowed and what forbidden can only be solved with the help of biologists working in many different fields: but primarily those investigating the natural behaviour of animals.'[40] Huxley and Thorpe were both actively concerned not only with conservation but also with animal welfare issues, and used their academic knowledge and standing to promote these. Huxley had much earlier commented on the cruelty of commercialised meat production;[41] as Secretary of the Zoological Society of London from 1935, he became concerned by the cramped conditions and boredom of the animals at the Zoo; and he speculated on the application of animal research techniques to human subjects when, with his brother, in 1955 he witnessed American work on the stimulation of the pleasure centres of the brain in rats.[42] Later, Thorpe served on the Brambell Committee on the keeping of domestic animals, and pioneered recognition of the cruelty of close confinement and beak-clipping (Hinde, 1987).[43]

In their popular literature, psychologists were keen to assure the general reader of good motives, intentions and practices. For example, P.L. Broadhurst emphasised the experimenters' responsibilities (to the welfare of their animals, to themselves and to their colleagues by maintaining a safe and sanitary environment, and to the legal and moral requirements of society), and confirmed that they were invariably met. He employed anthropomorphic descriptions to effect this reassurance, describing the life of the laboratory rat as one of leisured tranquillity, interrupted only by occasional concern about the arrival of its next meal or some moments of fairly acute discomfort. Small cages were supposedly excused if the animal was nocturnal. Another ethical aspect of animal psychology might be the applied results of such work, but in this speculative area there was little but optimism: 'whole crops may be harvested by ape labour in the future' and what was really a technology of animal behaviour offered food for thought for industrialists who might soon employ pigeon pilots and chimpanzee engine-drivers (Broadhurst, 1963).

There were occasional indications in the 1960s, however, of the disagreement that would later arise between 'experimenting' and some 'non-experimenting' psychologists (who happened very often, it was to prove, to be clinical psychologists). For example, M.B. Shapiro wrote in 1965: 'The infliction of injuries on animals for research purposes presents a special problem. It would seem to be impermissible to do these things for purely academic purposes. It is only where serious questions of health in man himself are involved that such operations may be justified' (Shapiro, 1965: 34). At this time he was working at the Maudsley Hospital's Institute of Psychiatry, where Broadhurst, his colleague, saw animal research in a much more enthusiastic light. Shapiro had warned a student, J.A. Gray, that there was little he could contribute to clinical psychology by doing fundamental research in the rat laboratory. Gray was awarded the 1983 Presidents' Award of the British Psychological Society and took the opportunity of attempting to demonstrate the relevance of animal work for clinical psychology and psychiatry, for example because of the similarity of the neurology of anxiety in man and rat, and because he believed in no dichotomy between cognitive and behaviourist psychology, their being 'two sides of the same coin' (Gray, 1985). Broadhurst had earlier commented: 'There is essentially only one basic scientific interest in the study of animal behaviour and that is to learn more about man himself. The pursuit of knowledge for its own sake is often spoken of but rarely practised in pure form' (Broadhurst, 1963: 13–14). But W. Sluckin said of British animal behaviour studies as they had developed by 1969: 'It should perhaps be noted that probably most research in the field of animal behaviour, whatever its roots and character, is carried out for its own sake rather than with reference to any human studies' (Sluckin, 1969).

Richard Ryder, senior clinical psychologist at the Warneford Hospital, Oxford, and between 1977 and 1979 Chairman of the Council of the Royal Society for the Prevention of Cruelty to Animals (RSPCA), did much to extend the debate within psychology to the public arena in the 1970s. Before the publication of his *Victims of Science* in 1975, he had asked in the *Sunday Mirror*:[44] 'Can we justify cruel experiments on animals on the grounds that psychologists can learn more about behaviour?', answering, 'I do not believe any of the suffering I have caused to laboratory animals – and, alas, there has been some – has helped humanity in the slightest.' Another psychologist, Alice Heim (1970), had written in her book *Intelligence and Personality: Their Assessment and Relationship* of 'the apparent callousness of much of the experimental work carried out on the lower animals', later comparing such experimentation with the practices of Nazism. She attributed such immorality to behaviouristic and mechanistic views of mind, and observed:

> The work on 'animal behaviour' is always expressed in scientific, hygienic-sounding terminology, which enables the indoctrination of the normal, non-sadistic young psychology student to proceed without his anxiety being aroused. Thus, techniques of 'extinction' are used for what is in fact torturing by thirst or near-starvation or electric-shocking. (Quoted by Ryder, 1975/1983: 55)

The first letter in a long series of correspondence (some of it later becoming rather acrimonious) on the ethics of the use of animals in behaviour research was published in the *Bulletin of the British Psychological Society* in August 1975 (Sperlinger, 1975). Over the next four years, letters from various correspondents (such as Shapiro, Ryder, A. Jolley, L.J. Holman and D.G. Boyle) covered a variety of aspects of the ethical question, including: the practical value of the research undertaken; whether the degree of stress involved should be left up to the experimenter; the comparative status, in terms of moral responsibility to be assumed by the experimenter, of human and non-human animals; the possible erosion of moral responsibility because of the effect of the allegedly uncaring laboratory ethos; the validity of evidence for suffering; humaneness and the lack of it; the justification of research which might be non-medical, or undertaken to achieve pure knowledge rather than knowledge directly applicable to the alleviation of suffering in humans; the necessity or prevalence of peer-group control of stressful experiments, or of their control by assessors including non-experimenters; whether all animals should have consideration, even, for example, protozoa; the nature of controversial experiments and the nature of the stocking of animals; the possible withdrawal of condonement of animal experimentation by the British Psychological Society; the comparison with other treatments of animals, such as eating or hunting them; and, if animals possessed sufficient similarities to human beings to make behavioural research on them valid, whether for that reason there was a moral requirement not to subject them to research involving suffering.

With regard to the last point, one of the similarities between animals and humans that began to suggest itself was altruism. On 9 September 1970, the

Daily Telegraph reported that S.J. Dimond, of the Department of Psychology at the University College of Wales, Cardiff, had discovered that a rat would press a lever to save another from drowning, and that a monkey would refuse a food reward if the reward resulted in an electric shock for another animal (cited by Ruesch, 1979: 55). The notion of altruism in animals would appear to be the kind of anthropomorphic weakness especially criticised by the behaviourists, but by this time alternative theories for animal (and human) behaviour based on the idea of 'kin selection' and 'inclusive fitness' were beginning to compromise the simple opposition of the earlier standpoints: it might be argued that immediate conscious behaviour in animals supported such long-term evolutionary theories.

At the annual general meeting of the British Psychological Society in Exeter in 1976, the above matters were discussed in a symposium, and as a result it was decided that the Society's Scientific Affairs Board should set up a working party whose terms of reference would be to examine: ways of ensuring that psychological advice was incorporated in Home Office assessments of licence applications; standards of training and supervision; the definition of 'animal' and possible categorisation for purposes of assessing 'ethical cost'; the scale and economy of animal use; the proper conditions for accommodation; the assessment of qualitative and quantitative 'ethical cost' in experiments, to be weighed against the likely benefits of findings; and the formulation of a set of guidelines for psychological teaching and demonstrations involving animals (British Psychological Society, 1976). In 1978, the working party presented its report (British Psychological Society, 1979). There were 215 licence holders in 38 departments of psychology. In 39 out of 57 departments, animals were used in undergraduate teaching. In considering the ethical implications of animal work, the working party found that, in spite of similarities between human and non-human animals, the differences justified the research, because, for example, animals lacked awareness and anticipation of the procedures being applied or planned; but 'these issues should continue to be the subject of public debate within the psychological community'. Broadly speaking, the aim should be maximum gain (in new knowledge or alleviation of human suffering) for minimum suffering. The working party recommended that a standing advisory committee on standards for psychological research and teaching involving animals be established by the British Psychological Society to liaise with the Home Office over implementation of the 1876 Act; to create guidelines for training graduate students; to liaise appropriately with similar committees of other societies; and to act as an ethical watchdog. Those who did not experiment on animals should also serve on the committee. The British Psychological Society declined an invitation to join the Research Defence Society, but at the end of 1983 it was announced by the Scientific Affairs Board that the newly formed Psychobiology Section of the Society was to be asked 'to advise on any role it might play in the identification of members willing to take an active part in considering the interests of psychologists conducting psychological research with animals' (British Psychological Society, 1983).

5 Conclusions

It is ironic that although during the course of the twentieth century the student of animal behaviour became best able to comment on the nature of animal experience, the result was often only criticism by sections of society about the nature of the research into that behaviour, instead of productive consultation. For example, Huxley and Thorpe denounced the failure of the Ministry of Agriculture to act on the recommendations of the Brambell Committee. But M.W. Fox applauded Thorpe as one who had 'contributed so outstandingly as an ethologist to establish the science of animal welfare'.[45] Now better use is made of this specialist knowledge, and we see in Bateson's report a turning of the tables: a distinguished specialist in scientific studies of animal behaviour has carried out an objective analysis of an activity (stag hunting with hounds) carried on by a section of society apart from science which can, as a result, be criticised for the suffering it causes (Bateson, 1997). Perhaps an eventual effect of comparative psychology and other forms of animal behaviour study will be to moderate our treatment of non-human species through having discovered more of the nature of shared sensation and motivation; but the necessary enquiries have so far involved some confusion and controversy along an uncomfortable and uncertain path.

Notes

1 *Dégringolade*: a tumbling down. George Bernard Shaw to Julian Huxley in 1942. Cited in Huxley (1970: 252).

2 The publication of Darwin's *The Expression of the Emotions in Man and Animals* in 1872 has been suggested as the time when the modern school of animal behaviour studies began (Thorpe, 1956).

3 The two major published histories addressing the development of British animal psychology have been written by psychologists who have opted for a traditional 'internal' treatment, and in them the progress of British work since Darwin has been set either in a more extensive historical timeframe, with other areas of psychology integrated into the account (Hearnshaw, 1964), or in a context which serves primarily to explain international progress (Boakes, 1984).

4 Although Pavlov had lectured on conditioned reflexes at Charing Cross Medical School in 1906, it was not until the translation of 1927 and that of his *Lectures on Conditioned Reflexes* of 1928 that his work became generally accessible in Britain (Pavlov, 1927).

5 B. Edgell, 8 December 1923, *Report to Council on the Needs for the Future Development of Psychology*. Royal Holloway University of London Archives, AR 334/10/1. Better facilities in the United States had recently tempted McDougall to emigrate, as Titchener had in 1892.

6 The vast education industry of the United States has been described as the powerhouse of the rapid growth of applied psychology there (Danziger, 1987: 26).

7 Mention was made of 'the enormous and hitherto unutilized scientific and technical resources which are available in America to an extent at present quite unobtainable in England or France. These resources comprise not only large numbers of highly skilled scientists and assistants with numerous large and well equipped laboratories, but also practically unlimited mechanical assistance for the manufacture of experimental

apparatus.' Report by Professor Sir Ernest Rutherford FRS and Commander Cyprian Bridge RN, on a visit to the United States in company with a French Scientific Mission, 19 May – 9 July 1917. BIR 28208/17. Public Record Office, London, ADM 293/10. American funding specifically for psychological work, as from the Rockefeller Memorial, improved dramatically in the 1920s (see Boakes, 1984: 237–239).

8 E.J. Allen, 1917, *Report upon Experiments on the Hearing Powers of Sea-Lions Under Water, and on the Possibility of Training these Animals as Submarine Trackers.* BIR 30051/17. London: Admiralty Board of Invention and Research. Public Record Office, London, ADM 293/5, pp. 450–469.

9 Sir Frederic Bartlett, *Report on the Support of the Rockefeller Foundation Since 1937*, Undated but *c.* 1945. Cambridge University Library Department of Manuscripts and University Archives. Add. MS 8076. D.1.4.

10 Much of the correspondence is preserved in the Bristol University History Collection (DM 128 and DM 612).

11 W.P. Pycraft, 1908, letter to C. Lloyd Morgan, 8 April. Bristol University History Collection, DM 128/179.

12 F.B. Kirkman, 1912–1913, letters to C. Lloyd Morgan, 10 September, 13 November and early July. Bristol University History Collection. DM 128/265, 277 and 288. E.S. Russell to C. Lloyd Morgan, 29 October, 1933. Bristol University History Collection, DM 612.

13 A survey of the postwar period ending in 1960 resulted in the identification of a total of 258 individual papers in the five principal British journals (*Bulletin of Animal Behaviour, British Journal of Psychology, Quarterly Journal of Experimental Psychology, British Journal of Animal Behaviour* and *Animal Behaviour*) and in *Behaviour* by 152 different authors, which were related to specific fields of interest as later categorised by *Animal Behaviour Abstracts*. Of these occasions, 48 concerned publication on sexual and reproductive behaviour; 33 on maintenance behaviour (foraging, ingestion, and so on); 27 on groups and social behaviour; and 21 on evolution and survival value. In the same way, mammals, excluding primates and usually signifying the rat or mouse, were the subjects of research on 132 of these occasions, insects on 78 and birds on 67. Other types of animal had very little use, and primates earned only three author attributions. Among 81 sites productive before 1960, the most active were Madingley (36 out of the 315 attributions), the Department of Zoology and Comparative Anatomy at Oxford (25), Rothamsted (22), the Institute and Department of Experimental Psychology at Oxford (17) and Birkbeck (13). The *British Journal of Psychology* had continued to reduce its coverage of British animal behaviour work, as in later decades (for example 1940–1959, 11 articles; 1973–1980, 10 articles). Meanwhile, the output of *Behaviour* became steady throughout the 1950s (1948–1959, 71 articles), but because the *Quarterly Journal of Experimental Psychology* remained concerned to provide a coverage representative of all forms of experimental psychology, its treatment of British animal work was relatively limited (1949–1959, 26 articles; 1973–1980, 41 articles). The dominant position was eventually taken over by *Animal Behaviour*, having evolved from the *Bulletin of Animal Behaviour*, which had managed to survive the war (1938–1951, 12 articles), and from its successor, the *British Journal of Animal Behaviour*, which itself achieved a very significant level of publication of British work in the mid-1950s (1953–1957, 95 articles). In its new role as an international forum for animal work, *Animal Behaviour* has subsequently remained the key journal for British research (1958–1959, 44 articles; 1973–1980, 171 articles). The general trend in British publication since the Second World War has shown a shift from the use of the traditional psychological journals to those with a greater orientation to zoology and ethology, together with the participation of international journals representing applied psychological research, as in pharmacology (such as *Pharmacology, Biochemistry and Behavior*, 46 British contributions between 1974 and 1980). See Wilson (1999).

14 L.C. Robbins (later Baron Robbins of Clare Market) was Chairman of the Committee on Higher Education (1961–1964), which was responsible for the major expansion and reforms of British university education in the 1960s. *Report of the Committee on Higher Education*, under the chairmanship of Lord Robbins, cmnd 2154, October 1963. London: HMSO.

15 The favoured fields of interest among the whole experimenting community in Britain in an ensuing period, between 1973 and 1980, as abstracted from all relevant international journals, can be compared (figures given in parentheses) with those for the period before 1960 (that is 1938–1959, using the five principal representative journals referred to under note 13). Author attributions for the later major areas of interest (as categorised in *Animal Behaviour Abstracts*) are as follows: chemical stimulation and drugs, 251 (9); brain lesions, 132 (6); sexual and reproductive behaviour, 117 (48); hormones, 116 (5); communication, 115 (10); maintenance behaviour (foraging, ingestion, and so on), 109 (33); and ontogeny, 108 (8). Throughout all periods, the rat and mouse remained the most frequently used animals. Birds overtook insects for second place; and primates became regarded as increasingly important experimental subjects. In the 1973 volume of *Behavioural Biology Abstracts*, 283 out of a total of 3,340 abstracts (8.47%) referred to papers describing work carried out in Britain; in the 1980 volume (now *Animal Behaviour Abstracts*), the figures were 517 out of 5,838 (8.86%). See Wilson (1999).

16 'Where ... researchers have a wide variety of legitimate audiences for their work, including educated laymen, and research skills are not highly standardized, as in many of the human sciences, the need to co-ordinate research results with those of a particular group of colleagues to gain positive reputations is limited, and so contributions to intellectual goals are relatively diffuse and divergent. Integration of task outcomes around common objectives is, therefore, not likely to be very high in such fields' Whitley (1984: 26).

17 Solly Zuckerman felt very differently and emphasised the inability either of early comparative psychology or of ethology to do this (Zuckerman, 1978). Thorpe's concern for the role of general science was shown by his inauguration at Cambridge of a scientists' lunch club in the 1950s, through which, like Zuckerman's prewar 'Tots and Quots', issues connected with the social responsibilities of science and scientists could be discussed. See Hinde (1987).

18 K. Danziger, personal communication, 19 January 1987.

19 Broadbent (1970) notes that the teaching system established by the 1930s by Frederic Bartlett at Cambridge 'produced a brilliant crop of students who, after the Second World War, held the lion's share of the Professorships of Psychology in Britain; and indeed quite a number elsewhere in the Commonwealth'. But Bartlett was critical of the all-embracing theories proposed by the behaviourists: the experimental strategies adopted for animal learning and behaviour studies in the United States 'might almost as well have been planned in the early 1900s' (Bartlett, 1955). In 1927, he had said of John Watson's *Behaviourism*: 'It signalled a great fall. The last remnants of caution have disappeared' (Bartlett, 1927).

20 External and internal variables persistently threatened to deceive the experimenter: if they were not recognised or catered for (and this was extremely difficult), the results, thought to be valid, would in fact be false. Eysenck (1965: 14) referred to this problem when rejecting stimulation–response psychology in *Fact and Fiction in Psychology*; and so did Broadbent (1961: 132), although he appeared to want to try to develop behaviourism rather than abandon it. Individual differences in organisms also created variation in results (Eysenck, 1966).

21 For example, Hinde (1966) and Thorpe and Zangwill (1961). 'If a rapprochement has been reached between the American and European "schools," it is largely due to the personal and intellectual efforts of Thorpe and Hinde and their pre- and

postdoctoral students (Peter Marler, Peter Klopfer, Patrick Bateson, John Fentress, among others)' (Gottlieb in Hearst, 1979: 167n). Furthermore, between the late 1950s and the 1980s behaviourism began to decline in the United States and 'cognitive science' to emerge.

22 Dewsbury (1984: 16) cites the following examples. '[The psychologist] has worked mainly with mammals – above all the white rat – and has devoted but little attention to interspecies differences or to the significance of his findings for behaviour in its natural setting. Indeed one may surmise that the psychologist has chosen to work with animals rather than with men largely on account of their lesser complexity and greater tolerance of the indignities of the experiment!' (Thorpe and Zangwill, 1961: x). 'Psychology tended to treat animals as if they were tiny men and so was subjective in approach' (Thorpe, 1979: ix). 'Comparative psychology, on the other hand, as the term has been used for the past fifty years or so, seems (temporarily one hopes) to have lost its identity and be on the wane' (Thorpe, 1979: 166). Thorpe also entitled a paper: 'Is there a comparative psychology? The relevance of inherited and acquired constraints in the action patterns and perceptions of animals' (Thorpe, 1974). He suggested that 'we are all ethologists in the new sense' (of adopting objective, experimental approaches to problems) and that the chapter to which he was then contributing should be renamed 'Ethology' (Thorpe, 1961). An example of the attempt to reassert the relevance of comparative psychology internationally is Tobach *et al.* (1973).

23 N. Tinbergen, correspondence with D. Lack, 26 February 1940. In The David Lack Papers, Edward Grey Institute, Oxford, item 155. Cited by Durant (1986).

24 In his Foreword to Konrad Lorenz's *On Aggression* (1963/1972), Julian Huxley referred to Lorenz's interpretation of vertebrate behaviour as composed of 'behaviour units' (just as anatomy is composed of structural units), having a genetic basis and having through evolution become modified by Darwinian natural selection.

25 Driscoll and Bateson (1988) thought that opponents of animal work should remember that such programmes were the result of ethological research.

26 This awareness was soon matched and articulated by the arrival of international pressure groups such as Friends of the Earth and Greenpeace, which harnessed the environmental idealism that began especially to permeate the educated and youthful elements of Western society from the 1960s. Rowan and Rollin (1983) refer to the legacy of the social criticism of the 1960s, affecting also philosophers and scientists, and to the growth of concern about various kinds of discrimination.

27 For example, Clark (1977), Lindzey (1976), Singer (1975/1976) and Ryder (1975/1983). The issue of non-human animals' interests within environmental ethics is addressed in an anthology edited by Elliot (1995).

28 N.J. Mackintosh, personal communication, 10 December 1986.

29 Guidelines for the use of animals in research (1985) *Bulletin of the British Psychological Society*, 38, 289–291; Guidelines for the use of animals in research (1981) *Animal Behaviour*, 29, 1–2; Guidelines for the use of animals in research (1986) *Animal Behaviour*, 34, 315–318; and Guidelines for the use of animals in research (1986) *Quarterly Journal of Experimental Psychology*, 38B, 111–116.

30 On 2 November 1978 *The Times* had reported, under the heading 'Reappraisal of animal experiments urged' (p. 6), that Bernard Dixon, editor of *New Scientist*, supported the critical comments of Alice Heim at a symposium of the RSPCA on animal experimentation. He called for a public enquiry and an examination of animal experimentation by the Commons Select Committee on Science and Technology, noting the 'poor level of discussion of the subject in the House of Commons' at the time.

31 Records of the British Union for the Abolition of Vivisection, University of Hull, Brynmor Jones Library, Archives and Special Collections, DBV/23.

32 Public Record Office, London, HO 45/25867.

33 Its replacement later took the form of the Animals (Scientific Procedures) Act of 1986.

34 The edition of 1974 advised that 'Procedures calculated to cause stress, including those designed specifically for behaviour studies require specific authority.... Conditioning by reward alone would not require the authority of the Act.... Intention to affect any of the special senses by damage or deprivation requires a detailed description and explanatory notes.... [For Certificate A work without anaesthetic, including] Exposure to sensory stimuli such as mild electric shock ... [state] intensity, duration, frequency, period of administration, and whether the animal is to have the facility of avoidance or not.... [An experiment within the meaning of the Act] must be calculated to give pain; the Home Office interpretation of this phrase is made in the widest sense as including the possibility of discomfort, distress, disease, or other disturbances of normal physical or mental health, [i.e.] any procedure which may interfere with the normal well-being of a vertebrate animal other than killing, if it be done for the purpose of experiment.' Students were advised that 'Procedures that may cause undue fear, fright or stress would be considered as calculated to cause pain. Examples of these procedures would be very loud noises, very bright lights, and the conditioning experiments such as Pavlov did where the reinforcement is painful.' It was acknowledged in the *Guidance Notes* of 1974 that: 'There has not been sufficient specific research into housing, lighting, nutrition, genetics, husbandry practices, and diseases of laboratory animals, with the result that there is as yet no consensus of opinion amongst the major users in this country as to what the ideal conditions should be in detail.' See Research Defence Society (1974).

35 For opposing views on the adequacy of this state of affairs, compare Blackman (1981: 85) with Ryder (1975/1983: 53).

36 Public Record Office, London, HO 285/13.

37 Public Record Office, London, HO 45/25867.

38 Copies of the annual reports of UFAW, together with much uncatalogued material, have been kept at its headquarters in South Mimms, Potters Bar, London. The previous London office, together with the earlier archives, was destroyed in the Blitz.

39 Blackman (1981: 87) notes that 'psychologists have long recognized that the experience of pain is both difficult to judge and dependent on the general circumstances in which a noxious stimulus may be presented. Similarly, psychologists are accustomed to evaluating the possible disruptive effects on psychological and behavioural well-being of environmental circumstances which do not necessarily give rise to pain as such. In short, psychologists should generally be more alert than some other scientists to the subtleties of how animals interact with their environmental circumstances, and are therefore in a position to heighten awareness of the possible impact of all experimental procedures.'

40 William Homan Thorpe Papers 1927–1984, Cambridge University Library Department of Manuscripts and University Archives, Add. MS 8784 / M13.

41 'Natural Selection', unpublished essay dated 'Oxford 1907'. Julian S. Huxley Archive, Woodsen Research Centre, Fondren Library, Rice University, Texas. Early Materials, Box 2: 1906–1909. Cited by Bartley (1995).

42 'We were stirred by a mixture of fascination and horror at the state of these poor creatures acting under a compulsive spell.... Was Aldous's Brave New World moving a step nearer?' (Huxley, 1970: 175.)

43 Towards the end of his life he noted with approval that 'the RSPCA has already embarked on the support of ethological and ecological research.... One of the most promising, admirable outcomes of this has been the work of Dr Marian Dawkins (1977) on the behaviour of battery-reared and farmyard chickens. This kind of support for research should be developed on a much wider and long continued scale.' William

Homan Thorpe Papers 1927–1984. Cambridge University Library Department of Manuscripts and University Archives, Add. MS 8784 / M13.

44 On 24 February 1974. Cited by Ruesch (1979: 255).

45 M.W. Fox to W.H. Thorpe, 28 April 1980, William Homan Thorpe Papers 1927–1984, Cambridge University Library Department of Manuscripts and University Archives, Add. MS 8784/M13.

13

Science in the clinic: clinical psychology at the Maudsley

Maarten Derksen

1 Defining clinical psychology

A prominent feature of the history of clinical psychology is the discussion about its definition and the related question regarding who is a bona fide clinical psychologist. Introductory texts have often mentioned the difficulty of defining clinical psychology, the variety of approaches to clinical psychology, its overlap with other health care professions and the debates concerning training, professional roles and accreditation. Authors sometimes resort to describing clinical psychology by the activities of clinical psychologists, remarking that the issue of definition has not prevented the growth of the field nor hindered practitioners in their work (see for instance Østergaard, 1962: 10; Rotter, 1964: 2; Garfield, 1974: 1). This is true, but it suggests that the debates concerning the proper definition and demarcation of clinical psychology have nothing to do with its practical development. This makes the vehemence of those debates incomprehensible, and obscures their practical importance.

In science, as in other parts of culture, demarcation is always a vital issue:

> Bounding a practice is a way of defining what it is, of protecting it from unwanted interference and excluding unwanted participants, of telling practitioners how it is proper to behave within it and how that behaviour differs from ordinary conduct, and of distributing value across its borders. (Shapin, 1992: 335)[1]

Much of this 'boundary work' is rhetorical in the sense that language is used to bound a practice. The discussions about the definition and demarcation of clinical psychology are not 'mere words', nor just an administrative effort to find the right label: rather, they are 'instrumentalities actively used to maintain social and cultural realities, to shift them in some desired direction, to say "good" and "bad"' (Shapin, 1992). Thus, the meaning of 'clinical psychology' as a concept is not independent of its meaning in practice, of the practices in which clinical psychologists are involved. The history of the term 'clinical psychology' is an important part of the history of clinical psychology.[2]

Boundary work creates space for practice, but practices need alliances as well as demarcations. Cultural boundaries differentiate *and* link domains. In science, the knowledge of one discipline is distinguished from the other, but facts, theories and methods often cross the boundaries: interdisciplinary projects are set up, sometimes leading to new disciplines with their own boundaries. Pure science is, often passionately, demarcated from applied science, yet equally important is the flow of knowledge from the latter to the former. The boundaries of science demarcate disciplines and regulate their interaction. They are, moreover, themselves the result of interaction, of the play of forces between disciplines, markets for their expertise, funding bodies and governments. The politics of demarcation and alliance result in a constantly changing map of science.

Clinical psychology has traditionally been caught between two disciplines that have often regarded it with some hostility.[3] Clinical psychologists have had to deal with the scepticism of their academic colleagues and the suspicion of psychiatrists, both groups insisting on demarcation and keeping clinical psychology 'in its place'. Yet, alliances between academic and clinical psychology, and clinical psychology and psychiatry, were also sought by all three disciplines. As a result, clinical psychology has been marked by a tension between science and practice, laboratory and clinic, scientist and clinician.

In this chapter I analyse the boundaries of clinical psychology as a combination of demarcation and alliance, focusing on the relations between clinical psychology and psychiatry. Furthermore, particular attention is given to the role of boundary rhetoric and the definition of the discipline in relation to its practical development, to answer just how the history of 'clinical psychology' is a part of the history of clinical psychology.

In this chapter I examine the development of clinical psychology at one site, the Department of Psychology of the Institute of Psychiatry at the Maudsley Hospital in London. The Maudsley was one of the three places where, shortly after the Second World War, psychology began to be applied in the context of the psychiatric clinic under the name of 'clinical psychology' (the other two were the Tavistock Clinic in London and the Crichton Royal Hospital in Dumfries). Of the three, the Department of Psychology at the Maudsley was the most influential in term of its research, its diagnostic and (later) therapeutic practice, the number and quality of the graduates on its training programme, and its boundary work. Most important in the context of this chapter is that Maudsley psychologists played a crucial part in the momentous shift in the balance between laboratory and clinic that took place in British clinical psychology in the 1960s. During this decade, clinical psychologists annexed part of the domain of treatment, which opened up a new field of professional activity, leading to a rapid growth of clinical psychology and a move towards a more clinical, less scientific role for clinical psychologists.

2   Origins

The association between psychology and clinic was first made at the end of the nineteenth century. Independently, two former students of Wilhelm Wundt sought to make psychological knowledge and methods relevant for clinical work. They developed very different practices, however, at opposite ends of the laboratory–clinic dimension that would continue to dominate the vicissitudes of the field.

Lightner Witmer was a pupil of J. McKeen Cattell at the University of Pennsylvania. Like Cattell and many of his contemporaries, he had been to Wundt's laboratory in Leipzig to study for his PhD. Upon returning in 1892 he succeeded Cattell as head of the Psychological Laboratory. His interest, however, soon turned towards the application of psychology. In 1896 he opened a 'psychological clinic' at the University where backward children were diagnosed and treated, and where he gave courses in 'clinical psychology' for the benefit of doctors and teachers.

Witmer's clinic was both an event and a locality. On the one hand, the psychological clinic was, as he put it, 'conducted' (Witmer, 1907: 248). 'The term clinical implies a method, and not a locality,' he wrote, attempting to wrest the concept away from its etymological roots (the Greek *klinè* means 'bed') and out of the hands of medical doctors. In the clinical method, 'the status of an individual mind is determined by observation and experiment, and pedagogical treatment applied to effect a change, i.e., the development of such individual mind' (Witmer, 1907: 251). On the other hand, the clinic was a site, characterised by the fact that it brought people and activities together: teachers, students and patients (Reisman, 1991: 39, 76), diagnosis, treatment and research. Witmer put special emphasis on this latter trio: the clinical psychologist examines a child with a single definite object in view – the next step in the child's mental and physical development' (Witmer, 1907: 251). He viewed the patient, moreover, as an experiment: as a scientist, his purpose was to discover the causal relations brought to light by his interventions: 'The pure and the applied science advance in a single front' (p. 249).

Emil Kraepelin, generally considered to be one of the founders of modern psychiatry, was among Wundt's first students and remained a lifelong friend. He came to Leipzig in 1882 and conducted research on word association. When he became Professor of Psychiatry at Heidelberg in 1890, he introduced two innovations (Shorter, 1997: 102): a system of cards on which details were kept of his patients' history, diagnosis, treatment and condition at discharge, and a psychological laboratory.

Kraepelin's laboratory was organised rather like Wundt's: Kraepelin gathered an extensive staff of assistants and graduate students around him and assigned them specific research projects (Roback, 1961: 308). They did studies on subjects such as association, fatigue and the effects of alcohol, tea and other substances on mental functions. All this work was part of one programme, which Kraepelin presented in the first issue of his own journal, *Psychologische Arbeiten*. It was high time, he announced, to replace speculation and theory in psychiatry with measurement, observation and fact by applying psychology to psychiatric questions (Kraepelin, 1896). Kraepelin's programme has been called a 'psychology in the clinic', to distinguish it from Witmer's clinical psychology (Pongratz, 1977: 22), but he did emphasise that psychology did not remain unaffected by its location in the clinic. The use of patients as research subjects requires special methods, and the fact that the psychiatrist is concerned with the whole person means that experiments have to form an integrated set. For both Witmer and Kraepelin, the association of clinic and psychology changed psychology's method. The difference is that in Witmer's case, clinical psychology was essentially pedagogic and thera-peutic, whereas for Kraepelin it remained an experimental laboratory science – one which, eventually, might have implications for treatment.

The example of Witmer's psychological clinic inspired the founding of similar clinics at other American universities, colleges and medical schools – 19 by 1914 (Reisman, 1991: 113). Soon, however, the medical profession began to protest against what it considered to be an intrusion on its territory. Psychiatrists claimed direction over clinics, and excluded psychologists from diagnosis and treatment. The child guidance clinics that emerged after the war set the model for clinical work with children: a team consisting of psychiatrist, psychologist and social worker, under the direction of the psychiatrist. Thus, clinical psychologists were relegated to an auxiliary role as 'technicians', administering mental tests (O'Donnell, 1979: 12; Richards, 1988). To the public and other professionals, clinical psy-chology became synonymous with the IQ test (Reisman, 1991: 135). Moreover, clinical psychologists were cold-shouldered rather than supported by academic psychologists, who feared this premature foray outside the laboratory might compromise psychology's as yet insecure status as a science.[4]

In Britain, too, psychologists were unable to gain a dominant position in the growing 'psychological complex' of interventions in family life (Rose, 1985). Cyril Burt published his own vision of a 'psychological clinic' in 1925, as an appendix to his *Young Delinquent* (Burt, 1925). This text, and the example of the Tavistock Clinic's Children's Department (Rose, 1985: 199), inspired the establishment of child guidance clinics, mostly maintained by local education authorities (Hearnshaw, 1964: 273–274). As in the United States, the clinics were soon under medical control. Psychologists played a subordinate role, 'testing but not diagnosing, supplying information but not directing treatment' (Rose, 1985: 208). Meanwhile, the psychological laboratory in a psychiatric clinic, as Kraepelin had devised it, remained rare (for the United States, see Popplestone and McPherson, 1984). In Britain, the most important site was the Maudsley Hospital, which during the 1930s always employed two psychologists, each half-time, to do research (Hearnshaw, 1964: 288).

3   Maudsley and Mill Hill

The Maudsley Hospital had been expressly set up as a research hospital. It was part of an attempt to shift the emphasis in psychiatry from long-term palliative care in asylums to short-term treatment in clinics. Henry Maudsley, one of the foremost nineteenth-century British psychiatrists, had put a large sum of money at the disposal of the London County Council (LCC) to establish a clinic for the treatment and study of insanity. Together with Frederick Mott, the pathologist for the LCC asylums, he campaigned to this end for many years. Inspired by Kraepelin's clinic in Munich, which Mott had visited, the hospital was to combine early treatment, research and teaching at one site and have an outpatient department. Building was finished in 1915, but the hospital was immediately put to use in the war effort. It finally opened in 1923 (for a history of the Maudsley, see Allderidge, 1991; Lewis, 1951).

When the Second World War broke out, the Maudsley Hospital was cleared for civilian casualties and most of its staff moved to the Mill Hill emergency hospital, to take care of military personnel suffering neuroses. Aubrey Lewis, its clinical director, in 1942 appointed the German émigré Hans Jürgen Eysenck to do psychological research at Mill Hill. Lewis shared Maudsley's goal of putting psychiatry on a secure scientific footing and deemed psychology essential in that regard. As he wrote in 1967: psychology 'is as much a basic science of psychiatry as physiology is a basic science of physical disease' (Lewis, 1967: 105–106).

At the end of the war, Eysenck followed Lewis back to the Maudsley. Lewis at this time was giving shape to the status of psychiatric postgraduate teaching at the Maudsley and was setting up the Institute of Psychiatry. The financial means to realise his plans for the Institute came when the Maudsley was amalgamated with the rich Bethlem Royal Hospital (Waddington, 1998). One of his plans involved clinical psychology. Via the Association of Scientific Workers (the scientists' trade union), psychologists had managed to secure recognition in the newly established National Health Service (NHS) and had been given a position on the Whitley councils. Lewis was one of the few psychiatrists who seized the opportunity: he asked Eysenck to head the Department of Psychology at the Institute, set up a training programme in clinical psychology, and establish the profession of clinical psychologist (Eysenck, 1990/1997: 107–109).

4   Boundary rhetoric

Faced with the responsibility of training clinical psychologists, Eysenck found it 'desirable to find some kind of definition of precisely what a clinical psychologist is' (Eysenck, 1949a: 138). Lewis sent him to the United States in 1949 to find an answer, but it seems Eysenck had his mind made up already. The article that appeared in the *American Psychologist* in 1949, 'Training in clinical psychology', setting out his views, had been submitted before he left (Eysenck, 1949b – the paper was received on 14 December 1948). His six-month study trip would not change his opinions. The texts he published after his return contain identical views set out in similar fashion (Eysenck, 1950a,b).

He was based at the University of Pennsylvania as a guest of Robert Brotemarkle and Morris Viteles, staff members of the psychological clinic that Witmer had established. Eysenck apparently took no notice of the clinic (Richards, 1983: 129). It is not mentioned in his articles, nor in his account of this trip in his autobiography. Perhaps out of courtesy, Eysenck was thankful for the kindness of his American hosts and 'impressed by the sincerity of those who are trying to transform clinical psychology into a genuine profession' (Eysenck, 1950b: 710), but he was not at all impressed by the direction taken by clinical psychologists in the United States. His main objection was that they did not restrict themselves to research and testing but were performing psychotherapy as well.

The war had offered many opportunities for American psychology and clinical psychologists had profited greatly. The mental test, the staple of clinical psychology, had given clinical psychologists a secure foothold in the military effort, but psychiatrists, swamped by servicemen with mental problems, had also been forced to delegate some of the treatment to psychologists (Capshew, 1999). After the war, the Veterans Administration began sponsoring training programmes in clinical psychology. The spectacular growth that its ample funds fostered forced the American Psychological Association (APA) to do boundary work and answer the same question that occupied Eysenck: what is clinical psychology? In 1947 the APA published a report in which therapy was confirmed as being part of clinical psychology. This was defended on the grounds that there was a clear social need and that, without training in therapy, diagnostic and research work would be seriously hampered (American Psychological Association, 1947: 548). Eysenck was indignant: 'Therapy is something essentially alien to clinical psychology,' he declared (Eysenck, 1949b: 173). This issue he saw as the principal difference between 'the American view' and 'the Maudsley view' (Eysenck, 1949a: 138).

The arguments that Eysenck put forward conspire to make his demarcation seem the only natural, logical and proper alternative. They are based on two principles. First, since specialisation is 'an inevitable condition for advance' (Eysenck, 1949b: 174), it is clearly better to divide tasks and leave psychiatrists in charge of treatment. Second, this division of labour should be based on the principle that clinical psychology is a science. If training in therapy were a precondition for doing clinical research, it would 'take the concept of research in this field right out of the realm of science into the mystical regions of intuition, idiographic "understanding", and unrepeatable experience' (Eysenck, 1949b: 174).

The greatest threat to clinical psychology's scientific mission came from psychoanalysis, at that time the only model for psychotherapy.[5] As a case in point, Eysenck quoted a particularly damaging recommendation from the APA report. The report advised 'intensive self-evaluation' as part of the training of the clinical psychologist, and then stated (p. 556): 'We are not prepared to recommend any special form of such procedures, but some of us believe that whenever possible this should take the form of psychoanalysis' (see Eysenck, 1949b: 174). This, to Eysenck, was simply indoctrination rather than scientific education.

Despite his severe criticism of US clinical psychology, Eysenck did forge a rhetorical link between his enterprise and the American parent. By combining American and local history he gave the Maudsley view an air of naturalness.

As he explained in the psychiatric *Journal of Mental Science*, the current practice of clinical psychology in Britain had 'grown organically from seeds planted long ago' (Eysenck, 1950b: 711). He then described the history of clinical psychology in the United States, starting with Witmer, 1896, and ending with the postwar expansion and the efforts to standardise and organise the discipline and profession. Next, he described the situation in Britain, where 'clinical psychologists … have almost exclusively worked with children' and were called 'educational psychologists' (Eysenck, 1950b: 713). As a result of this educational self-misunderstanding, therapeutic activities had been going on without adequate supervision, Eysenck warned the psychiatrists. Moreover, it had done nothing to remedy the 'lack of recognition of the inseparable destinies' of psychology and psychiatry. The Department at the Maudsley was established to 'facilitate such a rapprochement' (Eysenck, 1950b: 714).

Eysenck took recourse to linguistic reasoning to give the Maudsley 'concept of Clinical Psychology' a British history (Eysenck, 1950a: 175). The fact that clinical psychology had gone under the name of educational psychology he attributed to 'etymological reasons which will appear amusing to students of semantics, and which can hardly suffice to eliminate the semeiotic connotations it adumbrates' (Eysenck, 1950c: 48). Although 'clinical' originally referred to the hospital bed, in current medical practice the term was no longer limited to the care of bedridden patients. 'Today, "clinical" as applied to any specialty, means only that the person is being studied and regarded as an individual, not as a member of a larger group' (Eysenck, 1950c: 48). This, however, was exactly what had been practised in Britain for some time under 'the disguising flag of "educational psychology"' (Eysenck, 1950c: 48). Educational psychologists, 'a rather curiously named group of persons' (Eysenck, 1950a: 173), had in fact been clinical psychologists.[6] Although the term 'clinical psychology' was of 'obvious trans-atlantic parentage' and seemed 'new-fangled' (Eysenck, 1950a: 175), it was the proper name for something that had been there all along.

That Maudsley clinical psychology was *not* US clinical psychology also meant that it was *not* psychiatry. The sin of American clinical psychologists was that they had shaped themselves in their masters' image and acted as substitute psychiatrists, using their instruments (such as projective tests) and adopting their therapeutic role. In this way, the clinical psychologist had become a 'technician' rather than 'an independent scientist' (Eysenck, 1952, 1955a: 4). In order to articulate the clinical psychologist's proper role as an independent collaborator in the clinic, Eysenck emphasised research and downplayed testing. Administering a test was indeed a task that could 'often be handed over to a technician' (Eysenck, 1950b: 718). Selecting tests and interpreting the results, however, required the psychologist's skill. More important still was research. 'It is his skill in research methodology, more than any other ability or proficiency, which makes the psychologist a useful member of the psychiatric team' (Eysenck, 1950b: 718). Through fundamental research, psychology could become to psychiatry what physiology was to medicine: a basic science (Eysenck, 1950c: 51). This concept of clinical psychology, Eysenck told the assembled psychiatrists at his inaugural lecture, was originally formulated by a psychiatrist: Emil Kraepelin (Eysenck, 1955a).

Indeed, like Kraepelin, Eysenck defined clinical psychology as a laboratory in a clinic. Witmer's model was clearly anathema to him. To make treatment rather than experiment the basis of clinical psychology went against its scientific nature. In fact, Eysenck demarcated laboratory and clinic more strictly than Kraepelin. The principle of the division of labour meant that psychologist and psychiatrist could work together successfully only as long as they remained different. The clinical psychologist's specific contribution lay in the sphere of research, and was most worthwhile where it was furthest from the immediate practical concerns of the clinic: in fundamental research, not in the 'technical or ad hoc research' (Eysenck, 1950b: 718) that is concerned with standardising and intercorrelating tests, diagnoses and so forth. Rather than describing in detail how the clinical environment shaped psychological research, as Kraepelin had done, Eysenck extended the laboratory–clinic demarcation into the laboratory itself.

5   Psychology and psychiatry

Eysenck's boundary work was not a representation of the actual state of affairs. His concept of clinical psychology, however natural and obvious he considered it to be, was in the late 1940s only a concept. The practical role of psychologists at the Maudsley was to a large extent that of technicians carrying out diagnostic tasks. Eysenck had created a number of sections at the Psychology Department: Research, Statistical, Animal, and Clinical (Eysenck, 1951; see also Crown, 1949). He himself headed the Research Section and never did any clinical work. This was the task of the members of the Clinical Section, which was led by Monte Shapiro. Aubrey Yates, who was at this section between 1951 and 1957, has described their relation with the psychiatrists as involving a trade: in return for patients, needed in the training of clinical psychologists, the section 'provided a clinical service to the hospital' (Yates, 1970b: 16). This service consisted of administering tests of cognitive ability and of personality, including the projective tests that Eysenck despised (Gibson, 1981: 84; Schorr, 1984: 157).

This arrangement, continuing that of the prewar child guidance clinics, accorded with the status given to clinical psychologists in the NHS (Summerfield, 1958). The NHS provided the institutional context for the profession of clinical psychology, setting a career structure and salary scales, and later recognising training programmes – British clinical psychology has developed within the context of the NHS. The role expected of clinical psychologists was that of 'medical auxiliaries', analogous to radiologists and biochemists, doing prescribed work. 'The doctor would define the problems and prescribe the output he required and the psychologist, working as a highly skilled technician, would carry out the appropriate test.' In the Whitley system, the psychologist is an employee rather than a professional (Kat, 1985).

Psychiatrists were keen to keep psychology's expertise within these bounds. Their position regarding clinical psychology was rather ambivalent. Many psychiatrists, such as Lewis and his predecessor, Mapother, had a great interest in developments in psychology (Miller, 1996). The experiences with shell shock in the First World War gave a boost to psychological models in psychiatry and psychiatric jurisdiction had been expanded to include the neuroses as well as the psychoses (Richards, 1983; Rose, 1985; Pilgrim and Treacher, 1992: 9; Bourke, Chapter 6). Biological and psychological models, however, led a troubled co-existence, in part because psychological models threatened medical authority, as shown for instance by the debate over lay analysis.

It is not surprising, then, that psychiatrists asserted their dominance in the collaboration with psychologists. Testing was subordinate to diagnosis: the quantitative accuracy of clinical psychology could be usefully employed only if it was embedded within psychiatric concepts and categories, clinical judgement and experience (see, for instance, Mayer-Gross, 1951; Wilson *et al.*, 1952; McIntyre, 1953). The domain of therapy was defended even more fiercely. Independent treatment by psychologists was ruled out completely, a fact that Lewis made clear to Eysenck right from the start. At the Crichton Royal Hospital, psychiatrist Mayer-Gross and psychologist Raven agreed on this principle as well (Mayer-Gross, 1951; Raven, 1950).[7] At the Tavistock Clinic (which defined itself as a 'psychological clinic'), in contrast, demarcation seems hardly to have been an issue, psychologists and psychiatrists being united in a psychodynamic view of personality and psychological illness. 'Personal analysis and participation in treatment' formed an important component of the training of clinical psychologists (Sutherland, 1951: 109). Nevertheless, even at the Tavistock, clinical psychology was regarded principally as the bearer of science in the field of mental health (Richards, 1983: 152).

Eysenck's demarcation of clinical psychology from its US counterpart and from psychiatry served to convince the psychiatrists that Maudsley clinical psychology was not a threat. In the process, he made something of a straw man out of US clinical psychology. His depiction of clinical psychologists in the United States as pseudo-psychiatrists was rather one-sided. The APA report, for instance, was a careful compromise between different points of view on clinical psychology, balancing science and humanism, research and therapy. In his description, Eysenck left out the opinions that were closer to his own, such as the statement that part of the committee would prefer 'less indoctrinating' methods of self-evaluation during training than psychoanalysis (American Psychological Association, 1947: 556).[8] Equally, Eysenck did not dwell on the fact that according to the US view (as well as in his own), the clinical psychologist should be a scientist first, a practitioner second. This 'scientist-practitioner model', according to which clinical psychologists should have a doctoral degree based upon graduate education in clinical psychology, was adopted by the APA at the Boulder Conference in 1949. It was also the basis of the Maudsley training programme.[9]

By using US clinical psychology as a foil, Eysenck highlighted the fact that Maudsley clinical psychologists had no intention to encroach on the psychiatrists' domain of treatment. In fact, some psychiatrists had no objection to clinical psychologists performing psychotherapy, as long as it happened under psychiatric supervision (Committee on Clinical Psychology of the Group for the Advancement of Psychiatry, 1949; Mayer-Gross, 1951; Kennedy, 1951). Being critical of existing forms of psychotherapy, Eysenck willingly sacrificed more than necessary to placate psychiatrists. Eysenck's emphasis on the clinical psychologist's scientific role also confirmed the psychiatrists' expectations. It was generally agreed that psychology's distinct contribution to clinical work lay in the sphere of quantitative accuracy and objectivity. The 'objective efficiency of the scientist' could complement 'the informed kindliness and clinical art of the physician' (Kennedy in Wilson et al., 1952: 449). Aubrey Lewis made a distinction between psychiatric practitioner and psychiatric investigator; clinical psychologists were to help the latter. Thus Lewis split clinical from research work, preparing 'a controlled space for psychology within the NHS' (Richards, 1983: 145–146).

Eysenck's boundary rhetoric, rather than merely differentiating clinical psychology from psychiatry, itself combined demarcation and alliance. It did so by linking clinical psychology to its US counterpart and to prewar educational psychology, despite his criticism of both. More importantly, it advanced a view of psychologists and psychiatrists as independent and complementary, and played on the hopes and fears of psychiatrists to convince them of the value of this arrangement. Eysenck's concept of clinical psychology as a science fundamental to psychiatry was in keeping with the views of the most powerful psychiatrist at the Maudsley, and his strong emphasis on a division of tasks and his insistence that therapy is 'essentially alien' to clinical psychology allayed the fears of psychiatrists about a challenge to their medical authority.

The result of his rhetorical efforts was a tension between the boundaries of clinical psychology as Eysenck saw them, and as the NHS prescribed them (and many psychiatrists preferred them): between the clinical psychologist as an independent scientist and as a scientific auxiliary. In practice, clinical psychologists at the Maudsley played both roles, Eysenck devoting himself completely to research, the members of the Clinical Section providing clinical services as well as doing research. The Maudsley was unusual, however, in the emphasis on research – the psychologists who came into the mental health field in the 1950s and 1960s to work in other institutions were generally confined to the role of auxiliaries, administering the mental tests that the psychiatrists required. For them, working as a researcher remained 'a utopian dream' (Pilgrim and Treacher, 1992: 55).

Nevertheless, Eysenck's boundary work has been influential. Until the 1970s, British clinical psychology continued to define itself primarily as an applied science, grounded in experimental psychology (Pilgrim and Treacher, 1992; Richards, 1983). Training was based on the scientist-practitioner model. Apart from taking part in the debate about the definition of clinical psychology, Eysenck exerted considerable influence through the staff that he hired and through the training programme of the Maudsley. Shapiro, an early recruit, set up a course that strongly emphasised scientific theories, methods and attitude. Many of the psychologists who entered the clinics in the 1960s to do psychometric work had the dream of research instilled in them at the Maudsley. Moreover, most of the courses set up elsewhere during this period were led by its graduates (Pilgrim and Treacher, 1992: 33). Second, although testing was the main task of clinical psychologists, Eysenck had created a space for research. The laboratory in the clinic would prove to be a power base. Science was used as a lever to effect change in the psychiatric clinic.

6   Challenging psychiatry

The introduction of the dossier heralded a fundamental change in the history of medicine (the *locus classicus* is Foucault, 1973). In the words of Bruno Latour: 'The same medical mind will generate totally different knowledge if applied to the bellies, fevers, throats and skins of a few successive patients, or if applied to well-kept records of hundreds of written bellies, fevers, throats and skins, all coded in the same way and all synoptically present' (Latour, 1986b: 15). Eysenck understood this power of the dossier and had the statistical skills to bring it out (Rose, 1989, 1996b).

The psychiatrist Linford Rees, who worked with Eysenck at Mill Hill, has claimed that the whole of Eysenck's later career was based on the so-called 'item sheet', designed by Aubrey Lewis, on which the personal, family and social particulars of each patient were noted, as well as the psychiatrist's diagnosis and the treatment given (Gibson, 1981: 65). One of the first things Eysenck had done at Mill Hill was to assess the reliability of psychiatric diagnoses. This study had been facilitated by the fact that each patient was seen and diagnosed by more than one psychiatrist, each, moreover, noting his or her diagnosis and other findings on the item sheet. By comparing and analysing several thousand dossiers, Eysenck could show that there was less than 5% agreement between diagnoses. He claims the superintendent of the hospital refused him permission to publish these findings (Eysenck, 1991a: vol. 1, pp. 49–51).

At the Maudsley, assessing psychiatry became a powerful counter against the existing diagnostic practice, in which the clinical psychologists had to play the subordinate role of test administrators. The dossiers proved their value again. Psychiatric diagnostic categories were targeted with an analysis of the information on the item sheets and patients' scores on various tests using a new statistical method that Eysenck had developed, criterion analysis. In his inaugural lecture Eysenck presented the resulting graphs, which clearly showed that psychiatric theories about the relation between neurosis, psychosis and normality were incorrect (Eysenck, 1955a).

The reliability and validity of the tests that the psychologists had to administer came under close inspection as well. Shapiro led the members of the Clinical Section in a 'devastating critical analysis' of existing tests, 'from which little emerged with retained credibility' (Jones, 1980: 25). Eysenck had the Rorschach

administered to 50 normal and 50 neurotic patients and asked Maudsley psychiatrists to sort the resulting records. They were unable to do better than chance
(Eysenck, 1991a: 55). Yates analysed tests of brain damage and concluded they
were neither reliable nor valid (Yates, 1954). By confronting the psychiatrists
with these and similar results, the members of the Clinical Section persuaded
the psychiatrists to give up their reliance on the traditional instruments of clinical
psychology (Schorr, 1984: 158; Jones, 1984: 7).

Thus, the laboratory in the clinic possessed a power that Kraepelin had not
foreseen: it allowed critical scrutiny of the clinic by statistically combining and
comparing the results of its processes. The dossier played an important role, which
Kraepelin had not imagined either. He, like other physicians before him, had
used his cards to get a synoptic view of mental illness.[10] Eysenck and his colleagues
surveyed the clinic itself through the dossiers.

An important motive to challenge existing psychiatric procedures was the
perception that the results of psychological testing had very little influence on
subsequent clinical decisions. Psychologists at the Maudsley were frustrated by
'the futility of attempting to answer diagnostic questions posed by psychiatrists
(e.g. is this patient a hysteric or a schizophrenic; is this patient brain-damaged,
or deteriorated intellectually, and so on) when a diagnostic decision usually had
neither etiological nor treatment implications' (Yates, 1970a: 94). In the words
of Victor Meyer, another member of the Clinical Section in the 1950s, the testing
practice sometimes was 'a comedy': psychiatrists asked for tests, the results of
which they subsequently did not use or, when they did, used for the wrong
reasons.[11]

7   Dimensions

The psychologists at the Maudsley not only challenged psychiatric expertise, but
also began to develop alternatives to it. Applying psychology to the problems of
the clinic involved crossing the boundary between laboratory and clinic that
Eysenck had constructed. Eysenck had emphasised the importance of a division
of labour to ensure successful cooperation between psychologist and psychiatrist,
but had left open what form this collaboration should take. Somehow, the
demands of science had to be aligned with those of medicine.

The need for cooperation across different cultural domains tends to give rise
to what historian of science Peter Galison has called 'trading zones', areas where
cooperative ventures are negotiated and coordinated. These need not be distinct
physical spaces; instead, they can take the form of a committee dedicated to
negotiation, or a special phoneline. Trading zones produce and contain tools that
facilitate negotiation, such as a creole. Such tools have been termed 'boundary
objects', and their general function is to translate between the cultures participating in the trading zone (Galison, 1997; Star and Griesemer, 1989; Löwy, 1992).
Eysenck's vision of clinical psychology, a psychological laboratory in a psychiatric clinic, implied a trading zone, where the independent cultural domains of

psychology and psychiatry cooperated. Both the Research Section and the Clinical Section developed boundary objects to further this collaboration.

In his papers of the late 1940s and early 1950s, Eysenck never failed to emphasise the importance of taxonomy in the development of science. In his view, psychology had gone from observation straight to theory and application, without passing through a taxonomic phase. The absence of a proper taxonomy of personality was the reason why clinical psychologists had had to adopt obsolete psychiatric classifications such as Kraepelin's, thus giving up their scientific independence (Eysenck, 1950a: 178). Eysenck's alternative was the dimensional theory of personality.

The dimensional theory was the main result of his work at Mill Hill, and another proof of the value of the dossier. Eysenck selected 39 items of the item sheet that seemed of psychological interest, including such variables as 'irritability', 'unemployment', 'sex anomalies' and 'domestic problems' (Eysenck, 1947: 35). He applied factor analysis to 700 dossiers on these items and found two main factors: the primary factor accounted for 14% of the variance, the secondary factor for 12%. On the basis of the items that correlated most with each, he interpreted them as dimensions of 'neuroticism' and 'hysteria-dysthymia', respectively. The latter he then renamed 'introversion–extraversion', because of its correspondence to Jung's theory.

The dimensions as yet had no other support than subjective data: 'The evidential value of psychiatrists' ratings is, of course, strictly limited' (Eysenck, 1947: 60). Validation was first sought by constructing questionnaires and determining whether they, too, distinguished between groups scoring on the extremes of the factors. These questionnaires did indeed give independent confirmation of the psychiatrists' ratings, but their data, self-ratings, were equally subjective. To go from intersubjectivity to true objectivity, Eysenck correlated the dimensions with scores on 'objective tests', such as of intelligence, body build and suggestibility. Psychiatric assessments had been translated into psychological measures that were more powerful than the clinical gaze they replaced, since the 39 items on the item sheet, or more precisely 26% of their variance, were represented by only two dimensions.

The dimensional theory was the first product of a trading zone between psychology and psychiatry, of the 'close integration of psychiatric experience and theory, and psychological testing and research design' (Eysenck, 1950b: 718). In Eysenck's view of clinical psychology, the psychologist works closely with the psychiatrist 'by taking his theories seriously and by attempting to devise experimental tests for them' (Eysenck, 1950a: 181). The dimensional theory was the outcome of an experimental test of such psychiatric intuitions as 'Jung's extravert–introvert hypothesis' (Eysenck, 1950a: 181). Subsequently, the theory and its accompanying instruments (questionnaire, objective tests) functioned as a boundary object, allowing further laboratory work on clinical issues, such as 'the experimental study of the joint influence of heredity and environment, and the investigation of the results of different types of therapy on different types of patients'. In this way, Eysenck hoped to 'revitalize and revolutionize' psychiatry (Eysenck, 1950b: 718).

Soon, the full extent of the revolution became visible. The upshot of the analysis that he presented at his inaugural lecture was that normality, neurosis and psychosis are not qualitatively different, but are positioned in a three-dimensional space charted by the dimensional theory. A third dimension, inter-preted as 'psychoticism', had been added, and Eysenck showed that patients diagnosed as neurotics were high on the neuroticism dimension, psychotics high on both the neuroticism and the psychoticism dimension, and normals low on both. Eysenck boldly claimed that 'psychiatric procedures are at fault in diagnosing categories, such as "hysteria" or "schizophrenia"' and that one should determine each patient's position on the dimensions instead (Eysenck, 1955b). Assessment of personality held the key to the psychoses as well as the neuroses.

Bold as this proposal was, it still conformed to the model of psychology as an applied science, its role primarily concerned with diagnosis. Notwithstanding the extent of psychology's reach into one of the key areas of psychiatry, nosology, psychologist and psychiatrist were still complementary collaborators in a single clinical practice. Eysenck tried to move the boundaries of clinical psychology – no longer merely contributing to psychiatric diagnosis, but taking over diagnosis completely – but clinical psychology remained a psychological laboratory in a psychiatric clinic.

The same paper, however, in which he claimed that 'psychiatric procedures are at fault' also contained the first steps towards a new model. Eysenck proposed a theory that grounded the dimensions of personality in learning theory. Individual differences were now quantified differences in elementary psychological function-ing (Eysenck, 1957). Taken one step further, this meant that an individual's score on the dimensions could indicate how to proceed with a therapy, provided the treatment was based on the same principles from learning theory (Eysenck, 1957: ch. 8). Gradually, the dimensional theory was losing its character of a boundary object mediating between psychology and clinic, and changing into an instrument for a new clinical practice. Developments in the Clinical Section, meanwhile, went in the same direction.

8   The experimental approach

Eysenck's laboratory in the clinic was a trading zone between psychology and psychiatry of a rather abstract kind, in the sense that it hardly involved actual cooperation between psychologists and psychiatrists. Indeed, Eysenck was very unpopular with most psychiatrists because of his criticism of psychiatry and psychotherapy. The members of the Clinical Section, headed by Monte Shapiro, shared Eysenck's scientific ethos, but were obliged to find a practical way of turning their work for psychiatrists into work with psychiatrists. As one of them, R.W. Payne, explained, given the poor state of psychiatric theory and treatment, a role of subordinate technicians for clinical psychologists was unacceptable.

The preferred role, as Eysenck had said, had to be that of an applied scientist. However, the difficulty with this model, according to Payne, was the fact that there was as yet no science to apply. 'It is doubtful ... whether there exists what might be called a science of abnormal psychology at the present time' (Payne, 1953: 151). Eysenck in fact agreed: he presented the alternative approach, developed by Shapiro and his assistants, as a kind of intermediate solution while awaiting firmer results of his own fundamental, long-term research (Eysenck, 1955a: 25).

In the absence of an applicable theory, the members of the Clinical Section decided to apply the scientific method to clinical work. As in the case of Eysenck's dimensional theory, this cooperation between laboratory and clinic was based on a translation of a psychiatric procedure into a psychological one. In the article in which he first described the approach, Shapiro did this by 'making explicit the underlying principles' (Shapiro, 1951: 754) of diagnosis. In every diagnostic procedure, the following steps are taken: the available information about the patient is carefully considered and the problems he or she suffers from are formulated; next, hypotheses that explain these problems are advanced – 'this is in essence what the clinician always does, though at times he will not be inclined to admit it' (Shapiro, 1951: 755); finally, leaving out the hypotheses that would have no relevance for treatment, the remaining are tested. When the diagnostic process is reformulated like this, it becomes clear that the standardised psychological test is only one way of testing hypotheses. From the perspective of scientific method, it is simply a particular form of experiment. Many other ways of testing hypotheses are available, including simple observation. 'The methods open to the psychologist are many; the essential characteristics of the investigation are, however, always the same' (Shapiro, 1951: 755).

The experimental approach allowed a perfect alignment of the demands of the laboratory with those of the clinic. It was, in principle, the perfect boundary object. First, it did away with all the problems commonly associated with the use of standardised tests. The fact that tests are never completely reliable, for instance, means that there will always be patients misclassified. Thus, a reliability of 0.8 may be high for the psychometrician, but for the clinician it could still spell disaster. The experimental approach reduces this problem considerably, because it usually consists of a series of hypotheses and tests, with anomalous results leading to new hypotheses and tests. Moreover, another problem of standardised tests is solved as well: a test merely describes the current state of the patient, but does not indicate the cause of the condition. A series of experiments, however, will point to an explanation. Second, the experimental approach makes clinical diagnostic work relevant for general psychology and vice versa: 'clinical work can go hand in hand with research, research problems being suggested by experiments on individual cases, and the investigation of individual cases making use of general research findings' (Payne, 1953: 152). Thus, the experimental approach combines the clinical concern with the unique individual with the possibility of scientific generalisation.

The experimental approach was embedded in a communication strategy that was the practical analogue of Shapiro's general reformulation of the diagnostic process. Clinical psychologists had to be 'able to work effectively with other members of the psychiatric team, whose theoretical orientation may be very different from that of the psychologist' (Shapiro, 1955: 16). Every time a psychiatrist requested the services of a psychologist, it was therefore necessary to translate his psychiatric question into a psychological problem. It was a matter of 'helping the psychiatrist formulate clearly the question he is asking' (Payne, 1953: 153; Meyer interview[11]). First, the terms used by the psychiatrist were clarified, because the meaning of such labels as 'schizophrenia' and 'obsessional neurosis' differed from one psychiatrist to another. Then, the problem which had brought the psychiatrist to ask the psychologist for help was examined, because it could be meaningless. A request for a differential diagnosis between obsession and schizophrenia, for instance, would assume the two are qualitatively different, but there is no scientific basis for this. Finally, the psychologist enquired what the psychiatrist intended to do with the answer. If it turned out the point of the question was to decide whether psychotherapy was indicated or not, it was made clear to him that there is no evidence such treatment is effective. Once the question was 'shorn of its psychiatric terminology and its purpose made clear', it was ready for experimental investigation (Payne, 1953: 153; Meyer interview[11]; see also Yates, 1970b: 16).

Shapiro valued science as much as Eysenck, but his conception of scientific psychology in the context of the clinic was quite different. Shapiro's approach does not rely on a theory of personality and the accompanying tests to form fixed, standardised routes to connect laboratory and clinic and guide their cooperation. His boundary object is not a sorting device based on a method for measuring individual differences, but a general strategy for the experimental investigation of individuals. It left all the decisions to be made for each unique case. The course from clinic to laboratory, from vaguely formulated psychiatric problem to underlying psychological cause, had to be plotted each time anew.

Shapiro himself formulated the distinctive character of his approach in terms of an opposition with psychometrics:

> The current procedures often consist of obtaining a large number of test scores from various nosological groups. The psychologist then determines the way in which these test scores differentiate between groups and the way in which they inter-correlate.... The essence of the method of experimental control, however, is that the phenomenon under investigation is made to change in a given individual or group in accordance with controlled changes in circumstances. In this way causal elements can be more unequivocally identified, and processes are more directly observed. (Shapiro and Ravenette, 1959: 297)

The experimental method is about explaining and controlling phenomena, not about proving or disproving theories: 'it sometimes seems as if some psychologists look upon experimental method merely as the most convincing method of persuading people to accept their ideas' (Shapiro and Ravenette, 1959: 297).[12]

For Shapiro as well as for Eysenck, clinical psychology was a laboratory in a clinic, a place where psychologists cooperated with psychiatrists on the basis of a division of tasks between science and medicine. The principles of the experimental approach and the communication strategy described by Payne functioned as boundary objects facilitating this cooperation. But while Eysenck demarcated laboratory and clinic more strictly than Kraepelin had done, Shapiro's approach contained elements of Witmer's idea of clinical psychology in the emphasis on the individual case and on experimentation. Both Witmer and Shapiro considered each individual patient as an experiment, an experiment, moreover, that could be relevant for general psychology. Shapiro made research out of diagnosis, and resolved the tension between scientist and technician that lingered after Eysenck's boundary work.

The experimental approach to diagnosis was ultimately unsuccessful, however. The method had an inherent problem that proved to be its undoing: applying the experimental method took a lot of time. The phrase 'time-consuming' comes up a lot in Payne's description of the approach, where he also admits that 'Some of our studies have, in fact, taken as long as a year' (Payne, 1957: 191). The experimental method took many staff hours, was very demanding on the patients and delayed their treatment. It was soon considered 'an almost wholly impracticable technique in the settings in which clinical psychologists operate except for very simple questions' (Hamilton, 1964: 33). Moreover, the experimental approach did not give the laboratory more impact on the clinic. The actions of psychiatrists seemed as little influenced by diagnoses reached with this method as they had been by test results. 'Psychiatrists seldom acted on any of our recommendations' (Jones, 1984: 7).

9   A psychological clinic

Frustrated by their lack of influence on treatment decisions, and unimpressed by the effectiveness of psychotherapy, clinical psychologists at the Maudsley extended the experimental approach to include treatment. Therapy seemed to be the next logical step: if one could describe, measure and explain the patient's problem experimentally, why should not the same approach be applied to modifying the problematic behaviour (Ingham, 1961; Yates, 1970a,b)? Was not treatment equally a matter of observing, manipulating and controlling processes?

There is some debate among behaviour therapists about the respective influence of Eysenck and Shapiro on the development of behaviour therapy, and about the relevance of learning theory. Yates has claimed that behaviour therapy as it developed in England was an application of Shapiro's experimental method rather than of learning theory (Yates, 1970a); Eysenck himself has always described behaviour therapy as applied learning theory, and notes that Shapiro did not like behaviour therapy very much;[13] Meyer claims Eysenck 'didn't know anything about behaviour therapy', and that learning theory was irrelevant, Joseph Wolpe's techniques being the main inspiration;[14] Shapiro has said behaviour therapy grew out of discussions between him, Yates and Jones (see Gibson, 1981); and Jones acknowledges the importance of both Shapiro's method and Eysenck's theoretical work, with Wolpe having little influence in the early years (Jones, 1984).

The use of learning theories in the early attempts at behavioural treatment is undeniable, but equally clear is that the experiments depended on the trading zone created by Shapiro, and followed the principles of the boundary object that bore his stamp. Whereas virtually all Maudsley psychiatrists hated Eysenck (who did nothing to placate them), some were quite well disposed to the members of the Clinical Section and cooperated amicably with them. They allowed them to carry through the process of experimental diagnosis with children suffering cognitive and educational problems, into the treatment, remedial education, that the assessment pointed to (Jones, 1980, 1984). In the course of time, permission was granted to treat adult patients, and such treatment was even requested of the psychologists of the department. The early reports of these treatments all acknowledge the cooperation of the supervising psychiatrists (Jones, 1956; Meyer, 1957; Yates, 1958).

Moreover, the application of learning principles and other theories from experimental psychology followed the methodology developed by Shapiro. In the first place, each treatment was structured in accordance with Shapiro's phasing of the experimental process: first a precise statement of the problem,[15] then, drawing on whatever theory seemed appropriate, generating hypotheses regarding its cause and/or cure, and finally experimentally testing these hypotheses. In the famous case of Jones' 'peeing ballerina', the precise nature of the patient's 'abnormal bladder responses' was first determined, and subsequently a training programme was designed, drawing on experimental work in conditioning. After successfully completing the training, the same pattern was then followed for the accompanying anxiety response (Jones, 1956).

Second, the case reports show the emphasis on manipulation and control characteristics of Shapiro's approach. Yates' treatment of a patient suffering four different tics is a perfect illustration (Yates, 1958). Again, the treatment had three phases. First, a theoretical model was proposed of tics as learned responses, based on the theoretical work of O.H. Mowrer and C. Hull. Next, a method of treatment (so-called massed practice) was deduced from the model and its effects predicted. Finally, the treatment was described as a test of these predictions. But the therapy was more than an opportunity to prove a point, more than a testing ground for learning theory. It also offered the possibility to refine theory by observing the results of the therapist's interventions, leading to increased control: 'The optimum conditions of massed practice under which conditioned inhibition … may be expected to grow most rapidly and effectively are unknown with respect to the extinction of tics. The present experiments represent, therefore, an attempt to discover these conditions' (Yates, 1958: 176). As in the experimental approach to diagnosis, this attempt resulted in a series of hypotheses and experiments: five in all, requiring a total of 315 experimental sessions. A 'standard procedure' was used, consisting of two sessions per day, each consisting of five one-minute massed practice trials for each tic, with one minute's rest between each set of five trials. Variations were then tested on one or more tics, while the standard procedure was being applied to the others: increased duration, a period without practice, paying careful attention to the tic, and so on. These variations were then compared with the standard procedure, which functioned as a control condition. By thus varying the experimental manipulation, 'the optimum conditions for the production of conditioned inhibition' were suggested (Yates, 1958: 180).[16]

Among the ideas that failed the test was, ironically, Eysenck's proposed connection between the dimensional theory and treatment based on learning theory. The value of Eysenck's work on individual differences for behaviour therapy was nil (Jones, 1984).[17] The Maudsley Personality Inventory (MPI), a brief questionnaire measuring introversion–extraversion and neuroticism that Eysenck published in 1959, was in fact never used by the Clinical Section (Gibson, 1981: 159).[18] Shapiro stated in 1960 that 'There are as yet no tests that can be used for diagnostic purposes. The limitation of the present situation can to some extent be overcome by carrying out experiments on the single case' (Shapiro, 1960). The MPI did gain use elsewhere, but its clinical relevance has been contested.[19] Jones has explained the MPI's irrelevance in the clinic by the fact that 'in dealing with an individual case, idiosyncratic aspects and the effects of specific environmental influences assume a great importance' (Jones, 1984: 8–9). Shapiro's boundary object, attuning science to the unique individual, triumphed over Eysenck's, the dimensional theory.

The introduction of behaviour therapy amounted to a break with the model for clinical psychology that Eysenck had propagated from 1949 onwards.[20] Collaboration across the boundary between laboratory and clinic had proved difficult as long as treatment remained in the hands of psychiatrists. By extending the experimental approach to include treatment, a space had been created where diagnosis and treatment could be aligned using psychological method and theory. The practice of behaviour therapy created a psychological clinic not unlike Witmer's original clinic: a site which brought research, diagnosis and treatment together, where experimental methods were applied to individual cases and treatment took the pedagogical form of re-education, of the correction of behaviour.

Eysenck's boundary work changed accordingly to get the new, as yet unofficial practice within the boundaries of clinical psychology. In his 1958 lecture before the Royal Medico-Psychological Association, in which he introduced behaviour therapy to British psychiatry (and created a furore), he claimed the neuroses as the territory of clinical psychologists (Eysenck, 1959). Medical authority over this domain was to be kept to a minimum: the patient remained in 'the general medical care' of the psychiatrist, but the theory of neuroses, their diagnosis and treatment were the 'special competence' of the clinical psychologist (p. 74). Clinical psychology was still defined as an applied science, but it now also had its own object. The distinction between mental abnormality of organic origin and of psychological origin (learned responses) remained the basis of Eysenck's boundary work in subsequent years (Eysenck, 1975). Indeed, despite the initial fierce opposition from psychiatrists to psychologists performing therapy, behaviour therapy has proved to be eminently suited to an eclectic treatment practice, in which psychology and psychiatry concern themselves with different kinds of patients (Rose, 1986).[21]

Eysenck also took the lead in bounding behaviour therapy and its community of practitioners. He used the term 'behaviour therapy', coined at an informal gathering in his house and independently by Lazarus in South Africa, to emphasise its distinctiveness. In particular, it was *not* psychoanalysis, a point supported in typically Eysenckian fashion by a schematic summary of the ten main differences between the two approaches, which he presented at the 1958 lecture (Eysenck, 1959: 67). As illustrated in two columns of a table, behaviour therapy and psychotherapy were not merely different, but actually based on 'opposing viewpoints' (Eysenck, 1959: 67): good versus bad science, depth versus surface, history versus present, and so on. It has been noted that there are in fact similarities between behaviour therapy and psychoanalysis,[22] but Eysenck's oppositional rhetoric made clear that behaviour therapy was an applied science rather than a clinical art, and therefore fell under the authority of psychology.

Colleagues such as Jones and Yates were not so sure of Eysenck's claim that behaviour therapy was the application of a 'consistent, properly formulated theory' (Eysenck, 1959: 67) and stressed the theoretical questions that remained (Schorr, 1984: 167). Eysenck's 'ghost-image' of behaviour therapy was in fact more wish than reality (Schorr, 1984: 167), but it was also a rhetorical instrument to make the wish come true. By naming what was still an only loosely connected and geographically dispersed set of theories and practices he added, in appearance at least, to each separate theory and technique the power of all the others. Suddenly, psychiatrists at the Maudsley were confronted not by a few clinical psychologists claiming therapeutic results, but by an international movement with mutually supportive claims. While psychiatrists were busy testing these claims, Eysenck could continue creating his vision. Again, he showed his skill in drawing things together, in using theory and statistics to link together texts, numbers, practices and people into a powerful network, as he had done with the dimensional theory. In 1960 he edited a volume in which he united, under the title *Behaviour Therapy and the Neuroses*, classic studies such as Watson and Rayner's 'Little Albert' with the work of Wolpe, Lazarus and the Maudsley psychologists (Eysenck, 1960). Everything was held together by Eysenck's brief introductions, but by 1965 his work had developed into a full-fledged synthesising theory (Eysenck and Rachman, 1965). Eysenck never performed behaviour therapy, but his boundary work and advocacy were invaluable to its development.

10 Epilogue: rhetoric and practice

In his boundary rhetoric, whether for clinical psychology or for behaviour therapy, Eysenck throughout stuck to the model of applied science, of laboratory results put to use in the clinic. Clinical practice at the Maudsley, on the other hand, early on acquired elements of the Witmerian model of the psychological clinic, and the development of behaviour therapy created a practice that resembled Witmer's in several key aspects. Behaviour therapists have continued to resist the conception of their work as applied learning theory, arguing that 'much of what goes on in behaviour therapy cannot be said to derive in any obvious way from learning theory principles' (Beech, 1969).[23] Essential, rather, is the scientific approach.

That raises the question of what the relative contributions have been of rhetoric and practice to the changing boundaries of clinical psychology. It might seem Eysenck's rhetoric has lost out in the end, particularly given the fact that the influx of psychologists into psychotherapy, once behaviour therapy had paved the way, prompted a redefinition of the clinical psychologist as a practitioner rather than a scientist or technician (Pilgrim and Treacher, 1992; Richards, 1983). However, the concept of the clinical psychologist as an independent scientist, of which Eysenck was the most forceful proponent, played an important part in the development of the discipline away from its auxiliary status. It offered an identity (if not an actual role) where that of 'therapist' was unattainable except by becoming a psychoanalyst. And it offered a legitimisation for challenging medical authority, with far-reaching consequences. Behaviour therapy was developed on the basis of the experimental approach to diagnosis, which in turn was the result of the scientific assault on traditional tests mounted by Maudsley psychologists. Eysenck's subsequent formulation of behaviour therapy as an applied science fostered its growth, despite its inadequacy as a representation of the practice. In sum, I would suggest that the strength of clinical psychology at the Maudsley lay in the combination of the two models that shaped it, and that its influence on British clinical psychology was a result of both the rhetoric and the practices it produced.

Acknowledgements

This essay is based on research funded by the Wellcome Trust, grant number 041963. I would like to thank Trudy Dehue, Nik Rose, Douwe Draaisma, Hans Ettema, the participants in the conference of the History and Philosophy of Psychology Section of the British Psychological Society, York 1999, and the editors of this book for their valuable comments, and Jeffrey Gray, Victor Meyer and Barry Richards for answering my questions.

Notes

1 The term 'boundary work' has gained currency through the work of Thomas Gieryn (for instance Gieryn, 1999).
2 One informer used the term 'trade union disputes' when asked about territorial relations between clinical psychology and psychiatry, saying that in the end it does not matter who does what, as long as the work gets done (J.A. Gray, interview with the author, 22 April 1999). This chapter argues that, in fact, it has mattered a lot.

Whether it should have mattered is a question that falls outside its purview (if I may be allowed some boundary work of my own).

3 For this dynamic as it was played out in the United States, see Reisman (1991) and Capshew (1999).

4 Capshew (1999) chronicles the vicissitudes of the relation between academic and applied psychologists in the United States.

5 A new model, Carl Rogers' non-directive approach, was drawing attention in the United States. Eysenck does not mention it in his papers. In terms of boundary work, the fact that the new approach bore the name of 'counselling' rather than 'therapy' was significant.

6 Vernon (1940) referred to psychologists working in psychological clinics as 'Clinic psychologists', thus defining them by their location.

7 Like Eysenck, both further stressed the complementary relationship between psychologist and psychiatrist. However, in Raven's view, the specific contribution of the psychologist lay in empathic understanding of the person as an integrated whole, which he considered at odds with a therapeutic attitude to the patient.

8 This statement follows immediately after the point at which Eysenck breaks off the quotation. Eysenck also neglected to mention that there was considerable resistance from American psychiatrists to the independent practice of therapy by psychologists. See, for instance, Committee on Clinical Psychology of the Group for the Advancement of Psychiatry (1949).

9 Pilgrim and Treacher (1992) give a history of the scientist-practitioner model and its influence on British clinical psychology.

10 Shorter (1997) describes how each new edition of Kraepelin's *Compendium der Psychiatrie* was the result of a thorough inspection and reshuffling of the cards.

11 V. Meyer, interview with the author, 26 April 1999.

12 His readers will have taken these last remarks as a reference to and criticism of Eysenck, and that was probably Shapiro's intention. A personal conflict, the nature of which has never become clear, had grown between the two men in the early 1950s. See Gibson (1981).

13 He also tends to emphasise his own role. In Eysenck (1984: 3) he even fails to mention anyone else in his account of the origins of behaviour therapy. On Shapiro see Eysenck (1991b: 424).

14 Meyer, interview (see note 11). However, in Meyer (1970: 108) he does define behaviour therapy as an application of 'principles established in the field of learning', though not of 'learning theory', since there is no such thing.

15 See Crellin (1998) for the pervasive influence of the idea of 'formulation' in the history of British clinical psychology.

16 In the report, the ticqueur is presented at times as a patient, passively undergoing treatment and experimental manipulation, and at other times as an active participant, performing her own therapy under Yates' guidance. See Baistow (Chapter 15) for the historical development of the second role in behaviour therapy.

17 Also interviews with Meyer (see note 11) and Gray (see note 2).

18 Meyer did in fact redesign the treatment of one patient (after the original design failed) on the basis of his position on the extraversion–introversion dimension (Meyer, 1957).

19 McGuire (1962: 57) concludes that the MPI has 'no part to play in differential diagnosis, although the N-scale might be useful as a screening test'. Hamilton (1964: 31) considered Eysenck's dimensional descriptions of patients to have 'few implications for the treatment, prognosis or disposal of patients'. Watts (1985: 30) stated that 'There are ... only a few situations in which it assists clinical decision making to be able to place a particular patient on a general dimension of intellectual or personality functioning'.

20 Eysenck has claimed that it was always his intention to bring treatment into clinical psychology's remit, but that, given the absence of a scientific form of therapy and Aubrey Lewis' strong opposition, he decided to keep this to himself and bide his time (Eysenck, 1997: 137).

21 Behaviour therapy has also turned out to lend itself extremely well to contexts other than the clinic, and to application by a wide variety of professionals and lay people. See Baistow (Chapter 15).

22 For example, in both psychoanalysis and Wolpe's systematic desensitisation, 'anxiety' is a central concept, and language and imagination the main instruments (Schorr, 1984: 200–201).

23 See also Yates (1970a,b); Jones (1984: 12); Meyer (interview, see note 11). All were trained at the Maudsley.

14

'Our friends electric': mechanical models of mind in postwar Britain

Rhodri Hayward

As it reached its mid-point in the early 1950s, the century of psychology suddenly appeared imperilled. The wartime emergence of electronic calculators and self-governing automata seemed to threaten the intellectual distinctions that had separated lived identity and mental activity from the mundane operations of the material world. The six marks of behaviour which the great prewar psychologist William McDougall had used to define the purposive activity of living animals had now been successfully replicated by a number of mechanical impostors which had been developed in the laboratories and hospitals of wartime Britain.[1] McDougall's criteria – spontaneous movement, persistent activity, variation of methods, effective termination of goal-directed actions, anticipation and learning – could all be recognised in the behaviour of the new feedback machines and self-governing robots displayed in educational festivals and psychological congresses across Western Europe and the United States (McDougall, 1928: 43–46).[2]

Psychology was thus presented with a kind of Faustian bargain. The new technologies offered to the discipline the possibility of novel insights into the nature of mind and behaviour, yet at the same time they threatened the existence of the subject's very soul. As C.A. Mace, the Chair of Psychology at Birkbeck College, London, noted, the developments were at once both intriguing and terrifying.[3] Writing in the introduction to Wladyslaw Sluckin's *Minds and Machines* in 1954, Mace described how:

> … the great gulf that divides the mind of man from the machine has been con-
> siderably lessened in the present century. Calculations and deductions hitherto
> carried out only by minds can now be performed with greater speed and precision
> by a variety of mechanical and electronic contraptions. These machines are rather
> frightening. No one knows where their invasions of the territory of mind is going

to end [*sic*].… The machine, no doubt, still has a long way to go, but the pace of its progress is extremely hot. It behoves us all to keep an eye on these machines, and to try to understand them. This is the more important since to understand the machines is in some measure to understand ourselves. (Mace, 1954: 9)

Fifty years later, as the century of psychology moves to its close, Mace's warnings seem extremely well placed. The machine is now widely seen as the evolutionary counterpart of humanity, enjoying the fruits of intelligence, reproduction, learning and self-control. Commentators ranging from contemporary philosophers of mind through to wild-eyed enthusiasts of cyberpunk theory have all insisted upon the functional equivalence of man and mechanism (Gregory, 1971; Regis, 1991; Mazlish, 1993; Pepperell, 1997). Daniel Dennett, the American doyen of artificial intelligence, has insisted that consciousness be viewed as a virtual machine, a product of semi-independent programs running on the substrate of the brain (Dennett, 1993, 1998). The popular science writers Edward Feigenbaum and Pamela McCorduck have forecast the birth of a new generation of artificial intelligence machines, whose silicon architecture will allow them to learn and evolve in the same way as the human mind (Feigenbaum and McCorduck, 1983).[4] The critical theorist George Dyson has argued that such a process is already underway, with the 'primitive metabolism' of the World Wide Web evolving from the open-ended organisation of the Internet (Dyson, 1997: 215). According to the champions of the new technology, these developments must result in a reassessment of our relationship to the machine. They advocate a moral revolution in which we jettison the 'protein chauvinism' (Levidow, 1994) implicit within our anthropocentric understanding of mind and consciousness and instead embrace our silicon counterparts as fellow travellers and would-be mates on the long spiral of future evolution.

At one level, of course, such enthusiastic speculations can be located in a centuries-old tradition which has long associated the operations of mental life with the functioning of a machine.[5] As Graham Richards has made clear in his study of the development of psychological ideas in the years following the Scientific Revolution, there has been an ongoing popular uptake of mechanical metaphors ('getting steamed up'; 'going off the rails') which has inspired new models and programmes in psychological research (Richards, 1992b: 397–398).

Yet such metaphorical productions are quite distinct from our current insistence on human–machine analogies. In our contemporary writings, the relationship between machine and organism has transcended the level of mere metaphor to become one of identity. In this process, the metaphorical roots of this apparent equivalence have been obscured and the social achievement of the analogy disguised behind the claim of literal truth and natural knowledge (Haraway, 1991: 8–9). As Ulric Neisser noted as long ago as 1966:

The computing machine serves not only as a tool but as a metaphor, as a way of conceptualising man and society. The notion that the brain is like a computer, that man is like a machine, that society is like a feedback mechanism all reflect the impact of cybernetics on our idea of human nature.… Having taken deep roots and being partially unconscious it is invulnerable to evidence. (Neisser, 1966: 75–76)

This sense of self-evidence that we increasingly associate with mechanical models of mind and behaviour has had a twofold effect (Douglas, 1975). At one level, it obscures the very real struggles which surrounded the scientific and popular acceptance of the machine analogy. At a second and connected level, it leaves a whole series of critical questions unanswered. How did such models become acceptable? How do we link such idealised systems to real-life situations? What aspects of life experience are excluded in this equation? What new aspects of behaviour are made visible by this metaphor? The strategies and tactics behind the postwar establishment of this machine metaphor provide the focus for this chapter.[6]

1   Machine metaphors and their origin myths

Attempts to explain our faith in the functional equivalence of man and mechanism have usually taken one of two forms. The first, and more popular, attempts to naturalise the contemporary cultural position of machines by depicting their long evolution into a position of sophistication and self-government.[7] Such stories usually begin with the eighteenth-century development of feedback devices in engineering, with the paradigmatic example being Watt's invention of the centrifugal governor, although Alexandrian water clocks and Chinese drinking straws have been proposed as alternative candidates (Bolter, 1984: ch. 2; Beniger, 1986: ch. 5; Kelly, 1994: ch. 7; Mayr, 1970 on whom most authors draw). After this acquisition of self-control, the new machines have been depicted developing memory (through the invention of the punched card), senses of sight and sound (through the development of the valve amplifier and photoelectric cells) and a logic of calculation (with the invention of mechanical relays and integrated circuits). By holding up the capacities and abilities of twentieth-century man as the implicit telos of mechanical development, these historical checklists of mechanical acquisition reinforce the idea of an identity between human and machines.

Such attempts to explain our current fetishisation of the machine only deepen the mythic sense of their origins. In their insistence upon the identity of the machine as an 'evolving species' across the ages, they import the self-same biological analogies that they had sought to explain. By naturalising the current status of machines in disciplines such as artificial intelligence, these origin accounts disguise the political decisions and social interests which have sustained the naturalistic metaphor.[8]

Since the 1990s, however, more critical authors have begun to undermine the sense of historical inevitability associated with the developing idea of human–machine identity. The sociologists of science Peter Galison and Andrew Pickering have both argued that this proposed equivalence arose in a contingent set of historical circumstances specific to the Second World War (Galison, 1994; Pickering, 1995). They maintain that the identity thesis originated in the programmatic claims of the incipient discipline of cybernetics, a discipline whose organisation and investigations were dictated by the US military research agenda of the 1940s.[9]

At this level, their claims remain uncontentious. Certainly, cybernetics provided the first radical investigations based upon the machine–organism analogy, and its proponents were exceptionally candid about the military origins of their research (Wiener, 1956). Norbert Wiener, the American mathematician and self-styled inventor of the young science, claimed that the original inspiration for the human–machine analogy arose in his team's work on anti-aircraft gunnery in wartime Boston (Wiener, 1954: ch. 1). In their attempt to build a mechanical predictor of enemy airplane behaviour, Wiener's team had been faced with the problem of integrating a massive number of variables into a single calculation. Since any plane encountering ground fire would be likely to change course, the Boston group had to include factors as varied as the speed of the plane, the size of its turning curve, the intention of the enemy pilot and the sharpness of his reactions in any general calculation of the target's location. Moreover, since Wiener and his team were building automatic predictors which would be attached to anti-aircraft batteries, they also had to include the reactions of anti-aircraft gun operators in their equations. Target prediction thus encompassed the data of mathematics, engineering, physiology and psychology in its predictions. It incorporated the mechanisms of the plane, the anti-aircraft battery and the nervous systems of the pilot and the gunner into a single integrated whole (Galison, 1994: 229).

Wiener believed that this elision between the biological, the psychological, the mechanical and the mathematical provided the cornerstone for the new science of cybernetics. It held out the promise of a common approach to the problems of the physical and the life sciences. In 1943, he attempted to formalise this new integrated approach to the problems of biology and mechanics. In cooperation with his colleagues, the physiologist Atruro Rosenblueth and the engineer Julian Bigelow, he co-authored a paper entitled 'Behavior, Purpose and Teleology', which argued that the actions of men and machines could be explained through reference to a common process of feedback (Wiener *et al.*, 1943). Feedback is a mechanism whereby an effect acts back on one of its causes and thus initiates a process of self-control. Wiener, Rosenblueth and Bigelow argued that this process could be interpreted as purposeful behaviour insofar as it allowed a machine to continually monitor and adjust its performance in order to achieve a certain end.

It is easy to see how this reinterpretation of purpose led to the beginnings of that intellectual transformation which Mace had identified in the 1950s. The conflation of purpose with negative feedback robbed the term of its humanistic and vitalistic associations. Purpose was no longer seen as a characteristic specific to living organisms (as McDougall had once insisted); rather, it now encompassed all instances of self-adjustment, whether they occurred in animals or machines. Purpose was not some metaphysical force which dictated animal action; rather, it was simply a word used to describe any form of behaviour which seemed directed towards a certain goal.

As well as demonstrating the historical contingency of our intellectual faith in man–machine identity, Wiener's account also points to a wider set of moral concerns implicit within the intellectual movement. As Pickering and Galison have argued, the new science of cybernetics can be seen as encoding a specific view of mankind: a dehumanised view, which arose in the emotional adjustments of combat. Thus, Galison claims that the discipline was made intellectually possible by the Allies' hatred of the wartime enemy (Galison, 1994: 230). He argues that its equation of men with machines was simply a development of one of the more familiar strategies for demonising military and civilian opponents. Just as generals in the South Pacific had likened the Japanese to ants and beasts in order to justify their extermination, so too did Wiener reduce the enemy pilot to little more than a mechanical apparatus as he planned his future elimination. Galison believes that cybernetics appears at the point where this rhetoric of hatred escapes its intended target. It is in Wiener's repeated extension of this dehumanising metaphor of the mechanical man that cybernetics is born. As Galison writes:

> In fighting this cybernetic enemy, Wiener and his team began to conceive of the Allied anti-aircraft operators as resembling the foe, and it was a short step from this elision of the human and non-human in the ally to a blurring of the human–machine boundary in general. The servo-mechanical enemy became, in the cybernetic vision of the 1940s, the prototype for human physiology and ultimately, for all of human nature. Then, in a final move of totalization, Wiener vaulted cybernetics to a philosophy of nature, in which nature itself became an unknowable but passive opponent. (Galison, 1994: 233)

Thus, in Galison's account, cybernetics appears through the universal extension of a psychological hatred: a hatred which had supported the dehumanisation and hence the extermination of the wartime enemy.

Andy Pickering's work 'Cyborg History and the World War II regime' follows Galison in his analysis. Although the tone is more tempered, Pickering similarly argues that cybernetics is rooted in the global extension of a wartime rhetoric:

> Cybernetics … took computer controlled gun control and layered it in an ontologically indiscriminate fashion across the academic disciplinary board – the world understood, cybernetically, was a world of goal-oriented feedback systems with learning. (Pickering, 1995: 30)

In Pickering's view, this repeated extension of the rhetoric of cybernetics has led to a global economy in which humans are reduced to the role of limbs or organs in a massive capitalist machine. Such a vision reflects the dystopian analyses outlined at the beginning of this chapter.

The historical analyses offered by Pickering and Galison are intellectually persuasive and politically compelling. Yet they still embody the same mythic functions as the more naturalised stories of technological evolution outlined earlier. In their concentration on the programmatic claims of self-publicists such as Warren McCulloch and Wiener, they impoverish our understanding of mechanical modelling as a social phenomenon by reducing its historical complexity. At least some of this complexity can be restored if we return to the largely unacknowledged contribution of British wartime workers to the origin of cybernetics.

2   The cybernetic anticipation of Kenneth Craik

Despite the widespread propagation of Wiener's claim to be the founding father of cybernetics, it was in fact British workers who first pioneered these conceptions of behaviour and purpose as feedback-governed mechanisms (de Latil, 1956; Cordeschi, 1987: 119–129). The Cambridge psychologist Kenneth Craik and the Gloucestershire psychiatrist William Ross Ashby both promoted a new intellectual agenda, which insisted upon the theoretical possibility of a mechanical model of mental life.[10] Their contribution is worth stressing, not because of some misguided sense of intellectual patriotism, but because their research and achievements provide a counterpoint to the militaristic understanding of cybernetics advanced by Galison and Pickering. For while the research of both men was shaped by the demands and experience of war, their realisation of this new programme was guided by a far wider agenda, which ranged from the instability of the international situation through to the local economics of laboratory practice.

Craik was to be involved in war work from almost the beginning of his career. A former student of James Drever at Edinburgh, he embarked upon a doctorate at Cambridge in October 1936.[11] Nine months before the outbreak of war, his supervisor, Frederic Bartlett, had been drafted onto the Flying Personnel Research Committee, which had been convened by the Air Ministry with the assistance of the Medical Research Council (MRC).[12] Originally concerned with questions of personnel selection, the Committee had been forced to widen its brief as the initial enthusiasm of war developed into the long attrition of the Battle for the Atlantic (Bartlett and Mackworth, 1950; Green and Covell, 1953: 36–37). In 1941, subcommittees on the problems of vision and dazzle were formed, with Craik serving as a member on both.[13] By the end of the war, Craik was also serving on the Military Personnel Research Committee and had been appointed Chairman of the Target Tracking Panel organised by the Ministry of Supply.[14]

Kenneth Craik was a skilled technician. Upon first meeting Bartlett, he had amazed the older scientist by producing a tiny working model of an internal combustion engine from his waistcoat pocket (Bartlett, 1946: xiv; Zangwill, 1980: 2). Later, as he became engaged in war work, these mechanical skills were exploited to the full as Craik devised a number of technical devices, ranging from instruments for investigating fatigue and visual adaptation through to a full-scale experimental cockpit.[15] However, these technical skills did not simply lend themselves to a series of material achievements in the laboratory – they also inspired an intellectual approach which would enable Craik to recast philosophical questions as problems in engineering. In his research, Craik moved from the difficulties of assessing the human input in mechanical systems, through to the possibility of providing a mechanical model of such inputs, before reaching a new mechanistic conception of mental life as a process of model making.

At a primary level, Craik's wartime experiments developed from a similar problematic to that faced by Wiener and Rosenblueth. In his work for the Target Tracking Panel and the Servomechanisms subcommittee of the Ministry of Supply, he was immediately faced with the ergonomic problem of including man as a variable in mechanical control systems.[16] This was of course a fairly general question, which had traditionally been associated with the time-and-motion studies of industrial psychology and in wartime was being confronted by a number of research teams across Britain.[17] In Oxford, a group based around the neuroanatomist Wilfred Le Gros Clark investigated the improvement of working conditions in director control towers on behalf of the Royal Naval Personnel Research Committee.[18] In the MRC's newly established Armoured Fighting Vehicle Laboratories at Lulworth Cove (Green and Covell, 1953: 23–28), the Applied Psychology Unit (APU) findings on cockpit design and visibility (Rolfe, 1996) were extended in their application to the working conditions of tank crews (Bates, 1947: 298).

Craik's penchant for engineering inspired a material solution to these problems of human modelling. The young psychologist quickly realised that it would be possible to imitate the ballistic adjustments made by human operators engaged in tracking tasks using the positive feedback of a 'velodyne' (to maintain a movement), coupled to a condenser and amplifier which would transmit a corrective charge if an error voltage was received (Craik, 1947–1948a: 60). He suggested that the human operator in any control system could be modelled out of a short chain of electronic components consisting of a sensory device, a computing system, an amplifier and mechanical linkages (Craik, 1947–8b: 146).[19] Before Wiener and Rosenblueth, Craik pioneered the idea of human–machine equivalence in fighting systems.

Craik's use of mechanical models of human activity was not limited to problems of ergonomic integration. His original and abiding interest had always been in problems of visual adaptation, particularly the difficulties this created in attempts to calibrate human observation. In both his doctoral work and his military research, Craik continually drew analogies between the operation of the electrical photometer and the range-finding abilities of the human eye (Craik, 1940).[20] These metaphorical inspirations were not simply a product of his philosophical materialism; rather, they arose through his practical engagement in laboratory work. Although Craik's experimental practice requires further historical investigation, it seems clear that in the process of fine-tuning his experiments on the visual efficiency meter, Craik found himself confronted with the same problems as the adapting eye. Just as the eye had to adjust itself in response to target distance and light intensity, so Craik had to adapt his instruments to function despite the problems of focus and glare (for example Craik, 1941: 4–5).[21] Within this technical engagement we can see the beginnings of dialectical movement in which solutions to mechanical problems in the experimental apparatus suggested new models in the analysis of human vision.[22] It was a movement which revealed the origins of scientific inspiration in the practical labour of the laboratory worker.

It would be a mistake, however, to see Craik's faith in the possibility of mechanical models or man–machine integration as a straightforward product of his military research on the human operator in control systems. In his private writings, he revealed a more spiritual belief in the possibilities of technology as a key to self-transformation. In a personal meditation on the notion of claustrophobia, Craik contrasted the stifling atmosphere of the country village with the possibilities of extension and communion offered by 'the dark and airless laboratory':

> To me, this small, dark room, cluttered with apparatus and a tangle of wires, is a place of infinite possibilities and far horizons, full of pathways leading me into the unknown. Its instruments extend my eyes and limbs – allow me to see living cells, the sound waves of my voice, the impulses in a living nerve; its machines enable me to mould and carve metal as if it were putty. Through the books in it and the telephone I am in touch with a host of other minds, alive and dead and can converse with them. (Sherwood, 1966: 156–158; cf. Craik, 1943: 171)

Craik's writings are redolent of the utopian schemes promoted by the scientific Marxists of the 1920s and 1930s (on whom see Wersky, 1988). This self-same language of prosthesis and extension was used by authors such as J.D. Bernal and J.B.S. Haldane in their attempts to develop a humanist eschatology in which man would escape the fates of death and apocalypse by engaging in a project of scientific self-engineering (Bernal, 1929; Haldane, 1927).[23]

In his model of the human operator as a servomechanism, Craik prefigured an argument that was to become one of the foundations of cybernetic research. Yet his investigations went beyond this position, having a far wider and more reflexive implication. In a slim volume of philosophical analysis published in 1943, Craik suggested that this process of modelling was not simply a useful heuristic in psychology; rather, it was the basis of human mental life (Craik, 1943). He argued (p. 50) that reasoning consisted of three processes:

(1) 'Translation' of external process into words, numbers or other symbols.
(2) Arrival at other symbols by a process of 'reasoning', deduction, inference etc. and
(3) 'Retranslation' of these symbols into external processes (as in building a bridge to a design) or at least recognition of the correspondence between these symbols and external events (as in realising that a prediction is fulfilled).

By reducing the act of reasoning to this formulaic process of inference and comparison, Craik was able to emphasise the analogy between human and mechanical prediction. As he argued in *The Nature of Explanation*:

this process of prediction is not unique to minds, though no doubt it is hard to imitate the flexibility and versatility of mental prediction. A calculating machine, an anti-aircraft 'predictor' and Kelvin's tidal predictor all show the same ability. In all these cases the physical process which it is desired to predict is imitated by some mechanical device or model which is cheaper or quicker, or more convenient in operation. Here we have a very close parallel to our three stages of reasoning – the 'translation' of external processes into their representatives (positions of gears etc.) in the model; the arrival at other positions of gears, etc., by mechanical processes in the instrument; and finally the translation of these into physical processes of the original type. (Craik, 1943: 51)

Each of these mechanisms could be regarded as a model of external events insofar as they operated in the same way as the process they paralleled. In terms of function at least, Craik claimed that 'the only logical distinction' between the model and its object was 'on the grounds of cheapness, speed and convenience'. As he went on to explain:

The *Queen Mary* is designed with the aid of a model in a tank because of the greater cheapness and convenience of the latter; we do not design toy boats by trying out different plans on boats the size of Atlantic liners. In the same way, in the particular case of our nervous systems, the reason why I regard them as modelling the real process is that they permit the trial of alternatives, in e.g. bridge design, to proceed on a cheaper and smaller scale than if each bridge in turn were built and tried by sending a train over it to see whether it was sufficiently strong. (Craik, 1943: 52)

The economics of laboratory practice were thus reflected in the operations of mental life. The model-making heuristic was naturalised as the most efficient and effective means of arriving at knowledge of the natural world.

In this movement from using electrical models to elucidate the operations of the mind to his intellectual thesis of the mind as a modeller, Craik broke down the artificial distinction between the context of scientific discovery and the context of logical justification (Gigerenzer, 1992, 1996). This distinction had been promoted in the work of philosophers of science such as Karl Popper and R.B. Braithwaite, and the English biologist J.H. Woodger (Braithwaite, 1953; Woodger, 1937, 1939/1970). These authors had argued that philosophy was concerned solely with the logical basis of scientific claims, while the processes which led to scientific discovery were a matter for individual psychology or the sociology of knowledge. In Craik's work, however, modelling escaped its legitimising role and instead became a new heuristic, providing a fertile framework for imagining the processes of mental life. In this combination of legitimising philosophy, conceptual system, experimental practice, research programme and financial rationale, Craik demonstrated the deep interconnections which existed between the social, intellectual and the practical in the life of the individual scientist (cf. Lenoir, 1988).

For Craik, it seemed as if the experimental practice of the psychological laboratory was incarnated in the nervous tissue of the brain. His work on man–machine interfaces and his faith in the rhetoric of prosthetics rendered redundant the artificial distinctions between reason, nature, technology and action. In Craik's scheme the instruments of the laboratory and the heuristics of rational investigation were of one and the same form and nature. As he argued in *The Nature of Explanation*:

> Most of the greatest advances of modern technology have been instruments, which extended the scope of our sense organs, our brains or our limbs. Such are telescopes and microscopes, wireless, calculating machines, typewriters, motor cars, ships and aeroplanes. Is it not possible, therefore, that our brains themselves utilise comparable mechanisms to achieve the same ends and that these mechanisms can parallel phenomena in the external world as a calculating machine can parallel the development of strains in a bridge? (Craik, 1943: 61)

Craik's mental models had a real physical foundation. As friends and colleagues noted, his thought was essentially hylozoistic, with mental symbols and operations arising from patterns of neurophysiological organisation.[24] Oliver Zangwill, the experimental psychologist, who worked alongside Craik as a graduate student, argued that:

> His model is envisaged as a physical or chemical system which has a relation structure similar to that of the process it imitates. By 'relation structure' Craik means not some esoteric or non-physical entity but an actual physical working model operating in the same way as the process it parallels. (Zangwill, 1980: 7)[25]

Likewise, in a tribute to Craik at the conclusion of his 1946 Waynflete Lectures, the Nobel Prize-winning physiologist E.D. Adrian argued that Craik's system had escaped the need for mental phenomena.[26] In his scheme the application and transformation of cognitive models were achieved instead, through changing patterns of electrical organisation in the nervous system (Adrian, 1947: 94).

In his movement from psychological function to neural organisation, Craik was to encourage the formation of a series of new alliances between psychology, philosophy, neurophysiology and engineering.[27] It was a process which was to transform his work from being purely speculative exercise to the basis of a new programme of research and investigation.

3   New alliances

Craik was killed in a cycling accident on 18 May 1945, just after the war in Europe had drawn to a close. Yet, despite his untimely death, the new alliances which he had so ardently promoted quickly became established. In Britain, wartime contacts between the disciplines of psychology, neurophysiology, computing, psychiatry and engineering were maintained – most famously through the creation of the Ratio Club, an informal discussion group founded by John Bates in August 1949.[28] Although Bates was an old colleague of Craik's (having worked at the Armoured Fighting Vehicles Physiological Laboratories in Lulworth Cove) it would be wrong to attribute the club's establishment solely to Craik's inspiration. Rather, the club brought together a small number of researchers who had been engaged with problems of modelling and feedback control since the beginning of the war.

The idea of feedback control had been a recurring topic in physiological research since Claude Bernard's formulation of the notion of homeostasis (Langley, 1973; Cross and Albury, 1987). In the early part of the twentieth century it had been extended to cover the integrative work of the nervous and endocrine systems (Sherrington, 1906; Cannon, 1932). By 1940, it had entered the terrain of psychology, being held up as an explanation of adaptive and purposive behaviour (Pribram, 1992: 83). In a paper published in *Journal of Mental Science*, the Gloucestershire psychiatrist and future Ratio Club member William Ross Ashby had argued that the 'vague' and 'subjective' notion of adaptation be abandoned in favour of a more rigorous conception of 'stable equilibrium' (Ashby, 1940; the ideas were refined in Ashby, 1947a).

As a psychiatrist working on the homeostatic regulation of cortical enzyme levels, Ashby seized upon the notion of stable equilibrium as a concept which would bring together both the body's automatic reaction to changes in the internal environment (as in homeostasis) and the individual's psychological reaction to changes in the external world (Ashby, 1947b). From a modern perspective, these ideas of stable and unstable equilibria can be mapped on to the concepts of negative and positive feedback, respectively. Thus, Ashby defined his conceptions, arguing that 'a variable is in stable equilibrium if, when it is disturbed, reactive forces are set up which react back on the variable so as to *oppose* the initial disturbance. If they go with it then the notion is in unstable equilibrium' (Ashby, 1940: 479).

As with Craik's reformulation of reason and cognition in terms of symbolic model making, Ashby's adoption of the notion of stable equilibria as the key to behavioural adaptation opened up a previously occult process to the possibility of scientific representation. Just as Craik had argued that the tracking actions of human operators could be represented in mechanical systems, so Ashby embraced the possibility of modelling psychological health using electrical machines (Ashby, 1946a, 1952).

With the conclusion of the war in 1945, electronic components and technical expertise became available as they were suddenly released from military research and the armaments industry.[29] As a private psychiatrist with support for research, Ashby was able to draw upon this postwar glut in his attempt to build a mechanical model of human adaptation. In 1948, he announced the invention of the 'homeostat', a machine which seemed to mimic the hidden workings of the individual mind (Ashby, 1948; de Latil, 1956: ch. 13; Cooper and Bird, 1989: 42–45).

The homeostat's imitation was purely functional. In appearance it simply consisted of four units, each of which supported a magnetised needle. The four units were electrically interconnected, so that the disturbance of the needle on one unit would lead to an electrical change in the remaining units. These units in turn would feed back corresponding currents until the machine returned to a stable equilibrium. Moreover, Ashby's machine was endowed with a secondary feedback system that was triggered if the automata's basic wiring or organisation was interfered with. Reversing the polarities in the units would initially result in a positive feedback, which would destabilise the whole system. This destabilisation, however, would cause the machine to begin switching through a series of new possible arrangements until a state of stable equilibrium was again recovered.[30] This ongoing rearrangement of the system's internal connections allowed the homeostat to achieve what Ashby called 'ultrastability', as the machine moved between a number of potentially stable systems. The importance and uniqueness of Ashby's device lay in this secondary switching system (built from Post Office uniselectors) and the richness of the electrical interconnections which existed between the units. Each unit supported 25 possible points of connection, thus there were 25 to the power of 4, or 390,625, possible electrical arrangements within the homeostat as a whole (Ashby, 1952: 93–99; de Latil, 1956: 297–305). This complexity lent the device a certain plasticity: it was possible to rearrange the units in any way – and even mutilate the machine as a whole – yet it would always return to a state of stable equilibrium, although the internal arrangements which it used to achieve this could never be easily predicted (Ashby, 1950: 91).

Ashby believed that the secondary switching system deployed in the homeostat could be used to model more teleological notions, such as learning and purpose.[31] He argued that the repeated rearrangements of the system's internal connections could be compared to a 'step function' in which the machine altered its centre of equilibrium (Ashby, 1946b, 1960: 122–130). Although learning was traditionally seen as a highly complex process, this shifting equilibrium could be modelled in the simplest of mechanisms, such as a pendulum which achieved a new stable equilibrium every time its string broke. Ashby believed that such breaks could be 'considered to be an ordinary incident in the activity of one (more comprehensive) machine' (Ashby, 1947a).[32] It was a mechanism which allowed an automaton to transform itself into a new machine with a new purpose, or 'stable equilibrium', towards which it would adapt its actions.[33]

Although its intellectual origins were quite independent, Ashby's machine could be seen as a mechanical accomplice in the promotion of Craik's argument. It suggested that even the most capricious examples of human adaptation could be explained through reference to feedback mechanisms. Purpose did not belong to a realm which was somehow removed from the physical world – rather, it was a product of the rich levels of neural interconnection that existed within the organic body. The homeostat seemed to demonstrate that there was no fixed boundary between animals and machines; it was simply a gradient of internal complexity.

This extension of Craik's mechanistic hypothesis from the individual's capacity for cognition and ratiocination through to these more human qualities such as purpose and learning was continued in the work of a number of Ashby's British colleagues. Frank George at the University of Bristol built network machines capable of modelling belief and classification (George, 1957, 1961: 145–147). J.A. Deutsch at the Institute of Experimental Psychology, Oxford, suggested possible mechanisms which could achieve insight and pattern recognition (Deutsch, 1954, 1960). Grey Walter, Ashby's colleague at the Burden Neurological Institute, Bristol, attempted to build mechanical models of social behaviour.[34] Although each of these authors is deserving of historical investigation, the following discussion restricts itself to the example of Grey Walter, since much of his work was directed at the investigation and reinforcement of Craik's original conjectures.

Walter claimed that his enthusiasm for mechanical models had first been inspired by a meeting with Craik in the summer of 1944, when the young Cambridge psychologist had travelled down to Bristol to use the Burden's newly developed automatic frequency analysers (Walter, 1953/1960: 112).[35] The meeting was to reinforce the faith of both scientists in the possibility of electrical models of human behaviour. From Craik's point of view, the electroencephalograph (EEG) seemed to offer tantalising evidence for the cerebral scanning mechanism whose existence he had hypothesised in *The Nature of Explanation* and the self-maintaining positive feedback systems he posited in his work on the human operator (Craik, 1947–8a). For Walter, Craik's theories were to provide the basis for a new understanding of the data of electroencephalography.

Walter's electrical models were to have a far wider and more popular appeal than anything developed by Craik or Ashby. His creations were commonly known as the 'tortoises' and they were exhibited at meetings and exhibitions ranging from British Association conferences to the Festival of Britain (Fletcher, 1951; Stehl, 1955: 258; Cohen, 1966).[36] With frequent appearances in the press and on television, the tortoises could be seen as mechanical propagandists for the cybernetic argument.

The actual set-up and construction of the tortoises was fairly straightforward. Like Ashby, Walter's intention was to demonstrate that quite complex behaviour could emerge from extremely simple systems (Walter, 1950a,b, 1953/1960: ch. 7). Thus, the tortoises were designed as creatures limited to two nerve cells. They simply had two valves, two relays, two motors, two batteries and two condensers, which were connected to two basic forms of sense receptor. The first of these was a continually rotating photoelectric cell, which granted the organism sensitivity to light. The second was an electrical contact serving as a touch receptor that made the tortoise responsive to material obstacles (Walter, 1953/1960: 82f.).

Through the interrelation of these two simple circuits, Walter's tortoises seemed to exhibit behaviour such as speculation, discretion, moderation, self-recognition and mutual attraction. The scanning photoelectric cell was connected to the tortoise's steering mechanism, so that the creature engaged in a series of exploratory movements until it detected a source of light. Once a light signal had been located, the steering mechanism would lock and the tortoise would move towards the source. The very human qualities of self-recognition and mutual attraction were achieved by attaching a sensitive pilot lamp to the mechanical animals. This lamp would extinguish if it received a strong source of illumination, ensuring that the tortoises would at first be attracted and later repulsed by both their reflections and their potential companions (Walter, 1953/1960: ch. 5; Sluckin, 1954/1960: 62–63).

The design of the tortoises provided a bridge between Craik's speculative hypothesis and the data of neurophysiology. Craik had tentatively suggested that the EEG might represent a cerebral scanning mechanism in which a steady cortical carrier wave was modulated by incoming sensory signals. This idea was taken up and modelled by Walter in the rotating action of the tortoises' photoelectric cells. Just as the EEG was suppressed by the reception of visual information, likewise the scanning cell locked upon the location of a light source (Craik, 1943/1967: 73–75; Walter, 1950a; Wisdom, 1951: 16–17, 20–21; Jefferson, 1955: 81; Smythies, 1960: 251). Both actions were understood as evidence for the scansion hypothesis promoted by Craik. Through the actions of the tortoise and the EEG, the brain was now seen as a kind of electron-beam television camera, converting impulses of light into electrical signals (Walter, 1950c: 76–77; Thomson and Sluckin, 1954b: 120–121; Smythies, 1956: ch. 2).

This bridge – which the models provided between the feedback hypothesis and neurological data – was not simply limited to the normal operations of the brain. From the beginning of cybernetics, proponents had suggested that the discipline might elucidate some of the mechanisms of psychopathology. In his conclusion to *The Nature of Explanation*, Craik had remarked that neurosis could be modelled as a possible failure to adapt to the environment (Craik, 1943/1967: 91–92). Likewise, Wiener and Rosenblueth in their programmatic article had seized upon the similarity between the repetitive and ill-focused movements demonstrated by sufferers of cerebellar ataxia and the oscillatory process occurring when a feedback mechanism overshot its target and began 'hunting' (Wiener *et al.*, 1943). Such examples were easily multiplied, especially since the model mapped on to the traditional neurological problem of inhibition.[37] As the neurophysiologist Molly Brazier pointed out, many of the pathological actions produced through experimental lesions could be interpreted as resulting from the loss of inhibitive feedback control (Brazier, 1950: 36–37). The incessant swimming produced in cuttlefish and spinal dogfish after the removal of their higher nervous centres and the perpetual progressive movement in cats after decortication seemed to demonstrate the existence of a delicate balance in the nervous system between inhibitory and excitatory circuits.[38] Similarly, the catatonic states induced in animals with lesions in the mid-brain suggested that this neural balance could be upset in the opposite direction, with excitatory circuits being damaged or removed. Such feedback errors could also be induced electrically. Walter claimed that epileptic fits induced by stroboscopic lighting were a result of interference with the natural feedback rhythms of the brain (Walter *et al.*, 1946).

This pathological evidence was supplemented by histological data which seemed to suggest the existence of feedback relays at the level of the individual neurone. In the 1930s, the neurologist Lorente de No had suggested that neuronal organisation followed a 'law of the reciprocity of connections', which led to the creation of 'self re-exciting chains' (Lorente de Nó, 1933, 1938; Ashby, 1950: 80; Brazier, 1950: 37). Thus, when a group of nerve cells sent fibres into another group, there would always be other fibres which fed back (directly or indirectly) into the original group of cells. By the 1940s, a number of neuroanatomists had claimed to have isolated such systems. Ramon y Cajal's original work on the cerebral cortex and olfactory bulb had been supplemented by Walter Pitts and Warren McCulloch's studies on the visual system and J.Z. Young's research on cuttlefish (Sanders and Young, 1940).

These neuroanatomical findings provided a material framework for the cybernetic hypotheses of Craik and Ashby, yet their own significance was transformed in the process. In the writings of Ashby's contemporaries, a new vision of the brain as a probability calculator was developed. In this model, operation and function were no longer seen as products of local activities; rather, they arose through the combined actions of randomly distributed neurones reaching a state of statistical significance (Cogburn, 1951: 155; Uttley, 1955; Scholl, 1956). As Richard Gregory made clear, if such a conception of cerebral action was valid, then neuroanatomical investigations would have to be abandoned in favour of the electrical models pioneered by Craik and Ashby (Gregory, 1959: 669–680, especially 679–680; 1961).

It was, of course, easy to model these 'self-exciting' circuits in the machines developed by Walter and Ashby, and it was a happy accident that all their creations seemed to frequently suffer malfunctions. The homeostat frequently found itself trapped in a series of minor oscillations, too small to allow it to switch circuits but too large for it to achieve dynamic stability.[39] Likewise, Walter's tortoises, with their problematic reflections and unfulfilled attractions, often succumbed to a form of neurotic behaviour – spinning in circles or fixedly moving in repetitive patterns. These repetitive actions could be terminated only if the machine was turned off, rewired or recharged. For their creators, such behaviour had an obvious analogy with the cases they encountered in their medical work (Ashby, 1952: 40–41; 1954). It was a striking indication of the psychiatric origins of these first cybernetic machines that they suffered from debilitating neuroses yet responded well to surgery, rest cure and electroshock therapy (Walter, 1950a: 93).[40]

In their movements between stability and adaptation, learning and neurosis, the new cybernetic machines seemed to appropriate the fundamental characteristics of human life. At the same time, the language used to describe these characteristics was transformed. The work of Gilbert Ryle and others on the legitimate use of ordinary language facilitated these new analogies between human and machine behaviour (Ryle, 1949; Gregory, 1953–1954; George, 1956).[41] In their efforts to reject metaphysical conceptions and category mistakes, the ordinary-language philosophers began to adopt increasingly reductive and functionalistic definitions of mental phenomena. Thus, Ryle distinguished four forms of thinking: i) as belief or supposition; ii) being in a particular state of mind; iii) cogitating or puzzling out a problem; and iv) stating a conclusion. From this selection, he argued that only the last two definitions were valid, since thinking must be understood as a communicable process. As Ryle explained, 'it was not some peculiar shadow process which goes on behind the overt perform-ances of the thinker which is describable in special terms denoting mental acts' (Ryle, 1949). This restricted definition of thinking as a form of problem solving was increasingly adopted as standard in British psychology. In his synthetic work, the Cambridge psychologist George Humphrey was moved to define thought as 'what occurs in experience when an organism, human or animal meets, recog-nises and solves a problem' (Humphrey, 1951: 311).[42] In this movement of language which the philosophers mapped out, it was possible to see how Craik's theory had travelled from being an extreme and speculative hypothesis to become an idea at the centre of discourse.

4   Conclusions

By the end of the 1950s, Craik's theory seemed firmly established within British intellectual life. It had found allies in cognate disciplines ranging from neuro-anatomy through to linguistic philosophy. Increasingly, modelling came to be seen as the key to a whole series of activities. No longer restricted to experimental thought and practice, it was the secret behind intellectual success and social cohesion. In his contributions to the early American conferences on cybernetics, Ashby suggested that it would be possible to increase the intelligence of the general population if model building were employed as a universal heuristic. Model building would empower the individual by reducing the number of elements they would need to confront in their search for an answer (Ashby, 1958).

J.Z. Young went much further in the power he attributed to models. In his Reith Lectures for 1950, Young argued that our Christian idea of God could be understood as a model of social government which had been abstracted from the rule of the family and applied to society as a whole. It was the deployment of this model which allowed man to escape the primal urges of biology and begin on a life of coordination and cooperation with others (Young, 1951/1960: 94–99; Ashby, 1945; de Latil, 1956: 310–312; Deutsch, 1963).

Such assessments of the model-making heuristic remained curiously anthropo-centric. Although they recognised the mechanistic basis of thought, they still insisted on the role of humans as the model makers. By the end of the 1950s this final distinction was to disappear. The human project of constructing models (be it in the brain or the world) was now joined by a number of electrical actors. With the development of high-speed digital computers in the 1950s and the invention of linear programming, the computer moved from being a model of human cognition to become a modeller itself. With this Promethean gesture, the integrative research programme sketched out in the writings of Craik and his contemporaries came to an end. It was replaced by new sciences, cognitive psychology and artificial intelligence, in which the actions of the machines were no longer seen as pale imitations of human thought, rather they became the model of human psychology itself (Gardner, 1985; Mahoney, 1990: 551–552). Mace's fear was thus realised, as the human subject was displaced as the target of research in psychology. The very human hopes and efforts which Craik and Ashby had brought to the project of modelling were now disguised behind the apparent objectivity of the machine.

Acknowledgements

I should like to thank Roger Smith, Sandy Lovie and Richard Deswarte for their comments on this chapter. I gratefully acknowledge the support of the Wellcome Trust (Grant 047013) in financing the research and production of this chapter.

Notes

1 On William McDougall (1871–1938), Wilde Reader in Mental Philosophy at Oxford and later Professor of Psychology at Duke University, North Carolina, see McDougall (1930), Hearnshaw (1964: ch. 12).
2 Ironically, McDougall's definition of purposive behaviour has now inspired a research programme in artificial intelligence (see Boden, Chapter 18). For a survey of contemporary developments in popular robotics, see Chapuis and Droz (1958: 383f.) and Cohen (1966).
3 For Mace, see Who Was Who (1971–80): 492–493, and Carver (1962).
4 For a more tempered analysis of these developments, see Boden (1987: 475–478).
5 This tradition is usually traced back to La Mettrie's L'Homme machine (1747/1960) and then followed through nineteenth-century examples such as Huxley's (1894b) essay, 'On the hypothesis that animals are automata, and its history'. For an overview, see Young (1967: 122–127).
6 On the 'instrumental tactics' behind the establishment of a metaphor, see Gooding et al. (1989: 4f.) and Turbayne (1970: especially ch. 3, pt. 3). On the role of models in scientific research, see Hesse (1963, 1967), Wartofsky (1979), Latour (1990), Francoeur (1997), Hopwood (1999) and Sismondo (1999).
7 For the parallels between human and machine evolution, see Dyson (1997), who draws upon the classic work of Butler (1872/1932). Possible means for mechanical evolution were first explored in the early 1950s (Penrose, 1959).
8 On the political work of origin myths, see Latour and Strum (1986). On their role in disciplinary legitimisation, see Graham et al. (1983).
9 On the origins of cybernetics, see also Heims (1975: 368–373; 1980, 1993), Bowker (1993), Mahoney (1990) and Hayles (1999: ch. 4).
10 On Kenneth J.W. Craik (1914–1945), see Bartlett (1946) and Zangwill (1980, 1987). On Ashby, see obituary in The Times, 25 November 1972, p. 16h, and Asaro (1998).
11 On James Drever Snr (1873–1950), see his autobiographical account (Drever, 1948) and Hearnshaw (1964: 178).
12 On Frederic C. Bartlett (1886–1969), see his obituary in The Times, 1 October 1969), Broadbent (1970) and the Dictionary of National Biography (1961–70), pp. 77–79. On the constitution of the Flying Personnel Research Committee, see Green and Covell (1953: 32–33); Public Record Office, London (henceforth PRO), FD1/5350.

13 PRO ADM 212/8; PRO AIR2/8597.
14 PRO AVIA 22/2427.
15 Most of Craik's reports to the Flying Personnel Research Committee (FPRC) were never released into the public domain. See, however, FRPC report no. 119, *Fatigue Apparatus* (March 1940); FRPC report no. 188(a), *Effects of Anoxia on Manual Performance* (September 1940); FRPC report no. 193, *Form Perception During Dark Adaptation* (September 1940) (with M.A. Vernon); FRPC report no. 289, *Dark Adaptation and Night Vision* (April 1941); FRPC report no. 326, *Perception of Stationary and Moving Aircraft Silhouettes in Plain and Clouded Fields* (June 1841) (with M.D. Vernon); FRPC report no. 342, *Instrument Lighting for Night Use* (July 1941); FRPC report 359(a), *Glare from Searchlights* (October 1941) (with P.C. Livingston, E.A. Goldie and W.S. Stiles and also released as RA F Physiological Laboratory report 38/9); FRPC report 637, *Directions of Movements in Machine Controls* (August 1944) (with M.A. Vince). Most papers held at PRO AIR 14/1807.
16 On the history of ergonomics, see Murrell (1965) and Haraway (1992: ch. 8).
17 On the history of industrial psychology in Britain, see Hearnshaw (1964: 275–282) and Shimmin and Wallis (1994). On human engineering in general, see Rabinbach (1992).
18 On this work, see Le Gros Clark (1946: 39), Darcus and Weddell (1947) and Weddell and Darcus (1947: 77). For Le Gros Clark, see his autobiography (1968) and Zuckerman (1973).
19 This work drew upon the Military Personnel Research Committee report BPC 44/322, *Psychological and Physiological Aspects of Control Mechanisms* (written with M.A. Vince).
20 See also the list of Craik's publications compiled by S.J. Macpherson and reproduced in Sherwood (1966: 179–181).
21 FRPC 289.
22 For discussions of the interchange between intellectual models and craft practice in the sciences, see Hughes (1988) and Lenoir (1986).
23 Craik had expressed his admiration for Haldane in a personal note on 'The Marxist Philosophy and the Sciences' – see Sherwood (1966: 172–173).
24 On his hylozoism, see Craik (1943: 58). For a critical contemporary assessment see Barnes (1944).
25 For O.l. Zangwill (1913–1987), see Gregory (1991).
26 For E.D. Adrian (1889–1977), see Hodgkin (1979) and the *Dictionary of National Biography (1971–1980)*.
27 On this idea of alliances as the key to the success of scientific theories, see Latour (1986a, 1987: ch. 4).
28 On the formation of the Ratio Club, see Wellcome CMAC GC/179 B.1, and Hodges (1987: 411–412). The original members were: John Bates, Ross Ashby, H. Barlow, George Dawson, T. Gold, W.E. Hick, Donald Mackay, Thomas MacLardy, P.A. Merton, J.W.S. Pringle, Harold Shipton, D.A. Scholl, Albert Uttley, Grey Walter and J.A. Westcott. Later Alan Turing, F.A. Woodward, W.A.H. Rushton and I.J. Good joined the group.
29 For the flood of electronic components, see Williams (1994) and Monopolies and Restrictive Practices Commission (1956). On the connections between the thermionic valve industry and laboratory practice, see Hughes (1998).
30 Ashby drew upon the experiments of Marina and Sperry, who reversed the muscular organisation in the eyeballs and arms of apes and then traced the primates' gradual recovery of coordination (Sperry, 1947: 453). His model reflected Craik's belief that nervous organisation must arise from the effect of experience on reactive random connections (Craik, 1943: 115). Craik drew attention to Lashley and Stratten's work on the recovery of coordination (Lashley, 1938, 1942).

31 For similar learning machines using uniselectors, see Deutsch (1954) and Howard (1953). American psychologists, such as Edward Thorndike and Clark Hull, had long been working on attempts to build formal models of these processes (see Smith, 1986: 166).

32 For a criticism of this model of learning, see Kapp (1953–1954).

33 For a development of the theory of shifting equilibria, see Mace (1953) and Thomson and Sluckin (1954a,b). Cordeschi (1987: 126) argues that the increasingly extended use of the concept of homeostasis robbed the termed of its original meaning and explanatory power.

34 For Grey Walter, see Cooper and Bird (1989: ch. 4) and Kellaway (1990).

35 For the automatic analysers, see Walter (1943a,b).

36 The plans for the tortoises' role in the Festival of Britain are held at PRO WORK 25, 214 and 257.

37 The elision between the two topics was often resisted by senior neurologists (see Walshe, 1951).

38 For more examples, see Ashby (1955: 40–41).

39 Ashby, 'Cybernetics and insanity', MS, Wellcome CMAC: GC179/b.29.

40 See also Pavlovian breakdowns which Walter induced in IRMA and CORA, his machine models of learning, in Tanner and Inhelder (1971, part 2: 54).

41 On the rise of ordinary-language philosophy in Britain, see Smith (1997b: 827).

42 For Humphrey (1889–1966), see Zangwill (1966).

15

Behavioural approaches and the cultivation of competence

Karen Baistow

The starting point of this chapter is a paradox that raises interesting questions about the political and social role of psychology in contemporary Britain. In spite of the reported demise of behaviourism during the 1970s, and pessimistic assessments of behavioural psychology's intellectual and moral viability in the late twentieth century, behavioural approaches are alive and thriving.[1] While there has been ethical controversy surrounding behaviour therapy and doubts as to the efficacy of behaviour modification generally, the last 25 years have seen a widespread increase in their use by clinical psychologists for a range of anxiety-related problems. However, perhaps more significantly, during this period behaviour modification has spread beyond the clinic to non-clinical settings and problems. This expansion took place originally in prisons and residential institutions for young people, although subsequent publicised abuses of behaviour-modification techniques in these settings raised doubts among the media and the concerned public about the objectives and benefits of behavioural techniques. Less publicised but more widespread has been the expansion of behavioural approaches into the 'well' community during the last 20 or so years, where they are used by a variety of practitioners in health, welfare, social work and education as solutions to a range of individual and family problems. Health visitors, for example, routinely offer advice and guidance on the use of behavioural techniques in assisting parents to change the behaviour of their infants; nursery officers in day-care settings use them to manage their preschool charges; and family support workers help families to change their patterns of daily life by using behavioural approaches, training both parents and children in the process. Teachers, too, in mainstream as well as special education, have been encouraged by their local authorities to use these approaches, in particular to improve their pupils' social behaviour. With current debates about troublesome children focusing explicitly on behaviour problems, parental responsibility and the quality of 'parenting', professional interventions into family life are likely to increase. Indeed, the strategic development of such interventions became a priority of the New Labour government during its first 18 months in office.[2]

In addition, a reading of the professional literature and personal reports from the field point to several puzzling features of these community applications of behavioural approaches which do not accord with their previous reputation. These include the voluntary engagement of those in need of behavioural assistance, the empowering intentions of professionals who use behavioural approaches, and the enlistment of the former as 'partners' in a mutually negotiated and client-initiated programme of self-management, in which behavioural techniques are 'given away' to clients. Explicit emphasis is placed on building on strengths and optimising potential, with a view to enabling clients to 'take control' of their situation, their lives and so on. Given the erstwhile reputation of behaviour modification and the problems associated with behaviourism, recent expansions into the well community clearly raise social and political questions which have received little contemporary critical attention and which are not answered by earlier critiques of behaviourism.[3] The latter dismissed it intellectually, discredited it ideologically as mechanistic, dehumanising and reductive, and challenged the ethics of aiming to shape and control human material (see, for example, Ingleby, 1970). While there were some within the field, like Arnold Lazarus (1977), who were keen to put a distance between behaviourism and behaviour modification, critics tended to conflate them; behaviour modification was seen as punishment in the guise of treatment which involved changing people's behaviour against their will and, as such, a form of social control and a denial of basic civil liberties. By the late 1970s and early 1980s, however, behaviourism and behaviour modification were beginning to draw less critical attention on both sides of the Atlantic. The excesses of behaviour modification were apparently under control and there was confirmation of the demise of behaviourism, both as a cultural influence and within the discipline of psychology.[4] However, in spite of behaviourism's fall from grace, during the very same period behavioural psychologies, in theoretical and practical forms, expanded and diversified in new ways which rendered former problematisations of behaviourism and behaviour modification obsolete and warranted renewed attention.

These developments necessitated a different approach to the history, and to the present existence, of behavioural psychology, which problematised it new ways.[5] This involves asking how it has become possible for behavioural approaches to permeate the everyday lives of many 'ordinary people', given the decline of behaviourism and the controversial reputation of behaviour modification and considering the ways in which this has taken place during the last 20 or so years. To answer this question, this chapter examines the internal and external conditions of these more recent forms of behavioural psychology, first by tracing the discursive changes that have taken place within behavioural discourses in the postwar years, which, I suggest, had profound implications for the expansion and diversification of behavioural approaches; second by charting recent 'surfaces of emergence' in the well community in Britain, in relation to children; and finally by contextualising the spread and diversification of behavioural approaches in relation to contemporary political, economic and ethical discourses, in particular, the requirements of market economies.

1 The shifting conceptual ground

The period 1960–1990 was marked by several, associated shifts in the conceptual, strategic and technical emphases of behavioural psychology which were to lay the ground for the expansion and diversification of behavioural approaches in both America and Britain. Perhaps the most significant of these involved a move away from using behavioural approaches to modify the behaviour of others, towards developing ways of enabling people to manage their own behaviour. The emergence of the autonomous, self-managing behavioural subject during this period was closely connected with changing conceptualisations of personal power and control in American psychology, the historical home of behaviourism. Though these changing notions were most evident in American behavioural discourses, they had a profound impact on the development of behavioural approaches in Britain; behaviour therapy was well established in Britain, both institutionally and clinically by the late 1960s (see Derksen, Chapter 12), but I argue that it was these developments in the United States that established the discursive ground for behavioural approaches to move beyond the laboratory, clinic and institution and into the everyday lives of 'ordinary people', to be used in new ways on a wider range of people.[6]

However, this is not the whole story, for, as we shall see, the widespread use of behavioural approaches in Britain at the start of the twenty-first century is strongly connected with changing external conditions, in political, economic and ethical climates, as well as with changing conditions within behavioural discourse. Moreover, as this chapter aims to demonstrate, the two sets of conditions are not separate but interdependent. To begin with, therefore, we examine the condition of postwar American behavioural psychology.

1.1 *Problems of self-determinism*

Since the 1950s, behavioural psychology, in its various guises, has increasingly concerned itself with people's ability to control their personal environment. However, views on the importance of 'instrumentality' to human existence – the strength of connection between acts and their effects – have not been confined to behavioural psychology. White (1959), for example, in his influential critique of drive theories of motivation, postulated 'effectance motivation' as a biologically significant desire to have an effect on the environment; 'effectance motivation' in higher animals and especially humans was seen as having high survival value and experiences of 'competence' were viewed as being both adaptive and satisfying by producing a 'feeling of efficacy'.[7] Nevertheless, while the most evident interest in instrumentality came from behavioural psychology, this branch of the discipline was by no means homogeneous. Although, for several decades, the proponents of radical behaviourism continued to wage a campaign to re-establish its earlier dominance, it was no longer the most influential derivative of learning theory. A series of associated changes, under the rubric of social learning theory, extended the conceptual bases of behavioural psychology and broadened its explanatory powers.

Of fundamental importance were changing behavioural conceptions of the types of power which might be socially and ethically desirable. These new conceptions emphasised self-determinism rather than environmental determinism and the role that psychology might play in operationalising this ideal. The demise of radical environmental determinism was accompanied by a shift away from a view of the individual, whether child or adult, as essentially passive and subject to the shaping powers of external reinforcement, to interactional and transactional models which saw the individual as active, both affecting and being affected by the social environment. The 'reciprocal determinism' of Bandura's social learning theory laid emphasis on human agency in a new way, by focusing on the mutually shaping, transactional nature of the person–environment relationship and by arguing for a line of enquiry which examined the connection between self-beliefs and behaviour (Bandura, 1977). The problem that psychology needed to address, according to Bandura (1982), was that in spite of adequate knowledge, people 'often do not behave optimally'; the potential social contribution of psychology was to enable people, individually and collectively, to develop the capacity to produce and regulate events in their lives. The recognition and promotion of 'self-directing capacities' in behavioural discourses not only represented a substantial departure from a belief in the power of environmental control, they also marked a changing conception of power, away from power as control, to power as productive. Mastery of the self became the object of concern in psychological discourses, not only for the purposes of self-regulation (that is, subjecting the self to restrictions, adapting to requirements, and so on); self-management was seen to open up the possibilities of personal determinism.

The ground for the reintroduction of the person into behavioural psychology, at the theoretical and the ethical level, was laid by the 'cognitive revolution' of the 1960s, in which mentalistic constructs and explanatory models became reincorporated into mainstream academic psychology after almost half a century's exile, during the reign of radical behaviourism. Whereas radical behaviourists eschewed mentalism on ethical as well as conceptual grounds, exponents of social learning approaches drew on humanism, both to propose a connection between beliefs, actions and outcomes and to argue that individual and social change was best achieved through the promotion of capacities rather than by the elimination of deficits and by the adoption of explanatory models focusing on 'competency' rather than 'defect' (Bandura, 1974; Albee, 1980). The acquisition of behaviour and more importantly its performance, it was suggested, could best be understood in terms of its relation to people's beliefs about their own ability to make a difference to the outcome of a situation. Thus, people's beliefs about the locus of causality and variations in their explanatory styles regarding the relationship between their actions and outcomes began to be focused on as significant variables in learning, behaving and 'coping' (see, for example, Rotter *et al.*, 1972; Seligman, 1975; Kobasa, 1982; Bandura, 1982).

The seminal concept in the new amalgam of disposition and situation was that of 'locus of control', which distinguished between individuals' characteristic ways of attributing causality as either 'internal' or 'external'. According to Julian Rotter (1966), those with an internal locus of control believe that their own actions will, or can, make a difference to outcomes. Those with an external locus of control believe that outcomes are largely independent of their actions. Rotter's theory not only cast locus of control as a key variable in people's expectations about the outcomes of their own behaviour but also as highly significant in determining whether they acted or not. Thus, internal attributions were found to be more associated with action taking, based on the belief that outcomes are directly the result of one's own behaviour, or relatively enduring personal characteristics. In contrast, external attributions were more associated with feelings of powerlessness and an inability to act, characterised as helplessness and, by implication, an inability to take responsibility for outcomes. Early work in the 1950s in controlled laboratory settings was extended in the next two decades and applied beyond the psychological laboratory to explain more socially meaningful behaviour as well as personal health and happiness (see, for example, Rotter *et al.*, 1972; Kobasa, 1982; Lefcourt, 1966; Peterson and Stunkard, 1989).

The perceived 'uncontrollability' of events also lies at the heart of Seligman's theory of learned helplessness. People who experience learned helplessness are unlikely to act because they have learned through previous experiences that personal actions make little or no difference to the outcome of a situation. Their belief, therefore, in their own power is minimal, as is their self-esteem; the existential position is one of hopelessness. According to Seligman (1975), experimental studies on learned helplessness in animals could explain human depression. However, criticisms that the translation of animal helplessness into human depression was simplistic led to a reformulation of the theory in the mid-1970s which sought to cope with the more complex phenomena of helplessness in humans and to apply it to 'real-world', 'real-human', 'real-life' problems, raising the possibility that the alienating effects of learned helplessness might be reversed by teaching people that they could control things that had been previously uncontrollable (Abramson *et al.*, 1978).

Bandura's version of the connection between beliefs, actions and outcomes took the form of 'perceived self-efficacy', a belief in our own capability to take effective action to achieve a desired outcome. Inefficacy was seen as the product of a fundamental existential sense of futility, the sources of which were twofold, according to Bandura. On the one hand, there is our belief in our own ability to take action; on the other, there is our belief that particular actions will have the desired effect. Thus, we may have a belief in our own capacities but see little point in exercising them because we believe that they will not make any difference. A disinclination to take action, therefore, is reciprocally related to a sense of futility and perceived self-inefficacy (Bandura, 1982).

The discursive significance of these three constructs – locus of control, learned helplessness and self-efficacy – was the emphasis that they placed on the critical importance of self-perceptions of power and efficacy as the necessary conditions for actions through which competence might be established and confirmed. The reciprocal determinism of self-beliefs and behaviour, which they embodied, pointed to new types of solutions that a behavioural, rather than a behaviouristic, psychology might offer.

1.2 *A psychology for everyone*

While the reintroduction of the mind provided some of the discursive conditions for a broader basis to behavioural psychology, of equal importance in laying the conceptual ground that would enable behavioural approaches to be used in more diverse ways were the attempts, particularly evident in America, to formulate a more socially sensitive behavioural psychology. Critics of the more strident forms of radical behaviourism came from inside as well as outside behavioural psychology.[8] While no less environmentally determinist than B.F. Skinner, the former were both less convinced and more apprehensive of the sort of wholesale cultural engineering that he had recommended as behaviourism's contribution to society's salvation. Apart from its dubious ethics, the kind of radical behaviourism promoted by Skinner, for example in his 1971 book *Beyond Freedom and Dignity* and also associated in the public eye with the practices of behaviour modification, was giving psychology a bad name. The late 1960s saw the emergence of a socially sensitive behavioural psychology, whose advocates were keen to emphasise psychology's claim to being a positive and benign social instrument. In his presidential address to the American Psychological Association in 1969, George Miller described his vision of a novel relationship between psychology and society – what he described as the 'revolutionary potential of psychology', which would offer to the public at large 'a new and different public conception of what is humanly possible and what is humanly desirable' (Miller, 1969). According to Miller, this new 'conception of man' would have immediate implications for the most intimate details of people's social and personal lives. The imperative, however, was not scientific or technical but ethical: the obligation to solve human problems fell on the psychologist as citizen, not as scientist. A key element in this was that psychology had to be practised by non-psychologists; it had to be 'given away' to 'people who really need it – and that includes everyone' (Miller, 1969: 1071). Giving psychology away, according to Miller, was an educational process in which psychologists would have to relinquish their previous status as experts in favour of a learner-centred teaching role, working with 'ordinary people' who needed practical psychological to help them solve what they saw as their problems. Satisfying their urge to feel more effective would inevitably lead, in his view, to a change in people's conceptions of themselves and what they could do.

This transformation of behaviour psychology's social project, with its shift of emphasis away from the control of behaviour to its enhancement, found a further influential voice in Albert Bandura. In his presidential address to the American Psychological Association, in 1974, he examined the 'images of man' that had become associated with behaviourist social technologies. Like Miller, he sought to address public anxieties about the controlling features of these technologies by demythologising their 'fabled powers' and to reassure his audience of psychologists' concern for human rights and their desire to 'ensure that reinforcement techniques are used in the service of human betterment rather than as instruments of social control' (Bandura, 1974: 863). According to Bandura, current concerns were to provide people with an increased number of options and the right to exercise them: 'The more behavioural alternatives and social prerogatives people have, the greater is their freedom of action.... Freedom can be expanded by cultivating competencies ... restored by eliminating dysfunctional self-restraints' (Bandura, 1974: 865).

The ethical and legal issues raised by the use of behaviour modification and behaviour therapy on captive subjects were more in evidence in American behavioural psychology texts (and law courts) than in their British counterparts. Sceptics might suggest that this was not so much to do with moral concerns but was connected with the US constitution and the greater possibilities of prosecution if a constitutional freedom was suspected of being violated. Whatever the reason, behavioural psychologists in Britain were apparently less concerned with these ethical and legal problems of behaviour modification and behaviour therapy, and frequently invoked the well rehearsed proposition that the moral strength of behavioural treatments lay in their proven effectiveness (Sheldon, 1982).

A further thrust to the establishment of a new, responsive and responsible behavioural psychology came with the formulation of the 'constructional approach' by Goldiamond (1974). This offered a civil-libertarian, legalistic basis for a system in which the US constitution would serve as a guide for the ethical and legal issues that were raised by the use of behaviour therapy. Of particular practical as well as conceptual significance was his proposal for an explicit reorientation of behaviour modification so that it would be 'more in line with the basic principles of human rights'. This involved a shift away from the then prevalent concentration on eliminating 'undesirable' behaviour through aversive techniques, which he viewed as 'pathologically orientated', to a 'constructional orientation'. This constructional approach, so called because it 'builds repertoires' by 'focusing on the production of desirables through means which directly increase available options or extend social repertoires', emphasised the use of positive reinforcement (Goldiamond, 1974: 14). It proved to be influential not only in the United States; it became established during the 1980s in Britain, a time when the excesses of punitive institutional regimes based on aversive approaches were coming to light.

For its advocates in Britain, the constructional approach was applicable to a range of human problems to be found outside the clinic. By attempting to build adaptive behavioural repertoires rather than eliminating maladaptive ones, the constructional approach was seen not only to 'increase social competence' in clients but also to give them 'insight into their own behaviour by organising therapy in a concrete, achievable way' (Hattersley *et al.*, 1979; see also Cullen *et al.*, 1981).

The discursive significance of the constructional approach lay in the way in which it created the conceptual and technical conditions for behavioural psychology to operationalise, as well as recommend, the cultivation of competencies as its new goal. This explicit shift away from a pathological orientation to one which attempted to 'normalise' problems of behaviour formed the basis of Tharp and Wetzel's (1969) seminal text *Behavior Modification in the Natural Environment*, which was to be influential on both sides of the Atlantic in the succeeding decades. They argued for the depathologisation of abnormal behaviour, claiming that 'the laws of learning like the rains, fall upon us all'. Tharp and Wetzel advocated the de-psychiatrisation and de-professionalisation of the field of mental health, and suggested that the best setting for therapeutic interventions was the individual's 'natural environment', as it was here that everyday contingencies (or reinforcers) of their behaviour occurred. In addition, they argued that, if the reinforcers lay in these natural environments, then so did those who dispensed them. Using people who had a 'natural relationship' with the individual and 'talented sub-professionals' to work directly with the person not only placed psychiatrists and psychologists in new roles, it also altered the relationship between them and the recipients of their expertise. In contrast to the traditional dyadic model of doctor–patient/psychologist–client, Tharp and Wetzel proposed a triadic model of consultant–mediator–target, in which psychological professionals (psychologists, psychiatrists, social workers) were cast as supervisors and consultants rather than therapists. Their consultant role as 'contingency managers' was to rearrange environmental rewards and punishments, which strengthened or weakened specified behaviours. However, it was parents, spouses, siblings, friends, employers or others in the 'target's' natural environment who carried out the new reinforcement contingencies, who became the mediators or intermediaries between the psychologist and the target, and to whom psychology was to be given away. The triadic model, it was argued, made it possible for behavioural approaches to be deployed in almost any setting, by non-professionals and paraprofessionals as well as psychologists, on new groups of problematic, but not necessarily psychiatric, 'targets'.

While the injunction to 'give away' behavioural psychology might have an egalitarian, ethical ring to it, the possibilities of this happening were closely connected to the increasing emphasis being placed, on both sides of the Atlantic during the 1970s, on behaviour modification as pure technique (see, for example, London, 1972; Lazarus, 1977; Erwin, 1978). This was and continues to be a contested move within the field of behavioural psychology. In Britain, advocates agreed about the advantages of concentrating on behaviour modification as a technology for changing behaviour, arguing that understanding why it worked was not a prerequisite for its use (see, for example, Yule, 1975; Herbert, 1981; Hewitt, 1981; Hastings and Schwieso, 1981; Milne, 1986; Carr, 1988; Appleton *et al.*, 1989). According to these psychologists, training in the use of the techniques without having to gain knowledge of the underpinning theory or principles meant that behavioural approaches would be open to a range of non-specialists (teachers, nurses, parents and so forth) relatively quickly and easily; this would make help more available for those with problems and at the same time give health and welfare services wider access to them in a broader bid to deal with an increasing social problem.

For some, the self-evidence of the inadequacy of traditional strategies of direct therapist–patient contact was best illustrated by the low ratios of psychologists (and psychiatrists) to the population (Milne, 1986). The 'vacuum of need' created by the shortfall in therapeutic and economic resources meant that new solutions were necessary which, preferably, met constraints of cost while increasing the availability of therapeutic assistance. In such conditions, the appeal of giving behavioural psychology away to unpaid, motivated parents, or paraprofessionals in search of new professional roles, seemed very attractive. The shortfall between need and provision would thus be met and, furthermore, this could be done comparatively cheaply because not only were behavioural approaches time-limited (unlike psychodynamic approaches), in addition, the time of non-specialists cost much less than that of psychologists and psychiatrists. The scene was set for the emergence of the 'new behaviourists'.

However, other behaviourally oriented psychologists in Britain warned of the dangers of behaviour modification being taught to non-experts, divorced from its theoretical base. For Berger (1979), the possibility that it could become a 'mindless technology' outweighed the advantages that Yule had proposed four years earlier. He saw the problem stemming from a combination of two features: the idea that behaviour modification was merely a technology, with apparently simple, common-sense techniques; and the over-enthusiasm displayed by some psychologists for teaching the techniques to non-psychologists. The resultant dangers lay in trying to resolve complex problems by means of 'a few technical tricks', in the possible rejection of the whole approach if these failed, and in the undermining of the professional's sense of competence in such cases of failure. Wheldall (1982), though a long-time advocate of the use of behaviour modification in education, shared these concerns about oversimplification. Sounding a note of caution, he expressed concern about the 'bastardised version' of applied behaviour analysis being used in schools, which operated at a crude, and unnecessarily heavy-handed level of consequence management: 'we must replace the notion of a peanut pushing, smartie smothering, token trafficking, behaviour mod "enthusiast" with the concept of the skilled behaviour analyst' (Wheldall, 1982: 184).

In spite of these concerns, behavioural approaches were increasingly promoted, as they had been by earlier proponents of behavioural psychology, as practical and practicable technologies whose worth lay in their power to produce effects. Moreover, the emphasis on technique implied that the problems of behaviour that they were addressing were themselves technical, not pathological, deep-seated or due to unconscious motivation. The problems were, thus, in one sense, normalised. As we shall see later, this normalisation process was less than straightforward, for while there was a de-psychiatrisation of problems, they were nevertheless still construed as ones requiring professional attention. If they were to be successfully solved and if future recurrences or increases in severity were to be prevented, professional psychological advice and interventions would be needed. This simultaneous normalisation of the problematic and problematisation of the normal thus meant that typical, 'everyday' behaviour could increasingly come under the purview of psychologists and, as we will see in the next section, of other practitioners in health, welfare and education.

2   Giving away behavioural approaches

The conceptual transformations discussed above were associated with expansion and diversification in the practical activities associated with behavioural psychology, with a widening range of clients and problems seen as suitable for behavioural interventions, and the development of new techniques to be deployed by a broader range of behavioural technologists. In effect, the last 30 years in Britain have seen more aspects of living becoming behaviourally problematised and a wider range of people being seen as constituting behavioural subjects. During the 1970s, for example, the field of mental handicap was to be subjected to the conceptual and practical activities of behavioural psychology, such that, in due time, the problems of 'mental handicap' and 'mental subnormality' came to be replaced by 'learning difficulties', and behaviour modification techniques were routinely applied to deal with them. By the end of that decade, behavioural attention began to extend beyond 'restricted' environments and their inhabitants (prisoners, the mentally ill, young offenders and so on) into the 'natural environment' of a wider set of candidates for behavioural interventions, who were characterised by the more 'typical' and less obviously socially threatening nature of their problems – those whose behaviour jeopardised their health or those who had antisocial habits, disobedient and disruptive children, ineffective parents and teachers, underachieving schoolchildren. However, my analysis points not to an orderly, progressive shift or displacement of interest away from one arena to another, but rather to a widening of focus.

Of central interest to this discussion about the impact of psychology on our everyday lives at the turn of the century are those expansions into the 'well' community which were outlined in the introduction. The last 20 years have seen an increasing institutional interest on the part of psychology in becoming involved more directly with people to help them solve their everyday problems of living. This has involved not only the application of psychology to the 'real world', but also the formulation of new kinds of psychological approaches and the emergence of new types of psychologist, such as 'community psychologists', to work in these new settings (see, for example, Bender, 1976; McPherson and Sutton, 1981; Koch, 1986; Orford, 1992; Pilgrim and Treacher, 1992). During this period, the British Psychological Society began to take a more active interest in these community developments, particularly in terms of their implications for the discipline and profession of psychology (see, for example, British Psychological Society, 1988, 1990).

As well as consolidating an involvement in fields such as mental health, in which clinical psychology had a significant role to play, behavioural approaches have expanded into the area of family life in a number of key ways. It is to this involvement that we now turn, by examining some of these developments in more detail, focusing particularly on an old favourite of psychological expertise: child development, welfare and education.

The rearing of children, and especially the potential role of psychological experts to offer guidance in this respect, has been of long-term interest to the discipline. Assisting parents to do a better job has preoccupied such experts for at least a century, with the rationale that psychology could (and should) improve on parenthood in the name of better child health and development. The publication of manuals and child-rearing texts and lectures for parents, nurses and educators has, until recently, been the most visible manifestation of this desire to intervene (usually indirectly) in the most commonplace and intimate aspects of family life (see Beekman, 1977; Hardyment, 1983). While not the domain solely of psychological expertise (most child-rearing texts have been written by doctors), a noticeable trend during the twentieth century was the increasing psychologisation of child health and development (see Baistow, 1995a). This trend involved the application of many different sorts of psychology, and behavioural psychology was no exception. In his manual *Psychological Care of Infant and Child*, published in 1928, which sold more than 100,000 copies, J.B. Watson advocated, advised and demonstrated the benefits of a scientific, behaviourist version of child rearing, worked out by the 'patient laboratory methods' of the psychologist, to produce 'practical results that can be used in the home' (Watson, 1928: 7).

However, behavioural interventions into child rearing and child development took rather a different form in the late twentieth century. While, for their advocates, the systematic application of practical, scientifically derived techniques continued to be the main recommendation of these approaches, they no longer belonged only to behaviourist fantasies of a re-engineered society but were a feature of many families' lives. A key difference lies in the rise of professionals, such as health visitors and social workers as well as teachers and psychologists, whose job it is to monitor and foster child welfare and development, and whose responsibility (and sometimes statutory duty) it is to intervene if there are aspects of these that are causing concern. It is through their professional alliances and the implementation of the 'triadic model' that behavioural approaches have reached more children and parents than possibly even Watson imagined. In the next section, we go on to examine some of these activities and to chart their impact on children from infancy to school age.

2.1 Behaviour problems: children, parents and practitioners

Who are the children and parents who are likely to be on the receiving end of behavioural approaches? As might be expected from the discussion above, since the 1970s new childhood candidates for behavioural attention have emerged. For example, the age range of potential candidates has been extended back to early infancy. Moreover, the childhood candidates now include both a broader range of problem categories and a wider range of childhood behaviours. Originally there were, on the one hand, homogeneous categories of childhood 'targets', generally those with a psychiatric diagnosis such as autism or learning difficulties and, on the other, specific behaviours like enuresis, tantrums, head-banging and so forth, or constellations of disordered behaviour denoted by terms such as aggression, coercion, social withdrawal or the broader 'social and emotional difficulties' (see, for example, Herbert, 1974, 1987; Yule, 1991). These categories and behaviours were not mutually exclusive, and so there were many permutations of problem behaviours in need of modification.

During the 1970s and 1980s, new childhood behaviours were added to the list, as were new categories of problem. Most noticeable is the addition of more 'typical', some might say even normative, childhood behaviours that were seen to need systematic behavioural attention, particularly those of infants and preschool children (see, for example, Chazan et al., 1983; Douglas, 1989). During the 1970s and 1980s, Richman et al. charted the prevalence of behaviour problems in this group and developed the Behavioural Checklist for assessment purposes (Richman et al., 1975, 1982; McQuire and Richman, 1987). This work served as evidence to support the argument that more professional interest and concern for this age group and their families were needed. Though previous statistics did not exist and estimates of prevalence could give little or no firm indications of trends over time, they did suggest that present untreated troubles could develop into much more serious ones (for example, Stevenson et al., 1988). This concern was shared by other psychologists working in this field and, as we saw earlier, the question was raised as to whether and how existing services might deal with these new categories of troublesome children who could misbehave from birth onwards. As early as 1975, the social problematisation of childhood misbehaviour was being linked with the inadequacies of 'service delivery'. Thus Yule (1975: 4) argued that it was clear from recent epidemiological studies that 'there are too many children with significant behavioural problems for traditional methods of service delivery to be effective'; 14 years later the theme persisted: Appleton et al. (1989: 761) argued that, 'there is no escape from the fact that, with prevalence of moderate to severe pre-school behaviour problems running at 7% (and mild problems at 15%) current service levels and service structures are woefully inadequate'. Others used parental complaint as an index of the scale of the problem: 'it has been estimated for one health district with a pre-school population of 14,100 that each year parents of 751 nine month olds and 1025 two-year olds may seek advice about what they regard as behaviour problems in their child' (Hewitt et al., 1991).

What were these problems and who should deal with them? Research in Britain exploring the possibilities of using health visitors to deal with preschool behaviour problems, particularly using parent training, was well underway by the mid-1980s.[9] Towards the end of that decade there was sufficient interest in the use of health visitors as 'new behaviourists' for the Association of Child Psychology and Psychiatry (ACPP) to initiate a study on health-visitor-based services for preschool children with behaviour problems. It was claimed that the need to train health visitors in psychological treatment techniques was endorsed not only by epidemiological research but also by health visitors themselves (Association of Child Psychology and Psychiatry, 1989). A further critical consideration was that of economy and budgetary constraints, which, according to the study, pointed to the need for 'innovative service developments' involving the collaboration of health visitors with clinical psychologists or child psychiatrists to provide community-based services for such children. It was believed that they were in an ideal and unique position, through their routine contact with under-fives and their families, to monitor parenting, to identify behaviour problems and to engage in preventive behavioural parent training regarding child abuse, including antenatally, as well as remedial work (Hewitt, 1981; Stevenson *et al.*, 1988; Appleton *et al.*, 1989).

By the 1990s, health visitors were using behavioural approaches (the constructional approach was favoured) with individual families, offering group sessions for parents and increasingly running parent training 'clinics' to deal with common infant and toddler problems associated with sleeping (the child's inability to go to sleep at the desired time, on its own, in its own bed, frequent night-time waking, the need for parental presence), crying (too much, too often), eating (food fads, food refusal), overactivity, bed wetting, temper tantrums, attention problems (inability to concentrate on an activity for any length of time), disobedience and so on. Significantly, these difficulties were associated with a parental behaviour problem – 'ineffective child management' – and changing parental behaviour has become as much the object of behavioural approaches as has the preschool child. According to Hewitt and other authors, as well as being more effective, the constructional approach is more attractive to parents; because it is easier to apply and involves the use of positive reinforcement, parents find it more humane, less emotionally demanding and more ethically acceptable. While there are circumstances where parents and children may be subjected to behavioural training on a less voluntary basis, for example where there are child welfare concerns and social services are involved, an important aspect of the deployment of behavioural approaches by health visitors is that, on the whole, parents 'refer' themselves and are voluntary candidates for 'training'.

Where do older children in the 'well' community most typically experience behavioural approaches? The setting where this is increasingly likely to happen is the school. Both within the classroom and in the wider school, through the use of behaviourally inspired management techniques, pupils of all ages are more likely to be routinely on the receiving end of behavioural approaches than at any time since the advent of behaviourism in 1913. While there has been an

enduring preoccupation with controlling the behaviour of pupils since the inception of formal schooling, contemporary efforts differ in several ways. The most
notable of these is the strategic nature of current deployments, particularly
regarding the policy contexts in which they have developed. These are manifested
in a national emphasis on clearly defined 'positive' management techniques, to
encourage the development and maintenance of good behaviour rather than the
punishment of bad behaviour, through the introduction, by local education
authorities, of 'behaviour support plans', and through the implementation of
'whole-school' behaviour policies (see below).

Research in this field began in Britain in the early 1970s (see, for example,
Ward, 1971; Berger *et al.*, 1977). However, unlike the field of preschool care and
health visiting, the use of behavioural approaches in mainstream educational
settings during the last three decades has been characterised by caution on the
part of teachers. In an overview of behaviour modification in education, which
noted how few articles there had been in Britain, Ward (1976) forecast an increase
in interest in the application of behaviour modification to education. The late
1970s saw some confirmation of this trend. Harrop (1980) reported an increase
in the number of journal articles on the subject in education journals and in
1977 an entire issue of the quarterly *Bulletin of the British Association of Behavioural
Psychotherapy* was devoted to the subject. Conferences, the other indicator of
academic and professional interest, also began to take place around this time.[10]
However, in spite of the proselytising efforts of some key players like those at the
Centre for Child Study at the University of Birmingham, including Kevin Wheldall,
whose book *The Behaviourist in the Classroom* (1981) and numerous articles did
much to put behavioural methods on the map in some educational circles, the early
1980s saw little real change in the classroom. Indeed, there were disappointed
claims by Wheldall and his colleagues that these approaches were largely unheard
of or, at best, misconceived by most British teachers and educationists (Wheldall
and Congreve, 1980; Wheldall, 1981, 1987).

Sceptics and critical supporters, however, detected sufficient signs of the
expansion of behaviour modification practices in schools to express concern.
While some critics remained concerned about the explanatory value of the
theoretical bases of behaviour modification and their ethical implications, others
warned of the 'insidious and irreversible take-over of curriculum planning' by
the 'crass and insensitive use of behavioural objectives' which had begun to permeate educational practice (Clark, 1979; Wragg, 1982). Supporters, too, sounded
notes of caution – about the undesirable dilution of behavioural theory and
methodology involved in contemporary applications of behaviour modification
in schools and the dangers of using behavioural technologies divorced from their
knowledge base (for example, Berger, 1979; Harrop, 1980; Owens and Walter,
1980). Still others claimed that the real increase in the application of behavioural
approaches in education was not among teachers within the mainstream but
among the external support services, especially educational psychologists (Dessent,
1988).

Towards the latter half of 1980s, things began to change. As well as the continuing use of behavioural approaches in special schools, there was growing interest from the mainstream, particularly in the area of classroom management. The problem of pupil indiscipline was not a new one, but it was being recast by changing social and political conditions, which had a direct effect on the ways that schools were organised, funded and managed. Increasing public and governmental attention was being directed towards the effectiveness of schools, in terms of both academic achievement and pupil attendance and behaviour, and during the decade this was enacted in new legislation in the form of the 1981 Education Act, the 1988 Education Reform Act and in the 1989 *Report of the Elton Committee of Enquiry into Discipline in Schools*. This was mirrored in the reports of teacher concerns about the problems caused by pupils misbehaving, especially their power to disrupt the learning and social climate of the classroom. From the teacher surveys used in the Elton report and others (see Jones, 1989), it appeared that there was a continuum of behaviour that was causing problems in the classroom and within the school as a whole: on the one hand, there was the power of certain pupils to disrupt the classroom through their 'challenging' and antisocial behaviour and, on the other, less serious, relatively trivial but persistent misbehaviours, such as talking, fidgeting and moving around the classroom, which were seen to have a cumulatively disruptive effect both on learning and teacher competence and confidence. What were needed were strategies and techniques which would enable teachers to manage and control their pupils more effectively.

During this period, a range of courses appeared which provided teachers with (behavioural) training in behaviour management.[11] While these varied in the extent to which they recommended the systematic implementation of the principles of applied behaviour analysis, they had a common view of certain basic features which underpinned the behavioural approach to classroom management and which, in the succeeding decade, became central to the development of 'whole-school' approaches to discipline. At the heart of this approach was an ethical emphasis on 'positive behaviour' as a personal and collective goal, and the use of positive techniques to accomplish this, in particular, the systematic application of positive reinforcement. There was a move away from token-economy models, to ones which emphasised the value of using discriminatory praise, not only to change pupils' behaviour but to foster their self-esteem and cooperative social relations. Target setting, verbal praise, progress reports and letters to parents highlighting positive behaviour all formed part of a strategic and systematic focus on positive behaviour and an explicit move away from punishment as the institutional solution for improving behaviour. In addition, there was a broadening of the behavioural gaze, which could range from the individual, disruptive child to the whole class or, increasingly, the whole school.

An important part of these new approaches involved paying close attention to antecedent conditions as well as systematically changing contingent conditions. Drawing on behavioural ecology, training courses and behaviour management consultants encouraged teachers to assess and, if necessary, change the layout of the classroom, seating arrangements and other environmental features of the school, in order to improve the antecedent conditions for positive behaviour. Another important aspect of antecedent condition setting was the teacher's own expectations and behaviour in relation to pupils; joint teacher–pupil goal setting, adapting the curriculum to pupils' needs and modelling positive behaviour were all seen as vital components of positive behaviour management programmes.

The 1986 Education Act had begun to identify specific management responsibilities of governors, head teachers and local authorities in dealing with discipline issues; after the 1988 Education Reform Act, governors had a legal duty to ensure that discipline issues were effectively managed within their schools. The beginning of the 1990s saw not only an increase in the accountability of schools and local education authorities to central government and parents but also, with the recommendations of the Elton report, a burgeoning of strategic efforts to deal with the problem of disruptive behaviour. In the wake of the report and the legislative pressure on local education authorities, schools and teachers to demonstrate their effectiveness, a vacuum of need was again created in which behavioural approaches might prove to be useful. During the next decade the systematic behavioural management of children was extended beyond the classroom and into 'whole school' and across the whole of a local education authority's area. For example, by the end of December 1998 every local education authority had to produce a 'behaviour support plan', detailing its arrangements for the education of children with behavioural difficulties (covering the broad continuum between 'normal' though unacceptable, challenging behaviour and that which is indicative of mental illness). This had to set out current provision and future plans for the promotion of good behaviour and discipline from 'early years' until school leaving. While these behaviour support plans are by no means exclusively behavioural in approach, they draw substantially on behavioural language, concepts and techniques in their descriptions of 'positive teaching', whole-school behaviour policies, home–school contracts and in the establishment of behaviour support teams. The role of the last is to provide schools with advice, training and programmes for the management of difficult behaviour (both of individual pupils and of whole schools) in which all staff, including playground supervisors and dinner ladies, may be involved. Significantly, during the 1990s, these approaches proved to be adaptable solutions to a range of behavioural problems of teachers as well as their pupils. With the aid of in-service training courses, resource packs and behaviour support teams, teachers, like health visitors and parents in other contexts, are being behaviourally trained to manage themselves more effectively: to be 'in control'.

3   The power to produce effects

The expansions of the use of behavioural approaches with preschool and school-age children in the community, though taking place at different paces, nonetheless have several features in common: first, broadening notions of the type of problem and age of children amenable to behavioural solutions, characterised, in particular, by the 'typical' nature of the behaviour; and second, the use of non-psychologists (parents or professionals) to implement the techniques, who themselves were behaviourally trained. The most important common factor, however, was the instrumental role played by psychologists in enabling behavioural approaches to be used in these new ways. It is unlikely that their actions were governed solely by a desire to follow the injunction to give psychology away. Although the conceptual developments described in the first part of the chapter had a significant impact in opening up new possibilities for behavioural approaches, it was the substantial changes in the political and economic climate in the late 1970s and early 1980s which enabled these to be put into practice. By placing new requirements on the delivery of public services, these political and economic changes created the conditions for psychologists to expand and diversify their activities. They also made it possible for behavioural approaches to be construed as socially, economically and professionally useful. Put another way, the increased use of behavioural approaches in the 'well' community in recent years has been influenced by a number of pragmatic and instrumental considerations which are associated with the new organisational and economic rationalities of health, welfare and education.

These economic and organisational changes took place during the Conservative administrations of the 1980s and were associated most strongly with Thatcherism and the espousal of monetarism. They involved the application of market principles to the fields of health, welfare and education, and the creation of internal markets within each of these areas, as well as between them (Education Reform Act 1988; National Health Service and Community Act 1990). The purchaser–provider model was adopted, in which not only were health, welfare and education services to be bought and sold, but done so according to whether the agency involved was defined as a 'service provider' or 'purchaser' (in which case they were a 'budget holder'). These fundamental changes in the economy of service provision were accompanied by a number of organisational changes in service structure, for example the creation of National Health Service trusts (which might serve as both purchasers and providers of health care), which were reconstituted as collections of self-regulating units. The purchaser–provider model provided opportunities for clinical psychologists to diversify their activities and to 'sell' their expertise as (behavioural) consultants to a wide range of 'providers' through the establishment of autonomous community clinical psychology services. These operate not only in mental health settings but also in the 'community', in primary care and education, for example in child development centres and family centres, where, through their work with other practitioners, community clinical psychologists now have routine contact with children from birth to 16 years old.

While the introduction of the internal market into the public services meant that the cost of health, education and social care became an explicit and primary criterion of its appeal to purchasers (and providers), the quantifiably assessable and cost-related effectiveness of interventions became equally important requirements. The need to balance budgets meant that both purchasers and providers of services needed to find ways of calculating their worth. 'Effectiveness' has become the key basis on which services are evaluated, and so being able to demonstrate effectiveness is of critical importance not only to those who buy and sell services but also to those who work in them. Being able to demonstrate effectiveness justifies professional existence by satisfying managerial and organisational demands; at the same time, it can also bolster flagging professional confidence and help to counter public scepticism. In addition, the neo-liberal emphasis on consumer choice, both as a feature of citizenship and as a determinant of market value (and enshrined in the Citizens' Charter 1991 and in subsequent Patients' and Parents' Charters), has become associated with the emergence of 'quality' as the other vital criterion in evaluating the worth of services and practitioners.

Professionals working with children and their parents in health and education have in recent years had to adapt to these changing expectations of service delivery; in particular, they have to be seen to be cost-effective and accountable. In the face of these requirements, behavioural approaches have certain built-in features, notably their measurability, which coincide with the organisational emphases that are associated with new forms of managerialism and make them appealing to audit-conscious managers and purchasers in health, welfare and education, and to practitioners. These relate to: cost (they are cheap because they are time limited and may be implemented by paraprofessionals); the self-evaluation qualities of these approaches (they have built-in self-monitoring procedures and involve before-and-after comparisons); their efficacy (their ability to have an effect, however limited); and to their ability to demonstrate their own efficacy (practitioners, managers, purchasers can 'evaluate' their usefulness, in relation to desired effects, cost, 'quality assurance' and so forth, or can be held accountable). In their ability to be accessible to parents and a range of practitioners, including paraprofessionals, and in their perceived relevance to the difficulties of typical, everyday life, behavioural approaches offer reassurance that something can be done. In this way, they are a useful instrument for both 'targets' and practitioners, such as teachers, health visitors and social workers, who, in recent years, have suffered a crisis of professional identity. Furthermore, the emphasis on them as techniques and problem-solving 'tools' means that that they can be used pragmatically, in conjunction with other approaches, without the constraints of theoretical understanding or ideological commitment. In these contexts, their usefulness lies in their amenability to being used eclectically, as part of a problem-solving 'package' of approaches, tailored to specific circumstances. The technical eclecticism to which this contributes offers adaptability to health visitors, teachers, social workers and so forth, in the face of new problematisations and changing conditions which may threaten their professional existence.

A further factor affecting the spread of behavioural approaches in recent years is, surprisingly, their ethical appeal, as enabling and empowering. In previous incarnations of behaviour modification and in critiques of them, this mutual compatibility between behavioural approaches and empowerment would have been unthinkable. However, by tracing the internal changes in behavioural discourses, we can see how the shifts from deficit models to those emphasising the cultivation of competence and self-directing capacities, using constructional rather than aversive techniques, have made it possible for behavioural approaches to be thought of as empowering and for them to have found favour with policy makers, practitioners and managers, who see it as their job to 'empower' their clients to be 'in control'. Moreover, by promoting self-management in others and by using techniques that promise to make it a reality, they can feel that they are engaged in an ethically worthy exercise of power.[12] The goal of effective self-management, of learning to take control and responsibility, found a renewed political salience in the last decades of the twentieth century, as expressed in the neo-liberal ethic of 'regulated autonomy', advocated by New Labour as well as by the New Right. According to this ethic, as citizens we enter into contractual obligations with political authorities to regulate ourselves.[13] Behavioural discourse and practices converge with neo-liberal political rationalities concerning regulated autonomy in several ways. Both emphasise the personal and social benefits of self-management and behavioural approaches provide acceptable, 'democratising' strategies that accord with those rationalities and practicable techniques that enable us to act upon our own conduct.

4 Conclusions

This chapter has examined the expansion of behavioural approaches into new community contexts and has shown that, in spite of the intellectual and moral opposition to earlier forms of behaviour modification, contemporary versions are thriving. By tracing the transformations in behavioural discourses and by situating these in relation to other discourses, it becomes apparent that behavioural approaches are more in tune with postmodern conditions than might have been predicted. Their capacity to align with changing political, economic and ethical conditions has made it possible for them to serve as useful and versatile tools in fulfilling new regulatory expectations. While they may be effective in changing behaviour, their success lies as much in their confirmation of neo-liberal shifts in attention away from programmatic imperatives, towards more consensual relations between the citizen and political authorities, in which personal and social goals converge. By helping to operationalise the goal of self-management, through the cultivation of competence, behavioural approaches have found a new political and social role; as well as creating new possibilities for citizens, they also serve to regulate them.

Notes

1 By behavioural psychology, I refer to those discourses, strategies and techniques which formulate the person primarily in terms of her or his behaviour rather than in terms of mentalistic constructs like 'personality' and so forth. The best-known manifestations of behavioural psychology take the form of techniques which are designed to change

behaviour. These are based on the principles of behaviourism and learning theory, which hold that behaviour is the essential focus of a scientific psychology and that it is only through the systematic observation, measurement and manipulation of their behaviour, according to certain laws of learning, that people can become true objects of knowledge. While not wishing to overdraw behaviour modification, it may be useful here to provide a brief description of some of the key features of the behavioural approach. This maintains that the performance of behaviour is dependent upon antecedent and consequent conditions (reinforcement) that either strengthen or weaken that 'response', that is, make it more or less likely to be repeated. Effective behaviour change therefore involves changing these conditions. This in turn depends upon using certain empirical strategies and techniques to identify these conditions; it is argued that the basis of these lies in systematic analysis of the specified behaviour and of the antecedent and consequent conditions that support it (applied behaviour analysis). This systematic analysis involves the observation and measurement of the 'response' in question over time (for example in terms of its timing and frequency of occurrence). The term 'stimulus' refers to the antecedent condition and the term 'reinforcement' is used both to describe and explain the role of those consequences of a 'response' which serve to strengthen or weaken it. Thus reinforcement may be positive, negative or, indeed, aversive. Strategies and techniques of behaviour change are closely connected; strategies designed to change behaviour by eliminating 'unwanted' or 'undesirable' responses frequently depend upon aversive techniques to make the behaviour as unattractive as possible to the 'learner'. Strategies which aim to change behaviour by increasing rather than decreasing the learner's 'behavioural repertoire' use positive reinforcement to instil and strengthen responses by making them more attractive to the learner, usually by providing a 'reward' for their performance. A particular strategy, which I discuss at several points in the chapter, is the so-called 'constructional approach', which is intended to build on existing behavioural 'strengths' by the exclusive use of positive reinforcement.

2 For example the Crime and Disorder Act 1998, the Government Family Policy Consultation Paper November 1998, and 'Sure Start', the national early-intervention programme.
3 For contemporary histories see, for example, Hearnshaw (1987); from a critical perspective, see Richards (1996) and Kvale, (1992).
4 See for example Ingleby (1981), Lamal (1989) and Zuriff (1979). For a reformulation of the history of the behaviourist and cognitive 'revolutions', see Leahey (1992).
5 This approach draws on Foucaultian analyses of the human sciences and in particular the work of Nikolas Rose on the political and social role of psychology in Britain, including Rose (1985, 1988, 1989, 1996a).
6 Prewar behavioural psychology had had little impact in Britain, but, as Maarten Derksen demonstrates in Chapter 13, in the postwar years it found a home at the Maudsley Hospital under the aegis of H.J. Eysenck, where it played a major role in the development of clinical psychology by providing it with an entrance to the domain of treatment.
7 By the 1960s, the rubric of behaviour therapy had been established. The first general text on behaviour therapy, published in 1960, comprised a collection of readings edited by Eysenck, and included a range of behavioural treatment methods (desensitisation, aversion therapy, reinforcement contingencies) for a diversity of problems (neurosis, cat phobia, chronic frigidity, tics, stammering, asthma, childhood disorders, homosexuality) and, significantly, patient management. In 1963 the first journal devoted to behaviour therapy was published, *Behaviour Research and Therapy*, again initiated by Eysenck. Over the next 15 years, such journals proliferated on both sides of the Atlantic and an increasing number of articles on behaviour therapy appeared in journals of psychiatry, education, special education, law, health, social work and so on.

8 See Kazdin (1978). See also the 1976 address of Davison (in Erwin, 1978: 175), President of the Association for the Advancement of Behaviour Therapy.

9 See for example the work of K. Hewitt and colleagues based at Southmead Health District, including: Hewitt and Crawford (1988); Hewitt *et al.*, (1984, 1989, 1990); Thomas *et al.* (1982); Perkins and Winke (1984).

10 See *Bulletin of the British Association for Behavioural Psychotherapy*, 5 (3), 1977; and *Perspectives on Behaviour Modification in Education*, University of Exeter, 1980.

11 For some examples of these courses see: Wheldall (1987); Ainscow and Muncey (1987); Merrett and Houghton (1989); Kelly and Ronaldson (1989): Atherley (1990); Luton *et al.* (1991); Wheeler (1996).

12 For a discussion of empowerment discourses see Baistow (1995b).

13 For a fuller discussion of 'regulated autonomy' see Rose and Miller (1992).

Part II

Personal reflections

16

The development of social psychology in Oxford

Michael Argyle

Social psychology was an American invention: there had been almost nothing in Britain until the 1950s, and I had never met a social psychologist. When I started as a graduate student in psychology at Cambridge in 1950, people in the lab knew nothing about social psychology, but they were against it. I was supervised by the great Sir Frederic Bartlett, who had been interested in social aspects of psychology much earlier, was supportive and encouraging, but really knew very little about it. When I became a lecturer in the subject at Oxford in 1952 there was similar ignorance and prejudice.

I have often wondered why the experimental psychologists were so hostile. I think that the prejudice against social psychology may have been because psychology itself had great difficulty gaining acceptance in Oxford in particular; Gilbert Ryle was against it, and there are still some Oxford colleges that will not admit students to read psychology. The humanities dons may have been against it since their model of man was of free, rational agents, and they objected to the idea that their thoughts or behaviour could be predicted and explained. Scientists were against it as a new and untried kind of science; they had had trouble themselves, and some could recall the first chemistry lab in a converted bathroom at Balliol.

What some of my psychological colleagues did both at Oxford and Cambridge was to present themselves as physiologists, neurologists, engineers, philosophers, anything but psychologists. (Most of those subjects had once been rejected at Oxford.) Social psychology was admittedly new and therefore late in finding a rigorous methodology, so was an embarrassment to them. It made no pretence of being something more respectable, or of studying people who didn't matter, like children, animals or the insane, or topics which did not impinge on life much, like perception and psychophysics. It also looked rather like common sense, except that the latter often turned out to be wrong.

However, we got started, and this chapter describes how it came about. I may have been ignorant, but my mind was already prepared, in this way. I had a friend at school who was very shy and socially unskilled (as we would now say), and this obviously caused him difficulties and made him unhappy. But what was it that was wrong with him? This was one of a number of experiences which sensitised me to social interaction, and to the subtle cues and processes which make it up. It was one of the reasons that I abandoned the physical sciences for psychology, but it didn't tell me the answer. I studied social psychology, but that didn't provide any answers either. There was nothing at all in the social psychology of the time about how social behaviour was done, on the nature of social interaction, or what people were doing wrong who couldn't do it.

At Cambridge I had heard a lot about manual skills from Alan Welford and others. Many in the lab had a tracking machine to study them; I knew Ted Crossman and then we both moved to Oxford. We realised that we had a common interest, and that the skills of dealing with machines and with the other people at work had something in common, and hence social behaviour could be looked at as a kind of motor skill. So the 'social skills model' was born (Figure 16.1), which postulated a similarity between the two.

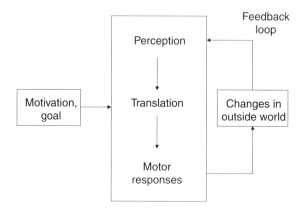

Figure 16.1 *The social skills model. (Source: Argyle, 1967.)*

In both cases the organism was seeking a goal consisting of responses from a physical object or a person, skilled behaviour was emitted, followed by feedback on its effects, and corrective action taken if necessary, all this taking place more or less automatically and at high speed. For example, to get another to talk more an interactor can reinforce whenever the other speaks by head nods, smiles or agreeing. If he then talks too much the reinforcement can be reduced or reversed, using head shakes, frowns or disagreement. Very rapidly and without thinking about it the other can be brought to speak exactly as much as is desired – just as a driver of a car can control its speed or direction very quickly and easily.

We thus had a theoretical interest in gaze since the motor skill model drew attention to the importance of feedback on the effects of action. We also had an interest in facial expression since that is where people look, probably because it is the main area for expressing emotions. Meanwhile, I had been studying the performance of industrial supervisors in factories, and this was the first social skill that I investigated. Later we were to study interviewers (and train them), cross-cultural skills, doctors, and sales staff.

An early research student, Adam Kendon, was very interested in cinematography; indeed, he called himself a 'cineaste' and saw several hundred films a year. He started filming social behaviour, using a time-lapse camera, taking two frames a second, and he then carried out a very painstaking frame-by-frame analysis. He soon saw that there was synchrony between speech and gaze, between both of these and gestures, and between the actions of the two interactors, who seemed to be having a 'gestural dance'. In the first of these studies he found that there was a prolonged 'terminal gaze' (Figure 16.2) by the speaker at the end of long utterances, and that if this was not given the other person did not reply; it followed that this gaze was acting as a full-stop signal to regulate speech – this was the first non-verbal synchronising cue to be isolated. We also assumed that it was used primarily to collect feedback on the effect of the utterance.

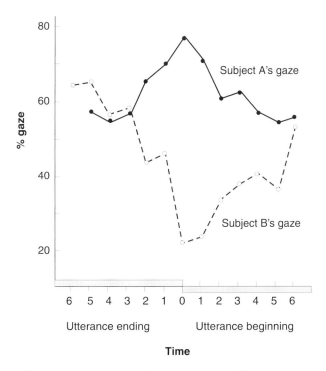

Figure 16.2 *Kendon's terminal gaze. (Source: Kendon, 1967.)*

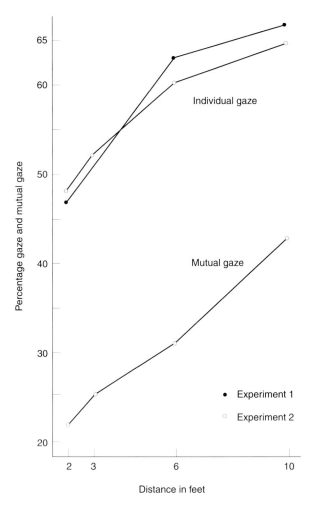

Figure 16.3 *Gaze (individual, top two lines, and mutual, bottom line) and distance. Experiment 1 involved two people, while experiment 2 involved three. (Source: Argyle and Dean, 1965.)*

From this point the whole project took off. Gaze had never been studied before as far as we knew, and this was the first aspect of social behaviour we investigated. An early paper, with an undergraduate, Janet Dean, on gaze and distance, became my most cited paper – after being turned down by several journals. What we found was that there was more gaze and more mutual gaze the greater the distance between two interactors (Figure 16.3), as we had predicted, in a theory about how intimacy was kept in equilibrium.

In fact, there was someone else working on gaze, Ralph Exline at the University of Delaware. We visited each other several times and he introduced me to

Americans studying non-verbal communication. We continued the gaze research and this led to a book with Mark Cook (Argyle and Cook, 1976).

This led to practical application in the development of videophones, since there is no loss of gaze here compared with the telephone. Lalljee and Cook ran experiments, and then Paul Guild and Ederyn Williams pursued this in connection with the Bell Labs and the Post Office. It was a major commercial issue for a time. It has come round again with the rise of mobile phones and e-mail as forms of communication. Another series of experiments found that non-verbal signals had a much greater effect than ingeniously equated verbal ones in expressing attitudes such as liking and dominance (Argyle *et al.*, 1972).

Our group expanded and we were awarded several research grants; indeed, we were generously supported by first the DSIR, later the Social Sciences Research Council and then the Economic and Social Research Council. We had postdoctoral research workers, many research students and many visitors, as well as a secretary, Ann McKendry, later to be the editor of the *Goat* book (see below), and a technician, Rad Babic. Without the financial support the whole enterprise could not have happened. We were lucky enough to have a number of very enthusiastic research students, like Mark Cook, Marylin Williams, Robert McHenry and Roger Ingham, who were busy with speech disturbances, proximity and other minutiae of social performance.

Two members became permanent: Peter Collett won a long series of research grants, and Mansur Lalljee became a lecturer in another Oxford department. I was the only faculty member in the Psychology Department for most of this period. In view of the huge demands for undergraduate teaching in social psychology, which was very popular, and the large number of graduate students, I saw a great need for a second person; many eminent people applied for vacant lectureships, but the departmental politics went against social psychology: there was a policy of appointing the 'best' applicant regardless of field –inevitably a more respectable field than ours. Many outstanding people were encouraged to apply and later had to be apologised to. I was advised that if I wanted a second social psychologist I would have to raise the money myself, and I was successful in raising money from the research councils for a series of postdoctoral research workers. During this time there were usually four faculty in physiological psychology and another four in perception.

However, though much later, Jos Jaspars, formerly a professor in Nijmegen, applied successfully, and this opened up a whole new area of social psychology. Lalljee had already been working on attribution theory and Jaspars attracted a strong group of research students in this and related areas of cognitive social psychology – including Miles Hewstone, Peter Lunt, John McClure, Denis Hilton and Frank Fincham. Some we supervised jointly, such as Ben Slugoski, who investigated Grice's famous rules of discourse, and Sonia Livingstone was the first to study television viewing as a social phenomenon.

The 'Oxford Social Psychology Group' lasted for about 35 years, and was quite large – 65 people were awarded DPhils while working in it, a number of them now professors elsewhere. At any one time there might be 20 people in this group, including the research workers and visitors. We had Friday seminars for 35 years, and these seminars were conducted in a spirit of cooperation and constructive comment – unlike the much less friendly seminars going on in the main Oxford department at this time. If one of our outside speakers gave a bad lecture this was taken as a challenge to see how best this unfortunate person could be helped. There were 'secret seminars' at which there was intense discussion of controversial issues behind closed doors. Members of this group came from all over the world, attracted by the combination of social psychology and Oxford. We were very lucky to have such a very talented and agreeable group. There were, of course, some real eccentrics, such as one who thought she was a princess and one who thought he was a spy. Perhaps they were, but then creativity is often found in rather unusual people. There were also diverse research interests – they didn't all have to work on the same things. However, they were welded together, perhaps by our rituals, perhaps by the hostility from outside.

The atmosphere of our group at this time, the 1960s and 1970s, was very interesting, in that the members were highly sensitised to the minutiae of social performance, and became capable of acting as experimental confederates, for example looking at another interactor in the region of the face 30% or 60% of the time, or varying the positivity or negativity of their non-verbal behaviour. Curiously, this sensitivity and these skills did not impair our behaviour with each other at all – we were a very close group. This social cohesion was sustained by various rituals – Monday morning coffee in my office, with 'news' and jokes, and after the Friday seminars there were often parties at my house, sometimes with party games, or noisy dinners at Indian restaurants. My wife, Sonia, worked very hard feeding all these social psychologists. Our offices were for some years in an old house in Keble Road, formerly the house of Warden Spooner, of Spoonerism fame, half a mile from the main department, and here we had most of our meetings, along with much coffee and tea. It was a delightfully eccentric house, with gargoyles in the hall, a servants' staircase and a first-floor conservatory. Our labs were first set up in the old Department of Experimental Psychology at 1 South Parks Road, with one-way screens, videotape recorders, and other recording gear. A notable event was the celebration in 1981 of our twenty-fifth successful DPhil student (Adrian Furnham), in the form of a grandiose party with speeches, cabaret and the presentation of a hilarious 'festschrift', satirising the work of the group, *The Psychology of Playing the Goat* (McKendry, 1981).

We got on very well, but some others were less happy with us and some at the time said they found it difficult and embarrassing talking to me, since they assumed that I was studying their behaviour in a special way, or they could not look me in the eye. A seminar that I gave on gaze experiments was found embarrassing; my colleagues were not accustomed to talking about such things.

There were several other intellectual inputs during this period. The most important was ethology, which was being created in Oxford at the time, and we used to go to the annual Tinbergen and Lorenz conferences. The work on the facial expressions, vocalisations, gestures and so on of non-human primates was of great interest to us. After all, they conducted their entire social life without talking at all, depending instead upon non-verbal communication; our studies suggested that much human social life is managed in the same way.

A little later the new linguistics was also prominent in Oxford, and Chomsky became an occasional visitor. This led to an interest in the sequencing of verbal behaviour seen as social behaviour, and was studied by David Clarke, who was looking for the deep structure of social interaction. Meanwhile, Kendon had been studying sequences of non-verbal behaviour, more with ethological models in mind. Peter Robinson, the first to get a DPhil and the first to become a professor, became a leading figure in the field of the social psychology of language.

Another influence was anthropology, though not really Oxford anthropology, which was unsympathetic to psychology at the time. Peter Collett was probably the first of our group to look for cross-cultural differences in non-verbal communication, and he was able to train Englishmen to interact successfully with Arabs. He collaborated with Desmond Morris and others to study the different gestures used around the Mediterranean (Morris *et al.*, 1979). In other studies we found a rich field of non-verbal differences in Italian and Japanese behaviour. Mary Sissons looked at social class differences in her famous 'Paddington Station experiment'.

Non-verbal communication was coming of age. In 1967 Ralph Exline and I organised the first international conference on this subject, in Oxford, financed by NATO, with many luminaries from ethology, and various branches of psychology and sociology, including Erving Goffman, Paul Ekman and Jane Goodall. My book *Bodily Communication* was first published in 1975.

However, our interests moved on. We couldn't do any more with gaze since we couldn't find an eye-movement recorder which allowed something like normal social interaction. (One exists now.) And non-verbal communication had moved so fast that it seemed to be becoming worked out. We became interested in the effect of the social situation on behaviour, and became part of another mini-movement, to study 'person–situation interaction'. There were three conferences on this in Stockholm run by Norm Endler and David Magnusson. For some members this was a kind of plot to overthrow personality psychology. I had a vision of a new kind of psychologist who could treat situations rather than people, but this has not come about; perhaps environmental psychologists come closest to it (Argyle *et al.*, 1981).

Two of our group became interested in violence. Peter Marsh became the national expert on football hooligans, and Anne Campbell was the first to study aggression in female delinquents, both of them using the ideas of our group but introducing new ones and studying real-life behaviour (Marsh *et al.*, 1978). David Pendleton penetrated doctors' consulting rooms and found how to train general practitioners in social skills.

We then became interested in social relationships, in which I was joined by Adrian Furnham and Monika Henderson; we held what was the first conference on this subject, in Britain at least, and this is now a flourishing field, with its own journals and conferences. But my particular interest in relationships lay in its importance for happiness, since that turned out to be one of the consequences of relationships. Happiness is also linked to our earlier interest in non-verbal communication, via the expression of positive emotions; most emotion researchers still study negative emotions only, but that is another story (Argyle, 1987).

We hosted most of the social psychology conferences going on in Britain, in the early days at least. We started the British Psychological Society Social Psychology Section conferences, and had the first three of them in Oxford, while I was Chairman. There were numerous more informal conferences, which usually had large attendances. We were in close touch with other social psychologists in Britain, and liked them to visit. I was the first social psychology editor of the *British Journal of Social and Clinical Psychology*. I edited two series of social psychology books, one for Penguin, the other for Pergamon Press; the second was later taken on by Peter Robinson.

During the early 1970s there was the famous 'crisis in social psychology', a lot of which was fought out in Oxford, partly because Rom Harré was one of the main players and Paul Secord a regular visitor (Harré and Secord, 1972). There was a vigorous critique of laboratory experiments as being unrealistic, unethical and so on. Our own work was not as vulnerable to this criticism as were some other varieties of social psychology, but this critique was enough to stop some from doing any research at all, or causing them to take an extra year or two over their thesis. There were a lot of dramatic graduate seminars, and several conferences, one of which led to a book, edited by Ginsburg (1979). The crisis became a major theme of the Social Psychology Section conferences.

From this we all modified our views a bit, and I learned about the importance of cognition in social behaviour, for example of social rules. In one of our studies of rules we wanted to know the effects of breaking them. We found some rules of friendship, and asked people to what extent any friendships they had lost had been the result of someone breaking these rules. Table 16.1 shows that this was indeed so.

There was a shift away from laboratory experiments to field studies, though still of a quantitative and well designed form. However, we were resistant to the new cognitive emphasis in social psychology, since we had been studying behaviour which was more akin to riding a bicycle than to thinking, and not accessible to introspection, though we always recognised the importance of cognition in skill.

We were greatly helped by our American visitors. In 1956 I went for the first time to the United States, to the University of Michigan, at the invitation of Ted Newcomb, and there were many of the famous names. We then had a string of wonderful American visitors in Oxford – Ralph Exline, Donald Campbell, Bob Zajonc, Ted Sarbin, Hob Crockett, Jerry Ginsburg, Ed Hollander, Paul Secord, Vernon Allen, Carl Backman, Len Berkowitz and Ross Buck, and many others for shorter visits. Some gave lectures or helped research students; all were a great

Table 16.1 *Friendship rules and break-up of friendships*

	Moderately or very important in breaking up friendship (%)	Slightly important in breaking up friendship (%)
Being jealous or critical of your other relationships	57	22
Discussing with others what was said in confidence with him/her	56	19
Not volunteering help in time of need	44	23
Not trusting or confiding in you	44	22
Criticising you in public	44	21
Not showing positive regard for you	42	34
Not standing up for you in your absence	39	28
Not being tolerant of your other friends	38	30
Not showing emotional support	37	25
Nagging you	30	25

Source: Argyle and Henderson (1985).

source of stimulation, information and help. Our group became an important channel for the transfer of American social psychology to Britain. And yet we kept a distance from American social psychology. They had colonised us, perhaps consciously, but we altered the message. We were impressed by their ingenious and well designed experiments, but we found them too artificial, insufficiently related to real behaviour. We could not see how this kind of research could be applied to real problems. We were looking for a different way of doing it. The way we favoured could also be found in several places in the United States, but not in the mainstream. The pressures to be more like life were increased by the crisis in social psychology, described above. We had been under other influences, from ethology, anthropology and linguistics.

There were also visitors from Australia, Canada, Japan, Belgium and Italy. They liked to come to Oxford, and some came several times. Wolfson College was very accommodating. I was one of the original members of that college; one of our aims was to look after such academic visitors and my visitors did very well out of this. I was one of the founders of the Oxford 'Newcomers' Club', which has been looking after the wives and families of visitors. An unexpected result of these visits was that some of us were invited back, and have had very enjoyable visits round the world. We may have been colonised by the Americans, but having altered the message we did our own colonising. The first outpost was next door, at the former Oxford Polytechnic, now Oxford Brookes University; most of the early faculty members came from our social psychology group – Peter Marsh, Roger Lamb, Robert McHenry, Mary Sissons and Giovanni Carnibella. Another of our mission fields was a bigger one – Australia; we provided many of the early social psychologists, including several professors – Joe Forgas, Peter Robinson for a time, Phil Pearce and Michael Walker. Adam Kendon was there, and other social psychologists, including Laurie Brown and Steve Bochner, have been frequent visitors; for several others I examined their theses. There were other centres throughout the Commonwealth and the Far East. We had collaborators in Italy, in Bologna and Padua, which was mutually beneficial for our cross-cultural work. We ran the European Association for Social Psychology Summer School, helped by Donald Campbell, Jerry Ginsburg, Willem Doise and Ragnar Rommetveit, and it was attended by many of the next generation of European social psychology professors, including my own successor, Nick Emler. Altogether I lectured in 35 different countries, often at the invitation of former students. While some became professors, others started their own firms of psychological consultancy – Robert McHenry, Peter Marsh and David Pendleton, for example.

We felt that there must be important practical applications of this work, and one of the implications of looking at social behaviour as a social skill was the likelihood that it could be trained in the same kind of way that manual skills are trained. This led to another project and team, based at an Oxford psychiatric hospital and with grant support from the Regional Hospital Board, to see if mental patients who couldn't cope with people or social situations could be treated by social skills training. Peter Trower, Bridget Bryant, Barbara Lalljee and I trained neurotic outpatients with great success, using the ideas and methods inspired by the experimental programme. The central method was role-play exercises. We made much use of the videotape recorder to give feedback on verbal and non-verbal performance, and we were probably the first to use it in this way. I happened to see one in a shop window in London, not having heard of the existence of such a device, and at once I saw its value for us. Some of these patients had a real need for help: one said that he had never had a friend for example, while others could not cope with situations at work. We carried out several controlled follow-up studies and found considerable success with our methods. Indeed, some individuals responded very fast and were in effect cured after two sessions (Trower *et al.*, 1978). I became aware that a considerable proportion of the world's population were handicapped by lack of social skills and that they could be treated quite easily.

The official end of the Social Psychology Group came with my retirement in 1992. It was marked by four parties or dinners; the grandest was run by the group itself, and included a real Festschrift (Collett and Furnham, 1995). There was also a hilarious spoof film biography of me, the commentary spoken in official deadpan tones by Donald Broadbent. That was not of course the end of social psychology in Oxford. My successor, Nicholas Emler, has taken it forward, but with different contents and style.

What were the later developments of all this activity? First, non-verbal communication has of course developed as a solid branch of social psychological knowledge, though it is not the central area in social psychology. It is very important in the study of emotions, including positive emotions, and a central part of happiness, one of my later concerns. Second, the study of sequences of social interaction, pursued by Kendon and Clarke, has made some recent progress, for example in the study of sequences of behaviour in happy and unhappy marriages. However, the goal of understanding and predicting long sequences has proved elusive. Third, social skills training is used for patients, in marital therapy and much occupational training, for lawyers, politicians, clergy, teachers, managers and many others. It has even been given to the unemployed, to help them get and keep jobs, and also for training people to work abroad. However, social skills training has not become generally accessible, although a proportion of the population clearly need it and could be trained quite easily.

I was very keen to let everyone know about this good news – that no one needed to be lonely, socially isolated or ineffective at work because of their social incompetence – and I tried to write books about it. The most popular was *The Psychology of Interpersonal Behaviour*, first published by Penguin Books in 1967, now in its fifth edition and in several languages: it has sold nearly a million copies. It has been sold mainly to people taking courses of one kind or another, to nurses, teachers, managers, and anyone else who has to deal with people in their work. It is an accident of fate that I had a facility for writing readable books, but did not have the facility for writing really popular ones, which might have had a greater impact on public social behaviour.

We had quite a lot of publicity. Sometimes we were deluged by telephone calls from the media, and there were a number of television programmes about our work. I think that our message must have penetrated quite a way into society. 'Social skills', 'social interaction' and 'eye contact' became household words. No one seems to be embarrassed by them any more. 'Attribution', 'equity' and 'cognitive balance' are probably less well known.

Sociologists of knowledge say that to run a successful intellectual movement you need three things – a supply of good graduate students, control of a journal and control of a learned society. We had all three. We also had strong financial support from the research councils. We had very good support from Methuen, later Routledge, and from Penguin Books, our two main publishers. Being at Oxford was very good in several ways, in particular in helping us to attract research students and visitors, and providing ready contact with leading members of other disciplines; it was also a very congenial place to work.

17

Memories of memory research

Alan Baddeley

I began studying psychology at University College London (UC) in 1953. As a schoolboy, I had sampled a number of psychology books, including one entitled *Listening with the Third Ear: The Inner Experiences of a Psychoanalyst*, and decided that psychology might be more interesting than my previous enthusiasm, geography. I saw ahead a career of delving into the unconscious and solving the problems of the world, but had enough youthful cunning to claim an interest in experimental and applied psychology during my UC interview. Ironically, I subsequently discovered that I was indeed much more interested in experimental psychology than in plumbing the depths of the unconscious.

It was an exciting time to be a psychologist, and to be at UC. Until the 1930s, Germany had been a major influence in the development of psychology. However, psychology rarely seems to find favour with totalitarian regimes and this, coupled with the fact that many psychologists were Jewish, led to the dissolution of psychology within Germany, and a diaspora of German psychologists to the United States and to Britain, including UC, which benefited from this trend in the case of Hans Eysenck. Another was a very charming and erudite psychoanalyst, Professor Carl Flügel, who regularly topped up the coffers of the student psychology society by participating in a showing of the classic 1928 surrealist film *Un Chien andalou* and providing a psychoanalytic interpretation.

In Britain, the war had stimulated the development of psychology, with Bartlett's influence leading to the application of experimental psychology to a wide range of practical problems, resulting in a generation of psychologists imbued with enthusiasm for combining theory and practice. The approach tended to be interdisciplinary, with clear links to engineering and to medical science, which in turn led to theoretical developments based on the newly developed computers as models of man (Craik, 1943). The information theory measures developed by

Shannon and Weaver (1949) were also influential, while medical influences led to a consideration of neuropsychological data and an interest in variables such as stress and arousal level.

At UC, Cyril Burt had been replaced by an American, Roger Russell, who brought in a much more relaxed style, as did a range of young lecturers. I knew almost immediately that psychology was what I wanted to spend my life doing. I am yet to change my mind.

In my first year, the only general experimental textbook available was that produced by Woodworth in 1938. During that year, 1953, Osgood published his classic text *Method and Theory in Experimental Psychology*. A comparison between the two illustrates the extent to which the war provided a watershed. Although many of the ideas that we encountered as undergraduates, such as those from Gestalt psychology or behaviourism, came from prewar days, by far the greatest proportion of the evidence we encountered was postwar. The tendency to forget anything done more than a decade ago has sadly continued to afflict psychology, but was even more pronounced in the 1940s and '50s.

As an undergraduate, theoretical discussion in the area of learning and memory was dominated by the work of Clark Hull (1943) and its rejection of Edward Tolman's (1932) more cognitive approach. This controversy formed the basis of my first published experiment, a successful attempt to show that rats are not as stupid as Hullian theory would predict, carried out during a year I spent at Princeton immediately after graduation. By the time it was published (Baddeley, 1960), the whole issue was dead, not because anyone had succeeded in achieving the mythical 'crucial experiment', but simply because the whole area had suddenly gone out of fashion, presumably because people realised that there was unlikely to be such an experiment. I was very struck by the capacity of psychological theory to change direction rapidly, apparently as a result of fashion rather than evidence. This led to the question, commonly raised at the time, as to whether psychological theory could ever be cumulative.

That experience has had a major influence on my own theoretical approach to psychology, causing me to favour theorisation based on relatively simple generalisations tied to robust phenomena. In choosing such a path, I was of course implicitly opting for a particular type of philosophy of science, a topic that was of considerable general interest at the time. In fact, four philosophy books appeared at about this time, all of which had a marked influence on views within psychology. Two of these, Ayer's (1936) *Language, Truth and Logic* and Ryle's (1949) *The Concept of Mind*, were influential in the way in which we talked about psychological theories, warning of the way in which thought may be influenced by the way in which language is used. We were also, however, much exercised about the philosophy of science, with opinions sharply divided between two opposing views. One was represented by the Cambridge philosopher Braithwaite (1953), who took Newtonian physics as the supreme example of scientific theory, presenting its logical structure as a model for all science. The opposing view was presented by Toulmin (1953), who argued that theories were simply useful artefacts, like maps, a view not dissimilar to the concept of a model as an explanation put forward by Kenneth Craik (1943) a decade earlier. I much preferred Toulmin's approach, and still see myself as a theoretical map maker, rather than aspiring to create the complex logical structure advocated by Braithwaite, or indeed by Clark Hull. A related issue was that of falsifiability, proposed as a crucial feature of a scientific theory by Popper (1959). Toulmin's views, on the other hand, would suggest that the usefulness and durability of a theory are of greater significance than its falsifiability. There is no point in throwing your map away until you have something better.

So what was it like to do research in the 1950s? First of all, it was much less formalised than it is today. Very few of the younger lecturers at UC had a PhD, although most of them were working on one at the time, most supervised by the professor and department head, Roger Russell. Many senior psychologists did not bother to complete a PhD, and it was not until the 1960s that this started to become a prerequisite for most university teaching posts.

There were in fact very few such posts in the late 1950s, and I was warned that planning to become a university lecturer was not a very promising employment strategy. After graduation, I took a summer job at the Medical Research Council's Applied Psychology Unit (APU) in Cambridge before taking a graduate fellowship at Princeton. I decided I would prolong my PhD research as long as possible, declining the opportunity of completing a PhD at Princeton. Instead, after a year, I returned to Britain, where I expected to spend two years as a national serviceman, hopefully at a military psychology establishment such as the Institute of Aviation Medicine, before going on to do a British PhD. When I was rejected on medical grounds I became a hospital porter and then a totally untrained schoolteacher. After six exhausting months teaching in a Yorkshire mining village, I moved to a research post at the Burden Neurological Institute in Bristol, tasked with discovering some positive effects of alcohol – on a grant from Guinness, which evaporated shortly after my arrival. Fortunately, as it did so an opportunity cropped up to take a research post at the APU.

The funding this time came from the Post Office, which was preparing for the introduction of postcodes to facilitate sorting by keyboard, rather than by manually assigning letters to pigeonholes. I was to be supervised by Conrad, an extremely good applied psychologist who was working extensively with the Post Office at this time, and who looked after the applied aspect of the project, leaving me to do basic research on 'coding'. I was to be paid a proper salary and allowed to do a PhD based on the research, provided the Cambridge University department would accept me. A year after I arrived I was interviewed by Oliver Zangwill, who stared fixedly at the ground throughout the interview, and his borzoi, who rested his head on my knees and gazed soulfully up at me throughout. I appeared to meet their joint approval and duly became a Cambridge research student.

I had become interested in Shannon and Weaver's (1949) information theory and its application to language, and devoted a good deal of my thesis to using the sequential redundancy within English words to generate letter sequences that varied in their memorability and ease of copying. At the time, the only source of statistical information was a prewar book on codes called *Secret and Urgent* that reported single-letter and *digram* frequencies. However, through Conrad's links with the Post Office we were able to use its computer to obtain more substantial norms based on analysis of the august leader columns of *The Times* newspaper and on the script of a radio soap opera, *Mrs Dale's Diary*.

Somewhat to my surprise, I found myself working on the learning of nonsense syllables and was able to demonstrate that a redundancy measure, which I called 'predictability', did a much better job in predicting ease of learning than the norms of meaningful associations that were universally used at the time. I wanted to publish these results but was discouraged on the grounds that it was unwise to publish before completing one's PhD. By the time my thesis was complete, two things had happened: two new sets of association values had been published, based on larger sample sizes, so that my previous carefully matched lists were no longer carefully matched; and Underwood and Schulz (1960) had published their book *Meaningfulness and Verbal Learning*, in which they also argued for the import-ance of language habits. I never did publish that part of my thesis. From a more practical viewpoint, I had accepted the challenge of generating postcodes for every British post town, using the statistical structure of English to make them maximally memorable. Having weeded out a number of accidental obscenities, this was forwarded to the Post Office, which showed no interest whatsoever, having already decided to opt for the current system. They could have done worse; the Canadian post office chose to alternate letters and digits, a pattern that leads to a greater error rate than any other number–letter sequence!

My interest in information-processing models led me to include a further set of experiments in my thesis, which aimed to vary the number of response alter-natives without requiring any difference in the range of stimuli. Subjects were simply required to generate a random sequence of letters from sets varying in size, producing results that were highly regular and lawful, but difficult to explain (Baddeley, 1966a). Anyone who has read Baddeley *et al.* (1998) will know that the phenomenon is still hard to explain.

The employment conditions at Medical Research Council units at the time were far from rigid. Research workers would start, typically without a PhD since there were very few PhDs around, on a series of three-year appointments. If things were going well, they would move on to five-year appointments, which would continue up to their fortieth birthday. At this point they would either be tenured, or given a final three-year appointment. In the meantime, we were expected to keep our sponsors happy, and chat from time to time to visiting Medical Research Council subcommittees, where I recall being told immediately before the visit whether, on that occasion, we should be 'pure' or 'applied' in our presentations. There was little pressure to publish. There was, however, a feeling of real intel-lectual excitement. We felt that we were at the forefront of a revolution – a revolution inspired by Kenneth Craik's insights (Craik, 1943), developed into a broad information-processing approach to the human mind as reflected by Donald

Broadbent, Director of the APU, in his highly influential book *Perception and Communication* (Broadbent, 1958).

I did, however, also see myself as part of an international group of people interested in human learning and memory, almost all using verbal material, and initially simply circulating our preprints to colleagues on a cyclostyled list that would be updated from time to time. Somewhat surprisingly, human verbal learning had taken over some of the theoretical leadership previously held by Hull and Tolman and their adherents. The list of 'verbal learners' gradually increased in length and then transformed itself into a journal, the *Journal of Verbal Learning and Verbal Behavior* (now the *Journal of Memory and Language*). I saw myself principally as someone who was interested in applying information-processing concepts to long-term memory (LTM) as reflected in the influence of language habits and redundancy.

About this time, Conrad took a year's sabbatical in the United States, leaving me to run a project concerned with using behavioural measures to assess the quality of telephone links. Our sponsor was due to build a piece of equipment that would add predetermined levels of noise to speech. We would then test intelligibility by requiring subjects to use the noisy link in performing some unspecified cognitive operation. I decided to start by using immediate memory as a task. This allowed me to incorporate an important phenomenon that Conrad had just discovered, namely the acoustic similarity effect (Conrad and Hull, 1964), reflected in the impaired recall of acoustically similar letter sequences (e.g. b, g, t, d, c, p). This, he suggested, demonstrated that short-term memory (STM) employed some type of acoustic or speech-based code. Perhaps, I thought, presenting acoustically similar items in noise would amplify this effect? I also felt it necessary to include a further control; perhaps any kind of similarity would impair immediate recall? I chose to vary semantic similarity, simply because it was easy to manipulate using verbal material. I found little or no effect of noise on memory, but dramatic differences between the major impact of acoustic similarity and a minimal semantic similarity effect (Baddeley, 1966b). I found that the pattern of effects reversed when a long-term rather than immediate memory paradigm was used (Baddeley, 1966c). I felt like the sorcerer's apprentice, trying out my supervisor's magic variable, with results that were more far-reaching than I dared anticipate. I had moved from LTM to STM, working along lines that I have continued ever since.

When Conrad returned, he left me free to work in my new area, with Pat Rabbitt, who had just joined the unit, taking over my old project but with newly arrived equipment.

I have described a simple story that I am sure must be inaccurate in detail. For example, alongside my STM project, I was carrying out a series of experiments concerned with the question of whether LTM and STM represent different systems. One study involved free recall; it was stimulated by a paper by Postman and Philips (1965) which interpreted the recency effect in free recall in terms of classic interference theory. I suggested that recency might represent items being held in STM, but again I was pipped at the post, this time by Glanzer and Cunitz

(1966), leading me to emphasise a rather different aspect of the data when I did eventually publish (Baddeley, 1968a).

A more successful line of publications was based on experiments contrasting acoustic and semantic coding in paired associate learning, carried out jointly with my friend and colleague Harold Dale. Harold had a contract from the army to look at the role in electronic maintenance of fault-finding and decision-making procedures. In connection with this, he was allowed to test groups of recruits at their base camp, adding further experiments if he wished. We had developed methods of testing 20 or more subjects at the same time, and might test anything up to 50 subjects on each of our fortnightly visits. The work I did with Harold Dale demonstrated the importance of acoustic coding for the STM procedure known as minimal paired associate learning, together with the importance of semantic coding for LTM (Baddeley and Dale, 1966). Although the immediate serial recall work is probably more quoted these days, I suspect that many of the ideas were developed jointly with Harold Dale on our drives down to Arborfield Camp, and during our snooker games in the officers' mess where we stayed.

I decided to investigate further the robust acoustic similarity effect, asking whether it influenced performance via encoding, storage or retrieval. The fact that it did not interact with presentation in noise seemed to rule out encoding, while the observation that similar items were not forgotten any more rapidly seemed to eliminate storage, leaving retrieval as a default interpretation (Baddeley, 1968b). While I was not able to find a good way of investigating retrieval in detail, a serendipitous finding allowed us to rule out at least one interpretation of the effect, namely the serial chaining hypothesis proposed by Wickelgren (1966). During Conrad's absence on sabbatical, his research assistant, Audrey Hull, and I had decided that we would try to get rid of the acoustic similarity effect by separating each of a succession of similar letters by a dissimilar letter (e.g., t, x, c, r, p, w). We found that this buffering procedure did not totally eliminate the similarity effect, a result that we initially thought was disappointing and put on one side. However, Wickelgren (1966) then obligingly published a theory proposing that serial order in STM reflected a process of chaining. The theory was inconsistent with our finding, thus providing a more interesting ending to my unsuccessful search for the location of the acoustic similarity effect (Baddeley, 1968b), and continuing to present a challenge for a whole series of later models of short-term serial recall based on chaining (Henson *et al.*, 1996).

At about this time, having spent nine years at the APU, I decided that it was time for a change. There were interesting jobs being advertised at Oxford and in the Department of Experimental Psychology at Sussex. Peter Bryant and I applied for both. Oxford chose Peter and Sussex chose me.

Both the university and the Experimental Psychology Department (oops, Sussex is not supposed to have departments) were relatively new. Stuart Sutherland was temperamentally an intriguing contrast to my previous boss, Donald Broadbent. Like Donald, however, he was committed to creating a first-rate research environment and, although somewhat eccentric and on occasions ferocious in his manner, he provided vigorous encouragement and support for staff and students. I was the only staff member who worked exclusively on people, but the intellectual atmosphere was lively and very broad, with the result that I did not feel at all isolated. I found that the requirement to teach forced me to broaden my approach, with very positive consequences.

Following Stuart's encouragement I took on a consultancy with the Ministry of Defence, advising them on training missile operators. Somewhat to my surprise I discovered that even though I could not claim any expertise in the area, my general background in psychology allowed me to understand the broad problems relatively easily – particularly as a number of them turned out to be difficulties in communication between different parts of the organisation. I discovered that I rather enjoyed interacting with a wide range of groups, from soldiers through to civil servants to engineers, and this fact encouraged me in due course to return to the APU.

During this period I also took my first steps into neuropsychology. I knew Elizabeth Warrington, who was at the Psychology Department at the National Hospital, Queen Square, London, from my undergraduate days at UC. She suggested I might be interested in working on amnesia; I was very sceptical, assuming that neuropsychological data would be very hard to interpret, but accepted her invitation to try out one of my tests on an amnesic patient. Results from the test in question proved uninteresting and I began to chat about what was supposed to be wrong with amnesic patients. I was told by Elizabeth that they had normal STM and impaired LTM, forgetting material immediately after it was presented. I pointed out that according to current theory, if their STM was intact then they should be able to perform the Peterson short-term forgetting task, in which material is retained over a brief filled delay. We decided to try, producing the material by cutting up postcards while our patient had coffee. She performed the Peterson task beautifully, and I rapidly became enthusiastic about neuro-psychology. We performed a range of other tasks of contemporary theoretical significance on a very carefully chosen group of patients, resulting in my first, and probably most quoted, neuropsychology paper (Baddeley and Warrington, 1970).

My teaching load was relatively light and I found that I was still able to keep up a reasonable rate of research, partly by utilising undergraduate projects and practicals, and partly by obtaining funding for a research assistant and subse-quently funding for my first postdoctoral fellow, Graham Hitch. After doing his first degree in physics, Graham had done the conversion course MSc in experi-mental psychology at Sussex, before going on to do a PhD with Donald Broadbent at the APU. He returned to Sussex on a joint grant to look at the relationship between LTM and STM. The grant coincided with a period when research on STM was suddenly falling out of fashion. The influential Atkinson and Shiffrin (1968) model was starting to encounter difficulties, both with its basic learning assumptions and with its capacity to deal with the recent neuropsychological evidence. Meanwhile, the literature had become filled with a large range of new STM techniques whose theoretical interpretation remained problematic.

We decided to take a step back and ask the simple question 'What function, if any, is served by STM?' We did not have access to patients with STM deficits but instead used the dual-task method to attempt to disrupt performance in various ways, studying a range of tasks that were assumed to depend upon STM, including learning, comprehending and reasoning. Our results suggested that there was indeed general involvement of STM in a range of complex tasks, but that its role was far less straightforward than that implied by STM models. We proposed a tripartite system, which we called working memory. We suggested that it comprised an attentional controller, the central executive, aided by two subsidiary systems, one concerned with verbal material, the articulatory or subsequently phonological loop, while the other, the visuospatial scratch-pad, subsequently sketchpad, was concerned with processing visual and spatial information.

In the midst of this research project I was offered a professorship by Stirling University, an even newer institution than Sussex. I visited initially out of curiosity, with no intention of moving, but was captivated by the beautiful environment and the exciting prospect of a new department that had established its teaching pattern and was determined to build up a major research reputation. At the time, 1972, they were talking about aiming for six chairs in psychology – in those days an incredibly ambitious undertaking – and wanted me to look after the research development of the department.

I accepted and moved up, accompanied by Graham Hitch and a PhD student, Neil Thomson, together with a new postdoctoral fellow from the APU, Duncan Godden, who had persuaded me to put in a research proposal on memory and divers. The next two years were probably the most productive of my whole career (so far!). Our new theoretical framework was proving extremely productive. In particular, the phonological loop was investigated further using the word-length effect, a very powerful relationship between word length and memory span that I investigated together with Neil Thomson (Baddeley *et al.*, 1975).

Meanwhile, we were finding ways of investigating the visuospatial component of working memory (Baddeley *et al.*, 1973; Baddeley and Lieberman, 1980). Further theoretical development was prompted by an invitation from Gordon Bower to write a chapter for the influential 'Recent Advances' series he edited. While we felt the model was not yet sufficiently developed, it seemed too good an opportunity to miss, a decision that in retrospect seems to have been the right one (Baddeley and Hitch, 1974). At the same time, the work on diver performance with Duncan Godden was demonstrating context dependency such that what was learned under water was best recalled under water and vice versa (Godden and Baddeley, 1975). Context-dependent memory was not, of course, a new phenomenon, but the magnitude of our effect was substantially greater than land-based equivalents.

Stirling University proved to be very congenial and intellectually seemed to hold great promise of further research development. Unfortunately, however, my move coincided with the end of the period of university expansion and the beginning of the long years of retrenchment, making the immediate prospect of six chairs totally unrealistic. Consequently, when I heard that Donald Broadbent was to give up the directorship of the APU I was tempted to apply for the post, and after much soul searching did so. It presented a whole range of new options and opportunities, together with the possibility of taking my research colleagues and indeed making no fewer than six new scientific appointments. It was followed by 21 years in an enviably well supported environment, surrounded by far more first-rate cognitive psychologists than one could reasonably expect in any university department. But that is another story.

18

Purpose, personality, creativity: a computational adventure

Margaret A. Boden

Even as a schoolgirl, I was fascinated by the human mind: how it works, how it relates to the brain and how it reflects our evolutionary heritage. Not least, I was perplexed by how it can go wrong – as in paranoia, multiple personality and automatisms. These interests led me first to study medicine (intending to become a psychiatrist), then philosophy and eventually psychology. Along the way, I added a further fascination: artificial intelligence (AI). For the computational approach to psychology offered a fruitful way of thinking about the phenomena that had puzzled me so much at school – including, believe it or not (most people do not!), human freedom and psychopathology.

I was especially puzzled by what I had read (in dusty old volumes bought on the Charing Cross Road) about psychosomatic phenomena such as hysterical paralyses and anaesthesias. In these cases, there is no bodily damage: under hypnosis, the 'paralysed' arm moves normally and the 'anaesthetised' skin is sensitive. Still more surprising, the bodily limits of the clinical syndrome are inconsistent with the gross neuromuscular anatomy and seem to be determined instead by what the lay-patient *thinks of* as an arm or a leg. For example, the movements that the 'paralysed' patient is unable to make do not correspond to any specifiable set of spinal nerves. They can be described only by using the ordinary person's concept of an arm, namely, a body part bounded by the line of a sleeveless shirt. It is *that* unit which cannot be moved (except under hypnosis) – yet from the anatomical point of view it is not a 'unit' at all. Normal voluntary action, I thought, was mysterious enough: how can the mind move the body? But in these pathological cases, the mind appeared not only to be influencing the body but even overcoming it. How could this be?

My medical studies at Cambridge (1955–1957) made the anatomical aspects of this problem clearer, but didn't help solve it. Nor did my first brush with cognitive science. My philosophy tutor (from 1957 to 1959) was Margaret Master-man, a pioneer of machine translation. She persuaded me that the structure of language and concepts might be modelled in computational terms, but did not try to model the psychological processes involved. Although I found her work intriguing, I couldn't see how to generalise it to the mind as a whole.

This state of affairs lasted for five years (including my time teaching philosophy at the University of Birmingham) but ended almost in a split second. Two days after arriving in the other Cambridge to study social and cognitive psychology with Jerome Bruner and Gordon Allport, I was browsing in a second-hand book-shop on Massachusetts Avenue when I picked up *Plans and the Structure of Behavior*, by George Miller, Eugene Galanter, and Karl Pribram (1960). Leafing through it in the bookshop, I made the conceptual leap from computation to psychology and to the mind–body problem. It seemed to offer a way to tackle just those questions which had bothered me as a schoolgirl.

Miller and his co-authors used the software–hardware distinction in explaining how an immaterial, abstractly conceived entity could cause changes in the physical world. And they applied specific computational ideas – hierarchies of test–operate–test–exit procedures, or TOTE units – to the whole of psychology. They focused on process as well as structure: how the mind works, not just what can be found in it. Even more to the point (for me), their discussion ranged from animal learning and instinct, through memory and language, to personality and psychopathology.

Their book was oversimplified, to be sure. This was inevitable, given the state of computational research at the time – their most influential source, besides Miller's work on formal grammars done with Noam Chomsky, was the 'general problem solver' (Newell and Simon, 1961). Worse, it was self-confessedly vague, and often careless to boot. I later discovered that wags familiar with the authors' previous work joked that 'Miller thought of it, Galanter wrote it, and Pribram believed it'. Nevertheless, it was a work of vision – and, for me, an intellectual intoxication.

Its computational ideas soon informed my own research. In 1963, I wrote a paper applying them to William McDougall's rich theory of the purposive structures underlying normal and abnormal personality (Boden, 1965). And I addressed one of my longstanding puzzles by outlining how a humanoid robot could have a paralysis conforming not to its wires-and-levers anatomy but to its programmed 'concept' of what an arm is. I argued that its behaviour would be best described in intentional terms, in the sense that what it was 'doing' could be stated only by reference to the descriptions and instructions in its program (Boden, 1970). My argument was not that the robot *really* wanted to move its left arm, nor that it was *literally* mentally inhibited from doing so. But this intentional vocabulary, insofar as it reflected the robot's program and data structures, was more helpful than descriptions of the hardware (e.g. the wires corresponding to the spinal nerves) in explaining, predicting and controlling the robot's behaviour.

The paralysed robot first hit the press in 1970 but had already featured in the manuscript of my first book, *Purposive Explanation in Psychology* (Boden, 1972: 315–320). Begun in 1964, this took me seven years to finish. (The publisher's advance copy reached me two days after the birth of my second baby: both were deep purple.) In it, I developed a fundamentally physicalist but non-reductionist account of purpose and other intentional concepts. I argued that psychology is irreducible to neurophysiology, much as descriptions of software are irreducible to talk about hardware. I compared my account of mind, and the mind–body relation, with a wide range of theories in psychology and philosophy. I discussed the treatment of purpose and freedom in psychologies as different as behaviourism and the Third Force personality theories. And I focused most closely on McDougall (1871–1938) – not as an unchallengeable guru, but as an intellectual sparring partner.

What had first excited me about McDougall was his deep insight into the complex structure of the human mind, and his many explicit arguments against psychological reductionism – most, but not all, of which I judged to be valid. It turned out later that there were several personal links, too. When I researched McDougall's life history, I discovered that, on completing his degree in medical sciences at Cambridge, he had taken up the same clinical scholarship at St Thomas's Hospital that had been offered to me a few years before. He, like me, had moved from medicine to psychology, and from one Cambridge to the other (he was Professor at Harvard for several years). Moreover, when I said to Bruner that instead of doing experiments on information density in disjunctive concepts (a less than fascinating research topic he had suggested) I wanted to study McDougall's theory of purpose, he told me – after a gasp of amazement – that McDougall had been his teacher at Duke University.

McDougall's broadly ranging psychology had been highly influential until it was suddenly eclipsed by behaviourism. He remained bitter about this for the rest of his life, gruffly warning the young Bruner of the intellectual corruption that awaited him at Harvard Graduate School. By the time I arrived there, some 25 years later, the behaviourist 'corruption' was less strong – in Bruner and Miller's new Center for Cognitive Studies, if not in the Psychology Department (whose denizens included Burrhus Skinner and Richard Herrnstein). Even so, McDougall's name had virtually vanished from the curriculum (hence Bruner's gasp of amazement). It survived only on a three-page mimeographed list of long-dead worthies, circulated by Allport as potential essay topics for his seminar on the history of social psychology.

Initially drawn to him by the title of his book *Body and Mind* (McDougall, 1911), I found that McDougall's ideas had a welcome subtlety and depth. They also showed a refreshing concern for real life, whether psychiatric syndromes or everyday pursuits. His psychology dealt not only with cognition but with motivation and emotion too – and with how these are integrated in individual personalities. Moreover, it seemed to me that his theory, including his account of psycho-pathology in terms of various types of 'dissociation', offered intriguing hypotheses and questions that were expressible in computational terms.

Besides these strengths, his writing abounded with insightful discussions of philosophical questions about mind, purpose and consciousness. Indeed, this was one reason why his work was considered passé, not fit for the psychological syllabus. Philosophical enquiry was anathema to most academic psychologists, who typically claimed – in the opening chapters of their textbooks, for example – that psychology had finally 'escaped' from philosophy. They seemed not to realise that their own (positivist) definition of psychology was itself a problematic philosophical position. But this was clear to me, and I responded positively (not positivistically!) to McDougall's concern with such matters.

However, that's not to say that I agreed with all of his philosophical arguments, still less that I accepted his robust defence of 'animism'. Despite writing a leading textbook on physiological psychology, McDougall had been combatively anti-mechanistic. So far, I thought, so good. For I, too, believed psychology to be irreducible to physiology. But he had even claimed that purposive behaviour requires a special form of energy (*horme*), intrinsically directed to a specific set of instinctive goals. That, for me, was a step too far. Purposive explanation is one thing, purposive energy quite another. But McDougall was no fool, and no mystic either. He realised how bizarre his hormic hypothesis appeared and would have avoided it if he could. So it was important to understand why, when considering purposive behaviour, he had said this. That done, one might be able to give a more acceptable account of the data he had explained by this strange hypothesis.

As part of my critique, I suggested that his many insights about personality and psychopathology could be simulated in computational terms. (I was well aware that he would be turning in his grave.) If this was indeed possible, then those insights could be saved, and even clarified, without positing any mysterious energy. And if it could be done for McDougall's avowedly antimechanistic psychology, it could in principle be done for any other, for McDougall was an extreme case. Freud, too, had theorised about purpose. But he was less suitable as a test case because, besides ignoring animal psychology, he had believed his theory of re-pression to be reducible to mechanistic physiological terms. McDougall was a harder philosophical nut to crack – and much the more worth cracking.

In sketching ways of simulating McDougall's psychology, I had to extrapolate from the computer models that already existed. In 1964, when the book was begun, there were only a handful of candidates. By the time it was finished, early in 1971, there were many more. These ranged from computer problem solving, through programs for vision and language, to models of analogy, learning and various aspects of personality.

These new examples were clearly relevant to my central claim: that purposive behaviour is intelligible in computational terms, and could in principle be simu-lated in computers. But although I was able to refer to a few of them, they were too numerous – and many were too late – for them all to be added to the already lengthy manuscript. So, even before *Purposive Explanation in Psychology* was completed, I decided to write an extended footnote to it. This would detail what psychological phenomena could, and what could not, be mimicked by computer modelling in the early 1970s, and what sorts of advance would be needed for the many remaining obstacles to be overcome. The resulting footnote, *Artificial Intelligence and Natural Man* (Boden, 1977), ran to 537 pages. Most readers thought of it as a stand-alone introduction to AI, albeit with a strong psychological slant (it was chosen as the set book for the Open University's first course in cognitive psychology). In fact, it was part of my initial project. Accordingly, the two penultimate chapters, focused on AI's implications for psychology and philosophy, related the programs discussed in earlier chapters to the theme and argument of my first book.

The prose in which the footnote was written, however, differed greatly from that of the main text. *Purposive Explanation in Psychology* (in essence, my PhD thesis) had been addressed to specialists in psychology and philosophy, and presupposed some scholarly knowledge. Now I wanted to reach a wider audience, since AI was potentially of widespread interest. This required a different rhetorical approach. Not only had most people never heard of AI, but those who had felt threatened by it. They saw computers as utterly mysterious and programming as rebarbatively difficult. And they regarded it as obvious that computer technology couldn't be used to throw light on human characteristics such as purpose, language, creativity or freedom. The very idea seemed to most people dangerously absurd. (To some, it still does.)

Accordingly, I tried to demystify computer programming – partly by comparing it to knitting, an activity no one doubts they could master if they tried. (A male colleague who read the manuscript complained that my knitting examples would not be understood by men. I replied that this matter was not negotiable: I myself was sick of reading examples assuming knowledge of radios or car engines, and rather enjoyed the prospect of bemused male readers running to consult their mothers or girlfriends.) Mostly, however, I relied not on knitting but on plain English. The book described, in non-technical language, just how the existing AI programs did what they did, and why they didn't do what they didn't do. It also suggested how they might be changed so as to do more, and contrasted superficial improvements with deeper ones, then way beyond the state of the art.

(Many of these improvements are still unachieved. And most of the comparisons with human abilities, scattered throughout the book, still stand. This explains why for the second edition, published ten years after the first, I added an up-date chapter but did not alter the main text.)

Insofar as *Artificial Intelligence and Natural Man* aimed to describe AI, most of the chapter topics were predictable. Obviously, AI work on language, vision, learning and problem solving would have to be discussed. Social interaction was less obvious, but had been insightfully addressed by the social psychologist Robert Abelson (1973), whose computational theories I detailed in Chapter 4. Two of my choices, however, struck many people as maverick, even perverse.

On the one hand, I included a chapter on creativity. 'But there isn't any AI work on creativity', some colleagues objected. I replied that there should be. Since AI aims to study intelligence in general, creativity must be discussed. It is too important, and too widespread, to be ignored. Moreover, it is a crucial aspect of human freedom, which (in my first book) I had analysed in computational terms. That claim usually elicited scornful dismissal: 'Nonsense! No computer could really be creative.' Anticipating similar scepticism in the reader, I countered that this was no more relevant than the fact that no computer could 'really' understand language, or 'really' see. In the Introduction and the philosophical chapter I repeated my belief (previously argued at length in *Purposive Explanation in Psychology*) that psychological vocabulary applied to computers should be interpreted metaphorically, with notional scare-quotes. My position was not that computers are really minds, but that psychologists can learn something illuminating about minds by comparing them with computers. (In the terminology later used by John Searle (1980), I was rejecting strong AI in favour of weak AI.) If the psychology of creativity – as opposed to language or vision – is so *wholly* unsuited to AI that no computer model could possibly teach us anything about it, so be it. But unless that could be specifically proven, creativity was grist for the AI mill just as language and vision were.

Moreover, the objection 'There isn't any AI work on creativity' was too quick. In the relevant chapter I showed that many AI projects were potentially pertinent, though not developed with creativity in mind. Granted, there were even more limitations in this area of AI research than in others and more challenges remaining for the future. Modelling creative processes would not be easy. In addition, the concept itself is slippery: it varies from person to person, and from moment to moment in the mouth of one person. Many discussions about creativity are therefore bedevilled with ambiguity. Nevertheless, there's no good reason to believe that creativity is an unfathomable mystery. (I promised myself then that, one day, I would return to this topic at much greater length; that day arrived some 15 years later (Boden, 1990, 1994a).)

On the other hand, I chose to devote the first two substantive chapters to a computer model of neurosis, written by the psychiatrist Kenneth Colby (1965). Based on one of his patients, a woman with an obsession about being abandoned by her father, it simulated the various defence mechanisms (denial, projection, displacement, etc.) distinguished by Freud. This program was already considered out of date. Indeed, even AI professionals were largely ignorant of it, often confusing it with Colby's model of paranoia (Colby, 1975). Why bother with it, then? My reasons for giving it so much attention, so early in the book, were both rhetorical and intellectual.

Colby's neurotic program (scare-quotes, of course!) was useful as a rhetorical device because its nitty-gritty details could be described in plain language, and followed through with pencil and paper. Readers unfamiliar with programming would thus get a sense of just how a program works, and just how precise its instructions must be. Some such nit-picking account had to be given, if only at the outset of the book. What's more, neurosis is interesting in human terms. To have described a chess program in comparable detail, or even a model of language or vision, would have struck many readers as forbiddingly tedious. But few could fail to be intrigued by Colby's work. Even if they were infuriated by its lack of subtlety, they would not be bored.

Moreover, this example showed that a computational model may clarify psychological questions despite, and partly through, its limitations. Colby's program was inadequate in many ways. I could point out its failings, suggest how they might be fixed, and recall this discussion in later chapters. Colby's procedure for finding analogies, for example, was painfully crude. If more powerful models of analogy (discussed in the creativity chapter) were incorporated in his program, it would better reflect the neurotic's generalisation from the father to other authority figures. This would require, I said, a program of a fundamentally different kind, involving a rich semantic network. If a persuasive computational model of analogy is unachievable, then no AI system will ever match the human neurotic's ability to generalise (or overgeneralise) from one class to another.

Even more important, to discuss Colby's neurotic program was to suggest that both normal and pathological personality might be illuminated by a computational psychology. This had been one of my main claims in *Purposive Explanation in Psychology*. Colby was not the only person who had tried to simulate personality (other examples, even cruder than his, had been mentioned in my earlier book). In doing so, he had been forced to consider motivation and affect as well as cognition. His research thus challenged the assumption (still widespread today) that if computational psychology is useful at all, it is suited only to dry matters such as rational problem solving and other aspects of cognition. Colby's work modelled irrationality and the effects of emotion on cognition (and vice versa). Distinct anxiety levels, for instance, would be aroused by different beliefs and would trigger different defence mechanisms.

Finally, Colby's program favoured psychological rather than physiological interpretations of psychoanalysis. It would not encourage anyone to think that repression is reducible to neurophysiology. To understand why the program repressed certain beliefs by denial and others by projection, one had to consider the semantic criteria it used. These intentional phenomena could not be similarly illuminated by talk about electrons buzzing through wires, or by programs simulating quantitative measures of the energies and cathexis supposedly involved, as had been developed by other Freudian psychologists (Boden, 1974: 250).

If I found the neurotic program so interesting, why was it 'out of date' and largely forgotten? The answer is that it had been hugely overambitious. The time was not yet ripe for such a project. (Nor is it ripe today: we still don't have sufficiently subtle computational theories of analogy or emotion, for example.) The psychologists who had turned away to model more tractable aspects of the mind had made a sensible decision. But I did not write programs. My aim was more general: to show that computational psychology, with or without fully implemented models, could in principle help us understand even the most personal aspects of human minds.

Another of my early interests was Jean Piaget, who – like hysterical paralysis – had caught my attention as a schoolgirl. Again, a second-hand bookshop played a crucial role, for I found his name in some volume on philosophy (or possibly biology) found in Foyle's treasure-house. A few weeks before starting as a medical student, I went to hear him lecture at the Sorbonne. He was already white-haired, then. To my pleasure, I met him 25 years later, a month before he died. Talking to me in his study, he suddenly unearthed a shell from the papers on his desk and invited me to admire 'une jolie petite limace'.

What attracted me to him in the first place was his attempt to combine biology and philosophy with psychology. In my own set of intellectual priorities, the hysterical paralysis took precedence. But Piaget remained smouldering in the background, and the spark was kept alive by my encountering his name in footnotes from time to time. In 1963 I read some of his work for Bruner's seminar. I promised myself then that I would eventually return to study it in greater depth, to see just what sense I could make of it.

In the event, my book on Piaget (Boden, 1979) devoted as much space to his biology and philosophy as to his psychology. And it discussed his psychological ideas, and his general commitment to formalism, in the light of AI modelling. In its attempt to integrate these four approaches to the mind, my third book resembled the first. But the psychological problems discussed were largely different, being concerned mostly with cognition, not motivation or personality.

The goal of 'seeing just what sense I could make of it' was primarily a challenge to my own powers of comprehension: could I get my head around his intellectually ambitious project? But it also reflected my doubts about whether any sense could be made of it. Notoriously, Piaget was no paragon of consistency or clarity. Others had complained that his views were so vague as to be irrefutable; even Bruner, who deeply admired him, had dismissed his core concept of equilibrium as 'surplus baggage' (Bruner, 1959: 365). Besides all that, there was the question of whether what he had said was true. In short, I was both highly intrigued by his work and sceptical about it.

Having thought about his work more seriously, both those attitudes survived. I ended my book by saying that Piaget's importance should be judged in the light of four questions: Has he been influential? Were his views more nearly correct than those of his contemporaries? Was he correct? Should someone starting from scratch today be advised to read him for his lasting intellectual contribution to psychology? And I argued that the answers to these questions are, respectively: Yes, very; Yes; Yes and no; and Yes, but … (Boden, 1979: 133). In the second edition of 1994, I reiterated these answers (Boden, 1994b). And I added that recent research has shown him to be both more wrong and more right than had appeared when my book was first written. It is now even clearer that he underestimated the cognitive organisation and domain-specificity of the baby's mind. But his biologist's emphasis on self-organisation and epigenesis is supported by neurophysiological evidence of the subtle interactions between inborn constraints and environmental pressures, and by current work in developmental biology and artificial life (A-life).

These three books of the 1970s, with my papers up to the late 1980s, comprise my 'early' research. The papers were scattered across journals of philosophy, psychology, biology, AI and sociology. Several dealt with the concept of intention or free choice (e.g. Boden, 1959, 1973, 1978). Most of the psychologically relevant items were gathered in two collections, *Minds and Mechanisms* (Boden, 1981) and *Artificial Intelligence in Psychology* (Boden, 1989).

All these publications focused on what was possible in principle. Empirical results, whether in psychology or AI, were treated as examples illustrating the possibilities – and difficulties – involved. I repeatedly claimed that future advances in computational psychology would provide specific theories about a wide range of phenomena. In short, this work abounded with promissory notes. My next book, *Computer Models of Mind*, commissioned by Cambridge University Press for its 'Studies in the Behavioural Sciences' series, asked to what extent these promises had already been fulfilled (Boden, 1988). It was essentially a progress report on other people's work. It argued that the greatest advances had been in the psychology of language and, especially, low-level vision. In addition, there were interesting results in the modelling of problem solving, learning and development. The advances were limited, to be sure, even in the most successful domains. I pointed out, for instance, that visual object recognition and open-ended reasoning were not adequately covered, and that creativity had hardly been touched.

The much-improved understanding of vision was due largely to the influence of David Marr, whose early work I had outlined in *Artificial Intelligence and Natural Man* and now described at much greater length. By the early 1980s, Marr's was not the only type of connectionism available. Another was parallel distributed processing (PDP). This methodology became widely known only after publication of the PDP 'bible' (Rumelhart and McClelland, 1986). But because Geoffrey Hinton had been a colleague at the University of Sussex I was already aware of it when planning my new book. A general theme of the volume, then, was a comparison of the – largely complementary – strengths and weaknesses of PDP and the symbolic approach.

Whereas there had been genuine advance in the modelling of cognition and learning, the same could not be said for motivation, emotion and personality. These remained recalcitrant – indeed, almost ignored. The most promising work, I said, was Aaron Sloman's (1987) outline of the computational architecture needed to generate emotions and to support their role in a multipurpose mind. This illuminated some of the issues I had addressed in my notional simulation of McDougall's personality theory. Since then, Sloman has deepened his account significantly, and directed some preliminary implementations of it (Wright *et al.*, 1996).

Looking back on my early research, I think it was going in the right direction. The advances described in my 'progress report' (not least, Sloman's work) indicate this. So, too, does the fact that the second editions of *Artificial Intelligence and Natural Man* and *Piaget* retained the original texts intact: what was required in each case was addition rather than alteration. Likewise, my later account of creativity in *The Creative Mind* (Boden, 1990) is entirely consonant with my earlier treatment, though significantly developed. And some of my early ideas about consciousness have been vindicated: the computational approach shows how it is possible for the mind to support the non-reciprocal co-consciousness typical of multiple personality (Boden, 1972: 254–259 1994c).

On one of my schoolgirl puzzles, however, I have made no advance at all – and in my view no one else has either. Computationalism explains how conscious experience (taken as given) can become dissociated in various ways. And neuroscience can often predict what conscious experience (again, taken as given) will happen. Occasionally, it can even explain why this experience rather than that one must happen. But how it is possible for any experience at all to occur when the neurones buzz in the brain remains profoundly unintelligible. To solve this conundrum will require parallel conceptual advances in philosophy and neuroscience that at present are fundamentally inconceivable (Boden, 1998).

The reason I don't need to repudiate my early work, despite the many exciting developments in cognitive science since then, is its level of generality. My research focuses on general principles, illustrated by specific examples. If the examples available change, thanks to scientific advance, the principles – and many of the challenges – do not.

In particular, although virtually all the computer models discussed in my early work were drawn from symbolic AI, I never claimed that this is the only possible form of computation. In *Purposive Explanation in Psychology*, for instance, I said that neural nets might simulate low-level psychological processes (Boden, 1972: 145, 303). And in *Artificial Intelligence and Natural Man* I outlined Marr's early approach and said that other radically different forms of computation might be developed. So to write about the recent methodologies of connectionism and A-life in the up-date chapters to my two second editions, or in my progress report, was to supplement my earlier ideas, not to contradict them.

My most recent publications include discussions of life, metabolism and self-organisation (Boden, 1996, 1999, 2000). This work picks up some loose ends originating in my days as a medical student, when I was enthralled by reading D'Arcy Thompson and Alan Turing on morphogenesis. It may seem wholly irrelevant to my psychological interests, but it is not. Many people (including McDougall) have argued – or more usually assumed – that life is a necessary precondition of mind. Computational psychologists need to consider whether this is true and what constraints its truth would put on our theories – and models – of mind. For the record, I see the current A-life methodologies as less well suited than symbolic AI to represent human freedom (Boden, 1995).

Some years ago, a member of the British Psychological Society's newly founded History and Philosophy of Psychology Group advised against their discussing computational psychology because the topic was 'too specialised'. Sociologically speaking, she was correct. Many psychologists – especially those concerned with social and motivational matters – were then, and are still, relatively ignorant of this approach. The hopes engendered in that magic moment on Massachusetts Avenue, and driving my work thereafter, will be fulfilled if such a remark from a professional psychologist becomes increasingly unlikely as the new century progresses.

19

The joys of psychology

David C. Duncan

This is an account of the sources of my continuing fascination with applied psychology; of what I expected and what actually happened; of the competences which I acquired in the course of my career in the field, and the opportunities which I had for exercising them.

My first reaction to joining the National Institute of Industrial Psychology (NIIP), in September 1953, was 'now here are some real problems for me to get my teeth into'. While my previous three years as a Management Trainee (Sales) had provided me with useful experience of the etiquette of visiting factories, shops and offices by appointment, it had not faced me with problems which demanded any depth of intellect.

The first competence which I had to acquire was in statistical analysis. In 1953 there were no computers to do correlations; calculations were done with the aid of slide rules and a factor analysis was a major project. I relearned my statistics from John Handyside, who was an enthusiast for 'state-of-the-art' calculators, and had a machine called a Friden, which multiplied and divided by winding a handle forward or back. We worked together to produce the validation of an NIIP selection procedure for supervisors (Handyside and Duncan, 1954). Having regained my statistics, I was eager to practise them and the selection procedure received far more analysis from me than was reported in the final paper. In analysing interview performance, for example, I found that the judgements of members of NIIP staff who had been trained in systematic interviewing were highly reliable and consistent with their colleagues, that personnel managers who received some training were rather less reliable, and that middle managers in a factory, untrained, showed poor reliability. This gave me the confidence I later needed when training supervisors, personnel managers and selection consultants in interviewing in later years. Even a short course in systematic interviewing using the Seven Point Plan (Rodger, 1952) could effect a significant improvement in the reliability of judgements about people. Eysenck's strictures on interviewing (Eysenck, 1953), based on research findings from untrained interviewers who did not know what they were looking for, were not describing an irremediable situation.

I also discovered that the reliability of judgements on performances in group discussions was at its best if, in choosing topics for discussion, (a) candidates knew something about the topic and (b) the assessors also knew something about the topic. This obvious finding taught me not to apologise if the results of statistical analysis looked like common sense – they were part of the definition of common sense as well as the test of it.

Research for the Medical Research Council on the selection, training and motivation of supervisors in industry met my expectations as being in line with my original interest in understanding and investigating morale and motivation in organisations. Supervisors in industry were an essential but neglected breed, not seen as part of management, but separated from the workers. Promotion to supervisor was not welcomed by factory workers; it paid more but had its costs, for it broke up social groups, established a new hierarchy and subjected the supervisor to new and unexpected pressures. Economists of that time were vociferous in their claims that there was no such thing as a science of management, and the application of science to management, of which supervision was an important part, had not much acceptance in industry. So supervisors were not trained and had to find their own methods of management. We were not concerned with developing advice for supervisors which would have wide generality so that it could be embodied into standard training courses; but I knew from my previous experience of industry that the application had to be tailored to suit the situation in which it was applied. The discrediting of Taylorism, which limited the scope for the NIIP by depriving it of trade union support in all but exceptional circumstances, arose from the application of perfectly good scientific techniques in ways which were unsuitable for the circumstances of their application.

In the 1950s, the most promising prospect for the development of supervisory training appeared to be the research into 'leader behaviour description' carried out by Hemphill and Fleischman for the US Office of Naval Research, and I addressed myself vigorously to the design of fully balanced questionnaires using Likert scaling. I used what would now be called a 360-degree approach, with 'what should you do?' and 'what do you do?' questionnaires, addressed in parallel to supervisors, their workers and their manager.

I ran a successful course for supervisors, and labour turnover, absence, survival and labour stability all improved, but a recession that started directly after my course was a much more significant cause of these, so the research was not published. The factory manager was credited with the improved productivity compared with other factories in the group, and the Hawthorne effect probably helped, so we had a satisfied client. Denis Healey, when Chancellor of the Exchequer, made a profound statement when he said, apropos the value of the pound, 'It isn't what the facts are that matters, it's what people think'. My researches into the integration of economics and psychology led Professor Alec Rodger to ask me to address the Department of Occupational Psychology at Birkbeck College on 'Economics for Psychologists'. On that occasion I took great pleasure in defining confidence as 'A situation in which people behave towards an expectation as if it were a reality', and pointing out that while economists attach great importance to confidence and use the term constantly without defining it, psychologists see it as the obverse of objectivity, avoid researching it and hope that it will not affect their researches. But it usually does.

This was never more clear than in the evaluation of training courses. Otto Klineberg, who was working for UNESCO (the United Nations Educational, Scientific, and Cultural Organization), visited the Institute and was instrumental in securing for the NIIP the UK survey and coordination of European research for a European Productivity Association survey, *Training Factory Workers* (NIIP, 1956). Significantly, the chapter on evaluation of training begins 'It was apparent from an early stage that statistical evaluation of training in the generally accepted sense of the word would not be possible'. The fact was that several training courses which had been carefully evaluated for results and had left records to prove it had vanished without trace, while courses which seemed to the investigator to have no evidence of effectiveness, but which had the confidence of management, were flourishing.

The NIIP plainly had a greater reputation internationally than in Britain, and we had some interesting overseas visitors. Isabel Blain, one of the Directors of the NIIP, had gained her PhD in the United States, and her tutor, Lillian Gilbreth, came to see us. She was by that time over retirement age and rather deaf, but still had a sharp analytical mind. From Dr Blain I learned the NIIP approach to Work Study for Training, which studied efficient working methods, but eschewed relating them to piecework payments. My most fascinating application of this was in a factory producing expensive greetings cards. 'If Mr. Duncan doesn't produce results for us, we'll have his guts for braces,' said the managing director amiably on my being introduced. Suitably motivated, I was able to prove within a month that systematic work study, selection and training of girls, in an assembly task involving feathers and glue, could produce, with two days' training, levels of output which to that point had taken six months to reach.

Gunnar Westerlund came from Sweden to discuss with us the future of functional supervision; and one highlight of my early years with the NIIP was my assignment to conduct a lady professor from the Sorbonne, Madame Suzanne Pacaud, on a survey, lasting a week, of supervisory training practices in British industry. Madame Pacaud spoke very little English, and my high-school French was sadly out of practice; so we made a pact, which worked out well in practice; as far as possible I would speak French and she would speak English. All went well until our visit to Glacier Metal, famous for its pioneering Managing Director Wilfred Brown and the subject of *The Changing Culture of a Factory* (Jaques, 1951). When Madame asked 'What do you make?', 'White metal bearings' was the answer, in which each word was comprehensible, but the combination baffling.

'Similar to a ball race' was the next explanation, which made matters even worse. Madame suggested that perhaps we ought to go and see a ball race, but we proposed that an apprentice would actually bring one to her. Meanwhile, we studied our respective dictionaries and found '*billes de l'engrenage*' – gear balls, which our hosts thought was by French standards logical, but unduly specific.

In 1956 Clifford Frisby, Director of the NIIP for many years, became the President of the International Association of Applied Psychology and the NIIP played host to a most impressive collection of psychologists from all over the world. Names which had a reality for us only from papers we had read suddenly became faces, people we could talk to and exchange ideas with. One memorable figure, who could be counted on for controversial interventions, appeared in the brown habit of a Capuchin monk. Only later did it emerge that this was Father Peter Dempsey, head of the Department of Applied Psychology in Cork, who had a notable reputation for settling industrial disputes in that region. Ten years later, when I worked in Dublin, he became a good friend, and as editor of the journal *Manpower and Applied Psychology* he published my paper 'The psychology of taxation' in 1967 (Duncan, 1967).

The archives at the NIIP were excellent. On the one hand, there was an excellent library containing reports dating back to the Industrial Fatigue Research Board investigations of the First World War, out of which industrial psychology was born, and these I read with interest. Problems which lent themselves to national surveys were the responsibility of the Industrial Health Research Board, but problems peculiar to one employer could be investigated by the NIIP. So there was also an array of filing cabinets containing reports on all the investigations carried out by NIIP staff since its inception in 1921. These had two consequences for me. The investigations files contained excellent reports on a variety of techniques used by Institute investigators engaged in solving problems of working conditions, training and working methods. One of the most interesting was the account of the product testing, design and pack development of the 'Black Magic' box of chocolates by the NIIP for Rowntree in 1933; this stimulated my interest in the application of psychology to consumer research (which by then had been declared ultra vires for the NIIP).

The other consequence was statistical. Efforts at improving the selection, training and motivation of supervisors were hampered by high labour turnover in an era of full employment, and the Labour Turnover Index tended to conceal any progress made in improving survival rates of newcomers and building up a stable workforce. From the library I was able to learn of the early investigations of Major Greenwood into the statistics of labour turnover. He it was who advised the government that it would be unnecessary to have a redundancy programme for women in munitions work. Natural wastage was so high that merely ceasing to recruit would solve the problem. He alerted me to the significance of survival rates, labour stability, even constituent rates of loss.

So in 1955 I developed a triangular matrix for recording the history of intake populations. Not only could it be used as a register of labour turnover but it also provided the basis for more significant calculations, such as labour stability and survival rates. My publication on tabular methods of recording labour losses (Duncan, 1955) so impressed the Director that, through the Institute of Personnel Management, he persuaded 50 member firms to keep tabular records of labour losses for four years.

These statistics became important in extreme cases where an intricate job necessitated a long training period, and losses were so high that too few survived the training. High labour losses provided the necessary numbers to apply chi-squared tests to generate advice. One employer discovered that the economic optimum for one task with a long training period was to recruit for it single women under 23 and over 28, and married women between these ages. The 'mirror test' was his selection test. 'You put a mirror under their nose. If it clouds, hire her, then allocate.'

When the NIIP was founded in 1921, Cyril Burt established its Vocational Guidance department and recruited Winifred Raphael to run it. The operation was never profitable, as those with most need for guidance were least able to pay for it, so Winifred Raphael soon found herself developing industrial investigations. In particular, in the 1920s, she developed attitude survey techniques for industry, which predated the much better publicised Hawthorne experiments. Alec Rodger succeeded her as head of Vocational Guidance in the 1930s and from his experience of career counselling borstal boys developed the 'Seven Point Plan' upon which NIIP approaches to vocational guidance, selection and job specification were founded.

When I joined the NIIP, Mary Stott and Margaret Grainger were the Vocational Guidance staff, so adult males seeking career guidance, for example retiring army or navy officers, were referred to me. One such was Godfrey Rampling, a gold medallist in the 1936 Berlin Olympics (and father of Charlotte). Another was a writer in the Royal Navy who found a new career in the production side of advertising. One was a member of the Greek royal family who became a landscape gardener. Another was the younger son of a duke, who by the age of 21 had a pilot's licence, had driven racing cars, was proficient in skiing, horse riding, golf and snooker, and who wanted advice on how to achieve, by the age of 30, a salary sufficient for him to pay for these pursuits. I discovered that although his basic intelligence was high, his formal education had been neglected and that he had the reading ability of a nine-year-old. I sent him on a remedial reading course, from which he greatly benefited.

I liked vocational guidance because, although it made use of my considerable experience of organisation of industry and commerce, it also provided subjects who were cooperative, honest and appreciative of the efforts one was making on their behalf. One had considerable freedom in the use of psychometric techniques. I gained there some skill in the interpretation of projective tests, such as Murray's Thematic Apperception Test and Crown's Word Association Test (Murray, 1938). Long term, there was gratification in discovering that a three-hour test battery, a one-hour interview with feedback and subsequent report could completely change the life of an individual for the better. However, vocational guidance, because it proceeds on a case-by-case basis, does not lend itself to statistical validation, so it is easy to write it off as unprofitable. After a year primarily in research, I was transferred to industrial investigations under Winifred Raphael.

My introduction to human–machine interaction took the form of involvement in problems of inspection in industry, in which I developed some expertise. My biggest assignment was an investigation into quality inspection of car tyres. Winifred Raphael accompanied me, and rather shocked me by apparently going to sleep as I interviewed the factory manager to survey the problem. When she awoke and asked some probing supplementary questions it was plain that although I had been given prime responsibility for investigation, she was well aware of what had been going on. The problem was that some police chases had been abruptly terminated by blowouts of the tyres of police vehicles, and quality improvements were needed.

The investigations raised numerous problems of environmental measurement. Tyre moulds produce heat, steam and carbon dust, so the workplace was hot, humid and dirty. It was also poorly lit. I interviewed all the inspectors and discovered that they became inspectors when they were too old to cope with the physically demanding task of tyre moulding. I tested their eyesight with a Stereosette machine and found that their eyesight needed attention. I used a lightmeter to test the light falling on the surface of the tyre they were testing and it registered 2 foot-candles. It was suggested that a sense of touch was more important than eyesight in detecting faults in tyres, but rubber retains heat well, and when I measured the surface temperature of tyres coming directly from the moulds they were plainly too hot to handle until about 20 minutes had elapsed. There was no mark on the tyre to show who had inspected it, so I instituted a marking system. This tripled the rate of rejection and brought the production line to a standstill within three hours, and was promptly discontinued. All of this told me that even with corrected eyesight they had too little light and too little time to inspect properly, and had also no clear idea of what they were looking for anyway. I asked the design and technical staff for a full list of likely defects, but was told that details of tyre construction were too confidential to be released to inspectors.

At this point I had to negotiate with top management. As a result I was able to insist on being provided with a set of tyres and tyre sections containing all known defects, and was able to use it first as a test of knowledge and competence of each inspector, and then as a basis of a training course for inspectors.

In my report to management I described a jig which I invented which would bring light to the workplace and mechanically grip the tyre, spread the beads to rotate it, and make the task of inspection less physically demanding. Visiting the factory some years later, I discovered that my report had lain in a drawer for two years, but was then fully implemented.

My very first industrial investigation, however, was an attitude survey of morale in a printing firm. The technique for this was non-directive interviewing covering satisfaction with a wide range of issues, but excluding pay and matters on which workers go on strike. We recorded the interviews in writing, on Kalamazoo cards with 120 holes round the edges. All top management were surveyed and a random sample from the workforce. Back at base, we conducted a content analysis of the material, developed a coding frame, punched the appropriate holes and used fine knitting needles to accumulate the frequencies. Very educative was a session in which Winifred Raphael counselled the managing director on faults in his management of which he was unaware, and advised him on how to be a better personnel manager. This was good experience in non-directive interviewing covering a defined field, in content analysis to develop a coding frame, and in data stacking to produce a coherent report, all of which I later used profitably in consumer research. But there we developed coding frames from pilot interviews to develop questionnaires; these could be plotted on to Hollerith or punched cards and analysed by computer.

By 1956, the NIIP had developed a substantial range of tests which were made available to psychologists and others attending NIIP courses. Industrial investigators were not allowed to use these tests but developed for each investigation work-sample tests or domain-referenced tests which were then regarded as the property of the commissioning client and not published. This is the origin of the collection of tests in the Science Museum.

An exception to this rule was the Engineering Apprentice Battery, which was originally developed for Metropolitan Vickers in 1928, and thereafter sold as a standard package, using some of the published tests of the NIIP. There was a fixed routine for installing this battery and training personnel managers to use it, and my early experience in training people to use psychometric tests came from installing these batteries in engineering works. In 1958, I was given the task of visiting all the factories in which the tests had been installed and collecting data which could be used to validate the battery. This was later the subject of an NIIP report (Frisby *et al.*, 1959).

My experience of training personnel managers in the field led to my being given the responsibility as Senior Tutor for running the courses held at the Institute. These typically lasted three weeks. The first week was devoted to job specification using the Seven Point Plan model, on the grounds that everyone involved in selection ought to have a way of defining what they were looking for. This gave me experience, useful later, in job specification. The second week was devoted to training in interviewing; it was considered that the high reliability resulting from good test design could easily be compromised by poor interviewing. It was accepted that, in spite of its unreliability, the interview would continue to be an essential part of any selection procedure, so that an improvement in interviewing standards would improve the predictive value of the procedure. Only when course members had proved that they were capable of conducting a competent interview were they allowed to attend the third week of the course, which was devoted to intelligence and aptitude testing. Personality testing was not seen as sufficiently reliable and dependable to be taught, other than as assessable by interview.

While the NIIP had a real expertise in assessing individual differences, it had limitations in applied social psychology and the collection of data by sample surveys and questionnaires. To extend my competences I joined Attwood Statistics Limited as statistician to their Household Panel of 2,000 housewives who reported weekly on their purchases during the week. I had an enjoyable month calculating the significance of the difference between two percentages, and using non-parametric statistics to assess repeat purchases and brand loyalty. However, around 1957 Vance Packard wrote a book called *The Hidden Persuaders*, a graphic account of the nefarious activities of psychologists in persuading people to buy things for which they had no need (Packard, 1957). Marketing managers were greatly impressed and insisted that any market research organisation of any size must have a psychologist for them to consult. So, after a month, I was made Manager of Ad Hoc Surveys, in charge of six graduate survey executives, a statistician and a production manager who controlled 25 analysts who spent their time on hand tabulations turning questionnaires into tables of figures.

In comparison with the NIIP there were tremendous freedoms for psychologists in the use of psychometric and statistical techniques. Consumers were flattered to think that their views on products were being sought and would readily give their time in providing them. But it became clear at an early stage that consumers were by no means the easy prey that Packard had suggested and believed only a fraction of what advertisers told them. I learned a lot of new techniques, some of them quite useless, and about questionnaire design and filtering, about sample size and design, and, most important, how to structure a statistical report at an early stage.

This required a new set of competences in time management. Clients would expect a fully costed proposal within 24 hours of providing a brief and this had to include a promised date for a first report. Executives had to be prevented from procrastination, motivated to produce, helped over hurdles, rescued from panic situations and encouraged to learn from experience.

Altogether, it was a hair-raising but enjoyable training in applied social science, and I kept in touch with developments in this field subsequently. But a number of influences drew me in 1960 into Management Selection Limited, a company established in 1956 to assist with executive appointments, one of whose founding directors was Alec Rodger. Executive selection and assessment were to be my main business for the next 30 years.

It might be expected that assessment of individuals would be the major competence of a psychologist in this work; but in fact a competence in job specification was more important. The more senior the appointment, the more people there were anxious to fill it, and a competence in organisational psychology was necessary to ensure that those short-listed were genuinely the most relevant for the situation. If competence in the psychological assessment of individuals was required, it was needed to assess clients, who wanted quick results and were not always clear about what their real requirements were. Even a promising applicant could fail if the client was not fully involved in the selection process.

Psychologists were a small minority in executive selection in 1960, but had a good record of success. After investigation of why this should be, I concluded that it was because they refused to believe that their client was mad. If a client behaved in an unexpected fashion, it would be because there was some underlying requirement which had not been explained. Discussion of the rejected short-listed candidates would cast light on this and would enable a successful appointment.

Life changed radically for me in 1975, when, by means of a 'management buyout', I became the owner of TEAM (Management Appointments) Limited, the company which had employed me. On the one hand, I could do exactly as I pleased, make a fortune or build up a conglomerate. On the other hand, it was like being unemployed; I had to set my own work objectives and decide how these would be achieved; I had to decide who I would accept as clients, colleagues, co-workers, or employees. My attachment to occupational psychology as a profession asserted itself, and for the next 25 years I was more concerned with exercising my competences over a full range of my preferred field than with making a fortune.

When one is exercising one's skills in a professional career which has been a deliberate choice, retirement is characterised, not so much as a cessation of work as by the arrival of pensions, so 'in receipt of pensions' is a more proper description than 'retired'.

I joined the British Psychological Society in 1957, and ever since the Society gained its Royal Charter I had argued that Chartered status was necessary to give psychology its proper place in public esteem. So I became a chartered occupational psychologist as soon as I could. I then learned that there is no escape from lifelong learning and that part of chartering is continued professional development. This now applies for me, training psychologists in the various applications of intelligence, aptitude and personality tests, supervising them on their way to chartered status, and assessing those whom I have not supervised. It also means making more effort to have published papers written in the past and neglected since.

20

The making of a psychologist: a late developer

Fay Fransella

Writing this chapter was particularly difficult because my life as a psychologist did not start until I was 34. So, to begin with, I have selected events that may have created the person who, in 1956, decided to study psychology. It all started on 1 October 1925. I was born in Jersey, in the Channel Islands, as Fay Feilden, when my mother was 25 years old and my father 54. My father had decided not to marry until he had enough money to keep a wife and family. To achieve this goal, he spent several years as governor of the Bahr el-Ghazal province in southern Sudan, for which double army pension was paid because of its extreme climate. He had already retired before I was born.

I mention all that to explain the trauma he must have experienced when my mother died. I was six and my brother one year old. The trauma was such that I do not remember seeing him for a long time. In fact, my memory of my whole childhood is patchy and I certainly have no memory at all of my mother. So, my life began when I was six, in a world I experienced as bleak and lonely. My brother and I were looked after by a series of professionally trained nurses who seemed to care more for a child's physical than psychological wellbeing. There were constant changes. Perhaps there were cuddles from one 'minder' when I was about ten years old, but I remember few others. My father loved us dearly, I know, but he was not a demonstrative man.

All that made me look inwards and take pleasure in my own company. But some positive early childhood memories stand out. For instance, my father bought me a steam engine which actually made enough steam to drive a train. He also helped me wire up my dolls' house for electricity and I was most annoyed because the only light switches available were too large. I suppose he bought me things that would now be seen as 'boys' toys'. Those experiences may have contributed to my lifelong pleasure in making machines work and, perhaps, even research.

When I was eight, my father decided that running a house was more than he could cope with and from then on our permanent home was a hotel.

Schooling was fairly disrupted. I went to boarding school in England as I was thought to need the company of children of my own age – then ten. In 1937, at the age of 12, I was sent to the Jersey Girls' College because of the unrest in Europe. At 14 we evacuated ourselves from Jersey to my aunt and uncle near Tunbridge Wells, because of the imminent invasion of the Channel Islands by the Germans. Back in my English boarding school I was put in the 'dunces' class for those not expected to pass the approaching School Certificate exams. We did not take Latin, geometry or algebra – arithmetic was considered not too difficult for us, but I even managed to fail that!

At some point at school I rebelled, quietly and privately, and decided to show them they were wrong about me. I did not consciously spell this out to myself, but I decided to use the near-photographic memory I seemed to have and to learn verbatim all my history notes – the head mistress taught history. I left school immediately after the exams, as I was not considered bright enough to go into the sixth form, so I received the validation of my efforts at home. Beside the distinction I got for history, my head mistress had scribbled 'you came top of the entire Middle and Upper Fifths with 92 marks!!' That was a landmark event in my life. I started to think I had some control over life and could achieve something if I set my mind to it.

Looking back on that personal history, I suppose these days someone would have sent me to a counsellor. I am sure that it would have made a difference to my life. But I have no doubt that I would now be a different person – and I would not want that.

My second rebellion, or behavioural experiment, in personal construct terms, was against the life mapped out for me – to look after my aged father and be a wife. I left home to train as an occupational therapist. My first job in 1945 was in a large psychiatric hospital then converted into a military hospital. When it reverted to being psychiatric again in 1947, I was able to stay on because I had qualified in both psychological and physical fields. It was there, at Horton Hospital, Epsom, that I learned about people with major problems, especially the long-stay person diagnosed as schizophrenic. I could easily relate that to some recognition of my own childhood loneliness and feelings of being cut off from the world. Those large hospitals were, indeed, asylums, but many of the treatments were harsh.

During one of my holidays, back in Jersey, I spent an enjoyable two weeks learning to fly a Tiger Moth. We stalled, dived, looped the loop – all with an open cockpit. My only fear was that I could never make out where the airport was. Quite difficult, I was repeatedly told, on a tiny island. Again, it was machines and the control of machines that was so exciting.

1   On the path to being a psychologist

My life then did not run smoothly. In 1948 I entered a disastrous marriage and, in 1949, was found to have pulmonary tuberculosis after a routine X-ray examination. I was also pregnant. That was all repeated a couple of years later. Each involved a termination, months in bed and a year off work. Back at work the second time and now divorced, there was something different. A dissatisfaction with life. Surely there must be something more. Here was I, Fay Fransella, a free woman, having a large staff and the largest occupational therapy department in the country and just 30.

I did two things that moved me towards becoming a psychologist. For some reason, I took an extramural evening course in social psychology, and much enjoyed the experience. At work I asked a crucial question: 'How do I know that anything we do in occupational therapy does any good?' Our clinical psychologist, Ricky Grygier, designed a piece of research to study the effect of the drug chlorpromazine on long-stay patients, all undergoing a 'total-push' programme of activity. The majority of patients improved in both the drug and placebo group, and some in the placebo group were actually discharged (Fransella, 1960).

What had I learned over those years as an occupational therapist? I learned the importance of listening and of interpreting non-verbal behaviours, and gained invaluable experience of working with those suffering a wide range of serious psychological problems. I had the skills to create and manage a large department. Importantly, I had discovered I wanted to be a psychologist who could design research projects. So, I decided to give up a well paid job and apply to go to university in my mid-30s. But there was a snag. I had neither A levels nor Latin. University College London offered me a place for 1958 if I got two A levels and O level Latin. So, after two more years as an occupational therapist, attending evening classes in three subjects, I started my degree course.

I had expected to learn about research, but I certainly did not expect to learn about the dance of the bees and the behaviour of sticklebacks – all of which I found truly fascinating. If that was what psychology was about, so be it. Apart from giving me an abiding interest in those non-human subjects, I got a very good grounding in research design, statistics and how psychology was the scientific study of behaviour. It was quite easy to enjoy those three years with such teachers as Bob Audley, Norman Dixon, Jonkheere and Professor Drew. I was delighted with the good upper second degree I got. Another landmark event was finding I had attained a very high mark for the three-hour essay. I still remember that sinking feeling on realising there was no question I could write on for 20 minutes let alone three hours! In desperation I chose the question: '"When the animal psychologist in America met up with the albino rat he softly and suddenly vanished away as a comparative scientist" (Beach)'. All those lovely bees and sticklebacks came into their own. But I construed the first-class mark I got as suggesting I might be able to write.

2   Being a psychologist

From University College I took up a place at the Institute of Psychiatry, London, to do clinical psychology. I learned about behaviour therapy but never met the man on the floor below – Hans Eysenck. I learned from Gwynne Jones not to take psychometrics too seriously and from Monte Shapiro the importance of face validity – 'no one ever complained they could not rotate their blocks in a test for "brain damage"'. There I also got my first chance to teach, an activity I have continued in one form or another to the present. After gaining the clinical diploma in 1962, I remained at the Institute for another three years as Assistant Lecturer and registered for a full-time PhD. It was my belief that no one would pay any attention to a middle-aged female psychologist without one. With Reg Beech as my supervisor, I used good experimental methods to study the speech of stutterers when speaking in time to a metronome. But I sneaked in a bit of repertory grid work to look at how my 'subjects' saw themselves. Vic Meyer, my external examiner, obviously thought that was all right. I thus started working with repertory grids well before I found that Kelly also had a theory of psychology. Reg Beech suggested that we co-author a book on stuttering. It was with some misgivings that I agreed. It looked, and was, a dull book (Beech and Fransella, 1968).

It was in 1964 that I got hooked on personal construct theory. Brunel University started a series of 'Kelly seminars' and Neil Warren wrote to George Kelly to ask if he knew of anyone interested in his work who would in be England during that academic year. Kelly said he would come himself – to everyone's amazement. His seminar was on 'The strategy of psychological research' (Kelly, 1965). Other seminars were given by Neil Warren, Don Bannister, Tom Ravenette, Miller Mair and Thelma Veness and myself. I chose to compare Kelly's grids and Osgood's semantic differential (Fransella, 1964). Participating in that event led me to read George Kelly's two volumes (Kelly, 1955).

While at the Institute I persuaded Don Bannister to work with me on the Grid Test of Schizophrenic Thought Disorder (Bannister and Fransella, 1966). It was not to be a diagnostic test but one that could identify early onset so that remedial action could be taken. Of course, it was used as a test and it certainly generated a wealth of journal papers showing that it was/was not valid, reliable/ unreliable. I am not proud of having used the repertory grid in that nomothetic way, and would not now do such work, but I was then seriously influenced by the psychometric tradition of the Institute.

In 1965, with my PhD achieved and approaching the end of my appointment, I was 40 years old and applied for a research grant to explore how personal construct theory could be used to understand and treat stuttering. I saw that as a harsh test of the theory's usefulness and range of convenience. I was both relieved and appalled when I got a Mental Health Research Fund grant for three years. I had once more launched myself into uncharted waters. Professor Arthur Crisp gave me a room in his St George's Hospital Department of Psychiatry, in which Gwynne Jones was a senior lecturer. After six months of head scratching and reading, my eventual hypothesis was that people stutter because they have no alternative – it is their way of life. To stutter enables them to predict how the other will react to them, whereas to be fluent would precipitate them into a world relatively devoid of meaning. My role in therapy therefore was to help people who stutter to construe themselves as fluent speakers. I used repeated implications grids (Hinkle, 1965) to measure changes in construing of the self as a stutterer and as a fluent speaker.

All in all, it was a wonderfully rewarding experience. I had never worked so closely with others before on a one-to-one basis. But it was demonstrating the link between construing and behaviour that was particularly exciting. As the person became more fluent, so the meaningfulness of being a fluent person increased. Personal construct theory says that it should be so, but here was evidence.

Not only did that research provide validation for the usefulness of personal construct theory but it also proved to be of use to many speech and language therapists. Subsequent work has built on my recommendation that, in a therapy setting, a personal construct approach is best when used in conjunction with techniques to reduce the disfluent speech. One result was linked to a finding in my first piece of published grid work (Fransella and Adams, 1966). A man in prison for committing acts of arson did not see himself as an arsonist but more as someone who was punishing wrongdoers. That same divorce between self-perception and behaviour appeared with many of my sample of those who stuttered – they did not see themselves as stutterers. It emerged again later with samples of obese people (e.g. Fransella, 1970) and alcoholics (Hoy, 1973). We can use stereotypes that others apply to us but we exempt ourselves from that stereotype. I tried to delve more deeply into that (Fransella, 1977) but there is still more to do there.

While at St George's, I ran psychology classes for the University Extramural Department to help improve my teaching skills. On one of the lecture tours I was now being invited to conduct, I stayed with the Kellys in Boston. At that time, George Kelly was Riklis Professor of Behavioural Science at Brandeis University. I taped an interview with him but was too nervous to ask interesting questions. My advice now is, if one gets an opportunity like that, use it.

The book on my stuttering research was not published until 1972 (Fransella, 1972). It was delayed because Don Bannister and I had started writing *Inquiring Man*, published in 1971 (Bannister and Fransella, 1971). Our target reader was the undergraduate psychology student. Three editions of that book kept it in print until March 1999. As our goal was 'to spread the word', I think we had some success.

In 1968 I married my second husband, Roy Hodson, exactly 20 years after my first marriage. Roy was then on the editorial staff of *The Times* and later on the *Financial Times*. Apart from the pleasures of being happily married, he introduced me to the excitements of sailing. On the principle 'if you can't beat them, join them', I went on a yachtmaster's course. Navigation is very interesting, especially when taught by ex-tanker captains. Sailing many times to France brought back to me my love of the sea. I also discovered what I would be like facing real physical danger, as well as the peace of a gently rocking boat on a mooring in a small foreign harbour.

At the end of the stuttering research, Arthur Crisp, internationally known for his work with those suffering from anorexia nervosa and obesity, gave me a year's research grant to work with him. We published a series of papers on changes in construing accompanying weight change in both groups of people (e.g. Fransella and Crisp, 1970). That was followed by a year working with Don Bannister's research team on helping those diagnosed as having schizophrenic thought disorder to become more 'thought ordered'.

I now had six years of full-time research behind me, plus three books and several chapters and journal papers. My areas of expertise were stuttering, personal construct theory repertory grid methods and weight disorders. In 1971 I was appointed Senior Lecturer at the Royal Free Hospital School of Medicine, London, and stayed there until 1982, by which time I was a Reader. It so happened that Professor Gerald Russell, in whose Department of Psychiatry I was, also had an international reputation in the field of weight disorders. I continued my research interests, including work on body image (e.g. Fransella, 1978), and was PhD supervisor to several people, including Eric Button, who applied my theoretical ideas and methods on stuttering to account for people with weight problems (Button, 1980). But teaching a hundred medical students at a time, half of whom did not really want to learn about 'psychology', was my main task and a very real challenge it was.

I am not conscious of being a writer-holic, but there do seem to be many books at this time. In 1975, *Need to Change?* (Fransella, 1975) was part of Peter Herriot's series on Essential Psychology and 'spread the word' about Kelly's psychology to six foreign countries – including a translation into Serbo-Croatian. In 1977 came *A Manual for Repertory Grid Technique* (Fransella and Bannister, 1977), which Don Bannister and I wrote because we were spending too much time helping people design grids and thought we might as well write a book for them – it stayed in print for 22 years. Also in 1977, Kay Frost and I published *On Being a Woman* (Fransella and Frost, 1977). I have never been an active campaigner for women's rights but privately have done my best to redress the obvious imbalance in society. All these writings had a personal construct slant.

The first public platform for personal construct theory in the United States was in 1975, exactly 20 years after it was published. Al Landfield arranged for that year's Nebraska Symposium on Motivation to be devoted to George Kelly's theory. After that, I managed to persuade Don Bannister and Miller Mair to join me in organising an International Congress in Personal Construct Psychology at Oxford University in 1977. Those congresses have continued biennially ever since at different venues around the world.

By the late 1970s, I was feeling real conflict between my work for the Medical School and the pressure to write and to give talks on personal construct theory internationally. That feeling was coupled with an increasing dissatisfaction with the psychology I was having to teach. Something had to give. So, in 1982, I took early retirement. Soon after leaving the Royal Free, I learned that the University had awarded me the title of Emeritus Reader in Clinical Psychology. That is something I take great pride in.

3   The founding of the Centre for Personal Construct Psychology

After leaving the university, I leaped into the unknown again by founding the
first centre devoted solely to the teaching and application of personal construct
psychology. My stated aim for the Centre was 'to give personal construct psychology to anyone who wants it'! Those who helped set up and then run the Centre
included Peggy Dalton (speech therapist), Gavin Dunnett (psychiatrist), Helen
Jones (counsellor), Chris Thorman and, of course, Don Bannister (psychologists).
All have continued to work with and write about the psychology. These people
make the point that George Kelly's psychology is not just for psychologists.

The Centre started by offering courses and a counselling and psychotherapy
service. But we unexpectedly tapped an interest in organisations. The head of
training at British Airways said he could not retrain the workforce before privatis-
ation until he knew how people viewed themselves and their work now. He had
read *Inquiring Man* in Australia and felt that personal construct psychology could
tell him. The 'diagnostic research' I developed for that work provided data on
how the various groups perceived their work, passengers, their management, the
company itself and so forth. The group profiles were used in British Airways'
retraining programme, Putting People First. Here I was able to combine my
interest in research with the psychology I espoused.

The Centre continues with such research work today. Much has been carried
out in Ireland with the help of Sean Brophy. The Centre also developed personal
construct methods to work with small groups and individuals within organisations.

A major achievement of the Centre has been becoming a member organisation
of the United Kingdom Council for Psychotherapy (UKCP). All those gaining
the Centre's diploma in personal construct psychotherapy can be registered with
the UKCP as 'PCP psychotherapists'. All that raised an interesting point for me.
For years I had been doing what could reasonably be called psychotherapy – and
was even teaching it! But, as I explained in Windy Dryden's book *On Becoming a
Psychotherapist* (Fransella, 1989), I have had training in behaviour therapy but
certainly not in psychotherapy. However, by the process of 'grandparenting' I
became registered as a PCP psychotherapist with UKCP.

I was not good at running a business. Philip Boxer, a director of the Centre
and on the staff at the London School of Management, forcibly said 'you are
paying people too much'. I am sure there were other factors involved, but we
were always chasing our own financial tails. In the end, the recession of the early
1990s put paid to our having a base of bricks and mortar in London and we
became a 'virtual organisation' with no fixed abode. The work the Centre had
built up over ten years was divided up. Ray Evans continued the courses from
his home in London, Fiorella Gatti-Doyle became the organiser of the psychotherapy service and I dealt with work for organisations.

Nick Reed then joined forces with me in 1997. He is a solicitor with much
experience working with and within organisations. He sees personal construct
psychology as having enormous value for management and organisational

development. We also continue to offer courses and have recently launched a six-module distance-learning programme. There are many people around the world interested in Kelly's ideas and his repertory grid who have no access to face-to-face courses.

4   Personal construct psychology now

Moving to the present, personal construct psychology is now well established and validated in Britain by being recognised as a specific psychotherapy. The constructivist and constructionist movements and, running alongside these, the growth of interest in qualitative as opposed to rigid quantitative methods of enquiry are of significance for how the psychology develops. Kelly, of course, did not invent constructivism, but there seems no doubt that it is he who was largely responsible for its resurgence in the 1980s and 1990s with his own philosophy constructive alternativism. In my opinion, Kelly did not base his ideas on the work of past philosophers but on the ideas he learned in his first degree courses, in physics and mathematics (Fransella, 1972, 1999). Again, qualitative methods are not new for those working within the personal construct framework, because Kelly showed how these can be combined with quantitative methods in the repertory grid.

My last book, *George Kelly* (Fransella, 1995), was part of a series on 'Key Figures in Psychotherapy'. Since psychotherapy is no more and no less than the application of his theory to those with a problem, the book allowed me to give my views on a number of matters. In particular, I explained why I thought the constructivist movement might result in Kelly's psychological theory being lost sight of. But I now think that unlikely. Too many people, not all psychologists, are using his theory of psychology in their day-to-day work. It is now clear to me that the constructivist movement and interest in qualitative methods have paved the way for a much wider acceptance of personal construct theory and repertory grid methods, and I see no reason why they will not continue to be accepted and used.

5   Personal construct psychology and the future

Where may people take Kelly's ideas in the twenty-first century? They will certainly continue to apply them to new areas. For instance, very recently they have been applied to autism (Procter, 1999), knowledge management (Sparrow, 1998) and literary criticism (Lee, 1999), and much else besides. But Kelly gave us an interesting pointer to the theoretical development of personal construct psychology. He suggested elaborating his fundamental postulate, which starts 'A person's processes are psychologically channelized…', to read, 'It is in the nature of life to be channelized by the ways events are anticipated'. He goes on to say 'while I am not prepared to defend this assumption with great skill or the weight of much evidence, it does intrigue me and I cannot help but wonder where we would be led if we ventured to start from such a premise' (Kelly, 1980). Back to the bees and sticklebacks? Perhaps even a new comparative psychology? I do hope someone does take up that idea and give it serious attention.

6   A personal overview

Looking back, I see that I have spent ten years as an occupational therapist, 20 years as a psychologist doing research or employed by the University of London and, within a few years and *Deus vale*, will have spent 20 years working solely with and for personal construct psychology in the Centre of that name. In those 40 years as a psychologist, I can but marvel at how lucky I have been in the people I have known and the chances I have had – particularly making contact with George Kelly and his ideas.

Apart from the lectures, workshops at home and abroad, journal papers, chapters and books, I am pleased to have shown how useful that psychology can be in my research on stuttering – research that is still exerting an influence (Stewart and Birdsall, 1999). I believe I have helped to establish personal construct psychology by inaugurating the international biennial congresses; founding of the Centre in London, with its work in organisations, and becoming a member of UKCP; and also in having found David Stonestreet at Routledge, who wanted to be the person 'who republished Kelly's two volumes' when Norton let them go out of print. Personal construct psychology has international recognition with active organisations, particularly in Australia, Germany, Italy, Serbia, Spain, and the United States and at the time of writing my *George Kelly* was being translated into Chinese.

A last question must be to what extent has personal construct theory influenced psychology? There is, of course, Walter Mischel, who, mistakenly, called George Kelly 'the first cognitive psychologist' (Mischel, 1980). More recently Rom Harré and Grant Gillett have acknowledged their debt to Kelly's ideas in *The Discursive Mind* (Harré and Gillet, 1994) and what has come to be called 'narrative psychology' also finds its origins in Kelly's work. Above all that, it seems that Kelly has influenced the whole movement of constructivism and the upsurge of interest in qualitative methods of measurement. I can but be proud if I have played some part in promoting that.

21

Adventures of a maverick

Richard L. Gregory

1   In the beginning – school and war

My father was a scientist – an astronomer – being the first director of the University of London Observatory. So I was brought up with optical instruments and also with the importance of making observations. My father measured the distances of the nearer stars for most of his life – using parallax from camera positions separated by the 186,000,000-mile diameter of the Earth's orbit around the Sun. These measurements are crucial for scaling the universe. Is it an accident that years later I tried to scale and explain distortions of visual space (Gregory, 1969a)?

At school I learned simple electronics in our radio club, as we built our own short-wave receivers, and then more in the Royal Air Force (RAF) at Number One Signal School at Cranwell. Cranwell had excellent teaching when I was there in 1941 and was highly civilised, with its drama and music societies.

I should have been posted to the Gold Coast, but a telegram recalling me from Christmas leave did not arrive in time so I was posted to Training Command in Canada. This was a year flying around the Bay of Fundy, sometimes testing radio communications and radar; then six months with the Fleet Air Arm at Kingston, Ontario, where I had my own boat and sailed among the Thousand Islands. During almost six years in the RAF I had time to read and think on physics and biology, and wrote a science column in a local RAF magazine. I also read C. G. Jung (developing a permanent allergy) and William James (who remains a hero). No doubt I absorbed some useful concepts from the technologies of radio and radar.

After the German war was over in 1945, and with the Japanese war near its end, the RAF offered me an unusual and useful experience. I was posted (mysteriously) directly by the Air Ministry to explain radar and communication systems to the public. This I did at an ambitious exhibition set up at the John Lewis bombsite in Oxford Street, London: the first jet plane (I actually saw its first flight, at Cranwell) and secrets were revealed. We explained how things worked, to all manner of people, especially factory workers, who made bits and pieces throughout the war but for secrecy reasons without knowing what they were for. We had four million visitors in six months. Is this a record? The experience was invaluable and great fun. Perhaps it led, 30 years later, to the founding of the Exploratory, the first hands-on science centre in Britain.

2   Cambridge and the influence of Kenneth Craik's engineering ideas

After the war, I was lucky to get a scholarship to Cambridge, by the imaginative scheme of the time, the Forces Preliminary Examination. Although Cambridge was a family tradition on both sides, my father thought it would be a waste of time and probably would not have made it possible without the scholarship. So the war did me a lot of good. Getting to Cambridge in 1947 was truly an impossible dream come true. I read moral sciences (for the first two years philosophy, ethics, logic and psychology). I just missed Wittgenstein, but was taught by Richard Braithwaite, C.D. Broad, Alfred Ewing and John Wisdom. Some of us spent an hour a week with Bertrand Russell (then aged 76), which was wonderful, though he was rather bored with mathematical logic and mainly concerned with the politics of immediately postwar Europe.

The third year was entirely psychology. This was 1949–1950, so I was among the last of Sir Frederic Bartlett's students. He was a major life influence, remaining in memory the revered intellectual grandfather. (Something of this is described in my 1999 Bartlett Lecture.) On the special occasions of his weekly lectures, he would share ideas that were interesting him, at that time the importance of prediction in skills. His favourite example was from cricket, which he loved: the batsman reading the present from his past knowledge, to predict the immediate future within his 'range of anticipation'. Such ideas countered the stimulus–response accounts of behaviourism that still dominated American psychology. Bartlett had the ability to ignore whole chunks of subjects, concentrating on what mattered. His judgement was right remarkably often, though perhaps he was too cavalier over statistics. I followed him in trying to save my students from the more idiotic ideas – especially the fashionable mathematical models of learning – though no doubt without his wisdom.

Cambridge psychology was deeply affected by Kenneth Craik's ideas, as presented in his short book *The Nature of Explanation* (Craik, 1943). Craik's premature death by an accident in 1945, when he was knocked off his bicycle outside his Cambridge college, was a major tragedy. His ideas inspired British psychology at that time and remain with us today. Much came from applying wartime technologies for considering the brain and the nature of skills. It is well known that Bartlett was greatly influenced by Craik's engineering concepts, and these were dominating ideas in the Department following Craik's death. In general, the concepts of servo-control and predicting, which were developed for anti-aircraft guns, led to cybernetic accounts of the nervous system and to Craik's crucially important notion of the brain representing perceptions, ideas and so on, by physical states.

For those of us who are guided by engineering principles, it seems somewhat paradoxical that engineering does not have a clue how to describe or explain consciousness – yet we look to engineering concepts for the answer. Perhaps most of us suppose that a sufficiently complicated artificial brain would be conscious; but we don't know how, or why, this would be. How we would recognise that it has sensations (or qualia) remains a puzzle; but this is also a puzzle for brain-based minds, other than our own.

A positive gain of the neuronal account of mind was active positing and testing of engineering-type accounts of intelligence, perception and learning. These were not, however, generally related to specific neural events. Indeed, many psychologists simply ignored the brain. The burgeoning fields of cybernetics and artificial intelligence (AI) were based on the assumption of brain-based mind, but so little was known of cortical function that this was generally recognised only implicitly. Exceptions were the very different ideas of Donald Hebb in Canada and Warren McCulloch at the Massachusetts Institute of Technology (McCulloch and Pitts, 1943). The great British exception was Kenneth Craik, with his 'internal models'. Surely the most important single idea in cognitive psychology is brain representation in physical terms. Craik (1943) wrote:

> By a model I do not mean some obscure non-physical entity which attends the model, but the fact that it is a physical working model which works in the same way as the process it parallels.... Thus the model need not resemble the real object pictorially; Kelvin's tide-predictor, which consists of a number of pulleys on levers, does not resemble a tide in appearance, but it works in the same way in certain essential respects – it combines oscillations of various frequencies so as to produce an oscillation which closely resembles in amplitude at each moment the variation in tide level at any place.

This is the basis of AI – except that computers came to be more symbolic as they became digital. No doubt the rise of computer technology has profoundly affected how we think of brain and mind; but now there is a considerable swing back to more analogue accounts of brain function. These had their start especially in the ideas of Donald Hebb (1949), which stressed the importance of slowly won inductive generalisations for learning and perception – with a specific neural hypothesis.

3   Internal models

I took Craik's internal models idea literally with the disturbance-rejecting telescope camera. From a working simulator, built with my technician Bill Matthews, this was developed and tested with the brilliant engineer Steven Salter. Salter built the final version and we tested it on mountains in New Mexico and Arizona.

This was supported by the Royal Society and the US Air Force. It started with the simulation, made in my room in the Cambridge Department of Psychology, using a randomly disturbed fish tank to play the part of the atmosphere. In a simple form, it embodied Craikian internal models. Perhaps it was an early example of AI, as it used knowledge from the past to improve perception of the present.

The method was, first, to take a long-exposure photograph of, for example, the moon, through the image-disturbing turbulence of the atmosphere. The positions of the contours were correctly placed, though blurred, in this photographic internal model. After rapid processing, the photographic plate was replaced in precisely the same position in the camera so the dynamically disturbed image fell on to its own time-averaged negative picture. When the image most nearly matched the negative, the least light passed through – so providing an auto-correlation signal from a photomultiplier which received the integrated light passing through the negative. This signal opened the shutter of a second camera, which received the moon's image directly; but only at moments when the disturbance was minimal, when the auto-correlation was high. This is when the disturbed present matches the average past (Gregory, 1964a, 1974a). So disturbances were rejected. A picture, better than the original, was built up in the second camera by many successive exposures selected in this way to have minimal disturbance. It might seem somewhat bizarre that a psychologist should spend time, and be allowed to spend time, on such a project. But it was possible to do just about anything in the Cambridge of that period. I hope this is still true!

It was also the influence of engineering ideas that made me question interpretations of experiments for localising brain functions. This was sometimes taken as a general criticism of what came to be called neuropsychology – inferring local functions from clinical symptoms of brain damage – but this is not quite right. I never claimed that it is impossible, only that there are severe logical difficulties to be considered, especially when adequate theoretical models of brain functions are not available. This 'attack' upset some friends, but they were generally tolerant of this eccentricity and did not simply dismiss it. These issues extend to how to interpret images from the wonderful positron emission tomography and functional magnetic resonance imaging techniques. Perhaps these difficulties are not considered sufficiently now.

Having done some electronics, I saw these issues in engineering terms – indeed, a paper was called 'The brain as an engineering problem' (Gregory, 1961). My first paper on this was 'Models and the localisation of function in the central nervous system', presented at the Mechanisation of Thought Processes Symposium (Gregory, 1959). Electronic systems have processes going on inside which are not in their outputs or 'behaviour', such as oscillators in radios or televisions. When detected, with a probing oscilloscope, they are mysterious if the principles of the circuits are not understood. To interpret brain waves traced on an electroencephalogram, we must know what processes they reflect and how this works. For problems of interpreting ablation experiments, I suggested an analogy from radio engineering, which has often been quoted since, as a potential trap (Gregory, 1959: 678):

> Suppose that when [a] condenser breaks down, the set emits howls. Do we argue that the normal function of the condenser is to inhibit howling? Surely not. The condenser's abnormally low resistance has changed the system as a whole, and the system may exhibit new properties, in this case howling.

Neurophysiologists, when faced with comparable situations, have sometimes postulated suppresser regions, but this may be entirely wrong. The problem is to analyse the new circuit – which may require very special, indeed unique understanding. What happens when bits go wrong, or are missing, can be unexpected and exceedingly hard to explain. In serial or closely coupled parallel systems, there is no simple one-to-one relation between internal component losses or failures and output behaviour or symptoms. It was just this kind of problem of interpretation from inadequate theoretical understanding that defeated the engineers of the Three Mile Island atomic power station, when the coolant failed.

4   Research and teaching at Cambridge (1950–1967)

I was fortunate in being kept on at Cambridge after graduating, by Sir Frederic Bartlett, first at the Medical Research Council's Applied Psychology Unit, which was then in the same building as the University Department of Psychology. Bartlett seconded me to the Royal Navy for a year to work on escaping from submarines, following the disaster of the *Affray*, when two crews were tragically lost. This was at the Royal Naval Physiological Laboratory at Portsmouth, using a large pressure tank with controlled levels of oxygen and carbon dioxide, with dummy escape gear. I designed and built a printing recorder (named Thoth, after the Egyptian god of writing) for recording what happened over ten or more hours. It was fun going on trips in the subs, and indeed this was a great experience with considerable responsibility. There is much to be said for combining practical and theoretical problems to work on.

   After three years, I was appointed as Demonstrator and shortly after Lecturer in the University Department of Psychology, under Professor Oliver Zangwill. The Department expanded with a new wing and I was very fortunate to be given the whole of the top floor, which I designed as the Special Senses Laboratory. This I ran with numerous British and American foundation grants and wonderful students. We worked on fascinating projects on vision and hearing, problems for astronauts for the forthcoming moon landing of 1969 (Gregory and Ross 1964a, 1964b), and designing various instruments, with our own workshop. This was a great time. There was a strong emphasis on engineering ideas, no doubt following Craik's lead; but this did not entirely dominate the Department. Notably, Alice Heim was developing her intelligence tests (AH4 and AH5), and there were strong links with animal behaviour in the Zoology Department, as well as clinical work with the local Fulbourn Fospital and the National Institute of Neurology at Queen Square in London.

We were in the same building as the Physiology Department. Following the heritage of Lord Adrian (I attended some of his demonstrations), we saw the physiologists as superior beings, with us rather low in the pecking order. The present effective sharing of ideas and cooperation over experiments came later, especially by the founding of the Craik Laboratory. Especially important were William Rushton, Horace Barlow (who very much combined physiology with psychology and still does), John Robson and Fergus Campbell. Fergus was the leader of grating experiments for investigating Fourier accounts of vision. Although this was important, I confess to finding its domination over a decade of visual research annoying, as it distracted from more cognitive concepts, which seemed fundamental – though at that time generally regarded as dubious science with little or no explanatory power. It is a great pleasure that this is now how much of perceptual research is developing. Of course the discoveries of physiology are incredibly exciting; but it is the linking of physiology with processes carried out by the machinery of the brain that gives deep insights into sight, and so much more. A great insight came from Claud Shannon's theory of information as surprise. What *might* happen affects perception and behaviour (Shannon and Weaver, 1949; Hick,1952), so stimuli are not all-important.

5   Recovery from blindness: the case of SB

A chance changed the way I came to think of perception: a rare case of recovery from blindness. This was the case of SB, studied with my colleague Jean Wallace (Gregory and Wallace, 1963). Jean saw in a Midlands local paper that a man who had been blind all his life was to receive corneal transplants at the age of 52. This presented a quandary: immediate action was essential; but we were very busy at the time, with teaching and other duties. Within an hour we packed every imaginable visual experiment into the car and set off for the hospital. It was the best decision I ever made.

Whatever we may have found of benefit to others, it was this investigation that set my path to vision, and phenomena of illusions, as among the most fascinating topics in psychology. In fact, this set up how I would think about perception and mind. We found that SB could see almost immediately objects already familiar to him, especially through touch, though he remained blind for a long time to unknown objects. The most striking example of this was that he could read upper case letters, which he had been taught to read by touch in the blind school, but not lower case letters, which were not taught in the school. Further, he could tell the time visually, without any help or practice. Here the touch experience was from a large pocket watch, with no glass. He could un-hesitatingly tell the time by touch. The conclusion was that object vision depends on knowledge derived from active exploration, giving meaning to the eyes' images. It showed, also, the importance of cross-modal transfer – knowledge from one sense being available to other senses. Our findings, especially extensive cross-modal transfer from touch to vision, were very surprising at that time. There is now confirming evidence from other cases (Valvo, 1971) in Italy and recently from Japan (cf. Gregory, 1997a).

Considering how eyes and other senses – together with brains – give knowledge of the world of objects is the central question. There are only two theories of perception: direct and indirect. Both go back to the Greeks, especially direct theories, which seemed plausible before the retinal image and the complexity of neural processing were discovered. These (it seems to me) make J.J. Gibson's direct pick-up theory impossible to accept literally. This was my conclusion shortly after graduating, but I greatly respected Gibson's experiments, and much liked Jimmy and his wife Eleanor personally. With his puckish grin he looked like a Walt Disney character, while Eleanor was stately and dignified. Jimmy would argue for hours on end. We stayed up all night in his house comparing insect with human vision. Jimmy allowed that insects had retinal image, but not humans. (Is this the sometimes misleading power of top-down belief on observation?)

As a student I was saturated in his direct theory of vision, as set out in his *Perception of the Visual World* (Gibson, 1950,). In fact, though, I spent too much time writing objections to direct theories of vision, as I came to hold a very different, essentially Helmholtzian, view of perception as being creatively intelligent – hence the title of my 1967 Royal Institution Christmas Lectures, *The Intelligent Eye* (Gregory, 1970). I couldn't then, and still do not, believe that perception of objects as solid things with causal properties can be given without a major contribution of knowledge of the world, gained from interactive experience, especially by handling objects. This is very different from Gibson's view that the information is simply out there, to be 'picked up'. Undoubtedly perception is adapted to the environment, through evolution, so his ecological optics makes a lot of sense; but it is striking that we can come to see and cope with new kinds of objects and situations, as in driving and flying. It amazed me that Gibson could deny retinal images (which, with the associated complex physiological processing, clearly makes vision indirect), and also that he could deny phenomena of illusions. They are, indeed, a traditional embarrassment for 'direct' theories. Gibson says that there are no illusions, except occasionally in special laboratory situations; but surely this is not the truth of illusions. They are all-pervasive, though not always recognised as distortions or whatever in normal situations. They become obvious in situations such as hill walking, or golf, where there are clearly noticeable errors. (A professional golfer wrote to me saying he would misjudge the length of a drive after tall trees near the green had been cut down.) For me, illusions are both strong evidence of the indirectness of perception and they are useful for investigating many physiological and cognitive processes (Gregory, 1966, 1998).

To accept an indirect account of perception, and spend time on illusions, was quite 'way-out' at the time, though I was certainly not the first to take illusions seriously: Hermann Helmholtz, W.H.R. Rivers, Adelbert Ames, Jerome Bruner and Donald Mackay, as well as Lionel and Roger Penrose with their wonderful impossible objects, made important discoveries by playing with illusions seriously. In Britain, Donald Mackay (at King's College in London and then at Keele) deserves special credit for seeing their importance and investigating and discovering a wide variety of illusory phenomena.

My approach was from epistemology. Indeed, this is an experimental epistemology, for the phenomena suggest answers to ancient philosophical questions of how we experience and know. Direct theories promise certainty (which has great appeal), while indirect theories give no such promise (which can be unsettling). John Locke's distinction between primary and secondary characteristics is germane here. It is disturbing to think that colours are created in the brain and projected into the world of objects – which themselves have no colour – though this is their most striking apparent reality.

Helmholtz's idea of perceptions as unconscious inferences was a far more appealing approach for me than Gibson's direct pick-up. Essentially following Helmholtz, it seemed to me that perceptions are predictive hypotheses. I have always found this a useful notion, especially as it suggests links between processes of perception to the methods by which science gains knowledge (cf. Gregory, 1981). The notion that perceptions are hypotheses gives a status for perceptions that seems right. It also gives phenomena of illusions a rational place – though they have to be played down or denied by direct accounts, which seems quite wrong. (These ideas are developed throughout my papers and books, especially: Gregory, 1963, 1968, 1969b, 1970, 1980, 1997a.)

6   Seeking truths through illusions

Illusions can be seen as trivial, as irritating, as dangerous, as amusing – or as significant phenomena for discovering perceptual processes, leading to the very nature of perception itself. Any of these can be true, though it is the last that justifies the remarkable attention they have now earned. Interest in illusions goes in fashions. They were deeply unfashionable when I was a student, though popular a century before.

It was the abnormality and general lack of illusions experienced by SB, following his recovery of sight, that attracted my attention to these phenomena and made me think of many of them as being more cognitive than physiological. Of course, physiology is always involved: the question is where the action is that generates the phenomenon. Generally, cognition seemed too vague a notion at the time: a view I did not share, but tried to make the ideas more concrete. This was greatly helped by the prevalence of computer errors due to inappropriate software though the hardware was working normally. This is the key concept, and not at all vague, for cognitive illusions.

The Müller–Lyer illusion was my chosen example, for it is very robust and readily measured. The idea came when I suddenly realised that the Müller–Lyer arrows are flat projections of corners – as inside rooms, or outside buildings, respectively. Then the Ponzo figure is obviously a perspective of receding lines. In all cases, features signalled as more distant are expanded. This is opposite to the optical shrinking of retinal images with distance. This suggested that the modus operandi of the distortions is size scaling, which normally compensates image shrinking with distance. But in a picture there is no shrinking, as it is flat, and so depth cues distort. What had probably hidden this before was the fact that the illusory figures generally appear flat. So the suggestion was that size scaling can be set directly by perspective or other depth cues even though depth is not seen, as when countered by the texture of the picture surface (Gregory, 1963). This led to experiments where the texture was removed, and to observations with luminous depth-ambiguous objects, such as wire cubes – which change shape as they flip in depth – the apparently further face appearing larger – though the retinal image is unchanged. This made it possible to separate bottom-up from top-down constancy scaling. (This was originally described neutrally as 'primary' and 'secondary' scaling.) The key was using ambiguous figures or objects, to separate bottom-up signals from top-down knowledge.

7   Edinburgh: the Department of Machine Intelligence and Perception

I left Cambridge in 1967, to help to found the Department of Machine Intelligence and Perception at Edinburgh with Donald Michie and Christopher Longuet-Higgins, FRS. Christopher and I joined Donald, whose idea it was, and who was already at Edinburgh. This was a brave dream which was generously supported by the University of Edinburgh, especially by its Vice-Chancellor, Sir Michael Swann, with funding by the Science Research Council (SRC).

It came at a bad time for me, as my Cambridge projects were going great guns. Edinburgh was a long way away from Cambridge, and I had to prepare apparatus for the six Royal Institution Christmas Lectures I was to give in London (the first to be presented on colour television), yet we did not even have electricity in the embryo workshop. This was the first of many snags. The first problem, however, was more amusing than tragic. Initially we were offered a deconsecrated Church of Scotland church for our laboratory and offices; but when they heard we were going to build a robot, it was withdrawn! The notion of minds in machines may indeed have theological implications, and can still be frightening.

The Department undertook a lot of theoretical work on vision and learning and problem solving, so the dream was in fair part fulfilled (cf. Michie, 1974; for general background, discussion and references, see Boden, 1977). I never became at all expert at programming, and I made very little contribution beyond something of the philosophy. This was pushing the importance of internal representations for prediction and gap-filling, rather than direct control from the inputs. Christopher Longuet-Higgens made a neat, very simple, wheeled model to show this. More important, Christopher developed fundamental ideas for neural nets. Unlike myself, Christopher learned to program. Jim Howe (who had been my graduate student at Cambridge) went on to run the Department for many years.

We, the founders, were criticised for overoptimism – expecting general intelligence by the end of the century – though without optimism we would never have started. What the early history of AI showed is that the brain is far more complicated and more subtle than had been realised. This was useful knowledge. It made the problems and aims of brain research more realistic and suggested some specific goals. The goal for me now (as then) is to give machines rich and rapidly available knowledge of the world. When a machine can draw interesting analogies – and make puns – it will have arrived.

Christopher and I left the Department after just a few years. This is regrettable. A major reason was the infamous Lighthill Report. The highly distinguished mathematician and fluid dynamicist Sir James Lighthill was commissioned by the SRC to write a report on the current state and likely future of AI. For right or wrong, this report had drastic effects on the new science of AI. Perhaps Lighthill was being wisely cautious, but it held up progress in one of the main activities that, surely, will mark out our time.

8   Bristol: the Brain and Perception Laboratory

I moved from Edinburgh to the University of Bristol in 1967, to start a new mini-department, funded by the Medical Research Council, in the Department of Anatomy in the Medical School. It was a great privilege to be able to run my own show, in prime laboratory space, with our own workshop and darkroom. The Brain and Perception Laboratory really started from an essay – an attempt to spell out an experimental philosophy of perception with a plan for progress. The emphasis was to be phenomena-based, for testing cognitive concepts with an eye on clinical implications. It ran for 20 years, was great fun and achieved much that was intended, together with several surprises.

One of the initial aims of the Brain and Perception Laboratory was to look at eye–hand tracking in Parkinson's disease, with gaps in the track, to see whether sufferers have reduced powers of prediction. This was taken up and studied over many years by Ken Flowers, who is now an established authority on Parkinson's disease. Robert Williams studied object recognition in dynamically noise-degenerated displays, measuring 'central' temporal integration. We studied many phenomena of illusions, including the cafe wall (Gregory and Heard, 1979, 1983) and illusory contours (Gregory and Harris, 1975; Harris and Gregory, 1975).

We also devised several instruments, including a heterochromatic photometer, a three-dimensional drawing machine and a speech processing hearing aid. The last should be useful, but was never manufactured, probably because at that time it could not be made sufficiently small to be inconspicuous. At any rate, this brought home the difficulty of developing techniques in the laboratory to a stage where industry might become involved.

9 Hands-on science – the Exploratory

Upon retiring, I was fortunate to be able to continue as an Emeritus Professor, with various small grants, especially Gatsby (the Sainsbury Foundation Trust), with the position of Senior Research Fellow. The University and the Department have been and still are generous, giving me space and time beyond my sell-by date. I am most grateful. This has allowed me to write papers and books (including revising my best-known book *Eye and Brain*) and to collaborate with colleagues in Britain and abroad, as well as giving umpteen lectures.

Presenting one's special knowledge and ideas more widely can be worthwhile and may repay the debt to society that supports research beyond its immediate payback. But for the public to be interested, there must be mutual learning for how to present and understand ideas and discoveries. So public understanding of science is important – but also scientific understanding of the public. The adventure of science should be a major basis of general culture. Psychology and perception are relatively easy to put across.

It was demonstrating RAF technologies to the public, at the end of the war, that initiated me into communicating with the public. This was confirmed by meeting Frank Oppenheimer in 1970 in San Francisco, when I gave the first Smith-Kettlewell Lecture, at the opening of the Eye Institute of this name. Frank had just opened the Exploratorium, a hands-on science centre. It was – it is – a revelation. Here, anyone can experiment and try out ideas. I helped him design perception experiments, and we spent many hours on the aims and philosophy of hands-on science.

The Exploratory was founded 18 years ago. Something of its philosophy is given in *A History of the Bristol Exploratory* (Gregory, 1987a) and in the last chapter of *Mirrors in Mind* (Gregory, 1997b). It put into practice the theoretical insight from SB's recovery of sight: that effective sight is immediately available when there is knowledge from touch – the idea being that infant learning by hand–eye experimenting may be continued, to enrich experience and understanding throughout life. The Exploratory attracted over two million visitors, and became an accepted Bristol institution with a wide reputation. Curiously and sadly, it has been killed by the massively funded local Millennium project. Money can destroy as well as create.

10 The great enigma: consciousness

Although eliciting experiences is what art, and most of living, is all about, consciousness has been a taboo topic for science until recently. So Francis Crick's book *The Astonishing Hypothesis* (Crick, 1994) is itself astonishing and most welcome. There are two major questions: How can a physical system, the brain, generate consciousness? What, if anything, does consciousness do? No plausible answer has so far been suggested for the first, except that consciousness is an emergent property of certain kinds of complexity. Emergent properties, such as those of water from combining oxygen and hydrogen atoms (and note how very different water is from these gasses), remain mysterious before we have a wide, embracing theory. Presumably this is what we seek for consciousness – to remove the mystery from this emergence from brain (or computer?) – physical functions to subjective sensations.

The second question seems to me to point to the special significance of the present moment. It is occasionally pointed out (cf. Humphrey, 1992) that consciousness is in the now. Surely this is right. It is interesting to compare the vividness of perception with the shadowy, quite dim awareness of memory and imagination. (Try looking at something, then shut the eyes and compare with the memory. The difference, surely, is dramatically striking.) If indeed perception depends to a very large extent on knowledge from the past, there must be a problem for distinguishing present from past. Yet this is essential for survival in the present. To confuse a green or red traffic light with a memory of a traffic light could be disastrous.

The present moment is signalled by real-time afferent inputs. This should be adequate for primitive stimulus–response behaviour – but for cognitive brains, such as ours, surely the real-time inputs could easily be confused or lost in the wealth of memory. So, perhaps the vivid sensations of perception flag the present, to avoid confusion with the past. What of the relatively dim consciousness of memory and imagination? These, also, are in the present; but they lack afferent inputs – which alone can signal the present. In both cases, the present moment seems to be a key to consciousness (Gregory, 1998). There is a hint here, but perhaps no more. Philosophy raises and can help to formulate questions but here, as elsewhere, we expect answers to come from experimental science.

22

The advent of the methodological critique

Rom Harré

In the summer term of 1966 an old friend, Stephen Toulmin, was visiting Oxford. At the time his work on the 'ideals of natural order' in the foundations of science was being widely discussed. He was invited to give a talk to the Friday social psychology research seminar, a well established institution under Michael Argyle's stewardship. Stephen invited me along. It was an occasion of mutual incomprehension. The budding social psychologists present knew no science and Toulmin, at that time, had no inkling of what an odd project these keen young people were engaged in. I was both baffled and intrigued. How could the project of creating a *scientific* psychology be undertaken by people who, however well intentioned, evidently had no inkling of what the natural sciences were like? I attended the seminar for the rest of the term. Determined not to be beaten by this paradox I spent a great deal of time that summer in the Radcliffe Science Library reading the standard social psychology texts and chasing up the seminal articles from the references. It was a revelation, though far from encouraging.

I was struck by several aspects of the research then being done that seemed to me to be thoroughly unsatisfactory, though I did not then fully appreciate the nature of the paradigm underlying them. For a start, it was assumed that social actors did not know what they were doing and why they were doing it. The 'experiments' made sense only if social responses were supposed to be the effects of environmental events, triggering mysterious mechanisms in individuals over which they had no control. The use of statistics to analyse the results of these studies was systematically fallacious, in a quite elementary way. It was clear to me that the mathematics was not understood. It is an elementary fallacy to infer an individual propensity to behave in a certain way from a statistical distribution of that way of behaving in a population. Whatever this work was, it was not psychology. Finally, even at the very beginning of my involvement in the work of the Oxford department, the gap between the overall 'social skills' approach, favoured by Michael Argyle, and the causal paradigm adopted in the research efforts of his graduate students was very obvious. A skill is normative! It necessitates a standard of better or worse performance. It is quite incompatible with the use of a causal metaphysics and methodology. It was some time before I could see how this intuition could be developed into an active research programme.

Henri Tajfel had long been a personal friend. He was a member of my college before he went to Bristol. I had discussed social psychology in a desultory way with him from time to time. He never tired of emphasising his commitment to the development of a European social psychology, in conscious opposition to the American influence, then at its height. Having begun to read up mainstream work in the field, I already had the feeling that there were very strong and local cultural assumptions animating research projects in the United States, for instance Lenny Berkowitz's studies of aggression and Leon Fetzinger's thesis of cognitive dissonance. Tajfel's studies of the foundations of intergroup conflict were methodologically no better than those emanating from America. The same dubious assumptions about causation and the same logical fallacies were evident in both. Tajfel's 'European' psychology was based on a distinction without a difference.

It soon became clear that there was indeed a pattern of tightly interwoven presuppositions that was serving as a paradigm. But from whence had it come? Certainly not from a generalisation of how people actually managed their social relationships. Then light dawned. I became aware of the paradox of individualism. Why, in the land of Thomas Jefferson and the enthronement of individual liberty, was so much emphasis placed on automatic, mindless functioning in social matters? Along with liberty goes responsibility. The greater the liberty, the heavier is the responsibility. No wonder that the search for causes was in full flood in the American universities. If one's behaviour is caused by environmental contingencies one is not responsible for it. Hence the rush to transform moral issues into medical and technical problems that is still so striking a feature of American life. Now I saw why the social psychology imported from the United States seemed so implausible. The patterns of European life were very much more collectivist. Families and long-running institutions, for example the 'public' schools that dominated English life, were the matrix of social life even in Britain and France, the two places where the cry of 'liberty' was first heard in the eighteenth century. The emphasis on training and the following of set procedures that one notices everywhere in North America shifts the burden of responsibility on to the training manual and away from the social actor. Naive experiments in an American context would indeed provoke responses that would look for all the world like the effects of causes. Social mores would reappear in the results of these studies in the guise of putative laws of psychology.

The third matter of importance that sparked my own later projects was the neglect of anthropology and social history by almost all the social psychologists I knew personally and whose work I had read. How could anyone make universalistic claims about gambling on the basis of a few 'experiments' in South Parks Road, Oxford, without at least a nodding acquaintance with Clifford Geertz's brilliant studies of Indonesian gambling? How could anyone carry out research into the psychology of remembering without a thorough study of ancient and mediaeval techniques for committing huge amounts of material to memory? Had anyone in the psychology department read the *Ad Herrenium*? Or looked into the patterns of eye contact between men and women, without taking account of the different patterns of gaze reported by anthropologists and discussed by social historians, for instance those inculcated in Catholic girls, or in the Puritan culture of Massachusetts? The point is not whether local studies are legitimate, but how they should be interpreted. It soon became clear to me that most social psychology had no claim to be a science in the sense of laying bare universal aspects of human social interaction. It was the anthropology of the local tribe. And given the reluctance of social psychologists to extract social actors' own accounts of what was going on, a resource no anthropologist would dream of neglecting, it was a pretty impoverished anthropology at that.

1   The advent of the methodological critique

I suppose I would have taken no further interest in what I had come to feel was a hopeless enterprise if chance had not led me to meet Willard Farnsworth Day. He had come to Oxford in the autumn of 1966 as a visiting scholar and was assigned to me as his mentor. His project was very simple. He wanted to learn as much about Wittgenstein's later philosophy as would suffice to provide a much-needed support for the 'radical behaviourism' of B.F. Skinner. At that time Skinner was beginning to attract very hostile attention from the emerging radical movement in the United States. His attack on freedom and dignity as the basis of a social dynamics, in favour of social operant conditioning administered by well meaning psychologists, was anathema to the new libertarians. I shared their view, since the Skinnerian programme, as I learned of it from Day, and from subsequent readings in the Skinnerian corpus, seemed to me eerily like the regime enforced in the early New England colonies by the notorious Governor Winthrop.

However, an unexpected result of the personal friendship between Willard and myself was an invitation to spend my next sabbatical term at Reno, Nevada, where chance had assembled a strong group of social psychologists and sociologists, including Paul Secord, Carl Backman, Gerry Ginsberg and Stanford Lyman. I found that Secord had come to feel the same doubts about mainstream social psychology as I had. The lack of attention to the symbolic dimension of personal interactions, the failure to take notice of participants' own accounts of what was going on, the failure of the 'experimental method' to meet elementary standards of rigour, the systematic refusal to acknowledge the role of individuals as the active sources of social acts, and much more, turned out to be common ground. Secord took his next sabbatical in Oxford, and there we set about writing a comprehensive methodological text (Harré and Secord, 1972). It was both critical and constructive. It was well received; indeed, it was celebrated as a 'Citation Classic' in the Citation Index. We hoped that 'new paradigm' studies would soon displace the old mainstream. In this we were to be disappointed. I will return to diagnose some of the reasons.

2   Oxford in the 1970s

Though Michael Argyle clung to some of the empiricist baggage of the old paradigm, he very quickly realised that the concept of 'social skills' sits ill with a cause–effect metaphysics. He encouraged a shift to explanatory schemes based on rules, conventions and even traditions. There were still distortions that inevitably followed the continued departmental requirement that there be some statistical analyses in doctoral dissertations, but that demand could be met by making use of the legitimate methodology of repertory grids, derived from Kelly. The arrival of Jerome Bruner from Harvard made a great, though as it turned out temporary, difference in the atmosphere (Bruner, 1983). The use of narrative analysis, the adoption of idiographic and intensive designs, the use of philosophical analyses of some of the leading psychological concepts, the adoption of such radical notions as Austin's speech-act analyses of conversational interactions, all opened up the orthodoxy to studies that began to look a little more like a science, that is a method of enquiry that produces reliable knowledge of phenomena of a certain kind and of how they are brought into existence. Expressing your observations numerically and using a naive cause–effect metaphysics to interpret them does not make your enterprise a science. Astrologers do the same thing!

If the methodological criticisms of the old paradigm were legitimate, and if the new paradigm proposals looked well founded, what would social psychological research look like? Ethnomethodology was already 'there', so to speak, but it was not easily accessible to anyone outside Harold Garfinkel's circle. I was very fortunate to be able to put the new paradigm to work as a support for the researches of several gifted graduate students. Peter Marsh and Elizabeth Rosser had both collected a great deal of material from young people who had been presented in the media as purveyors of 'mindless violence'. Marsh looked deeply into the nature of so-called 'football hooliganism', to find an orderly world, dominated by a working social hierarchy, and highly dependent on well understood, though largely tacit, rules. Rosser collected the accounts of adolescents who had disrupted classroom discipline to find that there, too, was a world where what had happened was both intelligible and, in the eyes of its perpetrators, also warrantable. In neither case was there 'mindless' violence. Behind the seeming disorder were firmly maintained systems of rules (Marsh *et al.*, 1978). Here, indeed, was work that exemplified a psychology of intentional actions, of meanings and rules, of social conventions and standards of correctness, even if those standards differed markedly from those of the majority of citizens. The young men who fought their status-determining battles at football grounds were active agents using the resources available to them to attain their ends.

Chatting with some of the students from the Department of Educational Studies, I remarked that nicknaming must have an effect on personality. Someone should look it up. Jane Morgan offered to do so, and drew a blank. After recruiting Chris O'Neill, the three of us began a massive study of nicknaming practices in several different cultural settings. Here was a neglected facet of social psychology. We found all sorts of interesting things, such as the use of multiple nicknames to forge and maintain a high-status group within a larger community. It was also clear that the repertoire of 'standard' nicknames revealed, in the negative so to say, the acceptable local forms of personality. The right to invent and assign these names was an important aspect of the power relations in small groups, not only of children but of musicians, footballers, convicts and so on (Morgan *et al.*, 1979). This important aspect of personality psychology was invisible to the mainstream. No manipulation of independent variables, correlated with variations in a dependent variable, could come anywhere near this phenomenon.

The nickname study was only a part of a larger project in which I was engaged. What were personality and character? Eysenck's work seemed to me to be unsatisfactory for the same reasons as the American work in social psychology. It was based on the presumption of fixed traits or dispositions, activated by environmental contingencies, which led to a display of the behaviour characteristic of the Eysenckian types. But looking around one at one's friends and monitoring one's own personality show that there is no such thing as one fixed personality per person. With Elizabeth Rosser and others I began to study 'personality' as a repertoire of 'parts', or roles, deployed for dramaturgical purposes. People differed a great deal in the degree to which they were knowingly deploying particular personalities for particular purposes. Again, this led to studies of single individuals, from which one could learn only the general truth that personality was a repertoire and one could get a glimpse of the local content of the repertoire. Who displayed what personality style in what circumstances was a highly contingent matter. From these studies it was a short step to joining the programme run by J.-P. de Waele in Brussels, to develop a new technique of personality assessment based on individual case studies. Like other workers at the time, I found myself involved both as a theoretician and as a commentator on and critic of the empirical work in which the new methods of autobiographical reconstruction were developed in studying the psychological styles of convicted murderers in the St Giles prison in Brussels (Van Langenhove *et al.*, 1986).

Friendship studies, too, seemed ripe for revision. The existing literature seemed to be exemplary of bad work in psychology. A glance at some of the assumptions of that work will help to make clear another difference between old- and new-paradigm social psychology. One form of experiment one sometimes finds in physics depends on analysing the conditions under which a certain phenomenon occurs and comparing the effect of the presence or absence of one of the component conditions on the existence of the phenomenon in question. Perhaps people get to like those they meet often. Let us then abstract 'frequency' from the conditions and vary it in relation to an abstracted aspect of friendship, say 'liking'. It has to be 'pure' liking, so it must be detached from the context of people. Perhaps we might use mock words. The experiment is to show participants pseudo-words at different frequencies and to find out which such word is *said to be* liked the most! Not surprisingly, it is the word most frequently seen. Therefore frequency of meeting causes friendship. This really is nonsense. So one turns to anthropology. There one finds the work of Mary Douglas, as she painstakingly records the ritual meals by which friendship is ceremonially advanced and ratified in our society (Douglas, 1972). Other cultures have other means of establishing that mutual regard and *commitment* that is the core of friendship. Friendship is not a free-floating relation into which people are conditioned. It is embedded within complex patterns of local moral orders and realised in narratives, both lived and told.

3   Feminism and the puzzle of the self

The English word 'self' was much in evidence in feminist writing in the 1970s. Many feminist authors made the claim that the self is different in men and in women, tending to be singular in the former and tending to be multiple in the latter. The self has also been as the focus of a philosophical debate on the criteria of personal identity that has run on for close to 400 years. Does the possession of a singular self explain the unity and identity of a person over time? Is there a Cartesian ego at the core of each human being, the 'real me'? Or is the uniqueness of personhood just a matter of continuous embodiment in one material thing? Is it a matter of the continuity of consciousness, or of memory? How is selfhood related to being a person? If a feminist author claimed that women's selves were multiple, overlapping and labile, did not this presuppose that one and the same person was at one time this and another time that? Unless there was a sense in which the self was singular, it would be impossible to realise that the self was multiple! The same weird wobble seemed to be visible in the way the concept of 'identity' was being used. How could one have *more than one* identity? It soon became clear that in that sense 'identity' meant 'type', not 'individual'. Someone could easily exemplify more than one type of person, in various ways and degrees, while retaining a personal identity, that is being one and same individual human being.

It seemed to me obvious that this morass was the result of conceptual confusions rather than the revelation of a genuine problem for psychologists to solve. Here was a prime case for the adoption of some of the techniques of analytical philosophy to deal with a pseudo-problem. But how to proceed?

'Self' and 'identity' were being used with several different meanings, the main variants being related to the distinction between 'type' and 'individual'. 'Person', on the other hand, seemed to be more stable and unified in its uses. The next step would surely be to study the symbolic means for the expression of personhood, with special attention to those devices by which a sense of personal identity, of being one and the same *person*, was expressed. A study of the uses of proper names and of pronouns looked promising, and so it proved. This work was a natural extension of the studies of personality presentation, since it was based on the metaphysical principle that people were actively engaged in intentional action, making use of the available grammar to perform various social tasks (Harré, 1983).

If pronouns expressed the sense of self, as a singularity, that is of being one and the same person, then if there were different pronoun grammars in use in different cultures it was a fair presumption that the sense of self that could thereby be expressed must be different. A study of grammar could offer some deep insights into the way the psychologies of alien folks worked. Peter Mühlhäusler and I began a massive study of pronoun usage in many very different cultural settings, looking for aspects of the general culture that would or should reflect the differences we noted in the pronoun grammars (Mühlhäusler and Harré, 1990). In the background to all this was a growing appreciation on my part of the work of Lev Vygosky (Vygotsky, 1962). Taking up the practices of one's culture inevitably determined in broad outline the cognitive possibilities open to a mind so shaped. In his famous controversy with Piaget it seemed to me that the Russian had all the aces.

One of the complaints levelled against mainstream psychology, and in particular old-paradigm social psychology, is its irrelevance to anything practical, for instance to the work of clinicians. Almost everything that came out of new-paradigm work had a more or less direct application. And yet it is clear that the old paradigm has still not been swept away. Even in Europe the main journals continue to publish and so to encourage research the theoretical basis of which has been demonstrated again and again to be indefensible. Why?

4   Social psychology of social change

The last project in which I became interested in the 1970s was the problem of the social psychology of social change. According to the new-paradigm picture of human psychology, people were to be taken to be active agents using local resources to accomplish projects that were locally defined as meaningful but not necessarily legitimate in the narrow legal sense. But it was obvious that both the projects and the rules and conventions for accomplishing them had been changing at different rates, although nevertheless inexorably, since records of human social life began. How did this happen? How *could* this happen?

Again, the feminist movement of the 1960s and '70s provided an ideal field of study. Well established sets of conventions according to which differential conduct was expected of the members of each sex were under attack. New conventions were being forged. Feminist movements were not new. In almost every century some version of a female protest movement had appeared. Why did these movements sometimes succeed in changing the social order and sometimes not? What conception of social change would be needed understand these matters? Plainly, historical and anthropological material was essential. At the time, mainstream social psychology offered nothing in this field. Nor could it, since it seemed to presuppose a fixed human nature, if its project was to find universal laws of human behaviour on the model of the laws of physics, which every material body obeys at all times and places. The only game in town was Marxism. But apart from its inherent implausibility it had no psychology. Historical reading soon made it clear that revolutionary politics hardly ever accomplished *social* change. New political regimes regularly and very shortly recreated the same sort of society that they had been dedicated to overthrowing. So there were two questions: What happened when social change was accomplished? Why was it that revolutionary movements, alternative utopias set up in the wilderness and other 'new ways' so often failed, returning to the very folk ways they originally repudiated? It was the latter question to which I turned (Harré, 1979).

What if there were a social order or orders, a repertoire of social practices, that existed among children, a culture passed on Vygotsky-wise from one generation to another, but that seemed to disappear as children entered into adolescence and learned the ways of the adult world? What if the change to adulthood was a transformation of content only, while the essential forms remained the same? What would a social psychology of the closed worlds of childhood reveal? Starting from the wonderful work of the Opies (Opie and Opie, 1972), I began to look into this fascinating matter. Helped by several generations of students at the local training colleges, I began to collect material. A couple of publications followed (Harré, 1974), but until recently no one has followed this up, to my disappointment.

5   What stalled the new paradigm?

As I look around at the contemporary scene, especially in Britain, France, Italy and Spain, I do see some reason for hope. Among clinicians, in the growing numbers of psychologists committed to qualitative studies and in one or two university departments new-paradigm work has taken root. But why is there any old-paradigm psychology at all?

Turning to the natural sciences for parallels, one is struck by the rapidity with which new styles of research and new general theories are accepted in physics and chemistry. One does not find the phlogiston theory of heat taught in some universities and the kinetic theory elsewhere. A new point of view may encounter resistance because it is more difficult to understand or to apply than the existing consensus. But even in the cases of relativity and quantum mechanics the resistance crumbled very fast. In the case of social psychology there is no doubt that the new paradigm was much more demanding than the old. It was metaphysically more complex. In replacing simple cause–effect relations by the idea of agents engaged in projects within the normative constraints of a local moral order, simplicity gave way to complexity. It also demanded a much wider knowledge of human affairs than the old paradigm. One must not only read the mainstream journals, but anthropology, history, literature and linguistics. Account analysis is a much more time-consuming methodology than that involved in conducting a simple two by two independent/dependent variable study and running the results through a statistical package. And no definite result can be guaranteed.

In biology the situation has been quite different. In the nineteenth century, Darwin's evolutionary theory threatened to undermine our view of ourselves much more directly than did the heliocentrism of Copernicus. In our time ethology, genetics and socio-biology touch on socially and personally sensitive matters. They take away responsibility. No wonder they are popular. New-paradigm social psychology forces us to contemplate our lives as our personal responsibility. We are not the passive spectators of causal processes from which our social lives emerge. We are active agents, using rules and conventions to accomplish things. Forced into passivity, trapped in conventions we had no hand in making, is a matter for protest, rebellion or even clinical collapse for most people. How much easier it is to locate responsibility for the shortcomings of our lives elsewhere, in patriarchy, the system, the risky shift (that is, being bolder in company than one would be by oneself), the effect of pure frequency on our affective experiences and so on! I am not the least surprised that old-style social psychology survives, and especially in the United States. However, I am comforted by the fact that innovations of the 1970s have shown that a truly scientific social psychology is possible.

23

Crossing cultures

Gustav Jahoda

Looking back over one's career is a challenging as well as, in my case, chastening task. Many of my peers, whose interests crystallised relatively early, went on to progress in a straight line, carrying out research in their specialty and perhaps elaborating theories. My own research history is rather more chequered, as is my personal one. I was born in Austria and lived in France for a number of years before coming to Britain. In France I began by studying engineering, switched to physics in London, but then dropped that in favour of sociology. Although gaining a qualification, it did not satisfy me, and so I ended up in psychology. Once again, even in this, my chosen field, I was never part of the mainstream and pursued a variety of different interests. This does not mean that I regard myself as a 'renaissance man', nor on the other hand as a mere dabbler. As I hope to show, certain dominant themes can be discerned in my various lines of research and writing.

With my background in sociology, it seemed a sensible course to become a social psychologist, and I obtained a lectureship in the subject at the University of Manchester. At that time – the late 1940s – the work of several talented American students of Kurt Lewin, such as Leon Festinger, had come to be known in Europe. It imbued the subject with a fresh air of vigour and excitement, which captured my imagination. Nonetheless, I was not content with sticking to a narrow line and read fairly widely. Thus I came to discover Piaget, not yet prominent in Britain at that time; and ventured into neighbouring fields, notably anthropology, which dealt with social behaviour in an entirely different way. I talked about this with Max Gluckmann, then head of the lively Anthropology Department at Manchester, and he was kind enough to invite me to their seminars. Since this might not be regarded as anything very unusual today, I should explain that at that period most British anthropologists kept psychologists at arm's length. The seminars provided a stimulating experience and, although I did not realise it at the time, they primed me for what was to come: a chance encounter that was radically to change the course of my professional life. A visitor from New Zealand passed through Manchester and the task of looking after him fell to me. He was Professor Ernest Beaglehole, distinguished in both psychology and anthropology. In the course of a walk he observed that in order to become a really good social psychologist one should have some experience of a non-Western culture. This thought struck home and after some initial hesitation I decided to apply for jobs that might be available in Africa. My colleagues in Manchester were astonished; leaving a tenured post for the unknown appeared to them a very eccentric thing to do. No doubt they were right: cross-cultural psychology did not yet exist as a recognised field.

Anyway, I departed to what was then the University College of the Gold Coast (now the University of Ghana), where I spent over four years. After returning to Britain I took up a Senior Lectureship at the University of Glasgow. From there I went on to establish a new department at the University of Strathclyde, where I have remained ever since. But it is important to mention that for about a quarter of a century after leaving Ghana I took every opportunity for research trips there, to other parts of Africa and, on a few occasions, to Asia. Accordingly, I propose to divide my sketch of work done into two sections. The first relates to the initial stay in the Gold Coast and subsequent fieldwork in Ghana and elsewhere, and the second to activities at home.

1   Fieldwork abroad

As the first – and for a few years the only – psychologist in the Gold Coast, the research opportunities were limitless. Such an *embarras de richesses* has drawbacks as well as advantages, for one does not know where to start. It seemed sensible to begin with one's students, trying to replicate some experiments in social psychology. Repeated lack of success gradually led to disenchantment, convincing me of the culture boundedness of experimental social psychology. Since there were so many other things to do at the time, I simply abandoned this line and it was not until many years later that I discussed the issues retrospectively (Jahoda, 1979a, 1988; cf. Amir and Sharon, 1987).

This did not mean that I had lost interest in social psychological problems, and one general topic that attracted me was the effect of rapid social change in what was still a predominantly traditional culture. It soon became evident that in such a setting the research methods I had been taught needed to be adapted, and I learnt a lot from an anthropologist colleague, David Tait. One problem that faced me was that of language. There were three main and numerous minor vernaculars, and while English was being taught at the later stages of education, reliance on that would have confined me to an atypical minority. I began by learning Twi, but before getting very far I realised that this would also restrict me to work with one ethnic group, sizeable but still only one of several. Accordingly, I decided to acquire some limited basic knowledge of the main vernaculars, just enough to show goodwill and facilitate rapport. Subsequently I trained students for work with young children and illiterates, and even my very limited command, together with paralinguistic cues, enabled me to make reasonably sure that things were done correctly.

Apart from language, it was also necessary to learn as much as possible about cultural norms, values and customs, some very basic. Thus, fairly early on, a formidable market woman taught me that it is exceedingly rude to tender money with the left hand. When one wanted to work in a remote village, one had to enter into a palaver with the chief and elders, who, naturally enough, wanted to know the purpose of the visit by the strange *oburoni* (literally 'red man'). It was no use trying to tell them about research in the service of the advancement of science! If they had encountered Europeans, it was in the roles of colonial officer, missionary, medical doctor or possibly teacher. It was important to avoid being identified with the first, otherwise one was liable to be asked to have a road built or a water supply laid on; 'teacher' was the safest bet. In order to obtain co-operation it was necessary to follow custom in providing a goat to be slaughtered or, at the very least, a supply of liquor (these raise some eyebrows when listed under 'research expenses'). In addition to such general prestations, small gifts were given to individuals who helped and some basic medicines made available to people in the village when needed.

There were plenty of other problems. Take, for instance, the seemingly simple matter of interviewing an individual in order to get his or her views. In a close-knit community this is a highly unusual situation, and was sometimes regarded with some suspicion; other people in the same compound would come and want to put their oar in. This was particularly tricky when an economist colleague and I decided to embark on a pioneering pre-election survey in Accra (Birmingham and Jahoda, 1955). It would be easy to multiply such examples, but enough has been said to show that radical adjustments are necessary when operating in a culture very different from one's own. This is, of course, commonplace for anthropologists, but relatively few psychologists appreciate it. Another lesson the experience in the Gold Coast taught me was the artificiality of disciplinary boundaries. When coming across an interesting problem, be it in social or developmental psychology, perception, or one more germane to sociology or anthropology, I pursued it. It was not the optimal way for advancing one's career and, as one visiting American psychologist told me, it was unscientific; but that did not bother me. Several years later I published, jointly with Nico Frijda (1966), a paper on methods in cross-cultural research that was followed by a conference on this topic at the University of Ibadan (Jahoda, 1968a). I also contributed a chapter on psychological approaches to a handbook, edited by Biesheuvel (1969), on methods in connection with the International Biological Programme.

Let me now turn to actual research carried out, beginning with the above-mentioned topic of social change. This included problems of adjustment of students to the radically contrasting settings of their home villages and university life, the emerging concept of 'romantic love' (Jahoda, 1959a), and the manner in which traditional healers modified their procedures, often adopting some of the external trappings of Western medicine (Jahoda, 1961a). One study of 'Westernisation' (Jahoda, 1961b, 1962a) anticipated what was later to become the burning topic of 'modernity' (Inkeles and Smith, 1974). In my contacts with a wide range of people, I noted early on widely differing responses to myself as a European 'stimulus object'. With highly educated Africans, social intercourse was at an easy level of equality. Those with limited schooling displayed an embarrassing subservience, not allowing me, for instance, to do any manual work, which they would take over without expectation of reward; but an underlying aggression sometimes rose to the surface. Illiterate villagers behaved with dignified detachment, but became very friendly on closer acquaintance. I kept a diary, as well as undertaking some relevant investigations and studying the historical record, in order to gain some understanding of these differences. The accumulated material later resulted in my first book, *White Man* (Jahoda, 1961c).

A topic that was being extensively discussed during the 1950s was the extent to which mental tests developed in the West were applicable in other cultures, and claims were being made for allegedly 'culture-free' tests of a non-verbal type. It was also believed not merely that tests of 'abstract behaviour' were culture free, but that non-Western peoples were deficient in this respect. One of my first studies in this area (Jahoda, 1956) demonstrated that so-called tests of abstract behaviour were no more culture free than intelligence tests. Furthermore, repeated administration of the Progressive Matrices (without feedback) produced a very substantial increase in scores. While this paper attracted attention as a novel approach, subsequent ones were submerged in an increasing stream.

Another phenomenon that greatly intrigued me was the prevalence and manifestations of various kinds of traditional beliefs in magic and witchcraft (Jahoda, 1961d, 1966a, 1968b). The last of these papers was concerned to show that, contrary to what was then widely believed, formal education does not eliminate traditional beliefs; it evoked a discussion in the pages of *Nature*. The psychological aspects of non-rational beliefs continued to interest me, eventually leading to the publication of *The Psychology of Superstition* (Jahoda, 1969a).

A comparative investigation of visual illusions on a worldwide scale had been undertaken jointly by two psychologists and an anthropologist (Segall *et al.*, 1963). This became a classic of cross-cultural psychology and was instrumental in putting the new subdiscipline on the map. Having seen a preliminary version of their findings, and taking advantage of eco-cultural variation within Ghana, I tested their hypotheses, which were only partially confirmed (Jahoda, 1966b). Experiential influences other than ecology were also explored (Jahoda and Stacey, 1970).

One related topic I pursued was originally prompted by a serendipitous observation. In a village where I worked there was an illiterate basket-maker whose products testified to his superb skill. Hence I asked him to make a basket as a present for my wife, leaving with him a picture in a catalogue as a model of what I wanted. When he had finished I was astonished to find that the basket, though very fine, bore scant resemblance to the model. Discussing this with colleagues in other disciplines, such as engineering and geology, I learnt that even very bright African students had difficulties in grasping complex two-dimensional representations of three-dimensional objects. Subsequent research in South Africa by Hudson (1967), which later became well known, suggested that unacculturated groups fail to understand pictorial depth. This led to a lengthy series of studies of pictorial and visual space perception, some undertaken jointly with Jan Deregowski, who became the most prominent authority in this field. For instance, it was shown that representations of simple objects were equally well understood by children as young as three years in both African and European cultures (Jahoda *et al.*, 1977), and in an educational context it was found across a range of different cultures that simple illustrations are equally effective everywhere (Jahoda *et al.*, 1976). Problems arise only with more complex representations of pictorial depth. As some of this work had practical implications, I made recommendations for the training of teachers in Ghana but do not know the extent, if any, to which they were implemented.

Changes in education did take place in Ghana, and evidence in a particular sphere suggests that they did have some effect. As mentioned previously, I had become interested in Piaget and tried out some of his approaches with African children, notably on animism and immanent justice (Jahoda, 1958a, 1958b), and on the mechanism of bicycles. On one of my return trips to Ghana some 13 years later I decided to replicate the bicycle study and found a highly significant improvement (Jahoda, 1969b). A few years after my initial work, cross-cultural Piagetian studies took off, with Pierre Dasen as the leading exponent. Yet the implications of cross-cultural findings for Piagetian theory still remain a moot issue.

My favourite developmental study also originated from a chance occurrence. I had given a talk on child development to a group of teachers, pontificating on the determinants of character. Some among my audience pointed out that I had omitted an important influence, namely the day on which the child was born. This referred to a belief among the Ashanti that the 'day name' given to a boy shapes his character. My initial scepticism evoked a flood of concrete examples, which made me pause and seek for a way of testing the claim. An empirical study (Jahoda, 1954) confirmed the belief, though my interpretation was along the lines of G.H. Mead rather than the traditional one. This paper used to be quoted in some texts, but has long been forgotten.

Before concluding this sketch of some of the major studies undertaken, one more general point will be made. In many of the studies, Scottish comparison samples were used and African children commonly did less well on Western-designed tasks. My purpose, however, was not that of documenting deficiencies but rather to explore the factors responsible for the differences. An obvious one is of course the lack of relevant experience, and a striking example of this will be cited later, since it was closely connected with some of the work in Scotland, to which I turn next.

2   Research at home

Alternating between cross-cultural studies and more usual research at one's home base appealed to me. Far from making an effort to pursue a single coherent line, I rather enjoyed variety: taking up something, leaving it for a while and coming back to it later; or dropping it altogether once it had become fashionable. Suffering from a tendency to get easily bored, I liked trying out something new.

My disillusionment with the pretensions of experimental social psychology, and consequent shift to another approach in the Gold Coast, has been mentioned above, as has my interest in Piaget. It occurred to me that 'modern' social psychology, unlike its predecessors (e.g. Murphy *et al.*, 1937), was preoccupied with the ideas, attitudes and beliefs of adults and ignored how these came about in the course of development. On the other hand, Piaget, apart from his early book on *The Moral Judgement of the Child* (1932) and a later article on children's conceptions of country and nationality (Piaget and Weil, 1951), concentrated mainly on advances in logico-mathematical understanding. So I embarked on a series of investigations on what is now known as the development of social concepts. One of the main challenges was that of elaborating ways of avoiding the usual predominantly verbal methods, since these are unsuitable for young children.

My first attempt in this direction was stimulated by the spontaneous talk of my own children and their friends, which occasionally seemed to indicate some awareness of social class differences. The method arrived at was to produce jigsaw pieces which could be physically fitted together in two different ways, only one of which was *socially* consistent. After any seemingly correct response the pieces were reversed and the child asked whether this would also be right; if the answer was negative children's comments were usually revealing (Jahoda, 1959b).

There followed a series of studies (Jahoda, 1962b, 1963, 1964) concerned with the development of children's ideas about countries and nationalities, addressing a range of different issues. For instance, one concerned the transition from knowledge of mere verbal labels, such as Glasgow, Scotland, England and Britain, to a grasp of the spatial relationships entailed by such names. Subsequently I teamed up with Henry Tajfel to conduct more ambitious cross-national explorations (Tajfel *et al.*, 1970, 1972). Perhaps the most important finding was that children come to associate a positive or negative affective tone with the names of countries well before they acquire even the most elementary objective information (e.g. that Russia is larger than Britain). A related topic was that of social or ethnic identity. For example, one question concerned the order of acquisition and relative salience of such symbols of Scottish identity as the flag, music, landscapes, dress, and so on. It turned out that Rabbie Burns was, at that time, the most salient symbol. Another study used a kind of identity kit to discover how children of Asian origin in Glasgow perceived themselves, and how they would have liked to be. This was done with equivalent samples by a Scottish investigator and an Indian one, with significantly different outcomes (Jahoda *et al.*, 1972), demonstrating a powerful experimenter effect.

Another sphere that attracted me was children's thinking about the economic world. An interesting aspect of this topic is that one deals with the functioning of *systems*. There is an analogy here to Piaget's logico-mathematical systems, except that in economic ones certain key aspects are not amenable to direct observation or manipulation. The technique employed was a 'shopping game' involving shopkeeper, supplier and customer, the critical feature being the price asked for by the supplier as compared with that for the customer. Most of the younger children took these to be equal, and the gradual progress to an understanding of the system was traced. It was not usually achieved by Scottish or Dutch children before the age of about 11 (Jahoda, 1979b; Jahoda and Woerdenbagch, 1982). Since many African children have personal experience of small trading, I predicted that in this respect they would be well in advance of European children, and this proved to be the case (Jahoda, 1983).

The research was also extended with secondary school children to the working of a bank. After being initially conceived as a kind of public service, the manner in which a bank makes a profit was only gradually understood by a minority, and by the end of schooling three-quarters of the adolescents still had not grasped it (Jahoda, 1981). Here again, relevant experience counts: a replication by Ng (1983) in Hong Kong exhibited closely similar stages, but Chinese adolescents there were well in advance of Scottish ones.

As already indicated in passing, some of the research reviewed had some practical implications, chiefly in the educational sphere. While this was not usually the reason why I embarked on it, sometimes application was the primary aim. This fitted in with the motto of John Anderson, the original founder of what was to become Strathclyde University, who wanted it to be 'a place for useful learning'. Thus I did pursue some directly applied projects, and in retrospect have come to realise that most of these were designed to correct some erroneous beliefs.

One study was concerned with what was then known as the Youth Employment Service (Jahoda and Chalmers, 1962a, 1962b). It showed that it functioned in a manner rather different, and less effective, than had been envisaged by its blueprint. When the Service came to be reorganised subsequently, some of the findings were taken into account.

During the early 1960s a number of satellite towns were established around Glasgow in order to reduce the population pressure, and people volunteered to move out. Politicians at the time claimed that a representative sample of Glaswegians were leaving, which seemed to me highly unlikely. On stating this view, I was challenged to provide evidence. Without any grant and only the help of a colleague, I did this by comparing the school marks of children who had left with those who remained, showing that the former had significantly better results. Publication (Jahoda and Green, 1965) brought down on my head the ire of local dignitaries, but the Chief Medical Officer, who had to deal with the consequent problems, gave me his support.

By contrast with this modest parochial exercise, a large project dealt with alcohol in relation to the young. I was asked by the Director of what was then the Scottish Health Education Unit to undertake a study of adolescent attitudes in this sphere (in the 1960s drugs were not yet prominent on the scene) with a view to dealing with the issue in secondary schools. On the basis of my work with younger children, outlined above, I suggested that it should be started in primary schools. This met with considerable scepticism, since it was then the conventional wisdom that primary school children are entirely ignorant of alcohol and in any case incapable of understanding anything about it. I managed to persuade the relevant committee to provide some extra funds, thereby enabling me to embark on one of my most demanding but also most rewarding pieces of research. New techniques had to be devised, relying minimally on verbal questioning and sufficiently game-like to motivate children in the first years of primary schools. An example will illustrate this. Children were presented one by one with series of small jars, masked to exclude visual cues, so that smell was the only one. The jars contained a range of liquids such as coffee, perfume, vinegar, and so on, but also alcoholic beverages. Children were first asked to indicate which of them they had smelled before; next, they were asked to say where they had smelled them. This simple procedure revealed that some three-quarters of six-year-olds were familiar with alcoholic drinks, though of course they did not know the term 'alcohol'. Publication of this study (Jahoda and Cramond, 1972) had some influence in changing views regarding primary school children. It was replicated by Fossey (1994), with closely similar results.

3   Changing perspectives

The emphasis in the present sketch has been on the first two decades of my professional biography, and a brief comment should be added on subsequent changes. Almost half a century ago, when I first began to embark upon research, the psychological landscape looked very different from today. Most of the areas with which I was primarily concerned barely existed at all. This applies particularly to cross-cultural psychology, where I might claim to have been a pioneer. It has now greatly expanded, without as yet being fully integrated with the mainstream, in spite of the fact that at least lip service is now paid to the importance of culture. It is also something of a disappointment to me that the style of the 'old guard', including John Berry, Pierre Dasen, Jan Deregowski and others, has become rare. We used to have direct personal contact with people on an individual basis, while the current trend is towards the administration of scales and questionnaires to large samples, sometimes by remote control. On the other hand, a new approach has emerged under the name of 'cultural psychology' which complements and to some extent rivals the 'cross-cultural' tradition (e.g. Cole, 1996).

As far as the development of social concepts such as nationality or social class is concerned, there has certainly been a great increase in activity, but it seems to me that the efforts remain scattered and await pulling together into a coherent account. By contrast, there has been a burgeoning of research into the development of children's economic ideas, which adds up to a more comprehensive picture (e.g. Berti and Bombi, 1988; Lunt and Furnham, 1996).

Looking back over my research career as a whole, I am aware that it must appear rather chequered and fragmented. Yet personally I found it exciting and rewarding to pursue whatever happened to capture my imagination, and so *'Je ne regrette rien'*.

24

Taking people seriously: psychology as a listening ear

John and Elizabeth Newson

Although we have been members of the British Psychological Society (BPS) ever since we graduated in 1951, and John chaired the newly formed Developmental Section, we have never really felt like BPS people (whatever they are), probably because we have often wanted to do the non-traditional things (like training educational and intending clinical psychologists together on an integrated developmental psychology MA course) and have had to negotiate serious, though not insuperable, obstacles. So it was an unexpected but very pleasurable honour to have the BPS turn to us in our still-busy seventies and ask 'How was it for you?'

We met at University College London (UCL) in the last two years of Cyril Burt's regime, when the College was almost taken over by men and women returning from the forces and wondering what to do with their lives and their demobilisation training grants; we don't recall them being called 'mature students' then. Elizabeth was one of only three students in her year coming straight from school; she remembers being interviewed by the Dean of the Arts Faculty, who openly regarded it as his job to dissuade an innocent girl from the 'rather morbid' subject of psychology.

It was a time of turmoil in the Psychology Department: Burt, 'about to retire' for over two years because no one had been found to replace him, was a distant and authoritarian figure, ruling over somewhat of an organisational shambles, in which students turned up for whatever lectures they fancied and nobody was ever expected to write an essay. At the end of the first year, a meeting was called by UCL to put forward the idea of managing the Department for an interim year through a consortium of professors from other departments in the university, not necessarily psychologists: C.A. Mace from Birkbeck, J.Z. Young, A.J. Ayer and a couple more; it sounded fun, but didn't come to anything. Then in 1950

Roger Russell whirled in from the United States in new-broom mood: the Department was scrubbed and painted, the lighting complained of and improved with unheard of speed, and ancient apparatus dumped. Russell himself chopped up the brains mouldering in formaldehyde which he found in a cupboard, and blocked the College plumbing, to everyone's excitement. Apparently the new order had arrived, and behaviourism joined the extraordinary mix of psychoanalysis (J.C. Flügel), work curves (S.J. Philpott), child guidance and child development (Grace Rawlings and Gertrude Keir), psychopathology (Max Hamilton) and philosophy (Stuart Hampshire) which was our psychological education. The Eysenck version of social psychology was replaced by Cecily de Monchaux's, an inspired and inspirational choice.

Surprisingly, through all this postwar chaos we worked very hard indeed at the things which interested us. It was acceptable, we found, for students of one college to turn up at another; Mace and J.A. Hadfield were lecturing at Birkbeck, and many of us spent an evening or two there each week; anthropology was on offer at Bedford College. Because our year seemed so much in transition, we went to *all* Burt's lectures, including postgraduate seminars, in our first year, and to all of Russell's in our third year. We turned up in the Philosophy Department to join a postgraduate seminar of Ayer's, who didn't even ask who we were and why we were gate crashing. Senate House library was clean, warm and comfortable, and full of anthropology – as was UCL's library once it had been rebuilt after bombing. It was in Senate House that we discovered Margaret Mead's and Gregory Bateson's *Balinese Character* (Mead and Bateson, 1942) – a seminal book for us, using as it did what had been a very new technology at the time, the rapid-winder camera, to illustrate and analyse sequences of behaviour, and so give vivid immediacy to the material underpinning their theoretical argument.

By the time we read Mead and Bateson we knew that anthropology attracted us, and we had started thinking about how we ourselves might get into that kind of research; we were going to get married immediately after our final examinations, and here was another couple already working the way we would like to work. That summer, the Professor of Anthropology was expecting to have a research assistantship to look at urbanisation in the Belgian Congo; we went to offer him two assistants for the price of one, with Elizabeth's French thrown in. It seemed a good bargain, he said, and we might well have disappeared into the violent maelstrom that the Congo became soon afterwards; fortunately for us, John was meanwhile offered an assistant lectureship at Nottingham by W.J.H. Sprott, and we couldn't afford not to take it. Nottingham was almost as unknown to us as the Congo, but we were told that it was an interesting and hospitable city, and so it proved to be.

1   The impetus

'Disinterested intellectual curiosity is the life-blood of real civilisation', wrote G.M. Trevelyan (1942). Perhaps; but one must wonder how often the motives that impel research workers to take the first step on a long-term commitment to a particular course of research are truly disinterested. It is clear enough that chance, circumstance and the concatenation of events play their part; but what about the personality, the domestic situation, the needs, doubts, ideals and whole lifestyle of the researcher? What degree of fit is necessary – or what disjunction tolerable?

Child rearing is a highly personal business, even though it happens within a web of culture that constrains parents more than they know; and it is perhaps appropriate that the impulse to begin our own study of child rearing was as much personal as it was academic. Both of us had completed PhD projects concerned with visual perception and coding, one with adult and the other with child subjects; and our curiosity, intellectual and otherwise, and not at all disinterested, was thoroughly taken up with our first baby. The baby himself, however, we soon realised, was also the focus and excuse (even before his actual birth) for a cultural bombardment designed by society to initiate us into our new role as young parents. Not only in terms of direct advice (though there was no shortage of that), but by means of the loaded comment, the unspoken assumptions, the 'of course' prefixed to somebody's value judgement, our culture enveloped us and our child.

Yet the culture did not speak with a single voice. We quickly became aware of subcultural norms which collided and conflicted. We already knew, both from reading and from professional contact, that there tended to be some division between medical and psychological opinion. Living in an area of Nottingham which for historical reasons is remarkable for its social class mix, we soon discovered differences of attitude among our neighbourhood acquaintances which were more than idiosyncratic. The swing of time was another factor. The baby's great-grandmother wrote to say how much she was looking forward to giving him a good cuddle – 'but', she added humbly, 'I know you modern mothers don't believe in picking them up too much, so I'll be careful to do as you think right': it was nice to be able to assure her that the Truby King era had passed and cuddling was in again. As far as baby-book advice was concerned, perhaps we were more conscious of changes in fashion than most young parents, as we thumbed our obligatory Spock: at three years old, one of us, in her role of responsible big sister, had studied every picture in the Truby King-inspired *Mothercraft Manual* (including the diagram for making a splint against eczema-scratching and thumb-sucking), and by the age of six had not only read the *Manual* from cover to cover but absorbed Susan Isaacs' rather different message in *The Nursery Years* (Liddiard, 1928; Isaacs, 1929b).

To be perfectly honest, we were finding that our academic training (though stronger in child psychology than many undergraduate courses) was rather less than adequate to answer the questions that naturally seemed to arise in the day-to-day practice of parenthood; and we were curious to know whether our own ways of dealing with quite ordinary issues were in fact typical. We just didn't know whether most people fed their babies on schedule or demand. We didn't know whether they potted the baby from the second day or the second year, nor what difference it made. When our son cried in the night and we hauled him into bed with us and sleepily sang him a song or muttered a nursery rhyme, we wondered whether we were quite alone in such indulgence: surely other people did not just ignore that plaintive howl, or perhaps they just spoke some firm words (what words?) which had the desired effect? Either way, we knew that the baby books invariably thought taking a child into bed was a Bad Thing with Unfortunate Consequences and, perhaps for this reason, parents didn't seem to discuss it much. (Later we found that 33% of one-year-olds' and 68% of four-year-olds' parents were actually prepared to do this, most of them expressing some guilt when talking about it.)

Over and above our curiosity, on an anthropological level, to know where we stood in the cultural scheme of things, we were intrigued by the degree of authority with which 'professional' advice on child rearing was vested. Words like 'ought' and 'should' seemed to be bandied about on issues which we were gradually coming to believe were matters of opinion; value judgements in terms of 'good', 'best', 'correct', 'harmful', 'faulty' were made with an assurance which, naively, we first assumed must stem from a well established body of knowledge. Is it characteristic of the enquiring mind that, precisely because of its respect for the research process, it imagines not only that its questions must have been asked many times before, but that there must also be answers already existing, a collated mass of documented evidence only waiting to be looked up? (We still find ourselves falling into this snare occasionally.) It took us some time to realise that if we seriously wanted answers to our questions, we would have to undertake some of the basic research ourselves.

Of course, there were a number of ways in which our academic background clearly did influence and help us. For instance, we were very aware of the theoretical controversies surrounding infant care practices, particularly those inspired by writers in the psychoanalytic tradition, which, despite intermittent sorties by the behaviourists, had for so long dominated the whole field of child development, including the anthropological studies which seemed closest to our own point of departure. Our scientific training had, however, made us critical concerning the nature of the evidence usually educed in order to cram child development into one theoretical framework or another; and we knew that the literature abounded with statements which could not all be true because many of them were implicitly contradictory. Nonetheless, we felt bound to take seriously the proposition that infant handling, whether in terms of a prevailing mother–child interaction climate or in terms of individual techniques of dealing with feeding, toilet training, wakefulness and so on, might have profound and irreversible effects upon a child's later personality development. As practising parents ourselves, we were caught in the usual trap: we dared not ignore theories, backed by a considerable weight of traditional orthodoxy, which suggested that if we did not follow expert advice we might irrevocably harm our own children. Perhaps we were even innocently optimistic (without being so aware as we are now of all the complications that bedevil research on such matters) that our own work might eventually shed some dramatic new light on which of the theories was correct.

Fortunately, however, we were from the outset more concerned to describe how a large and representative sample of mothers actually felt and behaved towards their babies than to concentrate on testing a string of theoretically derived propositions; and we would now strongly assert what we then only suspected, that wide-ranging descriptive studies of the hypothesis-*seeking* type are no less valuable to the general progress of psychology as an academic discipline than are the supposedly tightly controlled hypothesis-*testing* exercises which are still used as the central model in the scientific training of most psychologists. Our subsequent experience in repeated encounters with hundreds of mothers seen in their own habitats has made us more and more sceptical of the validity of drawing conclusions about real-life situations from laboratory studies of the experimental kind – particularly in the sphere of developmental social psychology, where generalisability from the laboratory model to the complex reality is likely to be very poor indeed. Increasingly, we found ourselves in sympathy with the philosophical standpoint of such writers as Roger Barker and Beatrice Wright, who tended to stress the need to adopt a broadly ecological approach to the understanding of human behaviour. In other words, we believe that it is essential to view child-rearing practices within a total context which subsumes such questions as the physical conditions under which people are constrained to live, the range of choices open to them, their work-style and time scale, and their beliefs, attitudes and values as members of a living community from which they can in no sense be isolated.

Making a deliberate decision to sensitise oneself, as it were, to the total life pattern into which the upbringing of an individual child is slotted has two immediate consequences, over and above the better understanding of the child development process. First, it swiftly removes the comfortable refuge of the easy value judgement. '*Tout comprendre, c'est tout pardonner*' – but it is not so much a matter of forgiving things, as of abandoning one's status as someone who has a *right* to forgive (with its implicit notion of a judgement made). In a research context which acknowledges the internal consistency of a variety of lifestyles, it becomes almost impossible to make dismissive comments about a particular style simply because it differs from what is acceptable in one's own frame of reference. (The researcher's own beliefs may indeed be suspect: how far does a theory appeal because of its good fit with his or her *emotive* preconceptions?) Thus, for instance, such a term as 'inadequate' applied to a mother or a family seems almost irrelevant once one has explored the pattern of constraints which have led this family to adopt the defences it does: the only way in which such a concept is usefully descriptive is in terms of the ways in which the family's defences are inadequate to master and transform those constraints.

Second, the more one becomes aware of how few choices certain groups of people actually have, and how far they are forced into behaviour patterns that happen to be maladaptive to their own progress in this society (thus completing an especially vicious circle), the greater the temptation is for the research worker to take a political stand and deliberately to work for change. This is not a contradiction of the last paragraph: one can respect the validity of many modes of child rearing as being the direct product of a total lifestyle, while at the same time deploring the convolution of circumstance which reduces to nil people's opportunity (or, insidiously, their wish) to consider alternatives. At this point, the researcher has to identify her role: if she is to remain an objective observer, she cannot range herself 'for' this and 'against' that. To put it at its simplest: if we went on record in the *Nottingham Evening Post* as saying that families in Blank Street live in appalling conditions, we could expect in the following edition a letter from Jim Smith of Blank Street suggesting that University people had better keep their noses out of Blank Street if they don't understand what a friendly neighbourhood it is. In other words, we would have distanced ourselves from life in Blank Street by showing how we disapprove of its material conditions, instead of simply accepting the subjective evaluation of people to whom Blank Street is home, and taking that as our point of departure in learning about it. Equally, we cannot make public statements about 'good' parenthood or 'bad' parenthood and then expect to talk to ordinary parents again on an equal footing: their awareness that you are in the labelling business, even if they do not remember just how you labelled what, cannot help distorting the information they give.

So we made no attempt, in this particular field, to instigate change or to become involved with policy making, because we did not see this as consonant with the long-term observer's role as we had chosen to play it. That is not to say that the two roles *cannot* be reconciled: in the same area, the National Children's Bureau is the supreme example of research and political functions successfully combined. But the Bureau's research, nationally mounted as it was, was (by the very factor of its size) set at a more impersonal level; our own, involving itself with a much narrower segment of population but at greater depth, had to continue to meet its respondents face to face.

Any effect the findings of our research may have had on social policy thus had to be indirect, in the sense that we provided ammunition for others rather than supplying the motive force for firing it. Once again, however, it is fair to ask how far we were finding good research reasons for a stance to which we were temperamentally suited anyway. Although we both sat on committees when it seemed we should, this was not an activity which gave either of us great joy or satisfaction. Convinced intellectually that social change at the grass roots must necessarily be backed up and given impetus by policy change at national level, we nevertheless chafed at the inevitable fatuities: perhaps the more high-powered the committee, the less tolerable its shortcomings. Obviously, we felt somewhat guilty at not being active political animals at that time, and we were occasionally accused of fence sitting; we remained reasonably certain that we could do a better research job from that position.

What gave us more pleasure was to feel ourselves a contributing part of a wider movement to take seriously the ideas and beliefs of ordinary people. This was always an essential feature of our research strategy. If we may quote ourselves:

The function of this research ... is simply to tap a rich source of information which already exists but which too often is ignored: the ordinary mother's ability to examine her own behaviour and her own feelings, and, if we only give her the opportunity, to share them with us. (Newson and Newson, 1968: 27)

2   Money and methodology

By 1957 we had planned what we wanted to do: to interview 700 Nottingham mothers in some depth every few years at what we regarded as key points in their sampled child's life: within a few weeks of the first, fourth, seventh, eleventh and sixteenth birthdays, and possibly later still. The one-year-old study could have stood on its own (though we didn't want that to happen); we had no money, and were afraid to embark on a long-term project with the kind of grant that would be needed, since we now had one child (with a disability), and another expected, and could not foretell whether we could commit ourselves fully to longitudinal research while being the kind of parents we wanted to be. We don't think the dual role of each of us could have worked if we had not both been committed to the *same* project: but, as things were, we were both motivated to be totally flexible, and had to be; we never had a nanny or an au pair, which was equally true of the mothers we were talking to.

For the first stage, the University paid for a portable tape recorder and our postage, and Elizabeth worked without salary; but we were also allotted health visitor time by a generous health authority to carry out 500 of the interviews. This brought its own (expected) problems (Newson and Newson, 1963), but we could not have got started without it. Once the one-year-old stage was finished, the Nuffield Foundation fully funded the next stage, followed by the Social Science Research Council on condition that the University finally took the funding over. This was agreed; we hardly think it would be nowadays.

The sample of 700 (topped up at each stage to make up any losses) was not just a figure plucked out of the air. We had a hunch, contrary to the received wisdom of the time, that social class might turn out to be important in determining child-rearing attitudes; and we needed to interview enough mothers in each class to be able to make statistically significant comparisons. Yet there was no information available as to the social class make-up of a random sample of mothers of one-year-olds. If we had simply taken a random sample of 700, we would have ended up with 350 skilled manual families and only 56 unskilled families, which would have been both wasteful and unsatisfactory; we needed at least 100 in each class group. In order to establish the effect of social class on specific attitudes, we had to take a random sample of 500, to establish actual proportions, stratify a further sample by class and add in 200 of the less well represented groups, finally weighting the sample to bring them back to a randomised total: 700 was the number needed for this operation.

It is difficult now to understand the social and academic climate in which we were attempting this work. We had two major problems to contend with: the belief (of the middle class), often expressed to us by members of the audience at conferences, that 'social class no longer exists'; and the very low esteem accorded to interviewing as a methodology at that time. As both we and the National Children's Bureau showed in our findings, occupational class is the biggest factor for good or ill that can be statistically shown; unemployment has changed this, but we would still need to 'build in' class if we were starting all over again. The myth of the demise of social class did make discussion of our work quite difficult at times: some critics thought it was 'not very nice' to talk about social class; and when television interviewers asked us beforehand about our main findings, and we said 'the effects of social class', they tended to say 'You can't possibly talk about *that!*' Ours was perceived as 'a class study', when in fact this had never been our major intention: we had only tried to make it possible for class (and gender, and neighbourhood, and birth order) to emerge *if it was significant in childhood experiences*. It seemed important to know how the cards were stacked in the society we lived in; but we were genuinely surprised at the magnitude of the class differences.

Academically, interviewing was seen as a very 'soft' and unscientific method to use. Attitude scales were the acceptable tool; although anyone who has ever submitted to an attitude scale, on a topic they care about, knows what a feeble travesty of their complex belief system is produced on that Procrustean bed. Observation, preferably experimentally constrained, might have been an approved option; yet what would be the effect of the psychologist taking notes in the corner? It seemed we would have to refine the interviewing method until it truthfully reflected our aim: to make it possible for mothers to talk at length about what their children did, what they themselves did, and what they thought about what they did.

The time was right; portable and non-intrusive tape recorders had just become available. Like Mead and Bateson, our methods were enabled by new technology (Newson and Newson, 2000). Tape recorders made it possible to use carefully structured yet truly open-ended questions, and freed us and our respondents from the tyranny of predefined, multiple-choice answers. Our interviewing technique would have owed much to Michael Argyle's studies on eye contact, distance and affiliation (Argyle and Dean, 1965), had they been published at that time; his experimental studies resonated closely with our practical attempts to produce a 'natural', user-friendly conversation in which the recorder and interview schedule would lose their prominence in the perception of the respondent. This technique has been very fully described elsewhere (Newson and Newson, 1976). Suffice it to say that allowing the respondent to give elaborate answers (including any red herrings that *she* thought relevant), during a conversational interchange that *she* thought natural, made a huge difference to our understanding, not only of what parents did in bringing up their children, but of the underlying reasons, feelings and attitudes that informed their practical decisions, their impulses, and the aftermath of either. Conversation as a methodological tool has the important advantage of allowing for surprises: the kinds of answers that ordinary people express do not necessarily coincide with the investigators' prior assumptions. And it is the disconfirmation of preconceptions which leads on to new advances in scientific understanding.

Genuine dialogue is possible only when we abandon all pretensions to being an authority on anything (especially, in this case, psychology!) and become respectful rather than respected, with the stated aim of truly comprehending the respondent's point of view. The name 'Child Development Research Unit' was coined simply to express what the respondents already knew, and for years we made sure not to be associated locally with 'Psychology', in which we were much helped by the *Nottingham Evening Post*, which understood our dilemma. The use of health visitors in the first stage, necessary as it was, broke the 'no identifiable status' rule, and some questions reflected this in being answered in terms of what the health visitor might like to hear rather than entirely frankly. When we started to suspect this, we asked each of the health visitors to complete a schedule in the way they thought ideal – which we were allowed to do only on condition we did not publish the results! So many years later, perhaps we can affirm that *all* the differences between the University interviewer's findings and the rest were accounted for in terms of health visitors' correctly perceived ideals. Elizabeth's genuine role as a young mother was enormously in her favour: when we were financially able to employ a team of interviewers, a prime qualification was their motherhood, so that this could be mentioned in the introductory letter; once contact had been made, we could all grow older together! The nature and length of the encounter (two to four hours, or more) seemed to have a bonding effect, as did the intimacy of the topic; and training new interviewers in achieving the skills we wanted was made possible by taping and thus closely supervising their first few (non-sample) interviews – not everyone could manage the degree of flexibility and sensitivity, nor the abrogation of status. Our favourite quotation (and we salute our long-term assistant, Dady Key, for getting so right the deceptive simplicity of the approach) was this one: 'I can sew … I don't say I'm clever … I'm not a *brainy* person … I couldn't do clerical work … I probably couldn't even do *your* job…'.

Perhaps it was unfortunate for us that, in our already bulky books, there was little room for a lengthy exposition of our interview technique; the long discussion published in a series of 'case studies' edited by Marten Shipman (1976) was separated from the reports of the work it referred to. We were also very anxious to give parents a real voice; and their vivid quotations, thanks to the tape recorder, illuminated the statistical framework of the research to a degree that was unusual at the time: possibly some people thought this made the research too easy. One reaction was 'What a good idea, to make the parents write half the book for you!', oblivious of the endless work of collation and selection; another was 'I so enjoyed that book, it's nice to read research that isn't full of tables', referring to a book that contained 69 of them! Accessibility doesn't necessarily enhance a scientific reputation. Of course, we were not the first to have quoted so extensively: both Henry Mayhew (1864) and the lesser known R.D. Grainger (1843), sub-commissioner to the Commission on Children's Employment, gave their respondents generous space; though they had fewer scientific constraints. Well received though our books were from the beginning, in journals as well as the broadsheets, there remained for a long time this doubt about our truly scientific status. When Elizabeth was, in 1980, appointed Scientific Advisor to the Mental Handicap Research Liaison Group of the Department of Health, she asked whether she had been recruited for her work in autism; the answer was, 'No – for your unrivalled experience in research interviewing'. Her face betrayed her astonishment, to the amusement of the senior civil servant involved, who correctly interpreted: 'Yes, you're respectable now!'

It was, however, the freedom with which mothers (later fathers too) were enabled to confide in us that led some of the voluntary societies for various disabilities to fund further projects; the then Spastics Society was the first to realise the possibilities, followed by several others. With funded research officers, we were able to carry out research on the experience of bringing up children with learning disabilities, cerebral palsy, deafness, blindness and autism – the last with a series of grants from the Department of Health. We discovered the possibilities of the marathon interview lasting two days, and the signed interview with deaf mothers. It was our interest in the experiences of both mothers and children living with disability, who were finding difficulties in so basic a right as the ability to play, that decided us to research the potential function of the 'toy library' as a support for families: at that time there was only one such library in the country, but this action research project was deliberately planned to release information and organise workshops as the research progressed, and by the end of the project there were over 200 nationwide, organising themselves under one umbrella.

Our teaching by 1970 had for some time been mainly with postgraduates, training to be educational or developmental psychologists with a specialism towards clinical aspects. We have always felt that the biggest influence in one's academic life must be one's students, who ask the difficult questions which force one to explain oneself: 'How do I know what I think till I hear what I say?' (variously attributed!). John was leading a research group on mother–baby interactions; parallel to this, with a strong two-way flow of ideas, Elizabeth had opened a weekly postgraduate training clinic specialising in children with communication disorders. Faced with such difficult children, she and her students developed the 'play-based assessment' – another endeavour which looks much easier, and less scientific, than it actually is. All we had learned about interviewing now fuelled the application of such principles in the two-hour clinical history taking carried out in teamwork with parents as they watched the entire playroom assessment via the kind of one-way screen that several people can sit comfortably behind. Our continuing concern was still to establish a 'language of partnership' with parents, even in situations where the parents' need to find expertise made the consultant's status much more obvious, requiring all our imagination to defuse its effects.

There seems to us now to have been a logical thread running through our lives: the pursuit of communication, negotiation and partnership, within a web that included parents, students, colleagues and other kinds of non-university professions, with children as the focal core. Many things might have distracted us into different kinds of life: in 1970 we opened both a family shop selling toys and ceramics (which lasted 25 years) and a school for autistic children (which is still very much alive, and internationally known under its Director, Phil Christie). We were involved in long-term toy consultancy (which educated us to the manufacturer's point of view, and gave us a still more rounded understanding of toys in practice); and we engaged in film making, television and a wide range of exhibitions with non-psychologist colleagues. We ran a charity – the Children's Play Activities Trust – originally set up by the pioneer toy-makers Paul and Marjorie Abbatt, and made over by Marjorie to our care – and were able to disburse many small grants that had big consequences for the recipients. We were frequently called upon by the courts as expert witnesses in child abuse, access and even toy patent cases. But in all of these diverse activities there remained the thread that tied everything together, and somehow made sense of what we were doing. And we enjoyed pretty well all of it.

When John retired at 65, he continued to take a full part in teaching and research until Elizabeth, too, retired from the University three years later; but at the request of the regional Society for Autism, she moved straight into the developmental diagnostic clinic which had been waiting for her. Over many years she had tried to pursue the notion of diagnosis coupled with immediate specific intervention through parents, and was equally interested in identifying specific syndromal clusters within the pervasive developmental disorders; the clinics (funded by the National Health Service) and these aspects of research continue to be her main full-time 'retirement career'. People who work with children are said to be long-lived; this is our hope, for we still have quite a lot to do.

Acknowledgement

Part of this chapter has been adapted from John and Elizabeth Newson (1976) Parental roles and social contexts. In M. Shipman (Ed.) *The Organisation and Impact of Social Research: Six Original Case Studies in Education and Behavioural Science*. London: Routledge and Kegan Paul. We are grateful to Routledge for permission to quote this passage.

25

The emergence of developmental psychopathology

Michael Rutter

When, having passed 'A' levels at 16 years of age, I left school to go to Birmingham Medical School in 1950, thoughts of psychiatry and psychology played no part in my career plans. Both my father and grandfather were general practitioners and I fully expected to follow them. Nevertheless, during the next five years, I became increasingly interested in the interconnections between brain and mind, with the academic thrust coming from books such as Grey Walter's *The Living Brain* (Walter, 1953/1960). Although I was not convinced by many of the specifics of the ideas in the book, I was certainly taken with the fascinating range of questions to which they gave rise, and I decided to specialise in psychiatry.

1 Postgraduate training in neurology, paediatrics and psychiatry, 1955–1961

Following advice, I obtained training in general medicine, neurology and neurosurgery first. The Maudsley Hospital was said to be the best place for psychiatric training and that is where I went. I hesitated at first because all trainees had to do a dissertation and I thought that research would not be for me. However, my brief period at the National Heart Hospital brought me in contact with Paul Wood, Britain's leading cardiologist at that time. He had a special skill in linking basic physiology with individual clinical manifestations. I became fully converted to the value of seeking to bridge basic science and clinical medicine and determined to try to apply that approach to psychiatry.

My three and a half years' psychiatric training at the Maudsley Hospital were wonderfully exciting. Professor Aubrey Lewis was a towering intellect and someone who especially fostered an enquiring, challenging, questioning approach from trainees. He encouraged all of us to read widely, to think deeply and never to accept anything without looking closely and carefully at the relevant empirical evidence. He was a powerful advocate of the importance of psychology and it was through him that my first strong interests in psychological issues were aroused.

At that time, psychology played the major role in the academic teaching that we received. Hans Eysenck gave many of the lectures and seminars and his brilliant teaching made a big impact. His view of what should be included in psychology was certainly idiosyncratically narrow and already his own particular brand of psychological evangelism was causing ex-students of his to make accusations that he manipulated research findings (Storms and Sigal, 1958). In the later years of his career, it became evident that there was indeed substance to these concerns (Pelosi and Appleby, 1992). I am indebted to Eysenck, and to the many bright and productive psychologists in his department, for firing my interest in psychology, but he is also responsible for my deep distrust of academic evangelists and my loathing of those who distort the evidence to support their own particular viewpoint.

Aubrey Lewis allocated particular papers for trainees to present at journal clubs. They were somewhat frightening occasions because of Aubrey's incisive questioning, but they were wonderfully stimulating. Aubrey had a rare gift of knowing just what would most interest each trainee and, in my case, he was right on target. One presentation was concerned with a series of psychological studies of individuals' responses to sensory deprivation (using water chambers) and this led to an abiding interest in the effects of different forms of deprivation on psychological functioning. The other dealt with an important epidemiological study by Buck and Laughton (1959) looking at associations between illness in parents and disorder in children. This led fairly directly to my own study for my doctoral thesis (Rutter, 1966), which provided the basis for later research to elucidate the range of genetic and environmental mechanisms involved in intergenerational continuities and discontinuities.

This got me fully hooked on empirical research and gave me a confidence that I might have the potential for a successful research career. Aubrey Lewis was hugely supportive but, rather to my surprise, decided that I should become an academic child psychiatrist. I had not been particularly impressed by the quality of clinical child psychiatry, but I recognised the research opportunities and I agreed to give it a go. I set about seeing some of the key experts in developmental research, agreeing with Aubrey's advice that it would be essential to have a year in the United States working full time studying child development. My choice on where to go was made immediately when I heard a talk on temperament by Herb Birch. Herb had started as a comparative psychologist working with primates under the direction of Schneirla, but then shifted to human studies with a prime interest in applying psychological methods to the study of children with developmental handicaps. He was a charismatic figure, absolutely brimming with ideas and tremendously responsive to those of other people.

2   Learning about child development in the United States, 1961–1962

My year in New York with Herb, Alex Thomas and Stella Chess constituted a
turning point for me. Alex and Stella were extremely helpful in allowing me to
develop various aspects of their longitudinal study, and I gained enormously from
the wide-ranging discussions with Herb (usually at 7 a.m.!) on all manner of
topics in psychology and child development. He was an argumentative man
without respect for authority, and I loved the cut and thrust of our discussions
as I learned to think for myself on developmental issues. Between them, Stella
and Alex seemed to know all the key figures in the field and they guided me on
whom to see, helping to arrange visits all over the country. Interestingly, although
Alex and Stella were clinical psychiatrists, many of the people they advised me
to visit were psychologists. I came back to Britain excited by the potential of
psychology but very disappointed in the generally poor standing of child psychiatry
in both countries.

Ernest Gruenberg and Ben Pasamanick, two highly creative, iconoclastic,
psychiatric epidemiologists, first impressed on me the utility of epidemiological
methods to tackle questions on causation, and not just to count heads to determine prevalence. Among the psychologists I spent time with, Jerry Kagan, Ed
Zigler and Harold Stevenson stood out. The other two people who played a key
role, both of whom became lifelong friends, were Lee Robins (a sociologist) and
Leon Eisenberg (a child psychiatrist). Lee was just beginning to report her pioneering long-term follow-up study of young people who had attended a child guidance
clinic during the 1930s. I was impressed by the power of long-term longitudinal
studies and she was influential in the great extent to which I subsequently made
use of this research strategy. Her findings were also important in indicating the
extent to which, through their own behaviour, people shaped their later experiences. Leon stood out as a beacon among child psychiatrists – immensely
thoughtful and intelligent, wonderfully articulate and questioning of the dogmas
that dominated the field. His own research showed the value of an empirical
approach and he was forthright in his insistence that research both incorporate
the very best of basic science and also concern itself with issues of policy and
practice.

3   The MRC Social Psychiatry Unit, 1962–1966

My four years in the Medical Research Council (MRC) Social Psychiatry Unit
constituted a further incomparable learning experience. From Beate Hermelin
and Neil O'Connor I learned about the value of experimental approaches. More
than anyone else in the world, they opened up the field of research into autism
and changed concepts in ways that have stood the test of time (Hermelin and
O'Connor, 1970). George Brown (a medical sociologist) and I worked closely
together to develop new methods of measuring family interaction and family
relationships, and developed, among other things, the concept and measure of

'negative expressed emotion' which has subsequently proved so useful. I continued working with Herb Birch, mainly in relation to his epidemiological studies in Aberdeen, and, most of all, I collaborated with Jack Tizard (a social psychologist), whose research opened up new avenues in a diverse range of fields spanning mental retardation, the study of institutions, the effects of malnutrition and the epidemiology of handicapping disorders. We worked most closely together in the planning and undertaking of the Isle of Wight epidemiological studies. Although, obviously, Jack was the expert, he was immensely generous in allowing me gradually to take over much of the leadership. Jack was passionately involved with political issues as they applied to the deprived and disadvantaged but he was a rigorous and conscientious methodologist who insisted that policy issues deserved nothing less than top-level dispassionate science.

The Isle of Wight studies were funded by government departments and their planning was shaped by discussions between the departments and Jack Tizard (and subsequently myself). What Jack had been asked to do was a relatively narrow study to check whether physical disability was associated with educational retardation in the way that it had been at the turn of the century. He succeeded in persuading those who held the purse strings that there was an opportunity for a much more ambitious study that could simultaneously be informative in the planning of services and also throw crucial light on the nature and origins of the common disorders of childhood. The studies were a great success (Rutter *et al.*, 1970/1981) and the findings remain influential today.

Because Aubrey Lewis did not think child psychiatry training was worth having, I returned from the United States to start immediately running my own clinical team, functioning as a consultant although paid as a trainee. Because I had got such good people to turn to for advice, that actually worked very well for me. I was pleased later on to play my part in improving child psychiatric training, and setting standards for it, but I regret that, in bringing up the standards of the weaker training programmes, a degree of rigidity and inflexibility in training requirements has since crept in.

The early 1960s was also the time when I started research into autism, initiating with Linda Lockyer, a Canadian clinical psychologist, a follow-up study with a comparison group of children with other forms of psychiatric disorder. The conceptualisation of what were then termed infantile psychoses seemed most unsatisfactory and it was not at all clear whether there was much validity in the diagnostic distinctions. Long-term outcome seemed one useful way to examine the matter. Our findings proved to be unusually interesting in several respects. The finding that about a quarter of the children with autism developed epileptic attacks during adolescence provided one of the first unambiguous indications that autism was likely to have its origins in some form of organic brain dysfunction. In parallel with the experimental findings of Hermelin and O'Connor, our results also pointed to the crucial role of cognitive deficits and especially of those that involved language in one way or another. I became fascinated by the many research and clinical issues that surrounded autism and their elucidation came to occupy an increasingly large part of my clinical practice, as well as my clinical research (Rutter, 1999).

4   Institute of Psychiatry, 1966–1984

The period from the late 1960s to the early 1980s, when I held successively the positions of Senior Lecturer, Reader and then Professor of Child Psychiatry, allowed me to put my research on a much firmer basis and also considerably to extend the range of topics tackled. In those days, the administrative load was miniscule, and there was huge freedom to develop one's own ideas together with a set of extremely high-calibre colleagues and a scintillating set of trainees. Provided one did a really good job, there were almost no constraints. Heady times indeed and wonderfully rewarding. I was fortunate to be able to establish a research career at a time of academic expansion and to do so within a supportive interdisciplinary setting. Regrettably, it would not be so easy today.

My studies of family influences during the 1960s led me to develop a strong interest in John Bowlby's ideas about 'maternal deprivation'. It seemed to me then that he had focused on a most important topic, that some of the claims were likely to prove valid, but that some of the ideas perhaps were more question-able. That led to my book on the topic, which made a substantial impact on both popular thinking and academic ideas. While writing the book, I first met Robert Hinde, then Director of the MRC Unit on the Development and Inte-gration of Behaviour. I had found his thinking about both animal behaviour and human development immensely helpful and I decided to ask if he would be willing to review my draft manuscript. It was typical of him that, although he knew me only slightly, he agreed to do so. What I got back was some 17 pages of closely argued comments! The book was incomparably better for his input and he helped me to take a broader biological perspective.

The 1970s saw substantial progress on several research fronts, but with some important lessons that had to be learned. A study comparing autism with severe developmental disorders of receptive language showed marked differences between the two and suggested that language abnormalities might not constitute a critical element in the underlying cognitive deficit associated with autism. Research over the subsequent two decades confirmed the basic finding but also indicated that deficits in language probably did play a central role in autism, albeit as part of a broader cognitive impairment (Bailey *et al.*, 1996). Our early research had shown the importance of organic brain dysfunction in autism but, in keeping with other commentators, I had concluded in a review in the 1960s that genetic factors were unlikely to be crucial because autism occurred in only some one in 50 of the siblings and because there have been no reports of autism transmitted from parent to child. Shortly afterwards, I realised that my reasoning had been mis-taken. The point was not that the rate of autism in siblings was low in absolute terms but, rather, that it was very high compared with the rate in the general population. The possibility of genetic factors had to be reassessed and this led to the first systematic population-based twin study of autism, undertaken with Susan Folstein. The findings of this first small twin study pointed to a strong genetic component but also indicated that the genetic liability probably extended well beyond the traditional diagnostic boundaries of autism. During the 1980s a larger twin study was undertaken with Ann Le Couteur and Tony Bailey, providing confirmation of both inferences (Rutter, 2000).

In the second edition of *Maternal Deprivation Reassessed* (Rutter, 1981), I concluded that it was unusual for adverse early experiences to have major long-term sequelae that were independent of later circumstances. Again, the finding has been confirmed by other research but I had posed the issue in a misleading way because, as I subsequently realised, one of the important consequences of early negative experiences was that they often led to a much-increased risk of later stresses and adversities. The notion of indirect chain reactions or developmental pathways came to the fore (Rutter, 1989).

Neither the epidemiological studies on the Isle of Wight nor the subsequent comparative study in inner London focused on school effects. Nevertheless, findings were striking in showing major differences among schools in the rates of both reading difficulties and emotional/behavioural disturbance, but it was unclear whether they simply reflected variations in intake or effects that stemmed from influences brought about by the school environment. Prompted by teachers who said that we absolutely had to go on to undertake research to find out whether the school differences were, or were not, a consequence of anything the schools themselves were doing, a working group of teachers and researchers was set up to plan what was needed and to take the research forward.

The results of our study of the progress of pupils through 12 secondary schools showed significant effects of the school environment on both behaviour and attainment, and provided pointers on which aspects of schooling were crucial in those connections. The research got a very positive reception from teachers and educational policy makers around the world but, at first, it was savaged by British social scientists. One group were offended because they felt that the finding that schools could make a difference detracted from the need for revolution. The other group focused on statistical issues and on the fact that, inevitably, there were aspects of the children's background that we had not been able to measure. The experience was a somewhat bruising one at the time but subsequent research by other independent investigators (using more sophisticated statistical techniques than were available at the time of our study) confirmed all our main findings (Mortimore, 1995). Numerous questions remain about school effects but no one now argues that schooling does not matter.

I look back on this as one of the most rewarding studies that I undertook. Collaboration with teachers was a real pleasure, as well as crucial to the success of the research, and I was exceptionally fortunate in the strong research team that I was able to recruit – Peter Mortimore, Barbara Maughan and Janet Ouston, who brought expertise and ideas from education, social administration and psychology. Again, it is noteworthy that support for the research came from the governmental department of education, which saw the importance of the topic and recognised that the research design that I proposed would work. It is clear from the hostile reception that we received later from British academics that there was no way that it would have survived peer review, particularly because I was not an educationalist and, at that time, had no track record in schools research. Although I remain a firm supporter of the value of peer review, because I know of nothing better, I am increasingly troubled by the extent to which it fosters conservatism and tends to suppress innovation, particularly if it comes from an unexpected quarter.

A further area of research during this time period comprised a series of studies of children with brain injury, in which epidemiological techniques were applied to circumstances that provided natural experiments, enabling causal hypotheses to be put to the test. I became convinced of the value of this approach and it came to play an increasingly large part in my research endeavours during the years that followed.

During the 1970s I was appointed to the Educational Research Board of what was then the Social Science Research Council (SSRC). Its membership spanned a wide range of disciplines and included policy makers and practitioners. It was a wonderful group of people with pioneers such as Sir Alec Clegg, one of the most creative directors of education in Britain, Alan Little, who directed the Inner London Education Authority Research Unit, and Basil Bernstein, whose ideas and findings on styles of language opened up thinking on how social class differences might operate.

A bit later, the SSRC and government departments jointly funded a major seven-year research programme to tackle the questions that derived out of Sir Keith Joseph's suggestions on transmitted deprivation (he was then Secretary of State for Social Services). The programme led eventually to some excellent research that did much to clarify thinking on the mechanisms involved in continuities and discontinuities (Rutter and Madge, 1976; Brown and Madge, 1982). Unfortunately, the initial reaction from British social and behavioural scientists proved to be very damaging. They were right to query the validity of Joseph's claims but it proved foolish to do so on ideological, rather than empirical, grounds. The fact that some researchers were governed more by political conviction than dispassionate science was primarily responsible for Joseph deciding that psychology and sociology were not science. The SSRC was renamed the Economic and Social Research Council and was provided with rather limited funding.

Fortunately, psychology was far from reliant on funding from the SSRC or ESRC because of the strong support for top-quality psychological research by the MRC: much psychology was included in the remit of the Social Psychiatry Unit; the Developmental Psychology Unit directed by Neil O'Connor and subsequently by John Morton (with the Unit renamed Cognitive Development) pioneered experimental studies, particularly in the fields of autism, reading/spelling difficulties and language; the Social and Applied Psychology Unit under the directorship of Peter Warr undertook a range of more applied studies; and the

Applied Psychology Unit under a series of most distinguished directors exerted world leadership over many years (see Baddeley, Chapter 17). The studies under-taken by Robert Hinde and Judy Dunn in Robert's MRC Unit were particularly important in the child development field.

5 The 1979/1980 year in California

During the early 1970s I first met Norman Garmezy, the American psychologist who did much to establish high-risk studies. We became close friends during the year that he spent in my department in the mid-1970s and we planned together a study group looking at stress coping and development to be held at the Center for Advanced Study of Behavioral Sciences at Stanford. That took place during the year 1979/1980, but with a membership more diverse than we had originally envisaged. Its heterogeneity proved hugely important and my experiences during that year constituted another turning point. The group included creative pioneers such as Jerry Patterson, Jerry Kagan, Lew Lipsett, Julie Sigel, Judy Wallerstein and Herb Liederman. During the year I also got to know Eleanor Maccoby much better. All our partners also got on well and a wonderful set of friendships, as well as research interactions, was established that has lasted through to today. The opportunity to be freed of administrative teaching and clinical responsibilities was hugely liberating and enabled me to rethink what I wanted to do in research. One result was the putting together of plans for an MRC research unit in which the most distinctive feature was to be a bringing together of developmental and clinical perspectives, with an interdisciplinary approach, in order to investigate the mechanisms involved in the cause and course of psychopathology.

6 The MRC Child Psychiatry Unit, 1984–1988

The Unit was established in 1984, very much along the lines that I had planned. I had wanted to call it a developmental psychopathology unit but it was decided that nobody would know what that meant and, instead, it was called the Child Psychiatry Unit. Nevertheless, the bringing together of developmental and clinical perspectives constituted its *raison d'être* and this research approach increasingly came to occupy a central role in the field (Sroufe and Rutter, 1984; Rutter and Sroufe, 2000). Particular use was made of long-term longitudinal studies of normal and high-risk groups of various kinds, with Barbara Maughan providing leadership for many (she is currently undertaking a follow-up of the Isle of Wight sample, now in their mid-40s). From the outset, I was aware that, if we were to achieve what I wanted, we were going to have to have top-level statistical involvement of a kind that could bridge and integrate conceptual and mathematical models. I was exceptionally fortunate in recruiting Andrew Pickles for this career scientist position and he played an absolutely key role in the success of all the Unit endeavours. At a personal level, too, I learned a lot from working with him.

By the 1980s it had become increasingly obvious that genetic research strategies were going to be crucial for the study of causal processes. From the outset, I participated in the Virginia Twin Study of Adolescent Behavioral Development, in which a large school-based sample of 8–16-year-old twins were followed over three waves of data collection. Lindon Eaves is the outstanding English geneticist who directs the study and the research team includes many other talented individuals in the fields of both psychology and genetics. The findings have proved informative on a whole range of issues but, most of all, they have highlighted the need to take seriously the effects of gene–environment correlations and interactions. It became increasingly clear to me that new approaches to the study of nature–nurture interplay were going to be required.

Genetic research in the field of autism proceeded apace with both twin and family studies, followed in the 1990s by a large international molecular genetic study of autism based on affected relative pairs. Collaboration built on a long-standing work with Cathy Lord, the American clinical psychologist, in the development of standardised interview and observation measures of autism was carried forward with Tony Bailey, an innovative child psychiatrist within my MRC Unit, joining up with Tony Monaco, the undoubted world leader in the field of molecular genetics as applied to developmental neuropsychiatric disorders. Playing a part in the running of a complex international collaborative group brought the usual sorts of difficulties associated with these enterprises but worked remarkably well and the research gave rise to positive findings that seem likely, in time, to lead to the identification of some of the genes associated with a liability to autism (Rutter, 2000).

7   The Social, Genetic and Developmental Psychiatry Research Centre, 1994–1998

My view that new approaches were needed for the study of the nature–nurture interplay led to the setting up of the MRC-supported Social, Genetic and Developmental Psychiatry Research Centre. British research in all three elements that constituted the name of the Centre had been highly productive in the past but it seemed that international recruitment was going to be essential to bring change. This got off to a good start with the appointment of Robert Plomin (a psychologist/geneticist) and Judy Dunn (a social psychologist) as research professors. Frankie Happé, from the Cognitive Development Unit, brought expertise in cognitive psychology; Ian Craig, Phil Asherson and David Ball greatly strengthened our molecular genetic expertise; and David Fulker (like Judy Dunn, another expatriate Brit) provided international leadership in the field of statistical genetics. It was a great loss when David died not long after getting new research launched at the Centre.

The last two recruitments were, in some ways, the most important of all. New approaches were desperately needed for the study of social and behavioural development. Two of the world's leaders in this field were Terrie Moffitt and

Avshalom Caspi, then working in Wisconsin. It seemed to me most unlikely that they would be willing to contemplate a move but you never know until you ask. To my surprise, and great delight, they were actually thinking about a move in order to bring together social, genetic and developmental research strategies. The situation was ideal and both of them joined the group of distinguished research professors in the Centre. As in any other form of recruitment, it is the starting that is most difficult. Once it is clear that you have a top-level team that is full of creativity and innovation, further recruitment is much easier.

8   Work with charities

During the 1990s, I was pleased to be able to contribute to the broader scientific endeavour by joining the Nuffield Foundation as Trustee, and the Wellcome Trust as Governor in 1996, becoming Deputy Chairman in 1999, and later also the Jacobs Foundation and Novartis Foundation. It was particularly good that these organisations span the social–biomedical range, as well as the policy–basic-research range. Each of them, in rather different ways, has been a major supporter of psychological research and it has been crucial for the field that that has been the case. The Wellcome Trust has proved a lifesaver for British biomedical science, including psychology. Its principal research fellowship scheme, targeted on supporting world leaders and freeing them from other responsibilities to engage full time in research, has been especially important.

9   Post-retirement years

In 1998, I stepped down from all my administrative posts in the University and the MRC but I feel very privileged to be able to continue with active research as well as my involvement in charitable foundations and in international organisations. When I first worked in the United States in 1961/1962, Americans scarcely ever quoted research by British psychologists and, although there was outstanding research, its international impact was quite limited. The situation has changed out of all recognition in the 40 years since then. British, as well as other European, research occupies a prominent place in meetings of the Society for Research in Child Development and, as a representative of that trend, I was pleased in 1999 to become the first non-North American President of that Society. The advent of the fax machine, and even more so of e-mail, has made communication across the world incomparably easier than it was when I first set out on my research career. This has made international collaborative research possible to undertake on the basis of daily interchanges that were inconceivable a few years ago, and it has also made the running of international organisations much easier. On the domestic scene, psychology has an important, albeit still rather small, role in the Royal Society. The last few years have seen the beginnings of an expansion of psychology in the British Academy. Also, one of the really encouraging aspects of the establishment in 1998 of the Academy of Medical Sciences was the firm commitment to an interdisciplinary approach, with psychology prominent in the first set of elected fellows. The future looks bright and I look forward to continuing involvement in that research progress. Looking back, however, I feel fortunate in having been able to build my career during times that were considerably easier than those now prevailing. On the other hand, the potential for research now is incomparably greater than it was 40 years ago.

26

Creativity in research

Peter Wason

1   Background

A propensity for doing research (above all else) might be related to scholastic achievement at a much earlier age. Psychoanalysts, for instance, would subscribe to the view that patterns of behaviour repeat themselves throughout life. Similarly, research workers are often faced with the funny question 'How did you ever think of it?', as if knowledge of the past explains the present. A brief account of my educational background may enable others, even experimental psychologists, to ponder the roots of originality.

My parents came from distinguished Liberal families, but this spirit hardly extended to the education of their children. I did enjoy my kindergarten more than any other school, perhaps because it was mainly populated by older girls. One report read: 'Very neat at scissor work'. This observation seemed to predict my later preference for cardboard stimuli in my experiments rather than expensive apparatus. At the age of eight, I was dispatched to a preparatory school in the Mendip Hills. I found it impossible to learn more about even those things which interested me, let alone things which bored me. In algebra lessons the maths master used to intone: 'You cannot add an apple to a banana'. This obvious falsehood assumed the significance of a Zen koan which was quite beyond me.

I failed exams (Common Entrance) with monotonous regularity. My next school, Stowe, was liberal, as public schools go – perhaps too liberal. I failed the School Certificate examination twice. Nowadays I would be considered a case for the educational psychologist.

But all bad things, even 10 years of boarding schools, come to an end: there was a war. After intensive selection procedures I eventually passed out of Sandhurst and was appointed (at the age of 20) a liaison officer to an armoured brigade in

Normandy. I do not suppose I had what is quaintly called a 'good war', but I never doubted that it was a just war. In 1945, I recovered in County Clare from the effects of a war which had, ironically, been therapeutic. Although severely injured I experienced a sense of spiritual freedom. In 1946 I went up to Oxford (New College) to read English and then became an Assistant Lecturer at the University of Aberdeen.

Dissatisfied with the humanities, I elected to read psychology at University College London (UCL) in 1950, and stayed there for over 30 years.

2   Creativity

Perhaps I was drawn towards the topic of reasoning because most things in life seemed unreasonable. At any rate, I should like to understand the relentless drive of research, which does not depend on reinforcement. But that is beyond my scope. There are several interesting theories of creativity, but the one I like best is Bruner's (1961) idea that the creative product arouses effective surprise. By searching between the lines of my papers and reliving the experience of research, I hope I may find I have met that criterion.

The significant moves in research seem as if they were done yesterday, but even the adventitious circumstances surrounding them retain a vividness of an almost hysterical intensity, and I touch on them because, in a minor way, they may reveal changing climates of opinion. Similarly, on just a few occasions I point to connections between experimental findings and everyday life.

3   Fakes and flukes

I start with a one-off problem, the roots of which may lie fairly deep. My interest in fakes was probably stimulated by an uncle. He had a vast collection of mathematical and mechanical puzzles as well as a scrapbook on fakes worldwide. The fascination of fakes is that the owner of one may passionately resist the suggestion that it is not authentic: a phenomenon related to the 2–4–6 problem.[1] Sam Fillenbaum, with diagnostic acumen, told me, 'I now see what drives you – things which are not what they seem'.

In collaboration with Shuli Reich (Wason and Reich, 1979), I investigated the understanding of a seemingly innocent sentence: 'No head injury is too trivial to be ignored'. It seems to mean that attention should be paid to all head injuries however trivial, but the sentence is a fake – it means all head injuries should be ignored however trivial. The puzzlement is not helped by considering the following sentence with the same syntax: 'No weather forecast is too plausible to be mistrusted'. That sentence means exactly what it seems to mean. We found that the fake is not exposed by any appeal to grammatical analysis. Linguists tended to offer different readings. Subsequently, I devised a thought experiment which creates an absurd world to match the absurd sentence.

'In our world,' said the Red Queen defiantly to Alice, 'we make a point of ignoring all head injuries.'

'Even the trivial ones?' murmured Alice.

'Of course, child,' retorted the Red Queen, 'No head injury is too trivial to be ignored.'

Effective surprise – the field is reorganised to mediate the meaning directly. The example is not unique. Much education is faked because it consists of memorising inauthentic bits and pieces that tend to block insights. We are all dominated by fakes that militate against understanding.

In addition to the deceptive influence of fakes, shifting climates of opinion affect the perception of problems. For instance, my views on the study which follows were not really acceptable to the Zeitgeist. At Harvard's Center for Cognitive Studies in 1963, I continued my chronometric experiments on negation. I aimed to determine whether pragmatic factors – the way in which negatives are generally used – would affect the ease with which they are grasped. George Miller and his students have been concerned with negation as a syntactical transformation, under the influence of Chomsky's early theory of grammar. My aim was to see whether contexts of plausible denial (e.g. 'a spider is not an insect') would facilitate understanding more than contexts of implausible denial (e.g. 'a herring is not a bird'). But in the experiment, conducted by Susan Carey, I rather perversely used abstract material to test the hypothesis. The results were promising, but there were methodological hurdles involved in their interpretation. I was told that the subtraction of reaction times was not on because it infringed the 'irreducible minimum'. And George Miller suggested I had 'carried out two experiments and thrown away the results of one'. In fact, I made the only valid *post hoc* comparison to throw further light on the confirmation of the hypothesis. Other critics said the results were a fluke, if not a fake. But some time later many seemed to agree (in my view rightly) that the results were not surprising at all – of course negatives are used to deny things which might otherwise be considered true. (I shall present a thought experiment on negation later to illustrate how the obvious can remain concealed.)

Psychologists, especially, suffer from changes in the climate of opinion. Iris Murdoch (1992: 43) relates something similar in philosophy. In 1940, A.J. Ayer's *Language, Truth, and Logic* was widely acclaimed, but today it may seem 'brilliant and ingenious, but also unsophisticated and dotty'. In our discipline we may wonder how, for instance, Clark Hull's mathematico-deductive theory of rote learning would be considered today.

4   Research strategy

'I am looking for a problem', a friend once said to me, surrounded by a pile of learned journals. This struck me, quite unfairly, as rather funny because I would not think of working in that way. For me, problems come when they are least expected. My own experience of 'creativity' is related to what others have experienced, so there may be little original (or creative) in my own account. Quite typically, the unconscious or, as Kubie (1958) would say, the preconscious (freed from distortion by the unconscious) becomes dominant. Phenomenologically, there is the impression of being guided. The distinctive criterion is one of passivity and the absence of intellectual effort. The will is not exercised; effort comes at a later stage when the problem is being formulated. All this has been described well by the analyst Masud Khan, in a comment on a case report: 'this is research into how to let oneself be used, become the servant of a process' (Milner, 1969).

I think there is an analogy here with the effective supervision of research. The balance between encouragement and criticism is often mishandled. Some supervisors are enthusiastic at the end of a research project, when they ought to be at the beginning. I frequently used to bombard my students with letters if I thought there was anything I could add to their ideas, thus giving time for digestion. An idea may be 'half-baked', as Y. Bar-Hillel said of a paper by Oliver Selfridge (1959) (see also Good, 1962), but 'half-baked' ideas, given careful attention, can become 'baked' in the course of time, rather than burned.

This suggests a general principle. In their development of the 2–4–6 problem (Wason, 1960), Ryan Tweney and his associates (1980) supplied an interesting correction. They argued that it is inefficient to try to disconfirm a hypothesis until it has been sufficiently confirmed. In a later development, they showed that if disconfirmatory evidence for one rule was made confirmatory evidence for another rule, then the task became dramatically easier. I had sent this 'half-baked' idea on the back of an envelope to Tweney without considering its implication in any way at all. After it had been tested, I saw again the link to supervision: avoid disconfirmation in the early stages and withhold criticism until later. Only once was I disappointed when a student wanted me to do his cooking for him. He asked for an idea on which to do research, but later rejected it on the grounds that 'it was not original enough'. Life is hard.

5   Methodology

'Physicists talk about physics,' said Poincaré, 'and sociologists talk about methodology'. He might as well have included psychologists, at least until recently. I like to keep my experiments as simple as possible. I have an intuitive dislike of complex statistics, especially the analysis of variance (invented by Fisher for the assessment of manure). It has been called 'robust', and it seems to me just too powerful for psychological data: like taking a magnifying glass for something which should be apparent to the naked eye. But then, of course, I am prejudiced and my views reflect my lack of mathematical sophistication. I prefer rank order tests, and have been fortunate because two of their leading exponents, A.R. Jonckheere and J.W. Whitfield, have been my friends at UCL.

I dislike group testing, which necessarily precludes 'introspections', so-called by neo-behaviourists who consider such information gratuitous or, at best, corroborative. Introspections can provide a key to a problem. For instance, in the early studies of negation (Wason, 1959, 1961; Wason and Jones, 1963), if I had been concerned only with the objective data (response latencies), I would not have captured the 'secret of negation': the mental deletion of the word 'not' in the sentence. The 'negation models' of Clark (1974) and Trabasso (1972) acknowledge this fact, but give it a rather arbitrary interpretation. At an information-processing level the rationale for the deletion is to yield an affirmative sentence, which requires fewer steps to verify, but at a psycholinguistic level it looks more like a recovery of the missing presupposition. A negative without a presupposition induces bafflement. This can be illuminated by a simple thought experiment. Verify in your mind the two sentences which follow, and see which is easier:

1. Six is even and five is not even.
2. Six is even and two is not odd.

This (partly) enabled me to write an article with the paradoxical title 'In real life negatives are false' (Wason, 1972) for Leo Apostel's 'Negation Project'. Negatives are used to falsify presuppositions rather than to maintain truth.

The simple statement of the solution belies the time and effort taken to arrive at it. In 1958, we were all puzzled. The curves of the response times in the first experiment were differentiated clearly over a large number of trials, and there was no sign of their convergence. 'You'll really learn something about the nervous system from that', said Ron Melzac, who was visiting, on entering my room. John Whitfield took the results to Canada to show them to Donald Hebb and his colleagues. 'It's always good to hear from young research workers even if their work is not ripe for publication', said the Chairman of the Experimental Psychology Society when I addressed them.

On the whole, I am against talking about an experiment before it has been carried out, although I violated this principle in my graduate seminars in the 1960s. It is true that consultation may reveal a flaw, but just as often it may distort the original idea, especially if it is only 'half-baked'. An experimental idea is like a poem. It would be odd to ask another person about it because nobody else would know what will emerge. This may seem a highly idiosyncratic way for a scientist to work, but that overlooks the affinity of discovery between arts and science. There is a time for discussion after the data cannot be altered and before the next experiment. I have been fortunate in having as a discussant and teacher A.R. Jonckheere, who has inspired countless graduate students for decades at UCL with his ideas, and sometimes with their own ideas.

6 Reporting research

It is obvious that there is a dialectic between thinking and experimenting, each modifying the other. I think that if thought is not externalised by experimental tests, then it is liable to distortion. But the same thing happens in writing: the concrete expression of thought in words modifies the ideas on the topic. The process of drafting and redrafting is like experimenting on a problem. Research has not been completed until it has been written up for publication. This is critically important for the research worker. I like Freud's comment: 'Write it, write it, put it down in black and white; that's the way to get it out of your system – outside you, that is; give it an existence independently of you' (Riviere, 1958).

I have presented my own practice in several articles (e.g. Wason, 1980; Green and Wason, 1982). It assumes that you do not know what you are really trying to say until you have said it. It consists in two phases. The first is an externalisation of thought without correction or criticism. There is an analogy with the confirmatory stage in the discovery of a rule in the 2–4–6 problem. I have called this kind of writing 'clearing the store' to make room for new ideas; it relieves mental congestion. The second, critical phase (analogous to disconfirmation) is an attempt to extract order and meaning from the 'zero draft'. But the process of concerted criticism brings with it new thought, memories and unforeseen connections.

I have called the conventional model of writing 'the tape in the head' because it implies a kind of pre-existent meaning which is run off, usually with stumbling corrections, as soon as pen is put to paper. The model for generative writing is a patchwork quilt, a crossword, or a jigsaw puzzle – a process of discovery devoid of serial order. The notion of generative writing has been independently expounded by Peter Elbow (1973) in his remarkable book *Writing Without Teachers*. I suspect, however, that it is rather difficult to make converts to this method. My hunch is that most students have an ingrained tendency to spell out the 'zero draft' in too committed a manner. Ask them to improve on what they have written and (in my experience) they will make a few perfunctory alterations. Their 'draft' simply does not catch alight. It is not sufficiently porous and undisciplined. In an effort to increase fluency, I have tried getting subjects to write about God in invisible ink, but the results were unclear. (The Editor of the *Quarterly Journal of Experimental Psychology* said he would be delighted to publish the excerpts so long as they remained in invisible ink.)

Some corroboration of the benefits of generative writing was obtained by David Lowenthal and myself (1977) in our survey of academics and their writing. One salient finding was that those who planned their writing in advance tended to dislike the process, but that those who used it to extend their thought generally enjoyed it. This was so regardless of academic discipline.

Personally, I enjoy academic writing because it is a sure way to get peace of mind, due no doubt to its ordering and creative functions. Indeed, I often have the fantasy that I may die before finishing a paper. This obviously inflates its importance, but suggests that unconsciously the paper is a part of myself. A similar irrational fantasy is rewarding and may be more common – the paper you are now writing will be the best you have ever written.

I dislike argument unless it is written down. Most face-to-face argument is a point-scoring game which proceeds from different premises. It is not conducive to peace of mind. In any case, it hardly contributes towards progress because the protagonists seldom change their minds about the issue under discussion.

7   A study in prejudice

Argument is a kind of debased criticism, but I take the latter fairly seriously. When people are criticised, they usually say they have been misunderstood, and usually they are right. It is my 2–4–6 studies which have given the most offence, and sometimes I wish the critics had actually done the experiment themselves. Perhaps I should have called the original paper (Wason, 1960) 'A study in prejudice', as a friend suggested at the time. Recently it has met with some interesting conceptual criticism.

The most influential idea underlying the experiment was Popper's concept of falsifiability in scientific methodology. But the English translation of *Logik der Forschung* was delayed until 1959, and I had to make do with a number of scintillating articles, especially one entitled 'Philosophy of science, a personal report' (Popper, 1957), which is less technical than his *magnum opus*. I attended one or two of Pepper's seminars at the London School of Economics, but found them rather above my head as well as disputatious. Popper's successor, Imre Lakatos, stopped me in the street with a rather ambiguous invitation: 'We've read everything you have written, and we disagree with all of it – do come and give us a seminar'.

Some misgivings about my original paper were raised as soon as it was published, although the more weighty ones were not made until the 1980s, at least 20 years after publication. On two different occasions an academic rather brusquely left the room when I was lecturing, and did so at precisely the same point: when I said that the correct rule cannot be proved, but any incorrect hypothesis could be disproved. In a similar way, when I said that the subjects seemed deeply moved after the experiment, someone retorted, 'That's only because it is you doing it'. And there is one individual who publicly proclaims that the erroneous solutions are justified because nearly all the subjects announce them. Perhaps this should be called the modal theory of truth. I should, of course, have tried to discover more about this interesting delusion.

In 1983 Jonathan Evans argued that there is no evidence that the subjects were trying to confirm their hypotheses, but only that they tended to generate positive instances of them. It seems to me, however, that when a subject writes down on the record sheet, 'to test this theory', accompanied by a positive instance of it, then that is *ipso facto* an attempt to confirm that hypothesis. Evans (1983: 143) writes: 'It is not that the subjects do not wish to falsify, it is simply that they cannot think of the way to do it'. But if a subject were not under the spell of a current hypothesis, it would surely be trivially easy to generate a negative instance of it. This could be tested by asking subjects, not to perform the task, but to comment on the protocol of another subject, or even a constructed one. Or, perhaps, possible ways of proceeding could be listed and the subject asked to put them into rank order with respect to efficiency. Simplest of all: instruct the subject to generate a negative instance and time the response.

Klayman and Ha (1987) argue that subjects are justified in using what they call 'a positive test strategy' (*pace* Francis Bacon, 1621) because in so doing they are unaware of the very general scope of the rule. The highly specific initial instance, 2–4–6, may cause them to think that the rule is also highly restricted.

Fenna Poletiek (1992) in her doctoral thesis also makes the same point. I concede that there may be some truth in these criticisms, and that I may have over-stated the case for confirmation, but as David Green and I have pointed out in an unpublished rejoinder to Klayman and Ha: 'A strategy implies a voluntary decision to generate evidence in one way rather than another, but many individuals in this task seem to behave as if the hypothesis which they entertain must be correct'. This is revealed by the extraordinary tendency merely to reformulate, and an-nounce, the same rule rather than seek an alternative. It suggests a commitment to truth rather than a plausible option. It is not, of course, claimed that every subject, at every opportunity, was a prey to this kind of conceptual blindness. The technology of the original experiment, and the absence of covert timing, did not allow any other indication of this tendency (other than reformulation and the obsession with past instances) of the extent to which there is an awareness that other hypotheses could be candidates for the rule. Stuart Sutherland (1992) in his provocative book *Irrationality* cites a pleasing glimpse of the surprises which may still occur with this task:

> I once put the problem to one of the most distinguished biologists in Britain, who proposed the rule, 'Any three numbers increasing by the same amount'. After being told he was wrong, he said, 'Well, it must be any three numbers in which, starting from the last number, each of the other two decreases by the same amount'. It is, of course, an identical rule.

It is just these ritualistic moves which convey far more about the kind of thinking adopted than any numerical analysis.

Some very recent informal reports suggest that students today do better than they did in 1959. I do not know whether to be pleased or sorry – both I suppose. However, Estelle Phillips (personal communication) has tested individuals outside the academic community (e.g. a carpenter and a businessman) who yielded typical results: their hypotheses tended to become more elaborate and difficult to de-cipher. (It is, incidentally, extremely uncommon for announced hypotheses of the same underlying rule to become shorter rather than longer. In the original paper I made the point that this recourse to verbal exactitude is analogous to the pronouncement of a spell in magic.) It would seem that my invitation to prejudice may be as valid today as yesterday.

8   The selection task as a picture of creative effort

In their definitive book *Human Reasoning,* Jonathan Evans and his associates (1993) state that I first described the selection task in 1966, but could hardly have suspected that in the next quarter of a century it would become the most intensively researched single problem in the history of the psychology of reasoning.[2] Correct. But as a minor contribution to the psychology of research, it would be interesting to plot the accelerating curve of publication dates over this period. Initially, the consumers of research may have caught something of the subjects' perplexities and suspicions. But today work on the task has been called a cottage industry.

The reason for the initial disdain and the subsequent enthusiasm may have something to do with a contradiction: the task is both simple in structure and difficult to solve. Only very recently a psychologist expressed surprise that although students could not solve it they were capable of writing a computer program for it. A few individuals in the early days called it a trick, while others called it 'irritating'. Some said it was divorced from everyday life. I felt like replying 'That is its saving grace'. We don't hear so much of that kind of talk nowadays. The fact that a simple structure, without semantic support, tends to defy our wits does have a definite appeal.

Actually, the selection task was conceived a few years earlier than 1966, probably in 1960 or 1961. I had become interested in Quine's (1952) elegant notation for determining validity in propositional calculus, but I experienced difficulty in understanding the truth functions of the conditional. So I constructed the familiar four cards, and presented the problem to two friends. Both solved it after some thought, and my assistant thought it lacked potential. I did not turn to it again until I found myself at the Center for Cognitive Studies in 1963. Here I found that sentences like 'If I go to Chicago, I catch a train' caused more hilarity than concentration. It is difficult to continue an experiment when the subjects collapse with laughter.

The first formal experiments, done partly in Scotland (Wason, 1968), met with grave looks from dedicated Piagetians: the subjects' responses were clearly incompatible with 'formal operations'. There was even the hint that there was something wrong with the experiment – a fluke or perhaps a fake. Furthermore, there were surprises – startling discrepancies between the selection of the cards and the inferences drawn from them when they were turned over. There were extraordinary cases of divided attention, which might have interested a clinician. Sometimes a single individual began to sound like two people talking. A further study (Wason, 1969) caught in my net the so-called 'Mensa Protocol', in which a member of that elite organisation reasoned, with assurance and precision, from premises which, according to Piaget, are typical of young children. I called the paper 'Regression in reasoning?'

In the 1970s, I had a fruitful collaboration with Phil Johnson-Laird, which culminated in our book *Psychology of Reasoning* (Wason and Johnson-Laird, 1972).

But at about this time I became aware of murmurs of disapproval in some quarters. On one occasion, someone suddenly said, perhaps half in jest, 'We're not having any more experiments on the selection task', as if the Department was in danger of being infected by some new virus. I should have met this oracular pronouncement by retorting, 'We've hardly begun'.

One thing that struck us was the invariable (and possibly blinding) effect of selecting the true antecedent (p). If it were to be removed from the task, the responses might be more rational. We considered the possibility of a three-card problem. I then suggested the additional removal of the false antecedent (p̄), leaving a binary choice between the true and false consequents (q and q̄). Phil greeted this as a stroke of genius, but it was really only a natural progression. In concrete terms, given the sentence 'All the rectangles are pink', with the task of proving it true as economically as possible, the solution is to inspect all non-pink objects to establish that they are not rectangles. Pink objects are vacuous. In our experiment (Johnson-Laird and Wason, 1970, experiment 1) all the subjects eventually solved the problem. After more than 10 years, David Green and I resuscitated it (Wason and Green, 1984) and investigated its potential in several ways. We called it the 'reduced array selection task' (RAST).[3]

The RAST has many advantages over the standard task. Its solution does not depend on an all-or-none decision but is seriated over a number of trials, each of which provides knowledge of results; it enables a variety of measures to be taken. The subjects usually start getting it wrong, but generally end up getting it right: an ideal situation. The RAST is so flexible that it has been used with good effect to study the thinking of children as young as seven (Girotto *et al.*, 1988; Light *et al.*, 1990).

The experiments we have done on the selection task have often been governed by chance occurrences, and the results have been surprising and non-linear. For instance, we tested the hypothesis that the phrase 'the other side of the card' could have been misinterpreted as the side which is face downwards, instead of referring to a symmetrical relation (Wason and Johnson-Laird, 1970). There was not a shred of evidence in favour of this hypothesis, but when all the information was revealed, the subjects' comments were saturated with self-contradictions which disclosed the sources of error, much to the astonishment of our assistant, Diana Shapiro. A similar serendipitous finding occurred in Wason and Golding (1974). The aim of the experiment was totally eclipsed by the subjects' inconsistent remarks (see also Wason, 1979).

Since the late 1980s, the selection task has had a liberating effect on research; it has lost its autonomy and become a catalyst which has resulted in a veritable intellectual ferment. The protagonists of social contract theory (Cosmides, 1989; Gigerenzer and Hug, 1992), pragmatic schemas (Cheng and Holyoak, 1985), mental models (Johnson-Laird and Byrne, 1993), deontic logic (Manktelow and Over, 1990), and heuristic-analytic theory (Evans, 1989) have used the task in the struggle for survival for their ideas.

The implications of social contract theory are particularly noteworthy because of their boldness, which (incidentally) should delight Popper. Gigerenzer and Hug (1992) have even claimed that the results obtained so far have helped to demolish the century-old assumption of Leibnitz that human reasoning can be reduced to a calculus. It has assumed instead that the mind is a bundle of Darwinian algorithms designed for survival in a clan of hunter-gatherers, rather than a reasoning machine (Cosmides, 1989; Gigerenzer and Hug, 1992). It remains to be seen whether further experimental tests will demand 'a new theory of mind', as a writer in *The Economist* (Anonymous, 1992) has suggested, but these assumptions will at least involve liaison between two disciplines – psychology and social biology. That is something for which we should be grateful.

Research on the selection task, from its earliest days, has revealed all the confusions, changes of perspective, accidental discoveries and insights which are typical of creative work. But what progress has been made, and what achievement will endure, has been due to the work of many hands. To have been a vehicle for such research, and to have watched it grow, has taught me, beyond question, that an apple can be added to a banana with impunity, and even with satisfaction. And that, perhaps, is what creativity is all about.

Acknowledgements

I would like to thank Rhena Bishop and Ann-Charlotte Scholey for easing my return to Oxford beyond the call of duty. This chapter is reprinted with permission from S.E. Newstead and J.St.B.T. Evans (Eds) (1995) *Perspectives in Thinking and Reasoning: Essays in Honour of Peter Wason*. Hove: Lawrence Erlbaum Associates. The editors would like to thank Professor Newstead for his assistance with this chapter.

Notes

1 In the 2–4–6 task, participants are told that the experimenter has chosen a rule which applies to groups of three whole numbers. Their task is to discover what the rule is by generating sequences of three numbers and receiving feedback on whether these conform to the rule. They are told that the sequence 2–4–6 conforms to the rule. Typically, people believe the rule to be 'numbers increasing by two', and even when told that this is not the rule they continue to generate sequences consistent with it (e.g. 1004–1006–1008) and thus often fail to discover what the rule is. If they were to attempt to disconfirm this rule, they would soon discover that the actual rule is 'any three numbers in ascending sequence'.

2 In the Wason selection task, participants are presented with four cards and told that these cards each have a number on one side and a letter on the other. They can see only the sides facing up, and these show E, D, 4 and 7. They are then presented by the experimenter with the rule 'If a card has a vowel on one side then it has an even number on the other side', and asked which cards they would need to turn over in order to determine whether the rule is true or false. Most people indicate they would need to turn over either just the E card or both the E card and the 4 card. In fact, it is necessary to turn over the E and the 7 cards. The rule would be falsified if the E card had an odd number on the other side and also if the 7 card had an E on its reverse side.

3 The reduced array selection task (RAST) is a variant on the standard Wason selection task in which participants are presented with fewer than four cards. For example, they might be given just the 4 and 7 cards and not the E and D cards in the example given above. This typically leads to improved performance, though the reasons for this are not fully understood.

Bibliography

A MEMBER OF THE PHRENOLOGICAL AND PHILOSOPHICAL SOCIETIES OF GLASGOW (1838) *The Philosophy of Phrenology Simplified.* Glasgow: W.R. M'Phun.

A VEGETARIAN CLERGYMAN (1905) The psycho-therapeutic revival. *Psycho-Therapeutic Journal, 4 (38),* 1.

ABELSON, R.P. (1973) The structure of belief systems. In R.M. Schank and K.M. Colby (Eds) *Computer Models of Thought and Language.* San Francisco: W.H. Freeman.

ABRAMSON, L.M.E.P., SELIGMAN, M.E.P. and TEASDALE, J. (1978) Learned helplessness in humans: critique and reformulation. *Journal of Abnormal Psychology, 87,* 49–74.

ADAMSON, R. (1884) Critical notice on James Sully. *Outlines of Psychology with Special Reference to the Theory of Education.* Mind, *9,* 429.

ADORNO, T. W., FRENKEL-BRUNSWICK, E., LEVINSON, D.J. and SANFORD, R. N. (1950) *The Authoritarian Personality.* New York: Harper.

ADRIAN, E. D. (1950) What happens when we think? In P. Laslett (Ed.) *The Physical Basis of Mind: A Series of Broadcast Talks.* Oxford: Basil Blackwell.

ADRIAN, E.D. (1947) *The Physical Background of Perception* (Waynflete Lectures for 1946). Oxford: Clarendon Press.

AHRENFELDT, R.H. (1968) Military psychiatry. In A.S. MacNalty and W. F. Mellor (Eds) *Medical Services in War. The Principal Medical Lessons of the Second World War: Based on the Official Medical Histories of the United Kingdom, Canada, Australia, New Zealand, and India.* London: HMSO.

AINSCOW, M. and MUNCEY, M. (1987) *Behaviour Difficulties in the Primary School.* Coventry: Drake Educational Associates.

ALBEE, G.A. (1980) Competency model to replace the defect model. In M. Gibbs, J. Lachenmeyer and J. Sigal (Eds) *Community Psychology: Theoretical and Empirical Approaches.* New York: Gardner Press.

ALEXANDER, S. (1920/1966) *Space, Time, and Deity: The Gifford Lectures at Glasgow 1916–1918,* 2 vols. London: Macmillan.

ALLDERIDGE, P. (1991) The foundation of the Maudsley hospital. In G.E. Berrios and H. Freeman (Eds) *150 Years of British Psychiatry, 1841–1991.* London: Gaskell.

AMERICAN PSYCHOLOGICAL ASSOCIATION (1947) Recommended training program in clinical psychology. Report of the committee on training in clinical psychology of the American Psychological Association submitted at the Detroit meeting of the American Psychological Association, September 9–13, 1947. *American Psychologist, 2,* 539–558.

AMIR, Y. and SHARON, I. (1987) Are social-psychological laws cross-culturally valid? *Journal of Cross-Cultural Psychology, 18,* 383–470.

ANDERSON, C. (1945) On certain conscious and unconscious homosexual responses to warfare. *British Journal of Medical Psychology, 20,* 161–174.

ANDERSON, J.R. (2000) *Learning and Memory: An Integrated Approach,* 2nd ed. Chichester: John Wiley.

ANGELL, J.R. (1908) The doctrine of formal discipline in the light of the principles of general psychology. *Educational Review, 36,* 1–14.

ANNAN, N. (1984) *Leslie Stephen: The Godless Victorian.* London: Weidenfield and Nicolson.

ANONYMOUS (n.d.) Real progress in the mental plane. *The Thinker, 81,* 322.

ANONYMOUS (1904) *New Thought, 2 (20),* 293.

ANONYMOUS (1923) Notice of annual meeting of the National Institute of Industrial Psychology. *Nature, 111,* 439.

ANONYMOUS (1924) Stray thoughts. *New Thought, 21 (110)*.
ANONYMOUS (1925) Editorial. *Practical Psychology, 1 (11)*, 2.
ANONYMOUS (1926a) The National Institute of Industrial Psychology. *Industrial Psychology, 1*, 14.
ANONYMOUS (1926b) Stray thoughts. *Applied Psychology, 26 (122)*.
ANONYMOUS (1927) Education and science. *Nature*, 23 July, 105–107.
ANONYMOUS (1930) *Applied Psychology, 28 (145)*, 57.
ANONYMOUS (1936) Editorial. *The Practical Psychology Magazine, 1*, 2.
ANONYMOUS (1937) Editorial. *Practical Psychology, 2 (9)*, 290.
ANONYMOUS (1938) Editorial. *You: The Practical Psychology Magazine, 3 (1)*, 4.
ANONYMOUS (1947) The influence of Sherrington on clinical neurology. *British Medical Journal, ii*, 825–826.
ANONYMOUS (1948a) Dr. Susan Isaacs, CBE. *Nature, 4127*, 4 December, 881.
ANONYMOUS (1948b) Obituary. *The Times*, 13 October, 6.
ANONYMOUS (1992) A critique of pure reason. *The Economist*, 4 July, 95–96.
ANSTIS, C.M., SHOPLAND, C.D. and GREGORY, R.L. (1961) Measuring visual constancy for stationary or moving objects. *Nature, 191*, 416–417.
APPLETON, P., DOUGLAS, J., FUNDUDIS, T., HEWITT, K. and STEVENSON, J. (1989) A trouble shared is a happy budget. *Health Service Journal*, 22 June, 760–761.
ARGYLE, M. (1967) *The Psychology of Interpersonal Behaviour*, 1st ed. Harmondsworth: Penguin. (5th ed. 1994.)
ARGYLE, M. (1987) *The Psychology of Happiness*. London: Methuen.
ARGYLE, M. and COOK, M. (1976) *Gaze and Mutual Gaze*. Cambridge: Cambridge University Press.
ARGYLE, M. and DEAN, J. (1965) Eye-contact, distance and affiliation. *Sociometry, 28*, 289–304.
ARGYLE, M. and HENDERSON, M. (1985) *The Anatomy of Relationships*. London: Penguin.
ARGYLE, M., ALKEMA, F. and GILMOUR, R. (1972) The communication of friendly and hostile attitudes by verbal and non-verbal signals. *European Journal of Social Psychology, 1*, 385–402.
ARGYLE, M., FURNHAM, A. and GRAHAM, J.A. (1981) *Social Situations*. Cambridge: Cambridge University Press.
ASARO, P. (1998) *Design for a Mind: The Mechanistic Philosophy of W. Ross Ashby*. Working Paper, Beckman Institute for Advanced Science and Technology. University of Illinois.
ASH, M.G. (1980) Wilhelm Wundt and Oswald Külpe on the institutional status of psychology: an academic controversy in historical context. In W.G. Bringmann and R.D. Tweney (Eds) *Wundt Studies: A Centennial Collection*. Toronto: Hogrefe.
ASH, M.G. (1983) The self-presentation of a discipline: history of psychology in the United States between pedagogy and scholarship. In L. Graham, W. Lepenies and P. Weingart (Eds) *Functions and Uses of Disciplinary Histories, Vol. VII*. Dordrecht: D. Reidel Publishing.
ASH, M.G. (1995) *Gestalt Psychology in German Culture, 1890–1967: Holism and the Quest for Objectivity*. Cambridge: Cambridge University Press.
ASHBY, W.R. (1940) Adaptiveness and equilibrium. *Journal of Mental Science, 86*, 478–483.
ASHBY, W.R. (1945) Effects of controls of stability. *Nature, 155*, 242.
ASHBY, W.R. (1946a) Dynamics of the cerebral cortex: the behavioural properties of systems in equilibrium. *American Journal of Psychology, 59*, 682–686.
ASHBY, W.R. (1946b) Principles for the quantitative study of stability in a dynamic whole system – with some applications to the nervous system. *Journal of Mental Science, 92*, 319–323.
ASHBY, W.R. (1947a) The nervous system as physical machine: with special reference to the origin of adaptive behaviour. *Mind, 56*, 44–59.
ASHBY, W.R. (1947b) The existence of critical levels for the actions of hormones and enzymes with some therapeutic applications. *Journal of Mental Science, 93*, 733–739.
ASHBY, W.R. (1948) Design for a brain. *Electronic Engineering, 20*, 379–383.
ASHBY, W.R. (1950) The cerebral mechanisms of intelligent action. In D. Richter (Ed.) *Perspectives in Neuropsychiatry*. London: H.K. Lewis.
ASHBY, W.R. (1952) *Design for a Brain*. London: Chapman and Hall.
ASHBY, W.R. (1954) The applications of cybernetics to psychiatry. *Journal of Mental Science, 100*, 114–124.
ASHBY, W.R. (1955) Ignorances in the physiological field. In J. M. Tanner (Ed.) *Perspectives in Psychiatric Research*. Oxford: Blackwell Scientific.
ASHBY, W.R. (1958) Design for an intelligence amplifier. In C. Shannon and J.E. McCarthy (Eds) *Automata Studies*. Princeton: Princeton University Press.

ASHBY, W.R. (1960) *Design for a Brain*, 2nd ed. London: Chapman and Hall.

ASSOCIATION FOR THE STUDY OF ANIMAL BEHAVIOUR (1981) Guidelines for the use of animals in research. *Animal Behaviour*, 29, 1–2.

ASSOCIATION FOR THE STUDY OF ANIMAL BEHAVIOUR (1986) Guidelines for the use of animals in research. *Animal Behaviour*, 34, 315–318.

ASSOCIATION OF CHILD PSYCHOLOGY AND PSYCHIATRY (1989) *Health Visitor-Based Services for Preschool Children with Behaviour Problems*. Occasional Paper 2. London: Association of Child Psychology and Psychiatry.

ATHERLEY, C. (1990) The implementation of a positive behaviour management programme in a primary school: a case study. *School Organisation*, 10, 213–229.

ATKINSON, R.C. and SHIFFRIN, R.M. (1968) Human memory: a proposed system and its control processes. In K.W. Spence and J.T. Spence (Eds) *The Psychology of Learning and Motivation: Advances in Research and Theory*, Vol. 2. New York: Academic Press.

AVELING, F. (1931) *Personality and Will*. London: Nisbet; Cambridge: Cambridge University Press.

AYER, A.J. (1936) *Language, Truth and Logic*. London: Gollancz.

BACON, F. (1621) *Novum Organum*. Oxford: Oxford University Press.

BACON, Rev. J.H. (1889) *A Complete Guide to the Improvement of the Memory, or the Science of Memory Simplified, with Practical Applications to Language, History, Geography, Music, Prose, Poetry etc.* London: Pitman.

BADDELEY, A.D. (1960) Enhanced learning of a position habit with secondary reinforcements for the wrong response. *American Journal of Psychology*, 73, 454–457.

BADDELEY, A.D. (1966a) The capacity for generating information by randomization. *Quarterly Journal of Experimental Psychology*, 18, 119–129.

BADDELEY, A.D. (1966b) Short-term memory for word sequences as a function of acoustic, semantic and formal similarity. *Quarterly Journal of Experimental Psychology*, 18, 362–365.

BADDELEY, A.D. (1966c) The influence of acoustic and semantic similarity on long-term memory for word sequences. *Quarterly Journal of Experimental Psychology*, 18, 302–309.

BADDELEY, A.D. (1968a) Prior recall of newly learned items and the recency effect in free recall. *Canadian Journal of Psychology*, 22, 157–163.

BADDELEY, A.D. (1968b) How does acoustic similarity influence short-term memory? *Quarterly Journal of Experimental Psychology*, 20, 249–264.

BADDELEY, A.D. (1976) *The Psychology of Memory*. London: Harper and Row.

BADDELEY, A.D. and DALE, H.C.A. (1966) The effect of semantic similarity on retroactive interference in long- and short-term memory. *Journal of Verbal Learning and Verbal Behavior*, 5, 417–420.

BADDELEY, A.D. and HITCH, G.J. (1974) Working memory. In G.A. Bower (Ed.) *The Psychology of Learning and Motivation*. New York: Academic Press.

BADDELEY, A.D. and LIEBERMAN, K. (1980) Spatial working memory. In R.S. Nickerson (Ed.) *Attention and Performance VIII*. Hillsdale, NJ: Lawrence Erlbaum Associates.

BADDELEY, A.D. and WARRINGTON, E.K. (1970) Amnesia and the distinction between long- and short-term memory. *Journal of Verbal Learning and Verbal Behavior*, 9, 176–189.

BADDELEY, A.D., EMSLIE, H., KOLODNY, J. and DUNCAN, J. (1998) Random generation and the executive control of working memory. *Quarterly Journal of Experimental Psychology*, 51A, 818–852.

BADDELEY, A.D., GRANT, S., WIGHT, E. and THOMSON, N. (1973) Imagery and visual working memory. In P.M.A. Rabbitt and S. Dornic (Eds) *Attention and Performance V*. London: Academic Press.

BADDELEY, A.D., THOMSON, N. and BUCHANAN, M. (1975) Word length and the structure of short-term memory. *Journal of Verbal Learning and Verbal Behavior*, 14, 575–589.

BAILEY, A., PHILLIPS, W. and RUTTER, M. (1996) Autism: towards an integration of clinical, genetic, neuropsychological, and neurobiological perspectives. *Journal of Child Psychology and Psychiatry Annual Research Review*, 37, 89–126.

BAILEY, S. (1858) *Letters on the Philosophy of the Human Mind*, 2nd series. London: Longman Brown.

BAIN, A. (1865a) *The Senses and the Intellect*, 2nd ed. London: Longmans, Green.

BAIN, A. (1865b) *The Emotions and the Will*, 2nd ed. London: Longmans, Green.

BAIN, A. (1875) *The Emotions and the Will*, 3rd ed. London: Longmans, Green.

BAIN, A. (1878) *Education as a Science*. London: Kegan, Trench and Trübner.

BAIN, A. (1893) George Croom Robertson. *Mind*, NS5, 1–14.

BAIN, A. (1904) *Autobiography*. London: Longmans, Green.

BAIN, A. and WHITTAKER, T. (Eds) (1894) *Philosophical Remains of George Croom Robertson*. London: Williams and Norgate.

BAISTOW, K. (1995a) From sickly survival to the realisation of potential: child health as a social project in twentieth century England. *Children and Society*, 9, 20–35.

BAISTOW, K. (1995b) Liberation and regulation? Some paradoxes of empowerment. *Critical Social Policy*, 14, 34–46.

BALDWIN, J.M. (1913) *A History of Psychology: A Sketch and an Interpretation* (2 vols). New York: Putnam.

BALLARD, P.B. (1913) *Obliviscence and Reminiscence*. British Journal of Psychology Monographs, 1 (2).

BANDURA, A. (1974) Behaviour theory and the models of man. *American Psychologist*, 29, 859–869.

BANDURA, A. (1977) *Social Learning Theory*. London: Prentice Hall.

BANDURA, A. (1982) Self-efficacy mechanism in human agency. *American Psychologist*, 37, 122–147.

BANNISTER, D. and FRANSELLA, F. (1966) A grid test of schizophrenic thought disorder. *British Journal of Social and Clinical Psychology*, 5, 95–102.

BANNISTER, D. and FRANSELLA, F. (1971) *Inquiring Man*, 1st ed. Harmondsworth: Penguin.

BARNES, W.H.F. (1944) Is the mind a calculating machine? *Nature*, May 20, 605.

BARRETT, P.N., *et al.* (Eds) (1987) *Charles Darwin's Notebooks, 1836–1844: Geology, Transmutation of Species, Metaphysical Enquiries*. Cambridge: Cambridge University Press.

BARTLETT, F.C. (1916) An experimental study of some problems of perceiving and imaging. *British Journal of Psychology*, 8, 222–268.

BARTLETT, F.C. (1920) Some experiments on the reproduction of folk-stories. *Folk-Lore, 31*, 30–47.

BARTLETT, F.C. (1923) *Psychology and Primitive Culture*. Cambridge: Cambridge University Press.

BARTLETT, F.C. (1926) Critical notice [of Henry Head, *Aphasia and Kindred Disorders of Speech*]. *British Journal of Psychology, 17*, 154–161.

BARTLETT, F.C. (1927) Critical notice. 'Behaviorism' by John B. Watson. London: Kegan Paul Trench, Trubner and Co. Ltd. 1925. *Mind, 36*, 77–83.

BARTLETT, F.C. (1932) *Remembering: A Study in Experimental and Social Psychology*. Cambridge: Cambridge University Press.

BARTLETT, F.C. (1936) Frederic Charles Bartlett. In C. Murchison (Ed.) *History of Psychology in Autobiography: Vol. 3*. New York: Russell and Russell.

BARTLETT, F.C. (1937) Editorial. *British Journal of Psychology, 27*, 343.

BARTLETT, F.C. (1945–1948) Charles Samuel Myers, 1873–1946. *Obituary Notices of Fellows of the Royal Society*, Vol. 5. London: Royal Society.

BARTLETT, F.C. (1946) Obituary notice: K.J.W. Craik. *British Journal of Psychology, 36*, 109–116. Reprinted in S. Sherwood (Ed.) (1966) *The Nature of Psychology: A Selection of Papers, Essays and Other Writings by the Late Kenneth J.W. Craik*. Cambridge: Cambridge University Press.

BARTLETT, F.C. (1951) *The Mind at Work and Play*. London: Allen and Unwin.

BARTLETT, F.C. (1955) Fifty years of psychology. *Occupational Psychology, 29*, 203–216.

BARTLETT, F.C. (1958) *Thinking: An Experimental and Social Study*. London: George Allen and Unwin.

BARTLETT, F.C. (1965) Remembering Dr. Myers. *Bulletin of the British Psychological Society, 18*, 1–10.

BARTLETT, F.C. and MACKWORTH, N.H. (1950) *Planned Seeing: Some Psychological Experiments*. Air Ministry Publication AP3139B. London: HMSO.

BARTLETT, F.C., GINSBERG, M., LINDGREN, E.J. and THOULESS, R.H. (Eds) (1939) *The Study of Society: Methods and Problems*. London: Kegan Paul, Trench, Trubner.

BARTLEY, M.M. (1995) Courtship and continued progress: Julian Huxley's studies on bird behaviour. *Journal of the History of Biology, 28*, 107.

BATES, J.A.V. (1947) Some characteristics of a human operator. *Proceedings of the Institutions of Electrical Engineer*, 94, 298–313.

BATES, J.A.V. (1949) Mind, machine and man. *British Medical Journal*, 16 July, 177.

BATESON, P.P.G. (1997) *The Behavioural and Physiological Effects of Culling Red Deer*. London: Council of the National Trust.

BEECH, H.R. (1969) *Changing Man's Behaviour*. London: Penguin.

BEECH, R. and FRANSELLA, F. (1968) *Research and Experiment in Stuttering*. London: Pergamon Press.

BEEKMAN, D. (1977) *The Mechanical Baby: A Popular History of the Theory and Practice of Child Raising.* Westport, CT: Lawrence Hill.

BELBIN, E. (1950) The influence of interpolated recall upon recognition. *Quarterly Journal of Experimental Psychology, 2,* 163–169.

BELLAH, J.W. and CLARK, A.F. (1943) The link trainer. *Infantry Journal, 52 (3),* 72–75.

BELOFF, H. (1985) *Camera Culture.* Oxford: Blackwell.

BENDER, M.P. (1976) *Community Psychology.* London: Methuen.

BENEDICT, R. (1935) *Patterns of Culture.* London: Routledge and Kegan Paul.

BENIGER, J. (1986) *The Control Revolution: Technological and Economic Origins of the Information Society.* Cambridge, MA: Harvard University Press.

BENJAMIN, M. (Ed.) (1991) *Science and Sensibility: Gender and Scientific Enquiry, 1780–1945.* Oxford: Basil Blackwell.

BERG, C. (1942) Clinical notes on the analysis of a war neurosis. *British Journal of Medical Psychology, 19,* 155–185.

BERGER, M. (1979) Behaviour modification in education and professional practice: the dangers of a mindless technology. *Bulletin of the British Psychological Society, 32,* 418–419.

BERGER, M., YULE, W. and WIGLEY, V. (1977) The teacher–child interaction project. *Bulletin of the British Association for Behavioural Psychotherapy, 5,* 42–47.

BERGSON, H. (1911) *Matter and Memory.* N.M. Paul and W.S. Palmer (Trans.). London: George Allen and Unwin.

BERNAL, J.D. (1929) *The World the Flesh and the Devil: An Enquiry into the Future of the Three Enemies of the Rational Soul.* London: Kegan Paul.

BERTI, A.E. and BOMBI, A.S. (1988) *The Child's Construction of Economics.* Cambridge: Cambridge University Press.

BIESHEUVEL, S. (1969) *Methods for the Measurement of Psychological Performance.* Oxford: Blackwell Scientific.

BILLIG, M. (1978) *Fascists: A Social Psychological Study of the National Front.* London: Harcourt, Brace and Jovanovich.

BILLIG, M. (1999) *Freudian Repression: Conversation Creating the Unconscious.* Cambridge: Cambridge University Press.

BIRMINGHAM, W. and JAHODA, G. (1955) A pre-election survey in a semi-literate society. *Public Opinion Quarterly, 19,* 140–152.

BLACKBURN, J. (1947) *The Framework of Human Behaviour.* London: Kegan Paul, Trench, Trubner.

BLACKMAN, D.E. (1981) Regulating psychological experimentation with animals in the United Kingdom. *Psychopharmacology Bulletin, 17 (2),* 84–88.

BLACKMAN, L.M. (1994) What is doing history? The use of history to understand the constitution of contemporary psychological objects. *Theory and Psychology, 4,* 485–504.

BLAIN, J. (1932) Psychology – a force or farce? *The Emblem, 1 (14),* 297.

BLITZ, D. (1992) *Emergent Evolution: Qualitative Novelty and the Levels of Reality.* Dordrecht: Kluwer.

BLUMENTHAL, A.L. (1975) A reappraisal of Wilhelm Wundt. *American Psychologist, 30,* 1081–1086.

BOAKES, R.A. (1984) *From Darwin to Behaviourism: Psychology and the Minds of Animals.* Cambridge: Cambridge University Press.

BODEN, M.A. (1959) In reply to Hart and Hampshire, *Mind, NS, 68,* 256–260.

BODEN, M.A. (1965) McDougall revisited. *Journal of Personality, 33,* 1–19.

BODEN, M.A. (1970) Intentionality and physical systems. *Philosophy of Science, 37,* 200–214.

BODEN, M.A. (1972) *Purposive Explanation in Psychology.* Cambridge, MA: Harvard University Press.

BODEN, M.A. (1973) The structure of intentions. *Journal for the Theory of Social Behaviour, 3,* 23–46.

BODEN, M.A. (1974) Freudian mechanisms of defence. In R. Wollheim (Ed.) *Freud: A Collection of Critical Essays.* New York: Anchor Books.

BODEN, M.A. (1977) *Artificial Intelligence and Natural Man.* Hassocks, Sussex: Harvester Press.

BODEN, M.A. (1978) Human values in a mechanistic universe. In G. Vesey (Ed.) *Human Values: Royal Institute of Philosophy Lectures 1976–77.* Hassocks: Harvester Press.

BODEN, M.A. (1979) *Piaget.* London: Fontana Press. (2nd ed., expanded, 1994.)

BODEN, M.A. (1981) *Minds and Mechanisms: Philosophical Psychology and Computational Models.* Hassocks: Harvester Press; Ithaca, CT: Cornell University Press.

BODEN, M.A. (1987) *Artificial Intelligence and Natural Man,* 2nd ed. London: MIT Press; New York: Basic Books.

BODEN, M.A. (1988) *Computer Models of Mind: Computational Approaches in Theoretical Psychology.* (Problems in the Behavioural Sciences.) Cambridge: Cambridge University Press.

BODEN, M.A. (1989) *Artificial Intelligence in Psychology: Interdisciplinary Essays.* Cambridge, MA: MIT Press.

BODEN, M.A. (1990) *The Creative Mind: Myths and Mechanisms.* London: Weidenfeld and Nicolson.

BODEN, M.A. (1994a) What is creativity? In M.A. Boden (Ed.) *Dimensions of Creativity.* London: MIT Press.

BODEN, M.A. (1994b) Preface to the second edition. In M.A. Boden. *Piaget.* London: Fontana Press.

BODEN, M.A. (1994c) Multiple personality and computational models. In A. Phillips-Griffiths (Ed.) *Philosophy, Psychology, and Psychiatry.* Cambridge: Cambridge University Press.

BODEN, M.A. (1995) Artificial intelligence and human dignity. In J. Cornwell (Ed.) *Nature's Imagination: The Frontiers of Scientific Vision.* Oxford: Oxford University Press. (Reprinted, slightly amended in M.A. Boden (Ed.), 1996: 95–108.)

BODEN, M.A. (1998) Consciousness and human identity: an interdisciplinary perspective. In J. Cornwell (Ed.) *Consciousness and Human Identity.* Oxford: Oxford University Press.

BODEN, M.A. (1999) Is metabolism necessary? *British Journal for the Philosophy of Science,* 50, 231–248.

BODEN, M.A. (2000) Autopoiesis and life. *Cognitive Science Quarterly,* 1, 115–143.

BODEN, M.A. (Ed.) (1996) *The Philosophy of Artificial Life.* Oxford: Oxford University Press.

BOLTER, D. (1984) *Turing's Man: Western Culture in the Computer Age.* London: Duckworth.

BOOTH, C. (1902/1980) *Life and Labour in London.* London: Macmillan.

BORING, E.G. (1929/1957) *A History of Experimental Psychology,* 2nd ed. New York: Appleton-Century-Crofts.

BORING, E.G. (1965) On the subjectivity of important historical dates: Leipzig 1879. *Journal of the History of the Behavioral Sciences,* 1, 5–9.

BOURKE, J. (1996) *Dismembering the Male. Men's Bodies, Britain and the Great War.* London: Reaktion.

BOURKE, J. (1999a) *An Intimate History of Killing: Face-to-Face Killing in Twentieth Century History.* London: Granta.

BOURKE, J. (Ed.) (1999b) *The Misfit Soldier. Edward Casey's War Story, 1914–1918.* Cork: Cork University Press.

BOWKER, G. (1993) How to be universal: some cybernetic strategies, 1943–70. *Social Studies of Science,* 23, 107–27.

BOWLER, P.J. (1988) *The Non–Darwinian Revolution: Reinterpreting a Historical Myth.* Baltimore: Johns Hopkins University Press.

BOZZANO, E. (1937) *Discarnate Influence in Human Life: A Review of the Case for Spirit Intervention.* London: International Institute for Psychical Research and John M. Watkins.

BRADLEY, B.S. (1989) *Visions of Infancy: A Critical Introduction to Child Psychology.* Cambridge: Polity Press.

BRAITHWAITE, R. B. (1953) *Scientific Explanation.* Cambridge: Cambridge University Press.

BRAZIER, M. (1950) Neural nets and the integration of behaviour. In D. Richter (Ed.) *Perspectives in Neuropsychiatry.* London: H.K. Lewis.

BRETT, G.S. (1912–1921) *A History of Psychology* (3 vols). New York: Macmillan.

BREWSTER SMITH, M. (1986) McCarthyism, a personal account. *Journal of Social Issues,* 42 (4), 71–80.

BRIERLEY, S. (1916) Authority and freedom. *Parents' Review,* 17.

BRIERLEY, S. (1918) Analysis of the spelling process. *Journal of Experimental Pedagogy,* 4, 239–254.

BRIERLEY, S. (1920) The present attitude of employees to industrial psychology. *British Journal of Psychology,* 10, 210–227.

BRIERLEY, S. (1921a) *An Introduction to Psychology.* London: Methuen.

BRIERLEY, S. (1921b) Science and human values in industry. *The Co-operative Educator,* January.

BRIERLEY, S. (1923) A note on sex differences, from the psycho-analytic point of view. *British Journal of Medical Psychology,* 3, 288–308.

BRITISH ASSOCIATION FOR THE ADVANCEMENT OF SCIENCE (1903–1909) *Reports of Committee to Inquire into the Conditions of Health Essential to the Carrying on of the Work of Instruction in Schools.* London: British Association for the Advancement of Science.

BRITISH ASSOCIATION FOR THE ADVANCEMENT OF SCIENCE (1911, 1912) *Mental and Muscular Fatigue. Reports.* London: British Association for the Advancement of Science.

BRITISH PSYCHOLOGICAL SOCIETY (1976) Working Party on Animal Experimentation, *Bulletin of the British Psychological Society*, 29, 377.
BRITISH PSYCHOLOGICAL SOCIETY (1979) Scientific Affairs Board: Report of the Working Party on Animal Experimentation. *Bulletin of the British Psychological Society, 32,* 44–52.
BRITISH PSYCHOLOGICAL SOCIETY (1983) Monthly report, Scientific Affairs Board. *Bulletin of the British Psychological Society*, 36, 326.
BRITISH PSYCHOLOGICAL SOCIETY (1985) Guidelines for the use of animals in research. *Bulletin of the British Psychological Society,* 38, 289–291.
BRITISH PSYCHOLOGICAL SOCIETY (1985) Scientific Affairs Board: Guidelines for the use of animals in research. *Bulletin of the British Psychological Society*, 38, 289–291.
BRITISH PSYCHOLOGICAL SOCIETY (1986) Guidelines for the use of animals in research. *Animal Behaviour*, 34, 315–318.
BRITISH PSYCHOLOGICAL SOCIETY (1988) *The Future of the Psychological Sciences: Horizons and Opportunities for British Psychology*. Leicester: BPS.
BRITISH PSYCHOLOGICAL SOCIETY (1990) *Psychologists and Social Services*. Leicester: BPS.
BROAD, C.D. (1925) *The Mind and Its Place in Nature*. London: Kegan Paul, Trench, Trubner.
BROADBENT, D.E. (1958) *Perception and Communication*. Oxford: Pergamon Press.
BROADBENT, D.E. (1961) *Behaviour*. London: Eyre and Spottiswoode.
BROADBENT, D.E. (1970) Frederic Charles Bartlett, 1886–1969. *Biographical Memoirs of Fellows of the Royal Society*, 16, 1–13.
BROADHURST, P.L. (1963) *The Science of Animal Behaviour*. Harmondsworth: Pelican.
BROADHURST, P.L. and MARTIN, I. (1961) Comparative and physiological psychology in Britain 1960. *Bulletin of the British Psychological Society*, 45, 41–55. (Also published as The study of higher nervous activity in Britain. *Activitas Nervosa Superior*, 3, 164–176.)
BROCK, A. (1992) Was Wundt a 'Nazi'? Völkerpsychologie, racism and anti-semitism. *Theory and Psychology*, 2, 205–223.
BROCK, A. (1993) Something old, something new: the reappraisal of Wilhelm Wundt in textbooks. *Theory and Psychology*, 3, 235–242.
BROCK, A. (1995) An interview with Kurt Danziger. *History and Philosophy of Psychology Bulletin, 7* (2), 10–22.
BROCK, A. (1998) Pedagogy and research. *The Psychologist*, April, 169–171.
BROKS, P. (1996) *Media Science Before the Great War*. London: Macmillan.
BROOKS, C.H. (1922) *The Practice of Autosuggestion*. London: George Allen and Unwin.
BROWN, A.W. (1947) *The Metaphysical Society: Victorian Minds in Crisis 1869–1880*. New York: Columbia University Press.
BROWN, J. (1954) The nature of set-to-learn and intra-material interference in immediate memory. *Quarterly Journal of Experimental Psychology*, 6, 141–148.
BROWN, J. (1958) Some tests of the decay theory of immediate memory. *Quarterly Journal of Experimental Psychology*, 10, 12–21.
BROWN, J. (1959) Information redundancy and decay of the memory trace. In *The Mechanisation of Thought Processes*. London: HMSO.
BROWN, M. and MADGE, N. (1982) *Despite the Welfare State: A Report of the SSRC/DHSS Programme of Research into Transmitted Deprivation*. London: Heinemann Education.
BROWN, W. (1927) Mental unity and mental dissociation. *Report of the British Association for the Advancement of Science*, 167–175.
BROWN, W. (1928) Mental unity and mental dissociation. *British Journal of Psychology*, 18, 237–248.
BROWN, W. (1936) Psychology at Oxford. In *Mind, Medicine and Metaphysics: The Philosophy of a Physician*. London: Oxford University Press. (First published in the *British Medical Journal*, 30 May 1936, *i*, 1121.)
BROWN, W. and THOMSON, G. (1921) *Essentials of Mental Measurement*. Cambridge: Cambridge University Press.
BRUNER, J.S. (1959). Inhelder and Piaget's *The Growth of Logical Thinking*: a psychologist's viewpoint. *British Journal of Psychology*, 50, 363–370.
BRUNER, J.S. (1961) The act of discovery. *Harvard Educational Review*, 31, 21–32.
BRUNER, J.S. (1983) *In Search of Mind*. New York: Harper and Row.
BUCK, C.W. and LAUGHTON, K.B. (1959) Family patterns of illness: the effect of psychoneurosis in the parent upon illness in the child. *Acta Psychiatrica et Neurologica (Kjobenhavn)*, 34, 165–175.

BURCHELL, G., GORDON, C. and MILLER, P. (Eds) (1991) *The Foucault Effect: Studies in Govern-mentality.* Chicago: University of Chicago Press.

BURT, C. (1925) *The Young Delinquent.* London: London University Press.

BURT, C. (1942) Psychology in war: the military work of American and German psychologists. *Occupational Psychology*, 16, 95–110.

BURT, C. (Ed.) (1945) *How the Mind Works*, 2nd ed. London: George Allen and Unwin.

BURTT, E. A. (1924/1932) *The Metaphysical Foundations of Modern Physical Science: A Historical and Critical Essay*, 2nd ed. London: Routledge and Kegan Paul.

BUSHAWAY, B. (1992) Name upon name: the Great War and remembrance. In R. Porter (Ed.) *Myths of the English.* Cambridge: Polity Press.

BUTLER, S. (1872/1932) *Erewhon, or Over the Range.* London: Dent.

BUTLER, S.V.F. (1988) Centers and peripheries: the development of British physiology, 1870–1914. *Journal of the History of Biology*, 21, 473–500.

BUTTON, E. (1980) *Construing and Clinical Outcome in Anorexia Nervosa.* Unpublished PhD thesis, University of London.

CALDER, A. (1969) *The People's War: Britain 1939–1945.* London: Cape.

CALDER, A. (1986) Introduction. In T. Harrisson and C. Madge (Eds) *Britain by Mass-Observation* London: Cresset.

CALDER, A. and SHERIDAN, D. (Eds) (1985) *Speak for Yourself: A Mass-Observation Anthology, 1937–1949.* Oxford: Oxford University Press.

CALDERWOOD, H. (1879) *The Relations of Brain and Mind.* London: Macmillan.

CAMPBELL, H.Y. (1910) *Practical Motherhood.* London: Longmans, Green.

CANE, V.R. and GREGORY, R.L. (1957) Noise and the visual threshold. *Nature*, 180, 1403.

CANGUILHEM, G. (1955/1977) *La Formation du Concept de Réflexe aux XVIIe et XVIIIe Siècles*, 2nd ed. Paris: J. Vrin.

CANNON, W.B. (1932) *The Wisdom of the Body.* London: Kegan Paul, Trench Trübner.

CANTRIL, H. (1934) The social psychology of everyday life. *Psychological Bulletin*, 31, 297–330.

CAPSHEW, J.H. (1999) *Psychologists on the March: Science, Practice, and Professional Identity in America, 1929–1969.* Cambridge: Cambridge University Press.

CARPENTER, W.B. (1875) *Principles of Mental Physiology: With their Applications to the Training and Discipline of the Mind, and the Study of Its Morbid Conditions*, 3rd ed. London: Henry S. King.

CARPENTER, W.B. (1877) *Mesmerism, Spiritualism &c. Historically and Scientifically Considered: Being Two Lectures Delivered at the London Institution.* London: Longmans, Green.

CARR, J. (1988) Giving away the behavioural approach. *Behavioural Psychotherapy*, 16, 78–84.

CARRUTHERS, M.J. (1990) *The Book of Memory.* Cambridge: Cambridge University Press.

CARSON, J. (1993) Army alpha, army brass, and the search for army intelligence. *Isis*, 84, 278–309.

CARVER, A. (1919) The generation and control of emotion. *British Journal of Psychology*, 10, 51–65.

CARVER, V. (Ed.) (1962) *C.A. Mace: A Symposium.* London: Metheun and Penguin Books.

CASSON, H.N. (1928) *Handbook for Foremen.* London: Efficiency Magazine.

CATTELL, R.B. (1937) *The Fight For Our National Intelligence.* London: P.S. King.

CHANCE, M.R.A. (1956a) Environmental factors influencing gonadotrophin assay in the rat. *Nature*, 177, 228–229.

CHANCE, M.R.A. (1956b) Social structure of a colony of *Macaca mulatta. British Journal of Animal Behaviour*, 4, 1–13.

CHANCE, M.R.A. (1957) The role of convulsions in behaviour. *Behavioral Science*, 2, 30–40.

CHAPUIS, A. and DROZ, E. (1958) *Automata: A Historical and Technological Study.* London: Batsford.

CHAZAN, M., *et al.* (1983) *Helping Young Children with Behaviour Difficulties.* London: Croom Helm.

CHENG, P.W. and HOLYOAK, K.J. (1985) Pragmatic reasoning schemas. *Cognitive Psychology*, 17, 391–416.

CHESTERTON, G.K. (1923) The game of psychoanalysis. *Century Magazine*, 106, 34–43.

CLARK, C. (1979) Education and behaviour modification, *Journal of Philosophy of Education*, 13, 73–81.

CLARK, H.H. (1974) Semantics and comprehension. In T.A. Sebeok (Ed.) *Current Trends in Linguistics. Vol. 12: Linguistics and Adjacent Arts and Sciences.* The Hague: Mouton.

CLARK, K.B. and CLARK, M.P. (1958) Racial identification and preferences in Negro children. In E.E. Maccoby, T.M. Newcomb and E.L. Hartley (Eds) *Readings in Social Psychology.* New York: Holt Reinhardt and Winston.

CLARK, S.R.L. (1977) *The Moral Status of Animals.* Oxford: Clarendon Press.

CLAUSEN, R.E. and DANIELS, A.K. (1966) Role conflicts and their ideological resolution in military psychiatric practice. *American Journal of Psychiatry, 123,* 280–287.

CLIFFORD, W.K. (1879) *Seeing and Thinking.* London: Macmillan.

CLINE, C.L. (Ed.) (1970) *The Letters of George Meredith.* Oxford: Clarendon Press.

COCKBURN, J.A. (1908) Address delivered before the London Child-Study Society on October 15, 1907. *Child Study,* 1, 1–3.

COGBURN, H.E. (1951) The brain analogy. *Psychological Review,* 58, 155–178.

COHEN, D. (1977) *Psychologists on Psychology.* London: Routledge and Kegan Paul.

COHEN, J. (1966) *Human Robots in Myth and Science.* London: George Allen and Unwin.

COLBY, K.M. (1965) Computer simulation of neurotic processes. In R.W. Stacy and B.D. Waxman (Eds) *Computers in Biomedical Research, Vol. 1.* New York: Academic Press.

COLBY, K.M. (1975) *Artificial Paranoia.* New York: Pergamon.

COLE, M. (1996) *Cultural Psychology.* Cambridge, MA: Harvard University Press.

COLLETT, P. and FURNHAM, A. (Eds) (1995) *Social Psychology at Work.* London: Routledge.

COLLIE, J. (1917) *Malingering and Feigned Sickness,* 2nd ed. London: Edward Arnold.

COLLINI, S. (1991) *Public Moralists: Political Thought and Intellectual Life in Britain 1850–1930.* Oxford: Clarendon Press.

COMMITTEE ON CLINICAL PSYCHOLOGY OF THE GROUP FOR THE ADVANCEMENT OF PSYCHIATRY (1949) The relation of clinical psychology to psychiatry. *Report of the Group for the Advancement of Psychiatry, no. 10,* July 1949.

CONRAD, R. and HULL, A.J. (1964) Information, acoustic confusion and memory span. *British Journal of Psychology,* 55, 429–432.

CONWAY, M. (1915) *The Crowd in Peace and War.* London: Longmans, Green.

COOPER, R. and BIRD, J. (1989) *The Burden: Fifty Years of Clinical and Experimental Neuroscience at the Burden Neurological Institute.* Bristol: White Tree Books.

COOTER, R. (1984) *The Cultural Meaning of Popular Science: Phrenology and the Organization of Consent in Nineteenth-Century Britain.* Cambridge: Cambridge University Press.

CORDESCHI, R. (1987) Purpose, feedback and homeostasis: dimensions of a controversy in psychological explanation. In S. Bem and H. Rappard (Eds) *Studies in the History of Psychology and the Social Sciences 4.* Leiden: Psychologisch Institut van de Rijkuinversiteit Leiden.

COSMIDES, L. (1989) The logic of social exchange. Has natural selection shaped how humans reason? Studies with the Wason selection task. *Cognition,* 31, 187–276.

COSTALL, A. (1991) Frederic Bartlett and the rise of prehistoric psychology. In A. Still and A. Costall (Eds) *Against Cognitivism: Alternative Foundations for Cognitive Psychology.* Hemel Hempstead: Harvester Wheasheaf.

COSTALL, A. (1992) Why British psychology is not social: Frederic Bartlett's promotion of the new academic discipline. *Canadian Psychology/Psychologie Canadienne,* 33, 633–639.

COSTALL, A. (1993) How Lloyd Morgan's canon backfired. *Journal of the History of the Behavioral Sciences,* 29, 113–124.

COSTALL, A. (1995) Sir Frederic Bartlett. *The Psychologist,* 8, 307–308.

COSTALL, A. (1998) Dire straits? Relations between psychology and anthropology after the Cambridge anthropological expedition of 1898. Paper to the conference on Psychology and Anthropology in Britain: the legacy of the Torres Strait expedition, 1898–1998, Cambridge, August, 1998.

COSTALL, A. (1999) Dire straits: the divisive legacy of the 1898 Cambridge Anthropological Expedition. *Journal of the History of the Behavioral Sciences,* 35, 345–358.

COTT, H.B. (1948) Camouflage. *Advancement of Science,* 4, 300–309.

COUÉ, E. (1922) *Self Mastery Through Conscious Autosuggestion.* London: George Allen and Unwin.

COUÉ, E. and ORTON, J.L. (1924) *Conscious Auto-Suggestion.* London: Fisher Unwin.

COX, E.W. (1863) *The Arts of Writing, Reading and Speaking: Letters to a Law Student.* London: Horace Cox.

COX, E.W. (1871, enlarged and revised 1872) *Spiritualism Answered by Science, with Proofs of a Psychic Force.* London: Longman. (1871 title: *Spiritualism Answered by Science,* without the additional phrase.)

COX, E.W. (1873, 1874) *What Am I? A Popular Introduction to the Study of Psychology* (2 vols). London: Longman.

COX, E.W. (1875a) *Heredity and Hybridism: A Suggested Solution of the Problem.* London: Longman.

COX, E.W. (1875b) *The Psychology of Memory and Recollection.* London: Psychological Society of Great Britain.

COX, E.W. (1878) _Monograph on Sleep and Dream: Their Physiology and Psychology._ London: Longman.

CRAIG, M. (1933) Mental hygiene in everyday life. _Mental Hygiene, 7,_ 61.

CRAIK, K.J.W. (1940) _Visual Adaptation._ Unpublished PhD thesis, Cambridge University.

CRAIK, K.J.W. (1941) Instruments and methods for testing sensory events. _Journal of Scientific Instruments, 18,_ 1–6

CRAIK, K.J.W. (1943) _The Nature of Explanation._ Cambridge: Cambridge University Press.

CRAIK, K.J.W. (1944) Medical Research Council Unit for Applied Psychology. _Nature, 154,_ 476–477.

CRAIK, K.J.W. (1947–1948a) Theory of the human operator in control systems: I. The operator as an engineering system. _British Journal of Psychology, 38,_ 56–61.

CRAIK, K.J.W. (1947–1948b) Theory of the human operator in control systems: II. Man as an element in a control system. _British Journal of Psychology, 38,_ 142–148.

CRAIK, K.J.W. (n.d.) _Man's Extension of Himself._ In S. Sherwood (Ed.) (1966) K.J.W. Craik, _The Nature of Psychology: A Selection of Papers, Essays and Other Writings by the Late Kenneth J.W. Craik._ Cambridge: Cambridge University Press.

CRAMPTON, C. (1978) _The Cambridge School: The Life, Work and Influence of James Ward, W.H.R. Rivers, C.S. Myers and Sir Frederic Bartlett._ Unpublished PhD thesis, University of Edinburgh.

CRELLIN, C. (1998) Origins and social contexts of the term 'formulation' in psychological case-reports. _Clinical Psychology Forum, 112,_ 18–28.

CRICK, F. (1994) _The Astonishing Hypothesis: The Scientific Search for the Soul._ Cambridge: Cambridge University Press.

CROLL, J. (1889) _Stellar Evolution._ London: Edward Stanford.

CROLL, J. (1890) _The Philosophical Basis of Evolution._ London: Edward Stanford.

CROOKES, W. (1926) _Researches in the Phenomena of Spiritualism Together with a Portion of his Presidential Address Given Before the British Association, 1898; and An Appendix by Sir A. Conan Doyle 1926._ Manchester: Two Worlds Publishing; London: Psychic Bookshop.

CROOKES, W., Dr HUGGINS, SERJEANT COX and LORD LINDSAY (1871) _Psychic Power – Spirit Power. Experimental Investigations._ London: E.W. Allen.

CROSS, R.C. (1970) The inaugural address: 'Alexander Bain'. _Aristotelian Society Supplementary, 44,_ 1–14.

CROSS, S.J. and ALBURY, W.R. (1987) Walter B. Cannon, L.J. Henderson, and the organic analogy. _Osiris, 2nd series, 3,_ 165–192.

CROWDER, R.C. (1993) Systems and principles in memory theory: Another critique of pure memory. In A.F. Collins, S.E. Gathercole, M.A. Conway and P.E. Morris (Eds) _Theories of Memory._ Hove: Lawrence Erlbaum Associates.

CROWN, S. (1949) The psychology department – Maudsley Hospital. _Bulletin of the British Psychological Society, 1,_ 57–58.

CRUIKSHANK, B. (1993) Revolutions within: self-government and self-esteem. _Economy and Society, 22,_ 327–344.

CULLEN, C., et al. (1981) Establishing behaviour: the constructional approach. In G. Davey (Ed.) _Applications of Conditioning Theory._ London: Methuen.

CULPIN, M. (1931) _Recent Advances in the Study of the Psychoneuroses._ London: J. and A. Churchill.

CULPIN, M. (1949) An autobiography. _Occupational Psychology, 23,_ 140–152.

DAIN, N. (1980) _Clifford W. Beers: Advocate for the Insane._ Pittsburgh: University of Pittsburgh Press.

DANIELS, A.K. (1969) The captive professional: bureaucratic limitations in the practices of military psychiatry. _Journal of Health and Social Behavior, 10,_ 255–265.

DANIELS, A.K. (1972) Military psychiatry: the emergence of a subspecialty. In E. Freidson and J. Larbour (Eds) _Medical Men and Their Work._ Chicago: Aldine Atherton.

DANZIGER, K. (1979) The positivist repudiation of Wundt. _Journal of the History of the Behavioral Sciences, 15,_ 205–230.

DANZIGER, K. (1982) Mid nineteenth-century British psycho-physiology: a neglected chapter in the history of psychology. In W.R. Woodward and M.G. Ash (Eds) _The Problematic Science: Psychology in Nineteenth-Century Thought._ New York: Praeger.

DANZIGER, K. (1987) Social context and investigative practice in early twentieth-century psychology. In M.G. Ash and W.R. Woodward (Eds) _Psychology in Twentieth-Century Thought and Society._ Cambridge: Cambridge University Press.

DANZIGER, K. (1990) _Constructing the Subject: Historical Origins of Psychological Research._ Cambridge: Cambridge University Press.

DANZIGER, K. (1993) Psychological objects, practice, and history. *Annals of Theoretical Psychology*, 8, 15–47.

DANZIGER, K. (1994) Does the history of psychology have a future? *Theory and Psychology*, 4, 467–484.

DANZIGER, K. (1997a) The historical formation of selves. In R.D. Ashmore and L. Jussim (Eds) *Self and Identity: Fundamental Issues*. Oxford: Oxford University Press.

DANZIGER, K. (1997b) *Naming the Mind: How Psychology Found Its Language*. London: Sage.

DARCUS, H.D. and WEDDELL, G. (1947) Some anatomical and physiological principles concerned with the design of seats for naval war weapons. *British Medical Bulletin*, 5, 31–37.

DARWIN, C. (1877) Biographical sketch of an infant. *Mind*, 7, 285–294.

DASTON, L.J. (1982) The theory of will versus the science of mind. In W.R. Woodward and M.G. Ash (Eds) *The Problematic Science: Psychology in Nineteenth-Century Thought*. New York: Praeger.

DAVENPORT-HINES, R. (1995) *Auden*. London: Heinemann.

DAVIS, D.R. and SINHA, D. (1950a) The effect of one experience upon the recall of another. *Quarterly Journal of Experimental Psychology*, 2, 43–52.

DAVIS, D.R. and SINHA, D. (1950b) The influence of an interpolated experience upon recognition. *Quarterly Journal of Experimental Psychology*, 2, 132–137.

DAWSON, S. (1917) The experimental study of binocular colour mixture. *British Journal of Psychology*, 8, 510–551.

DE LATIL, P. (1956) *Thinking by Machine*. Y. Golla (Trans.). Cambridge, MA: Riverside Press.

DENNETT, D. (1993) *Consciousness Explained*. London: Penguin.

DENNETT, D. (1998) *Brainchildren: Essays on Designing Minds*. London: Penguin.

DENNY-BROWN, D. (1932) Theoretical deductions from the physiology of the cerebral cortex. *Journal of Neurology and Psychopathology*, 13, 52–67.

DERKSEN, M. (1997) Are we not experimenting then? The rhetorical demarcation of psychology and common sense. *Theory and Psychology*, 7, 435–456.

DESMOND, A. (1994) *Huxley: The Devil's Disciple*. London: Michael Joseph.

DESMOND, A. and MOORE, J. (1991) *Darwin*. London: Michael Joseph.

DESSENT, T. (1988) Adapting behavioural approaches to the local authority environment. *Educational Psychology in Practice*, 3 (4), 24–28.

DESSOIR, M. (1912) *Outlines of a History of Psychology*. New York: Macmillan.

DEUSTCH, J.A. (1953) A new type of behaviour theory. *British Journal of Psychology*, 44, 304–318.

DEUTSCH, J.A. (1954) A machine with insight. *Quarterly Journal of Experimental Psychology*, 6, 6–11.

DEUTSCH, J.A. (1960) *The Structural Basis of Behavior*. Cambridge: Cambridge University Press.

DEUTSCH, J.A. (1963) Experiments on animals. In G. Humphrey (Ed.) *Psychology Through Experiment*. London: Methuen.

DEUTSCH, K. (1963) *The Nerves of Government*. London: Collier-Macmillan.

DEWEY, J. (1910) Review of *Eternal Values* by Hugo Münsterberg. *Philosophical Review*, 19, 110.

DEWSBURY, D.A. (1984) *Comparative Psychology in the Twentieth Century*. Stroudsburg, PA: Hutchinson Ross.

DOUGLAS, J. (1989) *Behaviour Problems in Young Children*. London: Tavistock/Routledge.

DOUGLAS, M. (1972) Deciphering a meal. *Daedalus*, 101, 61–81.

DOUGLAS, M. (1975) Self evidence. In *Implicit Meanings*. London: Routledge and Kegan Paul.

DREVER, J. (1921) *The Psychology of Everyday Life*. London: Methuen.

DREVER, J. (1948) An autobiography. *Occupational Psychology*, 22, 20–30.

DRISCOLL, J.W. and BATESON, P.P.G. (1988) Animals in behavioural research. *Animal Behaviour*, 36, 1569–1574.

DRUMMOND, W.B. (1907) *An Introduction to Child Study*. London: Edward Arnold.

DUNCAN, D.C. (1955) A new method of recording labour losses. *The Manager*, January.

DUNCAN, D.C. (1967) The psychology of taxation. *Manpower and Applied Psychology*, 1, 162–176.

DURANT, J.R. (1986) The making of ethology: the Association for the Study of Animal Behaviour, 1936–1986. *Animal Behaviour*, 34, 1601–1616.

DURBIN, E.F.M. and BOWLBY, J. (1939) *Personal Aggressiveness and War*. London: Kegan Paul.

DYSON, G. (1997) *Darwin among the Machines*. London: Allen Lane.

EARLE, F.M and GOW, F. (1930) *The Measurement of Manual Dexterities*. NIIP Report No. 4. London: NIIP.

EARLE, F.M. and MACRAE, A. (1929) *Tests of Mechanical Ability*. NIIP Report No. 3. London: NIIP.

EBBINGHAUS, H. (1913/1964) *Memory: A Contribution to Experimental Psychology.* H.A. Ruger and C.E. Bussenius (Trans.). Mineola: Dover Press. (Original work published 1885.)

EDGELL, B. (1913) The experimental study of memory. *Child Study,* 5, 84–89, 118–125.

EDGELL, B. (1924) *Theories of Memory.* Oxford: Clarendon.

EDGELL, B. (1929) Memory. In *Encyclopaedia Britannica,* 14th ed. London: Encyclopaedia Britannica.

EDGELL, B. (1947) The British Psychological Society: 1901–1941. *British Journal of Psychology,* 37, 113–132. (A slightly reduced version of this paper also appeared in H. Steinberg (Ed.). 1961: 3–21.)

EDWARDS, D. (1997) *Discourse and Cognition.* London: Sage.

EDWARDS, D. and MIDDLETON, D. (1987) Conversation and remembering: Bartlett revisited. *Applied Cognitive Psychology,* 1, 77–92.

EHRENREICH, B. and ENGLISH, D. (1979) *For Her Own Good: 150 Years of Experts' Advice to Women.* London: Pluto Press.

ELBOW, P. (1973) *Writing Without Teachers.* London: Oxford University Press.

ELLENBERGER, H. (1970) *The Discovery of the Unconscious: The History and Evolution of Dynamic Psychiatry.* New York: Basic Books.

ELLESLEY, S. (1995) *Psychoanalysis in Early Twentieth-Century England: A Study in the Popularization of Ideas.* Unpublished PhD thesis, University of Essex.

ELLIOT, R. (Ed.) (1995) *Environmental Ethics.* Oxford: Oxford University Press.

ELTINGE, L. (1918) *Psychology of War.* London: The Author.

ENGELS, F. (1845/1969) *The Condition of the Working Class in England.* London: Panther.

ERWIN, G. (1978) *Behaviour Therapy: Scientific, Philosophical and Moral Foundations.* Cambridge: Cambridge University Press.

ETZIONI, A. and WENGLINSKY, M. (Eds) (1970) *War and its Prevention.* London: Harper Row.

EVANS, G. and DURANT, J. (1989) The understanding of science in Britain and the USA. In R. Jowell, S. Witherspoon and L. Brook (Eds) *British Social Attitudes: Special International Report.* Aldershot: Gower, SCPR.

EVANS, J.St.B.T. (1983) Selective processes in reasoning. In J. St. B. T. Evans (Ed.) *Thinking and Reasoning: Psychological Approaches.* London: Routledge and Kegan Paul.

EVANS, J.St.B.T. (1989) *Bias in Human Reasoning: Causes and Consequences.* Hove: Lawrence Erlbaum Associates.

EVANS, J.St.B.T., NEWSTEAD, S.E. and BYRNE, R.M.J. (1993) *Human Reasoning: The Psychology of Deduction.* Hove: Lawrence Erlbaum Associates.

EXPERIMENTAL PSYCHOLOGY SOCIETY (1986) Guidelines for the use of animals in research. *Quarterly Journal of Experimental Psychology,* 38B, 111–116.

EX-PRIVATE X (1930) *War is War.* London: Victor Gollancz.

EYSENCK, H.J. (1947) *Dimensions of Personality.* London: Kegan Paul.

EYSENCK, H.J. (1949a) What is clinical psychology? *Quarterly Bulletin of the British Psychological Society,* 4, April, 138.

EYSENCK, H.J. (1949b) Training in clinical psychology: an English point of view. *American Psychologist,* 4, 173–176.

EYSENCK, H.J. (1950a) The relation between medicine and psychology in England. In W. Dennis, R.H. Felix, C. Jacobson, R.A. Patton, Y.D. Koskoff, P.E. Huston, N.W. Shock and H.J. Eysenck (Eds) *Current Trends in the Relation of Psychology to Medicine.* Pittsburgh, PA: University of Pittsburgh Press.

EYSENCK, H.J. (1950b) Function and training of the clinical psychologist. *Journal of Mental Science,* 96, 710–725.

EYSENCK, H.J. (1950c) Clinical psychology and its relation to industrial psychology. *Occupational Psychology,* 24, 48–53.

EYSENCK, H.J. (1951) Psychology Department, Institute of Psychiatry (Maudsley Hospital), University of London. *Acta Psychologica,* 8, 63–68.

EYSENCK, H.J. (1952) Discussion on the role of the psychologist in psychiatric practice. (With H. Wilson, O.L. Zangwill, H.J. Eysenck, and A. Kennedy.) *Proceedings of the Royal Society of Medicine,* 45, 445–450.

EYSENCK, H.J. (1953) *Uses and Abuses of Psychology.* Harmondsworth: Penguin.

EYSENCK, H.J. (1955a) *Psychology and the Foundations of Psychiatry.* London: Lewis.

EYSENCK, H.J. (1955b) A dynamic theory of anxiety and hysteria. *Journal of Mental Science,* 101, 28–51.

EYSENCK, H.J. (1957) *The Dynamics of Anxiety and Hysteria. An Experimental Application of Modern Learning Theory to Psychiatry*. London: Routledge and Kegan Paul.

EYSENCK, H.J. (1959) Learning theory and behaviour therapy. *Journal of Mental Science, 105*, 61–75.

EYSENCK, H.J. (1960) *Behaviour Therapy and the Neuroses: Readings in Modern Methods of Treatment*. Oxford: Pergamon.

EYSENCK, H.J. (1965) *Fact and Fiction in Psychology*. London: Penguin.

EYSENCK, H.J. (1966) Personality and experimental psychology. *Bulletin of the British Psychological Society, 19 (62)*, 1–28.

EYSENCK, H.J. (1967) *The Biological Basis of Personality*. Springfield, IL: Charles C. Thomas.

EYSENCK, H.J. (1975) *The Future of Psychiatry*. London: Methuen.

EYSENCK, H.J. (1984) Is behaviour therapy on course? *Behavioural Psychotherapy, 12*, 2–6.

EYSENCK, H.J. (1990/1997) *Rebel with a Cause: The Autobiography of Hans Eysenck*. Revised and expanded edition. New Brunswick: Transaction.

EYSENCK, H.J. (1991a) Maverick psychologist. In E. Walker (Ed.) *The History of Clinical Psychology in Autobiography, Vol. 1*. Pacific Grove: Brooks/Cole.

EYSENCK, H.J. (1991b) Behavioral psychotherapy. In E. Walker (Ed.) *Clinical Psychology: Historical and Research Foundations*. New York: Plenum.

EYSENCK, H.J. (Ed.) (1960) *Behaviour Therapy and the Neuroses:. Readings in Modern Methods of Treatment Derived from Learning Theory*. Oxford: Pergamon.

EYSENCK, H.J. and RACHMAN, S.J. (1965) *The Causes and Cures of Neurosis*. London: Routledge and Kegan Paul.

FANCHER, R.E. (1990) *Pioneers of Psychology*, 2nd ed. New York: Norton.

FARR, R. (1996) *The Origins of Modern Social Psychology*. Oxford: Blackwell.

FEIGENBAUM, E.N. and McCORDUCK, P. (1983) *The Fifth Generation: Artificial Intelligence and Japan's Computer Challenge to the World*. London: Michael Joseph.

FERRIER, D. (1876) *The Functions of the Brain*. London: Smith, Elder.

FERRIER, D. (1886) *The Functions of the Brain*, 2nd ed. London: Smith, Elder.

FEUDTNER, C. (1993) Minds the dead have ravished: shell-shock, history and the ecology of disease systems. *History of Science, 31*, 377–420.

FITZGERALD, G.H. (1922) Some aspects of the war neurosis. *British Journal of Psychology. Medical Section, 2*, 109–120.

FLECK, L. (1939/1979) *Genesis and Development of a Scientific Fact*. F. Bradley and T. J. Trenn (Trans.). Chicago: University of Chicago Press.

FLETCHER, K.H. (1951) Matter with mind: a neurological research robot. *Research, 4*, 305–307.

FLETCHER, R. (1991) *Science, Ideology and the Media: The Cyril Burt Scandal*. London: Transaction.

FLÜGEL, J.C. (1933) *A Hundred Years of Psychology, 1833–1933*. London: Duckworth.

FLÜGEL, J.C. (1939) Obituary of W. McDougall. *British Journal of Psychology, 29*, 321–328.

FLÜGEL, J.C. and WEST, D.J. (1964) *A Hundred Years of Psychology, 1833–1933*, 3rd ed. London: Duckworth.

FORMAN, P. (1991) Independence, not transcendence, for the historian of science. *Isis, 82*, 71–86.

FOSSEY, E. (1994) *Growing up with Alcohol*. London: Routledge.

FOUCAULT, M. (1972) *The Archaeology of Knowledge and the Discourse on Language*. A.M. Sheridan Smith (Trans.). New York: Pantheon Books.

FOUCAULT, M. (1973) *The Birth of the Clinic: An Archaeology of Medical Perception*. A.M. Sheridan-Smith (Trans.). London: Tavistock.

FOUCAULT, M. (1978/1990) *The History of Sexuality, Vol. 1: An Introduction*. R. Hurley (Trans.). New York: Vintage Books.

FOUCAULT, M. (1980) *Power/Knowledge: Selected Interviews and Other Writings 1972–1977*. C. Gordon (Ed.) and C. Gordon, L. Marshall, J. Mepham and K. Soper (Trans.). New York: Pantheon Books.

FOUCAULT, M. (1988) *Politics, Philosophy, Culture: Interviews and Other Writings 1977–1984*. L.D. Kritzman (Ed.) and A. Sheridan *et al.* (Trans.). New York: Routledge.

FRACKER, G.C. (1908) On the transference of training in memory. *Psychological Monographs, 9*, 56–102.

FRANCOUER, E. (1997) The forgotten tool: the design and use of molecular models. *Social Studies of Science, 27*, 7–40.

FRANSELLA, F. (1960) The treatment of chronic schizophrenia: intensive occupational therapy with and without chlorpromazine. *Occupational Therapy Journal*, September, 23.

FRANSELLA, F. (1964) A comparison of the methods of measurement of Kelly and of Osgood. In N. Warren (Ed.) *The Theory and Methodology of George Kelly*. London: Brunel University.

FRANSELLA, F. (1970) Measurement of conceptual change accompanying weight change. *Journal of Psychosomatic Research*, *14*, 347–351.

FRANSELLA, F. (1972) *Personal Change and Reconstruction: Research on a Treatment of Stuttering.* London: Academic Press.

FRANSELLA, F. (1975) *Need to Change?* London: Methuen.

FRANSELLA, F. (1977) The self and the stereotype. In D. Bannister (Ed.) *New Perspectives in Personal Construct Theory.* London: Academic Press.

FRANSELLA, F. (1978) *Our Body Shape – In Fact and in Imagination.* Bath: British Association for the Advancement of Science,.

FRANSELLA, F. (1983) What sort of person is the person as scientist? In J. Adams-Webber and J. Mancuso (Eds) *Applications of Personal Construct Theory.* London: Academic Press.

FRANSELLA, F. (1989) A fight for freedom. In W. Dryden (Ed.) *On Becoming a Psychotherapist.* London: Routledge.

FRANSELLA, F. (1995) *George Kelly.* London: Sage.

FRANSELLA, F. (1999) Personal construct theory and constructive mathematics. Paper given at the 13th International Congress on Personal Construct Psychology, Berlin.

FRANSELLA, F. and ADAMS, B. (1966) An illustration of the use of repertory grid technique in a clinical setting. *British Journal of Social and Clinical Psychology*, *5*, 51–62.

FRANSELLA, F. and BANNISTER, D. (1977) *A Manual for Repertory Grid Technique.* London: Academic Press.

FRANSELLA, F. and CRISP, A.H. (1970) Conceptual organisation and weight change. *Psychosomatics and Psychotherapy*, *9*, 265–271. (Reprinted in R.A. Pierloot (Ed.) (1971) *Recent Research in Psychosomatics*. Basel: S. Karger.)

FRANSELLA, F. and FROST, K. (1977) *On Being a Woman.* London: Tavistock.

FRENCH, R.D. (1975) *Antivivisection and Medical Science in Victorian Society.* Princeton: Princeton University Press.

FREUD, S. and BREUER, J. (1895/1974) *Studies on Hysteria.* A. Richards (Ed.) Pelican Freud Library, Vol. 3. Harmondsworth: Penguin.

FRIJDA, N. and JAHODA, G. (1966) On the scope and methods of cross-cultural research. *International Journal of Psychology*, *1*, 109–127.

FRISBY, C.B., VINCENT, D.F. and LANCASHIRE, R. (1959) *Tests for Engineering Apprentices: A Validation Study.* NIIP Report No. 14. London: National Institute of Industrial Psychology.

FROMM, E. (1984) *The Working Class in Weimar Germany.* Warwick: Berg.

FULLER, J.F.C. (1914) *Training Soldiers for War.* London: H. Rees.

FULTON, J.F. (1946) *Harvey Cushing: A Biography.* Springfield, IL: Charles C. Thomas.

FUSSELL, P. (1975) *The Great War and Modern Memory.* Oxford: Oxford University Press.

GALISON, P. (1994) The ontology of the enemy: Norbert Wiener and the cybernetic vision. *Critical Inquiry*, *21*, 228–266.

GALISON, P. (1997) *Image and Logic: A Material Culture of Microphysics.* Chicago: University of Chicago Press.

GALTON, F. (1883) *Inquiries into Human Faculty and Its Development.* London: Macmillan.

GALTON, F. (1887) Supplementary notes on 'prehension' in idiots. *Mind*, *12*, 79–82.

GALTON, F. (1908) *Memories of My Life.* London: Methuen.

GARDNER, D.E.M. (1969) *Susan Isaacs.* London: Methuen.

GARDNER, H. (1985) *The Mind's New Science: A History of the Cognitive Revolution.* New York: Basic Books.

GARFIELD, S.L. (1974) *Clinical Psychology: The Study of Personality and Behaviour.* London: Edward Arnold.

GAUCHET, M. (1992) *L'Inconscient cérébral.* Paris: Editions du Seuil.

GEISON, G. (1978) *Michael Foster and the Cambridge School of Physiology: The Scientific Enterprise in Late Victorian Society.* Princeton: Princeton University Press.

GENERAL MEDICAL COUNCIL (1910) *Report as to the Practice of Medicine and Surgery by Unqualified Persons in the United Kingdom.* London: HMSO.

GEORGE, F. (1956) Pragmatics. *Journal of Philosophy and Phenomenological Research*, *17*, 226–235.

GEORGE, F. (1957) Behaviour network systems for finite automata. *Methodos*, *9*, 279–291.

GEORGE, F. (1961) *The Brain as a Computer.* Oxford: Pergamon Press.

GEUTER, U. (1992) *The Professionalization of Psychology in Nazi Germany.* Cambridge: Cambridge University Press.

GIBB, J.W. (c. 1942) *Training in the Army.* London: War Office.

GIBSON, H.B. (1981) *Hans Eysenck: The Man and his Work*. London: Peter Owen.

GIBSON, J.J. (1950) *The Perception of the Visual World*. Boston, MA: Houghton Mifflin.

GIERYN, T. (1999) *Cultural Boundaries of Science: Credibility on the line*. Chicago: University of Chicago Press.

GIGERENZER, G. (1992) Discovery in cognitive psychology: new tools inspire new theories. *Science in Context*, 5, 329–350.

GIGERENZER, G. (1996) From tools to theories: discovery in cognitive psychology. In K. Gergen and C. Graumann (Eds) *Historical Dimensions of Psychological Discourse*. Cambridge: Cambridge University Press.

GIGERENZER, G. and HUG, K. (1992) Domain-specific reasoning: social contracts, cheating, and perspective change. *Cognition*, 43, 127–171.

GINSBURG, G.J. (1979) *Emerging Strategies in Social Psychology*. London: Wiley.

GIROTTO, V., LIGHT, P. and COLBOUM, C. (1988) Pragmatic schemas and conditional reasoning in children. *Quarterly Journal of Experimental Psychology*, 40A, 469–482.

GLANZER, M. and CUNITZ, A.R. (1966) Two storage mechanisms in free recall. *Journal of Verbal Learning and Verbal Behavior*, 5, 351–360.

GLOVER, W. (1914) *Know Your Own Mind: A Little Book of Practical Psychology*. Cambridge: Cambridge University Press.

GODDEN, D. and BADDELEY, A.D. (1975) Context-dependent memory in two natural environments: on land and under water. *British Journal of Psychology*, 66, 325–331.

GOFFMAN, E. (1961) *Encounters: Two Studies in the Sociology of Interaction*. Indianapolis: Bobbs-Merrill.

GOLDIAMOND, I. (1974) Toward a constructional approach to social problems. Ethical and constitutional issues raised by applied behavior analysis. *Behaviourism*, 2, 1–84.

GOOD, I.J. (Ed.) (1962) *The Scientist Speculates*. London: Heinemann.

GOODAY, G. (1990) Precision measurement and the genesis of physical teaching laboratories in Victorian Britain. *British Journal for the History of Science*, 23, 25–51.

GOODING, D., PINCH, T. and SCHAFFER, S. (Eds) (1989) *The Uses of Experiment: Studies in the Natural Sciences*. Cambridge: Cambridge University Press.

GOTTLIEB, G. (1979) Comparative psychology and ethology. In E. Hearst (Ed.) *The First Century of Experimental Psychology*. Hillsdale, NJ: Lawrence Erlbaum Associates.

GOULD, S.J. (1977) *Ontogeny and Phylogeny*. Cambridge, MA: Belknap Press of the Harvard University Press.

GRAHAM, L., LEPENIES, W. and WEINGART, P. (Eds) (1983) *Functions and Uses of Disciplinary Histories*. Dordrecht: D. Riedel.

GRAINGER, R.D. (1843) Contributions in *Children's Employment Commission: Second Report of the Commissioners on Trades and Manufactures*. British Parliamentary Papers series. Shannon: Irish University Press facsimile.

GRAUMANN, C.F. and GERGEN, K.J. (Eds) (1996) *Historical Dimensions of Psychological Discourse*. Cambridge: Cambridge University Press.

GRAVES, R. and HODGE, A. (1971) *The Long Weekend: A Social History of Great Britain, 1918–1939*. London: Penguin.

GRAY, J.A. (1985) A whole and its parts: behaviour, the brain, cognition and emotion. *Bulletin of the British Psychological Society*, 38, 99–112.

GREEN, D.W. and WASON, P.C. (1969) A rejoinder to Klayman and Ha. Unpublished manuscript.

GREEN, D.W. and WASON, P.C. (1982) Notes on the psychology of writing. *Human Relations*, 35, 47–66.

GREEN, F.H.K. and COVELL, G. (1953) *Medical Research*. History of the Second World War: United Kingdom Medical Series. London: HMSO.

GREGORY, R.L. (1953–1954) On physical model explanations in psychology. *British Journal of the Philosophy of Science*, 4, 192–197.

GREGORY, R.L. (1959) Models and the localisation of function in the central nervous system. In *Mechanisation of Thought Processes. Vol. 2*. London: HMSO.

GREGORY, R.L. (1961) The brain as an engineering problem. In W.H. Thorpe and O.L. Zangwill (Eds) *Current Problems in Animal Behaviour*. Cambridge: Cambridge University Press.

GREGORY, R.L. (1963) Distortion of visual space as inappropriate constancy scaling. *Nature*, 199, 678–691.

GREGORY, R.L. (1964a) A technique for minimising the effects of atmospheric disturbance on photographic telescopes. *Nature, London*, 203, 274.

GREGORY, R.L. (1964b) Stereoscopic shadow images. *Nature, 203,* 4952, 1407–1408.

GREGORY, R.L. (1966) *Eye and Brain: The Psychology of Seeing.* London: Weidenfeld and Nicolson. (5th ed. 1998. Oxford: Oxford University Press.)

GREGORY, R.L. (1968) Perceptual illusions and brain models. *Proceedings of the Royal Society, B171,* 179–296.

GREGORY, R.L. (1969a) Apparatus for investigating visual perception. *American Psychologist, 24,* 219–225.

GREGORY, R.L. (1969b) On how so little information controls so much behaviour. In C.H. Waddington (Ed.) *Towards a Theoretical Biology, Vol. 2.* Edinburgh: Edinburgh University Press.

GREGORY, R.L. (1970) *The Intelligent Eye.* London: Weidenfeld and Nicolson.

GREGORY, R.L. (1971) The social implications of intelligent machines. In B. Meltzer and D. Michie (Eds) *Machine Intelligence, Vol. 6.* Edinburgh: Edinburgh University Press.

GREGORY, R.L. (1974a) A technique for minimising the effects of atmospheric disturbance on photographic telescopes. In *Concepts and Mechanisms of Perception.* London: Duckworth.

GREGORY, R.L. (1974b) *Concepts and Mechanisms of Perception.* London: Duckworth.

GREGORY, R.L. (1980) Perceptions as hypotheses. *Philosophical Transactions of the Royal Society of London, B290,* 181–197.

GREGORY, R.L. (1981) *Mind in Science: A History of Explanations of Psychology and Physics.* London: Weidenfeld and Nicolson.

GREGORY, R.L. (1986a) On first reading Einstein. In *Hands-on Science: An Introduction to the Bristol Exploratory.* London: Duckworth.

GREGORY, R.L. (1986b) *Odd Perceptions.* London: Methuen.

GREGORY, R.L. (1987a) *A History of the Bristol Exploratory.* London: Duckworth.

GREGORY, R.L. (Ed.) (1987b) *The Oxford Companion to the Mind.* Oxford: Oxford University Press.

GREGORY, R.L. (1991) Zangwill, Oliver Louis (1913–87). *Dictionary of National Biography 1986–1990.* Oxford: Oxford University Press.

GREGORY, R.L. (1993) *Even Odder Perceptions.* London: Routledge.

GREGORY, R.L. (1997a) Knowledge in perception and illusion. *Philosophical Transactions of the Royal Society of London, B,* 1121–1128.

GREGORY, R.L. (1997b) *Mirrors in Mind.* Oxford: W.H. Freeman/Spektrum.

GREGORY, R.L. (1998) Brainy mind. *British Medical Journal, 317,* 1693–1695.

GREGORY, R.L. (1999) The Bartlett Lecture. From truths of Bartlett to illusions of vision. *Quarterly Journal of Experimental Psychology, 52A,* 801–812.

GREGORY, R.L. and DRYSDALE, A.E. (1976) Squeezing speech into the deaf ear. *Nature, 264,* 5588, 748–751.

GREGORY, R.L. and GOMBRICH, E. (Eds) (1973) *Illusion in Nature and Art.* London: Duckworth.

GREGORY, R.L. and HARRIS, J.P. (1974) Illusory contours and stereo-depth. *Perception and Psychophysics, 15,* 411–416.

GREGORY, R.L. and HARRIS, J.P. (1975) Illusion-destruction by appropriate scaling. *Perception, 4,* 203–220.

GREGORY, R.L. and HEARD, P.F. (1979) Border locking and the café wall illusion. *Perception, 8,* 365–380.

GREGORY, R.L. and HEARD, P.F. (1983) Visual dissociations of movement, position and stereo depth: some phenomenal phenomena. *Quarterly Journal of Experimental Psychology, 35A,* 217–237.

GREGORY, R.L. and ROSS, H.E. (1964a) Visual constancy during movement: 1. Effects of S's forward and backward movement on size constancy. *Perceptual and Motor Skills, 18,* 3–8.

GREGORY, R.L. and ROSS, H.E. (1964b) Visual constancy during movement: 2. Size constancy, using one or both eyes or proprioceptive information. *Perceptual and Motor Skills, 18,* 23–26.

GREGORY, R.L. and WALLACE, J.G. (1958) A theory of nerve deafness. *Lancet, i,* 83.

GREGORY, R.L. and WALLACE, J.G. (1963) *Recovery From Early Blindness: A Case Study.* Experimental Psychology Society Monograph No. 2. Cambridge: Heffers.

GREGORY, R.L., CANE, V. and WALLACE, J.G. (1956) Increase in neurological noise as a factor in sensory impairment associated with ageing. CIBA Prize Essay. (First published in R.L. Gregory (1974) *Concepts and Mechanisms of Perception.* London: Duckworth.)

GREGORY, R.L., WALLACE, J.G. and CAMPBELL, F.W. (1959) Changes in the size and shape of visual after-images observed in complete darkness during changes of position in space. *Quarterly Journal of Experimental Psychology, 11,* 54–55.

GRINDLEY, E.C. (1927) The neural basis of purposive activity. *British Journal of Psychology*, 18, 168–188.

GROSS, J. (1991) *Rise and Fall of the Man of Letters: Aspects of English Literary Life Since 1800.* Harmondsworth: Penguin.

GUTTRIDGE, M. (1937) *The Duration of Attention in Young Children.* London: Home and School Council of Great Britain.

GWYNNE JONES, H. (1969) Clinical psychology. *Supplement to the Bulletin of the British Psychological Society*, 22, 21–23.

HACKING, I. (1986) Making up people. In T.C. Heller, M. Sosna and D.E. Wellberg (Eds) *Reconstructing Individualism, Autonomy, Individuality, and the Self in Western Thought.* Stanford, CA: Stanford University Press.

HACKING, I. (1991) Double consciousness in Britain, 1815–1875. *Dissociation*, 4, 134–146.

HACKING, I. (1994) The looping effects of human kinds. In D. Sperber, D. Premack and A.J. Premack (Eds) *Causal Cognition: A Multi-Disciplinary Approach.* Oxford: Clarendon Press.

HACKING, I. (1995) *Rewriting the Soul: Multiple Personality and the Sciences of Memory.* Princeton, NJ: Princeton University Press.

HACKING, I. (1998) *Mad Travellers: Reflections on the Reality of Transient Mental Illnesses.* London: Free Association Books.

HALBWACHS, M. (1980) *The Collective Memory.* New York: Harper Row.

HALDANE, J.B.S. (1927) The last judgement. In *Possible Worlds.* London: Chatto and Windus.

HALE, M., Jr (1980) *Human Science and Social Order: Hugo Münsterberg and the Origins of Applied Psychology.* Philadelphia, PA: Temple University Press.

HALE, N.G., Jr (1971) *Freud and the Americans: The Beginnings of Psychoanalysis in the United States, 1876–1917.* New York: Oxford University Press.

HALE, N.G., Jr (1995) *The Rise and Crisis of Psychoanalysis in the United States: Freud and the Americans, 1917–1985.* Oxford: Oxford University Press.

HALL, G.S. (1899) Introductory words. *Paidologist*, 1, 9.

HALL, G.S. (1912) *Founders of Modern Psychology.* New York: Appleton.

HALL, G.S. (1919) Some relations between the war and psychology. *American Journal of Psychology*, 30, 211–223.

HALL, K.R.L. and OLDFIELD, R.C. (1950) An experimental study on the fitness of signs to words. *Quarterly Journal of Experimental Psychology*, 2, 60–70.

HALLAM, A. (1910) Perfect health: how to acquire it. *Health Record*, June, 66.

HALLAM, A.M. (1925) The threshold of practical psychology. *Practical Psychologist*, 1 (January), 1.

HAMILTON, V. (1964) Techniques and methods in psychological assessment. *Bulletin of the British Psychological Society*, 56, 27–36.

HAMILTON, W.D. (1964) The genetical evolution of social behaviour, I and II. *Journal of Theoretical Biology*, 7, 1–52.

HAMLEY, H.R., OLIVER, R.A.C., FIELD, H.E. and ISAACS, S. (1936) *The Educational Guidance of the School Child.* London: Evans Bros.

HAMLYN, D.W. (1976) A hundred years of *Mind. Mind*, NS85, 1–5.

HANDYSIDE, J.D. and DUNCAN, D.C. (1954) Four years later: an experiment in selecting supervisors. *Occupational Psychology*, 28, 9–23.

HARAWAY, D. (1991) Animal sociology and the natural economy of the body politic: a political physiology of dominance. In *Simians, Cyborgs and Women: The Reinvention of Nature.* London: Free Association Books.

HARAWAY, D. (1992) The semiotics of naturalistic field. In *Primate Visions.* London: Verso.

HARDYMENT, C. (1983) *Dream Babies.* London: Jonathan Cape.

HARRÉ, R. (1974) The conditions for a social psychology of childhood. In M.P.M. Richards (Ed.) *The Integration a Child into a Social World.* Cambridge: Cambridge University Press.

HARRÉ, R. (1979) *Social Being.* Oxford: Blackwell.

HARRÉ, R. (1983) *Personal Being.* Oxford: Blackwell; Cambridge, MA: Harvard University Press.

HARRÉ, R. and GILLETT, G. (1994) *The Discursive Mind.* Thousand Oaks, CA: Sage.

HARRÉ, R. and SECORD, P.F. (1972) *The Explanation of Social Behaviour.* Oxford: Blackwell.

HARRINGTON, A. (1996) *Reenchanted Science: Holism in German Culture from Wilhelm II to Hitler.* Princeton: Princeton University Press.

HARRIS, G. (1874) *Supernatural Phenomena: Tests Adapted to Determine the Truth of Supernatural Phenomena.* London: Ballière and Cox.

HARRIS, G. (1875a) *The Psychology of Memory*. London: Psychological Society of Great Britain. (Also included in *Proceedings*.)

HARRIS, G. (1875b) *Caligraphy [sic] Considered as an Exhibition of Character*. London: Psychological Society of Great Britain. (Also included in *Proceedings*.)

HARRIS, G. (1876) *A Philosophical Treatise on the Nature and Constitution of Man*, 2 vols. London: George Ball and Sons; Cambridge: Deighton, Bell.

HARRIS, J. (1993) *Private Lives, Public Spirit: A Social History of Britain, 1870–1914*. Oxford: Oxford University Press.

HARRIS, J.P. and GREGORY, R.L. (1973) Fusion and rivalry of illusory contours. *Perception*, 2, 235–247.

HARRISSON, T. (1937) *Savage Civilisation*. London: Gollancz.

HARRISSON, T. and MADGE, C. (1937) *Mass-Observation*. London: Frederick Muller.

HARRISSON, T. and MADGE, C. (1939/1986) *Britain by Mass-Observation*. London: Cresset.

HARRISSON, T., JENNINGS, H. and MADGE, C. (1937). Letter. *New Statesman and Nation*, 30 January, 155.

HARROP, L.A. (1980) Behaviour modification in schools: a time for caution. *Bulletin of the British Psychological Society*, 33, 158–160.

HARROWER, M. (1983) *Kurt Koffka: An Unwitting Self-Portrait*. Gainsville: University Presses of Florida.

HASTINGS, N. and SCHWIESO, J. (1981) Social technik: reconstructing the relationship between psychological theory and professional training and practice. *Oxford Review of Education*, 7, 223–229.

HATFIELD, G. (1992) Descartes' physiology and its relation to his psychology. In J. Cottingham (Ed.) *The Cambridge Companion to Descartes*. Cambridge: Cambridge University Press.

HATTERSLEY, J., BREWSTER, L., CULLEN, C. and TENNANT, L. (1979) A constructional approach to social problems. *Social Work Today*, 10 (40), 10–12.

HAYLES, N.K. (1999) Liberal subjectivity imperilled: Norbert Wiener and cybernetic anxiety. In *How We Became Post-Human*. Chicago: University of Chicago Press.

HAYWARD, R. (1995) *Popular Mysticism and the Origins of the New Psychology, 1880–1910*. Unpublished PhD thesis, University of Lancaster.

HEAD, H. (1920) *Studies in Neurology*. London: Hodder and Stoughton.

HEAD, H. (1923) The conception of nervous and mental energy. (II) ('Vigilance'; a physiological state of the nervous system). *British Journal of Psychology*, 14, 126–147.

HEAD, H. and SHERREN, J. (1905) The consequences of injury to the peripheral nerves in man. *Brain*, 28, 116–299.

HEARNSHAW, L.S. (1964) *A Short History of British Psychology 1840–1940*. London: Methuen.

HEARNSHAW, L.S. (1987) *The Shaping of Modern Psychology*. London: Routledge and Kegan Paul.

HEARST, E. (Ed.) (1979) *The First Century of Experimental Psychology*. Hillsdale, NJ: Lawrence Erlbaum Associates.

HEBB, D.O. (1949) *The Organization of Behaviour: A Neuropsychological Theory*. New York: Wiley.

HEIDBREDER, E. (1933) *Seven Psychologies*. New York: Appleton.

HEIM, A. (1970) *Intelligence and Personality: Their Assessment and Relationship*. Harmondsworth: Penguin.

HEIMANN, P. and ISAACS, S. (1943/1990) Regression. In P. King and R. Steiner (Eds) *The Freud–Klein Controversies 1941–45*. London: Routledge.

HEIMS, S.J. (1975) Encounter of the behavioral sciences with new machine organism analogies in the 1940s. *Journal of the History of the Behavioral Sciences*, 11, 368–373.

HEIMS, S.J. (1980) *John von Neumann and Norbert Wiener: From Mathematics to the Technologies of Life and Death*. Cambridge MA: MIT Press.

HEIMS, S.J. (1993) *Constructing a Social Science for Postwar America: The Cybernetics Group, 1946–1953*. Cambridge, MA: MIT Press.

HELLMAN, I. (1990) *From War Babies to Grandmothers*. London: Karnac.

HENSON, R.N.A., NORRIS, D.G., PAGE, M.P.A. and BADDELEY, A.D. (1996) Unchained memory: error patterns rule out chaining models of immediate serial recall. *Quarterly Journal of Experimental Psychology*, 49A, 80–115.

HERBERT, M. (1974) *Emotional Problems of Development in Children*. London: Academic Press.

HERBERT, M. (1981) *Behavioural Treatment of Problem Children: A Practice Manual*. London: Academic Press.

HERBERT, M. (1987) *Conduct Disorders of Childhood and Adolescence: A Social Learning Perspective*. Chichester: Wiley.

HERLE, A. and ROUSE, S. (Eds) (1998) *Cambridge and the Torres Strait: Centenary Essays on the 1898 Anthropological Expedition*. Cambridge: Cambridge University Press.

HERMELIN, B. and O'CONNOR, N. (1970) *Psychological Experiments with Autistic Children*. New York: Pergamon Press.

HESSE, M. (1963) *Models and Analogies in Science*. London: Sheed and Ward.

HESSE, M. (1967) Models and analogy in science. In P. Edwards (Ed.) *The Encyclopaedia of Philosophy, Vol. 5*. London: Collier Macmillan.

HEWITT, K. (1981) Overactivity in children: how health visitors can help. *Health Visitor*, 54, 276–278.

HEWITT, K., APPLETON, P., DOUGLAS, J., FUNDUDIS, T. and STEVENSON, J. (1990) Health visitor based services for pre-school children with behaviour problems. *Health Visitor*, 63, 160–162.

HEWITT, K. and CRAWFORD, W. (1988) Resolving behaviour problems in pre-school children: evaluation of a workshop for health visitors. *Child: Care, Health and Development*, 14, 1–7.

HEWITT, K., *et al.* (1984) *The Child Development Project*. University of Bristol: Early Child Development Unit.

HEWITT, K., HOBDAY, A. and CRAWFORD, W. (1989) What do health visitors gain from behavioural workshops? *Child: Care, Health and Development*, 15, 265–275.

HEWITT, K., MASON, L., SNELSON, W. and CRAWFORD, W. (1991) Parent education in preventing behaviour problems. *Health Visitor*, 64, 415–417.

HEYCK, T.W. (1982) *Transformation of Intellectual Life in Victorian England*. London: Croom Helm.

HICK, W.E. (1952) On the rate of gain of information. *Quarterly Journal of Experimental Psychology*, 4, 11–26.

HINDE, R.A. (1966) *Animal Behaviour: A Synthesis of Ethology and Comparative Psychology*. New York: McGraw-Hill.

HINDE, R.A. (1971) Obituary, James Fisher. *Animal Behaviour*, 19, 416.

HINDE, R.A. (1987) William Homan Thorpe 1 April 1902 – 7 April 1986. *Biographical Memoirs of Fellows of the Royal Society of London*, 33, 621–639.

HINDLE, E. (1947) Zoologists in war and peace. *Advancement of Science*, 4 (15), 179–186.

HINKLE, D.N. (1965) *The Change of Personal Constructs from the Viewpoint of a Theory of Construct Implications*. Unpublished PhD thesis, Ohio State University.

HOBHOUSE, L.T. (1901) *Mind in Evolution*. London: Macmillan.

HODGES, A. (1987) *Alan Turing: The Enigma*. London: Vintage.

HODGKIN, A. (1979) E.D. Adrian. *Biographical Memoirs of Fellows of the Royal Society*, 25, 1–74.

HODGKIN, A.L., *et al.* (1977) *The Pursuit of Nature: Informal Essays on the History of Physiology*. Cambridge: Cambridge University Press.

HOPE, E.W., BROWNE, E.A. and SHERRINGTON, C.S. (1913) *A Manual of School Hygiene*, revised ed. (first published 1901). Cambridge: Cambridge University Press.

HOPKINS, P.C. (1938) *The Psychology of Social Movements: A Psycho-Analytic View of Society*. London: Allen and Unwin.

HOPWOOD, N. (1999) 'Giving body' to embryos: modelling mechanism and the microtome in late nineteenth-century anatomy. *Isis*, 90, 462–496.

HOTHERSALL, D. (1995) *A History of Psychology*, 3rd ed. New York: McGraw Hill.

HOWARD, I.P. (1953) A note on an electro-mechanical maze runner. *Durham University Research Review*, 4, 54–61.

HOWITT, D. (1991) *Concerning Psychology: Psychology Applied to Social Issues*. Milton Keynes: Open University Press.

HOY, R.M. (1973) The meaning of alcoholism for alcoholics: a repertory grid study. *British Journal of Social and Clinical Psychology*, 12, 98–99.

HUDSON, W. (1967) The study of the problem of pictorial perception among unacculturated groups. *International Journal of Psychology*, 2, 89–107.

HUGHES, J. (1998) Plasticine and valves: industry, instrumentation and the emergence of nuclear physics. In J.P. Gaudillere and I. Lowy (Eds) *The Invisible Industrialist: Manufactures and the Construction of Scientific Knowledge*. London: Macmillan.

HUGHES, T.P. (1988) Model builders and instrument makers. *Science in Context*, 2, 59–75.

HULL, C.L. (1943) *The Principles of Behaviour*. New York: Appleton-Century.

HUME, C.W. (1949) *How to Befriend Laboratory Animals*. London: UFAW.

HUME, C.W. (1959) In praise of anthropomorphism. *UFAW Courier*, 16, 1–13.

HUMPHREY, G. (1951) *Thinking: An Introduction to Experimental Psychology*. London: Methuen.

HUMPHREY, N. (1992) *A History of the Mind*. London: Simon and Schuster.

HUNT, H.E. (1936) What can practical psychology do? *Practical Psychology Magazine*, *1*, 3.

HUNTER, I.M.L. (1998) 1891–1906: Creating a psychology lectureship at Edinburgh University. *Bulletin of the Scottish Branch of the British Psychological Society*, *26*, 6–9.

HUNTER, M. (Ed.) (1999) Psychoanalysing Robert Boyle: a special issue. *British Journal for the History of Science*, *32*, 257–324.

HURST, A.F. (1918) *Medical Diseases of the War*, 2nd ed. London: Edward Arnold.

HUXLEY, J.S. (1963) Foreword. In K. Lorenz *On Aggression*. M. Latzke (Trans.). (Reprinted 1972.) London: Methuen.

HUXLEY, J.S. (1970) *Memories*. London: George Allen and Unwin.

HUXLEY, T.H. (with the assistance of H.N. Martin) (1875) *A Course of Practical Instruction in Elementary Biology*. London: Macmillan.

HUXLEY, T.H. (1879) *A Course of Elementary Instruction in Practical Biology*. London: Macmillan.

HUXLEY, T.H. (1894a) On Descartes' 'Discourse Touching the Method of Using One's Reason Rightly and of Seeking Scientific Truth'. In *Method and Results*. *Collected Essays*, *Vol. 1*. London: Macmillan.

HUXLEY, T.H. (1894b) On the hypothesis that animals are automata, and its history. In *Method and Results*. *Collected Essays*, *Vol. 1*. London: Macmillan.

HYNES, S. (1990) *A War Imagined: The First World War and English Culture*. Oxford: Bodley Head.

IBANEZ, T. and INIQUEZ, L. (Eds) (1997) *Critical Social Psychology*. London: Sage.

INGHAM, J.G. (1961) Clinical psychology. *Bulletin of the British psychological Society*, *43*, January, 6–11.

INGLEBY, D. (1970) Ideology and the human sciences. *The Human Context*, *2*, 159–187. (Reprinted in T. Pateman (Ed.) (1972) *Counter Course*. Harmondsworth: Penguin; and J. Kovel (Ed.) (1978) *A Complete Guide to Therapy: From Psychoanalysis to Behaviour Modification*. Harmondsworth: Pelican.)

INGLEBY, D. (1981) The politics of psychology. *Psychology and Social Theory*, *2*, 4–18.

INKELES, A. and SMITH, D.H. (1974) *Becoming Modern*. London: Heinemann.

ISAACS, S. (1928/1948) The mental hygiene of the pre-school child. In *Childhood and After*. London: Routledge and Kegan Paul.

ISAACS, S. (1929/1948) Privation and guilt. In *Childhood and After*. London: Routledge and Kegan Paul.

ISAACS, S. (1929a) Review of *The Child's Conception of the World* by J Piaget. *Mind*, *38*, 506–513.

ISAACS, S. (1929b) [Critical review of three works by J. Piaget]. *Journal of Genetic Psychology*, *36*, 597–609.

ISAACS, S. (1929c) *The Nursery Years*. London: Routledge and Kegan Paul.

ISAACS, S. (1930) *Intellectual Growth in Young Children*. London: Routledge and Kegan Paul.

ISAACS, S. (1931) Review of *The Child's Conception of Causality* by J. Piaget. *Mind*, *40*, 89–93.

ISAACS, S. (1932) *The Children We Teach*. London: University of London Press.

ISAACS, S. (1933) *Social Development in Young Children*. London: Routledge and Kegan Paul.

ISAACS, S. (1934) Review of *The Moral Judgement of the Child* by J Piaget. *Mind*, *40*, 85–99.

ISAACS, S. (1934/1948) Rebellious and defiant children. A public lecture at the Institute of Psycho-Analysis. In *Childhood and After*. London: Routledge and Kegan Paul.

ISAACS, S. (1935) Bad habits. *International Journal of Psycho-Analysis*, *16*, 446–454.

ISAACS, S. (1935/1948) Property and possessiveness. In *Childhood and After*. London: Routledge and Kegan Paul.

ISAACS, S. (1937) *The First Two Years*. London: Home and School Council of Great Britain.

ISAACS, S. (1937/1948) The educational value of the nursery school. In *Childhood and After*. London: Routledge and Kegan Paul.

ISAACS, S. (1938/1948) Recent advances in the psychology of young children. In *Childhood and After*. London: Routledge and Kegan Paul.

ISAACS, S. (1939/1948a) Modifications of the ego through the work of analysis. In *Childhood and After*. London: Routledge and Kegan Paul.

ISAACS, S. (1939/1948b) Criteria for interpretation. In *Childhood and After*. London: Routledge and Kegan Paul.

ISAACS, S. (1939/1948c) A special mechanism in a schizoid boy. In *Childhood and After*. London: Routledge and Kegan Paul.

ISAACS, S. (1940/1948) Temper tantrums in early childhood in their relation to internal objects. In *Childhood and After*. London: Routledge and Kegan Paul.

ISAACS, S. (1942) Children of Great Britain in wartime. In S.M. Gruenberg (Ed.) *The Family in a World at War*. New York: Harper.

ISAACS, S. (1943/1948) An acute psychotic anxiety occurring in a boy of four years. In *Childhood and After*. London: Routledge and Kegan Paul.

ISAACS, S. (1943/1990) The nature and function of phantasy. In P. King and R. Steiner (Eds) *The Freud–Klein Controversies 1941–45*. London: Routledge.

ISAACS, S. (1945) Notes on metapsychology as process theory. *International Journal of Psycho-Analysis*, 26, 58–62.

ISAACS, S. (1945/1948a) Fatherless children. In *Childhood and After*. London: Routledge and Kegan Paul.

ISAACS, S. (1945/1948b) Children in institutions. In *Childhood and After*. London: Routledge and Kegan Paul.

ISAACS, S. (1948a) *Troubles of Children and Parents*. London: Methuen.

ISAACS, S. (1948b) *Childhood and After*. London: Routledge and Kegan Paul.

ISAACS, S. (1948c) The nature and function of phantasy. *International Journal of Psycho-Analysis*, 29 (2), 73–97.

ISAACS, S. (Ed.) (1941) *The Cambridge Evacuation Survey*. London: Methuen.

ISRAEL, J. and TAJFEL, H. (1972) *The Context of Social Psychology: A Critical Assessment*. London: Academic Press.

JACKSON, J.H. (1931–1932) *Selected Writings of John Hughlings Jackson* (2 vols). London: Hodder and Stoughton.

JACOBS, J. (1887) Experiments on 'prehension'. *Mind*, 12, 75–79.

JACYNA, L.S. (1981) The physiology of mind, the unity of nature, and the moral order in Victorian thought. *British Journal for the History of Science*, 14, 109–132.

JAHODA, G. (1954) A note on Ashanti day names in relation to personality. *British Journal of Psychology*, 45, 192–195.

JAHODA, G. (1956) Assessment of abstract behavior in a non-western culture. *Journal of Abnormal and Social Psychology*, 53, 237–243.

JAHODA, G. (1958a) Child animism, II. A study in West Africa. *Journal of Social Psychology*, 47, 213–222.

JAHODA, G. (1958b) Immanent justice among West African children. *Journal of Social Psychology*, 47, 241–248.

JAHODA, G. (1959a) Love, marriage and social change: letters to the advice column of a West African newspaper. *Africa*, 29, 177–190.

JAHODA, G. (1959b) Development of the perception of social differences in children from 6–10. *British Journal of Psychology*, 50, 159–175.

JAHODA, G. (1961a) Traditional healers and other institutions concerned with mental illness in Ghana. *International Journal of Social Psychiatry*, 7, 245–268.

JAHODA, G. (1961b) Aspects of westernization. Part I. *British Journal of Sociology*, 12, 375–386.

JAHODA, G. (1961c) *White Man*. London: Oxford University Press.

JAHODA, G. (1961d) Magie, sorcellerie et développement culturel. *Lumen Vitae*, 2, 334–342.

JAHODA, G. (1962a) Aspects of westernization. Part II. *British Journal of Sociology*, 13, 43–56.

JAHODA, G. (1962b) Development of Scottish children's ideas and attitudes about other countries. *Journal of Social Psychology*, 58, 91–108.

JAHODA, G. (1963) The development of children's ideas about country and nationality. *British Journal of Educational Psychology*, 33, 47–60; 143–153.

JAHODA, G. (1964) Children's concepts of nationality: a critical study of Piaget's stages. *Child Development*, 35, 1081–1092.

JAHODA, G. (1966a) Social aspirations, magic, and witchcraft in Ghana. In P. Lloyd (Ed.) *The New Elites of Tropical Africa*. London: Oxford University Press.

JAHODA, G. (1966b) Geometric illusions and environment: a study in Ghana. *British Journal of Psychology*, 57, 193–199.

JAHODA, G. (1968a) Some research problems in African education. *Journal of Social Issues*, 24, 161–178.

JAHODA, G. (1968b) Scientific training and the persistence of traditional beliefs among West African university students. *Nature*, 220, 1356.

JAHODA, G. (1969a) *The Psychology of Superstition*. London: Allen Lane.

JAHODA, G. (1969b) Understanding the mechanism of bicycles: a cross-cultural study of developmental change after 13 years. *International Journal of Psychology*, 4, 103–108.

JAHODA, G. (1979a) A cross-cultural perspective on experimental social psychology. *Personality and Social Psychology Bulletin*, 5, 142–148.

JAHODA, G. (1979b) The construction of economic reality by some Glaswegian children. *European Journal of Social Psychology,* 9, 115–127.

JAHODA, G. (1981) The development of thinking about economic institutions: the bank. *Cahiers de Psychologie Cognitive,* 1, 55–73.

JAHODA, G. (1982) *Psychology and Anthropology: A Psychological Perspective.* London: Academic Press.

JAHODA, G. (1983) European lag in the development of an economic concept: a study in Zimbabwe. *British Journal of Developmental Psychology,* 1, 113–120.

JAHODA, G. (1988) J'accuse…. In M.H. Bond (Ed.) *The Cross-Cultural Challenge to Social Psychology.* Newbury Park, CA: Sage.

JAHODA, G. and CHALMERS, A.D. (1962a) The Youth Employment Service, a consumer perspective. *Occupational Psychology,* 37, 20–43.

JAHODA, G. and CHALMERS, A.D. (1962b) School-leavers' recall of the interview with the Youth Employment Officer. *Occupational Psychology,* 37, 112–121.

JAHODA, G. and CRAMOND, J. (1972) *Children and Alcohol.* London: HMSO.

JAHODA, G. and GREEN, M. (1965) Does Glasgow overspill cream off the more able? *Scottish Journal of Political Economy,* 12, 293–296.

JAHODA, G. and STACEY, B. (1970) Susceptibility to geometric illusions according to culture and professional training. *Perception and Pychophysics,* 7, 179–184.

JAHODA, G. and WOERDENBAGCH, A. (1982) The development of ideas about an economic institution: a cross-national replication. *British Journal of Social Psychology,* 21, 337–338.

JAHODA, G., CHEYNE, M., DEREGOWSKI, J.B., SINHA, D. and COLLINGBOURNE, R. (1976) Utilization of pictorial information in classroom learning: a cross-cultural study. *AV Communication Review,* 24, 295–315.

JAHODA, G., DEREGOWSKI, J.B., AMPENE, E. and WILLIAMS, N. (1977) Pictorial recognition as an unlearned ability: a replication with children from pictorially deprived environments. In G. Butterworth (Ed.) *The Child's Representation of the World.* New York: Plenum Press.

JAHODA, G., THOMSON, S. and BHATT, S. (1972) Ethnic identity and preferences among Asian immigrant children in Glasgow: a replicated study. *European Journal of Social Psychology,* 2, 19–32.

JAHODA, M. (1941) Some socio-psychological problems of factory life. *British Journal of Psychology,* 31, 191–206.

JAMES, W. (1890) *The Principles of Psychology.* New York: Henry Holt.

JAMES, W. (1910/1971) The moral equivalent of war. In J.K. Roth (Ed.) *The Moral Equivalent of War and Other Essays and Selections from Some Problems of Philosophy.* New York: Harper Row.

JAQUES, E. (1951) *The Changing Culture of a Factory.* London: Tavistock.

JARDINE, N. (1992) The laboratory revolution in medicine as rhetorical and aesthetic accomplishment. In A. Cunningham and P. Williams (Eds) *The Laboratory Revolution in Medicine.* Cambridge: Cambridge University Press.

JEFFERSON, G. (1955) The search for mechanisms involved in thinking and talking. *Memoirs and Proceedings of the Manchester Literary and Philosophical Society,* 95, 81.

JENKINS, E.W. (1979) Sources for the history of science education. *Studies in Science Education,* 6, 52.

JENNINGS, H and MADGE, C. (1937) *Mass-Observation Day Surveys.* London: Faber and Faber.

JOHNSON-LAIRD, P.N. and BYRNE, R.M.J. (1993) Models and deductive rationality. In K. Manktelow and D. Over (Eds) *Models of Rationality.* London: Routledge and Kegan Paul.

JOHNSON-LAIRD, P.N. and WASON, P. (1970) Insight into a logical relation. *Quarterly Journal of Experimental Psychology,* 22, 49–61.

JONES, E. (1915) War and individual psychology. *Sociological Review,* 8, 167–180.

JONES, E. (1945) Psychology and war conditions. *Psychoanalytic Quarterly,* 14, 1–27.

JONES, E. (1956) Obituary: JC Flügel. *International Journal of Psycho-Analysis,* 37, 193–194.

JONES, G., CONNELL, I. and MEADOWS, J. (1978) *The Presentation of Science by the Media.* Primary Communications Research Centre, University of Leicester.

JONES, H.G. (1956) The application of conditioning and learning techniques to the treatment of a psychiatric patient. *Journal of Abnormal and Social Psychology,* 52, 414–419.

JONES, H.G. (1980) Appreciations: Monte Shapiro. *Newsletter of the Division of Clinical Psychology of the BPS,* 27, February, 25–26.

JONES, H.G. (1984) Behaviour therapy – an autobiographic view. *Behavioural Psychotherapy,* 12, 7–16.

JONES, N. (Ed.) (1989) *School Management and Pupil Behaviour.* London: Falmer Press.

JORAVSKY, D. (1989) *Russian Psychology: A Critical History.* Oxford: Basil Blackwell.

JOYNSON, R.B. (1970) The breakdown of modern psychology. *Bulletin of the British Psychological Society*, 23, 261–269.

JOYNSON, R.B. (1989) *The Burt Affair*. London: Routledge.

KAPP, R.O. (1953–1954) Review of Ashby, *Design for a Brain*. *British Journal for the Philosophy of Science*, 4, 171–172.

KAT, B. (1985) The emergence of clinical psychology as a profession. *Division of Clinical Psychology Newsletter*, 50, December, 20–30.

KAY, H. (1955) Learning and retaining verbal material. *British Journal of Psychology*, 46, 81–100.

KAY, H. and POULTON, E.C.P. (1951) Anticipation in memorizing. *British Journal of Psychology*, 42, 34–41.

KAZDIN, A.E. (1978) *History of Behaviour Modification: Experimental Foundations of Contemporary Research*. Baltimore: University Park Press.

KEIR, G. (1952) Symposium on psychologists and psychiatrists in the child guidance service: a history of child guidance. *British Journal of Educational Psychology*, 22, 5–29.

KELLAWAY, P.W. (1990) Grey Walter: a memoir of an extraordinary man. *Journal of Clinical Neurophysiology*, 7, 157–161.

KELLER, P. (1979) *States of Belonging: German–American Intellectuals and the First World War*. Cambridge, MA: Harvard University Press.

KELLY, G.A. (1955/1991) *The Psychology of Personal Constructs*. London: Routledge.

KELLY, G.A. (1965) The strategy of psychological research. *Bulletin of the British Psychological Society*, 18, 1–15. (Reprinted in B. Maher (Ed.) (1977) *Clinical Psychology and Personality*. New York: Krieger.)

KELLY, G.A. (1980) The psychology of optimal man. In A.W. Landfield and L.M. Leitner (Eds) *Personal Construct Psychology: Psychotherapy and Personality*. Chichester: Wiley.

KELLY, K. (1994) *Out of Control: The New Biology of Machines*. London: Fourth Estate.

KELLY, M. and RONALDSON, J. (1989) Emotional and behaviour management: the course and its outcomes. *British Journal of Inservice Education*, 15, 187–190.

KENDON, A. (1967) Some functions of gaze direction in social interaction. *Acta Psychologica*, 26, 22–63.

KENNA, J.C. (1969) Chairs of psychology in British universities. *Supplement to the Bulletin of the British Psychological Society*, 9–13.

KENNEDY, A. (1951) Psychologists and psychiatrists and their general relationship. *British Journal of Educational Psychology*, 21, 167–171.

KIGGELL, L.E. (1916) *Training of Divisions for Offensive Action*. London: War Office.

KLAYMAN, J. and HA, Y.U. (1987) Confirmation, disconfirmation, and information in hypothesis testing. *Psychological Review*, 94, 211–228.

KLEIN, M. (1921/1975) The development of a child. In *Love, Guilt and Reparation*. London: Hogarth.

KLEIN, M. (1927/1975) Symposium on child analysis. In *Love, Guilt and Reparation*. London: Hogarth.

KLEIN, M. (1932/1975) *The Psycho-Analysis of Children*. London: Hogarth.

KLEIN, M. (1935) A contribution to the psycho-genesis of manic–depressive states. *International Journal of Psycho-Analysis*, 16, 145–174.

KLEMM, G.O. (1914) *A History of Psychology*. New York: Scribner.

KNIGHT, R. (1961) The Society since 1941. In H. Steinberg (Ed.) *The British Psychological Society 1901–1961. Supplement to the Bulletin of the British Psychological Society*.

KOBASA, S. (1982) The hardy personality: toward a social psychology of health. In G. Sanders and J. Suls (Eds) *Social Psychology of Health and Illness*. New York: Lawrence Erlbaum Associates.

KOCH, H.C.H. (Ed.) (1986) *Community Clinical Psychology*. Beckenham: Croom Helm.

KRAEPELIN, E. (1896) Der psychologische Versuch in der Psychiatrie. *Psychologische Arbeiten*, 1, 1–91.

KUBIE, L.S. (1958) *Neurotic Distortion of the Creative Process*. Kansas: University of Kansas Press.

KUHN, T.S. (1964) *The Structure of Scientific Revolutions*. Chicago: Phoenix.

KUKLICK, H. (1991) *The Savage Within: The Social History of British Anthropology, 1885–1945*. Cambridge: Cambridge University Press.

KUSCH, M. (1995) Recluse, interlocutor, interrogator: natural and social order in turn-of-the-century psychological research schools. *Isis*, 86, 419–439.

KUSCH, M. (1999) *Psychological Knowledge: A Social History*. London: Routledge.

KVALE, S. (Ed.) (1992) *Psychology and Postmodernism*. London: Sage.

LA METTRIE, J.O. (1747/1960) *L'Homme machine: A Study in the Origins of an Idea*. Princeton, NJ: Princeton University Press.

LAIRD, J. (1925) *Our Minds and Their Bodies.* London: Oxford University Press, Humphrey Milford.

LAKATOS, I. and MUSGRAVE, A. (Eds) (1970) *Criticism and the Growth of Knowledge.* Cambridge: Cambridge University Press.

LAMAL, P.A. (1989) The impact of behaviorism in our culture: some evidence and conjectures. *Psychological Record, 39,* 529–535.

LAMPE, D. (1959) *Pyke: The Unknown Genius.* London: Evans.

LANGLEY, L.L. (1973) *Homeostasis: Origins of the Concept.* Stroudsberg: Hutchinson and Ross.

LAQUEUR, T.W. (1994) Memory and naming in the Great War. In J.R. Gillis (Ed.) *Commemorations: The Politics of National Identity.* Princeton, NJ: Princeton University Press.

LASHLEY, K. (1938) The mechanism of vision xv: preliminary studies of the rat's capacity for detail vision. *Journal of General Psychology, 18,* 123–193.

LASHLEY, K. (1942) The problem of cerebral organisation in vision. *Biological Symposia, 7,* 301–322.

LATOUR, B. (1986a) The powers of association. In J. Law (Ed.) *Power, Action and Belief.* London: Routledge and Kegan Paul.

LATOUR, B. (1986b) Visualisation and cognition: thinking with eyes and hands. *Knowledge and Society: Studies in the Sociology of Culture Past and Present, 6,* 1–40.

LATOUR, B. (1987) *Science in Action.* Cambridge, MA: Harvard University Press.

LATOUR, B. (1990) Drawing things together. In M. Lynch and S. Woolgar (Eds) *Representation in Scientific Practice.* Cambridge: Cambridge University Press.

LATOUR, B. and STRUM, S.C. (1986) Human social origins: Oh please, tell us another story. *Journal of Social and Biological Structures, 9,* 169–187.

LAWE, F.W. (1929) The economic aspects of industrial psychology. In C.S. Myers (Ed.) *Industrial Psychology.* London: Butterworth.

LAWRENCE, C. (1985) Incommeasurable knowledge: science, technology and the clinical art in Britain, 1850–1914. *Journal of Contemporary History, 20,* 503–520.

LAWRENCE, C. and WEISZ, G. (Eds) (1998) *Greater than the Parts: Holism in Biomedicine, 1920–1950.* New York: Oxford University Press.

LAWRENCE, D.H. (1921/1971) Psychoanalysis and the unconscious. In *Fantasia of the Unconscious and Psychoanalysis and the Unconscious.* Harmondsworth: Penguin.

LAWRENCE, E. (1960) Foreword. In N. Isaacs *A Brief Introduction to Piaget.* New York: Agathon Press.

LAZARUS, A. (1977) Has behavior therapy outlived its usefulness? *American Psychologist, 32,* 550–554.

LE BON, G. (1896) *The Crowd: A Study of the Popular Mind.* London: Fisher Unwin.

LE GROS CLARK, W.E. (1946) The contribution of anatomy to the war. *British Medical Journal, i,* 39–43.

LE GROS CLARK, W.E. (1968) *Chant of Pleasant Exploration.* Edinburgh: E.S. Livingstone.

LEAHEY, T.H. (1980) *A History of Psychology: Main Currents in Psychological Thought.* Englewood Cliffs, NJ: Prentice-Hall.

LEAHEY, T.H. (1992) The mythical revolutions of American psychology. *American Psychologist, 47,* 308–318.

LEARY, D.E. (Ed.) (1990) *Metaphors in the History of Psychology.* Cambridge: Cambridge University Press.

LEE, J. (1999) My tables, my tables. In J. Lee (Ed.) *Shakespeare's Hamlet and the Controversies of Self.* Milton Keynes: Open University Press.

LEFCOURT, H. (1966) Internal versus external control of reinforcement: a review. *Psychological Bulletin, 65,* 206–220.

LENOIR, T. (1986) Models and instruments in the development of electrophysiology, 1845–1912. *Historical Studies in the Physical and Biological Sciences, 17,* 1–54.

LENOIR, T. (1988) Practice, reason, context: the dialogue between theory and experiment. *Science in Context, 2,* 3–22. (Reprinted in *Instituting Science: The Cultural Production of Scientific Disciplines.* Stanford, CA: Stanford University Press.)

LEPENIES, W. (1988) *Between Literature and Science: The Rise of Sociology.* Cambridge: Cambridge University Press.

LEVENSTEIN, A. (1912) *Die Arbeiterfrage.* Munchen: Reinhardt.

LEVIDOW, P. (1994) *The Soft Edge: A Natural History of the Information Revolution.* London: Routledge.

LEWIS, A. (1951) Henry Maudsley: his work and influence. (The Twenty-Fifth Maudsley Lecture.) *Journal of Mental Science, 97,* 18–277.

LEWIS, A. (1967) Empirical or rational? The nature and basis of psychiatry. In A. Lewis (1979) *The Later Papers of Sir Aubrey Lewis*. Oxford: Oxford University Press. (Originally published in *Lancet*, 1967, 1–9.)

LIDDIARD, M. (1928) *The Mothercraft Manual*. London: Churchill.

LIGHT, P.H., BLAYE, A., GILLY, M. and GIROTTO, V. (1990) Pragmatic schemas and logical reasoning in six to eight year olds. *Cognitive Development*, 4, 49–64.

LIGHTHILL, J., SUTHERLAND, N.S., NEEDHAM, R.M., LONGUET-HIGGINS, H.C. and MICHIE, D. (1973) *Artificial Intelligence: A Paper Symposium*. London: Science Research Council.

LINDZEY, A. (1976) *Animal Rights*. London: SCM Press.

LONDON, P. (1972) The end of ideology in behavior modification. *American Psychologist*, 27, 913–920.

LORENTE de NÓ, R. (1933) Vestibulo-ocular reflex arc. *Archives of Neurology and Psychiatry*, 30, 245–291.

LORENTE de NÓ, R. (1938) Analysis of the activity of a train of internuncial neurons. *Journal of Neurophysiology*, 1, 207–244.

LORENZ, K. (1963/1972) *On Aggression*. M. Latzke (Trans.). London: Methuen.

LOVELL, A. (1902) Psycho-therapeutics and science. *Psycho-Therapeutic Journal*, 1 (2), 2–5.

LOVIE, A.D. (1998) The BPS and 2001: Centenary? What centenary? *Current Trends in the History and Philosophy of Psychology*, 2, 1–8.

LOWENTHAL, D. and WASON, P.C. (1977) Academics and their writing. *Times Literary Supplement*, 24 June, 781.

LÖWY, I. (1992) The strength of loose concepts; boundary concepts, federative experimental strategies and disciplinary growth: the case of immunology. *History of Science*, 30, 371–396.

LUBBOCK, J. (1911) *Marriage, Totemism and Religion. An Answer to Critics*. London: Longmans, Green.

LUNT, P. and FURNHAM, A. (1996) *Economic Socialization*. Cheltenham: Edward Elgar.

LUTON, K., *et al.* (1991) *Positive Strategies for Behaviour Management*. Windsor: NFER-Nelson.

MacCURDY, J.T. (1917) War neuroses. *Psychiatric Bulletin*, July, 250–254.

MacCURDY, J.T. (1918) *War Neuroses*. Cambridge: Cambridge University Press.

MacCURDY, J.T. (1928) *Common Principles in Psychology and Physiology*. Cambridge: Cambridge University Press.

MacCURDY, J.T. (1943) *The Structure of Morale*. Cambridge: Cambridge University Press.

MACE, C.A. (1953) Homeostasis: needs and values. *British Journal of Psychology*, 54, 200–210.

MACE, C.A. (1954) Foreword. In W. Sluckin *Minds and Machines*. Harmondsworth: Penguin.

MACE, C.A. and VERNON, P.E. (Eds) (1953) *Current Trends in British Psychology*. London: Methuen.

MACKSEY, K. and WOODHOUSE, W. (Eds) (1991) *The Penguin Encyclopaedia of Modern Warfare*. London: Penguin.

MacLEOD, R. (1980) Evolutionism, internationalism and commercial enterprise in science: the International Scientific Series 1871–1893. In A.J. Meadows (Ed.) *Development of Scientific Publishing in Europe*. Amsterdam: Elsevier.

MacNAGHTEN, H. (1922) *Emile Coué: The Man and his Work*. London: Methuen.

MacPHERSON, W.G., HERRINGHAM, W.P., ELLIOTT, T.R. and BALFOUR, A. (Eds) (1923) *Medical Services. Diseases of the War. Vol. II*. London: Oxford University Press.

MADGE, C. and HARRISSON, T. (1937) *Mass-Observation*. London: Frederick Muller.

MADGE, C. and HARRISSON, T. (Eds) (1938) *First Year's Work 1937–38, by Mass-Observation*. London: Lindsay Drummond.

MAHONEY, M.S. (1990) Cybernetics and information technology. In R.C. Olby, *et al.* (Eds) *Companion to the History of Modern Science*. London: Routledge.

MANDLER, J.M. and JOHNSON, N.S. (1977) Remembrance of things parsed: story structure and recall. *Cognitive Psychology*, 9, 111–151.

MANKTELOW, K.L. and OVER, D.E. (1990) Deontic thought and the selection task. In K.J. Gilhooly, M.T.G. Keene, R.H. Logic and G. Erdos (Eds) *Lines of Thinking, Vol. 1*. New York: Wiley.

MANSTEAD, A.S.R. and McCULLOGH, C. (1981) Sex-role stereotyping in British television advertisements. *British Journal of Social Psychology*, 20, 171–180.

MARDER, A.J. (1969) *From the Dreadnought to Scapa Flow: The Royal Navy in the Fisher Era, 1904–1919. Vol. IV. 1917: Year of Crisis*. London: Oxford University Press.

MARSH, P., ROSSER, E. and HARRÉ, R. (1978) *The Rules of Disorder*. London: Routledge and Kegan Paul.

MARTINEAU, J. (1876). Modern materialism: its attitude towards theology. *Contemporary Review*, 27, 323–346.

MAXWELL, W.N. (1923) *A Psychological Retrospect of the Great War.* London: George Allen and Unwin.

MAYER-GROSS, W. (1951) Psychologists and psychiatrists. *Quarterly Bulletin of the British Psychological Society*, 13.

MAYHEW, H. (1864) *London Labour and the London Poor.* London: Griffin.

MAYR, O. (1970) *The Origins of Feedback Control.* Cambridge, MA: MIT Press.

MAZLISH, B. (1993) *The Fourth Discontinuity: The Co-evolution of Humans and Machines.* New Haven: Yale University Press.

McCULLOCH, W.S. and PITTS, W. (1943) A logical calculus of the ideas immanent in neural nets. *Bulletin of Mathematical Biophysics*, 5, 115–137.

McDOUGALL, W. (1908) *An Introduction to Social Psychology.* London: Methuen.

McDOUGALL, W. (1911) *Body and Mind: A History and a Defense of Animism.* London: Methuen.

McDOUGALL, W. (1920) *The Group Mind.* Cambridge: Cambridge University Press

McDOUGALL, W. (1923) *The Outline of Psychology*, 1st ed. London: Methuen.

McDOUGALL, W. (1927) *Character and the Conduct of Life. Practical Psychology for Every Man.* London: Methuen.

McDOUGALL, W. (1928) *The Outline of Psychology*, 4th ed. London: Methuen.

McDOUGALL, W. (1930) Autobiography. In C. Murchison (Ed.) *A History of Psychology in Autobiography, Vol. 1.* Worcester, MA: Clark University Press.

McDOUGALL, W. (1931) *An Introduction to Social Psychology*, 22nd ed. London: Methuen.

McDOUGALL, W. (1943) *An Introduction to Social Psychology*, 25th ed. London: Methuen.

McDOWALL, R.J.S. (Ed.) (1927) *The Mind By Various Authors: A Series of Lectures Delivered in King's College, London, During the Lent Term, 1927.* London: Longmans.

McGUIRE, R.J. (1962) A study of the M.P.I. used with psychiatric in-patients. *Bulletin of the British Psychological Society*, 47, April, 56–57.

McINTYRE, J.L. (1904) A sixteenth century psychologist, Bernardino Telesio. *British Journal of Psychology*, 1, 61–77.

McINTYRE, W.M. (1953) Co-operation between clinical psychologists and psychiatrists. *Quarterly Bulletin of the British Psychological Society*, 19, January, 13–18.

McKENDRY, A. (Ed.) (1981) *The Psychology of Playing the Goat.* Oxford: Capra Press.

McPHERSON, I. and SUTTON, C. (1981) *Reconstructing Psychological Practice.* Beckenham: Croom Helm.

McQUIRE, J. and RICHMAN, N. (1987) *The Behaviour Checklist (BCL).* Windsor: NFER-Nelson.

MEAD, A.P. (1960) A quantitative method for the analysis of exploratory behaviour in the rat. *Animal Behaviour*, 8, 19–31.

MEAD, M. and BATESON, G. (1942) *Balinese Character: A Photographic Analysis.* New York: Academy of Sciences.

MEDICAL RESEARCH COUNCIL (1949–1950) *Progress Report on the Applied Psychology Unit, Cambridge.* London: MRC.

MEDICAL RESEARCH COUNCIL (1950–1953) *Progress Report on the Applied Psychology Research Unit, Cambridge.* London: MRC.

MEDICAL RESEARCH COUNCIL (1954–1960) *Progress Report on the Applied Psychology Research Unit, Cambridge.* London: MRC.

MEISEL, P. and KENDRICK, W. (1986) *Bloomsbury/Freud: The Letters of James and Alix Strachey 1924–1925.* London: Chatto and Windus.

MEREDITH LOGAN, H. (1923) Military training to-day. *The Army Quarterly*, 6, April, 58–76.

MERRETT, F. and HOUGHTON, S. (1989) Does it work with older ones? A review of behavioural studies carried out in British secondary schools since 1981. *Educational Psychology*, 9, 287–309.

MERRINGTON, M. and GOLDEN, J. (1978, 1st ed. 1976) *A List of the Papers and Correspondence of Sir Francis Galton (1822–1911) Held in The Manuscripts Room, The Library, University College London.* London: Galton Laboratory, University College London.

MEUMANN, E. (1913) *The Psychology of Learning: An Experimental Investigation of the Economy and Technique of Memory.* J.W. Baird (Trans.). New York: Appleton. (Original work published 1912.)

MEYER, V. (1957) The treatment of two phobic patients on the basis of learning principles. *Journal of Abnormal and Social Psychology*, 55, 261–266.

MEYER, V. (1970) Comments on A.J. Yates' 'Misconceptions about behavior therapy: A point of view'. *Behavior Therapy*, 1, 108–112.

MICHIE, D. (1974) *On Machine Intelligence.* Edinburgh: University of Edinburgh. (2nd ed. 1986.) Chichester: Ellis Horwood.

MIDDLETON, D. and EDWARDS, D. (Eds) (1990) *Collective Remembering.* London: Sage.

MILLER, E. (1996) Twentieth century British clinical psychology and psychiatry: their historical relationship. In H. Freeman and G.E. Berrios (Eds) *150 Years of British Psychiatry. Vol. II: The Aftermath.* London: Athlone.

MILLER, G.A. (1969) Psychology as a means of promoting human welfare. *American Psychologist,* 24, 1063–1075.

MILLER, G.A., GALANTER, E. and PRIBRAM, K.H. (1960) *Plans and the Structure of Behavior.* New York: Holt.

MILLER, P. and ROSE, N. (1988) The Tavistock programme: the government of subjectivity and social life. *Sociology, 22,* 171–192.

MILLER, P. and ROSE, N. (1994) On therapeutic authority: psychoanalytical expertise under advanced liberalism. *History of the Human Sciences, 7,* 29–64.

MILNE, D. (1986) *Training Behaviour Therapists.* Beckenham: Croom Helm.

MILNER, D. (1975) *Children and Race.* Harmondsworth: Penguin.

MILNER, M. (1938) *The Human Problem in Schools: A Psychological Study Carried out on Behalf of the Girls' Public Day-School Trust.* London: Methuen.

MILNER, M. (1969) *The Hands of the Living God.* New York: International University Press.

MISCHEL, W. (1980) George Kelly's appreciation of psychology: a personal tribute. In M.J. Mahoney (Ed.) *Psychotherapy Process: Current Issues and Future Directions.* New York: Plenum Press.

MOLLON, J.D. (Ed.) (1996) *The Experimental Psychology Society 1946–1996.* Cambridge: Experimental Psychology Society.

MONEY-KYRLE, R.E. (1937) The development of war. A psychological approach. *British Journal of Medical Psychology,* 16, 219–236.

MONOPOLIES AND RESTRICTIVE PRACTICES COMMISSION (1956) *Report on the Supply of Electronic Valves and Cathode Ray Tubes.* London: HMSO.

MORAWSKI, J.G. (1992) Self-regard and other-regard: reflexive practices in American psychology, 1890–1940. *Science in Context,* 5, 281–308.

MORGAN, J., O'NEILL, C. and HARRÉ, R. (1979) *Nicknames.* London: Routledge.

MORRIS, D. (1958) *The Story of Congo.* London: Batsford.

MORRIS, D., COLLETT, P., MARSH, P. and O'SHAUGHNESSY, M. (1979) *Gestures: Their Origins and Distribution.* London: Cape.

MORTIMORE, P. (1995) The positive effects of schooling. In M. Rutter (Ed.) *Psychosocial Disturbances in Young People: Challenges for Prevention.* New York: Cambridge University Press.

MOSES, W.S. [as M.A. Oxon] (1877) *Psychological Curiosities of Spiritualism.* Reprinted from *Human Nature* in reply to W.B. Carpenter's article in *Fraser's Magazine.*

MOSES, W.S. [as M.A. Oxon] (1889) *Second Sight: Problems Connected with Prophetic Vision.* London: London Spiritualist Alliance.

MOSES, W.S. (1902) *Spirit Identity.* London: London Spiritualist Alliance.

MOSES, W.S. (1930) *Pearls of Great Price: Selected Passages from Spirit Teachings.* London: London Spiritualist Alliance.

MOTT, F.W. (1919) *War Neuroses and Shell Shock.* London: Henry Froude/Hodder and Stoughton.

MOTT, F.W. (1922) Body and mind: the origin of dualism. *Mental Hygiene,* 6, 673–687.

MÜHLHÄUSLER, P. and HARRÉ, R. (1990) *Pronouns and People.* Oxford: Blackwell.

MÜLLER, G.E. and PILZECKER, A. (1900) Experimentelle Beiträge zur Lehre vom Gedächtnis. *Zeischrift für Psychologie* (Supplement 1).

MÜNSTERBERG, H. (1899) *Psychology and Life.* London: Archibald Constable.

MÜNSTERBERG, H. (1909) *Psychology and the Teacher.* New York: Appleton.

MÜNSTERBERG, M. (1922) *Hugo Münsterberg: His Life and Work.* New York: Appleton.

MURCHISON, C.A. (Ed.) (1930) *A History of Psychology in Autobiography.* Worcester, MA: Clark University Press.

MURCHISON, C.A. (Ed.) (1935) *Handbook of Social Psychology.* Worcester, MA: Clark University Press.

MURDOCH, I. (1992) *Metaphysics as a Guide to Morals.* London: Chatto and Windus.

MURPHY, G. (1929) *Historical Introduction to Modern Psychology.* New York: Harcourt Brace.

MURPHY, G. and KOVACH, J.K. (1972) *Historical Introduction to Modern Psychology,* 3rd ed. New York: Harcourt Brace Jovanovich.

MURPHY, G., MURPHY, L.B. and NEWCOMB, T.M. (1937) *Experimental Social Psychology.* New York: Harper and Brothers.

MURRAY, D.J. (1983) A History of Western Psychology. Englewood Cliffs, NJ: Prentice Hall.

MURRAY, G.G.A. (1940) Herd Instinct: For Good and Evil. London: George Allen and Unwin.

MURRAY, H.A. (1938) Explorations in Personality. New York: Oxford University Press.

MURRELL, K.H. (1965) Ergonomics. London: Chapman and Hall.

MUSCIO, B. (1920) Lectures on Industrial Psychology, 2nd ed. London: George Routledge.

MYDDLETON, W.W. (1925) Mental stature. Practical Psychology, 1 (3), 18–21.

MYERS, C.S. (1909) A Textbook of Experimental Psychology. London: Edward Arnold.

MYERS, C.S. (1911) A Textbook of Experimental Psychology, 2nd ed. Cambridge: Cambridge University Press.

MYERS, C.S. (1914) An Introduction to Experimental Psychology, 3rd ed. Cambridge: Cambridge University Press.

MYERS, C.S. (1918) Present-Day Applications of Psychology with Special Reference to Industry, Education, and Nervous Breakdown. London: Methuen.

MYERS, C.S. (1923) The influence of the late W.H.R. Rivers (President Elect of Section J) on the development of psychology in Great Britain [Presidential Address to Section J, 1922]. Reports, The British Association for the Advancement of Science, 179–192.

MYERS, C.S. (1932) On the nature of mind [Presidential Address, Section J]. British Association for the Advancement of Science: Report of the Centenary Meeting, London – 1931, 181–195.

MYERS, C.S. (1933) A Psychologist's Point of View. London: Heinemann.

MYERS, C.S. (1936) Autobiography. In C. Murchison (Ed.) A History of Psychology in Autobiography, Vol. 3. Worcester, MA: Clark University Press.

MYERS, C.S. (1937) In the Realm of Mind: Nine Chapters on the Applications and Implications of Psychology. Cambridge: Cambridge University Press.

MYERS, C.S. (1940) Shell Shock in France 1914–1918: Based on a War Diary Kept by Charles S. Myers, CBE, FRS. Cambridge: Cambridge University Press.

MYERS, F.W.H. (1886) Multiplex personality. Nineteenth Century, 20 November, 648.

MYERS, F.W.H. (1893a) Science and a Future Life with Other Essays. London: Macmillan.

MYERS, F.W.H. (1893b) The subliminal consciousness. Proceedings of the Society for Psychical Research, 9, 14–15.

MYERS, F.W.H. (1903) Human Personality and Its Survival of Bodily Death. London: Longmans.

NATIONAL INSTITUTE OF INDUSTRIAL PSYCHOLOGY (NIIP) (1956) Training Factory Workers. London: Staples.

NEISSER, U. (1966) Computers as tools and metaphors. In C.D. Dechart (Ed.) The Social Impact of Cybernetics. New York: Simon and Schuster.

NEISSER, U. (1967) Cognitive Psychology. New York: Appleton, Century and Crofts.

NEWELL, A. and SIMON, H.A. (1961) GPS – a program that simulates human thought. In H. Billing (Ed.) Lernende Automaten. Munich: Oldenbourg.

NEWSON, J. and NEWSON, E. (1963) Infant Care in an Urban Community. London: Allen and Unwin.

NEWSON, J. and NEWSON, E. (1968) Four Years Old in an Urban Community. London: Allen and Unwin.

NEWSON, J. and NEWSON, E. (1976) Parental roles and social contexts. In M. Shipman (Ed.) The Organisation and Impact of Social Research. London: Routledge and Kegan Paul.

NEWSON, J. and NEWSON, E. (2000) Castaways' corner: six books that influenced our professional development. Journal Clinical Child Psychology and Psychiatry, 5, 289–295.

NG, S.H. (1983) Children's ideas about bank and shop profit: developmental stages and the influence of cognitive contrasts and conflict. Journal of Economic Psychology, 4, 209–221.

NICHOLS, T.L. (n.d., c. 1873, Preface date) Esoteric Anthropology. Malvern: T.L. Nichols.

NIXON, S.R. (1946) Some Experiments on Immediate Memory. Paper No. 39. Cambridge: Applied Psychology Unit.

NOBLE, R.L. and COLLIP, J.B. (1942) A quantitative method for the production of experimental traumatic shock without haemorrhage in unanaesthetized animals. Quarterly Journal of Experimental Physiology, 31, 187.

NORTHFIELD, W. (1940) Curing Nervous Tension. London: The Psychologist, Practical Psychology Handbook No. 8

O'CONNOR, W.J. (1988) Founders of British Physiology: A Biographical Dictionary, 1820–1885. Manchester: Manchester University Press.

O'CONNOR, W.J. (1991) British Physiologists 1885–1914. Manchester: Manchester University Press.

O'DONNELL, J.M. (1979a) The Origins of Behaviourism in American Psychology, 1870–1920. Unpublished PhD thesis, University of Pennsylvania.

O'DONNELL, J.M. (1979b) The clinical psychology of Lightner Witmer: a case-study of institutional innovation and intellectual change. *Journal of the History of the Behavioral Sciences, 15*, 3–17.

O'DONNELL, J.M. (1986) *The Origins of Behaviorism: American Psychology, 1870–1920*. New York: New York University Press.

OESER, O.A. (1936) Critical notice [review of K. Koffka, *Principles of Gestalt Psychology*]. *British Journal of Psychology, 27*, 96–106.

OESER, O.A. (1937) Methods and assumptions of field work in social psychology. *British Journal of Psychology, 27 (4)*, 343– 363.

OGDEN, C.K. (1929) *The ABC of Psychology*. London: Kegan Paul, Trench, Trubner.

OLDFIELD, R.C. (1937) Some recent experiments bearing on 'internal inhibition'. *British Journal of Psychology, 28*, 28–42.

OLDFIELD, R.C. (1950) Psychology in Oxford, 1898–1949: Part I. *Quarterly Bulletin of the British Psychological Society, 1*, 345–353.

OLDFIELD, R.C. (1972) Frederic Charles Bartlett: 1886–1969. *American Journal of Psychology, 85*, 133–140.

OLDFIELD, R.C. and ZANGWILL, O. (1942a) Head's concept of the schema and its application in contemporary British psychology: Part I. *British Journal of Psychology, 32*, 267–285.

OLDFIELD, R.C. and ZANGWILL, O. (1942b) Head's concept of the schema and its application in contemporary British psychology: Parts II and III. *British Journal of Psychology, 33*, 58–64, 113– 129.

OPIE, P. and OPIE, I. (1972) *The Lore and Language of Schoolchildren*. Oxford: Clarendon Press.

OPPENHEIM, J. (1985) *The Other World: Spiritualism and Psychical Research in England, 1850–1914*. Cambridge: Cambridge University Press.

OPPENHEIM, J. (1991) *Shattered Nerves: Doctors, Patients and Depression in Victorian England*. Oxford: Oxford University Press.

ORFORD, J. (1992) *Community Psychology, Theory and Practice*. Chichester: Wiley.

OSGOOD, C.E. (1953) *Method and Theory in Experimental Psychology*. New York: Oxford University Press.

ØSTERGAARD, L. (Ed.) (1962) *Clinical Psychology*. Copenhagen: Munksgaard.

OWENS, R.G. and WALTER, A.J. (1980) Naïve behaviourism and behaviour modification. *Bulletin of the British Psychological Society, 33*, 312–314.

PACKARD, V. (1957) *The Hidden Persuaders*. London: Longman.

PANDORA, K. (1997) *Rebels Within the Ranks. Psychologists' Critique of Scientific Authority and Democratic Realities in New Deal America*. Cambridge: Cambridge University Press.

PARSONS, J.H. (1927) *An Introduction to the Theory of Perception*. Cambridge: Cambridge University Press.

PARSONS, J.H. (1928) Critical notice [of John T. MacCurdy, *Common Principles in Psychology and Physiology*]. *British Journal of Psychology, 19*, 102–105.

PASSMORE, J.A. (1952) Memoir: George Frederick Stout 1860–1944. In G.F. Stout *God and Nature*. Cambridge: Cambridge University Press.

PASSMORE, J.A. (1957) *A Hundred Years of Philosophy*. London: Duckworth.

PASSMORE, J.A. (1976) G.F. Stout's editorship of *Mind* (1892–1920). *Mind, NS 85*, 17–36.

PATON, W.D.M. (1979) Animal experiment and medical research: a study in evolution. Paget Lecture. *Conquest, No. 169*, 1–14.

PAVLOV, I.P. (1927) *Conditioned Reflexes: An Investigation of the Physiological Activity of the Cerebral Cortex*. G.V. Anrep (Trans./Ed.). Oxford: Oxford University Press.

PAYNE, R.W. (1953) The role of the clinical psychologist at the Institute of Psychiatry. *Revue de Psychologie Appliquée, 3*, 150–160.

PAYNE, R.W. (1957) Experimental method in clinical psychological practice. *Journal of Mental Science, 103*, 189–196.

PAYNE, S. (1952) Obituary: Dr John Rickman. *International Journal of Psycho-Analysis, 33*, 54–60.

PEAR, T.H. (1911a) The experimental examination of some differences between major and minor chords. *British Journal of Psychology, 4*, 56–88.

PEAR, T.H. (1911b) The classification of observers as 'musical' or 'unmusical'. *British Journal of Psychology, 4*, 89–94.

PEAR, T.H. (1914a) The role of repression in forgetting. *British Journal of Psychology, 7*, 139–146.

PEAR, T.H. (1914b) The analysis of some personal dreams, with reference to Freud's theory of dream interpretation. *British Journal of Psychology, 6*, 281–303.

PEAR, T.H. (1918) The war and psychology. *Nature, 102*, 88–89.

PEAR, T.H. (1922) *Remembering and Forgetting.* London: Methuen.
PEAR, T.H. (1931a) Grafton Elliot Smith 1871–1937. *Bulletin of the John Rylands Library, 21,* 4–6.
PEAR, T.H. (1931b) *Voice and Personality.* London: Chapman and Hall.
PEAR, T.H. (1939a) Obituary notice: Professor Samuel Alexander 1859–1938. *British Journal of Psychology, 29,* 317–320.
PEAR, T.H. (1939b) *The Psychology of Conversation.* London: Thomas Nelson.
PEAR, T.H. (1940a) The psychology of psychologists. *Bulletin of the John Rylands Library, 24,* 101–120.
PEAR, T.H. (1940b) The trivial and the popular in psychology. *British Journal of Psychology, 31,* 115–128.
PEAR, T.H. (1942) The social status of the psychologist and its effect upon his work. *Sociological Review, 34,* 68–81.
PEAR, T.H. (1943) *Are There Human Instincts?* Manchester: Manchester University Press.
PEAR, T.H. (1944) Psychology for medical students [review of *Sane Psychology: A Biological Introduction to Psychology,* by Prof. R.J.S. McDowall, London: John Murray, 1943]. *Nature, 154,* 411–412.
PEAR, T.H. (1945) Psychological implications of the culture-pattern theory. *Bulletin of the John Rylands Library, 29,* 201–224.
PEAR, T.H. (1947) Charles S. Myers. *British Journal of Educational Psychology, 17,* 1–5.
PEAR, T.H. (1948a) Industrial psychology as I have seen it. *Occupational Psychology, 22,* 107–117.
PEAR, T.H. (1948b) The relations between psychology and sociology. *Bulletin of the John Rylands Library, 31,* 277–294.
PEAR, T.H. (1953) Social psychology of everyday life. In C.A. Mace and P.E. Vernon (Eds) *Current Trends in British Psychology.* London: Methuen.
PEAR, T.H. (1954) The place of the psychologist in the community. *Rationalist Annual.* London: Watts.
PEAR, T.H. (1955a) *English Social Differences.* London: Allen and Unwin.
PEAR, T.H. (1955b) The Manchester University Department of Psychology (a) 1909–1951. *Bulletin of the British Psychological Society, 26,* 21–30.
PEAR, T.H. (1960) Some early relations between English ethnologists and psychologists. *Journal of the Royal Anthropological Institute of Great Britain and Ireland, 90,* 227–237.
PEAR, T.H. (1962) Personalities in the early days of the British Psychological Society. *British Journal of Psychology, 53,* 223–228.
PEAR, T.H. and WYATT, S. (1914) The testimony of normal and mentally defective children. *British Journal of Psychology, 6,* 387–419.
PEARSON, K. (1901) Paedometry. [Letter to the editor.] *Educational Times,* 21 February.
PEARSON, K. (1924) *The Life, Letters and Labours of Francis Galton, Vol. 2.* Cambridge: Cambridge University Press.
PELOSI, A.J. and APPLEBY, L. (1992) Psychological influences on cancer and ischaemic heart disease. *British Medical Journal, 304,* 1295–1298.
PENFIELD, W. (1957) Charles Sherrington, poet and philosopher. *Brain, 80,* 402–410.
PENROSE, L.S. (1959) Automatic mechanical self reproduction. *New Biology, 28,* 92–117.
PENROSE, R. (1990a) *The Emperor's New Mind.* Cambridge: Cambridge University Press.
PENROSE, R. (1990b) Précis of *The Emperor's New Mind: Concerning Computers, Minds, and the Laws of Physics. Behavioral and Brain Sciences, 13,* 643–705.
PEPPERELL, R. (1997) *The Post Human Condition,* 2nd ed. Exeter: Intellect.
PERKINS, T.S. and WINKE, S. (1984) Management of behavioural disorders: a joint approach by parents, health visitors and psychologists. *Health Visitor, 57,* 108–109.
PERRY, W.J. (1918) *War and Civilisation.* Manchester: Manchester University Press.
PETERSON, C. and STUNKARD, A. (1989) Personal control and health promotion. *Social Science and Medicine, 28,* 819–828.
PETERSON, L.R. and PETERSON, M.J. (1959) Short-term retention of individual items. *Journal of Experimental Psychology, 58,* 193–198.
PFISTER, J. and SCHNOG, N. (Eds) (1997) *Inventing the Psychological: Toward a Cultural History of Emotional Life in America.* New Haven: Yale University Press.
PIAGET, J. (1931) Review of *Intellectual Growth in Young Children* by S Isaacs. *Mind, 40,* 137–160.
PIAGET, J. (1932) *The Moral Judgement of the Child.* London: Routledge and Kegan Paul.
PIAGET, J. and WEIL, A. (1951) The development in children of the idea of the homeland and of relations with other countries. *International Social Science Bulletin, 3,* 561–578.
PICKERING, A. (1995) Cyborg history and the World War II regime. *Perspectives on Science, 3,* 1–48.
PICKSTONE, J. (1992) Introduction: a centre of intelligence. In C. Field and J. Pickstone (Eds.) *A

Centre of Intelligence: The Development of Science, Technology and Medicine in Manchester and its University. Manchester: John Rylands University Library of Manchester.

PIÉRON, H. (1927) *Thought and the Brain.* C.K. Ogden (Trans.). London: Routledge and Kegan Paul.

PILGRIM, D. and TREACHER, A. (1992) *Clinical Psychology Observed.* London: Routledge.

PINES, M. (1991) The development of the psychodynamic movement. In H. Freeman and G. Berrios (Eds) *150 Years of British Psychiatry.* London: Gaskell.

PLUMPTRE, C.J. (1861) *The Principles and Practice of Elocution.* Oxford and London: J.H. and Jas. Parker.

PLUMPTRE, C.J. (1870, 1876, 1881, 1883) *King's College Lectures on Elocution.* London: variously T.J. Allman or Trübner.

PLUMPTRE, C.J. (1874) *The Culture of Voice and Speech.* London: T.J. Allman.

PODMORE, F. (1902) *Modern Spiritualism: A History and a Criticism.* London: Methuen.

POLE, J. (1948) Susan Isaacs. *New Statesman and Nation,* 23 October, 350.

POLETIEK, F. (1992) *Toektsen.* Amsterdam: Lemma.

PONGRATZ, L.J. (1977) Einleitung: Geschichte, Gegenstand, Grundlagen der Klinische Psychologie. In K. Gottschaldt, P. Lersch, F. Sander ane H. Thomae (Eds) *Handbuch der Psychologie. Vol. 8.* L.J. Pongratz (Series Ed.) Klinische Psychologie. Göttingen: Hogrefe.

POPPER, K.R. (1957) Philosophy of science: a personal report. In C.A. Mace (Ed.) *British Philosophy in the Mid-Century.* London: Allen and Unwin.

POPPER, K.R. (1959) *The Logic of Scientific Discovery.* London: Hutchinson.

POPPLESTONE, J.A. and McPHERSON, M.W. (1984) Pioneer psychology laboratories in clinical settings. In J. Brozek (Ed.) *Explorations in the History of Psychology in the United States.* Lewisburg: Bucknell University Press.

PORTER, N. (1868/1872) *The Human Intellect with an Introduction upon Psychology and the Soul.* New York: Scribner; London: Strahan.

PORTER, N. (1870) *The Human Intellect.* New York: Scribner.

POSTMAN, L. and PHILIPS, L.W. (1965) Short-term temporal changes in free recall. *Quarterly Journal of Experimental Psychology,* 17, 132–138.

POTTER, J. and WETHERALL, M. (1987) *Discourse and Social Psychology: Beyond Attitudes and Behaviour.* London: Sage.

POULTON, E.C.P. (1950) Perceptual anticipation and reaction time. *Quarterly Journal of Experimental Psychology,* 2, 99–112.

PRESSMAN, J.D. (1988) Sufficient promise: John F. Fulton and the origins of psychosurgery. *Bulletin of the History of Medicine,* 62, 1–22.

PRESSMAN, J.D. (1998) *Last Resort: Psychosurgery and the Limits of Medicine.* Cambridge: Cambridge University Press.

PRIBRAM, K. (1992) From metaphors to models: the use of analogy in neuropsychology. In D. Leary (Ed.) *Metaphors in the History of Psychology.* Cambridge: Cambridge University Press.

PRITCHATT, D. (1966) Comparative psychology as an undergraduate practical course. *Bulletin of the British Psychological Society,* 19 (65), 25–27.

Proceedings of the Psychological Society of Great Britain 1875–1879 (1880) London: privately printed.

PROCTER, H. (1999) Explanations in autism. Paper given at the 13th International Congress on Personal Construct Psychology, Berlin.

PSYCHOLOGICAL BULLETIN (1918) Courses in Psychology for the Students' Army Training Corps. *Psychological Bulletin,* 15, 130.

PSYCHOLOGIST (1936) *Nervousness: Its Causes, Prevention and Cure.* London: The Psychologist, Practical Psychology Handbook No. 3.

QUETELET, L.A.J. (1870) *Anthropometrie.* Brussels: C. Muquardt.

QUINE, W.V.O. (1952) *Methods of Logic.* London: Routledge and Kegan Paul.

QUINTON, A. (1976) George Croom Robertson: Editor 1876–1891. *Mind, NS* 85, 6–16.

RABINBACH, A. (1992) *The Human Motor: Energy, Fatigue, and the Origins of Modernity.* Berkeley: University of California Press.

RAMACHANDRAN, V.S. and GREGORY, R.L. (1978) Does colour provide an input to human motion perception? *Nature,* 275, 55–56.

RAMACHANDRAN, V.S. and GREGORY, R.L. (1991) Perceptual filling in of artificially induced scotomas in human vision. *Nature,* 350, 699–702.

RAND, B. (Ed.) (1912) *The Classical Psychologists: Selections Illustrating Psychology from Anaxagoras to Wundt.* New York: Scribner.

RAPP, D. (1988) The reception of Freud by the British press: general interest and literary magazines, 1920–1925. *Journal of the History of the Behavioural Sciences*, 24, 191–201.

RAPP, D. (1990) The early discovery of Freud by the British general educated reading public, 1912–1919. *Social History of Medicine*, 3, 217–249.

RAVEN, J. (1950) What is clinical psychology? *Quarterly Bulletin of the British Psychological Society*, 7, 282–285.

REES, G. (1925) Society news. *Practical Psychology*, 1 (5), 27.

REES, J.R. (1945) *The Shaping of Psychiatry by War.* London: Chapman and Hall.

REGIS, E. (1991) *Great Mambo Chicken and the Trans-Human Condition.* London: Viking.

REID, B.H. (1987) *J.F.C. Fuller: Military Thinker.* London: Macmillan.

REISMAN, J.M. (1991) *A History of Clinical Psychology*, 2nd ed. New York: Hemisphere.

RESEARCH DEFENCE SOCIETY (1974) *Guidance Notes on the Law Relating to Experiments on Animals.* London: Research Defence Society.

RICHARDS, B. (1983) *Clinical Psychology: The Individual and the Welfare State.* Unpublished PhD thesis, North East London Polytechnic.

RICHARDS, B. (1988) Lightner Witmer and the project of psychotechnology. *History of the Human Sciences*, 1, 201–219.

RICHARDS, E. (1989) Huxley and women's place in science: the woman question and the control of Victorian anthropology. In J. Moore (Ed.) *History Humanity and Evolution: Essays for John C. Greene.* Cambridge: Cambridge University Press.

RICHARDS, G. (1987) Of what is history of psychology a history? *British Journal for the History of Science*, 20, 201–211.

RICHARDS, G. (1989) *On Psychological Language: And the Physiomorphic Basis of Human Nature.* London: Routledge.

RICHARDS, G. (1992a) Reflexivity problems in psychology: too embarrassing even to talk about. *British Psychological Society History and Philosophy Section Newsletter*, 15, 7–22.

RICHARDS, G. (1992b) *Mental Machinery: The Origins and Consequences of Psychological Ideas. Part 1: 1600–1850.* London: Athlone Press.

RICHARDS, G. (1995) 'To know our fellow men to do them good': American Psychology's continuing moral project. *History of the Human Sciences*, 8 (3), 1–24.

RICHARDS, G. (1996) *Putting Psychology in its Place: An Introduction from a Critical Historical Perspective.* London: Routledge.

RICHARDS, G. (1997) *'Race', Racism and Psychology: Towards a Reflexive History.* London: Routledge.

RICHARDS, G. (2000a) Britain on the couch: popularising psychoanalysis in Britain 1918–1940. *Science in Context.*

RICHARDS, G. (2000b) Psychology and the Churches in Britain 1919–39: symptoms of conversion. *History of the Human Sciences*, 13, 57–84.

RICHARDS, R.J. (1977) Lloyd Morgan's theory of instinct: from Darwinism to neo-Darwinism. *Journal of the History of the Behavioral Sciences*, 13, 31–32.

RICHARDS, R.J. (1987) *Darwin and the Emergence of Evolutionary Theories of Mind and Behavior.* Chicago: University of Chicago Press.

RICHMAN, N., STEVENSON, J. and GRAHAM, P.J. (1975) Prevalence of behaviour problems in three year old children: an epidemiological study in a London borough. *Journal of Child Psychology and Psychiatry*, 16, 277–287.

RICHMAN, N., STEVENSON, J. and GRAHAM, P.J. (1982) *Preschool to School: A Behavioural Study.* London: Academic Press.

RICKMAN, J. (1950) Obituary: Susan Sutherland Isaacs. *International Journal of Psycho-Analysis*, 31, 279–285.

RIVERS, W.H.R. (1918) War neurosis and military training. *Mental Hygiene*, 11, 513–533.

RIVERS, W.H.R. (1922) *Instinct and Unconscious: A Contribution to a Biological Theory of the Psycho-Neuroses*, 2nd ed. Cambridge: Cambridge University Press.

RIVIERE, J. (1958) A character trait of Freud's. In J.D. Sutherland (Ed.) *Psychoanalysis and Contemporary Thought.* London: Hogarth.

ROBACK, A.A. (1961) *A History of Psychology and Psychiatry.* New York: Greenwood.

ROBERTSON, G.C. (1866/1894) Psychology in philosophic teaching. Abstract of his inaugural lecture on appointment as Professor of Philosophy of Mind and Logic in University College London. Reprinted in A. Bain and T. Whittaker (Eds) *Philosophical Remains of George Croom Robertson.* London: Williams and Norgate.

ROBERTSON, G.C. (1868/1894) Philosophy as a subject of study. (Introductory lecture at University

College London). *Fortnightly Review*, December 1868. (Reprinted in A. Bain and T. Whittaker (Eds) *Philosophical Remains of George Croom Robertson*. London: Williams and Norgate.)

ROBERTSON, G.C. (1874) *Prospectus to* 'Quarterly Review of Mental Science', MS add. 88, Manuscripts and Rare Books, Science Library, University College London.

ROBERTSON, G.C. (1875) *Prospectus to* 'Mind: a Quarterly Review of Scientific Psychology and Philosophy', MS add. 88, Manuscripts and Rare Books, Science Library, University College London.

ROBERTSON, G.C. (1876) Prefatory words. *Mind*, 1, 1–6.

ROBERTSON, G.C. (1876/1894) Philosophy in London. *Mind*, 1, 531–545. Reprinted in A. Bain and T. Whittaker (Eds) *Philosophical Remains of George Croom Robertson*. London: Williams and Norgate.

ROBERTSON, G.C. (1878/1894a) The physical basis of mind. *Mind*, 3, 24–42. (Reprinted in A. Bain and T. Whittaker (Eds) *Philosophical Remains of George Croom Robertson*. London: Williams and Norgate.)

ROBERTSON, G.C. (1878/1894b) Philosophy in education. *Mind*, 3, 241–252. Reprinted in A. Bain and T. Whittaker (Eds) *Philosophical Remains of George Croom Robertson*. London: Williams and Norgate.

ROBERTSON, G.C. (1882/1894) The action of so-called motives. Privately circulated Metaphysical Society paper. Reprinted in A. Bain and T. Whittaker (Eds) *Philosophical Remains of George Croom Robertson*. London: Williams and Norgate.

ROBERTSON, G.C. (1883/1894) Psychology and philosophy. *Mind*, 8, 1–47. Reprinted in A. Bain and T. Whittaker (Eds) *Philosophical Remains of George Croom Robertson*. London: Williams and Norgate.

ROBERTSON, G.C. (1887/1894) Psychology. *Mind*, 12, 439–443. Reprinted in A. Bain and T. Whittaker (Eds) *Philosophical Remains of George Croom Robertson*. London: Williams and Norgate.

ROBERTSON, G.C. (1890) George Grote. *Dictionary of National Biography, Vol. 23*. London: Smith, Elder.

ROBINSON, J. (1986) Autobiographical memory: an historical prologue. In D.C. Rubin (Ed.) *Autobiographical Memory*. Cambridge: Cambridge University Press.

RODGER, A. (1952) *The Seven Point Plan*. NIIP Paper No. 1. London: National Institute of Industrial Psychology.

ROFFEY, G.W. (1925) Speed, bonnie boat. *The Practical Psychologist*, 1 (1), 7

ROISER, M.J. and WILLIG, C. (1995) The hidden history of authoritarianism. *History of the Human Sciences*, 8, 77–97.

ROLFE, J. (1996) Craik and the Cambridge cockpit. *The Psychologist*, 9 (2), 69–71.

ROMANES, E. (1896) *The Life and Letters of G.J. Romanes*. London: Longmans, Green.

RORTY, R. (1980) *Philosophy and the Mirror of Nature*. Oxford: Blackwell.

ROSE, N. (1985) *The Psychological Complex: Psychology, Politics and Society in England, 1869–1939*. London: Routledge and Kegan Paul.

ROSE, N. (1986) Psychiatry: the discipline of mental health. In P. Miller and N. Rose (Eds) *The Power of Psychiatry*. Cambridge: Polity.

ROSE, N. (1988) Calculable minds and manageable individuals. *History of the Human Sciences*, 1, 179–200.

ROSE, N. (1989) *Governing the Soul: The Shaping of the Private Self*. London: Routledge.

ROSE, N. (1992) Engineering the human soul: analyzing psychological expertise. *Science in Context*, 5, 351–369.

ROSE, N. (1996a) *Inventing Our Selves: Psychology, Power, and Personhood*. Cambridge: Cambridge University Press.

ROSE, N. (1996b) Psychology as an individualizing technology. In *Inventing Ourselves: Psychology, Power and Personhood*. Cambridge: Cambridge University Press.

ROSE, N. (1999) *Governing the Soul: The Shaping of the Private Self*, expanded 2nd ed. London: Free Association Books.

ROSE, N. and MILLER, P. (1992) Political power beyond the state: problematics of government. *British Journal of Sociology*, 43, 173–205.

ROSS, E. (1993) *Love and Toil: Motherhood in Outcast London, 1870–1918*. Oxford: Oxford University Press.

ROTH, M.S. (1989) Remembering forgetting: maladies de la mémoire in nineteenth-century France. *Representations*, 26, 49–68.

ROTTER, J.B. (1964) *Clinical Psychology*. London: Prentice Hall.

ROTTER, J.B. (1966) Generalised expectancies for internal versus external control of reinforcement. *Psychological Monographs*, 80, 1–28.

ROTTER, J.B., *et al.* (1972) *Applications of a Social Learning Theory of Personality.* New York: Holt, Rinehart and Winston.

ROWAN, A.N. and ROLLIN, B.E. (1983) Animal research – for and against: a philosophical, social, and historical perspective. *Perspectives in Biology and Medicine, 27,* 1–9.

ROWNTREE, B.S. (1901/1980) *Poverty: A Study of Town Life.* London: Garland.

RUESCH, H. (1979) *Slaughter of the Innocent.* London: Futura.

RUMELHART, D.E. and McCLELLAND, J.L. (Eds) (1986) *Parallel Distributed Processing: Explorations in the Microstructure of Cognition.* Cambridge, MA: MIT Press.

RUSE, M. (1996) *Monad to Man: The Concept of Progress in Evolutionary Biology.* Cambridge, MA: Harvard University Press.

RUSSELL, E.S. (1934) Presidential address: the study of behaviour. *British Association for the Advancement of Science, Reports,* Section D, 83–98.

RUTTER, M. (1966) *Children of Sick Parents.* Oxford: Oxford University Press.

RUTTER, M. (1981) *Maternal Deprivation Reassessed,* 2nd ed. Harmondsworth: Penguin.

RUTTER, M. (1989) Pathways from childhood to adult life. *Journal of Child Psychology and Psychiatry, 30,* 23–51.

RUTTER, M. (1999) The Emanuel Miller Memorial Lecture 1998. Autism: two-way interplay between research and clinical work. *Journal of Child Psychology and Psychiatry, 40,* 169–188.

RUTTER, M. (2000) Genetic studies of autism: from the 1970s into the millennium. *Journal of Abnormal Child Psychology, 28,* 3–14.

RUTTER, M. and MADGE, N. (1976) *Cycles of Disadvantage: A Review of Research.* London: Heinemann Educational.

RUTTER, M. and SROUFE, A. (in press) Developmental psychopathology: concepts and challenges. *Development and Psychopathology.*

RUTTER, M., TIZARD, J. and WHITMORE, K. (1970) *Education, Health and Behaviour.* London: Longmans. (Reprinted 1981: Melbourne: Krieger.)

RYDER, R.D. (1975/1983) *Victims of Science. The Use of Animals in Research.* London: Davis-Poynter Ltd and National Anti-Vivisection Society Ltd.

RYLE, G. (1949) *The Concept of Mind.* London: Hutchinson.

SALMON, T.W. (1917) The care and treatment of mental diseases and war neuroses 'shell shock' in the British army. *Mental Hygiene, 1,* 509–547.

SAMSON, F. and ADELMAN, G. (Eds) (1992) *The Neurosciences: Paths of Discovery, Vol. II.* Boston: Birkhauser.

SANDERS, F.K. and YOUNG, J.Z. (1940) Learning and other functions of the higher nervous centres of *Sepia. Journal of Neurophysiology, 3,* 501–526.

SAVAGE, G.H. (1916) Mental disabilities for war service. *Journal of Mental Science, 62,* 653–657.

SCARFF, A.B. (1938) Mental disorders: principles of psychotherapy. *Practical Psychology, 2,* 374–375.

SCHAFFER, S. (1994) *From Physics to Anthropology and Back Again.* Cambridge: Prickly Pear Press.

SCHMITT, C.B. (1988) The rise of philosophical textbook. In C.B. Schmitt, *et al.* (Eds) *The Cambridge History of Renaissance Philosophy.* Cambridge: Cambridge University Press.

SCHMITT, F.O. (1992) The Neurosciences Research Program: a brief history. In F. Samson and G. Adelman (Eds) *The Neurosciences: Paths of Discovery, Vol. II.* Boston: Birkhauser.

SCHOLL, D.A. (1956) *The Organisation of the Cerebral Cortex.* London: Methuen.

SCHORR, A. (1984) *Die Verhaltenstherapie: Ihre Geschichte van den Anfängen bis zur Gegenwart.* Weinheim: Beltz.

SEARLE, J.R. (1980) Minds, brains, and programs. *Behavioral and Brain Sciences, 3,* 417–424.

SEDGWICK, P. (1982) *Psycho Politics: Laing, Foucault, Goffman, Szasz and the Future of Mass Psychiatry.* London: Harper and Row.

SEGALL, M.H., CAMPBELL, D.T. and HERSKOVITS, M. (1963) Cultural differences in the perception of geometric illusions. *Science, 139,* 769–771.

SELFRIDGE, O.G. (1959) Pandemonium: a paradigm for learning. In D.V. Blake and A.M. Uttey (Eds) *Proceedings of the Symposium on Mechanisation of Thought Processes.* London: National Physical Laboratory.

SELIGMAN, M.E.P. (1975) *On Development, Depression and Death.* New York: W.H. Freeman.

SERPELL, J. and PAUL, E. (1994) Pets and the development of positive attitudes to animals. In A. Manning and J. Serpell (Eds) *Animals and Human Society – Changing Perspectives.* London: Routledge.

SHANNON, C.E. and WEAVER, W. (1949) *The Mathematical Theory of Communication.* Urbana: University of Illinois Press.

SHAPIN, S. (1992) Discipline and bounding: the history and sociology of science as seen through the externalism–internalism debate. *History of Science*, 30, 333–369.

SHAPIRO, M.B. (1951) An experimental approach to diagnostic psychological testing. *Journal of Mental Science*, 97, 748–764.

SHAPIRO, M.B. (1955) Training of clinical psychologists at the Institute of Psychiatry. *Bulletin of the British Psychological Society*, 26, 15–20.

SHAPIRO, M.B. (1960) Approaches to clinical psychology. In Abstracts of a symposium held by the Northern Branch of the BPS, 14 May. *Bulletin of the British Psychological Society*, 42, 95.

SHAPIRO, M.B. (1965) An approach to the social responsibilities of the clinical psychologist. *Bulletin of the British Psychological Society*, 18 (59), 31–36.

SHAPIRO, M.B. and RAVENETTE, A.T. (1959) A preliminary experiment on paranoid delusions. *Journal of Mental Science*, 105, 295–312.

SHELDON, B. (1982) *Behaviour Modification*. London: Tavistock.

SHEPHARD, B. (1996) The early treatment of mental disorders: R.G. Rows and Maghull 1914–1918. In H. Freeman, G.E. Berrios (Eds) *150 Years of British Psychiatry. Vol. II: The Aftermath*. London: Athlone.

SHEPHERD, F. (1937) *The Baby Who Does Not Conform to Rules*. London: Home and School Council of Great Britain.

SHERRINGTON, C.S. (1902) Report of lecture to teachers on fatigue. *British Medical Journal*, ii, 1371.

SHERRINGTON, C.S. (1904) On binocular flicker and the correlation of activity of 'corresponding' retinal points. *British Journal of Psychology*, 1, 26–60.

SHERRINGTON, C.S. (1906) *The Integrative Action of the Nervous System*. New York: Charles Scribner's Sons.

SHERRINGTON, C.S. (1913) The sight tests of the Board of Trade [Letter to the Editor]. *Lancet*, i, 1691.

SHERRINGTON, C.S. (1923) Some aspects of animal mechanism [Presidential Address, 1922]. *Reports, British Association for the Advancement of Science*, 1–15.

SHERRINGTON, C.S. (1933) *The Brain and Its Mechanism* [The Rede Lecture]. Cambridge: Cambridge University Press.

SHERRINGTON, C.S. (1940) *Man on His Nature*. Cambridge: Cambridge University Press.

SHERRINGTON, C.S. (1961) *The Integrative Action of the Nervous System*, 2nd ed. New Haven: Yale University Press.

SHERRINGTON, C.S. (1963) *Man on His Nature*, revised and abridged 2nd ed. London: Cambridge University Press.

SHERWOOD, S. (Ed.) (1966) *The Nature of Psychology: A Selection of Papers, Essays and Other Writings by the Late Kenneth J.W. Craik*. Cambridge: Cambridge University Press.

SHIMMIN, S. and WALLIS, D. (1994) *Fifty Years of Occupational Psychology in Britain*. Leicester: British Psychological Society.

SHIPMAN, M. (Ed.) (1976) *The Organisation and Impact of Social Research*. London: Routledge and Kegan Paul.

SHIRLEY, W. (1916) *Morale: The Most Important Factor in War*. London: Lifton, Praed.

SHOPLAND, J.C. and GREGORY, R.L. (1964) The effect of touch on a visually ambiguous three-dimensional figure. *Quarterly Journal of Experimental Psychology*, 16, 66–70.

SHORTER, E. (1997) *A History of Psychiatry: From the Era of the Asylum to the Age of Prozac*. New York: Wiley.

SHOTTER, J. (1990) The social construction of remembering and forgetting. In D. Middleton and D. Edwards (Eds) *Collective Remembering*. London: Sage.

SINCLAIR, H.M. (1984) Sherrington and industrial fatigue. *Notes and Records of the Royal Society*, 39, 91–104.

SINGER, P. (1975/1976) *Animal Liberation*. New York Review and London: Jonathan Cape.

SINGLEY, K. and ANDERSON, J.R. (1989) *The Transfer of Cognitive Skill*. Cambridge, MA: Harvard University Press.

SISMONDO, S. (1999) Models, simulations and their objects. *Science in Context*, 12, 247–260.

SKINNER, B.F. (1971) *Beyond Freedom and Dignity*. New York: Alfred A. Knopf.

SLATER, P.J.B. (1979) The two sides of ethology. *Trends in Neuroscience*, February, 33–35.

SLEIGHT, W. (1911) Memory and formal training. *British Journal of Psychology*, 4, 386–457.

SLOBODIN, R. (1978/1997) *W.H.R. Rivers: Pioneer Anthropologist, Psychiatrist of* The Ghost Road. Stroud: Sutton.

SLOMAN, A. (1987) Motives, mechanisms, and emotions. *Journal of Emotion and Cognition*, 1, 217–233.

SLUCKIN, W. (1954/1960) *Minds and Machines*. Harmondsworth: Penguin.

SLUCKIN, W. (1969) Animal behavioural and ethological work. *Supplement to the Bulletin of the British Psychological Society*, 22, 35–36.

SMILES, S. (1859) *Self Help, with Illustrations of Character, Conduct and Perseverance*. London: Murray.

SMITH, G.E. and PEAR, T.H. (1917) *Shell Shock and its Lessons*. Publications of the University of Manchester, No. 111. Manchester: Manchester University Press; London: Longmans, Green.

SMITH, L. (1985) *To Understand and to Help: The Life and Work of Susan Isaacs (1885–1948)*. Cranbury, NJ: Associated University Presses.

SMITH, L. (1986) *Behaviourism and Logical Positivism: A Reassessment of the Alliance*. Stanford: Stanford University Press.

SMITH, R. (1988) Does the history of psychology have a subject? *History of the Human Sciences*, 1, 147–177.

SMITH, R. (1992) *Inhibition: History and Meaning in the Sciences of Mind and Brain*. Berkeley: University of California Press; London: Free Association Books.

SMITH, R. (1997a) History and the history of the human sciences: what voice? *History of the Human Sciences*, 10, 22–39.

SMITH, R. (1997b) *The Fontana History of the Human Sciences*. London: Fontana. Also published as *The Norton History of the Human Sciences*. New York: W.W. Norton.

SMITH, R. (1998) The big picture: writing psychology into the history of the human sciences. *Journal of the History of the Behavioral Sciences*, 34, 1–13.

SMITH, R. (2000) The embodiment of value: C.S. Sherrington and the cultivation of science. *British Journal for the History of Science*, 33, 283–311.

SMYTHIES, J. (1956) *Analysis of Perception*. London: Routledge and Kegan Paul.

SMYTHIES, J. (1960) The stroboscopic patterns III: further experiments and discussion. *British Journal of Psychology*, 51, 247–255.

SOFFER, R.N. (1978) *Ethics and Society in England: The Revolution in the Social Sciences 1870–1914*. Berkeley: University of California Press.

SOKAL, M.M. (1972) Psychology at Victorian Cambridge – the unofficial laboratory of 1887–1888. *Proceedings of the American Philosophical Society*, 116, 145–147.

SOKAL, M.M. (Ed.) (1981) *An Education in Psychology: James McKeen Cattell's Journal and Letters from Germany and England, 1880–1888*. Cambridge, MA: MIT Press.

SOKAL, M.M. (1997) Baldwin, Cattell and the *Psychological Review*: a collaboration and its discontents. *History of the Human Sciences*, 10, 57–89.

SOUTHARD, E.E. (1919) *Shell-Shock and Other Neuro-Psychiatric Problems. Presented in Five Hundred and Eighty-Nine Case Histories from the War Literature, 1914–1918*. Boston: W.M. Leonard.

SPARROW, J.H.A. (1949) *Morale*. London: War Office.

SPARROW, J. (1998) *Knowledge in Organizations: Access to Thinking at Work*. London: Sage.

SPEARMAN, C. (1937) *Psychology Down the Ages*. London: Macmillan.

SPENCER, H. (1870) *Principles of Psychology*, 2nd ed. London: Williams and Norgate.

SPENDER, H. (1987) Mass-Observation. *Camerawork*, 11: 6. London: Half-Moon.

SPERLINGER, D. (1975) Correspondence. *Bulletin of the British Psychological Society*, 28, 356–357.

SPERRY, R.W. (1947) Effect of crossing nerves to antagonistic limb muscles in the monkey. *Archives of Neurology and Psychiatry*, 58, 452–473.

SROUFE, A. and RUTTER, M. (1984) The domain of developmental psychopathology. *Child Development*, 55, 17–29.

STAR, S.L. and GRIESEMER, J.R. (1989) Institutional ecology, 'translation' and boundary objects: amateurs and professionals in Bekeley's museum of vertebrate zoology, 1907–1939. *Social Studies of Science*, 19, 387–420.

STEHL, R. (1955) *The Robots are Amongst Us*. London: Arco.

STEINBERG, H. (Ed.) (1961) *The British Psychological Society 1901–1961*. Leicester: BPS.

STEKEL, W. (1943) Active psychotherapy in war-time. *Individual Psychology. Medical Pamphlets – No. 23*, 21–27. Rochford, Essex: C.W. Daniel.

STEPHEN, L. (1892) Obituary of George Croom Robertson. *The Spectator*, 1 October.

STEPHEN, L. (1896) George Croom Robertson. *Dictionary of National Biography, Vol. 48*. London: Smith, Elder.

STEVENSON, J., BAILEY, V. and SIMPSON, J. (1988) Feasible intervention in families with parenting difficulties: a primary preventive perspective on child abuse. In K. Browne, C. Davies and P. Stratton (Eds) *Early Prediction and Prevention of Child Abuse*. London: Wiley.

STEWART, T. and BIRDSALL, M. (2000) A review of the contribution of personal construct psychology (PCP) to stammering therapy. *Journal of Fluency Disorders* (submitted).

STOCKING, G., Jr (1965) On the limits of 'presentism' and 'historicism' in the historiography of the behavioral sciences. *Journal of the History of the Behavioral Sciences*, 1, 211–218.

STONE, M. (1985) Shell-shock and the psychologists. In W.F. Bynum, R. Porter and M. Shepherd (Eds) *The Anatomy of Madness: Essays in the History of Psychiatry. Vol. 2, Institutions and Society*. London: Routledge.

STORMS, L.H. and SIGAL, J.J. (1958) Eysenck's personality theory with special reference to 'The Dynamics of Anxiety and Hysteria'. *British Journal of Medical Psychology*, 31, 228–246.

STOUT, G.F. (1892) Prefatory remarks. *Mind*, NS 1, 1–2.

STOUT, G.F. (1896) *Analytical Psychology*. London: Swan Sonnenschein.

STOUT, G.F. (1898) *A Manual of Psychology*. London: University Tutorial Press.

STOUT, G.F. (1904) *A Manual of Psychology*, 4th ed. London: University Tutorial Press.

STOUT, G.F. (1952) *God and Nature*. Cambridge: Cambridge University Press.

STURDY, S. (1992) The political economy of scientific medicine: science, education and the transformation of medical practice in Sheffield, 1890–1922. *Medical History*, 36, 125–159.

SULLY, J. (1874) *Sensation and Intuition: Studies in Psychology and Aesthetics*. London: H.S. King.

SULLY, J. (1877) *Pessimism: A History and a Criticism*. London: H.S. King.

SULLY, J. (1881) *Illusions: A Psychological Study*. London: C.K. Paul.

SULLY, J. (1882a) *The Saturday Review*, 3 June, 706–707.

SULLY, J. (1882b) Critical notice on *Die Seele des Kindes. Beobachtungen über die geistige Entwickelung des Menschen in den ersten Lebensjahren* by W. Preyer. *Mind*, 7, 416.

SULLY, J. (1882c) *Outlines of Psychology*. London: Longmans, Green.

SULLY, J. (1884) *Outlines of Psychology with Special Reference to the Theory of Education*. London: Longmans, Green.

SULLY, J. (1885) Introduction. In B. Perez *Child Psychology*. A.M. Christie (Trans.). London: Sonnenschein.

SULLY, J. (1886) *The Teacher's Handbook of Psychology*. London: Longmans, Green.

SULLY, J. (1892a) *The Human Mind: A Text-Book of Psychology*. London: Longmans, Green.

SULLY, J. (1892b) *Outlines of Psychology with Special Reference to the Theory of Education*, 2nd ed. London: Longmans, Green.

SULLY, J. (1895/1903) *Studies of Childhood*. London: Longmans, Green.

SULLY, J. (1897) *Children's Ways*. London: Longmans, Green.

SULLY, J. (1912) *Italian Travel Sketches*. London.

SULLY, J. (1918) *My Life and Friends: A Psychologist's Memories*. London: T. Fisher Unwin.

SUMMERFIELD, A. (1958) Clinical psychology in Britain. *American Psychologist*, 13, 171–176.

SUTHERLAND, J.D. (1951) The Tavistock Clinic and the Tavistock Institute of Human Relations. *Quarterly Bulletin of the British Psychological Society*, 2 (14), October, 105–111.

SUTHERLAND, S. (1992) *Irrationality: The Enemy Within*. London: Constable.

SUTTON, J. (1998) *Philosophy and Memory Traces: Descartes to Connectionism*. Cambridge: Cambridge University Press.

SWAZEY, J.P. (1969) *Reflexes and Motor Integration: Sherrington's Concept of Integrative Action*. Cambridge, MA: Harvard University Press.

SYKES, M. (1947) *Rabindranath Tagore*. London: Longmans, Green.

TAJFEL, H., FLAMENT, C., BILLIG, M.G. and BUNDY, R.P. (1971) Social categorisation and intergroup behaviour. *European Journal of Social Psychology*, 1, 149–178.

TAJFEL, H., JAHODA, G., NEMETH, C., CAMPBELL, J.D. and JOHNSON, N. (1970) The development of children's preference for their own country. *International Journal of Psychology*, 5, 245–253.

TAJFEL, H., JAHODA, G., NEMETH, C., RIM, Y. and JOHNSON, N.B. (1972) The devaluation by children of their own national and ethnic group: two case studies. *British Journal of Social and Clinical Psychology*, 11, 235–243.

TANNER, J.M. (1981) *A History of the Study of Human Growth*. Cambridge: Cambridge University Press.

TANNER, J.M. (1993) Galton on human growth and form. In M. Keynes (Ed.) *Sir Francis Galton FRS. The Legacy of His Ideas*. London: Macmillan.

TANNER, J.M. and INHELDER, B. (Eds) (1971) *Discussions on Child Development*. London: Tavistock.

TAYLOR, W.S. (1947) Remembering: some effects of language and other factors. *British Journal of Psychology*, 38, 7–19.

TEEAR, C.H. (1939) *The Art of Making Friends*, Practical Psychology Handbook No. 15. London: The Psychologist.

TEEAR, C.H. (1941) *Mastering Shyness*, Practical Psychology Handbook No. 20. London: The Psychologist.

THARP, R.G. and WETZEL, R.J. (1969) *Behavior Modification in the Natural Environment*. New York: Academic Press.

THOMAS, J.A., BIDDER, R.T., HEWITT, K. and GRAY, O.P. (1982) Health visiting and preschool children with behavioural problems in the county of South Glamorgan: an exploratory study. *Child: Care, Health and Development*, 8, 93–103.

THOMSON, M. (1995) Mental hygiene as an international movement. In P. Weindling (Ed.) *International Health Organisations and Movements, 1918–1939*. Cambridge: Cambridge University Press.

THOMSON, M. (1998a) Before anti-psychiatry: 'mental health' in wartime Britain. In M. Gijswijt-Hofstra and R. Porter (Eds) *Cultures of Psychiatry in Postwar Britain and the Netherlands*. Amsterdam: Rodopi.

THOMSON, M. (1998b) *The Problem of Mental Deficiency: Eugenics, Democracy and Social Policy in Britain, 1870–1959*. Oxford: Oxford University Press.

THOMSON, M. (forthcoming) Psychology and the consciousness of modernity in Britain, 1900–1950. In M. Daunton and B. Reiger (Eds) *The Consciousness of Modernity*. Berg.

THOMSON, R. (1968) *The Pelican History of Psychology*. Harmondsworth: Penguin.

THOMSON, R. (1993) Introduction to James Sully *Studies of Childhood*. London: Routledge/Thoemmes Reprints.

THOMSON, R. and SLUCKIN, W. (1954a) Cybernetics and mental functioning. *British Journal for the Philosophy of Science*, 4, 130–146.

THOMSON, R. and SLUCKIN, W. (1954b) Machines, robots and minds. *Durham University Journal*, 46, 116–127.

THORPE, W.H. (1956) Some implications of the study of animal behaviour. *Advancement of Science*, 13 (50), 42–55.

THORPE, W.H. (1961) Comparative psychology. *Annual Review of Psychology*, 12, 27–50.

THORPE, W.H. (1974) Is there a comparative psychology? The relevance of inherited and acquired constraints in the action patterns and perceptions of animals. *Annals of the New York Academy of Sciences*, 223, 89–112.

THORPE, W.H. (1979) *The Origins and Rise of Ethology: The Science of the Natural Behaviour of Animals*. London: Heinemann.

THORPE, W.H. and ZANGWILL, O.L. (Eds) (1961) *Current Problems in Animal Behaviour*. Cambridge: Cambridge University Press.

THOULESS, R.H. (1925) *Social Psychology: A Text Book for Students of Economics*. London: W.B. Clive.

THOULESS, R.H. (1937) *General and Social Psychology*. London: University Tutorial Press.

TITCHENER, (1898) A psychological laboratory. *Mind*, NS 7, 311–331.

TOBACH, E., ADLER, H.E. and ADLER, L.L. (Eds) (1973) Comparative psychology at issue. *Annals of the New York Academy of Sciences*, 223, 28 December.

TOLMAN, E.C. (1932) *Purposive Behavior in Animals and Men*. New York: Century.

TOULMIN, S. (1953) *The Philosophy of Science*. London: Hutchison.

TOULMIN, S. (1972) *Human Understanding. Vol. 1: General Introduction and Part I*. Oxford: Clarendon Press.

TRABASSO, T. (1972) Mental operation in language comprehension. In J.B. Carroll and R.O. Freedle (Eds) *Language Comprehension and the Acquisition of Knowledge*. Washington, DC: Winston.

TREVELYAN, G.M. (1942) *English Social History*. London: Longmans, Green.

TROSCIANKO, T. and GREGORY, R.L. (1984) An assessment of two amplitude-compression hearing aid systems, especially in high ambient noise. *British Journal of Audiology*, 18, 89–96.

TROTTER, W. (1916) *Instincts of the Herd in Peace and War*. London: T.F. Unwin.

TROWER, P., BRYANT, B. and ARGYLE, M. (1978) *Social Skills and Mental Health*. London: Methuen.

TURBAYNE, C. (1970) *The Myth of Metaphor*. Columbia, SC: University of South Carolina Press.

TURNER, F.M. (1993) *Contesting Cultural Authority*. Cambridge: Cambridge University Press.

TURNER, J.C. and GILES, H. (Eds) (1981) *Intergroup Behaviour*. Oxford: Blackwell.

TURNER, T. (1996) James Crichton-Browne and the anti-psychoanalysts. In H. Freeman and G. Berrios (Eds) *150 Years of British Psychiatry. Vol. II: The Aftermath*. London: Athlone.

TUSTIN, A. (1953) Do modern mechanisms help us to understand the mind? *British Journal of Psychology*, *44*, 24–37.

TWENEY, R.D., DOHERTY, M.E., WAMER, W.J., PLISKE, D.B., MYNATT, C., GROSS, K.A. and ARKELIN, D.L. (1980) Strategies of rule discovery in an inference task. *Quarterly Journal of Experimental Psychology*, *32*, 109–123.

UNDERWOOD, B.J. and SCHULZ, R. (1960) *Meaningfulness and Verbal Learning*. Chicago: Lippincott.

UNGERSON, B. (1953) *Personnel Selection*. London: War Office.

UTTLEY, A.M. (1955) The conditional probability of signals in the nervous system. *RRE Memorandum*, 1109.

UTTLEY, A.M. (1959) Conditional probability computing in a nervous system. *Mechanisation of Thought Processes*, National Physical Laboratory Symposium 10. London: HMSO.

UTTLEY, A.M. (1961) The engineering approach to the problem of neural organisation. *Progress in Biophysics and Biophysical Chemistry*, *11*, 25–52.

VALENTINE, C.W. (1942) *Principles of Army Instruction with Special Reference to Elementary Weapon Training*. Aldershot: Gale and Polden.

VALENTINE, C.W. (1943) *The Human Factor in the Army: Some Applications of Psychology to Training, Selection, Morale, and Discipline*. Aldershot: Gale and Polden.

VALENTINE, C.W. (1960) *Psychology and Its Bearing on Education*, 2nd ed. London: Methuen.

VALENTINE, E. (1991) William James's *The Principles of Psychology*: 'A seemingly inexhaustible source of ideas'. *British Journal of Psychology*, *82*, 217–227.

VALENTINE, E. (1997) *Psychology at Bedford College London 1849–1985*. London: Royal Holloway, University of London.

VALENTINE, E. (1999) The founding of the Psychological Laboratory, University College London: 'Dear Galton … Yours truly, J Sully'. *History of Psychology*, *2*, 204–218.

VALENTINE, E. (forthcoming) Beatrice Edgell: an appreciation. *British Journal of Psychology*.

VALVO, A. (1971) *Sight Restoration Rehabilitation*. American Foundation for the Blind, 15 West 16th St, New York, NY 10011.

VAN DER EYKEN, W. and TURNER, B. (1969) *Adventures in Education*. London: Allen Lane.

VAN LANGENHOVE, L., DE WAELE, J.M. and HARRÉ, R. (1986) *Individual Persons and their Actions*. Brussels: Pers van Vreij Universiteit.

VARLEY, R. (1987) *Mass-Observation*. Brentford: Watermans.

VATIN, F. (1999) *Le Travail, sciences et société: essais d' épistémologie et de sociologie du travail*. Brussels: Editions de L'Université de Bruxelles.

VERNANT, J-P. (1965/1991) History and psychology. In F.I. Zeitin (Ed.) *Mortals and Immortals: Collected Essays*. Princeton, NJ: Princeton University Press.

VERNON, H.M. (1921) *Industrial Fatigue and Efficiency*. London: Routledge.

VERNON, P.E. (1940) *The Measurement of Abilities*. London: University of London Press.

VICKERY, A. (1993) Golden age to separate spheres? A review of the categories and chronology of English women's history. *Historical Journal*, 36, 383–414.

VYGOTSKY, L.S. (1962) *Thought and Language*. Cambridge, MA: MIT Press.

WADDINGTON, K. (1998) Enemies within: postwar Bethlem and the Maudsley Hospital. In M. Gijswijt-Hofstra and R. Porter (Eds) *Cultures of Psychiatry and Mental Health Care in Postwar Britain and the Netherlands*. Amsterdam: Rodopi.

WAKE, C.S. (1868) *Chapters on Man, with the Outlines of a Science of Comparative Psychology*. London: Trübner.

WAKE, C.S. (1878) *The Evolution of Morality: Being a History of the Development of Moral Culture*. London: Trübner.

WAKE, C.S. (1882) *The Origin and Significance of the Great Pyramid*. London: Reeves and Turner.

WAKE, C.S. (1888) *Serpent-Worship, and Other Essays, with a Chapter on Totemism*. London: G. Redway.

WAKE, C.S. (1889/1967) *The Development of Marriage and Kinship*. London. Reprinted (Ed. and Intro.) R. Needham. Chicago: University of Chicago Press.

WAKE, C.S. (1904) *The Geometry of Science Diagrammatically Illustrated*. Chicago: privately printed. (Reissued 1907 as *Vortex Philosophy; or the Geometry…* etc. Chicago: privately printed.)

WALKERDINE, V. (1984) Developmental psychology and the child-centred pedagogy. In J. Henriques, W. Hollway, C. Urwin, C. Venn and V. Walkerdine (Eds) *Changing the Subject*. London: Methuen.

WALSHE, F.M.R. (1947) A foundation of neurology [review of Sherrington, *The Integrative Action of the Nervous System*, 2nd ed.] *British Medical Journal*, *ii*, 823.

WALSHE, F.M.R. (1951) The hypothesis of cybernetics. *British Journal for the Philosophy of Science,* 2, 161–163.

WALTER, W.G. (1943a) An automatic low frequency analyser. *Electronic Engineering,* 16, 9–13.

WALTER, W.G. (1943b) An improved low frequency analyser. *Electronic Engineering,* 16, 236–238.

WALTER, W.G. (1950a) An electro-mechanical animal. *Discovery, March,* 90–95.

WALTER, W.G. (1950b) An imitation of life. *Scientific American,* 182, 42–45.

WALTER, W.G. (1950c) Features in the electro-physiology of mental mechanisms. In D. Richter (Ed.) *Perspectives in Neuropsychiatry.* London: H.K. Lewis.

WALTER, W.G. (1953/1960) *The Living Brain.* Harmondsworth: Penguin.

WALTER, W.G., DOVEY, V. and SHIPTON, H. (1946) Analysis of the electrical response of the human cortex to photic stimulation. *Nature,* 158, 540–541.

WAR OFFICE COMMITTEE OF ENQUIRY INTO 'SHELL-SHOCK' (1922) *Report.* London: HMSO.

WARD, J. (1885) Psychology. In *Encyclopaedia Britannica,* 9th ed. Edinburgh: Black.

WARD, J. (1904) On the definition of psychology. *British Journal of Psychology,* 1, 3–25.

WARD, J. (1926) *Psychology Applied to Education.* G. Dawes Hicks (Ed.) Cambridge: Cambridge University Press.

WARD, J. (1971) Modification of deviant classroom behaviour. *British Journal of Educational Psychology,* 41, 304–313.

WARD, J. (1976) Behaviour modification in education: an overview and model for programme implementation. *Bulletin of the British Psychological Society,* 29, 257–267.

WARD, T.H.G. (1949) An experiment on serial reproduction with special reference to the changes in the design of early coin types. *British Journal of Psychology,* 39, 142–147.

WARNER, F. (1897) *The Study of Children and Their School Training.* London: Macmillan.

WARTOFSKY, M.W. (1979) *Models: Representations and Scientific Understanding.* Dordrecht: D. Reidel.

WASON, P.C. (1959) The processing of positive and negative information. *Quarterly Journal of Experimental Psychology,* 11, 92–107.

WASON, P.C. (1960) On the failure to eliminate hypotheses in a conceptual task. *Quarterly Journal of Experimental Psychology,* 12, 129–140.

WASON, P.C. (1961) Response to affirmative and negative binary statements. *British Journal of Psychology,* 52, 133–142.

WASON, P.C. (1965) The contexts of plausible denial. *Journal of Verbal Learning and Verbal Behavior,* 4, 7–11.

WASON, P.C. (1968) Reasoning about a rule. *Quarterly Journal of Experimental Psychology,* 20, 273–285.

WASON, P.C. (1969) Regression in reasoning? *British Journal of Psychology,* 60, 471–480.

WASON, P.C. (1972) In real life negatives are false. *Negation, Logique et Analyse,* 57–58, 17–38.

WASON, P.C. (1979) Self-contradictions. In P.N. Johnson-Laird and P.C. Wason (Eds) *Thinking: Readings in Cognitive Science.* Cambridge: Cambridge University Press.

WASON, P.C. (1980) Specific thoughts on the writing process. In L.W. Gregg and E.R. Steinberg (Eds) *Cognitive Processes in Writing.* Hilisdale, NJ: Lawrence Erlbaum Associates.

WASON, P.C. and GOLDING, E. (1974) The language of inconsistency. *British Journal of Psychology,* 65, 537–546.

WASON, P.C. and GREEN, D. (1984) Reasoning and mental representation. *Quarterly Journal of Experimental Psychology,* 36A, 597–610.

WASON, P.C. and JOHNSON-LAIRD, P.N. (1970) A conflict between selecting and evaluating information in an inferential task. *British Journal of Psychology,* 61, 509–515.

WASON, P.C. and JOHNSON-LAIRD, P.N. (1972) *Psychology of Reasoning: Structure and Content.* London: Batisford.

WASON, P.C. and JONES, S. (1963) Negatives: denotation and connotation. *British Journal of Psychology,* 57, 413–418.

WASON, P.C. and REICH, S.S. (1979) A verbal illusion. *Quarterly Journal of Experimental Psychology,* 31, 591–597.

WATERHOUSE, E.S. (1930) *Psychology and Religion: A Series of Broadcast Talks.* London: Elkin Mathews and Morrot.

WATKINS, A. (1927) The school's teaching – some of its distinctive features. *Thought and Action,* 4, December, 32.

WATSON, J.B. (1928) *Psychological Care of Infant and Child.* New York: Arno Press.

WATT, H.J. (1910) Some problems of sensory integration. *British Journal of Psychology,* 3, 323–347.

WATT, H.J. (1911) The elements of experience and their integration: or modalism. *British Journal of Psychology*, 4, 127–204.

WATT, H.J. (1913) The main principles of sensory integration. *British Journal of Psychology*, 6, 239–260.

WATT, H.J. (1920) A theory of binaural hearing. *British Journal of Psychology*, 11, 163–171.

WATTS, F.N. (1985) Clinical psychology. *Health Trends*, 17, 28–31.

WAVELL, A. (1948) *The Good Soldier*. London: Macmillan.

WEDDELL, G. and DARCUS, H.D. (1947) Some anatomical problems in naval warfare. *British Journal of Industrial Medicine*, 4, 77–84.

WEIDMAN, N. (1999) *Constructing Scientific Psychology: Karl Lashley's Mind–Brain Debates*. Cambridge: Cambridge University Press.

WELCH, H.J. and MYERS, C.S. (1932) *Ten Years of Industrial Psychology: An Account of the First Decade of the National Institute of Industrial Psychology*. London: Pitman.

WELFORD, A.T., ARGYLE, M., GLASS, D.V. and MORRIS, J.N. (1962) *Society: Problems and Methods of Study*. London: Routledge and Kegan Paul.

WERSKY, G. (1988) *The Visible College: A Collective Biography of British Scientists and Socialists of the 1930s*. London: Free Association Books.

WESTROPP, H.M. and WAKE, C.S. (1875) Introduction. In *Ancient Symbol Worship*. Additional notes and an appendix by Alexander Wilder. London. (Reprinted 1972. London: Curzon Press and New York: Humanities Press.)

WHEELER, S. (1996) Behaviour management: rewards or sanctions? *Teacher Development*, 5, 51–55.

WHELDALL, K. (Ed.) (1981) *The Behaviourist in the Classroom*. London: Allen and Unwin.

WHELDALL, K. (1982) Behavioural pedagogy or behavioural overkill? *Educational Psychology*, 2 (3 and 4), 181–184.

WHELDALL, K. (Ed.) (1987) *The Behaviourist in the Classroom*, 2nd ed. London: Allen and Unwin.

WHELDALL, K. and CONGREVE, S. (1980) The attitude of British teachers towards behaviour modification. *Educational Review*, 32, 53–65.

WHITE, R.W. (1959) Motivation reconsidered: the concept of competence. *Psychological Review*, 66 (5), 297–333.

WHITEHEAD, A.N. (1926/1953) *Science and the Modern World*. Cambridge: Cambridge University Press.

WHITLEY, R. (1984) *The Intellectual and Social Organization of the Sciences*. Oxford: Clarendon Press.

WICKELGREN, W.A. (1966) Associative intrusions in short-term recall. *Journal of Experimental Psychology*, 72, 853–858.

WIENER, N. (1954) *Human Use of Human Beings*. New York: Doubleday and Anchor.

WIENER, N. (1956) *I am a Mathematician*. London: Victor Gollancz.

WIENER, N., ROSENBLUETH, A. and BIGELOW, J. (1943) Behavior, purpose, teleology. *Philosophy of Science*, 10, 18–24.

WIGAN, A.L. (1844) *A New View of Insanity. The Duality of the Mind Proved by the Structure, Functions and Diseases of the Brain*. London: Longmans, Green.

WILLIAMS, M. (1994) *The Precision Makers: A History of the Instruments Industry in Britain and France*. London: Routledge.

WILSON, D.A.H. (1999) *Encouragements and Constraints in the Development of Experimental Animal Behaviour Studies in Great Britain Since the Late Nineteenth Century*. Unpublished PhD thesis, University of Leicester.

WILSON, E.O. (1975) *Sociobiology: The New Synthesis*. Cambridge, MA: Harvard University Press.

WILSON, H., ZANGWILL, O.L., EYSENCK, H.J. and KENNEDY, A. (1952) Discussion on the role of the psychologist in psychiatric practice. *Proceedings of the Royal Society of Medicine*, 45, 445–450.

WINCH, W.H. (1908) The transfer of improvement in memory in school-children. *British Journal of Psychology*, 2, 284–293.

WINCH, W.H. (1910) The transfer of improvement in memory in school-children: II. *British Journal of Psychology*, 3, 386–405.

WINCH, W.H. (1911) Some relations between substance memory and productive imagination in school children. *British Journal of Psychology*, 4, 95–125.

WINTER, J. (1995) *Sites of Memory, Sites of Mourning: The Great War in European Cultural History*. Cambridge: Cambridge University Press.

WISDOM, J.O. (1951) The hypothesis of cybernetics. *British Journal for the Philosophy of Science*, 2, 1–24.

WITMER, L. (1907) Clinical psychology. *American Psychologist, 51,* 248–251. (Originally published in *The Psychological Clinic, 1,* 1–9.)

WOODGER, J.H. (1937) *The Axiomatic Method in Biology.* Cambridge: Cambridge University Press.

WOODGER, J.H. (1939/1970) The technique of theory construction. In O. Neurath, R. Carnap and C.W. Morris (Eds) *Foundations of the Unity of Science.* Chicago: University of Chicago Press.

WOODWARD, A.G. (1938) *Personnel Management.* London: Efficiency Magazine.

WOODWORTH, R.S. (1931) *Contemporary Schools of Psychology.* New York: Ronald Press.

WOODWORTH, R.S. (1938) *Experimental Psychology.* New York: Henry Holt.

WOODWORTH, R.S. (1950) *Experimental Psychology.* London: Matthew.

WOOLDRIDGE, A. (1994) *Measuring the Mind: Education and Psychology in England, c. 1860–c. 1990.* Cambridge: Cambridge University Press.

WORDEN, F.G., SWAZEY, J.P. and ADELMAN, G. (Eds) (1975) *The Neurosciences: Paths of Discovery.* Cambridge, MA: MIT Press.

WRAGG, T. (1982) Fever pitch. *Times Educational Supplement,* 11 June, 80.

WRIGHT, I.P., SLOMAN, A. and BEAUDOIN, L.P. (1996) Towards a design-based analysis of emotional episodes. *Philosophy, Psychiatry, and Psychology, 3 (2),* 101–137.

WUNDT, W. (1920) *Völkerpsychologie: Eine Untersuchung, der Entwicklungsgesetze von Sprache, Mythus und Sitte.* Leipzig: Engleman.

WYATT, S. (1950) An autobiography. *Occupational Psychology, 24 (2),* 65–74.

WYNDHAM, H. (1937) *Mr Sludge, the Medium. Being the Life and Adventures of Daniel Dunglas Home.* London: Geoffrey Bless.

YATES, A.J. (1954) The validity of some psychological tests of brain damage. *Psychological Bulletin, 51,* 359–379.

YATES, A.J. (1958) The application of learning theory to the treatment of tics. *Journal of Abnormal and Social Psychology, 56,* 175–182.

YATES, A.J. (1970a) Misconceptions about behavior therapy: a point of view. *Behavior Therapy, 1,* 92–107.

YATES, A.J. (1970b) *Behavior Therapy.* New York: Wiley.

YATES, F.A. (1966) *The Art of Memory.* London: Routledge Kegan and Paul.

YELLOWLEES, H. (1943) Mental hygiene in modern life. In *Out of Working Hours: Medical Psychology on Special Occasions.* London: J.A. Churchill.

YELLOWLEES, H. (1955) *To Define True Madness: Commonsense Psychiatry for Lay People.* London: Penguin.

YOUNG, J.Z. (1951/1960) *Doubt and Certainty in Science: A Biologist's Reflections on the Brain, Being the BBC Reith Lectures for 1950.* Oxford: Oxford University Press.

YOUNG, M. (1982) *The Elmhirsts of Dartington.* London: Routledge and Kegan Paul.

YOUNG, R.M. (1966) Scholarship and the history of the behavioral sciences. *History of Science, 5,* 1–51.

YOUNG, R.M. (1967) Animal soul. In P. Edwards (Ed.) *The Encyclopaedia of Philosophy, Vol. 1.* London: Collier Macmillan.

YOUNG, R.M. (1970) *Mind, Brain and Adaptation in the Nineteenth Century: Cerebral Localization and its Biological Context from Gall to Ferrier.* Oxford: Clarendon Press.

YOUNG, R.M. (1985) *Darwin's Metaphor: Nature's Place in Victorian Culture.* Cambridge: Cambridge University Press.

YOUNG, R.M. (1989) Persons, organisms … and primary qualities. In J.R. Moore (Ed.) *History, Humanity and Evolution: Essays for John C. Greene.* Cambridge: Cambridge University Press.

YULE, W. (1975) Teaching psychological principles to non-psychologists. *Journal of the Association of Educational Psychology, 10 (3),* 5–16.

YULE, W. (1991) The changing face of behavioural psychotherapy: children's problems. *Behavioural Psychotherapy, 19 (1),* 88–91.

ZANGWILL, O. (1937a) An investigation of the relationship between the processes of reproducing and recognizing simple figures, with special reference to Koffka's trace theory. *British Journal of Psychology, 27,* 250–276.

ZANGWILL, O. (1937b) A study of the significance of attitude in recognition. *British Journal of Psychology, 28,* 12–17.

ZANGWILL, O. (1938) The problem of retroactive inhibition in relation to recognition. *British Journal of Psychology, 28,* 229–247.

ZANGWILL, O. (1939) Some relations between reproducing and recognizing prose material. *British Journal of Psychology, 29,* 370–382.

ZANGWILL, O. (1950a) Amnesia and the generic image. *Quarterly Journal of Experimental Psychology*, 2, 7–12.

ZANGWILL, O.L. (1950b) *An Introduction to Modern Psychology*. London: Methuen.

ZANGWILL, O.L. (1964) Physiological and experimental psychology. In J. Cohen (Ed.) *Readings in Psychology*. London: Allen and Unwin.

ZANGWILL, O.L. (1966) George Humphrey (1889–1966). *Quarterly Journal of Experimental Psychology*, 4, 280–281.

ZANGWILL, O.L. (1972) Obituary notice, R.C. Oldfield, 1909–1972. *Quarterly Journal of Experimental Psychology*, 24, 375–377.

ZANGWILL, O.L. (1977) Obituary, G.C. Grindley (1903–1976). *Quarterly Journal of Experimental Psychology*, 29, 1–3.

ZANGWILL, O.L. (1980) Kenneth Craik: the man and his work. *British Journal of Psychology*, 71, 1–16.

ZANGWILL, O.L. (1987) Craik, Kenneth John William (1914–45). In R. Gregory (Ed.) *The Oxford Companion to the Mind*. Oxford: Oxford University Press.

ZENDERLAND, L. (1998) *Measuring Minds: Henry Herbert Goddard and the Origins of American Intelligence Testing*. Cambridge: Cambridge University Press.

ZUCKERMAN, S. (1973) W.E. Le Gros Clark. *Biographical Memoirs of Fellows of the Royal Society, Vol. 19*. London: Royal Society.

ZUCKERMAN, S. (1978) *From Apes to Warlords: An Autobiography 1904–46*. London: Hamish Hamilton.

ZUCKERMAN, S. (1988) *Monkeys, Men and Missiles. An Autobiography 1946–1988*. London: Collins.

ZURIFF, G.E. (1979) The demise of behaviourism – exaggerated rumour? *Journal of the Experimental Analysis of Behaviour*, 32, 129–136.

Index